North Korean
Nuclear Operationality

North Korean
Nuclear Operationality

Regional Security & Nonproliferation

Edited by
GREGORY J. MOORE

Foreword by
GRAHAM T. ALLISON

Johns Hopkins University Press
Baltimore

Johns Hopkins University Press
2715 North Charles Street
Baltimore, Maryland 21218-4363
www.press.jhu.edu

Library of Congress Cataloging-in-Publication Data
North Korean nuclear operationality : regional security and
nonproliferation / [edited by] Gregory J. Moore ;
[foreword by] Graham T. Allison.
   pages cm
Includes bibliographic information and index.
ISBN-13: 978-1-4214-1094-4 (hardcover)
ISBN-13: 978-1-4214-1095-1 (electronic)
ISBN-10: 1-4214-1094-X (hardcover)
ISBN-10: 1-4214-1095-8 (electronic)
1. Nuclear disarmament—Korea (North)   2. Nuclear nonproliferation—
Korea (North)   3. Nuclear nonproliferation—East Asia.   4. Security,
International—East Asia.   I. Moore, Gregory J.
JZ6009.K7N66   2013
327.1'747095193—dc23   2013012246

A catalog record for this book is available from the British Library.

Special discounts are available for bulk purchases of this book.
For more information, please contact Special Sales at 410-516-6936 or
specialsales@press.jhu.edu.

Contents

Contributors

Graham T. Allison
Harvard University
Cambridge, Massachusetts, USA

Jong-Yun Bae
Yonsei University
Seoul, South Korea

Scott Bruce
Nautilus Institute
San Francisco, California, USA

Jong Kun Choi
Yonsei University
Seoul, South Korea

Katsuhisa Furukawa
National Graduate Institute for Policy
    Studies
Tokyo, Japan

Peter Hayes
Nautilus Institute
San Francisco, California, USA

Hajime Izumi
University of Shizuoka
Shizuoka City, Japan

David Kang
University of Southern California
Los Angeles, California, USA

Andrei Lankov
Kookmin University
Seoul, South Korea

Gregory J. Moore
Zhejiang University
Hangzhou, China

Maria Rost Rublee
Australia National University
Canberra, Australia

Georgy Toloraya
Russian Academy of Science
Moscow, Russia

Daniel Twining
German Marshall Fund
Washington, DC, USA

Jing-dong Yuan
University of Sydney
Sydney, Australia

Foreword

This volume highlights the most inconvenient truth about the global nuclear order: one of the poorest and most isolated states in the world, North Korea, has repeatedly violated the rules of the nuclear nonproliferation regime with impunity. Even more telling is that the nation has done so in direct defiance of the explicit demands of the United States and China, presumptive guardians of the regime.

These brute facts are hard to believe but impossible to deny. When President George W. Bush entered office in 2001, North Korea had two bombs' worth of plutonium, eight thousand spent fuel rods that contained plutonium for six additional bombs locked securely in warehouses monitored around the clock, and a frozen reactor at Yongbyon. Today, it has an arsenal of ten bombs and has conducted thee nuclear weapons tests as well as a series of long-range missile tests. It has also developed a uranium-enrichment facility at Yongbyon that will be capable of producing two bombs' worth of highly enriched uranium each year, and it is likely operating a covert uranium program that will soon be producing additional bomb-usable material.

If that were not enough, North Korea has also demonstrated its readiness to proliferate nuclear-weapons technologies, most dramatically when it sold to Syria a plutonium-producing reactor plus starter fuel for its own nuclear weapons (the facility was destroyed by an Israeli air attack in September 2007).

From the perspective of the nuclear nonproliferation regime, two stark questions arise. First, does Pyongyang believe that North Korea could get away with selling a nuclear weapon to Al Qaeda or Iran? The fact that North Korea sold Syria a reactor that is thousands of times larger than a bomb suggests that it does. Second, what are the consequences for the Nuclear Non-Proliferation Treaty if one of the world's weakest states can violate the rules of the regime with impunity and defy the demands of those states charged with its enforcement?

Although Kim Jong-il's appearance and antics were ridiculed by most Western observers, his success in negotiations over the past two decades suggests that he may have been crazy like a fox. By adopting a cyclical strategy, described by former U.S. director of national intelligence Michael McConnell as "negotiate, prevaricate, escalate, and renegotiate," Kim managed to expand North Korea's nuclear program steadily while maintaining a façade of openness to negotiations and extracting payments whenever he returned to the negotiating table.

Risks to regional and global stability have grown in recent years. Following North Korea's sinking of the *Cheonan* in March 2010 and its shelling of Yeonpyeong Island later the same year, South Korean president Lee Myung-bak warned that his country would respond forcefully to any future North Korean attack. Such a response could escalate rapidly into a war in which the United States would be fighting alongside our South Korean allies. Furthermore, in an updated U.S. assessment presented in Beijing in January 2011, then–secretary of defense Robert Gates also warned that North Korea is becoming a "direct threat" and would be able to strike the U.S. homeland with a nuclear-armed intercontinental ballistic missile within the next five years.

Professor Moore's introductory chapter to this book reminds us that failure to confront this nuclear challenge could have "horrifying implications for peace on the Korean Peninsula and for regional peace and security," as well as "alarming implications for the nuclear nonproliferation regime worldwide." Organizing a coherent strategy to address these urgent threats must begin with a comprehensive assessment of the North Korean nuclear threat. The contributors to this volume take an important step in this direction.

Graham T. Allison

Acknowledgments

As with any good project, successful results come only with the work and support of many hands. This project is no exception. Thanks are due to all the authors in this collection, who worked hard, met numerous shifting deadlines, and endured many ups and downs, including the death of Kim Jong-il as this project neared completion—leading to further editing of their contributions.

I would like to thank my home institution, Zhejiang University and its College of Public Administration and Department of Political Science, as well as the Zhejiang University Humanities Interdisciplinary Maritime Project (浙江大学文科海洋交叉项目; No. 188050+193415801/02) and the Zhejiang University Post-Graduate English Language Development Programme (浙江大学的全英文项目; No. 188310*193226101), the Australia National University, the Institute for Far Eastern Studies at Kyungnam University (Seoul), and the University of North Korean Studies (Seoul) for support that helped enable this study. I am also grateful to the China Institutes for Contemporary International Relations, which helped arrange interviews in Beijing and always made their own experts available for interviews.

Thanks are also due to Geoffrey Burn, Cal Dunlap, Stephan Haggard, Kongdan Oh Hassig, Jin Canrong, Li Xin, George Meese, Liu Ming, Chung-in Moon, Marcus Noland, Shi Yinhong, Yu Xunda, Mark Valencia, Peter Van Ness, Zha Daojiong, Zhang Liangui, Zhang Xizhen, Suisheng Zhao, and a number of others not listed here (including a number of anonymous reviewers and Chinese interviewees), for support and helpful comments on various aspects of this volume and the writings herein.

Last and most importantly I thank my lovely wife, Chenchen, who made many sacrifices in supporting me to see this project through to completion.

North Korean
Nuclear Operationality

The Problem with an Operationally Nuclear North Korea

GREGORY J. MOORE

Miss Sasaki went back to her office and sat down at her desk. She was quite far from the windows, which were off to her left, and behind her were a couple of tall bookcases containing all the books of the factory library, which the personnel department had organized. She settled herself at her desk, put some things in a drawer, and shifted papers. She thought that before she began to make entries in her lists of new employees, discharges, and departures for the Army, she would chat for a moment with the girl at her right. Just as she turned her head away from the windows, the room was filled with a blinding light. She was paralyzed by fear, fixed still in her chair for a long moment. . . . Everything fell, and Miss Sasaki lost consciousness. The ceiling dropped suddenly and the wooden floor above collapsed in splinters and the people up there came down and the roof above them gave way; but principally and first of all, the bookcases right behind her swooped forward and the contents threw her down, with her left leg horribly twisted and breaking underneath her. There, in the tin factory, in the first moment of the atomic age, a human being was crushed by books.[1]

Although crippled for life, Miss Toshiko Sasaki survived the atomic bomb blast that struck Hiroshima on August 6, 1945, destroying the East Asian Tin Works where she was employed a little less than a mile from the blast's center. Some one hundred thousand other citizens of Hiroshima did not survive. Nor did tens of thousands of other Japanese citizens in Nagasaki, which was bombed three days later. At the time of this writing, these incidents are history's only two examples of the use of nuclear weapons. As horrifying as the aftermath was of the explosions of "Little Boy" and "Fat Man"—the names euphemistically given to the bombs dropped on Hiroshima and Nagasaki, respectively—today's nuclear weapons are many times more powerful.

A bit closer to home for most of us, September 11, 2001, is a date that exemplifies the power of asymmetrical warfare—of the strong as strangely vulnerable. National defense was once conceived almost exclusively as a military matter with clearly demarcated national boundaries defended by long green lines and naval armadas, such conceptualizations of national defense are no longer apropos or at least no longer complete. The enemy today may be a lone figure with a car bomb in Times Square, as was the case in May 2010. Worse yet, the enemy might possess some sort of suitcase-size nuclear weapon. Russian national security adviser General Alexander Lebed told a visiting U.S. congressional delegation in 1997 that the Russian military possessed such weapons and had managed to lose track of one hundred of them. Steve Kroft of television's *60 Minutes* had this exchange with Lebed:

> GENERAL LEBED: It [the nuclear weapon] is made in the form of a suitcase. It is a suitcase, actually. You could carry it. You can put it into another suitcase if you want to.
>
> KROFT: But it is already a suitcase.
>
> GENERAL LEBED: Yes.
>
> KROFT: I could walk down the streets of Moscow or Washington or New York, and people would think I'm carrying a suitcase?
>
> GENERAL LEBED: Yes, indeed.
>
> KROFT: How easy is it to detonate?
>
> GENERAL LEBED: It would take twenty, thirty minutes to prepare.
>
> KROFT: But you don't need secret codes from the Kremlin or anything like that?
>
> GENERAL LEBED: No.
>
> KROFT: You are saying that there are a significant number that are missing and unaccounted for?
>
> GENERAL LEBED: Yes, there are. More than a hundred.
>
> KROFT: Where are they?
>
> GENERAL LEBED: Somewhere in Georgia, somewhere in Ukraine, somewhere in the Baltic countries? Perhaps some of them are even outside those countries? One person is capable of triggering this nuclear weapon—one person.
>
> KROFT: So you are saying these weapons are no longer under the control of the Russian military.
>
> GENERAL LEBED: I'm saying that more than 100 weapons out of the supposed number of 250 are not under the control of the armed forces of Russia. I don't

know their location. I don't know whether they have been destroyed or whether they are stored or whether they've been sold or stolen. I don't know.[2]

The Russian government later denied Lebed's claims, but this exchange underlines the notion that better securing and ultimately reducing the world's stockpiles of nuclear weapons and materials are certainly among the world's most pressing issues.

Just as important is keeping nuclear weapons out of the arsenals of states such as the Democratic People's Republic of Korea (DPRK; North Korea). Even more troubling than the likelihood of North Korea's eventual ability to marry its nascent nuclear capabilities to its better-proven missile capabilities is the possibility that North Korea could proliferate these technologies to state or non-state actors. North Korea has proven itself capable of initiating acts of war (e.g., the 1950–53 Korean War), acts of terrorism (e.g., the 1987 bombing of a Korean Air Lines flight), and acts of assassination (e.g., the 1983 Rangoon assassination attempt on South Korean president Chun Doo-hwan, which while missing the president, left twenty-two dead, including South Korea's foreign minister and a number of other cabinet members). North Korea has been on both the giving and receiving ends of nuclear proliferation (e.g., receiving from the A. Q. Khan network, and proliferating to Iran, Syria, and other nuclear aspirants), so the nation is clearly not a reliable keeper of such capabilities.

The North Korean nuclear issue has been one of the most intractable problems in international security circles in the past two decades and potentially one of the most explosive—pun intended. This crisis broke onto the global scene for the first time in 1993–94, when Pyongyang announced that it would withdraw from the Non-Proliferation Treaty (NPT) and later that it had unloaded fuel rods from its Yongbyon reactor that could be converted into plutonium suitable for nuclear weapons. With the intervention of former U.S. president Jimmy Carter, the United States and North Korea struck an eleventh-hour deal, even as contingency plans were being discussed for U.S. surgical strikes on North Korea. The resulting Agreed Framework seemed to be a real breakthrough, yet it unraveled quickly. By late 2002 the United States accused Pyongyang of breaking its 1994 promises, after which North Korea responded by kicking out International Atomic Energy Agency (IAEA) inspectors and restarting its Yongbyon reactor, announcing that it would withdraw permanently from the Nuclear Non-Proliferation Treaty. In 2003 China began organizing the Six Party Talks, which seemed to help the parties (the United States, North Korea, China, South Korea, Japan, and Russia) move toward a resolution. By October 2006, however, international observers confirmed that North Korea had conducted a nuclear test, though of very low yield and questionable success. The test led to a more concerted effort to address the issues; the six parties reached an agreement in 2007 that would see North Korea's Yongbyon nuclear facility closed and IAEA inspectors return in exchange for heavy fuel oil and other benefits for Pyongyang. Mutual recriminations between Pyongyang, Washington, and Seoul led to a breakdown in this agreement during 2007 and 2008, and in April 2009 North Korea again tested its Taepodong II intercontinental ballistic missiles. In May 2009 another nuclear test followed. International condemnation and UN Security Council sanctions followed, leading to a complete breakdown in the Six Party Talks. Add to this chain of events the sinking of South Korea's naval ship *Cheonan* and North Korea's shelling of the South Korean island Yeonpyeong in 2010, and the North Korean nuclear issue once again is in a dangerous state of irresolution.

As the studies in this volume establish, North Korean capabilities at present put Pyongyang on the cusp of nuclear operationality, and North Korean leaders have said they are pursuing operationality and membership in the club of the world's nuclear weapons states. In October 2006 and May 2009 the DPRK conducted underground tests of a little less than one and four kilotons, respectively.[3] While considered a success in the sense of ushering North Korea into the club of nuclear states—as Moore, Hayes and Bruce, and others in this collection note—both tests were lower yield than planned and much lower than the U.S. bombs dropped in 1945 on Hiroshima and Nagasaki, which were thirteen to eighteen and twenty-one kilotons, respectively. In addition to its nascent nuclear capabilities, North Korea also has two families of medium- and long-range missiles, the No-dong and Taepodong missiles, with ranges of 1,250 and between 2,500 and 3,700 miles, respectively, putting all of South Korea, Japan, and possibly Alaska in range. Most Western observers contend that the North Koreans have not yet been able to successfully marry a nuclear payload to these missiles, nor make a "Little Boy"- or "Fat Man"–type bomb. When North Korea is able to do either of these things or create another means of delivering such a weapon to its target, the nation will have achieved nuclear operationality.

Before moving further, we should define "nuclear operationality" as used here. When an underground nuclear test is conducted, as North Korea has done twice, a nation has "weaponized"; bombs, after all, are not for nuclear energy production. As a result, as of at least October 2006, when the first test was conducted, North Korea has had nuclear weapons capabilities in their most basic form. If the DPRK could go to a parking garage in a tall building in New York City and set up the test it conducted in its underground facility, it could detonate a bomb that could do serious damage. By that standard, North Korea has weaponized its nuclear capability. It has a bomb. This sort of scenario would not likely occur, of course, because the New York City authorities would catch those setting up the device long before they could detonate it. This weaponized form is not yet, then, truly operational in any practical sense; it is not ready to be delivered to a target.[4] Subsequently, the argument here is that North Korea has already *weaponized* its nuclear capability, but it has not *operationalized* its capability in the sense that it can realistically deliver such a weapon to a target of choice outside North Korea. "Nuclear operationality," for our purposes, can be defined as the ability to marry a nuclear bomb to a missile that could be directed toward an intended target, fashion a nuclear bomb that could be dropped out of an airplane, or miniaturize a nuclear bomb into a suitcase bomb or another kind of explosive device that could be transported surreptitiously to the intended target and detonated. Because North Korea has not achieved any of these technological breakthroughs to date, it has not achieved nuclear operationality as we use the term here.[5]

The question posed for consideration in this volume is as follows: What is at stake for Northeast Asian regional security and for the international nuclear nonproliferation regime if North Korea was to successfully develop nuclear weapons capability and marry it to its missile technology or another potential delivery system, thus achieving nuclear operationality? I have invited experts from different national and experiential perspectives to contemplate the question from political, security, and economic perspectives. Some additional questions could be posed here, too: Would Japan then go nuclear? Would South Korea as well? What about Taiwan? Would a regional arms race result? Which side would China take if North Korea attained nuclear operationality? Would China engage in, support, or refuse to be a party to sanctions or attacks on North Korea? Would the United States do nothing and even give its blessing to DPRK nuclearization as it ultimately has India, or would it pursue a more robust policy line, such as attempting surgical strikes inside North Korea? Would an international sanctions regime against North Korea follow, and what would be such sanctions mean? Would it all lead to war? What would be the implications of North Korean nuclear operationality for the nuclear nonproliferation regime? Is there a way out of this morass?

This general issue area is vital for Northeast Asia, U.S. policy in the region, and the international nuclear nonproliferation regime. Northeast Asian security directly involves the world's three most powerful military powers (the United States, Russia, and China) and the world's three largest economies (the United States, China, and Japan). It also includes one of the world's most dangerous flashpoints—the Korean Peninsula—and one of the world's most unpredictable nations: North Korea. Pyongyang's pursuit of an operational nuclear capability is strangely understudied and underappreciated in the academy and in security circles. In addition to regional security implications, the status of the global nuclear nonproliferation regime is at stake—and vitally important. North Korean success in thwarting the efforts of this regime could embolden Iran, Syria, and other nuclear aspirants in their own nuclear weapons pursuits, which could destroy the nuclear nonproliferation regime and make the world much more dangerous.

AN OVERVIEW OF THE BOOK

This volume begins with an introductory section that addresses North Korea's present operational status and then offers an overview of U.S. policy toward North Korea and the path Pyongyang has taken to nuclear weaponization.

In chapter 1, Peter Hayes and Scott Bruce make the case that North Korea has a number of strategic uses for the nuclear capabilities the nation already possesses. The DPRK could detonate a nuclear bomb at sea or in or near the demilitarized zone (DMZ) to signal displeasure with South Korea—including a pop-up attack by means of a tunnel on the South Korean side of the DMZ—or could attack forces that might invade North Korea. Pyongyang thus already has a deterrent, albeit one of very limited use. In exploring a number of other delivery options, Hayes and Bruce conclude that North Korea is not yet in a position to deliver a weapon to a target of choice outside of its borders. For these authors, the only realistic solution to the North Korean nuclear impasse is establishing a regional nuclear-weapon-free zone.

I argue in chapter 2 that U.S. policy since the first North Korean nuclear crisis in 1994 has been a failure. U.S. goals have been to prevent North Korea from developing nuclear weapons and from proliferating nuclear materials, know-how, or anything related to its nuclear program to other states. Pyongyang has, however, developed and tested nuclear weapons as well as proliferated nuclear materials, know-how, and other elements related to their missile and nuclear programs to Iran, Syria, Pakistan, and possibly Burma and pre-2003 Iraq. I argue that what worked with China in the early 1970s should be tried with

North Korea: preemptive recognition with up-front offers of trade and better relations between North Korea and the United States before resolving the nuclear issue. If Pyongyang then balks and continues to arm and proliferate, the way would be open for more forceful measures if necessary. Washington might then have China more fully on board, for Beijing would be frustrated also if the Pyongyang leadership scuttled such a chance for peace. The goal of the policy is to give Pyongyang's leadership the security, the face, and the way out many believe they have been seeking. In the long run, such an approach can only work toward the good of reformers in Pyongyang and, ultimately, bring about a greater promise of regional security, maintenance of the nuclear nonproliferation regime, and peace on the Korean Peninsula.

The next section of the book surveys the reactions of North Korea's neighbors—South Korea, China, Japan, and Russia—to the potential of North Korean nuclear operationality and its regional security implications. Jong-Yun Bae and Jong-Kun Choi argue in chapter 3 that, given Seoul's proximity to the North Korean border (thirty-plus miles) and the four hundred to five hundred pieces of DPRK artillery pointing into the city—each of which can fire some ten thousand rounds per minute—North Korea does not need nuclear weapons to check South Korea. Its conventional capabilities are more than sufficient. Because of this conventional threat to Seoul, Bae and Choi conclude that the only real option for South Korea in the long run is engagement with North Korea. The authors maintain, though, that Seoul would and should follow a policy of containment of North Korea if the North moves to operationalize its nuclear capabilities. Little support in South Korea would exist, though, for more robust responses to North Korean nuclear operationality, nor would there be support for any moves toward South Korean nuclear weapons—either or their own or placed on their soil. Bae and Choi explain that South Korean president Kim Dae-jung's Sunshine Policy of engagement with North Korea, continued under President Roh Moo-hyun, was bearing fruit and that the tension in North-South relations under President Lee Myung-bak has played into the hands of Pyongyang hardliners and strengthened their positions, making resolution of the tensions more difficult.

In chapter 4, I show that China's relations with North Korea since the onset of the contemporary North Korean nuclear crisis have been more complicated than Beijing's amicable Cold War history with Pyongyang would suggest. Beijing is clearly against Pyongyang's acquisition of any nuclear capabilities, let alone having nuclear operationality. Beijing has joined in international condemnation of North Korean ballistic missile and nuclear tests in recent years and in some cases used rather harsh language toward its neighbor. Beijing policymakers have come to view the North Korean leadership as a liability to China and have increasingly shown a willingness to join the international community in condemning Pyongyang's provocative behaviors. (A possible exception came in 2010, when Beijing refused to condemn North Korea's sinking of the South Korean ship *Cheonan* or the shelling of the South Korean island of Yeonpyeong.) China's interests have dictated a two-pronged strategy of discouraging North Korea's nuclear policy while supporting North Korea economically. China wants to avoid the collapse of the DPRK regime, which would likely lead to political chaos and an enormous inflow of North Korean refugees into northeastern China.

Katsuhisa Furukawa and Hajime Izumi explain in chapter 5 that North Korea's nuclear ambitions have not, thus far, pushed Japan toward acquiring its own nuclear weapons. Abduction of Japanese citizens by North Korean agents over the years remains a more important issue to Japan than North Korean nuclear weapons; moreover, the Japanese are even more concerned about China's rise. Japan's position on North Korean nuclear weapons remains closely tied to its security relationship with Washington. As long as the Japanese believe that the United States is committed to Japan's defense, Japan has little incentive to pursue nuclear weapons at this time or in the near future.

Georgy Toloraya discusses the likely Russian response to operational North Korean nuclear weapons. Toloraya writes in chapter 6 that North Korea is not going to give up its newfound status as a member of the nuclear club anytime soon, despite all the efforts of China and the other members of the Six Party Talks. In his view, North Korean nuclear operationality is not necessarily going to increase the danger of escalation of tensions on the Korean Peninsula, although the possibility exists. Russia is concerned about the danger that North Korean nuclear weapons pose to regional security and the nonproliferation regime, as well as North Korean nuclear know-how or weapons being sold into the hands of terrorists or separatists who could threaten Russia's security or territorial integrity. Russia's policymakers, though, remain opposed to using force to resolve the issue. Toloraya maintains that Russians look to Washington to jump-start the process with a fresh approach to the North Korean nuclear issue, rooted in engagement with economic incentives.

In chapter 7 David Kang argues that while China has proven helpful in many ways in bringing Pyongyang to the table, Washington is overly optimistic that China is going to put the necessary pressure on Pyongyang to achieve any real results. For U.S. policymakers, invasion of and military strikes on the DPRK would not be realistic because of the threat that North Korea poses to Seoul. Kang says that Washington should pursue economic engagement with Pyongyang, but he acknowledges that more than forty U.S. laws restricting economic relations with North Korea make that policy difficult, which leaves "rhetorical pressure, quiet diplomacy, and mild sanctions" against Pyongyang. Kang is not optimistic that Washington can find a solution to the problems on the Korean Peninsula.

An investigation of North Korea's interests in the nuclear issue and conclusions about the implications thereof are Andrei Lankov's focus in chapter 8. Lankov states that North Korea will not give up its newfound nuclear prowess under any circumstances. He believes that China wants to maintain the status quo on the Korean Peninsula and, therefore, will do nothing (nor tolerate anything) that would bring about either regime change or collapse in Pyongyang, or a war on the peninsula that could have the same result. In Lankov's view, Beijing prefers to keep North Korea as a buffer state, fearing that a unified Korea would become a U.S. ally on China's doorstep. At stake for North Korea are the security and longevity of what Lankov calls the Kim Family Regime, not the good of the North Korean people. Unless the United States is willing to ensure the security of the Kim Family Regime—not just offer "security assurances"—no way is available to reconcile the interests of the parties in this conflict, leaving Lankov to conclude that the world will have to learn how to live with a nuclear North Korea.

The last section of the book presents three chapters that consider the implications of an operationally nuclear North Korea on the nuclear nonproliferation regime. In chapter 9 Daniel Twining responds to the obvious question of why the United States blessed Indian nuclear operationality, after a brief sanctions regime, but North Korea is chastened for pursuing a nuclear capability. Twining maintains that India is worthy of the international nuclear acceptance it has ultimately secured and that North Korea and India are not comparable. He points out that India never signed the Non-Proliferation Treaty as Pyongyang did; India was thus not in violation of the treaty when it tested its nuclear weapons. Moreover, since acceding to the club of nuclear weapons nations, India has acceded also to the key parts of the nuclear nonproliferation regime, including trade with the Nuclear Suppliers' Group, and it has an agreement with the IAEA in which IAEA inspectors regularly inspect all of India's civilian nuclear facilities. Twining argues that these actions plus India's stands against nuclear proliferation and the recent U.S.-India Civil Nuclear Cooperation Agreement have all made India a respected nuclear power in the international community and have strengthened the nuclear nonproliferation regime.[6]

Maria Rost Rublee stresses in chapter 10 the need for coordination between descriptive norms ("Watch what I do") and injunctive norms ("Listen to what I say"). She argues that North Korea is more likely to pay attention when the speaker's actions are consistent with its words, which is true of Iran and other nuclear aspirants as well. The Iranians argue that Israel and India are treated differently than North Korea and Iran, for instance, and what they view as a double standard is likely to be seen as a reason not to take these nuclear norms seriously. Rublee argues that if North Korea achieves nuclear operationalization without paying any cost for its transgressions, the nuclear nonproliferation regime would be devastated and Iran and other aspirants would be heartily emboldened, leaving significant negative ripple effects.

Jing-dong Yuan argues in chapter 11 that the unchallenged operationalization of North Korea's nuclear capability, should it occur, would indeed be a grave blow to the nonproliferation regime. Never before has a nation acceded to and then withdrawn from the NPT, let alone then gone on to develop nuclear weapons, as has North Korea. The NPT regime would in that case appear toothless, which Yuan states is a serious problem, for the NPT remains the last, best hope against a very dangerous world of nuclear weapons states and other states and non-state actors that seek such capabilities.

In the final chapter, I summarize the findings in the volume and their implications for regional security and the nonproliferation regime. Then I discuss international relations (IR) theory, its implications for the North Korean nuclear issue, and insights into the North Korean nuclear issue that IR theory offers. The Realists' approaches do not lend themselves to much optimism for peaceful resolution of the impasse over Pyongyang's nuclear program. Neoliberal institutionalism's notions of complex interdependence might ameliorate the tensions, but according to most authors in this study (with the possible exception of Toloraya), without solving the tensions on the Korean Peninsula, Pyongyang will not likely implement economic reforms that might allow interdependence to have its positive effects on regional peace and security. Constructivism, done at the second level of analysis, offers perhaps more hope for peaceful resolution, although it does not see such an outcome as foreordained. Maintaining that Realist assumptions about security-maximizing behavior and mutual distrust as norm are not necessarily accurate, constructivist approaches lend themselves to more options for creative solutions. The chapter ends with a discussion of such options, and a number of possible ways forward toward resolving the North Korean nuclear dilemma—all found in chapters in this volume. These include discussion of a nuclear-weapon-free zone (Hayes and Bruce); a Nixon-Kissingeresque approach to Pyongyang, akin to Washington's China policy in 1971–72 (Moore); and a security architecture based on the Six Party Talks (Toloraya, Moore), as ways to move the Six Party Talks toward resolution.

BOMBS AWAY?

What does the future hold for the North Korean nuclear crisis? Will it be "bombs away" as North Korean leaders launch a future nuclear strike, or as they proliferate their nuclear weapons, technology, or know-how to state or non-state actors in the future? Will it be U.S. bombardiers crying "Bombs away" as they launch surgical strikes on North Korean nuclear installations or weapons sites? Will North Korean leaders put their newly developing nuclear bombs away and even disavow nuclear weapons entirely? Or will something else happen? In answering these and other questions, this volume offers a venue for experts on the North Korean nuclear issue from a number of different countries and types of institutions to knock their heads together, so to speak, in an attempt to work toward better understanding of and possible solutions to one of the world's most difficult and dangerous security quandaries. Failure to resolve the North Korean nuclear dilemma has potentially horrifying implications for peace on the Korean Peninsula, for regional peace and security, and for the nuclear nonproliferation regime worldwide, given North Korea's history of proliferation and its potential to proliferate in the future. We hope that the insights offered in this volume might contribute to better understanding and the ultimate resolution of this dilemma.

PART ONE

The North Korean Nuclear Dilemma

CHAPTER ONE

Translating North Korea's Nuclear Threats into Constrained Operational Reality

PETER HAYES AND SCOTT BRUCE

To examine the current operational doctrine and practices of the DPRK military when it comes to its nuclear weapons, we begin by outlining what is entailed in developing an operational nuclear doctrine in a nuclear-armed state—a set of requirements that does not vary, although the arrangements made to respond to the imperatives may differ by nation. We then examine carefully the DPRK's potential to deliver nuclear weapons outside of the DPRK to targets such as the Republic of Korea (ROK; South Korea), Japan, or China, concluding that such attacks are still purely hypothetical and would not be undertaken with existing means by a rational decisionmaker. Moreover, if taken irrationally, such attacks would most likely fail.

We find that in some narrowly defined circumstances, the DPRK might explode its nuclear weapons, either as a warning shot to slow or stop a war from developing, or in actual military use to stop a conventional force heading north over its borders. For reasons explained in this chapter, however, we argue that the DPRK's usage in this manner would be limited to its own territory, presenting a narrow, direct nuclear threat to its adversaries, friends, and neutral third parties except during an invasion, proliferation worries aside. Nonetheless, this contingency does present an operational challenge to the DPRK military, and we believe that they will have attended to this issue with their customary vigor, that is, making careful plans to maximize the security of their nuclear weapons and preparing where, when, and how the weapons would be used.

We conclude that measures are urgently needed to stabilize the DPRK political relationship with South Korea and the United States, and we suggest that a regional nuclear-weapon-free zone offers a way to create the required confidence by increasing transparency with respect to both DPRK and U.S. nuclear capacities in Korea.

INTRODUCTION

Scholars and practitioners of nuclear weapons strategy have long distinguished between the declaratory policy of a country with respect to nuclear weapons and its operational policies and practices. The latter may be embodied in and revealed by the type of research and development undertaken in a nuclear-armed country and manifested as the amazing variety of nuclear weapons and their effects:

- Electromagnetic "strikes" induced by atmospheric and exo-atmospheric explosions
- Atmospheric, submarine, and underground testing of nuclear weapons
- Testing and deployment of delivery systems
- Creation and training of nuclear-specific units and personnel, including the certification thereof
- The security and control of nuclear warheads by deployment forces
- Nuclear targeting and nuclear annexes to nuclear war plans
- Alert levels and force mobilization
- Warning and assessment sensors of nuclear attack
- Nuclear command authority, release authority, delegation of such, and the organizational cybernetics of such complex control systems
- The command-and-control and communications and intelligence systems required to achieve actual deployment or delivery of nuclear weapons to targets

Operational doctrine also encompasses the truly dismal dimensions of nuclear war, such as implementing preemptive strikes to decapitate the leadership of nuclear adversaries, nuclear defenses, the technical analysis and targeting-deployment requirements of city-busting and retaliatory nuclear strikes as the basis of "stable" mutual nuclear deterrence, grappling with the irresoluble dilemmas of nuclear war termination, and finally the horrors of post-nuclear-war reconstitution of nuclear-armed states.[1]

The terrors of nuclear war and its planning also motivated nuclear-armed states to create and implement a subset of nuclear operations called "arms control." This field of nuclear operations took the form of highly technical procedures and codified organizational routines to limit or dismantle nuclear weapons or delivery systems in order to increase confidence between nuclear adversaries, based on monitoring and verification systems, and thereby stabilize the nuclear balance of terror. Thus, in addition to compellence and deterrence, nuclear operations also set out to evoke reassurance, between adversaries as well as between the United States and its allies upset that they might be sacrificed in a limited nuclear war between the nuclear superpowers.

Almost always, a divergence, sometimes dramatic, exists between what a country's leaders say and what its nuclear war planners and military units do. This dissonance is not because the latter are somehow rogue or out of control, but because in the largely and thankfully mostly imaginary world of nuclear war, words and symbols matter as much with respect to the psychology of threat on which the realization of deterrence, compellence, and reassurance effects are based as the physical and organizational reality of the actual weapons. Of course, the latter are needed at some level of visibility to lend credibility to the words—even if it is a nuclear-armed state, such as Israel, that seeks the deep ambiguity of total opacity with respect to intentions and capacity.

However, nuclear weapons states can use declaratory policy to gain leverage from words as well as offer insight into the intention of the leaders who control these weapons. The capacities can lend credibility to these words or provide useful ambiguity as to their significance, even in cases where the capacities themselves may be weak or overstated. Declaratory doctrine can provide clues about the a state's likely operational doctrine, on the assumption that a degree of consistency between intention and capacity is likely to be desirable and necessary for the leaders of a nuclear-armed state to achieve its goals. In addition, the status of the operational doctrine combined with an estimate of the physical nuclear warhead and delivery capacities controlled by that state can also provide clues about its leaders' intentions and the extent to which they are able or striving to leverage political or other gains by threatening to act in an incredible way—that is, to detonate nuclear weapons against actual targets.

During the Cold War, rivers of ink were spilled in endless reports on topics such as net assessment of nuclear forces, counterforce exchange, relative nuclear superiority, how many warheads could fit on the head of a missile, and other near-metaphysical nuclear-related questions to which there were no right answers—the reason being that only a global nuclear war could provide real data, but no one would be around to collect it after such a war because most nuclear analysts lived in cities that were likely targets and would be dead or dying. Thus, analysts were free to make outrageous statements—in one notorious case during the Reagan administration, calling for deployment of cardboard missiles in Europe on the grounds that satellite imagery by the Soviets would lead to strategic deception to U.S. advantage. In many respects, the Star Wars missile defense system was just such a threat, resting not on any physical reality or credible strategy but rather on Soviet fears of U.S. technological prowess—that is, the image of precision-guided missiles U.S. pole-vaulting past their clunky missiles carrying gigantic nuclear warheads.

North Korea's leaders have watched this game for decades, studying U.S. nuclear doctrine and practice in the South in great depth, as well as its global and regional nuclear doctrines and practices, and also that of other nuclear-armed states, such as Israel, China, Russia, and more recently, Pakistan and India. Clearly, strategic ambiguity verging on opacity with regard to both intention and capacity was the basis for the DPRK's slow-motion proliferation action accompanied by an evolving arsenal of threat rhetoric in the 1990s. Thus, the presence of International Atomic Energy Agency (IAEA) inspectors was allowed at key points in the nuclear crisis not to encourage confidence in the DPRK's intention to cooperate henceforth with monitoring and safeguards but rather to send a message of threat with regard to both the DPRK's intentions and slowly increasing capacity to accumulate sufficient material to make one or more plutonium-based weapons.

Now that the DPRK has tested twice (the 2006 test was a less-than-one-kiloton dud, while the 2009 test was a sure-fire, rather small nuclear explosion by the standards of other testing states), it has removed some of the ambiguity that obstructed a clear view of its intentions and capacities since 1987, when the issue of DPRK nuclear weapons potential first erupted onto the radar screen of U.S. policymakers. We now have slightly more information on the DPRK's ostensible declaratory doctrine than we do with respect to its operational doctrine, due to its many pronouncements of nuclear threat and its specific attempt to match the U.S. Nuclear Posture Review in April 2010 with a DPRK Nuclear Posture Review later that month.[2]

Nonetheless, the laws of physics and logistical and operational aspects that arise from capacity and constraints thereon provide indications of how North Korea's operational doctrine will evolve, regardless of its declaratory doctrine. Putting it bluntly, the North Korean leadership or foreign ministry is free to air their opinions in whatever way they see fit at the moment, but the military has to plan for the secure and reliable operation of nuclear weapons in a serious, calculated, and purposeful manner. Analysts can infer much from what is already known about its past and current military posture and practices, its level of technology and its various delivery and logistical systems, and its command-and-control structure and related technical supporting systems such as communications and intelligence infrastructure. We develop below our best guess of the practical options open to the DPRK military for creating a nuclear operational doctrine as they weaponize or deploy their fissile material.

TECHNICAL AND LOGISTICAL CONSTRAINTS
ON DPRK NUCLEAR OPERATIONS

Some facts about North Korea's nuclear capacities are now known and more or less uncontested. First, we know that the DPRK has a limited maximum stock of plutonium with which to make more nuclear explosives, thereby setting an upper limit on the number of warheads they can deploy on delivery vehicles. This limit is roughly ten to twelve crude nuclear devices, of which two weapons' worth of plutonium have already been used in the two tests.

Second, the probabilities are that the DPRK has a crude nuclear device that is large and heavy, on the order of a ton, not a small warhead that can be deployed easily on a missile or aircraft.[3] The possibility is faint that the small yield of its second nuclear test signifies that it achieved unprecedentedly brilliant scientific shortcuts to miniaturize its warhead, which none of the other states that have developed or tested nuclear weapons have achieved, or that they had some rented foreign professional help, perhaps from footloose nuclear scientists and technicians from another nuclear-armed state, although this scenario is not probable based on public information. Generally, the DPRK's military and civilian technology is decades old—some of it harking back to the 1950s—and is clunky, primarily mechanical in nature, and artisanal in production. North Korea is very poor on systems engineering for reliable, complex machines, as anyone who has worked in its industrial plants or stood up close to one of their weapon systems can attest. "Brute force" and "heavy metal" are terms that come to mind. For ideological reasons, DPRK production units work at high speed with centralized command, based on the notion that fast failure and rapid recovery is better than slow, precise assembly of seamlessly integrated modules that lead to reliable performance under extreme conditions.

Nuclear operations are characterized by extreme conditions. For example, reentry vehicles carrying warheads returning to earth at about thirteen thousand miles per hour must survive tremendous shock loadings and vibration induced by atmospheric buffeting.[4] The DPRK is decades away from achieving such capacity, which would take scores of tests per missile system. If they ever create a sufficient system to test, after testing technology and components, they would need to perform the following:

- Research and development tests (typically twenty to thirty tests for missile types in the United States)
- Initial operational tests (typically thirty to forty tests for U.S. missiles)
- Demonstration and shakedown operational tests (typically two to ten tests for U.S. submarine and air force missiles)
- Operational follow-up tests (typically three to six tests per year per missile type for U.S. submarine and air force intercontinental missiles)[5]

The former Soviet Union and Russia today require similar levels of testing. Even China, with a much smaller nuclear missile force, conducts many tests of its missiles.

So far, the DPRK has tested three long-range, multistage rockets, none of which launched a reentry vehicle, and all of which have failed.[6] Put simply, if we give each warhead a fifty/fifty probability of successful detonation based on tests to date, and each missile a few percent probability of successful launch of a warhead to somewhere outside the territorial airspace of the DPRK into the upper atmosphere or outer space, and a further estimate of zero probability of successful reentry (as the DPRK has never tested a reentry vehicle), the probability of a successful intermediate or long-range missile-delivered nuclear warhead (assuming one exists with a fuse and navigation system that can survive the ride) would therefore be 50% times 2% times 0%, equaling a 0% probability of success.

Like their long-range cousins, DPRK intermediate- and short-range missiles are notoriously unreliable at launch and inaccurate in impact. For this reason alone, we judge that proposals to deliver scarce and precious nuclear warheads by missiles to be insufficiently credible to pass a laugh test for a national nuclear commander with any level of rationality. And if he or she is irrational and decides to launch a nuclear attack using a missile, the probabilities are that it will blow up on the ground or mid-air somewhere over the DPRK, over international waters, or somewhere other than the intended target. North Korea is clearly not prepared to launch a nuclear missile attack.

In a strictly theoretical sense, the DPRK has a limited delivery capacity. North Korea's nuclear warheads are likely large and heavy. In principle, they can be delivered to a detonation site by a bomber, by sea in a surface or submarine vessel, by truck, or by rail. Each of these delivery systems is sufficiently reliable in a mechanical sense to transfer a warhead to a location with a high degree of confidence, provided the vehicle is not under attack and is well-serviced or travels in convoy with immediate redundancy if one unit fails, although this approach entails keeping heavy lifting equipment in the convoy.

The DPRK does possess some old bombers from the 1950s, 1960s, and late 1970s—about twenty imported Soviet Frogfoot SU-25s—capable of hauling a large nuclear bomb and dropping it over a target, either in a suicide mission, as the explosion could envelop the plane, or in a parachute-delayed drop while the plane tries to escape.[7] Yet there is no evidence that the DPRK has bombers capable of toss-bombing, in which the plane uses its velocity in a dive or in pulling up at time of release to impart an upward direction to the bomb, thus making it a separate ballistic object upon release. In principle, a DPRK bomber could try to loft a nuclear weapon from the North's side of the DMZ in a surprise attack onto the South or combined forces in or south of the DMZ, but no evidence exists that the DPRK has pilots or planes with this capacity.

Moreover, the idea that the DPRK would start a war by lobbing a nuclear bomb over the DMZ when the reliability of the warhead inside the bomb is dubious— currently fifty/fifty at best, in a static instrumented test underground, not to mention a dynamic ballistic trajectory from a bomb tossed from a plane above the DMZ—strains credulity. That the U.S. and ROK air defenses would allow a DPRK aircraft to approach the DMZ directly at high speed—leaving no time to veer away before crossing the DMZ before firing on it—is also incredible, although slightly less so perhaps than the notion that the DPRK would ever attempt to deliver a nuclear strike in such a manner.

The same argument of incredibility applies to the notion of a high-altitude electromagnetic strike by the DPRK against combined forces in the ROK.[8] In both cases, simply too much risk of failure is present for a rational decisionmaker to launch such a strike. Nuclear weapons states developed electromagnetic pulse (EMP)–specific nuclear warheads based on considerable atmospheric and, after 1962, extensive underground nuclear testing.[9] The effects of EMP are very complex, perhaps generating electromagnetic peak radiation that is converted into strong electric currents and high voltages that damage or disable electrical and electronic equipment and systems. The EMP footprint of atmospheric weapons varies greatly with altitude; for example, a weapon exploded at a few miles affects a radius of about three miles, whereas a ground burst has a much smaller effect. With only one underground test and no atmospheric tests to date, the DPRK has little capacity to launch an EMP attack. Moreover, the vulnerability of DPRK technology to EMP effects relative to those of U.S.-ROK systems is unknowable, but one should not assume that the advantage lies with the DPRK due to its reliance on underground or electromechanical devices. Many of the U.S.-ROK systems were hardened during the Cold War against EMP effects, and upgrades are already under way. Claims that the DPRK projects a plausible electromagnetic pulse threat from an airburst nuclear explosion at this stage of primitive warhead development verge on the ludicrous, yet such claims appear in authoritative Western reference materials.[10]

Seaborne delivery is more credible but still unlikely. Admittedly, the DPRK has a large fleet of high-speed patrol boats, small and midget submarines, and a fish-trawling fleet that could move a nuclear weapon into place for detonation, presumably a suicide mission. Again, though, the chances of detection and capture well before such a vessel reaches its coastal or port-city target are finite given the number of such vessels that have been captured or attacked and destroyed by U.S.-ROK forces over the decades. ROK and U.S. naval forces are more alert than ever to DPRK naval and submarine incursions after the attack on the ROK warship *Cheonan* in March 2010.

Given the limited number of nuclear weapons that the DPRK may be able to field and the consequences that would follow discovery and capture, we do not believe that Pyongyang would approve prepositioning a nuclear weapon in South Korea or overseas. Moreover, nuclear communications for exercising command and control over such a delivery unit would be susceptible to interception and to disruption by jamming or equipment failure. That North Korea's leaders would predelegate authority to such a unit to deliver a nuclear strike outside of the DPRK is not credible. Too many things could go wrong, and the consequences of failure could be catastrophic to the DPRK leadership. The same applies, only more so, to possible use of non-state actors or terrorists to deliver proxy attacks that are deniable but sourced from the DPRK against the United States, Japan, or other targets. This view does not preclude the possibility that the DPRK may share or trade its nuclear capacities, such as test data, with another state (such as Iran, as Maria Rost Rublee suggests in her chapter in this volume), but the notion that the DPRK's leaders, in command of the most controlling political system in human history, would hand over their most precious security asset to non-state actors that they do not control is also not credible. That they might somehow spirit whole, usable nuclear weapons over borders and into targets such as U.S. cities or islands in the west Pacific is also incredible, for the same reason that seaborne attacks by North Korea do not make sense.

One other possibility is worth mentioning: the DPRK could use an undiscovered tunnel under the DMZ to conduct a surface "pop-up" surprise nuclear detonation south of the DMZ in ROK territory. However, the exit point of such a tunnel is unlikely to coincide with a U.S. or ROK military facility or other high-value site. These tunnels were intended for moving large numbers of ground forces into the ROK and needed to survive concealed indefinitely, so the exits of tunnels—at least those discovered to date—tend to be in relatively unpopulated areas. Such a use would have noteworthy shock value and is worthy of serious consideration by South Korean and Western planners, but the option does not appear to be attractive to DPRK planners. As similar usage in an unpopulated zone just north of the DMZ would have a similar psychological effect without inviting immediate retaliation by virtue of exploding a nuclear weapon on ROK territory, we see little marginal value and therefore little likelihood that DPRK war planners would emplace nuclear weapons south of the DMZ.

DELIVERY OF NUCLEAR STRIKES INSIDE THE DPRK

The DPRK is not limited to using nuclear weapons outside the DPRK. Even in its present rudimentary form, the DPRK now has a very basic nuclear deterrent that it could use against attackers who cross into the North. We should consider the possibility of both offensive and defensive use of nuclear weapons inside the DPRK itself. An offensive use would involve nuclear explosions in the DPRK coupled with conventional attack on the ROK, while defense use could include nuclear explosions coupled with defensive operations against U.S.-ROK attack, either in preemption or in a retaliatory strike in response to a conventional DPRK attack. We analyze these strategic options below, but first we describe how the DPRK might logistically support deployment of nuclear weapons for such an explosion.

Our culling of the list of hypothetical delivery systems for the DPRK's small number of nuclear weapons brings us to truck or rail delivery—or a combination of the two—to sites inside the DPRK itself. In principle, either system could be used to move nuclear weapons around North Korea. However, using rail transport is unlikely compared to trucks for many reasons, not least of which are the susceptibility of trains to surveillance and attack; trucks can disperse very quickly, but trains are sitting ducks for modern weapons, especially drones and cruise missiles, and the DPRK railway system mostly does not go to where the DPRK would likely deploy its weapons.

Whereas the fissile material was developed outside of the Korean People's

Army (KPA), the DPRK military now almost certainly controls the nuclear warheads as well as the delivery systems—most likely a dedicated fleet of specially trained security and transport crews and vehicles. Trucks can be camouflaged, and North Korean convoys do not yet present a distinctive pattern unique to DPRK nuclear transport. U.S. and Soviet nuclear transport logistics did reveal such patterns over time, but at this time, unless a nuclear weapons convoy departs significantly from standard practice or can be identified immediately upon egress from a rear storage location—most likely underground—a nuclear transport unit would likely not be distinguishable from a standard KPA truck convoy. U.S. intelligence may have already monitored the logistics of moving material from Yongbyon to other sites and have prepared a list of possible storage sites based on tracking of transport vehicles from Yongbyon to known KPA military sites. The same type of tracking may have been done for the transport vehicles used to deliver equipment to nuclear test sites in the DPRK's northeast mountains. Of course, the DPRK military is intensely aware of close U.S. monitoring and may have already conducted deception tactics designed to confuse or mislead U.S. intelligence by creating decoys.

At this time, we can only speculate about the location of KPA nuclear weapons units. Given the density of underground sites in the DPRK, it seems likely that the devices are stored deep underground in caves with multiple exits in case of attack. The weapons units are also likely stored in two or three locations in order to minimize the risk of successful preemptive attack by the ROK or the United States, although multiple sites also present greater requirements for elite security forces and increase the probability of unique signatures that various types of intelligence may identify. One site may be impossible to find; three may be obvious. Furthermore, we conclude that the KPA controls these sites, which are most likely located in northern rear areas, especially in the mountains where tunnels can be dug horizontally, thereby creating an easily transited infrastructure for such convoys combined with almost immediate massive overhead protection, plus multiple entry-exit points.

An important operational issue is whether the plutonium pits or shaped fissile material used in a warhead are co-located with the warhead itself or are stored separately to enhance controls against unauthorized release and usage. This situation presents increased vulnerability in some respects because a successful attack on or loss of control of the stock of pitless warheads renders the pits useless for military purposes; however, co-location of the pits with or integrated into warheads presents obvious risk of premature release and usage due to command or communication errors. Our guess is that, given the likelihood that rear storage is preferred in non-wartime or routine operations, the pit and warheads are kept separate.

NORTH KOREA'S NUCLEAR USE OPTIONS

Recognizing all the constraints outlined above and considering the strategic imperatives that drive the DPRK's political and military options in wartime or at the brink of a war, we see only two possible operational strategies for the DPRK's actual use of nuclear weapons under present conditions.[11] Both entail pre-emplacement, likely early in a crisis to minimize vulnerability in the transport operation, in tunnels or holes in the attack corridors across the DMZ north and northeast of Seoul.

The first possible usage is pre-war but at the brink of a crisis in which the two sides have already exchanged blows across the DMZ. In this situation, the DPRK might use nuclear weapons at these sites in tunnels or holes in the attack corridors across the DMZ north or northeast of Seoul to signal the danger of the situation—the risk of all-out war, including the faint but conceivable possibility of all-out artillery and rocket attack on ROK population centers or U.S.-ROK military forces massing along the DMZ—and to invoke the intervention of China and Russia to slow the northward advance of U.S. and ROK forces. However, a serious problem with this scenario would be that a subterranean or ground-level nuclear explosion would create an immense cloud of radioactive material that could, depending on winds, either drift over the DPRK itself, killing or rendering useless its own forces and population, or over the ROK, leading to powerful pressures for U.S. and ROK forces to accelerate rather than to back off from a conventional attack against the DPRK.

A variant on this scenario would be to deploy one or more weapons to the coastal waters of the DPRK and explode them at sea. As a method of ringing a very loud alarm bell, this approach would be slightly less hazardous than ground bursts north of the DMZ. Sea deployment would entail, however, a less secure route with possible interdiction and is therefore unlikely to be used.

An acute dilemma that this approach implies is that if the DPRK does not pre-deploy forward weapons required for the second use of the land-mines option (see below—the use of nuclear warheads to create impassable craters or to demolish attacking forces heading north), then moving these weapons into place after the early-warning shots due to their vulnerability to discovery and attack during deployment may not be possible. Early forward deployment also poses the risk of seizure by U.S.-ROK forces in an actual war, which would be highly undesirable for the DPRK for two reasons: if it were already facing a substantial loss of territory but not yet forced to surrender, and because of the intelligence gains that recovery of a DPRK nuclear device would give the United States and South Korea. This problem suggests that the command might forward deploy only one or two, given how unreliable they may be in DPRK configurations, and keep most of its small nuclear arsenal rear-based, recognizing that no actual usage option serves the DPRK's military strategy in actual combat.

In this regard, the Korean People's Army is a latecomer to nuclear war and may not have played an important role in nuclear activities that produced usable fissile material, other than providing perimeter security. In many respects, the KPA is a conservative organization that may not take kindly to concepts of nuclear operations that invite attack and divert resources from conventional operations. The KPA has had a patently inadequate nuclear operations strategy against U.S. nuclear attack in past decades. The core of this strategy was to fortify installations and dig tunnels to protect occupants from radiological contamination if attacked with nuclear weapons; soldiers sitting underground aren't fighting. The soldiers above ground were told to take cover, and then rise, put on a gas mask, and return to fighting—as if nuclear explosions or their after-effects would somehow go away.[12] We are doubtful that the KPA at this time has embraced detailed nuclear war planning and operations, let alone serious exercises and training. In some respects, the KPA's likely cautious approach restrains the political command in the DPRK, but it also encourages possible improvisation in the midst of crisis—a dangerous dynamic with possible loss of control or inadvertent usage.

Assuming that the DPRK's plutonium arsenal was not held in reserve or exploded as warning shots to slow or stop a war, then a second possible use of DPRK nuclear capability is to explode the weapons for direct military purposes, as opposed to the warning or deterrent use described in option one. This second option is physically similar to the first, although the purpose is quite different. In case a few warning shots did not stop a war, the command could order that the remaining emplaced warheads be fired en masse as enemy ground forces crossed into North Korea. Ground-level explosions would decimate ground forces with direct and indirect blast effects, create large and impassable craters in the corridors, and eject into the atmosphere massive amounts of highly radioactive material that, depending on wind direction, could further reduce the ability of U.S. or ROK ground forces to use these corridors for preemptive or retaliatory attacks by armored mobile ground forces. U.S. nuclear artillery and gravity bombs were envisioned in the late 1970s to produce just such an effect on DPRK offensive ground forces. At that time, detailed studies were done to determine the effects of various levels of U.S. nuclear attack on target arrays presented by DPRK divisions that managed to make shallow and deep incursions into combined forces south of the DMZ.

Why U.S. and ROK forces would put themselves at risk to this obvious possible use of DPRK nuclear weapons as land mines is not clear. Moreover, the DPRK would need to use all of its nuclear weapons to make the corridors impassable; one or two would be insufficient. Perhaps the high command would keep one warhead rear-based and in reserve in such a strategy, but most warheads would be used simultaneously and in a concentrated area in order to achieve a meaningful effect, because the DPRK has only eight to twelve devices in the first place.

We do not see any credible option for rapid intrawar deployment of rear-based nuclear warheads around the DPRK to block highly maneuverable U.S. forces poised to come ashore in an amphibious operation, standing offshore to occupy a port city such as Wonsan or Nampo, or to attack air-mobile special forces as they land in the DPRK at key points. The only means fast enough—cargo aircraft, bombers, or helicopters—would be too vulnerable to ROK and U.S. attack and could not reliably deliver nuclear warheads for use against incoming or already established combined forces.

The wartime attack described above would be a truly desperate act by the KPA, more of a delaying tactic than a strategic use of nuclear weapons. However, leaving such usage until U.S. and ROK forces are already moving into, over, around, and under DPRK territory via submarines in an all-out envelopment would also be problematic; the central command could easily lose communication and control connectivity with the nuclear field units. Such an intended usage thus implies that the national command is willing to predelegate use of the weapons to the judgment of nuclear unit commanders on an individual basis in a nuclear suicide mission. We are dubious that the high command would adopt such a strategy, which is contrary to the extraordinarily centralized nature of KPA control systems, organizational control structures, and strategic logic.

This usage is also inherently problematic from a military perspective. Ironically, U.S. and ROK forces are far better equipped and trained to operate under radiologically dangerous conditions than DPRK forces, and any North Korean troops caught in the fallout would find themselves at great disadvantage in attempting to continue to fight incoming U.S. and ROK ground forces.

Such attacks would also risk a nuclear retaliatory response on an annihilative scale by the United States against the DPRK leadership—not an inviting prospect to the national commanders involved, no matter how loyal or committed they are to the regime, especially those commanders like the Kims themselves who personify the regime through the ubiquitous presence of their images in offices, classrooms, and so forth. But once forward deployed, and after a warning nuclear explosion or two, moving the remaining warheads back from the attack corridors should a war continue would be immensely risky. Not firing them would mean that the warheads would fall into the hands of the U.S. and ROK forces, which suggests that the high command would have to predelegate use authority on the basis of use-them-or-lose-them—a dilemma that worried U.S. security officials when they discovered that nuclear weapons were deployed at the DMZ itself in 1971, leading first to their removal from the DMZ, then to relocation at bases further south and, finally, storage at Kunsan Air Base, from where they were finally withdrawn in February 1992. For this reason alone, we are doubtful that the North Korean leadership would adopt this choice, but it is the logical outcome of the only military-use option that we believe to be even marginally credible given what we know about the KPA, its command-and-control system, its posture, its nuclear warheads and related delivery systems, and the countervailing forces to which it must respond.

CONCLUSION

As noted earlier, we have not addressed in this chapter the rhetorical dimension of declaratory doctrine that bears heavily on North Korea's nuclear intent (we have tackled that task in a separate paper[13]). Here, we note that the aggressive tone of DPRK nuclear threat statements should not be interpreted to imply that the DPRK's operational doctrine is similarly careless. Words are cheap; nuclear actions are expensive—in terms of the operational demands on organizations, security requirements, logistical imperatives, and above all, the risks implied by actual use in the midst of a real or imagined military crisis.

By the same token, we should not automatically assume that the DPRK has obtained the military capacity to match its threats, that "those who seek to bring down the system in the DPRK . . . will fall victim to the unprecedented nuclear strikes of the invincible army and the just war to be waged by all the infuriated service personnel and people."[14] The DPRK nuclear rhetoric is dangerous and should be taken seriously, but the DPRK's nuclear force does not yet represent a major military threat to anyone but itself—in that it diverts resources away from conventional forces that are its real strength and the regime could only explode its nuclear weapons on DPRK territory, to their own detriment. As Jong-Kun Choi and Jong-Yun Bae argue in this volume, a conventional threat already exists, and little marginal military deterrence is gained by the crude nuclear capacity that the North presently controls. Making countervailing nuclear threats is not helpful in clarifying DPRK intentions; such threats evoke highly provocative nuclear threat statements from the DPRK that have little to do with its nuclear weapons capacity. One implication of the study this chapter is that, over time, everything should be done to help the DPRK adjust its declaratory policy to be consistent with its limited nuclear armament, and to suggest that a minimalist doctrine is more realistic and credible than a flamboyantly overstated doctrine that suggests capacities that do not exist.

If our argument is correct—that the sole use of nuclear weapons in the DPRK would be defensive in the context of all-out war—then Georgy Toloraya's implicit thesis by in chapter 6 that North Korea's nuclear weapons have a stabilizing effect cannot be correct.[15] Nor, for the same reason, can we accept the North Koreans' assertion that the DPRK's possession of nuclear weapons has had a "deterrence effect" whereby "the danger of the outbreak of a war has noticeably reduced."[16] The DPRK's rhetoric is provocative and destabilizing, and its recent military actions have also destabilized the peninsula. But its actual nuclear military capacities have little to do with that effect, which derives from the perceptions of the North's intentions as defined symbolically, not by virtue of credible deployed nuclear weapons capacities and development of a North Korean operational nuclear doctrine. Thus, we also concur with the conclusions of Jong-Kun Choi and Jong-Yun Bae in this volume that the DPRK's nuclear capacities add nothing to the ability of its conventional forces to attack Seoul, and similarly, to its ability to deter attack on the DPRK itself. At this time, the DPRK's nuclear weapons are almost completely symbolic-psychological threats and are therefore amenable to a political and psychological rather than military response from the United States and South Korea.

In this regard, we point to a vexing issue that pertained during the Cold War between the former Soviet Union and the United States but was never adequately theorized nor addressed. As Paul Bracken pointed out at the time, nuclear weapons organizations are complex entities that often distort outcomes intended by high-level decisionmakers, or lead to perverse, unintended actions that are invisible to those at the top.[17] At that time, Soviet nuclear forces were directed by an extraordinarily centralized command-and-control system, one that tended to go on to high levels of alert in response to stimulus at its territorial edges, and then tended to amplify error by rapid mobilization with inevitable loss of control and implementation.

U.S. nuclear and conventional forces, on the other hand, were organized into devolved, self-contained, unified geographic and regional functional-service commands, a system that tended to dampen the propagation of error from one loosely coupled system to another. The problem of instability arose not because of the existence of either system per se, although each had intrinsic propensities toward first use based on the nature of nuclear weapons and delivery systems that drives commanders towards preemptive first use at the brink of a crisis. Rather, the problem of instability arose because of the interaction of the two systems; U.S. forward deployed forces were constantly probing at the edges of the Soviet system, and the Soviet system was constantly mobilizing and propagating error during the Cold War, a game of risk taking that could have ended human life on the planet had it spun out of control.

The same problem exists today in Korea on a much smaller scale. What steps might U.S.-ROK forces take to reduce the probability of DPRK first use in any circumstance? Hotlines, agreements to keep naval forces separate (as were signed between the Soviet Union and the United States), understandings with regard to alert levels, and technology to ensure that warheads are controlled in all circumstances are just a few of the measures that must now be considered to ensure that the probability of nuclear first use or loss of control is pushed toward zero. Even a tiny probability of possible first use or loss of control is too high, given the stakes involved in Korea to all the parties in the ongoing Korean conflict.

In this regard, a higher degree of transparency about the reality of U.S. nuclear weapons and war planning with regard to the DPRK is an important possible stabilizing factor. In spite of its still-vast nuclear arsenals, like North Korea the United States actually has only a few options for delivering and detonating a nuclear weapon in the DPRK.[18] To fire an intercontinental nuclear missile or missiles at the DPRK would present an immediate threat to Russia and China, and neither would agree nor stand by if the United States were to prepare for such an attack. The only other options, such as a bomber flying all the way from the United States, are too slow.

The only way for the DPRK to obtain a meaningful guarantee that the United States is no longer targeting the DPRK and will not attack the DPRK with nuclear weapons is for the DPRK to be a part of a treaty-based, nuclear-weapon-free zone.[19] In such a zone, the DPRK (like other parties) would have access to a regional monitoring and verification scheme assuring that U.S. nuclear weapons are not deployed in either the ROK or Japan. The reciprocal opportunity would be available to the ROK and other parties to a regional nuclear-weapon-free zone.

A nuclear-weapon-free zone would assure the DPRK that the United States has irrevocably removed the explicit nuclear threat from the Korean peninsula. We cannot imagine the resumption of authentic, meaningful negotiations over the DPRK's nuclear program between the United States and the DPRK without the provision of a legally binding U.S. guarantee of nonuse of nuclear weapons against the North. Either the ROK or Japan could initiate dialogue for a nuclear-weapon-free zone with regional states, leaving the door open for a denuclearized DPRK to join at a future date. Alternately, the DPRK could join at the onset on a provisional basis but delaying full compliance with the zone, as was the case with Argentina and Brazil and the Treaty of Tlatelolco.[20]

A Korea-Japan nuclear-weapon-free zone would also reinforce the commitment of Japan and the ROK to forever be non-nuclear-weapon states, an issue of particular concern to China. It would also reinforce the U.S. security commitment to the ROK, as it would necessitate a more explicit reliance on conventional military forces to support the U.S.-ROK security alliance and avoid any tendency to substitute cheap nuclear deterrence for proper conventional force planning and deployment.

Such a zone might take years to develop and result in the denuclearization of the Korean Peninsula, or it might emerge quickly as a neat solution to a messy set of security dilemmas in the region. Creating the zone should be attempted because it is the only way for the DPRK to obtain a legally binding negative nuclear security assurance from the United States were the North to denuclearize—something that the United States has not put on the table in nearly two decades of dialogue. Although it is not a panacea and is insufficient by itself to induce the DPRK to denuclearize, even slowly, we believe that this gradual approach is more likely to result in the eventual denuclearization of the Korean Peninsula than the brinksmanship; on-again, off-again negotiations; or strategic neglect that have characterized U.S.-DPRK relations for years. We believe that a nuclear-free-zone is the only peaceful way to resolve the North Korean nuclear crisis. All efforts should be made to pursue that zone at the earliest date.

CHAPTER TWO

North Korean Nuclear Weaponization: A U.S. Policy Failure

GREGORY J. MOORE

Given North Korea's nuclear tests in 2006, 2009, and 2013, it is clear that the United States' North Korea nuclear policy since at least the late 1990s has been a failure. U.S. policy goals regarding North Korea's nuclear programs have focused primarily on deterring North Korea from developing nuclear weapons and preventing North Korea from proliferating to other states technology, know-how, or materials related to its nuclear program. Yet since 2002 North Korea has withdrawn from the Nuclear Non-Proliferation Treaty (NPT), ejected international inspectors from its plutonium processing facilities, removed monitoring devices, and declared itself a nuclear-weapons-club member by testing with marginal success a rudimentary nuclear device. The DPRK has shown itself not only willing to proliferate nuclear technology and materials, as well as the missile hardware and technology to potentially deliver them, but to have already done so to Iran, Pakistan, and Syria, and perhaps Myanmar/Burma as well.[1] In short, the administrations of Presidents Bill Clinton, George W. Bush, and Barack Obama have failed to deter North Korea from developing and testing nuclear weapons, and they have failed to keep North Korea from proliferating nuclear weapons technology and materials to states of concern to the United States.

The United States has made several noteworthy efforts to address the North Korean nuclear issue. The 1994 Agreed Framework was a good attempt to address the issue, although it ultimately failed. Former assistant secretary of state for East Asian and Pacific affairs Christopher Hill's attempts via bilateral meetings within the Six Party Talks to draw North Korea into agreement with the United States during the George W. Bush administration were also admirable.

Moreover, U.S. flexibility—shown in the February 13, 2007, agreement reached with North Korea and the October 2008 removal of North Korea from the list of state sponsors of terrorism were good-faith efforts on Washington's part and certainly moves in the right direction. Unfortunately, they were still too little, too late.

As has been the case with U.S. policy toward Cuba, the United States has preferred to isolate North Korea rather than pursuing the path it followed with China—then another isolated state—in the 1970s: recognizing and engaging constructively with it. Despite its imperfections today, China and Chinese foreign policy behavior have changed remarkably since the change in U.S. policy toward it. This is not true of Cuba, however, nor is it true of North Korea, which begs the question: Why doesn't the United States try something truly novel in its dealings with North Korea? In this sense, today's U.S. policymakers have much to learn from Richard Nixon and Henry Kissinger, who exhibited fortitude and creativity in forging a radically new policy toward China in the early 1970s during the height of the Vietnam War and the Cold War.

In this chapter I first provide a brief overview of U.S. policy toward the Democratic People's Republic of Korea (DPRK) in its attempt to resolve the North Korean nuclear issue. Second, I discuss the problems—within the George W. Bush administration in particular—that led to policy failure. Finally, I conclude with a discussion of a new approach for U.S. North Korea policy. The new approach embraces two ideas: the need for a permanent multilateral security mechanism in Northeast Asia and the need for a preventive or preemptive U.S. action toward North Korea. Such action should involve what might be called "preemptive normalization" of relations with the DPRK, in other words a U.S. move that would preempt North Korean nuclear operationalization and the potential nuclear proliferation that could come therewith. North Korea should perceive normalization not as a reward for finally accepting American demands, but as the starting point of a new bilateral relationship and a means to the end of North Korean denuclearization.

U.S. NORTH KOREA NUCLEAR POLICY
AND THE SIX PARTY TALKS
The Lead-Up to Agreement in 2007

The first North Korean nuclear crisis erupted in 1993 when North Korea stopped cooperating with the International Atomic Energy Agency (IAEA). Pyongyang had only recently signed the NPT, which the IAEA enforces. North

Korea's action prompted the IAEA to refer North Korea to the U.N. Security Council. After more than a year of ups and downs and grave tensions, the United States and North Korea worked out a compromise in October 1994 called the Agreed Framework. It was agreed that the DPRK would disable its nuclear reactors and that the South Koreans (primarily) would provide a number of light water reactors for North Korea's energy needs—both steps making nuclear proliferation more difficult. The United States would also provide fuel oil to help meet North Korea's energy needs until the new light water reactors were operational.

The 1994 Agreed Framework nearly collapsed in the later years of the Clinton administration, and its fate was sealed with the election of George W. Bush in 2000. Rather than accept Clinton's policy on North Korea, the Bush administration did a complete policy review in 2001 to determine its own options regarding North Korea. When South Korean president Kim Dae-jung visited Washington in March 2001, President Bush disappointed and embarrassed him, stating that he had serious doubts about North Korea's leader and the workability of any deals with his regime. Bush thus effectively dismissed Kim's Sunshine Policy toward the North. The Bush administration had decided that North Korea was not a reliable partner and put a freeze on all talks with Pyongyang, putting President Kim in an awkward position, because his Sunshine Policy was ultimately unworkable without Washington's support.

After the September 11, 2001, attack on the United States and the U.S. shift in focus to the "war on terror," U.S. attention focused away from the Korean peninsula, and U.S.-DPRK relations deteriorated again. As a result, Kim Jong-il turned to his nuclear weapons program to serve the threefold purpose of getting Washington's attention, giving him a bargaining chip with the United States, and potentially providing him with a powerful deterrent and security enhancer regarding any potential U.S. aggression. This last purpose became even more important to him in the face of the 2003 U.S. invasion of Iraq, when Kim reportedly went into hiding for a period of time, fearing an attack with the same bunker-busting munitions the United States was using to ferret out Saddam Hussein.

However, the more recent North Korean nuclear crisis began in the fall of 2002 when a North Korean diplomat told U.S. diplomat James Kelly in Beijing that North Korea was pursuing a uranium enrichment program,[2] confirming what many U.S. observers had concluded for some time. While Chinese observers were skeptical at the time of Pyongyang's claim, becoming believers only after North Korea's 2006 nuclear test, the Chinese were worried enough about the deterioration of U.S.-DPRK ties that they came forward with an initiative to deal with the North Korean nuclear issue. This initiative became known as the Six Party Talks, which China hosted, and which included China, North Korea, South Korea, the United States, Japan, and Russia. While under the Bush administration the United States had generally taken a rather unilateral approach to foreign policy matters, it insisted on a multilateral approach regarding North Korea. U.S. policymakers did not trust North Korea and had concluded that the only way to make Pyongyang accountable was in a multilateral context.

The Six Party Talks have been a limited success. The Chinese hosted round one of the talks in Beijing in August 2003, and while this round did not achieve much in terms of resolving the crisis, the important precedent of bringing the six parties together in one place was valuable in and of itself. A second round was held in Beijing in February 2004, a third in June 2004, and after little progress a fourth was held in stages in July, August, and September 2005. During this fourth round an apparent breakthrough was achieved in that North Korea promised to end its nuclear weapons programs in exchange for a U.S. pledge of nonaggression, U.S. and South Korean assistance in meeting the North's energy needs in lieu of its nuclear reactors, U.S. and Japanese pledges to move toward normalization of relations with the DPRK, and formal U.S. and South Korean declarations that they had no nuclear weapons on the Korean Peninsula. The United States had removed U.S. tactical nuclear weapons from South Korean soil in 1991 under President George H. W. Bush.

That fall the Six Party Talks stalled again with a new stipulation from Pyongyang that unless it was first given a light water reactor it would not begin disabling its nuclear facilities; another reason for the stability was North Korean unhappiness with U.S. actions and Chinese cooperation against the Banco Delta Asia, a bank in Macau that held North Korean funds. The United States argued that the funds were acquired by illegal North Korean activities, including money laundering and counterfeiting. The Six Party Talks were at an impasse throughout 2006, during which time the North conducted a series of live-fire missile tests and the test of a nuclear device, bringing tensions between North Korea and the United States to a new high.

The Six Party Talks would certainly have to have been judged a failure had they ended at this point. Yet despite the missile and nuclear tests in 2006, the talks continued in 2007; an agreement was reached—what came to be known as the February 13th (2007) Agreement—which seemed then to be the beginning of the end of the impasse, comprising the final phase of the fifth round of Six Party Talks. According to the February 13th Agreement, the DPRK would first halt operations at its Yongbyon facility, after which it would receive 50,000 tons of heavy fuel oil to assist in its energy needs. After closing its Yongbyon facility, the DPRK would make a full disclosure of all of its nuclear programs and close all other related facilities, after which it would receive another 950,000 tons of heavy fuel oil or its equivalent. Following that, the United States would being the process of removing North Korea from its list of state sponsors of terror and no longer apply the provisions of the U.S. Trading with the Enemy Act.[3] The details were worked out in a series of sixth-round meetings later in 2007, which also included the return of its Banco Delta Asia funds. As a result, the North not only closed and disassembled the Yongbyon facility, but destroyed its cooling tower in late June 2008. In October 2008, after a series of fits and starts, the United States took North Korea off its list of supporters of state-sponsored terrorism, removing an important obstacle to improved relations from the DPRK perspective. Things went downhill in 2009, however, with the North Korean missile tests in April and the second nuclear test in May, followed by UN resolutions and sanctions against Pyongyang, after which it said it would not return to the Talks. Pyongyang continues to seek bilateral talks with the United States but did tell visiting Chinese diplomats in the fall of 2009 that it would return to the Six Party Talks at some point. With the sinking of the South Korean naval ship *Cheonan* and the shelling of South Korea's Yeonpyeong Island in 2010, Seoul and Washington put a freeze on further talks with Pyongyang for the time being. Kim Jong-il's death in December 2011 provided another delay in progress toward resolution, but the Leap Day Agreement between the DPRK and the United States was reached in February 2012 under Pyongyang's new leadership, only to be derailed soon thereafter by Pyongyang's botched attempt to launch a satellite into space using banned long-range-missile technology. At the time of writing a resumption of the Six Party Talks appeared likely in the future, but the time is not certain.

U.S. Policy Failure

While the Six Party Talks have brought about some noteworthy achievements, and the United States has made a number of good efforts at resolving the crisis over the years, U.S. policy toward North Korea since 2000 (or even the mid-1990s) must be judged a failure for several reasons. First, of course, is that despite deterrent strategies, diplomatic efforts, ultimatums, and U.S.-sponsored UN Security Council resolutions, the United States has not prevented North Korea from acquiring and testing nuclear capabilities, nor have they kept

Pyongyang from developing enrichment capabilities.[4] In October 2006 North Korea joined the small club of nuclear nations with a low-yield underground nuclear test that was confirmed by Western, Chinese, and other sources, a feat repeated in May 2009 with slightly better results.[5]

Moreover, the United States has not prevented North Korea from transferring its nuclear technology to Iran, Pakistan, and Syria in recent years, and Pyongyang may be covertly helping Myanmar acquire nuclear capabilities as well. In some cases North Korea did so even as it was participating in multilateral talks to disarm, and despite its vows neither to develop nor transfer nuclear weapons technology.[6] All of this activity has been well-documented. For example, according to U.S. and Israeli sources, in September 2007 Israeli intelligence tracked a North Korean ship laden with nuclear material to a port in Syria, and then followed the cargo as it was delivered to a site in northeastern Syria. Israeli commandos snuck into Syria and took soil samples that, they say, proved the cargo was nuclear. Israel then bombed the site a few days later, destroying the building there and the cargo in question.[7] The site had already been under close surveillance by U.S. and Israeli observers, and being built there was a facility that had the "structural DNA" of North Korea's Yongbyon facility. Moreover, North Korean workers had been spotted at the site. According to Seymour Hersh, a senior Syrian military officer confirmed the military nature of the site, and this officer as well as a Syrian government official confirmed the presence of North Korean construction workers at the site.[8] Since the destruction of the site, Syrian officials bulldozed it, erected a new structure on it, and have refused to allow international inspectors to visit—all of which, intelligence analysts say, Syria would do to erase the site's nuclear footprint if in fact the site had been nuclear.

North Korea is also on record as having sold to Pakistan uranium hexafluoride, a compound that can be enriched to produce weapons-grade uranium. Pakistan then sold it to Libya, although it is not known if North Korea was aware of the product's final destination.[9] The Pakistan connection went both ways for Pyongyang, as intelligence now reveals that then–Pakistani prime minister Benazir Bhutto had agreed to supply North Korea with the know-how to develop highly enriched uranium when she visited North Korea in 1993.[10] The father of Pakistan's nuclear program, A. Q. Khan, also went on record prior to his arrest in 2004 as saying he and senior colleagues in Pakistan's military provided nuclear know-how to North Korea, and revelations in the fall of 2010 made it clear beyond doubt that North Korea has an advanced uranium enrichment program, something it long denied but about which it now boasts.[11]

North Korea has also been a proliferator of record to Iran, both in missile and nuclear technology. Reliable sources reveal that Iran had helped finance North Korea's nuclear program in exchange for nuclear technology, equipment, and cooperation on enriching uranium.[12] Iran and North Korea have also been cooperating on the joint development of nuclear warheads that could be married to North Korean No-dong missiles that North Korea and Iran were also jointly developing,[13] and Iran seems poised to follow North Korea's footsteps in developing and testing its own nuclear capabilities.[14] While President Bush had emphasized that "we are committed to keeping the world's most dangerous weapons out of the hands of the world's most dangerous people,"[15] all of these North Korean activities took place on his watch and have the makings of the post-9/11 nightmare scenario that U.S. policymakers have been striving to avoid. As Leon Sigal points out, no progress has been made under the Obama administration either, because of the U.S. decision to identify with South Korean president Lee Myung-bak's hard-line approach to Pyongyang—which Sigal argues drove North Korea further away—rather than crafting a more creative and proactive approach.[16] While U.S. leaders cannot be blamed for North Korean dishonesty, duplicity, and intransigence, the events outlined above provide evidence all the same of nothing less than a grave U.S. policy failure in regards to North Korea, a failure spanning the tenure of three presidents to date.

WHY HAS AMERICA'S NORTH KOREA POLICY BEEN UNSUCCESSFUL?

U.S. policy toward North Korea has been unsuccessful in recent years for a number of reasons. In this assessment of Washington's North Korea policy under the George W. Bush and Barack Obama administrations, I consider the reasons for the lack of success in resolving the standoff with Pyongyang as well as Pyongyang's own brinkmanship and intransigence.

The first source of policy failure was found in the Bush administration's initial ABC (Anything But Clinton) approach to foreign policy, documented by frustrated sources in the State Department during the first two years of the Bush presidency.[17] While some evidence existed that South Korean president Kim Dae-jung's Sunshine Policy had made headway in softening Pyongyang's position on a number of important international issues, a continuation of the Clinton-era Agreed Framework principles was a nonstarter for the new Bush team, which was in no mood to flow with South Korea's policy in 2001–2, when the time may have been truly ripe for a deal with Pyongyang.

Second was what might be called the neoconservative takeover of U.S. foreign policy during the George W. Bush years, as many sources document.[18] Of particular note here are the hawkish and influential roles of Dick Cheney as vice president, Donald Rumsfeld as secretary of defense, Paul Wolfowitz as deputy defense secretary, and Richard Perle as chairman of the Defense Policy Advisory Board. All of these men exercised important influence over the U.S. policy process and shared a view of the world that one might call, "democratic peace theory's shotgun wedding with offensive realism on steroids." These individuals were too often successful in pushing to the side the more rational, calculated views of first-term secretary of state Colin Powell. With the Obama administration this particular issue has gone away for the most part, needless to say.

Third, the Bush administration tended not to trust experts in their various fields of expertise, but to rely on generalists loyal to the administration. For example, in 2002–3, once the decision had been made to invade Iraq, experts on Iraq were boxed out of Iraq decisionmaking.[19] Instead, the Bush team tended to rely upon inexperienced but loyal foot soldiers of the administration for too many key posts and as consultants on too many important issues. My research leads me to conclude that this was the case with Washington's North Korea policy as well, as arms control experts took the lead on North Korea rather than persons with deeper Korean and East Asian area studies experience.[20]

Finally, one of the hallmarks of the Bush administration's approach to North Korea was a serious division within it on how to deal with the DPRK. During the first four years of the administration there was a general divergence in views between Secretary of State Colin Powell and the administration's neoconservatives. On North Korea there was perhaps an even deeper split, personified in the earlier years of the Bush administration in the divergence of views among the special envoy for talks with North Korea, Charles L. (Jack) Pritchard, and the hawkish Bob Joseph, undersecretary of state for arms control at the time.[21] In the second term of the Bush administration, the divergence in policy opinions on the DPRK continued with divisions between the State Department's lead DPRK negotiator, Christopher Hill, and Bush's ambassador to the United Nations, arms control specialist John Bolton, who maintains to this day that the bilateral meetings, the overall 2007 agreement with North Korea, and the removal of the DPRK from the state-sponsored terror list were all mistakes and a giveaway. The divisions within the Bush administration on how to deal with North Korea certainly played some role in explaining why Washington seemed engaged at some points and disengaged at others. This division in Washington over whether the carrot or the stick, engagement or containment, is the right approach to North Korea exists to this day.

The same holds true with the Obama administration. President Obama clearly extended a hand to Kim Jong-il, saying in the early days of his presidency that he would bring a fresh approach to Washington's North Korea policy. Though he was sincere in his desire to take a fresh approach to North Korea, according to Washington insiders,[22] North Korea made things more difficult for him Pyongyang responded with missile firings and another nuclear test in the first half of 2009, and the sinking of South Korea's navy corvette *Cheonan* and the bombardment of South Korea's Yeonpyeong Island in 2010. On top of these developments, South Korea's conservative Lee Myung-bak administration and Japan's recent governments have taken a harder line on Pyongyang, making a return to any kind of Sunshine Policy all but impossible. Moreover, as Victor Cha argues, what North Korea really wants is the deal the United States gave India: recognition as a nuclear power. As Cha also points out, and Dan Twining elaborates upon more deeply in his chapter in this volume, the United States will not likely give the India accommodation to the DPRK.[23] While Barack Obama had the desire to forge a new approach to North Korea, little progress is evident to date.

A major reason for Washington's lack of success in resolving the North Korean nuclear standoff is clearly Pyongyang's policies itself. While the Republican Congress that took office in late 1994 made it difficult if not impossible for the Clinton administration to keep all of the promises it made in the Agreed Framework, Pyongyang began cheating on its commitments early in the game and ultimately did not keep its agreements but rather moved forward with its nuclear program. In 2002 Pyongyang told U.S. diplomats it had a uranium enrichment program, which violated all its previous commitments, and then proceeded to withdraw from the Nuclear Non-Proliferation Treaty. Again in September 2005 an agreement was reached as a part of the Six Party Talks, but Pyongyang backed out. Pyongyang backed away from its commitments again with the February 2007 agreement in the Six Party Talks. In February 2012 the DPRK reached an accord with the United States in the Leap Day Agreement, but again in effect killed the deal with its April satellite/missile launch, which violated UN Security Council resolutions and Pyongyang's previous commitments. Its missile launches and nuclear tests between 2006 and 2013 were grave blows to any remaining goodwill in the international community toward North Korea. Certainly, the DPRK has not been an easy partner with which to reach an international agreement on its nuclear weapons programs, to say the least, and

Washington cannot be held responsible for Pyongyang's own dishonesty and intransigence.

Pyongyang's policies have posed a great dilemma for U.S. policymakers, yet Washington has made its mistakes in its approach to Pyongyang as well. Given the lack of presidential leadership on or attention to the issue during the Bush administration, the distractions posed by the Iraq and Afghanistan wars, the election of a very conservative president in South Korea (Lee Myung-bak), continued divisions in Washington's North Korea and arms control policy circles under the Obama administration, and North Korea's own penchant for brinkmanship and some decidedly unconstructive behavior, Washington's DPRK policy has seemed at times nuanced and accommodating and at other times harsh and inflexible.

With a view toward better understanding this divide over Washington's North Korea policy, observers note within the U.S. foreign/security policy community in Washington not only differences in approach to North Korea but different goals for North Korea policy. Jack Pritchard explains that this divergence has often translated into confusing and counterproductive policy: "The inexperience of most [Bush] administration officials in dealing with North Korea and the discrepancy between the administration's stated goal of negotiating a peaceful resolution and its desire to see the regime collapse have been significant contributors to policy failure."[24] People in Washington who believe that engaging North Korea and pursuing bilateral dialogue are a waste of time tend to argue that regime change in Pyongyang is the only hope for resolving the nuclear dispute and achieving peace on the Korean Peninsula. On the other hand, for people who believe that engaging North Korea and meeting North Koreans bilaterally is worthwhile, they also tend to have hope of negotiating a peaceful resolution of the conflict short of regime change (though even with them, regime change would not be an unwelcome phenomenon). These contradictions in U.S. goals and approaches as they relate to North Korea have made and continue to make it difficult for Washington to articulate a logical and consistent North Korea policy. What Washington needs is a new approach to North Korea, with a strong dose of presidential leadership.

THE NEED FOR A NEW U.S. APPROACH TO NORTH KOREA

North Korea presents the United States with a true quandary. Allowing North Korea to continue to develop its nuclear weapons capabilities is not an option for Washington, given the possibility that Pyongyang might sell such weapons or technologies to terrorists or those connected to them, not to mention the possibility that the regime could use them itself or threaten to use them for purposes of blackmail. Yet as argued elsewhere in this volume, taking out North Korea's nuclear capabilities with military strikes is not feasible, even if the U.S. military could be certain where they all are. In response to any military incursion, conventional North Korean artillery and missiles would likely turn Seoul, a city of 14 million just thirty miles from the North Korean border, into rubble. Pyongyang has indeed threatened to reduce Seoul to "a sea of fire" under such circumstances.

Sanctions are not an attractive option either. First, they have not been effective to date because of "leaks"—that is, countries not fully upholding the sanctions. North Korea is highly isolated and therefore less vulnerable to such sanctions than most regimes; moreover, North Korea simply tightens its belt, so to speak. Second, even if North Korea's neighbors (China in particular) could be persuaded to plug the leaks, North Korea has declared that sanctions are the equivalent of a declaration of war and would respond accordingly—again, a grave threat to Seoul. In other words, continuing with the status quo simply gives Pyongyang more time to develop its weapons, and resorting to a military option is virtually unthinkable, given the threat to Seoul.

Two New Policy Options and Likely Outcomes

Two new options could together address U.S. interests in North Korea.[25] First is the institutionalization of the Six Party Talks into a regional security framework or organization. Such a move would provide a regularized, ongoing forum in which to discuss Northeast Asian security issues, as well as a way of holding North Korea accountable to regional powers. In addition, Pyongyang could feel that the United States, Japan, and South Korea are being held accountable also. China has been leading the way in strengthening the Six Party Talks as a forum to promote dialogue and avert disaster on the Korean Peninsula, and this forum has been a useful way for Washington to address its concerns with North Korea. The fact that these six parties include the world's most powerful nation (the United States), the world's three most powerful nuclear powers (the United States, Russia, and China), the world's three most powerful economies (the United States, China, and Japan), and the parties to the world's most potentially explosive unresolved civil war (North Korea and South Korea, and their respective backers, China and the United States), underline the importance of such an institution. Continued discussion among these six parties is crucial even if the immediate crisis of North Korean nuclearization is resolved. These talks have been instrumental in facilitating the face-to-face time that North Korea and the United States needed to finally seal a deal in 2007. If and when the present issues eventually are resolved, this sort of ongoing forum would have continuing usefulness.

The call for institutionalizing the Six Party Talks into a nascent regional security framework is not new. Many in China,[26] the United States,[27] and elsewhere[28] have called for the Six Party Talks to be extended beyond the present crisis. Given tensions between China and Japan, the two Koreas and Japan, China and the United States over Taiwan, and unresolved territorial disputes between Japan and Russia, the importance of a regional security framework or organization is manyfold. The Six Party Talks, or something like them, must remain a factor in Northeast Asian regional security.

The second policy recommendation may be viewed as radical by neoconservatives and others in Washington but is in fact a far more effective preemptive move than some of the preventive measures those neoconservatives have advocated recently. Preemptive strikes are strikes against an adversary just as they prepare to launch an attack. The much more controversial preventive strikes are made against an adversary—not in the presence of an immediate, imminent threat, but rather in the clear and present danger of attack or war in the long run, or a major negative shift in the balance of power, such that waiting until an attack is imminent is considered too dangerous. Here, the idea is that North Korean nuclear operationality is clearly imminent; the policy proposed is, in a sense, a preemptive, frontal assault on this imminent nuclear operationalization, done in the name of preserving the peace on the Korean Peninsula.

What characterizes this preemptive move? In addition to the agreements' details worked out in 2007 by way of the Six Party Talks, and to pave the way for a real breakthrough in the North Korea nuclear dilemma, the United States should offer North Korea full diplomatic recognition, including the opening of a U.S. embassy in Pyongyang and permission for a North Korean embassy in Washington. As part of this move, the United States should also offer to turn the 1953 Korean War armistice into a full-fledged peace agreement, formally ending the Korean War. These moves should be done without preconditions but with the clearly communicated message that denuclearizing the Korean Peninsula is still the goal. Such a policy would not require a retreat from any of the other agreements the United States and its partners presently have in place regarding North Korea's disabling of its nuclear facilities, full disclosure of all nuclear activities, or ending its nuclear proliferation activities, nor is it a retreat from any U.S. commitments to help defend South Korea. This latter point is quite important, in particular as it regards the ultimate need to sell such a policy in Seoul. This new approach to Pyongyang may also be seen as a confidence-building measure—another step toward resolving the North Korean nuclear issue, North Korea eventually abandoning its nuclear weapons programs, and restoring a nuclear-free Korean Peninsula.

The newness of this approach is that rather than making the normalization of U.S.-DPRK relations and the establishment of diplomatic missions in each other's countries a prize to be won when the nuclear issue is resolved, the proposal is that the United States—as the most powerful party to the North Korean nuclear issue—should make the first move. This sort of move could only be made in a more amicable season of U.S.–North Korean relations, particularly when Pyongyang is reaching out positively. It should not be pursued soon after events such as the sinking of the *Cheonan* or the shelling of Yeonpyeong Island, lest the danger that it be seen as a desperate measure done in weakness.[29]

While criticism would likely come from both sides of the political spectrum in Washington, such an approach is not actually as radical as it at first sounds. First, the closest U.S. ally, Great Britain, opened an embassy in Pyongyang in mid-2001 after establishing diplomatic relations with North Korea in late 2000, following progress in relations between South Korea and the DPRK. North Korea reciprocated, opening its own embassy in London in late 2002. From its mission in Pyongyang the British operate jointly funded humanitarian projects in North Korea, including those in Pyongsong, South Pyongan Province, and Wonsan. In addition, the British provide four English teachers at universities in Pyongyang and offer human rights and English-language training to North Korean officials in Britain.[30] Second, the United States had already talked about opening a liaison office in Pyongyang and eventually opening full diplomatic relations with North Korea as a part of the 1994 Agreed Framework. In fact, in the 2007 agreement, full normalization of relations was stated as part of the endgame for U.S.-DPRK bilateral relations. This approach simply moves up the timetable for what has already been discussed, offering the endgame as a foretaste of the peace to come, again as a confidence-building measure.

Before announcing such an approach, the United States would need to consult closely with South Korea. The South's agreement would not be as easy to achieve under a conservative South Korean government as it would have been under the previous Kim Dae-jung or Roh Moo-hyun administrations. However, as long as South Korea is assured that opening a U.S. embassy in Pyongyang and establishing a peace treaty with North Korea does not entail any weakening of the U.S. commitment to the defense of South Korea, or rejecting the requirement that North Korea lay down its nuclear weapons and end its proliferation activities, Seoul might be persuaded. After all, this sort of U.S. approach was exactly what the previous two South Korean presidents had hoped for from Washington but could not bring about, and such a U.S. policy then and would still enjoy a considerable level of popular support in South Korea.

If it chose to pursue such a policy, the United States would also need to consult closely with Japan to avoid a replay of the 1971 Nixon shock, when the Japanese learned about the U.S. opening toward China only after the fact, via international news coverage. Moreover, in addressing Japan's primary concerns —resolving the issue of North Korean agents abducting Japanese citizens over the past few decades and the North Korean missile threat—the United States would have to reassure the Japanese that Washington would not retreat from its commitment to defend Japan or hold North Korea accountable more generally. Moreover, U.S. policymakers would probably need to invest some extra political capital in addressing the abduction issue, perhaps offering to host dialogues between North Korean and Japanese authorities on the matter once the U.S. Embassy in Pyongyang is in place. In fact, U.S.-DPRK normalization would make it easier to resolve the DPRK's outstanding issues with Japan; normalization would effectively end the Cold War in Northeast Asia, which could only help improve DPRK-Japan relations. Washington should stress to Tokyo that recognizing Pyongyang is not a concession or a compromise but a confidence-building measure, a means to finally resolving the issues that have long plagued relations between both the DPRK and the United States and the DPRK and Japan.

The United States would have little to lose in taking this new approach, for several reasons. If North Korea responded favorably to the new U.S. overtures, two general streams of events might follow. First, if a peace treaty was signed, the U.S. Embassy opened in Pyongyang, and all sides continued to meet their commitments, these new developments would presumably lead to an environment in which the North Korean leadership might feel secure enough to lay down its nuclear weapons and terminate is nuclear weapons programs. This policy would directly address what North Korea pronounces as its reason for acquiring nuclear weapons in the first place: a perception of "U.S. hostility."[31]

A second possibility is that if North Korea accepted the new U.S. approach and, as was the case with the 1994 Agreed Framework, the agreement began to unravel, the United States would still be better off than it is now. Just as in the days of the Cold War standoff with the Soviet Union, the United States would have a listening post at its embassy inside North Korea, which the United States obviously does not have now. Moreover, this U.S. policy position would be viewed favorably in Beijing, Seoul, and Moscow, giving the United States more diplomatic capital with each. Building such capital is important in the wake of the unpopular Iraq War and the perceived unilateralism of the Bush II years, not to mention the fact that a number of potential U.S. policy options for North Korea would be impossible to realize without support from these three border nations, or China and South Korea at a minimum.

If North Korea were to refuse such a novel approach, the United States would find itself with several advantages as well, as compared to the status quo. North Korea's refusal would work against what North Korea itself has long said it desires: to be treated as a normal country by the United States and to see hostilities between Pyongyang and Washington finally laid to rest. The U.S. offer would thus put North Korea in a truly difficult position, perhaps making the North look even more like the intransigent troublemaker many believe it to be. The United States, on the other hand, would occupy the moral high ground, having made a good-faith effort to resolve the impasse surrounding Pyongyang's nuclear weapons. The policy proposed here could be particularly strategic if it became clear that sanctions or other actions were needed toward North Korea at some point in the future. Washington could then say to the Chinese, the Russians, or any other potential naysayers, "We tried normalization and look what it got us. Now we have to move in the direction of more robust sanctions or other contingencies."

Discussions with some of China's top strategic thinkers on North Korea between 2004 and 2012 indicate that Beijing would welcome such a U.S. approach. China has increasingly come to see North Korea as a brotherly pain in the neck.[32] Beijing's patience with Pyongyang is running thin, even more so since the 2009 nuclear test. If Pyongyang were to reject a U.S. offer this gracious, Beijing would be more likely to shift further toward the U.S./ROK position on the matter, further isolating North Korea. A decision by Beijing to truly put the squeeze on North Korea is a difficult one, given China's proximity to North Korea and the effect that a collapsing North Korea could have on China's border regions. However, Beijing would have little choice but to take a firmer stand against North Korea if North Korea rejected such an offer, and China still has considerable leverage over North Korea.

In the end, the most favorable outcome of such a fresh approach to North Korea from the U.S. perspective would be reducing tensions on the Korean Peninsula; a standing down of North Korea on the nuclear issue; a DPRK commitment to cease proliferation activities to Syria, Iran, and others; a significant improvement in U.S.-DPRK relations; and a general relaxation of tensions in the region. This outcome is also the most likely. Pyongyang has few options on its plate. The late Kim Jong-il stated continuously that his greatest concern was security and that the United States was North Korea's greatest threat.[33] Available evidence suggests that the death of Kim Jong-il has not changed North Korea's security calculus or its policy on nuclear weapons. A reasonable conclusion is that this approach would be as workable after consolidation of the new Kim Jong-un iteration of the Kim Family Regime, to use Andrei Lankov's terms, as it was before Kim Jong-il's passing.

The notion that Pyongyang perceives its greatest security threat as Washington, and that the sort of approach outlined here holds the greatest promise for resolving the North Korean nuclear issue, is the majority view of China's North Korea experts in my experience, and the view of many other North Korean watchers as well, including Jack Pritchard, Siegfried Hecker, and Leon Sigal.[34] Removing or significantly diminishing the U.S. security threat the North Korean regime faces might give North Korea's leaders the "face" and the political capital to do what the United States actually wants them to do. While giving the North some face or in any other way helping this problematic regime is not attractive, if it helps resolve the yet more disturbing potential for North Korean nuclear proliferation or war on the Korean Peninsula, such policy seems well worthwhile. Moreover, in the long run, the openness that would likely accompany resolution of the North Korean nuclear issue could prove to be the greatest hope to date for reform in North Korea.

One of the most important advantages that this new confidence-building approach could bring is establishing an elementary level of trust between Washington and Pyongyang. Trust has been lacking between the DPRK and the United States during its entire relationship—an enormous obstacle to resolving the recent nuclear dilemma—and significant evidence exists that lack of trust is the dilemma's root cause. Kim Jong-il feared the United States and concluded that his only source of security was nuclear weapons. His son can only feel more insecure, given his youth and inexperience. A U.S. policy such as the one outlined here would be the first step in addressing this most fundamental North Korean international security concern. In turn, a measure of trust between the two parties could result, perhaps enabling an end to the North Korean nuclear dilemma—and even possibly, in the longer run, opening doors that could lead to reunifying the Korean Peninsula. On the other hand, if, as some argue, nuclear weapons are primarily a domestic political issue in North

Korea and the Kim Family Regime is not willing to give them up at any cost because of their need to impress or appease military leaders whose support they need to rule, this policy would call Pyongyang's bluff and force its leaders to lay their cards on the table. This outcome is less ideal than Pyongyang's full cooperation and peace on the peninsula, but it is still a better outcome for U.S. policy than the status quo.

CONCLUSION

Richard Nixon and Henry Kissinger's rapprochement with Communist China in 1971 was considered a radical departure from previous U.S. policy. Remember that in 1971, when Nixon and Kissinger began pursuing this strategy, the United States was mired in a war in Vietnam and the Cold War was in full swing. Carrying out a broad rapprochement with any member of the Communist bloc was not even considered by most, especially on the Republican right; lest we forget, Nixon was a Republican with solid Cold Warrior credentials. While Democrat Lyndon Johnson was reported to have discussed such a move with China, only the strongly anticommunist Republican Richard Nixon had the political capital to make such a move. President Clinton discussed an opening to North Korea in the late 1990s but was unable to carry it out because of a combination of North Korean intransigence and moves in Congress by Republicans that undermined the 1994 Agreed Framework. Because George W. Bush and the Republican Party controlled Congress until 2006 and President Bush had the conservative credentials to preclude any attempts to label him as being soft on tyranny, he was in a position to take a radically different approach to North Korea just as Nixon did with China. He did not. Nor has the Obama administration been able to bring about any change in the dynamics of the North Korean nuclear crisis, despite early intimations and attempts at a fresh approach. Jeffrey Bader, one of the Asia policy advisory team members for the Obama administration, makes it clear that President Obama really wanted a new approach to North Korea as he came into office.[35] Given North Korean missile and nuclear tests, the election of more hawkish leaders in Seoul and Tokyo, the sinking of the *Cheonan*, the North Korean shelling of Yeonpyeong Island, and the death of Kim Jong-il, among other things, Obama was dealt a difficult hand and was not able to push forward anything truly new with North Korea as of the time of this writing. Nor is it clear that his North Korea policies were anything significantly different than the Bush Administration's.

The United States should now take a new approach to resolving the North

Korea nuclear dilemma, and I have proposed here an option the United States should seriously consider. After all, the U.S. approach to China in 1971–72 played an important role in paving the way for China to embark on the reforms that it undertook after Mao Zedong's death in 1976, allowing the much more pragmatic Deng Xiaoping to rise and lead China out of its totalitarian past. While North Korea today and China then are quite different in many ways, a similar U.S. policy of opening toward Pyongyang might create shifts in the North Korean political landscape such that more reform-minded leaders might rise to the fore.

The alternative, of course, is that Washington might continue to model its North Korea policy on its Cuba policy—relying on isolation, nonrecognition, hostility, and containment. In North Korea's case, however, this option is no longer possible given the proliferation threat that North Korea poses, an indicator that the old U.S. approach to North Korea has failed. North Korea is a true proliferation threat and is now a member of the world's club of nuclear nations. The United States should, therefore, consider applying the Nixon-Kissinger approach to North Korea. It worked in China's case. It just might work in North Korea's case as well. Even if it does not, however, the United States would still be in a better position to deal with Pyongyang. All that is needed is the boldness and intestinal fortitude in Washington to break with an obviously failed policy. May it come before it is too late and a war breaks out on the Korean Peninsula—or by way of North Korean nuclear proliferation "the world's most dangerous weapons" end up "in the hands of the world's most dangerous people."

What's at Stake for Northeast Asia?

CHAPTER THREE

The Implications for Seoul of an Operationally Nuclear North Korea

JONG KUN CHOI AND JONG-YUN BAE

Beyond doubt, in the post–Cold War era, one of South Korea's most serious security concerns has been keeping the Korean Peninsula free of nuclear weapons. This policy stance still continues even after North Korea's newly amended constitution on April 13, 2012, declared that North Korea is a nuclear weapons state. As the most visible threat to the Nuclear Non-Proliferation Treaty (NPT) and the regime that has grown up around it, North Korea's stubbornness and brinkmanship have been countered by U.S. determination to keep the nonproliferation regime intact, China's desire to keep its neighborhood trouble-free, and South Korea's drive to keep the peninsula nuclear-free. Since 1994 North Korea's nuclear adventure has been at the center stage of Northeast Asia's security politics, featuring numerous multilateral and bilateral negotiations, international sanctions, UN resolutions, and nuclear tests in 2006, 2009, and 2013. North Korea has skillfully crossed and pushed further a nuclear red line. It has variously withdrawn from the NPT, thrown out the International Atomic Energy Agency (IAEA) inspectors, and then turned on and off its research reactor at Yongbyon. Subsequently, the crisis intensified with three North Korean nuclear tests and a number of missile launchings. Consequently, prospects for potential conflict on the Korean Peninsula and in Northeast Asia are contingent upon the ways that the nuclear problems are resolved. The ongoing standoff over North Korea's nuclear program has become a constituent part of regional politics in Northeast Asia.

In the midst of North Korea's nuclear antics, South Korea has been searching for a policy aimed at overcoming the strategic uncertainty that the North's nuclear policies have thrust upon it, ranging from full-blown engagement to coordinated cooperation with the United States. Seoul's objectives are to prevent North Korea from developing nuclear weapons and to maintain a nuclear-free Korean Peninsula through a peaceful resolution of the dilemma. South Korea has tried to lure North Korea into peacefully resolving the nuclear problem by providing material and political incentives in the name of the Sunshine Policy for the ten years of its liberal governments' reign, even if it meant risking its alliance with the United States. Yet even during this era, Seoul often condemned and punished North Korea for its stubborn brinkmanship by enacting sanctions on the North. South Korea had to hedge, balance, and align with its neighboring states in order to underwrite military options, mobilize multilateral cooperative platforms, and maintain its policy initiatives. On the other hand, the obstinacy demonstrated by North Korea's nuclear ventures has generated divisions in South Korea that have erupted into fierce political struggles between the right and left wings of the Korean intelligentsia and policy circles.[1] Divisions over how to deal with North Korea have ruptured South Korean society for two decades, crosscutting between hawks and doves, conservatives and liberals, and pro-nationalist and pro-alliance groups. As of this writing, inter-Korean communication does not show any signs of reconciliation. The prospects for resurrecting the Six Party Talks are not presently bright. In short, little room for optimism exists in the region regarding the North Korean nuclear issue, and the potential for a way out seems dim.

In this chapter we present an unpalatable and undesirable, but now not-so-improbable, situation: the prospect of North Korea finally acquiring operational nuclear capabilities. In other words, we deal with a big "if" question: What would South Korea's strategic options be if North Korea emerged as a state armed with fully operational nuclear weapons? The emergence of a new nuclear power in Northeast Asia would present a significant change in the regional security environment, requiring a series of new policy choices for regional actors, most critically South Korea. South Korea faces the nearest and most immediate nuclear threat from an operational North Korean nuclear capability, and an operationally nuclear North Korea could rattle South Korea's general sense of security, inevitably inviting some serious soul searching in Seoul about its policy responses. Should South Korea condemn outright and enact containment policies toward North Korea? Should it seek to accept the new reality and learn to live with it? Or should it find new approaches to contain the immediate situation and upgrade its defense postures by strengthening its defensive capabilities and tightening its military alliance with the United States? In this chapter we offer an overview of what is at stake for Seoul in the event of North Korean nuclear operationality, and a discussion of the consequent policy options Seoul would have and likely embrace toward North Korea and its neighboring states.

The arguments of the chapter are as follows. First, we argue that in the years since 1994 and the beginning of the North Korean nuclear issue as we know it, South Koreans have become accustomed to a wide array of new, related security contingencies, and that through it all the public has been consistently supportive of an engagement policy toward the North. The reaction of the South Korean stock market, especially from the financial sector, has been prudent and nonpanicked. Capital flight, for example, has been a nonissue. To substantiate our arguments, we analyze public opinion for engagement with North Korea as well as the performance of the Korea Stock Market Index (KOSPI) in the 1994–2009 period. We then lay out South Korea's short- to mid-term options with the advent of an operationally nuclear North Korea. Here, we argue that for its initial course of action, South Korea would choose to prevent further proliferation of North Korea's nuclear capabilities beyond the Korean Peninsula. We also discuss South Korea's range of policy options related to the United States, China, and Japan. In short, we argue that South Korea would try not to discard multilateral cooperative platforms such as the Six Party Talks. Finally we argue why and how a policy of engagement will inevitably remain as the most preferable policy option for South Korea, the United States, and other states in resolving the situation—conditions that remain in a post–Kim Jong-il era.

FROM 1994 TO THE PRESENT: NORTH KOREA'S NUCLEAR VENTURE AND SOUTH KOREA

What impact would North Korea crossing the nuclear threshold have on South Korea? Would North Korea's operational nuclear capability create an unimaginable and unprecedented sense of fear among South Koreans? Would it bring about panic in the Korean economy and generate capital flight out of the KOSPI? Would it raise the probability of military conflicts initiated by North Korea as it possesses more favorable asymmetrical nonconventional capability over South Korea? Our estimation of South Korea's reaction to the eventuality of North Korea's confirmed nuclear capability is that it may not induce great chaos, but it would more likely be addressed with prudence in a context of relative stability; in essence, South Korea's society may have already developed a tolerance for the chronic North Korean threat.

The emergence of an operationally nuclear North Korea would not come as a total surprise to South Koreans, nor would it create a great sense of panic there, because the reality of dealing with an operationally nuclear-armed North Korea would not have come out of the blue. The lingering ordeals of the North's nuclear crisis since 1994 have almost become normal in the sense that the crisis has consistently made headlines in the major South Korean media outlets.[2] South Korea may have already developed a tolerance for North Korean provocations after three nuclear tests and numerous security threats from North Korea over the years, such that an operationally nuclear North Korea may not create much of a social or psychological panic.

Logically speaking, North Korea's nuclear capability has to be definitive and distinguishable as a clear and present danger for South Koreans to feel great fear. In fact, such danger is not clear and present. Since the Korean War ended in 1953, South Koreans, especially those residing in Seoul, have lived continuously with both an implicit and explicit threat of attack and the potential devastation of a "sea of fire" from North Korea's conventional weapons, especially the North's long-range artillery stationed along the demilitarized zone (DMZ). Seoul is within artillery range of the North, and the North is believed to have about four hundred to five hundred artillery tubes in a position to fire upon Seoul, and each tube can fire ten thousand rounds per minute.[3] Therefore, to South Koreans, the risk of nuclear attack from that of conventional weapons may be not so qualitatively different in its potential for destruction. In this sense, even if North Korea's nuclear capability becomes the ultimate weaponized reality, South Koreans may not see it as the end of the world.

South Koreans differ in their views of North Korea's nuclear ambitions. Like the U.S. debate over policy toward the Soviet Union during the Cold War, the differing views essentially come down to varying interpretations of Pyongyang's ideology, material capabilities, and willingness to attack. Moreover, the peculiarity of the Korean case presents an additional complexity: the idea of a Korean nation suggests a notion that the two Koreas constitute a shared cognitive, ethnic, cultural, and historical identity.[4] The security crisis presented by North Korea generates stimulating debates in the South, with conservatives perceiving North Korea's nuclear threat as the primary concern while liberals tend to argue that North Korea's defiant behaviors are confined to the context of U.S.-DPRK relations as a response to a historically aggressive U.S. policy toward the North. Although the international community approaches North Korea principally as a threat to the NPT regime, requiring prompt reactions for North Korea's nuclear action, South Koreans may approach the North in the particular context of inter-Korean relations, which requires peaceful coexistence for South Korea's continued survival. Therefore, regardless of their threat perception, South Koreans generally agree that brothers should not fight each other, as it means mutual destruction for both Koreas.[5]

While one may argue that South Korea's general perception of North Korea may be lacking the threat perception as conventional explanations of realism in international relations would expect, assuming that South Korea has not prepared for this security contingency may be a fatal mistake. Since 1994 South Korea's military has focused on enhancing its conventional deterrence capacity in addition to securing the extended deterrence from the United States. The various governments of South Korea, regardless of their ideological orientation, have exerted enormous efforts to modernize and upgrade South Korea's military capabilities and have responded to North Korea's limited provocations with strategic decisiveness, as was made clear in the three naval skirmishes of 1999, 2002, and 2009 in the Northern Limit Line of the West Sea,[6] as well as Seoul's robust response to North Korea's shelling of Yeonpyeong Island in November 2010. Furthermore, South Korea's foreign policy has generally been focused on securing a comprehensive political engagement with North Korea and maintaining its alliance with the United States, while upgrading its cooperative relationship with China and Japan.[7] Although North Korea's nuclear crisis has placed South Korea under tremendous pressure to restrict its engagement policy, South Korea has not shut all doors to North Korea and remains willing to continue negotiations under the multilateral framework of the Six Party Talks, in addition to bilateral negotiations. If South Korea exercises punitive behaviors, Seoul would be essentially closing the door to possible negotiations, because Pyongyang consequently would certainly not be willing to meet. This situation has not yet occurred, even after the second nuclear test in 2009. Thus, the emergence of an operational North Korean nuclear capability is not likely to rattle South Korea to the extent that South Korea chooses any punitive actions, as we discuss further below.

Since the first nuclear crisis in 1994, the North's nuclear program has generated many debates in the South as to how South Korea should work toward peaceful resolution. Our analysis, however, indicates a stable and formidably strong support for a policy of engagement throughout the 1990s and 2000s, despite the naval skirmishes between the North and the South, the North's nuclear tests, Pyongyang's inordinate provocations, and a general South Korean fatigue from the lingering nuclear problems.

Figure 3.1 indicates the public opinion trends from 1998 to 2009 regarding South Koreans' preference toward engagement with North Korea. The engage-

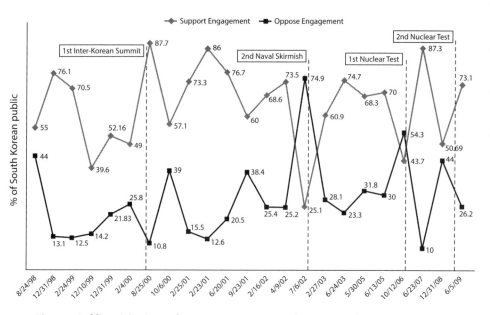

Figure 3.1. Public opinion in South Korea on engagement policy with North Korea, 1998–2009. Source: Compiled by the authors from the various data sources listed below. August 24, 1998: *Munwha Daily*; December 31, 1998: Korea Institute of National Unification (KINU); September 24, 1999: *Hangyeoreh Daily*; September 12, 1999: *Kookmin Daily*; December 31, 1999: KINU; February 4, 2000: *Chonsun Daily*; August 25, 2000: *Munwha Daily*; October 6, 2000: *Kyunghyang Daily*; February 2, 2001: Ministry of Unification; February 23, 2001: *Kyunghyang Daily*; June 20, 2001: Ministry of Unification; September 9, 2001: Ministry of Unification; February 16, 2002: *Munwha Daily*; April 9, 2002: Ministry of Unification; July 6, 2002: Korea Gallup; February 27, 2003: *Munwha Daily*; June 24, 2003: Korea Society Opinion Institute; May 30, 2005: Korea Broadcasting Company; June 13, 2005: Munwha Broadcasting Company; October 12, 2006: Korea Society Opinion Institute; June 23, 2007: *Chosun Daily*; December 31, 2008: KINU; June 5, 2009: East Asia Institute.

ment policy was a polarizing issue, dividing the society into the pro- and anti-engagement groups. As the data from the summer of 1998 indicates, public opinion was almost evenly split, even when an engagement policy had not yet begun in full force; the support for engagement was still 55% while the opposition to the policy was 44%. However, after the first inter-Korean summit in 2000, public opinion for the Sunshine Policy increased to 87.7%, the highest recorded during the twelve years studied.

South Koreans have lived through the ten-year Sunshine Policy (1998–2007) as well as endured the near-continuous tensions of the North Korean nuclear crisis since 1994. Throughout the ten years when South Korea's engagement was in full swing, public support was generally strong, even in the face of the more notable North Korean provocations. For example, in 2002 a fatal naval clash took place between the two Koreas in the West Sea, resulting in numerous casualties on both sides, bringing high military tension to the peninsula, and raising the opposition to engagement to 74.9% and lowering support to 25.2%. The first nuclear test itself was a critical point for the durability of support for South Korea's engagement policy. While the government was slammed with criticisms and public opinion against government policy rose to 54.3%, public support for engagement decreased from 70% to 43.7%. Public opinion on engagement, however, normally regains its momentum after security crises. With this in mind, the engagement policy begun in 1998 has been broadly and undeniably popular, even after the three nuclear tests. Thus, an engagement strategy with North Korea may remain acceptable to the general population of South Korea even with eventual North Korean nuclear operationality.[8]

South Korea is one of the most rapidly emerging markets for portfolio investment, comparing favorably with financial markets in the most developed nations. Because portfolio investment is sensitive to geopolitical risk, the North's nuclear crisis has functioned as one of the most significant catalysts of ups and downs on the KOSPI. Analysts had expected that a North Korean nuclear test would likely have a significant negative effect on the South Korean economy, and in particular that South Korea would likely "suffer from capital flight, consequent declines in asset prices and investments, and possibly a minor budgetary loss" after a North Korea nuclear test.[9] However, our analysis suggests quite to the contrary: while two nuclear tests by North Korea did in fact result in a short-term plunge of the KOSPI, nothing like capital flight nor a major decline in investment occurred.

Figure 3.2 indicates that following North Korea's announcement of the test in 2006, the KOSPI plunged 3.6% to 1319.40 on Tuesday, October 10, 2006 —following North Korea's October 9 nuclear test—from 1352.00 on Friday, October 6.[10] Yet the market rallied beginning on October 11 and recovered to the earlier level by the end of the week, ending at 1348.60. In other words, the market's reaction did not show any panic given the magnitude of the event itself.

As for the second nuclear test, the same pattern appears in Figure 3.3. The KOSPI fell by 2.2% from 1400.90 on May 25 to 1372.02 on May 26, and continued to plunge for a few days. The nuclear test came, however, when investors had already been worried about possible capital flight on profit taking after the KOSPI had increased more than 40% since early March 2009. Counting the nuclear test in May on its own as disastrous to the Korean stock market is dif-

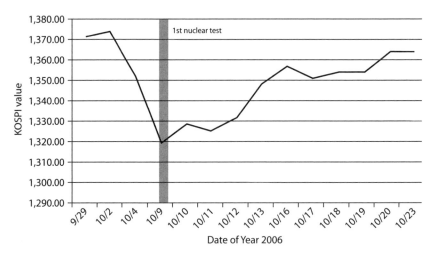

Figure 3.2. Reaction of the Korea Stock Market Index (KOSPI) to the first nuclear test by North Korea, on October 9, 2006.

ficult. As it rebounded to the pre–nuclear test level on June 1 with the KOSPI at 1415.10, the plunge was short-lived. Moreover, we did not see any panic-generating capital flight out of the Korean investment market. Foreign stock buyers, whose trading patterns influence local markets in a significant way, remained net buyers of some 62 billion won (US$68.2 million) worth of South Korean stocks, even after the North's second nuclear test. It seems that neither nuclear test had an immediate impact on South Korea's long-term foreign credit ranking. Despite all of the hoopla surrounding the nuclear tests, South Korea's credit rating remained at grade A, the sixth-highest in Standard and Poor's credit ranking system.[11] What matters more to the portfolio markets is not the nuclear tests themselves, but seemingly any potential for uncertain and dramatic changes in the security environment on the Korean Peninsula.

North Korea emerging as an operationally nuclear power is bad for the Korean Peninsula, and it certainly exacerbates the South's general sense of insecurity. Having to learn to live with a nuclear power such as North Korea is not pleasant by any means. However, the impact of such an event apparently is not as catastrophic as one might expect. As the public opinion and KOSPI data indicate, reactions from the public and the financial market have been prudent and tolerant of the nuclear turmoil. South Korea has achieved economic recovery from the 1997 Asian financial crisis, with continuous economic growth fueled by cutting-edge technological innovations and globalization initiatives.

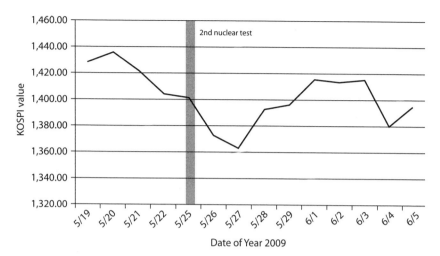

Figure 3.3. Reaction of the Korea Stock Market Index (KOSPI) to the second nuclear test by North Korea, on May 25, 2009.

Therefore, if North Korea emerges as an operationally nuclear power, South Korea is not likely to experience any major public panic or market disorder.

SOUTH KOREA'S FORMULATION OF SHORT- AND MID-TERM RESPONSES

Broad consensus exists in South Korea on three indisputable matters of the nation's interests regarding its policies toward Pyongyang: intolerance of an operational North Korean nuclear capability, the desirability of resolving the nuclear issue in a peaceful and diplomatic manner, and maintaining a proactive stance in dealing with the crisis.[12] These three doctrines have been institutionalized as the idea of *war aversion*. South Korea has categorically rejected the idea of war as a means of resolving the nuclear crisis. Thus, any policies toward North Korea by the South have at their core a desire to prevent a second Korean War. South Korea is thus more likely to rule out any coercive means, including surgical strikes on the nuclear sites, even if North Korea becomes operationally nuclear. In this sense, South Korea's choices in the post–operationally nuclear North Korea era may be limited even as the intensity of policy debates increases in Korean society. Ultimately, Seoul's response is likely to come down to initiating a set of containment policies at the initial stage for short-term punitive measures.

In the event of a certified weaponized North Korean nuclear capability,

South Korea would initially join the rest of the international community in condemning North Korea and would participate in some sanction regimes, as was the case after North Korea's second nuclear test. As for short- and mid-term policy choices, Seoul may try to contain further proliferation of nuclear technology beyond the borders of North Korea, upgrade its alliance posture with Washington, and tighten its defensive stances against further possible provocations by Pyongyang. Seoul would also be sensitive to Beijing, as Seoul's closer cooperation with Washington may endanger its cooperative relationship with China. Seoul would thus likely promote the idea of multilateral platforms to pressure Pyongyang to come back to the Six Party Talks.

Alliance Politics

An operationally nuclear North Korea may inevitably require a tighter South Korean alliance with the United States, especially with a conservative South Korean president in office, such as Lee Myung-bak. Seoul would need symbolically and substantially improved cooperation with Washington so that it would be able to send signals to Pyongyang that the ROK-U.S. alliance is firm and strong. Hence, North Korea would hardly be able to venture any military adventures against South Korea. While it would unilaterally strengthen its defensive capabilities in order to enhance its deterrence measures, South Korea would attempt to beef up its alliance with the United States in terms of intelligence gathering and any joint military exercises. The most important objective would be to focus on maintaining operational compatibility even after the transfer of wartime command in 2015.

South Korea also needs to make sure that Washington remains firmly committed to resolving the issue without resorting to forceful measures. Moreover, Seoul needs to send a strong signal to Washington that the ROK-U.S. alliance is firmly committed to denuclearizing the Korean Peninsula through multilateral cooperative platforms. In other words, as in 1994, Seoul must prevent any spiraling nuclear crisis from leading to U.S. attempts to use force, including surgical strikes.[13] The case in point for Seoul is that Seoul and Washington must both remain calm and rationally formulate action plans for short and mid-term responses free of the use of force. At the same time, Seoul would have to make sure that South Korea remains under a strong commitment of extended deterrence by the United States.

The fatal mistake for South Korea, however, would be to discuss bringing U.S. tactical nuclear weapons onto South Korean territory, which would only provide North Korea further justification for expanding its limited nuclear capabilities. Moreover, South Korea remains firmly under U.S. extended deterrence, as stated in the joint remarks by President Obama and President Lee Myung-bak on June 19, 2009. Any tactical nuclear weapons moved onto South Korean territory may not provide any further deterrence capability but would likely result in jeopardizing the South's relations with China. South Korea needs good relations with China for reinitiating any regional cooperative platforms. South Korea would have to work with the United States to reopen the multilateral cooperative platforms among the four other participating states in the Six Party Talks, moving toward a consensus that North Korea's nuclear capability is unacceptable and denuclearizing the Korean Peninsula is still the top priority.

In the event of North Korea becoming operationally nuclear, Seoul and Washington must not recognize the North as a legitimate nuclear power. Such recognition would be a fatal blow to the viability of the nonproliferation regime and trigger domestic political chaos in each capital. Seoul, though, could not ignore the reality that North Korea has nuclear bombs that explode and rockets that can deliver the bombs, for these realities would require realistic actions for resolution. While containing North Korea's nuclear capabilities, South Korea and the United States must make sure that normal diplomatic relations would be impossible for Pyongyang without resolving the nuclear issue. An imperative set of policy tools for persuasion would include terminating North Korea's international financial transactions, forbidding and blocking North Korea's arms trade, and scrutinizing its cargo transports under UN Security Council Resolution 1874. Ensuring the immediate containment of North Korea's nuclear capability does not mean acquiescing to the nuclear programs confined within its territory. North Korean nuclear operationality would put South Korea in a position of having to maintain a real balancing act between deterring any forceful military action against the North and making sure that the United States does not come to accept a nuclear-armed status for North Korea as it did for India and Pakistan. The possibility that North Korea might receive the Indian/Pakistan treatment would jeopardize not only the durability of the ROK-U.S. alliance but also the general stability of Northeast Asia and the NPT.

Containing Nuclear Proliferation beyond the Korean Peninsula

South Korea's initial reaction to North Korean nuclear operationality should be a policy of containment.[14] It should focus at the initial stage on continuing to deter further North Korean conventional provocations and preventing the proliferation of North Korea's weapons of mass destruction beyond its borders. Containing North Korea's nuclear and missile programs—including nuclear materials, technology, and know-how—should become the primary policy objective at the initial stage so that its nuclear program or end products cannot be transferred to other states or terrorist organizations. In particular, South Korea would need to completely block any potential linkage of North Korea's nuclear capability with other regions of the world so that resolving the issue would remain within South Korea's policy purview.

South Korea must make sure that Pyongyang recognizes that Seoul and Washington may not be able to detect all the nuclear materials hidden in underground facilities, but the allies can surely detect and prevent any attempts to transfer nuclear materials beyond its borders. South Korea and the United States should ensure that a transfer of nuclear material out of North Korea would be very risky if not suicidal for the Kim regime, and that the regime knows this, as the regime seems to value its own survival above all else.[15] A containment policy by South Korea, including temporary termination of inter-Korean economic projects and active participation in the Proliferation Security Initiative (PSI), would be pursued as a way to make North Korea liable for endangering the durability of the NPT regime. Such a policy would signal that South Korea remains committed to denuclearizing the Korean Peninsula.

Nevertheless, South Korea's efforts to contain North Korea do not mean that it seeks the North's collapse. South Korea is well aware of the fact that a sudden collapse of North Korea would create an uncertain future for the Korean Peninsula, not to mention the unimaginable social and economic costs of unification that Seoul would shoulder. Sanctions would not achieve the ultimate goal of denuclearizing North Korea. As we have seen for many years, North Korea has persevered under every type of international pressure and has often responded with acts of dire nuclear brinkmanship. The containment policy envisioned here is merely a series of short-term punitive actions that would serve to cool down the immediate impact of an operationally nuclear North Korea. South Korea would thus view sanctions and the halting of inter-Korean exchanges as a necessary and useful means of pressuring North Korea to return to the denuclearization process.

The Use of Military Force to Thwart North Korean Provocations

Some analysts argue that North Korea's acquisition of operational nuclear capability would serve as a catalyst for a nuclear domino effect on the Korean

Peninsula and in Northeast Asia.[16] However, while public discussion might take place about the desirability of South Korea's going nuclear, South Korea's nuclear option would not likely be seriously discussed at the governmental level. The exercise of South Korea's nuclear option would be irrational and ineffective even in the aftermath of North Korean nuclear operationality. As long as North Korea lacks second-strike capability, the development of nuclear weapons in South Korea remains unlikely. In addition, South Korea is constrained by formidable antinuclear social norms, as well as an alliance structure that has discouraged their development.[17] Even if North Korea's nuclear capability became operational, it would lack a second-strike capability and hence would not dramatically improve the North's conventional military capabilities.[18] Therefore, it is hard to imagine North Korea launching a nuclear first strike,[19] which would also clearly be its last.

Moreover, North Korea's nuclear capability does not make a conventional attack by Pyongyang more likely or successful. Strictly speaking from the deterrence point of view, unless the leadership in Pyongyang becomes radically irrational and completely suicidal,[20] the probability of war on the Korean Peninsula is likely to remain low, as the North would face the combined force of South Korea and the United States. Seoul's acquisition of nuclear capabilities would add little value to its deterrence capabilities, as it enjoys a number of strategic advantages already, and Seoul's going nuclear would only lead to instability in Northeast Asia, which would be disadvantageous for South Korea.

South Korea's primary military response would focus on thwarting North Korea's conventional threat, as North Korea may mistakenly assume that South Korea would capitulate to any demands of Pyongyang after it acquires a fully weaponized nuclear capability. Therefore, Seoul's defense posture would be to indicate its willingness to put up with any North Korean military provocations. At the same time Seoul would seek to showcase its defensive capabilities, signaling that it is staying on course with its defense upgrade program both in maritime and air power. South Korea also needs to create a more effective, elite, high-tech force with a rapid-response capacity to deter North Korea's more limited provocations, especially at the Northern Limit Line along the west coast. More broadly, South Korea should be able to acquire a cutting-edge surveillance capability for more independent intelligence analysis and technology-intensive military power better suited to curtail any North Korean adventurism. Strengthening South Korean forces, including the creation of a rapid-response system against North Korea's nuclear, chemical, and biological weapons, is a core issue for bilateral cooperation between South Korea and the

United States in the event of an operationally nuclear North Korea, and would be even more important for Seoul after the 2015 transfer of wartime operational control to ROK forces.

Regional Politics: Six Party Talks and Cooperation with China and Japan

In the event of North Korea's acquisition of operationally nuclear capability, in addition to seeking to reaffirm its security commitment with the United States, Seoul would need to rally the support of its neighboring states for peaceful denuclearization of the Korean Peninsula and to pressure North Korea to return to the Six Party Talks process. Since 2003 the Six Party Talks have been testing the sincerity of North Korea's willingness to trade its nuclear weapons for other incentives, and the Talks have in some cases stretched the patience of the other five participants near their breaking points. Ascension of North Korea to the status of nuclear power would imply that the Six Party Talks as a multilateral remedy have failed and that North Korea has successfully manipulated the process and deceived the international community. A disappointed Russia, a frustrated China, an angered Japan, and a betrayed United States may not see much need to revitalize the Six Party Talks under such conditions. In fact, any arguments for returning to the Six Party Talks might easily be shot down, for any such multilateral measures might only remind the parties of past failures.

The Six Party Talks have been successful, though, in at least a number of ways. A South Korean–Chinese collaborative partnership has emerged, and there would be no reason to discontinue such a collaborative relationship simply because of North Korea's nuclearization.[21] Seoul and Beijing share the common interest of integrating North Korea into Northeast Asia's regional economy by peaceful means. Therefore, they both have sought to work around Pyongyang's exaggerated sense of threat to persuade it to partake in the Six Party Talks.[22] On the other hand, Seoul and Beijing pressured the United States under the Bush administration to adopt a de facto bilateral negotiation framework with Pyongyang aside from the Six Party Talks. Underlying such facilitating roles was their shared strategic mind-set that the peaceful denuclearization of the Korean Peninsula was the key to a stable Northeast Asia.[23] In this spirit, South Korea would need to hold on to such collaborative relations with China even in a nuclear North Korea era.

Moreover, for the sake of South Korea's national interests—especially with China but also for the sake of Northeast Asia's stability—multilateral measures such as the Six Party Talks cannot be put aside. Thorough multilateral platforms such as the Six Party Talks, South Korea can mobilize international support, especially from China, for managing the new situation. As discussed above, an operationally nuclear North Korea inevitably would strengthen the cooperative alliance between South Korea and the United States, which would not serve China's strategic interests. The Six Party Talks are China's flagship diplomatic invention, and North Korea's operational nuclear capability would indicate a grand failure for China. Therefore, South Korea needs to revitalize multilateral platforms in which China and South Korea can facilitate new solutions for the North Korean nuclear issue. In other words, through the Six Party Talks, South Korea can maintain cooperation with China by pressuring North Korea to return to the negotiating table for denuclearization while strengthening its alliance with the United States.

If North Korea is able to weaponize its nuclear capability, one of its priorities would be demanding bilateral talks with the United States, as it has done since its first nuclear test in October 2006. This demand would essentially limit South Korea's and China's roles in the process. Therefore, while encouraging bilateral talks, Seoul should cooperate with China, and both should demand that any significant discussion on the future of the North's nuclear capability should be discussed and negotiated at the Six Party Talks. Because China would want to continue to use the Six Party Talks—through which China's influence and importance can be projected to the world—South Korea would have to continue to support the multilateral process even in the nuclear North Korea era despite its strengthened alliance with the United States. Furthermore, with the emergence of an operationally nuclear North Korea, South Korea may not be able to afford to be a reactive regional actor, as the nuclearization of the peninsula itself marks its gravest national security threat. By trying to sustain any types of multilateral platforms, South Korea may be able to actively mobilize international support for peacefully resolving the problem of a nuclear North Korea and seek a prominent role so as to prevent descending spirals of conflicts on the Korean Peninsula.

As for South Korea and Japan, they would closely collaborate with each other, especially on how to prevent further proliferation of North Korea's nuclear capability. As quasi-allies through their alliances with the United States, Seoul and Tokyo would be active in coordinating their actions toward North Korea. However, the emergence of an operationally nuclear North Korea would deepen Japan's perception of North Korea as a threat, which would play into the hands of the Japanese right and their push for Japan's bid for normal-state status. North Korea's launching of a Taepodong missile over Japanese territory in 1998 essentially jump-started what could be called Japan's remilitarization. Moreover, North Korea's nuclear tests and its long-range rocket launchings have generated greater domestic support in Japan for a more active Japanese role in Northeast Asian security. Certainly, North Korea's operational nuclear capability would bring greater panic to Japanese society than we saw in 2009, and it may eventually motivate Japan to seek more active and independent defensive capabilities, including its own nuclear deterrence. For South Korea, this situation is not desirable. Obviously, as for South Korea, Japan's going nuclear is not going to happen easily given its alliance with the United States and its pacifistic and antinuclear domestic cultural norms.

However, if North Korea's nuclear capability functions as a catalyst for any significant changes in Japan's security mind-set, then South Korea would again press for multilateral platforms such as the Six Party process as a way to address Japan's concerns with the result that Japan might be less likely to respond to North Korea by going nuclear or building up its own defenses. South Korea would ultimately need a multilateral cooperative approach to the North Korean problem in order to curtail any unintended outcomes in Northeast Asia.

FORMULATING A RESPONSE: IS ENGAGEMENT POSSIBLE IN THE ERA OF AN OPERATIONALLY NUCLEAR NORTH KOREA?

If South Korea must eventually face the reality of an operationally nuclear North Korea, then what kinds of options along a coercion-engagement continuum does South Korea have relating to ending the North Korean problem? If Pyongyang does not agree to abandon its nuclear capabilities, then how should South Korea, along with its allies and partners, formulate its ultimate response? Can engagement work again? Or should policy gears shift toward tougher punitive actions so that North Korea might disavow its nuclear capabilities? In the scenario described here, North Korea would undoubtedly be going through even tougher economic hardships, a deteriorating international situation, and deeper isolation. Consequently we may need to reframe our questions as follows: If North Korea is trying to strike a better deal with the United States by pushing Washington to the limit, if North Korea is willing to bear any international pressure despite its harsh economic conditions, and if North Korea is showing serious resolve to hold onto its nuclear capabilities, then what leverage do we have against North Korea in resolving this lingering problem? What options do we have? What can South Korea, Japan, China, the United States, Russia, and the United Nations do with this troublesome regime?

The international relations literature offers several choices in the range between coercion and engagement that might be useful to consider.[24] The first is for the United States or its allies and the international community to wage a major war against North Korea to bring down the regime. The second is to punish the regime by military actions specifically targeting nuclear sites. The third is to impose economic sanctions. Fourth would be to again negotiate with the North in the continued hope that Pyongyang will give up its nuclear weapons in return for certain compensation. Obviously, these four options are ideal types and may overlap to some extent. Some have already been implemented (e.g., economic sanctions), and some thus far rejected (e.g., surgical strikes on North Korean sites). At any rate, we conclude this chapter by evaluating the feasibility of each option. Putting aside our anger, sense of betrayal, indignation that North Korean crimes have not been but should be punished, and above all our feelings of well-deserved mistrust for North Korea, we argue that negotiations are ultimately the only realistic and rational option for delivering all Koreans from the worst-case scenario of renewed war on the peninsula. In this section we also analyze the leverage that South Koreans have in order to bring about solutions to North Korea's nuclear adventurism.

Option 1: Full-Scale War

Waging and winning a full-scale war against North Korea would bring the complete end to the lingering global security problems that North Korea has generated since the end of the Korean War. However costly the price associated with such a war would be, including an unimaginable number of civilian and military casualties and a great deal of economic destruction, some would argue that the long-term benefits of waging and winning such a full-blown war would offset such costs since it would bring about Korean unification and make the peninsula a zone of democracy, capitalism, and—above all—denuclearization.

However, this option is strategically unrealistic, morally repugnant, and therefore inconceivable. The majority of the North's military capabilities are deployed near the DMZ, just thirty miles from Seoul. Seoul accounts for about a quarter of South Korea's population (48 million) and boasts nearly half of its economic wealth. Even if the allied force could preemptively attack the North and win such a war, assuming such a victory may be too unrealistic. Given its military commitments in the Middle East, the United States could not afford to commit sufficient forces to the Korean Peninsula any time soon. Moreover, the United States could not initiate such a full-scale war without sufficient support from Seoul and Tokyo and consent from Beijing, all of which are unlikely. Part of this option's moral repugnance relates to countless North Korean artillery tubes and their firepower. Unleashed on metropolitan Seoul, the resulting "sea of fire" would certainly cause millions of civilian casualties, not to mention serious economic damage. Full-scale war is, therefore, inconceivable.

Option 2: Surgical Military Strikes

Surgical strikes against nuclear sites in North Korea were seriously considered back in 1994, and some analysts are renewing the call today. Surgical strikes against North Korea's nuclear facilities in Yongbyon and elsewhere in Hambuk Province may be strategically possible given the U.S. satellite surveillance and stealth bombing capabilities, and they may successfully destroy nuclear facilities, including buildings, nuclear generators, and known storage depots. However, destroying these facilities is one thing, while denuclearizing North Korea is another. In other words, one crucial blindside of such an option is that surgical strikes may not actually help achieve denuclearization of the Korean Peninsula. Even if South Korea and the United States successfully strike the known nuclear sites, what about the unknown nuclear sites? What about the plutonium and highly enriched uranium? Finally, what about the nuclear devices that the North has already?

This option would ultimately mean only the end of the current turmoil and signal the beginning of mid- to full-scale conflict on the Korean Peninsula. The North may retaliate by firing its short-range missiles at the Incheon International Airport, Seoul, and other major cities in the South, and its middle-range Nodong missiles at the Japanese islands, which again would not only cause grave damage to South Korea and Japan but also invite countermilitary measures from the allied forces. In short, surgical strikes against North Korea would be unrealistic, dangerously naïve, and unproductive at least, and would invite much the same response from North Korean as a full-scale military attack.

Option 3: Economic Sanctions and Embargoes

Economic sanctions have been one policy area consistently mentioned as a way to respond to North Korean provocations, and they are presently being executed against North Korea. Economic sanctions can and have included trade embargoes, bans on cash transfers and loans from U.S. and its allies' financial institutions, and measures that prevent access to its own assets in international banking institutions. The policy design of sanctions is to influence North Korean behavior by inflicting unacceptable economic costs upon the Kim regime. The logic behind the policy is to strangle North Korea's economy, weaken the domestic political legitimacy of the regime, and eventually force North Korea to concede to the United States and the international community. Such a punitive action by the sanctioning nations would be backed by a conviction that economic leverage works.

Unfortunately, economic sanctions against North Korea may have virtually no impact at this time. The Kim regime is designed to sustain external economic sanctions. North Korea has minimal economic relations with the United States and Japan; economic leverage from these two nations would only be symbolic rather than substantial. South Korea may have more leverage than the United States and Japan, as the South built up stronger economic relations with the North during the liberal governments preceding the Lee administration. Even if the South completely terminates its economic relations with the North, including the Kaesong Industrial Complex, it wouldn't do too much damage to Pyongyang but would only aggravate the current situation, as South Korea's leverage in fact decreased during the Lee administration.

China may be the only North Korean trading partner with sufficient economic leverage to effect the North, and only if it implements full-scale economic sanctions, including Sino-DPRK border trade. China may be angered by the North's nuclear test for causing many unanticipated problems in Northeast Asia. However, China would be unlikely to agree to full-scale economic sanctions until the North concedes to the U.S. and South Korea's denuclearization demand, which would be quite long enough to cause regional economic problems in Manchuria. Moreover, China's economic policy toward the North is designed to keep Pyongyang stable through economic assistance. Expecting that China would bluntly go ahead with economic sanctions is unrealistic, and without China, sanctions could not possibly work.

Economic sanctions also have a strategic problem in that they do not weaken the regime in power but rather victimize North Korea's civilians. The Kim regime would manipulate the sanctions to offer evidence to suffering North Koreans that the United States and South Korea are the real threats. Logically, if analysts know that the hostile external security perceived by the regime in Pyongyang has in fact strengthened North Korea's drive for nuclear-power status, and if we know that North Korea's military has been in the driver's seat pushing for more aggressive strategies, sanctions create an even more hostile environment out of which North Korea's military can only grow more influential. In short, economic sanctions would add to strategic uncertainty, raising an even greater likelihood for further stubborn brinkmanship from North Korea.

Option 4: The Inevitability of Engagement and Why It Works

The policies reviewed so far—from full and limited military actions to economic sanctions—are unrealistic, aggravating, and naively dangerous, and they will not achieve denuclearization. Consequently, is promoting the idea of engagement toward North Korea logically justifiable just because the hard-line policies are not expected to work? Despite North Korea's nuclear and missile ventures, not to mention the lingering negotiations since the first nuclear crisis in 1994, only one option remains for achieving the denuclearization of North Korea: engagement.

Many observers argue that the constructive engagement policy of the Kim, Clinton, and Roh administrations (and perhaps the last three years of George Bush's presidency) not only failed to work but also further encouraged North Korea's nuclear ambitions by not holding it accountable for its criminal behaviors.[25] Analysts maintain that an engagement policy has only spoiled the regime, and the time has come to teach it some lessons. The world is also disappointed with North Korea's surreal behavior, exaggerated threat perception, and truly medieval succession politics. Nonetheless, despite this anger and sense of betrayal, constructive engagement may remain the only viable option.

The North Korean system was designed to withstand pressure. History shows that it has survived critical junctures of international and regional change, including the end of the Cold War. What drives the North's more aggressive external and cohesive internal policies has been the hostile environment North Korea has endured since the Korean War. On the other hand, the North has no defense against friendly engagement stances from the outside.[26] If the North is built to sustain external pressure and has functioned well in hostile international environments, then the only logical course of action from the rest of the world is to be friendly. If North Korea has no defense against friendly behavior, then rational actors should stick with a friendly engagement policy toward the North.

The conventional wisdom holds that North Korea enjoyed ten years of constructive engagement from the South, and during those ten years the North built up its nuclear arsenals. We would argue that it is not, however, the engagement policy causing North Korea's pursuit of nuclear capabilities, but the duration of engagement, which was too short to expect any substantial changes. The North did not talk to the Kim Dae-jung administration for two years after its inauguration in 1998. There was also a serious naval skirmish between the two Koreas in 1999. Only in 2000 was the first inter-Korean summit held and was the engagement policy in full swing. In 2003, the first year of the Roh Moohyun administration, Seoul appointed a special prosecutor for illegal money transfers to the North in return for the 2000 summit. As a result, the North harshly criticized the Roh administration and halted any inter-Korean contacts for one year. Moreover, the Kim and Roh administrations had to deal with the Bush administration from 2001 to 2008, which was critical of the engagement policy.[27] Moreover, South Korea changed its policy stance away from constructive engagement in 2007, labeling the previous two administrations as the lost decade. In other words, blaming the engagement policy for the so-called lost decade and the failure to resolve the North Korean nuclear dilemma is essentially misleading. The engagement period was simply too short, unbearably bumpy, and continuously inconsistent for the policy to have any hopes of bringing about any real change within and from North Korea.

Nevertheless, constructive engagement by South Korea alone during the two liberal governments did in fact bring visible and significant changes within the North. In July 2002 North Korea launched economic reforms after the 2000 inter-Korean summit, which allowed North Koreans to test-drive and get a glimpse of liberal economic mechanisms. The initiation of the Kaesong Industrial Complex was a monumental achievement of engagement. In order to install the complex, the forward-based military just south of Kaesong City had to move north, signifying a monumental political victory for the reformers in Pyongyang. The Kaesong industrial park hosts ninety-three South Korean companies employing forty thousand North Koreans, about 20% of the Kaesong population. These workers have been exposed to the benefits of the modern South Korean working environment. On any given day, three hundred to four hundred South Korean vehicles go across the DMZ to North Korea, along with about six hundred to one thousand people crossing the same DMZ on the west and east coasts of the peninsula. Kaesong was even opened for South Korean tourists. Reunions of separated families, NGOs and private entrepreneurs networking with the North's counterparts, and cultural exchanges became trends signifying an optimistic future for the Korean Peninsula.

The Mount Kumgang project was another victory for engagement. North Korea's Mount Kumgang has been turned into a leisure resort for what the North used to call the class enemy of communism, the South Korean middle class. The engagement strategy linked the two economies to an unprecedented degree. As many as 1.8 million South Koreans have visited Mount Kumgang. At the end of 2009, total inter-Korean trade reached US$1.82 billion, accounting for 40% of North Korea's trade, despite nuclear tests, missile and rocket launchings, and continued shutdown of the Mount Kumgang tour.[28]

The fundamental problem was that South Koreans failed to maintain a consistent commitment to engagement, not delivering enough of the much-needed support to the reformers in Pyongyang, who always had to craft their political maneuvers carefully to satisfy the military and hard-liners. Reformers are the minority in North Korea, and they have taken great risks, even to their own lives. Thus, they have needed consistent success and confirmation from the outside on their nonthreatening intentions so that they could convince their leadership to stay on course.

In addition to shortcomings in Seoul's policies toward Pyongyang, a series of unfortunate events further complicated matters: the breakdown of the Korean Peninsula Energy Development Organization (KEDO), Washington's continuous verbal attacks on the North Korea leadership (e.g., President Bush's comments on the "tyranny of evil," Kim Jong-il as a "pygmy," "axis of evil," "loathing" Kim, etc.), disputes over and then the freezing of North Korean financial assets in the Macao-based Banco Delta Asia after the September 2005 agreement, and Japan's fixation on the abduction issue are only a few examples. Response to these issues by the United States and other members of the Six Party Talks needed better coordination and timing, for in some cases they threatened to derail all the progress that had been made. Additionally, the U.S. removal of North Korea from the list of terror-sponsoring states was painstakingly slow and proceeded only after Washington had made new demands upon new demands. Thus, the reformers in Pyongyang have been marginalized and the hard-liners returned to center stage. Kim Jong-il did not have many reasons to support the reformers, and neither does Kim Jong-un. In short, North Korean perceptions of threat and betrayal have only increased in recent years. When the Lee administration essentially reversed what it regarded as the ineffective and unconditional policy of engagement, Pyongyang only had to respond by personally dishonoring President Lee Myung-bak as "anti-unification," a "puppet of the U.S. warmongers," and "fascist." Obviously, attributing the current situation entirely to South Korea, the United States, and others is also unfair.

North Korea exaggerated its own perception of threat, did not show much of a swift commitment to denuclearization, and employed very stingy strategies in negotiations with the South and the United States. No matter whose fault it is, the political environment on the Korean Peninsula has become the worst since the end of the Cold War, exacerbated by the *Cheonan* sinking and the shelling at Yeonpyeong Island in 2010.

The North ultimately has no choice but to leave its isolation and engage the rest of the world; its economy will collapse otherwise. The DPRK will have to reinstate new reforms while strengthening its domestic power base. If such actions are inevitable, the outside must signal its readiness to cooperate along with its resolve for denuclearization. But external pressure only raises threat perception in Pyongyang, increases its regime cohesiveness, and aggravates its current aggressive external behavior. Unless South Korea and its allies can invade and win, continue to sanction, accept North Korea as a nuclear state, or endure at least another twenty years of North Korea's nuclear misadventures, then the only option is constructive engagement with North Korea. We need to empower the reformers in Pyongyang once again by returning to where we were at the turn of the century. In our opinion, the death of Kim Jong-il in December 2011 has not changed this calculus. If we continue on the current course of gridlock, we will end up with no future for reform and opening in North Korea, a more aggressive and paranoid Pyongyang, and above all, profound security instability in Northeast Asia. By supporting the reformers in Pyongyang and giving constructive engagement another chance, the other five parties and everyone engaged with the North can gradually shape North Korea into becoming economically interdependent with the outside, politically stable, behaviorally more predictable, and more communicative and amicable. Time is on our side, not North Korea's.

CONCLUSION

From the beginning, the North Korean nuclear crisis has presented a profound dilemma for South Korea. The emergence of an operationally nuclear North Korea would only provide a new urgency to an old problem. Obviously, an operational North Korean nuclear capability would have a serious impact on the security of South Korea and the stability of Northeast Asia. Although using force to neutralize North Korea's nuclear capability may be theoretically plausible, such an action would only mean another catastrophic war on the Korean Peninsula, and is therefore unlikely. Therefore, although it may be unpleasant, unwanted, and unacceptable, South Koreans may have to learn to live with an operationally nuclear North Korea. This strategic dilemma will limit South Korea's range of options, confining them to prudent engagement with the North. On the other hand, North Korea is no terrorist organization. The North has a return address with a long list of potential target sites north of the DMZ. Therefore, unless North Korea is completely delusional, the material capabilities of South Korea and the United States together would prevent the North from using any newfound capabilities it might develop.

Perhaps the NPT is one of the very few international institutions living up to its founding purposes. It has been largely successful in preventing proliferation of nuclear weapons beyond the official members of the nuclear club. On the other hand, one may argue that significant defections have indeed occurred. India, Pakistan, and perhaps North Korea have clearly demonstrated that when states want nuclear capabilities badly enough, they will press forward and the NPT seems not so effective.[29] States do what they can, not what they want. In this case, North Korea has pursued, and may well soon possess, nuclear weapons not simply for leverage but for the same reason that other states arm themselves: to deter an adversary. North Korea's main adversary happens to be the most powerful state in the world, armed with nuclear weapons.

All in all, an operationally nuclear North Korea would be very unpalatable to South Korea as well as to the international community. Even more unpalatable is that engagement remains the only viable option in the long term. Remember that the world has lived with "a nuclear China, the country once viewed as the ultimate rogue,"[30] for decades. South Korea's ultimate choice will most likely be to continue with its engagement policy for peaceful denuclearization while establishing orderly containment strategies. The combination of these two strategies is aimed at preventing further proliferation and deterrent postures, making sure the North knows the price it will have to pay if it goes ballistic.

CHAPTER FOUR

Beijing's Problem with an Operationally Nuclear North Korea

GREGORY J. MOORE

Speaking on North Korea's test of a nuclear device on October 9, 2006, official statements from the government of one of the permanent five members of the UN Security Council (UNSC) claimed that "the DPRK ignored [the] universal opposition of the international community and flagrantly conducted the nuclear test," and that this government "is resolutely opposed to it." Moreover, an expert on North Korea working in the defense sector of the same nation told the author he thought the Kim Jong-il regime was "scary" and "despotic," and that Kim maintained his rule by "brainwashing" his people. Hearing such words about North Korea from a senior Pentagon or South Korean official would certainly not be surprising. Yet, strange though it might seem to some, the views expressed came from official Chinese statements,[1] and the defense expert was one of China's most senior North Korea watchers, one with many years of experience in both Koreas.[2]

These statements express different Chinese sentiments toward North Korea than the language used by former People's Liberation Army marshal Zhu De, who once said that relations between the People's Republic of China (PRC) and the DPRK were as close as "lips and teeth," referring to relations during the Korean War era. In the last two decades, however, a subtle but quite remarkable transformation has taken place in the relations between the two countries, a transformation that has made China an important partner in U.S. and international efforts to roll back North Korea's weapons acquisitions programs.

What, really, is China's position on North Korea's acquisition of nuclear capabilities? The question is posed as such because a study of China's recent policy behavior toward North Korea reveals what might seem to be a measure of duplicity. On the one hand, China joined the other members of the UNSC in passing a resolution condemning North Korea's July 4 and October 14, 2006, missile tests, and joined UNSC members again in voting to condemn North Korea's October 9, 2006, nuclear tests. Again, after Pyongyang's second nuclear test on May 25, 2009, Beijing voted for another UNSC resolution condemning the test and imposing a series of sanctions, including bans on heavy weapons and nuclear- and missile-related items for North Korea, financial sanctions on North Korean companies working with the government on the test, and the imposition of a tougher inspections regime on shipping into and out of North Korea.

Yet China also seems to be increasing its economic engagement with North Korea even as Pyongyang goes further down the road toward nuclear operationality. In 2005 China accounted for more than five hundred thousand tons of cross-border food aid to Pyongyang,[3] and some $1.5 billion in bilateral trade with North Korea.[4] Despite Chinese opposition to the nuclear tests, those numbers increased after the first nuclear test in 2006; by 2008 China's trade with North Korea was some $2.8 billion (73% of Pyongyang's total trade for that year).[5] While numbers dipped a bit in 2009 because of UN sanctions following North Korea's second nuclear test in 2009, Sino–North Korean trade increased to $3.5 billion in 2010[6] and has only risen since.[7] Consequently, China is North Korea's number-one source of both aid and trade.

In this chapter I seek to answer the following questions: What explains the seeming paradox posed by China's pronounced discontent with North Korea's desire to acquire nuclear weapons and long-range missiles, and yet its continuing willingness to serve as North Korea's foremost source of aid and trade? Are the Chinese trying to bring North Korea to heel, or are they trying to prop it up?

The answer to the second question is "Both." Chinese policy is to bring North Korea to heel *and* to prop up its struggling economy. Odd though it might seem, this behavior is not at all duplicitous or contradictory but is based on a careful calculation of China's national interests. While the Chinese government goes to some pains to express affection and solidarity with North Korea, and while, as one Chinese military expert on North Korea put it, "The traditional friendship between China and North Korea is not empty talk,"[8] China's relations with North Korea have often been tense in recent years, resulting in this two-pronged approach. First, the Chinese have been working hard to dissuade North Korea from advancing its long-range missile and nuclear weapons programs because they have great potential to threaten some of China's most fundamental interests—namely, regional stability and possibly even China's economic modernization program if worst came to worst. Second, China continues to support North Korea economically and at times diplomatically because a complete collapse of North Korea is not in China's interest either. Both potentialities would create enormous problems for China.

Though some of the rhetoric of "lips and teeth" and friendship forged in blood is still tossed about and North Korea still has its supporters in Beijing, more and more Chinese experts and policymakers see North Korea as an anachronistic irritant and a potential catalyst for a series of events that could threaten China's most fundamental economic and security interests. Those holding the latter view have come to see North Korea's quest for nuclear weapons as China's gravest near-term security threat. In fact, many Chinese experts, such as Tsinghua University's Yan Xuetong—one of China's best-known foreign policy experts and a hawk regarding the United States—have argued that North Korea's pursuit of nuclear weapons has provoked the most recent North Korean nuclear crisis, not the United States.[9]

SOURCES OF TENSION IN SINO–NORTH KOREAN RELATIONS

What precipitated increased tension and the souring in the relationship between China and the DPRK in recent years? Most fundamentally, the key issues have been China's changing interests, changes in the region, the deterioration of the ties that used to bind China and North Korea together, and what Chinese policymakers have viewed as North Korea's increasingly provocative foreign policy behavior. Each of these laid the foundations for a souring Sino–North Korean relationship, and I consider each one below, followed by a number of the more striking examples of the increase in tension in the Sino–North Korean relationship in recent years.

An important part of the changing dynamics in Sino–North Korean relations is the fact that China has undergone a metamorphosis in recent decades in its understanding of its interests and its place in the world, moving from Maoist radicalism to Dengist hyperpragmatism, stressing the national interest above all in its foreign relations.[10] Today the number-one goal of Chinese policymakers is building and developing a strong economy and thereby modernizing and strengthening China. Chinese leaders concluded in the late 1970s that this was the way that China could attain both a higher level of development for its people and greater security in the long run. Consequently, China has a concomitant interest in terms of its foreign policy—regional stability—and North Korea has the power to disrupt China's plans for economic growth and regional stability in a number of ways.

Additionally, a number of regional changes have altered and in some cases put pressure on the Sino–North Korean relationship. The end of the Cold War and the demise of the Soviet Union removed an important source of potential support for North Korea's regime. China had to take up the slack, adding pressure to the relationship.[11] The end of the Cold War also coincided with new developmental dynamics in China and South Korea and greater post–Cold War economic integration between China, South Korea, Japan, and the United States. All of this has left North Korea feeling more isolated, as well as more dependent on and demanding of China.

In the last couple of decades, the ties that once bound China and North Korea together have also deteriorated. China's relations with North Korea are today much more complicated than they were in the years of "lips and teeth" when the two countries shared not only a common border, a long symbiotic historical relationship, a Confucian heritage, and a history of Japanese occupation but also a Marxist-Leninist ideology, "divided state syndrome," a history fighting U.S. and UN forces in the Korean War, pariah status in the international community, and refusal of diplomatic recognition by all but a few nations. The Cold War is gone and the Korean War a distant memory, and the two no longer share co-pariah international status, ideological affinity, or common interests relating to South Korea.

One of the most important sources of change in Sino–North Korean relations is the loss of ideological affinity, a change that is fundamental to their differing interests today. Both countries have long since departed from orthodox Marxist-Leninism, but while China has moved forward past it, most Chinese and Western observers agree that North Korea has moved backward toward feudalism, becoming a "post-modern dictator[ship]"[12] with "dynastic succession."[13] Indicative of the demise of DPRK/PRC ideological affinity was the decline of the governing role of the Korean Workers' Party (KWP) and the rise of the North Korean trinity of Father, Son, and Holy Notion (*Juche*).[14] Oh and Hassig among others argue that the DPRK formally became a military dictatorship in 1998 when Kim Jong-il was reelected chair of the National Defense Commission and began to rule the country from that position, which was then (and is still now, ostensibly) called "the highest post of the state."[15] This was a departure from past practice, wherein Kim Il-sung ruled from the position of general secretary of the Korean Workers' Party as well as president. However, whereas in other communist states, leaders ruled through the party and bodies like the Politburo, the KWP's Politburo Presidium had only one member under Kim Jong-il: Kim Jong-il himself. The KWP was not a significant source of ruling authority under Kim Jong-il, given that it only met twice under his rule (in 1980, when Kim Jong-il was named heir to his father's power, and again in late 2010, when Kim Jong-un was named Kim Jong-il's heir apparent). Instead Kim chose to rule through the National Defense Commission.[16] Because of these changes, analysts in the United States and China, including myself, conclude that North Korea is not communist[17] but is a totalitarian, dynastic, one-man military dictatorship, something that Chinese communist leaders have had trouble countenancing.[18]

Also gone are China and North Korea's former unifying antipathy toward South Korea, for China's interests have shifted. Though tensions remain between China and South Korea over the historical legacy of Koguryo[19] and China's positions on the 2010 *Cheonan* and Yeonpyeong Island conflicts between Seoul and Pyongyang,[20] most Chinese dealing with the Koreas find the South much easier to deal with than the North.[21] South Korea today is one of China's most important trading partners. Between 1992 and 1997, trade between the two nations quadrupled, to $23.7 billion per year. In 1997, China's trade with North Korea had shrunk to just $656.3 million.[22] China became South Korea's top trading partner in 2004, and bilateral trade passed $100 billion in 2005,[23] increasing to $207 billion in 2010; trade between China and North Korea stood at $3.5 billion in 2010.[24]

Moreover, because of the increasingly large volume of trade between China and South Korea and the great potential for trade between a reformed North Korea and China, leaders from China's northeastern provinces have been urging Beijing to pressure North Korea for reform, making North Korea policy a domestic political issue in Beijing as well.[25] Given China's 870-mile-long border with the North, many in China see much money to be made in trade with a reformed North Korea, and Pyongyang's anachronistic leadership has been the primary obstacle to boosting their region's economy. One Chinese North Korea expert said that politicians and businesspeople in Northeast China "hate" North Korea and its policies for this reason. Consequently politicians and businesspeople are pressuring Beijing to compel Pyongyang to open up and reform as China has done, so that they can make a living.[26] With China's present level of openness, economic development, and political decentralization, Beijing is less able to ignore such pleas than in the past.

Another reason that relations between China and North Korea soured in recent years was North Korea's provocative behavior after Kim Jong-il took over the North Korean leadership, the transition beginning in 1980 and made complete with the death of his father, Kim Il-sung, in 1994. As a responsible stakeholder in the international system, China had become increasingly weary of North Korean provocations under Kim Jong-il. The Chinese have come to embrace a clear disdain for a number of practices of the North Korean regime, from dynastic succession and the functional decline of the Korean Workers' Party as discussed above to Kim Jong-il's historical penchant for terrorism, illegal drug trade, the production and trade of counterfeit U.S. and Chinese currency, and the practice of extortion as discussed below. All played a part in the downward slide in the bilateral relationship.

The start of the decline in PRC-DPRK amity coincided closely with the rise in authority of Kim Jong-il in the late 1980s and early 1990s and was sealed with the passing of Kim Il-sung in 1994. In fact, contact between Beijing and Pyongyang broke down almost completely between 1994 and 1999.[27] A number of examples of Kim Jong-il's actions that affected relations between China and the DPRK are as follows.

One concerns the Dear Leader's interest in terrorism early in his rise to power. In 1983, North Korean agents planted a bomb in the ceiling of a room in Rangoon where a high-level diplomatic meeting was to take place between Burmese and South Korean leaders. The bomb killed most of South Korea's cabinet and narrowly missed South Korea's president, who was late for the meeting. Two North Korean Army officers were captured and tried by the Burmese government. Another example is the 1987 DPRK downing of a Seoul-based Korea Air Lines passenger plane with a bomb smuggled onboard by a female North Korean agent posing as a Japanese tourist, who then deplaned before the bomb exploded. The agent was captured soon after the bombing and confessed her guilt. Both events were linked directly to Kim Jong-il and condemned by the Chinese.

Kim Jong-il's willingness to affront his giant neighbor more directly was evidenced in 1990–91 when China, in line with its more pragmatic reform-era foreign policy, established relations with South Korea and voted to have it admitted to the United Nations. Pyongyang responded by establishing contact with Taiwan and made a deal whereby Pyongyang would be paid to take waste from Taiwan's nuclear power program.[28] The deal was eventually abandoned under Chinese and international pressure but was clearly meant as a jab at Beijing, signaling the North's displeasure over Beijing's establishing relations with Seoul.

Relations between Beijing and the new Kim regime deteriorated further in 1994 when the nation's saber rattling and threats to withdraw from the Nuclear Non-Proliferation Treaty brought about the first North Korean nuclear crisis, a crisis more serious than many realized at the time. Beijing temporarily cut off its supply of food exports to North Korea to show its displeasure. Perhaps partly because Beijing's relations with the new Kim regime were so poor, and partly because Beijing was also displeased with the new Clinton administration, Chinese leaders did very little to help Washington and Pyongyang find an accommodation at this time, though the United States and North Korea did reach an agreement later that year.

Relations between China and North Korea grew even worse when Kim Jong-il in 1996 tried to extort aid from China. Originally disclosed in Hong Kong's *Hsin Pao*, this incident began with North Korea asking Beijing for two hundred thousand tons of grain. China responded that this was too much, offering twenty thousand tons. Kim Jong-il reportedly went into a rage, threatened to play his Taipei card and made six additional demands, including Chinese weapons and mutual state visits by the two countries' heads of state. Beijing responded by saying it would only be able to send the secretary-general of the State Council to Pyongyang because China's top leaders were too busy. In response to Pyongyang's demands, Beijing responded, "We shall try our best, but we are still unable to meet the DPRK's demands." In an apparent attempt to quench the crisis, China later gave North Korea $59 million in material aid and $20 million in interest-free loans.[29]

Two more sources of bilateral tension came in 1997. When Chinese agricultural experts in the UN Development Programme in Pyongyang publicly encouraged North Korea to adopt Chinese-style reforms to help solve its economic problems, Pyongyang criticized them and called Deng Xiaoping a traitor to socialism. Beijing responded angrily, saying that it was considering cutting off food aid to North Korea. Pyongyang countered by opening discussions with Taiwan regarding direct flights between Taipei and Pyongyang. Taiwan is reported to have promised 500 million tons of food aid to North Korea to seal the deal, but it was scuttled after China backed away from its threats to cut off food aid.[30]

The other event that year deepened bilateral tensions and proved to be a grave blow to Pyongyang's leaders. In February, a top North Korean leader—former party secretary Hwang Jang-yop, creator of Pyongyang's *Juche* ideology—defected to the South Korean embassy in Beijing. After Beijing's initial refusal to let Hwang leave China, it eventually stood quietly by as he was spirited away to the Philippines and then on to Seoul, where he provided a treasure trove of information to South Korean and U.S. authorities. Hwang's defection and Beijing's refusal to intervene in the end brought about huge protests from Pyongyang and a temporary closing of the North Korean border with China.

After a slight improvement in China–North Korea relations in the late 1990s and early 2000s following the demise of the Soviet Union and U.S. actions in Kosovo, Afghanistan, and Iraq, Sino-DPRK relations took a turn for the worse again in late 2002 and early 2003, starting with North Korea's admission to U.S. diplomat James Kelly in October 2002 that it was indeed pursuing a uranium enrichment program.[31] In a policy paper presented to the Politburo after Pyongyang's disclosures, China's Vice Foreign Minister Wang Yi is reported to have expressed stern words about North Korea, calling North Korea's moves "diplomatic adventurism."[32] According to a participant at a regular meeting of top-level Chinese Foreign Ministry heads in November 2002, Chinese officials spoke freely about "cutting energy and food aid, and even opening the border to let more refugees in." Later, China signaled that Kim Jong-il was not welcome in China for the time being.[33]

Another provocation to China was Kim's proposed free-trade area in North Korea's Sinuiju, on China's border at Dandong, where the bulk of Sino–North Korean trade takes place. Kim's proposal to make Sinuiju a gambling city using U.S. dollars and catering primarily to wealthy Chinese, and his choice of Yang Bin to oversee the project, left Beijing feeling discomfited.[34] Yang was one of China's richest men but also a man wanted by Chinese authorities on charges of tax evasion and other crimes. Much to Kim Jong-il's disappointment, Yang was sent to jail in October 2002 and the Sinuiju project was put on ice.

In 2003 two other interesting developments occurred that suggested the souring of Sino-DPRK relations. In February, after North Korea had told the United States it had nuclear weapons, China shut down the oil pipeline between China and North Korea for three days,[35] a move that many observers in China and the U.S. interpreted as a strong message to North Korea. China provides the bulk of North Korea's oil, and given North Korea's dire economic straits and its massive energy shortages, any interruption in its oil supplies could be devastating. Then, in September 2003, China is reported to have deployed some 150,000 People's Liberation Army (PLA) troops to the China–North Korea border. While Chinese officials have admitted that the PLA has taken over for regular border guards there, it has denied any deeper implications, saying that the deployment was a "normal adjustment." Chinese military expert David Shambaugh viewed it differently: "The Chinese traditionally move troops to the borders to send signals to others. . . . This looks like a signal to North Korea."[36]

On February 21, 2004, in another sign of Sino–North Korean tension, China, acting on a request from the U.S. Central Intelligence Agency, prevented a train passing through China from proceeding to North Korea. The train was carrying a shipment of tributyl phosphate, a chemical used to extract weapons-grade plutonium from spent nuclear fuel rods—a sensitive matter given North Korea's 2002 removal of eight thousand spent fuel rods from international surveillance and previous suspicions of its trying to reprocess the rods for weapons-grade plutonium.[37]

The year 2004 seemed to mark an improvement in bilateral relations given an increase in high-level exchanges between Beijing and Pyongyang, including a visit to China by Kim Jong-il. Bilateral tensions deepened again in 2005, however, when North Korea announced to the world on February 10 that it possessed nuclear weapons and did not intend to continue participation in the Six Party Talks or any other regional forum with the United States. In covering North Korea's announcement, the Chinese news media was unusually unsympathetic toward North Korea, broadcasting international statements of condemnation and calls for North Korea to return to the Six Party Talks. According to Shi Yinhong, a North Korea watcher from China, "The Chinese government is really angry in their hearts about the declaration of North Korea, so they take a permissive attitude toward the media" (that is, allowing greater criticism of North Korea).[38] I heard comparable statements in a visit to Beijing at the time, when an interlocutor with good connections to the Chinese side of the DPRK-PRC relations nexus told me that the Chinese government had made a decision not to give any further financial aid in the form of cash payments to the DPRK because of Chinese frustrations with the North and the lack of accountability in how the aid was spent. Rather, China would limit support to grain, oil, and other kinds of aid.[39] This shift in approach has become common knowledge in recent years.

North Korean counterfeiting has also caused strains in the Sino–North Korean relationship. In 2005 the U.S. Treasury Department designated Macau's Banco Delta Asia (BDA) as a "primary money laundering concern" under the PATRIOT Act,[40] followed by a U.S.-ordered freezing of North Korean assets there valued at approximately $25 million. Beijing cooperated with the United States in freezing North Korean assets at BDA, which the United States accused of helping North Korea launder counterfeit U.S. one-hundred-dollar bills, as well as linking North Koreans to illegal weapons shipments and drug production and sales.[41] Interestingly, U.S. "sanctions" on North Korea in this case were "actually just a U.S. warning followed by a Chinese regulatory action," indicating full Chinese cooperation with the United States.[42] In July 2006 China continued to work with the United States to check illicit North Korean behavior by freezing North Korean assets at the Macau branch of China's own Bank of China because of charges of North Korean counterfeiting of not only U.S. hundred-dollar bills but Chinese currency as well.[43]

With North Korea's provocations in 2010 (the sinking of the ROK Navy's *Cheonan* and the shelling of the ROK military base and surrounding areas on Yeonpyeong Island), China took a more agnostic, even protective posture toward Pyongyang, saying it wasn't sure who was to blame for either incident. Interviews I conducted in China afterward led me to the conclusion that Beijing truly may not have been sure who to believe about the sinking of the *Cheonan*. Chinese interlocutors noted that while an international panel of experts concluded in a report that Pyongyang was to blame (saying a North Korean midget submarine was responsible), other reports indicated problems with this report and that, in the end, evidence was lacking as to Pyongyang's ultimate culpability. The Chinese thus thought it unfair to punish Pyongyang for an act for which it might not have been responsible. Regarding the Yeonpyeong Island incident, a Chinese expert on Korea whom I interviewed in Beijing in 2012 told me that Chinese analysts saw South Korea's artillery exercises in waters disputed by Pyongyang and Seoul as highly provocative. The shells landed in territorial waters that North Korea claims as its own, so from North Korea's perspective, Seoul's artillery practice was targeting North Korean territory.[44] Still, he said that the Chinese did not agree with Pyongyang's escalation, in other words, the shelling of Yeonpyeong Island and the consequent killing of innocent civilians.[45] Though Beijing refused to go along with Seoul and the Western countries in condemning Pyongyang for its role in these events, neither does China have great love for the conservative Lee Myung-bak administration in Seoul.[46] Beijing clearly did not enjoy being put in the position of having to defend or answer for Pyongyang, and these events have only deepened the misgivings among many Chinese officials and North Korea experts about China's role as North Korea's guarantor.[47]

There has also been evidence of Pyongyang taking advantage of on Chinese companies doing business in North Korea, which has angered Beijing as well. An important example is the experiences of China's Xiyang Group, which invested $40 million in a mining venture in North Korea. Xiyang leaders say that after four months of operations in North Korea, just when North Korean technicians in the venture had mastered the technology that China had brought in, the company's assets were seized by the DPRK government and its Chinese management and workers kicked out. Xiyang pressed Pyongyang for $31.2 million in damages, but at the time of writing the issue was not resolved.[48] Actions such as those in 2010 and those experienced by the Xiyang Group have deepened the divide in the Chinese foreign policy community between the traditionalists supporting Pyongyang and the more strategic thinkers who have concluded that Pyongyang is a liability that Beijing should no longer defend.[49]

North Korea's greatest affront to Chinese interests and sensibilities, however, has been its weapons tests and weapons acquisition programs. In August 1998 North Korea launched a long-range missile in a test over Japanese airspace, causing an uproar in Japan and the region. Consequently, Japan announced it would join the United States in research on a regional missile defense system, and the missile launch helped the Japanese right in its argument for normalizing Japanese defense policy. These events concern China to no small degree. International observers in June 2006 noticed the readying of several more North Korean missiles for launch, and Chinese officials publicly warned North Korea not to launch them.[50] North Korea ignored Beijing's warnings, however, and on July 4 test-launched seven missiles over the Sea of Japan. In a July 7 *People's Daily* article, the Chinese authorities printed a series of world reactions to the North Korean tests, all condemnatory in nature—again, not previously the norm in Beijing's handling of information on North Korea.

Truly unusual was what occurred in New York several days after the missile launches. Along with the other fourteen members of the UN Security Council, China voted for UNSC Resolution 1695, expressing "grave concern" about North Korean actions and the need for restraint so as to avoid further tension. The resolution also reminded North Korea of its obligation to avoid proliferation of weapons of mass destruction, and "deplor[ed]" North Korea's pursuit of nuclear weapons. China did not exercise its veto or abstain but uncharacteristically voted for this resolution.

North Korea tested the mettle of China, the United States, and the neighboring countries in a truly profound way in October 2006 when it announced that it had successfully tested a nuclear weapon. China's response to North Korea's test is significant. In the run-up to the actual test, Beijing's ambassador to the United Nations, Wang Guangya, said, "No one is going to protect" the DPRK if it commences with "bad behavior . . . I think if North Koreans do have the nuclear test, I think that they have to realize that they will face serious consequences."[51] Interestingly, a number of sources reported a cutoff of Chinese oil supplies to North Korea in September 2006, before the test.[52] Discussing this Chinese cutoff of oil, He Jun, an energy expert and consultant based in Beijing, observed, "It is a sharp and sudden reduction at a sensitive time, so political considerations cannot be ruled out. . . . China could be sending a clear signal."[53] Perhaps even more interesting is the report that all of China's oil exports in September 2006 (125,185 tons of crude) were exported to the United States,[54] an important message to Pyongyang suggesting which side Beijing was taking in this particular instance.[55]

Following Pyongyang's nuclear test, China's response was swift, condemning the test in no uncertain terms. "The DPRK ignored [the] universal opposition of the international community and flagrantly conducted the nuclear test on October 9. The Chinese government is resolutely opposed to it."[56] The word "flagrantly" here is *hanran* in Chinese, a term normally reserved in its use in the official Chinese lexicon for China's enemies or rivals—historical examples being when the Japanese prime minister visited the Yasukuni Shrine, or when the United States bombed the Chinese embassy in Belgrade.[57] Zhang Liangui, a North Korea watcher at China's Central Party School, said, "China has tried to persuade North Korea that talking with the outside world is in its interest. . . . Now China will have to demonstrate that there is a price to pay for ignoring that advice." He said North Korea's decision to test its nuclear device, in spite of Chinese admonitions not to, amounts to a slap in the face for the Chinese.[58] The Dear Leader's decision to go ahead with the nuclear test despite China's clear and emphatic admonitions not to do so took the Sino-DPRK relationship to a new low.

On October 14, 2006, China displayed its displeasure by standing with the other members of the UN Security Council in passing a resolution to denounce North Korea's nuclear test, with China's UN ambassador even calling for "punitive actions" against the DPRK.[59] After the nuclear test, China was reported to have been searching trucks crossing the DPRK-China border, but China has not been keen on searching ships at sea, for fear that such searches could provoke armed conflicts with North Korea. Also China has not fully endorsed the U.S.-initiated Proliferation Security Initiative (PSI). Still, one report says that Beijing is seriously considering adopting the PSI and has been quietly cooperating on interdiction issues involving North Korea, including those at sea.[60] In addition, China was reported to have instructed its four largest banks to halt all financial transactions with North Korea after the nuclear test. "All transactions are blocked, whether it's company-to-company or person-to-person," said a Bank of China employee in Dandong, China, on North Korea's border at the time.[61] Although China did work to make sure the resolution required that any military response to events in North Korea would require further discussion and votes at the Security Council, and that inspections of North Korean cargo ships and vehicles were voluntary and not required, Beijing's seriousness about its opposition to the DPRK's moves should not be doubted.

After Pyongyang's second nuclear test in May 2009, China's patience with Pyongyang was further strained. China strongly condemned the test and voted in favor of UNSC Resolution 1874, which included the following further sanctions against the DPRK: a large-scale arms embargo (excluding small arms); an embargo on any items related to ballistic missile, nuclear, or other WMD programs; an embargo on the export of luxury goods to North Korea; and a number of sanctions that target individual assets and entities in North Korea, including a ban on travel for those individuals. While China's enforcement of such sanctions on its own borders with North Korea appears to be quite lax, particularly regarding loose definitions of "luxury goods," it appears that China has tightened its inspections of exports to North Korea, as a number of examples are available of its intercepting shipments of weapons-related materials that were being trans-shipped through China into North Korea.[62] Japan's *Asahi Shimbun* reported that Beijing again used oil shipments to North Korea as leverage to send a message signaling China's displeasure, reducing the flow of oil into North Korea for a time following the tests.[63]

In this section of the chapter I have documented the reasons for the slide in China–North Korea relations and evidence of the depth of that slide. While the elder Northeast Asian socialist brother has made good for himself, the younger has been somewhat of a black sheep for some time. Even as China has joined almost all of the international governmental organizations, including the International Monetary Fund and the World Trade Organization, and is now a yet imperfect but well-respected citizen in world affairs, North Korea has remained for the most part in *Juche* autarky mode and has moved forward with nuclear weapons and missile programs despite warnings from the international community and China not to do so. While China has entered the global mainstream, North Korea has in the last two decades drifted downstream.

NORTH KOREA'S THREATS TO CHINA'S INTERESTS

Simply put, North Korea has become "a liability"[64] to China. Some specific actions of North Korea and situations it can provoke threaten some of China's most fundamental interests. Two stand out, however, as being the biggest problems for China: North Korea's weapons acquisition programs and the possible collapse of North Korea either because of a lack of reform or external pressure, or both. These two issues also explain China's seemingly duplicitous policy toward North Korea—holding the North Korean regime to account for its rogue weapons programs while propping up North Korea's economy.

North Korea's Weapons Programs

North Korea's moves to acquire nuclear weapons and longer-range ballistic missile systems, and the potential that it might transfer these materials or technologies to other countries fundamentally threaten China's most basic interests. The majority of China's North Korea experts agree that "it is unacceptable"[65] for North Korea to acquire nuclear weapons.[66] Beijing has been clear on this point as well.[67] In this section I discuss the specific ways that North Korea's weapons programs threaten China.

First and perhaps foremost, North Korean long-range ballistic missile and nuclear weapons programs elicit in Chinese policymakers the fear that North Korea could provoke a military intervention from the United States or other powers in its own backyard. China's concerns have been that were North Korea to successfully acquire and test nuclear weapons or proliferate them aggressively, the United States, Japan, and others would condemn North Korea and might move to forcefully disarm it at some point, perhaps including strikes on the Yongbyon facility. Though the United States discussed these options during the 1994 crisis and Japanese officials discussed such strikes in October 2006,[68] the United States and others have exhibited restraint after the 2006 and 2009 tests. However, if conditions deteriorated and the United States or Japan were to launch preemptive strikes against North Korean facilities, North Korea might respond with an artillery barrage against Seoul, leading to a general outbreak of hostilities on the Korean Peninsula. However unlikely such a scenario might appear at present, the possibilities remain real for China. The Chinese do not want a war in their backyard, particularly one that could bring U.S. troops again to China's border with Korea. Nor, for a number of reasons, does China want to see international sanctions against North Korea. In one author's words, "Beijing recognizes that the real potential for conflict lies with North Korea, not South Korea or the United States."[69]

The second way that North Korea's weapons programs pose a threat to China is that they could harm China's relations with the international community. Either international military action or comprehensive sanctions against

North Korea could put China in the awkward position of having to choose sides between its old ally and neighbor or the international community. China has worked hard to revitalize its international image since the Tiananmen Square incident of 1989, even winning accession to the World Trade Organization and putting on a superbly run 2008 Olympics. Given continued international questions about China's human rights situation, tensions involving the status of its minorities, and its treatment of dissidents, among other issues, failing to stand with the international community on the North Korea issue could have negative political and economic implications for an increasingly interdependent China, particularly as it regards three of its four most important trading partners: the United States, Japan, and South Korea, all parties to the North Korea crisis.[70]

North Korean activities threaten China in a third way in that the DPRK's acquisition and deployment of nuclear weapons might lead to major realignments in the regional balance of power, wherein Japan, South Korea, and even Taiwan might either seek nuclear weapons themselves or at least more actively seek military cooperation with the United States, including participation in its missile defense shield. All of the Chinese North Korea experts consulted for this chapter mentioned this factor to some degree, which has several dimensions.

For example, many Chinese fear that a nuclear North Korea could elicit greater pressures on the Japanese government to more fully rearm or become a nuclear power. That North Korea's launching of the Taepodong missile over Japan in 1998 played an important role in Japan's decision to join the United States in building and deploying a missile shield in the region is well established. Moreover, some politicians in Japan (e.g., Shintaro Ishihara, former prime minister Yasuo Fukuda, and former Democratic Party of Japan chairman Ichiro Ozawa) are already on record as saying that Japan should consider having nuclear weapons. In fact, Ozawa has stated that Japan already has enough plutonium to make three thousand to four thousand nuclear weapons.[71] Japan's well-developed nuclear energy program gives it the fissile material it needs to make nuclear weapons,[72] and it certainly has the technology to weaponize the fissile material it possesses. While Japan has not made any official moves toward becoming a nuclear power since the North Korean nuclear tests, then Japanese foreign minister Taro Aso and others tried to initiate a debate on acquiring nuclear weapons for Japan after the 2006 test,[73] a suggestion squelched by then prime minister Shinzo Abe. Still, Japan continues to use its "recessed nuclear status" (the possibility of going nuclear) as leverage in its relations with its neighbors,[74] and Pyongyang's tests certainly add gravitas to Japan's nuclear debate.[75]

South Korean public and official positions on nuclear weapons could change as a result of North Korean accession to a state of nuclear operationality as well. In the early 1970s South Korea sought to acquire nuclear weapons,[76] but U.S. pressure stopped it. More recently, in 2004 it was disclosed that South Korean scientists had continued doing research with plutonium and enriched uranium despite South Korea's official anti–nuclear weapons stance. In October 2006, opposition Grand National Party former chair Lee Hoe-chang said that South Korea should research the feasibility of acquiring nuclear weapons to counter North Korea's new capabilities.[77] While former president Roh Moo-hyun was staunchly against such policies, the December 2007 elections brought the more conservative Lee Myung-bak to power, along with his tougher policy on North Korea, although he shows no signs of changing Seoul's policy on nuclear weapons. In any case, South Koreans clearly have nuclear energy and the resources to become a nuclear power presently should they choose to do so.[78] The Chinese certainly prefer a nuclear-free Korean Peninsula, whether those weapons belong to Seoul or Pyongyang.

Taiwan is another factor in Chinese thinking on North Korean nuclear operationality. Chinese policymakers worry about what impact North Korean and potentially Japanese nuclear weapons development could have on Beijing's relations with Taiwan. In fact, Taiwan had an advanced nuclear weapons program in the 1970s but gave it up under U.S. pressure. Taiwan appears to have continued to experiment with plutonium in the 1980s,[79] and according to some sources could easily restart its nuclear weapons program using the plutonium-rich fuel rods from its six extant nuclear reactors.[80] A North Korean nuclear threat could make talk of Taiwan's need for nuclear weapons common in Taipei, particularly if Japan and perhaps South Korea acquire them. More likely is the possibility that a nuclear North Korea could start an East Asian arms race that would drive Taiwan closer to the United States, possibly making Taiwan put more pressure on the United States and Japan to let it be a full participant in the missile defense system under development. Given China's lack of sufficient amphibious capabilities to successfully invade Taiwan[81] and its reliance on a conventional missile-based deterrence system against Taiwan independence at present, any moves by Taiwan to acquire a nuclear deterrent or become a full participant in the Japan-U.S. missile defense system would be disastrous for Beijing.

Even if North Korea's further tests or deployment of nuclear weapons did not elicit similar moves in Japan, South Korea, or Taiwan, they might spark a *conventional* arms race in East Asia, giving all the more impetus for a reenergized U.S. presence in the region, likely reinvigorating alliances between the United States, Japan, South Korea, and possibly Taiwan. They would also likely deepen commitments to research, development, and eventual deployment of military technologies capable of countering North Korean, and potentially Chinese, nuclear missiles. Japanese prime minister Abe was in Seoul at the time of the October 2006 North Korean nuclear test. In discussing the test at the time he said that it was "unpardonable," and that Japan and the United States would step up their cooperation on the missile defense system they have been working on together since North Korea's 1998 missile test over Japanese waters.[82] Such outcomes are exactly what China fears could flow from development of North Korea's weapons programs.

The fourth way that North Korea's weapons programs threaten China comes from the uncertainty they bring in China's own relations with its unpredictable neighbor. Few consider it probable that North Korea would threaten China with its nuclear weapons, but Chinese concerns are palpable regarding even this possibility. According to the official *People's Daily*, "It is not impossible that China may be confronted with nuclear blackmail [from North Korea] over some issue one day."[83] Likewise, as a Chinese North Korea watcher told me, North Korea's acquisition of nuclear weapons would "cause some problems, not only in relations with the U.S. and the U.K., but that is also a threat to China, especially during tense periods between China and North Korea, because China doesn't know what North Korea wants to do when the tension is between them."[84] The Chinese themselves are not necessarily any more certain of North Korean intentions than their U.S. counterparts. In fact, when George W. Bush asked Chinese President Jiang Zemin at their summit at Bush's Crawford, Texas, ranch in 2002 if he thought Kim Jong-il was a "peaceful man," switching into English Jiang replied, "Honestly, I don't know."[85]

Fifth, North Korean weapons programs are a potential threat to China because of the likelihood that a war on the peninsula or a collapse of the hermit kingdom could bring on an onslaught of refugees, known in China as *tuobeizhe* (or *tuoli beichaoxian zhe* [lit., persons fleeing North Korea]). This threat is also one of the primary reasons that Beijing has done so much to prop up North Korea in recent years. A collapse could be catastrophic in human terms and in terms of what it could cost Beijing to harbor so many *tuobeizhe*. Approximately 2 million Koreans live in Manchuria (northeast China) as Chinese citizens, half of them in the Yanbian Autonomous Region of Jilin Province, and most have not assimilated into Chinese society and continue to speak Korean. Some sixty thousand to one hundred thousand North Korean refugees are in China as well, though human rights groups put the number as high as three hundred thousand. Some refugees, including high-profile cases such as that of Hwang

Jang-yop, have even made it to Beijing and have forced their way into South Korean, Japanese, or other embassies seeking asylum. The refugees put China in an awkward position, for while North Korea demands their return, China hesitates to do so because of concerns about their safety and the attention of Western governments and human rights organizations. Yet by letting them all stay, China fears encouraging thousands more to come, just as many people in the United States near the Mexican border fear that loosening U.S. immigration laws will encourage yet more immigrants to come to the United States. China's concern is that these refugees could spur Korean nationalism in northeast China in such a way that China might face the sort of problem with Koreans that the former Yugoslavia faced with Albanians in Kosovo. The *tuobeizhe* could also pose as protagonists in labor movements and other dramas that Beijing does not want to play out in northeastern China's rust belt, where unemployment is relatively high. Moreover, North Koreans in northeastern China have also historically had a reputation of participating in the criminal underworld there, given their ambiguous status.[86] In recent years, the flow of illegal North Korean immigrants into China has caused tension between Beijing and Seoul as well, as Beijing tends to deport them back into North Korea, where they are likely tortured and imprisoned.

Last, given the dependence of the Chinese Communist Party on continued economic growth for its legitimacy, perhaps hitting closest to home for Chinese leaders is the serious potential that North Korean actions could cause major economic disruption in East Asian and Chinese markets because of war or comprehensive sanctions against the DPRK. China's economy is now heavily dependent on trade, and trade requires stability—particularly when three of China's top four trading partners over the last few years, the United States, Japan, and South Korea, in that order (in 2010, Hong Kong was number three), would likely be party to the conflict.[87] Add the cost of any support China might be obliged to offer North Korea, whether during or in the aftermath of a war, and it becomes clear that a war or serious conflict on the Korean Peninsula, even if China did not support North Korea or remained neutral, could have a huge impact on regional trade and on China's economy.

The gravity of these matters for China arises from the intimate link between regional stability and trade on the one hand, and China's domestic economic growth and domestic political stability on the other. According to one Chinese observer, "The North Korean nuclear crisis is a severe challenge to China's efforts to keep the Korean Peninsula nuclear free, for the Korean Peninsula is China's strategic northeast security buffer,[88] and any tension on the Peninsula will wreck the region's peace and stability—no security on the Peninsula means no realization of China's ultimate goal of modernization."[89] War or serious conflict involving North Korea could cause a disruption of trade and investment in the region or a flight of portfolio investment, dollars, yen, and euros from China and the region toward safer, more stable environs in the Americas or Europe, as occurred in 1997. All of this could be devastating to Chinese economic development, particularly if it seriously disrupted China's surging exports, given that the United States, Japan, and South Korea are China's number-one, -three, and -four top export markets, totaling $283.3 billion, $121.1 billion, and $68.8 billion, respectively, in 2010.[90] Disruptions could cause economic slowdowns leading to layoffs, bank collapses, and other problems, which could ultimately shake China's domestic political stability and, if prolonged, could even threaten the rule of the Chinese Communist Party—given that the CCP's legitimacy today rests primarily on successful economic development.

As Susan Shirk and many others have observed, China's economy is in a very sensitive stage of development,[91] a sensitivity that is even more acute following the global economic recession starting in 2008, the color revolutions in Central Asia, and the Arab Spring of 2011. Yu Xintian, a well-respected observer of Chinese politics and international affairs, has said, "China is in a phase where instability from domestic contradictions is a frequent occurrence" because of "the transition from a centrally planned to a market economy." Therefore, "if it is not handled well, it can bring about social unrest."[92] She notes that many political movements in Chinese history in the last century were prompted by events outside of China, so the Chinese government watches the situation in North Korea closely. If the Chinese economy is battered or stalls for some reason, the CCP will face the wrath of laid-off workers, the poor left behind by the reforms, and the "I-told-you-sos" of neo-leftists. Such persons are already highly disillusioned by China's economic reforms, and major breakdowns in the economy could bring them out into the streets. Chinese leaders have no interests more fundamental than keeping this potential scenario from playing out. Any action by leaders in Pyongyang that could have an adverse effect on China's domestic political stability is a serious matter for leaders in Beijing.

The Danger to China of a North Korean Collapse

Besides the dangers of its weapons acquisition programs, North Korea poses another threat to China: the danger that North Korean foot dragging on reform and human rights abuses, and popular discontent on other issues, might cause the hermit kingdom to collapse. Each of the Chinese North Korea experts I consulted for this chapter told me that they thought North Korea needed to reform. Most opined that one of China's greatest worries about its neighbor was its lack of reform and the problems this could bring China. These experts are not alone. According to the Failed States Index, North Korea's economy was the second-worst in the world; as a candidate for state failure, North Korea was in "critical" condition, one of the world's worst states.[93] A North Korean collapse would create a myriad of potential problems for Beijing.

The dangers posed to Beijing by a Pyongyang collapse overlap significantly with the scenarios discussed above regarding North Korea's weapons programs. A collapse could bring a refugee flow to Northeast China and all that would entail for the Chinese if unrest were to break out in the DPRK. A civil war within the North or a power vacuum could result such that China might find it necessary to intervene militarily in North Korea to protect its borders,[94] or it could raise the specter of a violent South Korean or U.S. takeover of the North. China would prefer not to have to intervene, and Beijing does not fancy the notion of North Korea as a Northeast Asian version of present-day Somalia, the pre-2001 Taliban-ruled Afghanistan, or China itself during its own Warring States Period. No one knows how a unified Korea would treat China, which way it would lean internationally, or how it would handle the Koguryo and Paektusan disputes.[95] Nor is China keen on seeing U.S. troops on its border. Another possibility in the event of a North Korean regime collapse is a large financial drain on Beijing, as it might have to commit resources to aid, rebuild, and stabilize the new Pyongyang regime or a reunified Korea—providing for thousands (millions?) of North Korean refugees in China or Korea, funding a peacekeeping force in the North, or spending resources to secure a potentially more chaotic Sino–North Korean border due to a collapse of authority in Pyongyang or the stationing of troops belonging to third parties. For these reasons, the Chinese experts I consulted for this chapter maintained that while Chinese policymakers are not fans of the North Korean style of regime, they would rather see an orderly economic reform and power transition in Pyongyang than a dramatic and potentially cataclysmic regime change.

Consequently, Chinese officials have been counseling North Korean leaders to embark on cautious political and economic reform for some time, along the lines of the Vietnamese model.[96] Recent studies of the North Korean economy reveal that trade between China and North Korea, and Chinese investment in North Korea, is accelerating at a rapid pace as China tries to shift its relations with the DPRK to a for-profit mode for its own benefit and to spur growth and reform in North Korea. In one excellent study of Chinese investment in North Korea, Jae-Cheol Kim concludes that the Chinese central government has been working hard to encourage Chinese entrepreneurs to invest in North Korea, such that Chinese investment in North Korea accounted for 85% of all direct foreign investment in the DPRK in 2004, focused primarily on restaurants, stores, manufacturing, and mining.[97] The pace of Chinese economic activity with North Korea has only increased in recent years, and in 2010 a $10 billion Chinese investment project in North Korea was announced that alone accounted for 70 percent of North Korea's total gross domestic product and 60% of its total incoming foreign investments in 2010.[98]

North Korea's economic dependence on China is remarkable. Should Beijing withdraw its economic assistance, "The DPRK would likely collapse"[99] or at least become highly unstable. Thus, because Beijing deems North Korea's collapse not in its interest and because North Korea is so heavily dependent upon China, Chinese policymakers believe they must continue to prop up the regime, at least in a minimalist sense, until reforms are sufficient to keep the North Korean economy on its own feet. Haggard and Noland note that "although China has continued reservations about North Korea's economic strategy and nuclear ambitions, it has equally significant concerns about economic pressure that would lead to political upheaval, a second economic collapse, and a flood of refugees."[100] This explains China's reluctance to allow robust sanctions regimes against Pyongyang or other attempts to pull the rug out from under North Korea's regime economically. China isn't enthusiastically propping up an anachronistic totalitarian despot but rather is trying to avoid the catastrophic collapse of a near-failed state on its borders and the disaster that would be ensue.

Beijing has a lot to worry about regarding North Korea. The DPRK is playing a game of its own making, with its own rules, and it does not march to the tune China plays, if it ever did. Consequently, Beijing has come to view North Korea through lenses that are quite different than those through which it viewed the DPRK during the Cold War. North Korea's weapons acquisition programs and its reluctance to reform pose significant dilemmas for China, with the potential to impact China in profoundly adverse ways.

THE SIX PARTY TALKS AND CHINA'S EVOLVING ROLE IN NORTHEAST ASIA

The matters discussed above explain why China went from the sidelines in 1994 during the first North Korean nuclear crisis to the front lines in 2003 and after in the struggle to bring North Korea to the negotiating table in pursuit of an agreement with the United States and others regarding its weapons programs. In 1994 China did little to help resolve the nuclear crisis, as it viewed that chiefly as the responsibility of the United States, which did eventually get North Korea to the negotiating table, first with Assistant Secretary of State Robert Gallucci and later with former president Jimmy Carter, who is credited with the breakthrough that led to the 1994 Agreed Framework.

When in the early years of the new millennium it became apparent that the Agreed Framework had broken down and North Korea was proceeding with its weapons programs, however, China began to take a more active international role in seeking a solution to the North Korean dilemma. This decision ultimately culminated in the Six Party Talks, comprising North Korea, South Korea, China, the United States, Japan, and Russia. Because of the growing sensitivity of peace and stability on the Korean Peninsula to China's economic and political interests, "China very directly exerted its energy to kick off multilateral talks concerning the North Korean nuclear crisis."[101] In 2003 Beijing initiated and hosted talks between the United States and the DPRK, and then took the lead in arranging and again hosting the several rounds of Six Party Talks by which these parties have been working to resolve the North Korean nuclear issue since 2003, convening the first round of Six Party Talks in Beijing in August of that year.

The Six Party Talks have been significant in the evolution of Chinese foreign policy, for "never in the diplomatic history of the PRC has the country been so deeply or extensively involved in a controversial regional issue to which it was not a direct party."[102] What was the source of the dramatic new foreign policy posture for China? The answer is in the understandable evolution of China's changing interests. The statement of one of China's senior U.S. watchers while observing Pyongyang and Washington slip toward conflict in 2002–3 is illuminating: "One of the two [the D.P.R.K. or the United States] might go crazy. This would cause big problems for China. So China had to do something."[103] And so China has.

While the first round of Six Party Talks in August 2003 failed to achieve much in terms of resolving the nuclear crisis, it did establish the important precedent for the talks themselves.[104] The Chinese facilitated a second round of talks in February 2004, a third round in June 2004, and a fourth round in July, August, and September 2005. The fourth round of talks brought about what seemed to be a breakthrough on September 19, 2005, in which North

Korea promised to dismantle its nuclear weapons programs in exchange for U.S. and South Korea assistance with its energy needs, a U.S. assurance that it had no intention of attacking North Korea, U.S. and Japanese commitments to work toward normalizing relations with North Korea, and South Korean and U.S. declarations that they had no nuclear weapons on the Korean Peninsula. Korea expert and adviser to the Bush administration Victor Cha notes that he was surprised that the United States agreed to this negative security assurance (i.e., "We promise not to attack you"), for as the Russian delegation to the talks noted, throughout the Cold War the Soviet Union sought such an assurance from Washington and never received it.[105] Now it was offered to Pyongyang—no small feat.

As good as all of this sounds, a day after the fourth round concluded, North Korea threw cold water on prospects for success by stating that unless it was first supplied with a light water reactor to meet its power needs, it would not dismantle its nuclear weapons program. A fifth round of Six Party Talks convened in November 2005 but reached a further snag, and the Talks completely stalled with North Korean unhappiness over U.S. actions freezing North Korean funds at Macau's Banco Delta Asia. The fifth round of talks were stalled as well through most of 2006, a year capped by North Korea's testing of a nuclear device on October 9.

Things brightened in late December 2006 when U.S. and North Korean envoys met in Berlin and began to make progress on a deal that was formalized on February 13, 2007, in the final phase of the fifth round. North Korea would shut down its Yongbyon nuclear facilities and fully disclose all of its nuclear programs in exchange for 1 million tons of fuel oil and a U.S. promise to release the BDA funds as well as begin discussions of normalizing relations between the United States and the DPRK. This agreement seemed to be the one the parties had been looking for—for the most part. Unlike the September 2005 agreement, which began to fall apart the next day, the February 2007 agreement appeared to have staying power and address all the major issues regarding the nuclear impasse. A sixth round of Six Party Talks commenced in March 2007 to work out some of the details, and the BDA issue was finally resolved in June when the Federal Reserve Bank of New York received the funds from BDA, transferring them to the Russian central bank and then to a North Korean account in Russia. The sixth round of the Six Party Talks saw the parties reaching a successful outcome on October 3, 2007, when Pyongyang agreed to disable its nuclear facilities at Yongbyon and give a complete accounting for its nuclear activities by year's end. While that full accounting never came, Pyongyang did destroy the main cooling tower of the Yongbyon facility on June 27, 2008, an event captured in dramatic images projected to media around the world.

With the incoming Obama administration in Washington, there seemed to be renewed hope for progress on the North Korean nuclear impasse. Obama promised to negotiate with regimes in Pyongyang and Tehran. With Pyongyang his new special envoy for North Korea, Stephen Bosworth, told North Korean interlocutors that the new administration was hoping to move forward to resolve the impasse with the DPRK.

Obama's outstretched hand was met, however, with North Korea's April 5, 2009, test of a Taepodong-2 missile, and its second nuclear test on May 25, 2009. North Korea walked away from any prospect of returning to the Six Party Talks as a result of the UN Security Council resolutions and sanctions passed against it. In late 2009 North Korean diplomats expressed to Chinese diplomats a willingness to return to the talks, and they met with special envoy Bosworth in December 2009. However, what little progress was being made was stymied by the events of 2010. The sinking of the *Cheonan* and the shelling of Yeonpyeong Island so frayed relations between Pyongyang and the Seoul/Washington/Tokyo nexus that reconvening the talks was impossible for a time. Coolness between the parties continued through 2011.

With the death of Kim Jong-il in late 2011, the prospects for renewed talks—after a transition period for Pyongyang—seemed to brighten if only a bit with hope that progress might be made with the new leadership after a consolidation period. This was particularly evident when, on February 20, 2012, a surprise Leap Day Agreement between the DPRK and the United States was announced; in exchange for 240,000 tons of foodstuffs, Pyongyang agreed to a moratorium on uranium enrichment at its Yongbyon facility and plutonium reactor.[106] While Pyongyang does reportedly have other enrichment facilities, the agreement showed that the new leadership appeared to be in a position and possibly a mood to make deals. However, a failed move by the DPRK to launch a "satellite" in April using a long-range ballistic missile banned under UN Security Council resolutions brought new tension, condemnation from almost all quarters, and effectively did in the Leap Day Agreement. As of the time of writing, the Six Party Talks had not recommenced. It seems likely that at some time in the future, the Six Party Talks will eventually recomence, barring any further nuclear or missile tests on Pyongyang's part.

The Six Party Talks can only be as successful as any agreement they broker, it would seem. Despite the successes of 2007–8, the additional nuclear tests in 2009 were a major setback to the process. Obviously many issues remain, such as the full disclosure of all North Korean nuclear activities, including its stealthy enrichment program, the latter of which was fully disclosed in late 2010 when North Korean officials showed their enrichment facilities to U.S. nuclear expert Siegfried Hecker.[107] Some Chinese North Korea watchers like Lin Limin are cynical about Pyongyang's intentions. "To build and deploy nuclear weapons is a goal North Korea is actively pursuing, a goal it will not abandon even if it reaches the very end of its rope" (*shan qiong shui jin*).[108] Yet whatever their views of Pyongyang's motives or the likelihood of a successful outcome of the Talks, Chinese policymakers must be given credit for making the Talks happen. China has certainly found the Six Party Talks to be an important part of its interest calculations as it regards North Korea and Northeast Asian security.

CONCLUSIONS: CHINA'S INTERESTS AND ITS TWO-PRONGED NORTH KOREA POLICY

What are China's interests in North Korea today? "Maintaining the Korean Peninsula's peace and stability is China's basic policy."[109] Continued economic development is the Chinese leadership's most fundamental interest and its best hope for continued political stability at home. It is *not* in China's interest nor is it China's policy to allow North Korea to acquire and deploy nuclear weapons, for this could set in motion a series of events that would threaten to undermine China's most fundamental interests. Thus, while China has not supported instances or threats of heavy-handedness in Washington's dealing with North Korea, like the United States, China is seriously committed to a nuclear-free Korean Peninsula.

So why has China not sanctioned Pyongyang but instead increased its food aid to North Korea after Pyongyang's nuclear tests, and its trade and investment more recently? Why does it continue to host visits by North Korean leaders to China? Why has it protected the DPRK from the full brunt of a more robust UN Security Council sanction regime? The primary reasons are that China does not want North Korea to collapse nor to start a war in retaliation for international sanctions. China perceives clearly the prickly, unstable nature of present-day North Korea. China is propping up the North Korean economy in a minimalist sense while pressuring North Korean to reform its economy so that China and South Korea will not be left with the bill, in financial and security terms, for cleaning up after a collapsed North Korean state.

Moreover, by drawing the North closer and making it more dependent on China by way of its aid, trade, and investments, China can wield greater influence over North Korea so that it would be more costly for Pyongyang to harm China's interests presently or in the future.[110] Though it disagrees with "dynastic succession," China's embrace of Kim Jong-un appears to be consistent with this line of thinking. All of this fits an old East Asian cultural pattern related to the concept of *guanxi* [relationship, connections], wherein one does something for another with expectations of reciprocity. Helping another, then, makes the helped beholden to the helper, even entrapping the helped into doing the helper's bidding to some degree. The more China helps North Korea, the closer it gets; the more dependent Pyongyang is on Beijing, the more levers Beijing has to influence North Korea's behavior. This approach is at least part of China's intention in growing its aid to and trade with North Korea in recent years.[111]

Many people in the United States, neoconservatives in particular, overestimate China's support for North Korea and underestimate China's resolve to see North Korea lay down its nuclear weapons program,[112] perhaps because they do not understand China's two-pronged approach to North Korea. In Beijing's military and party circles, some still defend North Korea with great gusto. Those voices are increasingly being drowned out by those who are tired of Pyongyang's provocations and the political and economic costs they bring to Beijing. China clearly did not want North Korea launching missiles in 1998, 2006, 2009, or 2012, nor did it want North Korea testing nuclear weapons in 2006, 2009, or 2013. China does not want to see a U.S. attack on North Korea, refugees flowing across its borders, sanctions against North Korea, economic instability, Northeast Asian arms races, or any of the other scenarios I have discussed in this chapter. If, absent any explicit provocations from the United States, North Korea is found to have continued to develop, test, or deploy nuclear weapons, the United States can expect to see China continue to stand with the international community in holding North Korea accountable via the United Nations, and to continue to put the squeeze on North Korea when needed, as illustrated by its timely (though temporary) cutoffs of oil, capital, and food supplies. Where China will stand beyond this, though, is not clear. The Chinese experts interviewed for this chapter correctly predicted that China might participate at some level in sanctions if North Korea developed its nuclear capability, but they unanimously agreed that China would not support the international use of force against North Korea.

China's hope is that North Korea will lay down its weapons programs and follow Deng Xiaoping's lead by cautiously opening up and reforming North Korea. The present situation—a North Korea that is dragging its feet on reform, milking China for vast amounts of aid, and playing a game of chicken with the United States over its nuclear weapons and missile programs—is definitely not in China's interest. The Chinese believe that a continuation of Kim Jong-il's failed policies will lead to disaster for North Korea and potentially for China as well. Pyongyang has undoubtedly enacted some economic reforms from time to time,[113] but most observers felt that Kim Jong-il could not bring himself to carry out the kinds of reforms China and Vietnam have carried out, because he feared most what happened to Romania's Nicolae Ceaucescu in 1989 at the hands of his disaffected people.[114] It is too early to say what approach North Korea's new leadership will take, but most bets are on continuity for the foreseeable future, given the lack of experience of Kim Jong-un, North Korea's new leader, and the continuity in North Korea's uncertain security environment.[115] China's leaders are no strangers to fears of meeting the fate of Ceaucescu or facing the more recent revolutions that spread around the world in 2011. They might, however, be willing to coach the young Kim Jong-un through some of the difficulties of reform if in time he proves willing to go more boldly down the road to real reform than his father was, while, China hopes, laying down his nation's nuclear weapons capabilities and programs. A reformed, nonnuclear North Korea will be a better candidate for peace and security in the region than the bristling basket case that North Korea now represents. Herein lay Chinese hopes, as well as those of North Korea's neighbors and ultimately the United States, for the alternatives for any of the parties are truly unattractive.

CHAPTER FIVE

Japan's Responses to North Korea's Nuclear and Missile Tests

KATSUHISA FURUKAWA AND HAJIME IZUMI

After North Korea declared it would withdraw from the Nuclear Non-Proliferation Treaty (NPT) in January 2003, there was considerable foreign speculation that Japan might be prompted to develop its own nuclear weapons arsenal. Such speculation mounted as North Korea continued its provocations with multiple nuclear weapons and missile tests since 2006.[1] In the end, however, these views have not reflected the restrained reaction in Japan itself. Surely, in Japan, some discussions took place about indigenous nuclear options in the mid-2000s, primarily triggered by the North's provocations, but any serious discussion on this subject became almost invisible by 2012. North Korea's past provocations, including nuclear and missile tests, helped break a public taboo on discussing the possibility of Japanese nuclear capability, but little serious desire to replace the U.S. nuclear umbrella with a homegrown nuclear option is apparent in Japan. On the contrary, by 2012 Japan seemingly has become more confident about the credibility of U.S. extended deterrence than before, through official dialogues with the United States on extended deterrence and multiple joint military operations, such as those witnessed during the responses to the great earthquakes in eastern Japan, the tsunami disasters, and the Fukushima Daiichi nuclear accidents in 2011. Public opinion polls indicate that a majority of the Japanese public positively views the Japan-U.S. alliance as contributing to Japan's defense. In fact, even the past discussions of Japan's nuclear options were often aimed in part at shoring up the credibility of U.S. extended deterrence, which suffered a number of challenges in recent years with the changes of administration in both countries.

All in all, for Japan, North Korea's nuclear and missile threats are deemed serious but not its sole security challenge. As the security environment surrounding Japan changed significantly—especially with a renewed prospect of catastrophic earthquakes and tsunamis, the rise of China, and various other imminent transnational threats in the midst of a rapidly aging Japanese society—the direction of Japan's security strategy has been increasingly characterized by a pragmatism that seeks ways to allocate an increasingly limited amount of resources to meet various challenges in the most optimal way. Comparatively, the pursuit of indigenous nuclear options could bring about too many uncertainties for Japan and would most likely fail to address the above security challenges, such as confrontation over territorial waters and islands with neighboring countries. Tokyo's calculus is to avoid an adventurous, revolutionary course of action that might bring about high risk and uncertain results for Japan.

In this chapter we aim to explain Japan's restrained response to North Korean provocations, especially after 2006, and why indigenous nuclear options are not deemed as an answer to Japan's security challenges, including North Korean threats. We argue that Japan's restrained response is a product of its confidence in the credibility of U.S. extended deterrence and its rational adaptation to a shifting security environment, whereas North Korean threats are assessed in terms relative to various other security challenges, under conditions of the serious resource limitations available to Japan for security affairs. The consists of six sections. First, we present an overview of Japan's restrained response to those provocations, and explains the domestic political and social environment behind Japan's restrained response. In the second section we explain the changing security environment wherein North Korean problems are positioned as only one of the many grave challenges that Japan faces. We then analyze the strategic aspects of Japan's nuclear options, including sketching out a brief history of the past examinations of nuclear options, explaining why indigenous nuclear options would not be able to address the above-mentioned security challenges from a strategic perspective. Next we study the nonstrategic aspects of Japan's nuclear options, focusing on technical, societal, political, and institutional impediments for such options. We look at technical limitations to achieving these options, and how institutional inertia at the governmental level could hamper a drastic shift of security policy toward indigenous nuclear options, especially when political conditions remain unstable. Our subsequent point of focus is Japan's pursuit of an alternative pragmatic security strategy instead of the extreme nuclear options to address its security challenges, including those posed by North Korea. We conclude the chapter with an analysis of the specific conditions that would be required for Japan to decide on the extreme nuclear options, which are unlikely to materialize for the foreseeable future.

For Japan, North Korea has surely been one of the important triggers to its pursuit of a pragmatic security strategy but never its sole determinant. Foreign concerns over Japan's nuclear options after North Korean provocations have seemingly overestimated the extent to which North Korean threats have shaped Japan's security strategy. North Korea's nuclear and missile threats are deemed grave, but many Japanese tend to view—rightly or wrongly—that such threats are somewhat manageable through diplomatic efforts, given what are viewed in Japan as the political objectives of the North's provocations.

NORTH KOREAN NUCLEAR AND MISSILE TESTS AND JAPAN: A VERY RESTRAINED RESPONSE

North Korea has, since the late 1990s, carried out a series of provocative moves, including the testing of nuclear weapons and various types of missiles. Japan was surely shocked by these actions, but as North Korea continued with them, Japan's response became even more restrained, as evident in the results of various opinion polls presented below.

Since the 1990s, Japan's national security policy and the Japan-U.S. alliance have evolved every time a crisis arose on the Korean Peninsula. For example, after the North Korean crisis of 1993–94, Japan decided to redefine its roles and missions within the alliance, announcing the 1996 Japan-U.S. Joint Declaration on Security and creating the new Japanese-U.S. defense guidelines in 1998. When North Korea launched the Taepodong missile over Japan in 1998, Japan decided to embark on joint research into missile defenses with the United States. After the September 11, 2001, terrorist attacks and the new North Korean crisis since 2002, Japan strengthened its alliance with the United States by demonstrating its support for U.S. military operations in Afghanistan and for the reconstruction of postwar Iraq. In addition, since the October 2006 North Korean nuclear test, Japan has become more forthcoming in cooperating with NATO and other U.S. allies as well as other friendly countries in jointly tackling issues of regional and global security.

North Korea's 2006 nuclear tests also significantly affected the security thinking of the Japanese public and defense establishment. According to an opinion poll by TV Asahi in October 2006, while 90% of the respondents felt that North Korea's acquisition of nuclear capabilities was a threat, 54% did not think that "a war was imminent."[2] Furthermore, 82% said Japan should sustain its "Three Non-Nuclear Principles," which prohibit Japan from manufacturing, possessing, or permitting the entry of nuclear weapons into the air, land, or sea controlled by Japan. On the contrary, only 10% said Japan should have a nuclear weapon, and 46% opposed even the discussion of Japanese nuclear options. Similarly, even after North Korea's second nuclear test in 2009, according to another poll, the top concern among the Japanese respondents was a pandemic of A/H1N1 influenza (31.6%) while North Korea's nuclear and missile tests ranked second (22.2%).[3] Japan's response to the North's second nuclear test was even more restrained than it was to the first.

After November 2006 the Japanese media's coverage of North Korea focused more on Pyongyang's decades-long abduction of Japanese citizens than on any concern over North Korea's present nuclear weapons programs. Accordingly, in various public opinion polls, the abduction issue has been consistently rated as the top North Korea–related concern.[4] In April 2012 media focus on North Korea's missile programs became even more restrained after North Korea launched a rocket (characterized as a long-range ballistic missile), a test that ended up in failure.

The Japanese government itself has also been restrained in its response to the tests. Although it imposed sanctions on North Korea, Tokyo appears to have consistently placed a higher priority on the abductions issue. Since 2006, Japanese administrations have maintained an office within the Cabinet Office to address the abductions, and issue that receives bipartisan support. On the contrary, no prime minister ever created an equivalent office to address Pyongyang's nuclear or missile programs, despite the government's repeated statements that North Korea's nuclear weapons presented the gravest threat to Japan. Not surprisingly, the DPRK was unhappy with Japan's continued hardline position on the abductions, repeatedly demanding that Japan be excluded from the Six Party Talks.

Furthermore, none of the Japanese administrations since 2006 appear to have made any noteworthy efforts to negotiate with North Korea on its ballistic missile development and deployment, although Japan is the country that should be most concerned about Pyongyang's medium-range ballistic missile programs. Interestingly, despite North Korea's continuous provocations, the figures in Japan's defense budget have steadily decreased from 2003 through 2012.[5] Even considering Japan's economic deflation, Japan did not adopt significant counterbalancing measures against the DPRK's increasing military actions, contrary to the realist expectations of international relations theory.[6]

For the Japanese government, one of its top priorities has been reducing its large budget deficits, already almost 220% of Japan's gross domestic product in fiscal year (FY) 2012. The looming national fiscal crisis is deemed more serious and urgent than a decreasing defense budget.

As a result, the Japanese Self-Defense Forces have been constrained from expanding personnel and procurement, despite the December 2010 publication of the *National Defense Program Guidelines for FY 2011 and Beyond* (hereafter, the 2010 NDPG) which stated that Japan had "a Dynamic Defense Force that possesses readiness, mobility, flexibility, sustainability, and versatility."[7] Originally, after the DPRK's first nuclear test, a number of conservative Japanese politicians argued for developing offensive capabilities to strike North Korea's missile-launching sites preemptively. However, this discussion has become almost nonexistent by 2012. In the wake of North Korea's missile and nuclear tests, the Japanese public in general did not demonstrate an active interest in taking steps to strengthen preparedness or preventive measures for nuclear warfare, such as constructing underground shelters, nor to substantially increase the number of ballistic missile defense (BMD) interceptors. Again, the response has been calm.

Japan's restraint has been evident in other ways as well. Even in the immediate aftermath of North Korea's second nuclear test in May 2009, Japan did not respond at all when U.S. defense secretary Robert M. Gates stated, "I do not think that North Korea's nuclear program at this point represents a direct military threat to the United States."[8] From a strategic point of view, such a comment could have been viewed as representing a decoupling between Japan and the United States over the assessment of the North's missile threat, which primarily aims at targets in Japan and South Korea. In fact, however, scarcely any serious voice of protest or concern was heard in Tokyo. Also, in mid-November 2010, as a number of media sources began reporting on North Korea possibly preparing for a third nuclear test, then–chief cabinet secretary Yoshito Sengoku of the Kan administration simply stated, "At this point, under the current situation, our country's safety is not affected"; he added that Japan's firm position was not to allow North Korea's nuclear development and that Japan would strengthen its cooperation with the United States and South Korea.[9] Furthermore, in June 2011, even when Secretary Gates stated on the contrary to his statement two years before, "North Korea is in the process of becoming a direct threat to the United States,"[10] hardly any public debate in Japan arose. Likewise, despite the revived concern for the possibility of North Korea preparing for a third nuclear test in mid-2012, such information is almost absent from Japanese media headlines. While the Korean Peninsula was historically considered "Japan's backyard," today such statements are rarely heard from Tokyo.

These nonreactions, in fact, most likely reflect Japan's increasing confidence in the credibility of U.S. extended deterrence. Since February 2010 Japan and the United States have been conducting official dialogues on deterrence, enabling a regular mutual exchange of views and information that contributed significantly to improving confidence in the U.S. commitment to protect Japan. Such confidence was further reinforced during the responses to Japan's earthquakes and tsunami disasters and the Fukushima Daiichi nuclear accidents of 2011. Multiple opinion polls indicate that about 80% of the Japanese public positively evaluate the role of the Japan-U.S. alliance to protect Japan.[11]

Moreover, despite its antinuclear rhetoric, whether Japan has invested in significant diplomatic resources for operationalizing various ideas for nuclear disarmament is subject to question. In April 2009, after North Korea's missile tests, then–Japanese foreign minister Hirofumi Nakasone announced the "Eleven Benchmarks for Global Nuclear Disarmament," which stipulated a specific proposal to enable conditions toward achieving "Global Zero."[12] However, the successor Democratic Party of Japan–led administrations have virtually ignored this proposal. Nuclear disarmament seemed more of a political issue. Also, Japan has played little role to date in shaping an international consensus over practical matters, such as verification procedures for nuclear disarmament, or in deploying novel technologies for nuclear nonproliferation, which the International Atomic Energy Agency (IAEA) aspires to have. Neither has Japan demonstrated leadership in shaping the verification mechanism for the future disarmament of North Korea's nuclear weapons and missile programs, nor exhibited significant interest in designing a cooperative threat-reduction program toward the DPRK.

Japan has been overwhelmed by its own domestic political instability over the past several years. After the 2006 retirement of Prime Minister Junichiro Koizumi, the successive Japanese administrations experienced political crises and governmental instability, and most prime ministers left office after a year. The fluid political situation has seemingly become a structural trend of Japanese politics, and weak political leadership has seriously undermined Japan's efforts to address problems with North Korea. The Japanese public has been preoccupied with the nation's political instability and the national crises, triggered by such events as the 2008 global economic crisis, the 2011 earthquakes, tsunami, and consequent Fukushima Daiichi nuclear power plant's disasters, and an increasing number of security challenges from other countries, especially the so-called gray-zone confrontations over territory, sovereignty, and economic interests that fall short of war. Such confrontations include territorial disputes with South Korea, China, and Russia. All these factors make it less likely that North Korean issues may rise high in the eyes of the public without some unexpected and shocking event.

Even when Japan and North Korea held their government-to-government consultation in August 2012, the first such consultation since August 2008, a majority of the Japanese media and public focused almost exclusively on the abduction issues. (The direction of this consultation is still unclear as of October 2012.) In such an environment, politicians have not been able to spare the political resources necessary to tackle the broad aspects of challenges from North Korea.

Convincing evidence that the Japanese public feels so gravely threatened by North Korea's nuclear program and concerned by the reliability of the U.S. extended deterrence that they would pursue nuclear options as an alternative response to the existing policy, however, is hard to locate. Most Japanese regard as exaggerated foreign countries' concerns about Japan's future as a nuclear-weapon state. In fact, the Japanese media rarely conducts extensive or serious discussion about Japan's nuclear weapons capabilities or an associated nuclear doctrine if it were to pursue such options. Similarly, there barely exist any thorough assessments of Japan's capability to produce nuclear weapons. Rather, the Japanese government has been pursuing an alternative deterrence strategy, as we discuss later.

One notable exception in recent years is the single internal assessment of Japan's capability to produce a small nuclear warhead, conducted by a senior Japanese official after North Korea's July 2006 ballistic missile launches.[13] Though politicians denied the existence of this internal assessment, it most likely exists.[14] Reportedly, this 2006 internal study came to the conclusion that Japan would need three to five years to produce a prototype of a functional small nuclear warhead. Note that this assessment was initiated in response to the North's ballistic missile tests in July 2006 and completed in September 2006, prior to North Korea's first nuclear test in October.

In addition, in June 2012 some suspicions were raised over Japan's possible ambition for military use of nuclear programs when the Japanese government amended its Atomic Energy Basic Law by adding a new provision which states, "[The principle to secure nuclear safety] should be . . . aimed at contributing not only to defending people's lives, health, and assets and protecting the environment but also to *Japan's national security* (emphasis added). The media was alarmed by the inclusion of the term "national security," since it was deemed as implying possible future nuclear options. However, this provision was attached to another key provision, which clearly states, "The use of nuclear power is limited to peaceful objectives." The Japanese government explained that the words "national security" are related to nuclear security and the prevention of nuclear proliferation. As far as Japan's declared policy on the peaceful use of nuclear energy is concerned, it is hard to observe any change, despite concerns among some observers.

Concerns were raised on another occasion regarding Japan's "Innovative Strategy for Energy and the Environment" issued in September 2012, which states that Japan will "mobilize all possible policy resources to such a level as to enable zero operation of nuclear power plants in the 2030s" but also announced that Japan would "continue its present nuclear fuel cycle policy to engage in reprocessing projects." These seemingly contradictory statements effectively mean that Japan may likely continue to accumulate plutonium in the coming decades. The U.S. government is seriously concerned about this prospect. The Japanese government has explained that they have been trying to accommodate the public's call to decrease their reliance upon, or abolish totally, nuclear power, while also trying to keep the government's promise with Aomori Prefecture, a relatively poor prefecture that has accepted the nuclear fuel cycle program in exchange for a significant amount of government subsidies, by which the government has promised that nuclear fuel cycle policy would be promoted consistently and steadfastly in the medium and long terms.

In the societal context after the nuclear disaster of March 11, 2011, however, voices opposing the peaceful use of nuclear energy remain strong and persistent, which may likely continue for some time. At a minimum, most of the Japanese public supports decreased reliance on nuclear power. It is difficult to find any serious opinion in support of Japan's nuclear options in this social context, even despite the rising tensions with China over the Senkaku Islands (which China calls the Diaoyu Islands) in 2012.

THE CHANGING REGIONAL SECURITY ENVIRONMENT

In general, speculation about North Korean threats triggering Japanese nuclear options overstates the influence of North Korea on the thinking of the Japanese national security community and public. Although North Korea's WMD programs certainly represent one of the major threats to Japan's national security, the DPRK challenge is not necessarily regarded as the primary factor shaping Japan's national security strategy. For a majority of the Japanese, domestic challenges—such as a rapidly aging society, the ongoing economic crisis, and large governmental deficits—are deemed as the most imminent problems that directly affect the Japanese national security strategy. Not only does Japan still have a long way to go in its recovery from the significant damage caused by the earthquakes and tsunamis of March 2011, but Japan has to prepare for other such earthquakes and tsunamis to come in the near future, especially the Nankai Trough earthquakes, which the Japanese Cabinet Office estimates could lead to up to 323,000 casualties, not to mention the significant economic loss they could incur.[15] Preparedness and damage limitation for natural disasters have become another priority issue for Japan's national security.

The 2010 NDPG enumerated other major security challenges for Japan, including a global shift in the power balance with the rise of powers such as China, India, and Russia, along with the relative change of U.S. influence, as well as a growing number of gray-zone disputes, such as confrontations over territory, sovereignty, and economic interests that are not likely to escalate into wars.[16] The 2010 NDPG also lists a number of other priority areas, such as ensuring the safety of the seas and airspaces around Japan and responding to attacks on offshore islands, cyber attacks, guerrillas and special operations forces, and ballistic missile attacks. The NDPG noted that these multiple security threats can materialize simultaneously or consecutively, that the nature of a respective threat may change as the situation develops, and that Japan will likely be forced to respond flexibly to these threats.[17]

In particular, China, not North Korea, is actually deemed to present the most important strategic challenges for Japan's defense planners, who are increasingly concerned about the growing capabilities of China's People's Liberation Army (PLA), its lack of transparency, and its uncertain intentions.[18] Of particular concern is the expansion of missile forces that can strike targets in Japan, as well as the growth of the PLA's antiaccess and area-denial capabilities relating to the deployment of U.S. forces in Asia. Japan and other Asian countries are also concerned about the expansion and intensification of Chinese maritime activities in East and Southeast Asia that fall short of military confrontation. Often, the Chinese maritime behaviors are seen as unilateral and carried out in ways inconsistent with the spirit of the Law of the Sea treaty. China has clearly violated this pact, such as the PLA Navy's submarine intruding into Japan's territorial waters near the mainland without notification. Alerted by the increasing confrontation between Japan and China over the Senkaku Islands beginning around 2010, the Japanese Ministry of Defense has prioritized defending offshore islands as one of the key pillars of Japan's territorial defense.[19]

However, while China continuously modernizes its military forces and is seen by Japan as behaving provocatively, China has also become Japan's largest trading partner since 2007. China truly presents a complicated matrix of strategic challenges for Japan. Japan's nuclear options are not considered as an appropriate tool to address these complex Chinese challenges, especially when most of these strategic issues would fall short of escalation into war. Threatening to develop or use nuclear weapons as a response to Chinese intrusion into Japan's territorial waters would likely not seem credible to China. If Japan had such resources to spare for nuclear weapon programs, it would seem more rational for the nation to invest the money to strengthen the capabilities of its coast guard and Maritime Self-Defense Forces. Besides, given that many Japanese policymakers feel that U.S. extended deterrence combined with Japan's extant deterrence posture has effectively forestalled Chinese strategic attacks on Japan so far, it is rational for Japan to focus on strengthening its alliance with the United States to improve the reliability of U.S. extended deterrence as a cost-effective way to ensure Japan's security.

All in all, Japan has improved confidence in the U.S. commitment to protect it. Japan's nuclear options would not be able to address the complex matrix of various security challenges the nation faces. Rather, such options would absorb the resources necessary to develop the conventional measures that are seen in Japan as more effectively addressing its diverse security challenges.

THE STRATEGIC ASPECTS OF JAPAN'S NUCLEAR OPTIONS

In the past, at times of significant change in the strategic environment, the Japanese government quietly reexamined its nuclear options on several occasions. The most notable examples were in the 1960s, when China conducted its first nuclear test, and again in the 1990s, when the first nuclear crisis occurred on the Korean Peninsula.[20] However, all such examinations have reached the same conclusion: Japan's possession of its own nuclear arsenal would have few strategic advantages given the costs it would entail. All of these studies concluded that a nuclear Japan could motivate a number of other countries to pursue nuclear development, and Japan could not secure a location to store nuclear weapons safely given its geographic limitations. Similarly, the option to base nuclear weapons on submarines with high survivability could not be completed in less than a decade[21] and would require an enormous amount of investment that would significantly reduce the available defense budget for Japan's conventional forces.

A view has emerged over the past several years, however, that counters some

of the key conclusions above. Some argue that limited nuclear deterrent capability would be sufficient for Japan, since Japan's primary focus is no longer
massive nuclear attacks from the Soviet Union (as was the case during the Cold
War) but the far smaller number of nuclear weapons of China and North Korea.
According to this view, even if Japan could not possess a credible second-strike
capability, its nuclear arsenal might sufficiently complicate the calculation of
an adversary who might attempt to drive a wedge between the United States
and Japan by threatening Japan but not the United States.[22] They argue that
other nuclear weapons states, such as France, the United Kingdom, Pakistan,
and Israel, have pursued nuclear weapons even without a second-strike capability.[23] This perspective challenges some of the key conclusions in government
examinations of nuclear options during the Cold War.

Even so, however, in their past examinations of nuclear options, Japanese
policymakers have tended to pursue a robust deterrence strategy with a credible second-strike capability rather than a half-baked strategy with an insufficient second-strike capability. Perhaps for bureaucratic reasons or fear of uncertainty of the consequences, no politician or government official was ready
to take the blame for leading Japan to embark on a nuclear weapons program
without an assured second-strike capability, for the consensus was that such an
approval would fail to provide Japan with a credible deterrent.

Most of the relatively pragmatic thinkers who supported examining, though
not necessarily pursuing, Japan's nuclear options have favored the continuation of a strong Japan-U.S. alliance.[24] They justified their position by saying that
Japan even seriously discussing its nuclear options could in itself increase pressure on the United States to continue its commitment to provide Japan with extended deterrence.[25]

Almost every serious Japanese study of possible Japanese nuclear options
(few as they have been) has come to the same conclusion: the costs of attaining nuclear weapons for Japan would far outweigh the expected benefits.[26] All
of these studies, however, are based on the core assumption that U.S. extended
deterrence will continue to protect Japan. Japan has been pursuing various measures to make sure of the U.S. commitment in this regard, as explained later.

THE NONSTRATEGIC IMPEDIMENTS TO
JAPAN'S NUCLEAR OPTIONS

Putting aside strategic discussions, many other impediments exist to achieving
Japan's nuclear options, including technological limitations and those derived

from domestic factors. From a purely technical point of view, observers outside Japan have maintained that Japan has for some time had sufficient technology to produce nuclear weapons. Japan does have a nuclear fuel-cycle program that can produce plutonium, but this material is only reactor-grade plutonium in the form of mixed oxide (MOX), which can only be used for civilian purposes and is regularly inspected by the International Atomic Energy Agency (IAEA). As noted, the quietly done study mentioned above concluded that it would take at least three to five years for Japan to produce a prototype of a small nuclear warhead, which would also require a significant investment, not easily forthcoming under the existing fiscal conditions. However, the frequently heard assessment in the United States has been that it would take only one or two years, maximum, for Japan to develop nuclear weapons.[27]

As potential vehicles for a nuclear warhead, Japan possesses H-IIA and H-IIB rockets that are sufficiently technologically advanced to carry nuclear warheads, should Japan choose to develop them.[28] Japan also has solid-fuel-propelled M-V rockets, capable of placing a 1.8-ton payload into orbit, though these are privately owned and operated after completion of the government's research and development phase. Japan is also developing the Epsilon Launch Vehicle, a three-staged solid-propellant launch vehicle based on the M-V rockets.[29] In the early 2000s Japan reportedly made at least a preliminary inquiry into a cruise missile option, but there is no indication of any serious consideration of this option subsequently. Japan does not appear to have made any serious attempts to explore the development of ballistic missiles or even of the infrastructure or basic policies and doctrines that would be necessary to build, operate, and maintain nuclear weapons.

If Japanese leaders decided to pursue nuclear weapons, they would be confronted with a number of challenges.[30] First, Japan's use of any nuclear material is strictly regulated by a web of domestic regulations and laws as well as bilateral and international treaties, not to mention that it is illegal for Japan to use its plutonium for weapons purposes without the consent of its treaty counterparts. Unless Japan dared to follow the brinksmanship strategy of North Korea, it would be highly risky for Japan to ignore those legally binding obligations since the nation could be placed under international sanctions. Whether or how long the Japanese public, which has enjoyed a high quality of life for several decades, could endure the hardship of such sanctions is doubtful. Even the few proponents of a Japanese nuclear weapons program acknowledge that Japan would not be able to develop such weapons without the approval and cooperation of other countries—most importantly, the United States—because of

Japan's legal obligations for peaceful use of nuclear power under bilateral treaties. In addition, Japan is vulnerable to a potential embargo of fissile materials because of its very limited reserves of natural uranium.

More important, efforts to undermine the international rule of law and international institutions would run counter to Japan's diplomatic strategy to address its broader national interests, especially those related to its economy. Given that Japan's national power is highly dependent on the international economic system, but that its relative power has been declining constantly, Japan deems it essential to enlarge the rule of laws internationally; to establish multilateral, regional, and international institutions to implement these laws; and to use these institutions for the sake of its own national interest. The view of Japanese policymakers is that Japan's diplomatic standing in the world is essential for shaping the international system in various policy fields in ways that fit Japan's national interests. In this respect, Tokyo's decisionmakers regard Japan's international reputation as a precious asset that the country has nurtured since the end of World War II. They regard it as too valuable to throw away simply for the sake of the challenges posed by North Korea.

Because of those international legal frameworks, Japan's legal and administrative systems have been predicated on a complicated web of legally binding mechanisms and institutions that also serve as self-restraining factors for Japan's activities. Foreign concerns over Japan's nuclear options underestimate the enormous challenges associated with efforts to fundamentally alter such institutionalized, internalized legal systems and institutions. Likewise, such foreign concerns overestimate the courage and capabilities of Japanese politicians and officials to carry out such revolutionary tasks to fundamentally change laws and institutions, despite continuing political instability.

Moreover, due to the obvious decay in the popularity of nuclear research among the students over the past years, the Japanese nuclear industry has already been facing a deepening shortage of skilled human resources, generating the daunting prospect of a gradual decay of the quality of the nuclear power industry's infrastructure.[31] Because of the Fukushima Daiichi nuclear accidents after the earthquake and tsunami of March 2011, this challenge has become more serious. In the coming decades, as Japan may continuously reduce its reliance on nuclear energy, such challenges could become ever more serious. This domestic situation is certainly not conducive to any pragmatic discussion of Japan's nuclear options.

Japan's scientific and academic communities remain deeply within the pacifist tradition, despite Japan's general trend toward becoming a more normal country in terms of national security strategy. It would take an enormous effort, investment, and time to establish a working relationship between these communities and the national security community in the event of a move toward Japanese acquisition of nuclear capabilities. The lack of a cooperative working relationship between the defense sector and the scientific community would invariably make it difficult for Japan to mobilize resources essential for the construction of any sophisticated nuclear weapon. Indeed, in developing a functioning nuclear weapon, a range of scientific and technical problems would emerge that require the development of both explicit and tacit knowledge that would need to be applied to the local context at any nuclear weapons complex.[32] This kind of knowledge could be produced only by integrating a wide range of relevant interdisciplinary knowledge and practices across Japan's relevant stakeholders, which is not presently forthcoming.

Given the mature nature of democracy and civil society in Japan, the NIMBY ("not in my back yard") principle makes the prospect of even agreeing upon a location for nuclear weapons facilities difficult to imagine, as evidenced by the government's difficulties to simply secure locations for radioactive waste storage sites over the past decades. After the 2011 nuclear disasters, the Japanese public's rejection of radiological waste has become even stronger. The 2011 Fukushima nuclear accidents triggered a surge in negative opinion about nuclear power plants. The extent to which this might affect anti-nuclear-weapon sentiment in Japan is yet unknown. At a minimum, however, such developments are never a positive factor for those few espousing nuclear weapons in Japan. Nuclear reactors themselves are seen as a source of grave security risk. If the nuclear industry experiences difficulty sustaining its skilled human resource pool and quality infrastructure in the coming years, the public risk perception of nuclear programs may deepen, making a social consensus on the location for a nuclear weapon complex even more difficult to construct.

JAPAN'S STRATEGIC POSTURE

Japan has no other choice as it weighs various security threats but to pursue a more pragmatic and feasible option to respond to various security challenges, including North Korea's threats, rather than its indigenous nuclear options. Japan's security strategy is increasingly characterized by a "balanced pragmatism"[33] to pursue effective measures to address a diverse set of security challenges in a cost-effective way. Broadly, the strategy focuses primarily on three objectives: (1) strengthening Japan's deterrence, (2) strengthening the

Japan-U.S. alliance, and (3) developing multilayered security cooperation with other countries.

Looking at each of these a bit more deeply, first, Japan has developed a multifaceted national security posture that incorporates the concepts of assurance, dissuasion, deterrence, denial, defense, damage confinement, and crisis management, which are expected to reinforce Japan's nonnuclear position.[34] Since 2010 Japan has concentrated on operationalizing its "dynamic deterrence" posture, as stipulated in the NDPG, which focuses on generating a deterrent effect by highly responsive, maneuverable forces, instead of the traditional "static deterrence" posture that focuses mainly on the quantities and size of weapons and troops. In contrast to the traditional deterrence concept that focuses on "the deterrence effect of the existence of defense forces per se," the new concept focuses on the deterrence effect expected from "displaying Japan's defense capabilities in action."[35] For example, in order to prevent intrusion into Japan's territorial waters by a neighboring country, the NDPG states the importance of clearly demonstrating the national will and strong defense capabilities through timely and tailored military operations.[36] Dynamic deterrence places particular emphasis on creating the perceptions among other countries about Japan being "without deficiencies" through regular, continuous, and strategic operations of its forces.[37] Dynamism is deemed essential to effectively deter and respond to various contingencies, according to this NDPG.

The NDPG also stresses the importance of national capabilities to deal with all stages of a contingency seamlessly in order to respond in a harmonized manner to multiple contingencies simultaneously or consecutively.[38] Contingencies could emerge in a complex form, triggering other contingencies, as was the case where East Japan mega-thrust earthquakes caused huge tsunamis that led to the Fukushima Daiichi nuclear power plant disasters. The self-defense forces were required to execute their normal duties while responding simultaneously to both the earthquake and tsunami disasters and the Fukushima Daiichi nuclear disasters. Similarly, if attacked by ballistic missiles, Japan would also need to be able to respond to various contingencies, such as collateral damage on critical infrastructure, including nuclear power plants or national transportation systems. For this purpose, Japan intends to enhance its capability to respond to complex, multiple security challenges by improving its capabilities in decisionmaking, joint military operations, logistics, surveillance, and coordinating responses together with local governments, other NGOs, the private sector, and other countries.[39]

Second, despite the tension in the Japan-U.S. alliance over the relocation of the Futenma military base in Okinawa Prefecture—one of the key issues in the realignment of U.S. global military posture—Japanese policymakers are determined to strengthen deterrence by further institutionalizing the bilateral alliance with the United States. This point is particularly important, given Japan's decreasing defense budget. Japan believes that the credibility of deterrence is elastic since reassurance is political by nature,[40] and the nation has consistently striven to ensure the credibility of U.S. extended deterrence. In fact, as one senior Japanese diplomat stated, Japan plays the critical role in "defend[ing the] U.S. forward military presence in Asia."[41]

In June 2011 Japan and the United States issued a joint statement, "Toward a Deeper and Broader U.S.-Japan Alliance: Building on 50 Years of Partnership," expanding on security and defense cooperation in various fields.[42] In this statement, the United States has clearly taken the stance of focusing on Asia, which is seen as further reassuring Japan's defense planners.[43] Based on this joint statement, Japan and the United States are focusing on further institutionalization of alliance cooperation by improving mutual interoperability in order to enable harmonized responses to multiple threats.

With regard to the question of whether to deploy U.S. nuclear weapons to Japan, there were discussions in Japan on several occasions to revisit Japan's Three Non-Nuclear Principles, which prohibit the presence of U.S. nuclear weapons *in* or their transit *through* Japanese ports. In recent years, it was disclosed that the Japanese government had for a long time tacitly permitted the entry of U.S. naval assets with nuclear weapons into Japan.[44] The August 2010 report by the Council on Security and Defense Capabilities in the New Era suggested that Japan reconsider the validity of the Three Non-Nuclear Principles in the current security environment.

Two views commonly held among Japanese strategists regarding the relationship between U.S. nuclear forces being stationed in Japan on the one hand, and the U.S. assurance to defend Japan in the event of a crisis on the other.[45] Some Japanese strategists argue that U.S. nuclear forces should be posted farther from Japan for their own protection, given Japan's geographical proximity to potential conflict areas in East Asia. Such positioning would add to Japan's confidence in the credibility of U.S. extended deterrence assured by a secured U.S. second-strike nuclear capability, the argument goes. Another view, however, is that the psychological assurance provided by the physical presence of U.S. nuclear forces in Japan is actually the key to maintaining U.S. commitment to Japan, as a symbol of credible assurance. In any event, a majority of the Japanese public continues to express its support for continuing the Three Non-Nuclear Principles, making the option to base U.S. nuclear forces in Japan difficult.

This approach is not necessarily inconsistent with the U.S. nuclear posture. In 1991 the U.S. had already declared that it would withdraw most and eliminate many of its nonstrategic nuclear weapons.[46] Also, as stated elsewhere,[47] because of provisions in the United States–Soviet Union Intermediate-Range Nuclear Forces Treaty,[48] the United States has given up the intermediate-range nuclear weapons it maintained prior to the treaty, and consequently there are no nuclear missiles the U.S. could deploy in Japan that could attack targets in China or North Korea in the event of a crisis.[49]

In March 2010, in a discussion with members of the Lower House of Japan's Diet, Japanese foreign minister Katsuya Okada described a hypothetical scenario in which Japan might permit U.S. nuclear weapons–carrying ships into Japanese ports in case of an emergency if Japan's security could not be ensured without them.[50] Japan, however, is not likely to change the Three Non-Nuclear Principles in the near future, given their popularity among the public. In August every year, Japanese prime ministers have stated during their Hiroshima visits that Japan would not change the Principles.[51] The NDPG has also reaffirmed them.

As another key deterrent tool, ballistic missile defense constitutes a core component of Japan's denial strategy and is deemed highly important both in institutionalizing the alliance and in complementing U.S. extended deterrence, with the continued development of Japan's extant Aegis-based Patriot Pac-3 and potential future Japanese-U.S. cooperative efforts in this area. The 2004 Prime Minister's Council on Security and Defense Capabilities Report clearly made this point, stating, "Although the U.S. forces continue to provide effective deterrence against the threat that nuclear weapons and ballistic missiles capable of delivering them pose to Japan, the introduction of ballistic missile defense systems will likely reinforce its credibility,"[52] and "By relying on a ballistic missile defense system, Japan can complement America's nuclear deterrent."[53]

Third, Japan has been making various efforts, mostly in cooperation with the United States, to build and institutionalize trilateral, regional, and multilateral security cooperation frameworks, such as strengthening trilateral cooperation with both Australia and the Republic of Korea, and strengthening security cooperation with the Association of Southeast Asian Nations (ASEAN) and India. Japan also aspires to sustain its diplomatic standing in the world, especially in Asia, in order to counterbalance China's rising political influence. To do so,

Japan has been seeking to lead regional integration and institutionalization in Asia, through such vehicles as the Asia Pacific Economic Cooperation (APEC) or the Association of Southeast Asian Nations (ASEAN), with the aim of shaping rather than reacting to the global and regional security environment. The strengthening of the Japan-U.S. alliance has been implemented in tandem with those efforts as well. For example, Japan and the United States have conducted multilateral joint exercises and training with other U.S. allies and friendly countries.

The strengthened Japanese deterrence posture and Japan-U.S. alliance, supplemented by multilateral security institutions and networks, is expected to constitute an indispensable basis for stability and confidence building in the Asia-Pacific region. In the view of Japanese security policymakers, Japan's nuclear options are simply deemed as not fit to address those complex security challenges.

CONCLUSION

Japan's domestic reactions to North Korea's nuclear tests have been much more restrained than some foreign observers predicted. Similar predictions followed China's nuclear tests in the 1960s and the North Korea nuclear crisis of 1992–94. So far, all of these predictions have proven ill founded. Even in the midst of increasing tension between Japan and China over the Senkaku Islands since 2010, no serious public debate about nuclear options has occurred in Japan.

It is difficult to find in Japan any national leader who strongly advocates Japan's pursuit of its own nuclear options or who fundamentally questions the credibility of U.S. extended deterrence. Shifts in Japan's regional security environment and strategic culture from pacifism to realism over the past decade have ended the taboo on discussing publicly the possibility that Japan might pursue nuclear options. After North Korea's October 2006 nuclear test, Japanese media highlighted remarks by a limited number of Japanese politicians, including cabinet members, who argued in favor of a public discussion about Japan's nuclear options. Others countered that such a discussion could provoke regional concerns about Japan's nuclear intentions. Many Japanese decision-makers are concerned that such a discussion might undermine the trust it has fostered with its neighbors since the end of World War II. These political leaders deem retaining this trust to be of greater value to Japan than developing an indigenous nuclear deterrent against North Korea.

As of 2012 the surge in antinuclear sentiments after the Fukushima Daiichi nuclear accidents became another impediment to Japan's nuclear options. Moreover, the emergence of various security challenges, which indigenous nuclear options cannot address, requires significant resources. Japan must use its limited resources to meet these challenges in the most pragmatic and yet effective way. As Japan has had improved confidence in the credibility of U.S. commitment to protect Japan in recent years, it remains practical and cost-effective for Japan to strengthen the bilateral alliance with the United States to ensure its security. Thus, Japanese national security stakeholders focus on operationalizing the new "dynamic deterrence" posture, strengthening and institutionalization of the Japan-U.S. alliance, and developing multilayered security cooperation with other countries.

Given these observations, Japan's going nuclear could be conceivable only under an extreme scenario. Multiple conditions would seem essential before Japan would decide to develop its own nuclear weapons capability.[54]

1. The Japanese public would need to hold, for a sustained period of time, a far graver threat perception toward neighboring states, especially China and North Korea, than any other security challenges.

2. Perception of the credibility of U.S. extended deterrence would need to deteriorate significantly, leading the Japanese public to believe that U.S. extended deterrence would no longer defend them. Such a worst-case scenario would most likely materialize where Japan came under attack or was under imminent attack from neighboring states, and the United States failed to protect Japan.

3. Japan would need to conclude that the merits of its nuclear option would overwhelm its demerits, even considering the likely international sanctions following a Japanese decision to acquire nuclear weapons. The Japanese public would have to be willing to tolerate a degradation of the quality of their lives under the sanctions for a time. Considering that Japan is a democratic country, any assumption about Japan's nuclear options would have to assume public support for a sustained period (a few to several years, at a minimum, or most likely over a decade) despite their significant costs.

4. Given that the political power of the local governments has been strengthening considerably in various policy fields relative to that of the national government, a majority of these local governments would also have to be willing to collaborate with the national government's call for a nuclear weapons program, especially in terms of selecting the location for a nuclear weapons complex, knowing that such a complex might likely become a target of military attack

from other countries. These local governments must be willing to store a certain amount of dangerous radiological materials, in contrast to their strong opposition to the national government's call for accepting radiological contaminated waste after March 11, 2011.

5. Japan's scientific community would also have to be willing to collaborate with the government on developing nuclear weapons. They would have to jettison their pacifist character and stop excluding defense practitioners from the scientific community, as they have done since the end of World War II.

6. Given that Japan's nuclear options would considerably undermine (or possibly destroy) the international regimes for international security, arms control, and nonproliferation, the Japanese government would also need to conclude that these regimes had become obsolete, meaningless, and worthy of collapse, after decades of significant investment by Japan. Japan would have to judge that any significant damage that its nuclear options might cause upon these regimes would outweigh the potential merit those regimes have brought about.

7. Strong political leaders and capable bureaucrats in Japan would need to be able to construct a national consensus on Japan's nuclear options and to fundamentally alter all regulations, laws, and institutions related to the peaceful use of nuclear energy, in order to enable a nuclear-armed Japan. For this task, Japan's political situation would need to become stabilized for a considerable period of time—a break from the norm in the post-Koizumi era—until the nuclear option could be implemented.

8. Most importantly, foreign suppliers of nuclear technologies and materials, especially the United States, would have to be able to tolerate Japan's nuclear options, given that their nuclear technologies and materials would constitute the essential basis of Japan's nuclear programs.

All or most of the above conditions would have to be satisfied before Japan could make a decision to go nuclear. The authors consider this scenario highly unlikely.

On the contrary, the consensus in Japan today continues to favor reliance on the U.S. nuclear umbrella and BMD while strengthening Japan's new deterrence posture, the Japan-U.S. alliance, and multilateral security cooperation with other countries. The credibility of U.S. extended deterrence is the most important factor among them. Japanese political leaders and strategic planners aspire to secure the credibility of U.S. extended deterrence into the foreseeable future. In their minds, the answer to the North Korean security challenge is not Japanese nuclear options but adoption of a new deterrence posture to meet a variety of security challenges seamlessly, including those posed by the North. North Korean security challenges are grave but not the sole threat to Japan. Besides, Japan's nuclear options would have fairly marginal utility in addressing those diverse security challenges while consuming resources for conventional measures to address those challenges. Given the limited resources available for security affairs, the nuclear weapon programs would be in a tradeoff related to conventional programs. North Korean provocations have not changed this strategic calculus in Japan to date. Full North Korean nuclear operationality would likely not do so either, unless the aforementioned extreme conditions were realized.

CHAPTER SIX

Russia's De Facto Nuclear Neighbor

GEORGY TOLORAYA

North Korea appears unwilling to give up its nuclear capability any time soon. This is not to say that denuclearization, or at least the liquidation of the militarized nuclear component, is impossible, but it will certainly take a long time, and many conditions difficult to swallow by both Pyongyang and the other members of the now-defunct Six Party Talks would have to be met.[1] This creates a new strategic reality for all the countries, including Russia. North Korea's neighbors may not want to recognize North Korea as a nuclear power, but for a considerable period of time they will have to live side by side with a de facto nuclear state. While the United States is across an ocean from North Korea, Russia and China are just across a river and South Korea just across a demarcation line. How are all the parties concerned going to treat this situation and this North Korean culprit?

Although the DPRK becoming a de facto nuclear power probably has not increased an immediate risk of conflict in the region, further escalation of tensions is not impossible. Additional grave dangers are nuclear proliferation and the emergence of new regional and extraregional nuclear players as a result of North Korea's moves and the relative weakness of the international response. A discussion of this effect is noticeable already in many regional capitals; in Tokyo, for example, talk of Japan joining the nuclear club has become more pronounced in recent years as a result of North Korean missile and nuclear tests.[2]

The only prescription against these threats is keeping the diplomatic process going, as fruitless as it may seem at times. Sanctions and additional pressure on North Korea may actually result in further provocative actions by

Pyongyang, including new weapons of mass destruction (WMD) programs, WMD technology proliferation, or even military actions near the southern border (although probably limited)[3] meant to discourage its opponents and prevent their resorting to more pressure. Such a spiral of tension, which might eventually lead to an open conflict, should be averted by the other five parties in the Six Party Talks reengaging the DPRK. After the death of Kim Jong-il and the new leader Kim Jong-un's attempts to modernize the country and reestablish dialogue with the West (in early 2012 Kim Jong-un even decided to postpone another nuclear test, as was ordered by his late father), the timing seems perfect, even if it would mean making the West taking the first step. Actually, a choice is available between a hostile and cornered nuclear North Korea and a nuclear North Korea engaged, acting responsibly, and searching for compromise. Isolated and cornered, North Korea might resort to irresponsible behavior, such as exporting nuclear technologies, while a North Korea engaged in dialogue with the international community would be more likely to play by the rules.

At the same time, while the efforts for denuclearization via the Six Party Talks, the International Atomic Energy Agency (IAEA), and other actors should continue, new responses and approaches should be considered. In Russia's case a bilateral response may vary—from doing nothing and continuing business as usual with North Korea to sanctions and beefing up its military capabilities to prevent a nuclear strike. However, support for a military option is highly doubtful. Russia has repeatedly made it clear that only a negotiated, diplomatic solution taking into account the interests of all concerned parties is the answer,[4] although Moscow dutifully—though belatedly, because of domestic bureaucratic delays—joined the international sanctions regime.[5]

CONSEQUENCES FOR RUSSIA OF NORTH KOREAN NUCLEARIZATION

In an article on Russian foreign policy published in February 2012, Russian leader Vladimir Putin expressed concern about North Korea's nuclear ambitions, stressing that "DPRK nuclear status is unacceptable for us." However, he called for this problem to be solved exclusively by diplomatic means and stressed the need for the soonest possible resumption of the Six Party Talks. Putin noted, however, that not all "DPRK partners" share the understanding on the need for exclusively diplomatic means when dealing with North Korea and called "inadmissible" any attempts to "test the strength of the new leader," which could provoke "ill-considered countermeasures" from North Korea. The Russian leader promised to continue active dialogue with the leaders of this neighboring country and developing relations while promoting a solution for the nuclear problem. He also called for resumption of inter-Korean dialogue.[6] After his return to the presidency in May 2012 Putin made it clear that a nuclear North Korea is in principle unacceptable to Russia, but stopped short of explaining any steps Russia might unilaterally take to reach this goal, meaning that the traditional line of engaging the DPRK would continue. In fact, the basic Russian military and political approaches remain rather static, although high-level rhetoric criticizing Pyongyang's behavior reached an unprecedented level after the second nuclear test, as well as after the rocket launch in 2012.

First, a de facto DPRK acquisition of nuclear weapons would deal a severe blow to the nonproliferation regime, which could have dangerous consequences for Russian security in the Far East as well as quite distant areas.[7] This position was clear cut even before the DPRK declared its possession of nuclear weapons. Russia maintains that the Korean Peninsula should be free from all nuclear weapons and that Moscow would not formally recognize the DPRK as a nuclear state.

At the same time, Russia strongly opposes any attempts to solve the nuclear issue through pressure or sanctions and would use its influence to prevent external attempts for a regime change. Denuclearization at any price is not Russia's slogan. Synchronization is needed so that the nuclear issue can be solved in conjunction with the broader issue of Korean security guarantees.

Today, however, it is permissible to speak about some new nuances among Russian political and academic circles for approaching the North Korean nuclear issue; I address them below. The traditional approach, which still more or less determines practical policy in this area for Russian policymakers, can be summarized as follows: Stability in neighboring areas is a first priority, and a diplomatic solution giving North Koreans incentives—primarily security guarantees—to make them agree to abandon nuclear weaponization should be sought, even though few optimists believe that would happen any time soon. Under no circumstances would military action be taken to rein in the nuclear program or attempt to change the regime, which would effectively wipe the North Korean state from the political map. Sanctions would not help either; only a compromise could lead to a breakthrough. The status quo is a better option than the risk involved in changing the situation forcefully, even if it means living side by side with a de facto nuclear-weapon state. However, recognizing North Korea as a member of the nuclear club of nations remains out of the question. By this logic, maintaining amicable relations between Moscow and Pyongyang is imperative both for Russia's ability to preclude dangerous developments and to influence Pyongyang to be more receptive to compromise.

Such an approach is well suited to the core Russian strategy, based on its national interests, and is also in tune with the policies of Moscow's strategic partner, China. The approach is also useful to contain potentially hostile Western ambitions in a vital area, where Russian positions have never been strong enough. Therefore, Russia's seeming passivity sometimes causes the United States and its allies' displeasure. The goal of denuclearization is subordinate to other Russian interests and under current conditions remains elusive. Speaking cynically, deep in the heart of many a Russian policymaker the idea of a nuclear North Korea (even an operationally nuclear one) is less appalling than that of a destroyed North Korea dominated by the United States and all the catastrophic consequences for Russian interests, and those of the other nations in the region, this outcome could entail.

RUSSIAN REACTION TO THE CRISIS OF 2009–11

Since 2009 Pyongyang's provocative behavior and its pursuit of nuclear and long-range missile capabilities have almost overfilled the cup of the Kremlin's patience and have given rise to a less lenient approach to the DPRK's adventurism by then–president Medvedev's administration. Its global interests, including that of preserving the nonproliferation regime, are considered in the framework of such an approach more important for Russia than appeasing the whims of an abhorrent regime. The distant possibility of Japan, South Korea, or Taiwan aspiring for nuclear capability would be particularly worrisome, as it would change the power equation against Russia's favor and would require costly countermeasures. A reset of relations with the United States, then high on the Russian leadership's agenda, prompted it to sacrifice the interests of good relations with Pyongyang for the sake of closer cooperation with Washington in vital security areas, especially in strategic arms limitation and counterproliferation activities. Iran, where Russian interests are much deeper than in Korea, should not be forgotten either. Maintaining a delicate balance in the dance around Tehran's nuclear program is more essential to Russian interests than keeping an unruly Pyongyang out of trouble. Such an approach presupposes that effective measures to guard against the potential implications of an operationally nuclear North Korea might be necessary, including increased military preparedness in the Russian Far East as well as a more supportive approach to international sanctions against North Korea.

Would Russia resolutely change its practical strategy toward North Korea because of its newly acquired nuclear status? The answer depends on whether the strategy change would bring about a real change in North Korea's policies in nuclear-related matters. Regardless of Russia's actions, Pyongyang will not change its behavior unless U.S. policies change. Only if meeting the conditions they would want in exchange would be possible would Pyongyang's leaders make a decision to give up nuclear weapons. This scenario is beyond Russia's control, so Moscow feels no need to rush. The status quo, which is actually not deleterious to Russia's overall regional position and which can only be considered an indirect challenge to its global priorities, suits Russia's own interests.

In 2008–11, however, the dangerous maneuvers of the DPRK's leaders annoyed Moscow because they actually constituted a clear break with the status quo and contributed to the deterioration of Russia's security situation in the Far East. After Kim Jong-il's death, though, the situation seem to be changing. It is a promising sign that Kim Jong-un, using the traumatic experience of the international consequences of the rocket launch, managed to postpone his father's decision on another nuclear test despite objection from the military. But Kim Jong-un had to show that DPRK's patience is not unlimited—and that if North Korea would not get positive signals soon from the United States, the North's new leader would have to give up to the hard-liners and reconsider the nuclear issue.

Russia still boasts a decades-old school of Korean studies, uniting Russia's Academy of Science (with a record of excellence in Korean studies more than a century long), former diplomats, party and state officials, university professors, and other experts having spent decades in the DPRK. This expertise results in a deeper understanding of North Korean leaders' thinking and motives than may be the case elsewhere outside of East Asia, which in many cases accounts for the differences in Russian prognoses of the North Korean situation from those of other analysts.

The latest cycle of tensions leading to the emergence of the DPRK as a de facto nuclear weapons state started sometime in late 2008. What caused the high-level decision on the change of strategy from dialogue to confrontation? The causal factors seem to be more external than internal. Most likely the North Koreans became disappointed with the lame-duck George W. Bush administration's true intentions in the ongoing diplomatic process, which could be read as procrastinating and giving Pyongyang tangible security guarantees in anticipation of the regime's meltdown, which many experts suspected.[8] The Six Party Talks seemed to Pyongyang to have exhausted their potential to help solve the central issue: regime survival. Tit-for-tat bargaining has not brought North Korea much closer to that prize. Pyongyang agreed to reign in its nuclear program, but received in return reluctant and ultimately insignificant aid and halfhearted half steps on a long and winding road to normalization. At the same time, further down the road Pyongyang would have to discuss—and probably be pressed for concessions on—something really tangible, such as reprocessed fissile materials and actual nuclear weapons.

Is Pyongyang totally to blame for the failure of the Talks? Although deeply irritated with Pyongyang's decision to quit the diplomatic process yet again, Moscow also puts blame on the United States and its allies in Tokyo and Seoul, which tried to force new concessions from Pyongyang without adequate reciprocity. Russian foreign minister Sergey Lavrov noted in September 2008,

> Differently from some other members of the Six Party Talks, we are acting in a team spirit fashion, collectively, as was agreed initially. We try to avoid unilateral steps. . . . The purpose is denuclearization of the Korean Peninsula, not solving the bilateral problems of some participants. . . . It would be fruitful if all the members of the Six Party Talks would fulfill their obligations by the letter of the agreements reached and not file some other requests without consulting other partners. And of course it would be important that all the DPRK's partners in the Six Party process would actually participate in providing economic assistance to Pyongyang. That, I think, would constitute a package that would enable forward movement.[9]

Officially Moscow indirectly blamed the United States and sometimes Japan for dragging its feet on fulfilling its obligations and thereby complicating the peace process.[10]

Russian experts understand North Koreans became frustrated; their actual gains from the multiparty process were marginal. They did not come much closer to getting substantial security guarantees; even a largely symbolic and easily reversible delisting of the DPRK as a terrorist state caused much controversy in the United States and abroad, and new concessions were demanded in exchange from North Korea, which Pyongyang saw as a breach of trust. As to the modest economic assistance promised when the accord was sealed, only the United States and Russia carried out their obligations (two hundred thousand tons of heavy oil), while other countries either totally abstained (Japan) or moved sluggishly. From their perspective, the DPRK felt that its concessions were neither fully recognized nor valued. Hawks in Pyongyang might have suspected that the West perceived these concessions as a sign of weakness and testimony to Pyongyang's pressing need to normalize relations. The turn since early 2008 of Lee Myung-bak's administration to a hard-line policy, effectively dismantling almost all the achievements of the North-South rapprochement under the liberal governments of Kim Dae-jung and Roh Moo-hyun, was seen as yet another precedent of untrustworthiness of the negotiation partners and became a major setback for those in the Pyongyang leadership who put diplomacy in front of the policy of *songun* [military first].

Small wonder that the voices in Pyongyang saying that engagement policies were ineffective became louder. While external factors and internal factors led to Pyongyang's turn to a hard-line policy, the crucial catalyst probably was the reported illness of Kim Jong-il in 2008–9, which came as a shock to the elite; without Kim Jong-il's guidance the North's elite were too scared to continue the elaborate chess game with the West, while reform would present a real and immediate danger for the ruling class. Consequently, the turn to a strategy of increasing tensions and raising the stakes became imminent. Reversing the promises to dismantle the nuclear facilities and move toward denuclearization along the lines agreed to in the September 19, 2005, Statement of the Six Party Talks—the substance of which is the peace-for-nukes formula[11]—was a natural choice for Pyongyang, which considered that its adversaries were the first to break their earlier promises.

This moment was also seen as an opportunity to move one step closer to becoming a member of the global nuclear club without any particular danger of retaliation from the world community. (The United States was busy with the transition between administrations, Iraq and Afghanistan, and later the financial crisis.) At the same time, from a pragmatic point of view, gaining the attention of the world and the new U.S. administration and raising stakes for a future diplomatic contest were easily achievable through raising tensions. Kim Jong-il probably concluded that the incoming Obama administration would not take North Korea seriously enough and decided that he would continue his slow-burning tit-for-tat bargaining. However, this piece-by-piece approach would not deliver the regime the sustainability guarantees it needed. Pyongyang decided to tame the new U.S. leaders and teach them a lesson, regardless of the possibilities of more liberal intentions from the incoming U.S. leaders.

Kim Jong-il's new message was that Obama would have to talk to an established nuclear weapons state.

Another goal of this new strategy was to harness the North Korean population, who were becoming increasingly wary of hardships, by restoring the besieged-fortress mentality. The country followed the familiar pattern of closing up and tightening the screws as demanded by the military and ideologues.

From the start of this policy turn Russia became increasingly critical of the DPRK's rhetoric and actions. Moscow expressed its "concern with the escalation of tensions"[12] before the missile test in April 2009 and "repeatedly recommended to the DPRK not to conduct the rocket experiment." Russia supported the U.N. Security Council presidential statement condemning North Korea's rocket launch, adopted on April 13. However, that maneuver backfired. As Russia had previously emphasized the right of all nations to conduct satellite tests, this inconsistency turned out to be unexpected to Pyongyang and caused it displeasure, which was bluntly communicated to Russian foreign minister Sergey Lavrov during his April 2009 visit to Pyongyang, perhaps the last high-level contact between the two capitals for some time to come. Lavrov was not granted a meeting with Kim Jong-il, and North Koreans made it clear that they were not going to take into account the Russian position on the need to abstain from further tests and return to the negotiation process. In November a visiting Speaker of the upper chamber of the Russian Parliament was also not given the normally expected meeting with Kim Jong-il.

The nuclear test of May 25, 2009, caused indignation in the Kremlin, which called it "irresponsible," "absolutely unacceptable," and "unpardonable." Natalya Timakova, chief spokeswoman for President Dmitry Medvedev, said the test was a "direct violation" of U.N. Security Council resolutions, adding, "Initiators of decisions on nuclear tests bear personal responsibility for them to the world community," and, saying the test "deals a blow to international efforts to strengthen the global regime of nuclear nonproliferation."[13] The Russian military—probably acting on orders from above—went as far as to suggest deploying Russia's sophisticated S-400 air defense system in its far eastern region to protect against any potential test mishap near its border with the DPRK.[14] The Russian permanent representative to the United Nations stressed that Russia "regards the second nuclear test in the DPRK as a serious blow to international efforts to strengthen the nuclear non-proliferation treaty . . . action, seriously threatening security and stability in the region."[15]

After the condemnatory UN Security Council resolution was adopted, Russia "called on the partners in the DPRK to rightfully accept the will of the international community, expressed in the resolution, denounce nuclear weapons and all the military nuclear-missile programs, return to the NPT, the CTBT and the IAEA safeguards regime, and resume participation in the Six Party Talks aimed at finding a mutually acceptable solution of the current knot of contradictions."[16] Russia also denounced North Korean intentions to proceed to uranium enrichment, and President Medvedev signed a decree implementing intensified UN Security Council sanctions against Pyongyang's nuclear programs. The presidential decree banned purchases of weapons and relevant materials from the DPRK by government offices, enterprises, banks, organizations, and individuals currently under Russia's jurisdiction. It also prohibited the transit of weapons and relevant materials via Russian territory or their export to the DPRK. Any financial aid and educational training that might facilitate Pyongyang's nuclear program and proliferation activities were forbidden as well.[17]

These events, however, have not led to a basic reappraisal of Russian strategy toward the North Korean problem. Moscow doesn't blame Pyongyang solely for the failure of the diplomatic process of 2003–8.[18] Russia also sees the George W. Bush administration, as well as the Japanese Liberal Democratic Party governments and South Korea's Lee Myung-bak administration, as bearing responsibility for dragging their feet on fulfilling obligations, complicating the peace process, and making excessive demands on Pyongyang.

The tragic *Cheonan* incident in March 2010 became a severe test for Moscow's Korean policy. Moscow suspected that Seoul used the campaign implicating North Korea as the culprit to achieve its long-term policy ambitions of further isolating and pressuring Pyongyang in order to weaken the regime and gain a competitive edge over it while trying to disrupt Chinese support of the DPRK.[19] In the UN Security Council, Russia was supportive of China.[20] At the same time, Russian naval experts, sent to Korea by President Medvedev at the request of President Lee Myung-bak, could not support the South Korean version of events.[21] As a result of these events, starting with the *Cheonan* sinking, Russia's interests suffered. First, tensions near its borders increased. Second, the Six Party Talks, which Russia sees as the vital mechanism to maintain its involvement in Korean and Northeast Asian affairs, lost a chance for swift resumption, thus affecting Russia's interest in peacefully addressing its nonproliferation concerns. Third, relations with both Koreas, China, and the United States were strained by the *Cheonan* incident and the controversy surrounding the investigation that followed.

Russia was even more concerned about the North Korean artillery's shelling of Yongpyeong Island. The Russian Foreign Ministry stated, "The Russian side resolutely condemns any manifestations of force in relations between states and believes that all existing controversial issues should be dealt with solely by peaceful, diplomatic, and political means."[22] However, Foreign Minister Sergey Lavrov noted, "The incident was preceded by the information that North Korea asked South Korea not to conduct training, not to fire, but the training took place nevertheless." He stopped short of condemning North Korea but demanded that no such incidents should take place in the future.[23]

In December 2010, during DPRK foreign minister Park Ui-chun's visit, Russia condemned the shelling, which led to the loss of life. In UN Security Council deliberations, Russia thus went further than China, which stopped short of condemning North Korea's actions.[24] At the same time Russia was also opposed to South Korea's actions and, on December 17, demanded that the ROK abstain from planned live ammunition training to avoid further escalation of tensions in Korean Peninsula.[25] However, this appeal was ignored.

Russia is urging North Korea and South Korea to restart the dialogue without preconditions, thus being implicitly critical of the South's demand for prior "apologies" from the North, which are certain not to follow.[26] During ROK foreign affairs and trade minister Kim Sung-hwan's visit to Russia in August 2011, Moscow expressed its desire to restart the Six Party Talks, for which the improvement of DPRK-ROK dialogue is essential.[27] Russia made it clear that it does not view as realistic the approach of "denuclearization first, rewards later," and some experts suspect that this stance is just a cover for promoting the hidden agenda of undermining the North Korean regime. Russian experts,[28] therefore, see North Korean denuclearization as only one of the tasks in the comprehensive settlement to the decades-old Korean security problem, not the end in itself. Russia has always suggested that the Korean nuclear issue should be solved through multiparty diplomacy and was instrumental in bringing about the Six Party Talks started in 2003 and a package deal:[29] to put it in the nutshell, "peace and aid for nukes." North Koreans did not evade discussing these problems with Russia, even stating at times that the DPRK does not actually want to develop nuclear potential as it is burdensome for the country, but such actions are necessary because of the "hostile policy" of the United States and South Korea. North Koreans also were always blaming the United States and South Korea for the stalemate in the diplomatic process.

Actually, what could really affect Russia's interests is not the current nuclear status of North Korea but a further expansion of North Korean nuclear programs and improvement of its nuclear weapons and delivery means. Consequences of those actions eventually could endanger Russia's national security, mostly because of an increased regional answer to these developments, which would require countermeasures. The possibility of North Korea's WMD technologies falling into terrorists' hands should not also be totally discarded. Russia's interest in stopping any such developments coincides, therefore, with the interests of the United States, Japan, and South Korea.

But the full denuclearization of Korea under the current rules of the game seems to be unattainable, especially in the wake of the intervention in Libya after Qadaffi had voluntarily given up his nuclear weapons program in a deal with the West. For Russia the more viable option is trying to rein in the DPRK nuclear potential—that is, to "manage the risks," silently agreeing to the temporary preservation of the current situation. This feasible option can be achieved through the diplomatic process, although the goal of actual denuclearization would move over the horizon.

During his visit to Pyongyang in March 2011 Russian deputy foreign minister Alexei Borodavkin urged Pyongyang to take constructive steps: "announce its readiness to return to the Six Party Talks without preliminary conditions; impose a moratorium on production and testing of nuclear weapons, and on launches of rockets with ballistic technologies; agree on the inspection by IAEA experts of facilities for enriching uranium and on the inclusion of North Korea's uranium dossier into the agenda of talks; invite IAEA inspectors to the nuclear center."[30] Pyongyang officials responded that North Korea is not opposed to discussion of its uranium enrichment program as part of nuclear talks and could return to the Six Party Talks, but the North would count on a principle of reciprocal actions, and that other Russian requests could also be discussed and settled in the course of implementing past agreements. However, South Korea rebuffed this offer. Nevertheless Russia's comments laid the foundation for the 2011–12 DPRK-U.S. talks that resulted in the Leap Day Deal of February 2012, which formalized these obligations in exchange for U.S. aid and promise for talks on normalization and lifting of sanctions. Although this deal was brought down by Pyongyang's rocket launch, the ideology is still relevant for future dealings with the DPRK.

A RETROSPECTIVE ON THE NUCLEARIZATION OF NORTH KOREA: LESSONS FOR A FUTURE SETTLEMENT

Speculating on Russia's possible response to the emergence of a de facto nuclear neighbor, it should be noted that North Korea going nuclear was not totally unexpected for Russia. Pyongyang was long suspected of having such ambitions, even in Soviet times, although Russian technical experts familiar with the DPRK's nuclear program had long doubted the North's technological ability to master a nuclear charge. It was established knowledge in the Soviet Union that North Koreans, bombed heavily during the Korean War, were over-concerned with security and considered the policies of the United States—supported by former colonial power Japan and South Korea—to be a menace to its very existence, while they did not consider the Soviet and Chinese umbrellas reliable enough. Throughout the Cold War, acquiring a relatively cheap and accessible "nuclear strategic equalizer" looked like the most tempting and optimal solution for *Juche* proponents in Pyongyang, regardless of Moscow's attempts to prevent it. Pyongyang pushed to acquire its own deterrent not least because North Korea did not have any moral obligations to abstain; the North knew about U.S. plans to use nuclear weapons against it during the Korean War and even after the war (up to the 1970s at least), and the regime still suspects the U.S. military of planning to use next-generation miniature nuclear munitions against vital DPRK targets.[31] The North remembers well the introduction of U.S. nuclear weapons into South Korea in 1958.[32]

North Korea might have fulfilled its dream of constructing a nuclear bomb as early as the early 1960s and, some experts suggest, even had it tailored especially for its technicians, who were trained on Soviet reactors in preparation to work on the IRT-2000 research reactor that the USSR built in 1965; the actual plutonium for the bomb was produced at another reactor and facilities, reassembled by North Koreans without Soviet consent or even knowledge. Nuclear research had been going on in North Korea since the early 1960s, and in the 1970s the DPRK embarked on creating its own plutonium weapons.[33] According to Soviet intelligence data, by the end of the 1980s Moscow knew about the DPRK's nuclear weapons aspirations[34] in 1990 Moscow heard about it directly from then–foreign minister Kim Young-nam, who told Soviet foreign minister Eduard Shevardnadze that, in response to the USSR's establishment of relations with Seoul, "In the conditions of the presence of nuclear weapon in South Korea we, in this case, inevitably will develop a corresponding counter-weapon and will have to leave the Treaty on the Non-Proliferation of Nuclear Weapons."[35]

Leaving aside the decades-long twists and turns of the negotiation on denuclearization, I would point out that Russia was still never entirely sure that North Korea was capable of delivering on its menacing promises. For example, in February 2005, when the DPRK Ministry of Foreign Affairs issued its first-ever statement on manufacturing the "nuclear deterrent,"[36] the Russian reaction was rather calm. Official Russian representatives expressed concern mainly about Pyongyang's decision to stop participation in the Six Party Talks for an indefinite period, although "accumulation of nuclear military potential" was also mentioned, accompanied by a statement that such a decision does not correspond to the goal of denuclearizing the Korean Peninsula that the DPRK also shares. Moscow called for discussing and settling existing problems at the negotiation table with the interests of all sides taken into consideration. Even when the danger of the DPRK acquiring nuclear weapons became imminent, no major diplomatic action was taken, as most experts considered the move a North Korean bluff; the reaction was mostly rhetorical. Not long before the first DPRK nuclear test, Russia's then–military chief of staff General Yuri Baluyevsky stressed, "It is necessary to do everything possible in order not to allow North Korea to conduct [nuclear] tests. It is necessary to do everything for the resumption of the Six Party Talks on this problem. It is necessary to do everything in order [that] the Korean Peninsula never becomes an arena of the use of nuclear weapons,"[37] but no active measures occurred. Russian experts privately doubted that the first nuclear test was successful and did not take seriously the ability of North Korean technicians to miniaturize a successful sample small enough to mount on a missile.

Nevertheless, the very fact of the nuclear test made reassessing the situation necessary. Russia's diplomatic response was clear: it dutifully supported UN Resolution 1718 and later, in April 2007, the sanctions regime. However, the restart of the Six Party Talks reassured Russian policymakers that things were under control and no special measures endangering relations with the capricious Pyongyang leaders were necessary.

This logic becomes clear if we pose a practical question: Has the immediate danger to Russian territory or national interests increased as a result of North Korea's nuclearization? Probably not much, as the danger of a military conflict near Russian borders has actually diminished with the appearance of a nuclear deterrent in the DPRK, whatever its actual operationality might be. The implications of a nuclear North Korea for Russia lie mostly in the spheres connected to nonproliferation and Moscow's geopolitical strategy with the United States and China to preserve its own interests and positions in Asia.[38]

RUSSIA'S PRIORITIES IN LIGHT OF NORTH KOREAN NUCLEARIZATION

Russia's political priorities in Northeast Asia have not changed much over the last decade, although the DPRK can now be considered as a nuclear-weapons state. Preventing any conflict that might lead to a nuclear catastrophe only became more urgent. Russia's priorities in light of North Korean nuclearization can be summed up as follows.

Russia sees its number-one priority as stability and regional development in order to create conditions for Russia's own deeper integration into the global economy and the regional and international division of labor. Such stability and development are important for the economic prosperity and security of the Russian Far East, so as to prevent its distancing from the federal center. Also important is carrying through the Russian strategy of advancing in Asia and the Pacific as proclaimed in July 2010,[39] and reaffirmed as a result of the Asia Pacific Economic Cooperation (APEC)-2012 Summit in Vladivistok, a highly symbolic first meeting in Russia of Asian heads of state. Therefore, preventing any conflict or increase of tension in Korea is fundamental to Russian interests.

Other Russian priorities are that the Korean Peninsula should be free of all weapons of mass destruction, the DPRK should obey the NPT rules and return to compliance with the IAEA, and verification and guarantees of denuclearization should be based on international law. A nuclear arms race in the region and globally could change the balance of power in a manner detrimental to Russian interests. However, unlike the United States, Russia thinks that all countries have the right to develop modern energy technologies, including nuclear energy; Russia was thus never against development of a peaceful nuclear program in the DPRK, including the possible construction of light water reactors, although after the Fukushima disaster this stance is no more than a declaration of principle.

Moscow is certain that the ultimate solution to the Korean issue should be found within a multiparty diplomatic process and that the idea of a package solution, first suggested by Moscow in 2003 and strikingly similar to the agreements reached by the Six Party Talks in 2005–8, should become the basis for it. Guaranteeing security and sustainability of the DPRK is actually a precondition for achieving the goals of nonproliferation, demilitarization, and stability, although Russia admits that these goals might take a long time. Achieving these goals does not depend solely on the DPRK's actions but is the responsibility of other countries as well.

Russia sees as imperative good relations with the DPRK and cooperation with other major players in order to achieve these goals. In Moscow's view, the international process, comprising major powers, should not be regarded as a zero-sum game. The idea of a regional type of Cold-War-era division on Korean affairs (3+3—i.e., Russia, China, and North Korea on one side, and the United

States, Japan, and South Korea on the other) has no appeal for Moscow, especially after the recent growth of U.S.-Chinese tension due to a more assertive Chinese foreign policy in its neighborhood. A concert of powers is more attractive and could be formed on the basis of the existing multiparty mechanism of nuclear talks.

Throughout modern history Russia has supported North-South reconciliation and cooperation without outside interference. Eventual Korean reunification in a form agreed upon by both North and South is a distant goal and not on today's agenda. A unified, peaceful, and prosperous Korea that is friendly to Russia is the utmost dream. Such a country would be one of the most important partners of Russia in Asia, helping to build a more balanced system of international relations in the Far East, which is now dominated by the U.S.-Japan-China triangle. At the same time, Korea could become a growing market, especially for resources of the Russian Far East.

A unified Korea dependent on either the United States or China would be detrimental to Russian interests, and Russia would strive to prevent such a development. Absorption of the North by a pro-U.S. South Korea could be harmful both to the Korean nation and regional security, and Russia would probably join China in opposing such a scenario. Neither is a China-dominated North Korea desirable, as such a regime would probably be unstable and would cause containment efforts aimed at China as well as increased military tensions in the area. A new security system in and around the Korean Peninsula should take into account the legitimate interests of all the parties and should not be used for purposes other than maintaining peace and stability and achieving development. Such an approach suits well the core Russian strategy based on its national interests and is also in tune with the policies of its strategic partner, China.

While Pyongyang's behavior in 2009–13—pursuit of nuclear and missile capabilities, as well as provocations on the border—has tested the Kremlin's patience and given rise to a less lenient approach to the DPRK's adventurism in Moscow's top echelons of power, engagement remains the code word for Russia to deal with its prickly neighbor, even if that neighbor is nuclear armed. What should engagement of the DPRK entail to make it successful? Any new round of the diplomatic process, which is sure to replace confrontation at some stage, must from the start set objectives coordinated among all the parties and evaluate different ways of attaining them.

Could such talks yet again be perceived (as some in Washington, Seoul, and Tokyo do) simply as a tool to prevent further provocations and the increase of

WMD and the military capabilities of the North Korean side, while in fact waiting for the regime to collapse? Such a strategy would mean granting no major concessions to Pyongyang, while keeping it at bay with promises. "Denuclearization first, rewards later" seems to be the core of such a strategy. The oft-repeated declaration that North Korea should be "rewarded" by economic assistance and strategic reassurances *after denuclearization* would be taken seriously neither by the North Koreans nor its allies. The sequence should be reversed to avoid losing the chance to achieve the DPRK's deweaponization. In other words, engagement, political and economic, should precede phased denuclearization. Such an approach also has a hidden agenda: that the possible expansion of cooperation with the West and South Korea would soften and undermine the regime. Such thinking seem delusional. Oversuspicious North Koreans see these dangers and would not accommodate such treatment by their adversaries. Periodic resurgences of tensions and provocations would be almost certain.

I believe that the gambit should be totally different. The only hope for denuclearization is to promote a substantial evolution in North Korea for it to become a normal country that could live without nuclear weapons. Is it feasible? Official Russian documents give little clue as to how Moscow would like to see the situation on the Korean Peninsula develop. This issue is sensitive, because it inevitably includes discussing the future of North Korea, and any such speculations might cause a harsh reaction from Pyongyang and damage the relationship. While Russia does not want to witness an implosion or abrupt change of the North Korean regime, Moscow might still welcome the regime gradually changing and transforming, making its neighbor a more conventional country. The unprecedented de facto admission by the authorities in March 2010 of the failure of the November 2009 currency reform initially meant to curtail market forces, well illustrates this point, despite the drama added by the scapegoating and execution of former planning commission chairman Park Nam-gi for "damaging the people's economy."[40] With the new leadership firmly in place, the clock cannot be turned back.

The possibility of North Korea's collapse is generally seen in Russia as remote, although the internal and external crises in which the DPRK has found itself since 2008 have increased such a likelihood. Unlike China, Russia has neither a desire to support nor is there any possibility it would actively support the current regime, although preserving stability does correspond to Moscow's interests, and political support of efforts in this direction can be expected. Pragmatic new leadership for the DPRK may, while anxious about preserving the system, nevertheless try to reinvigorate the country, starting with the cautious adoption of a new economic guidance system.

Is a positive evolution of North Korea's regime possible? The current power structure seems to be rather unlikely to accommodate such a consideration. The DPRK's political and economic system should be assisted in undertaking a positive evolution that could ensure a smooth transition to a new generation of leaders and conventionalization of the country. Such a changed North Korea would feel that militarization, including WMD, as a deterrent and a guarantee of preserving its statehood is redundant and would lead to the denunciation of WMD and a decrease in military potential.

Such a vision presupposes that denuclearizing the Korean Peninsula should remain as a vital final goal, but it cannot become the sole issue under discussion with North Korea. As prior experience has shown, without taking into consideration the DPRK's legitimate interests, no progress from such a discussion can be expected. The "denuclearization first, cooperation later" scenario is implausible.

The agenda of the talks should be comprehensive, including the issues of a Korean and regional security and peace regime, nonproliferation, and economic cooperation, not just "the nuclear issue."[41] Maybe a convention of completely new talks with a broader agenda could be considered, provided that all the parties proclaim adherence to the agreements reached in the course of the Six Party Talks, including the September 19, 2005, statement. However, the format should be the same: the original six parties, plus maybe UN representatives and observers from the European Union and other interested parties. The talks should discuss the modalities of phased denuclearization and the building of a new security regime.

A number of experts in member countries of the Six Party Talks, including Russia, have long advocated such or similar approaches, which have sometimes served as a basis for practical policies. These policies were moderately successful in freezing and at times even halting the DPRK nuclear program, although so far they have always resulted in false starts for a variety of reasons. The single most important reason is the absence of a genuine commitment by North Korea's opponents to coexist with the regime. Insincere and halfhearted partial engagement with an underlying intent of regime change does more harm than good. A strategic decision to coexist with the DPRK's only existing regime should be adopted in the capitals of Pyongyang's adversary countries—

followed by Pyongyang's own strategic decision to forgo nuclear weapons when relations are normalized. This approach really could provide the basis for a future package deal or grand bargain.

POSSIBLE NORTH KOREAN REFORMS AS THE CATALYST FOR DENUCLEARIZATION

Would this manner of engagement stimulate the conventionalization of the country? In the nascent Kim Jong-un era, this does not seem impossible. The soil is now fertile for a gradual transformation of the DPRK's political economy,[42] regardless of what the diehard orthodox communist segment of the leadership, obviously being slowly replaced, might think about it. Even before the death of Kim Jong-il, the hard-line strategy of closing up and tightening the screws—demanded by the military and ideologues and based on fear rooted in Kim Jong-il's sudden illness—and the efforts to reestablish centralized control of the population were not equally successful in every sphere of life. Increasing political and ideological pressure causes no major domestic opposition, and even the number of people who want to leave the country seems not to be on the rise. However, the attempts, noticeable since 2005 but reinforced since 2008, to limit the economic aspects of marketization from below became less evident after the failures of the economic crisis of the 1990s and the "150 days" and "100 days" "battles"—mass-mobilization campaigns—wherein people actually could not leave their workplaces for the designated time. The strangely political restoration of Kim Il-sung–era governance methods augmented by militarization (i.e., the military first or *songun* ideology and especially the catastrophic currency reform of 2009) proceeded against the background of grassroots economic liberalization, which tends to become irreversible. As a sign of the times, cell phones, knock-off Kentucky Fried Chicken restaurants and pizza are now in vogue in Pyongyang, while markets thrive with imported goods, regardless of sanctions. After gaining full power in 2012 Kim Jong-un, although retaining the dictatorial political system, immediately started looking for ways to modernize the economy through market mechanisms.

The Pyongyang elites themselves need a transformation unless the North Korean leaders are willing to risk driving their nation into a corner—a geopolitical impasse that could eventually lead to catastrophe. Many Russian experts support this opinion.[43] Such a scenario fits well with Russia's security and economic goals in the region, as the views of one well-respected Russian-born researcher indicates: "Indeed, the position of a reformed North Korea in the newly emerging map of economic interests can be surprisingly strong. The DPRK is located at the very center of the world's most vibrant and dynamically developing region. By playing his cards shrewdly North Koreans might create conditions for socio-economic revitalization of the North that will be a positive contribution to the eventual unification of the Korean Peninsula."[44]

In June 2012 Kim Jong-un made a first step toward a more normal economy by instructing the cabinet to introduce a de facto "family contract system" in agriculture. The changes[45] should start with gradual marketization of the DPRK economy—first on the microeconomic level, which is already happening, and later on a macroeconomic level under state control (a "guided market economy"—and evolution toward multisectoral production and trade conglomerates resembling South Korean *chaebols*. Such conglomerates are to be the centerpiece of engagement, which should go on disregarding the periodic setbacks in the diplomatic process. Economic sanctions only impede the return to normality. As the Kaesong zone experience has shown, the ideology-obsessed North Koreans' unreasonable and overly politicized demands tend to eventually subside and give way to a more sound economy-based approach, even if the ideologues are not so happy with it. The 2012 agreements to restart economic zones with China is a testament to that.

A successful policy of engagement will be evident when the North Koreans feel the benefits of economic development and enjoy a more peaceful environment. Unconditional economic assistance is not the answer: any assistance should be aimed at developing the marketized sector in the economy, which, as the Chinese example has shown, the DPRK leaders should not perceive as an automatic threat to their power. Rather, this sector should be brought out of the shadows and produce resources—via taxation, increased employment and incomes, corresponding growth in demand, and in other forms—for the development of strategic industries that the government now wants to keep state-owned and -controlled, but which are typically unprofitable.

All of these actions could lead to structural economic transformation. This shift would include the decline of outdated and noncompetitive economic activity and the emergence of industries based on North Korea's comparative advantages, such as cheap and relatively well-educated labor, mineral resources, an excellent central East Asian location with transit potential, and the potential for easy access to foreign capital (chiefly of South Korean, Chinese, and maybe even Japanese origin). Economic growth would bring about sociopolitical stabilization that, in parallel with alleviating the DPRK's security concerns, would enable the authorities to soften their grip on the population.

Communist ideology might eventually give way to social nationalism and patriotism (maintaining the sacred role of the founder of the state) as the foundation of societal mentality. The political system in the long run might evolve into a sort of constitutional monarchy or a collective leadership with much greater feedback from the grassroots level for Kim Jong-un. A corresponding decrease of tensions and of DPRK confrontation with the outside world (Myanmar-style) would set the ground for military confidence-building measures and eventual creation of a multilateral system of international arrangements for Korean security, such as checks and balances cross-guaranteed by the United States, Japan, China, and Russia). Of course, such developments are likely a long time away. However, embarking on this road offers the only chance that North Korean leaders might conclude that they no longer need a nuclear deterrent and would voluntarily abandon their nuclear and other WMD ambitions and reduce their level of militarization. For comparison, consider the South African variant, when the elite voluntarily gave up existing secret nuclear potential when the threat from African neighbors disappeared upon dismantling the apartheid regime.

This option, however long it might take (one or two decades at least), is actually the international community's only realistic peaceful way to achieve the goals of denuclearization and peace on the Korean Peninsula. This variant also corresponds with North Korea's own interests.

The responsibility for embarking on this road largely lies with the United States. The denuclearization-first requirement that Washington normally includes as a part of this package would probably block the way, but the idea itself could become the sound basis for a future change of U.S. strategy. The expectations existed in many capitals in 2008–11 that any possible turmoil in North Korea due to a succession crisis may lead to its implosion and a South-led unification, thus solving all the problems. Such expectations date back to the Clinton administration's 1990s approach, which failed. The Obama administration, enraged by North Korean provocations ("a slap in the face," "a fist in exchange for an outstretched hand"), was unable to decipher the meaning of these actions and chose a wait-and-see approach, enforcing sanctions without proposing any coherent vision for resolving the crisis. The sort of vision described above is sorely needed as a prerequisite for the talks. The reluctant U.S. resumption of contacts with Pyongyang started only in 2011, however, close to the end of Obama's first presidential term, and led to a considerable breakthrough evidenced by the deal of February 29, 2012. The failure of the Leap Day Deal due to the rocket launch in April 2012 (actually ordered before his death by

Kim Jong-il, who figuratively turned the ignition key from his grave) postponed moving along this road. As a result of new pressure North Korea threatened to "reconsider the nuclear issue"—probably meaning denouncing the September 19, 2005, Statement providing for staged denuclearization. With such a scheme being the only viable option for the international community, all the partner countries should restrain the DPRK from making such a denunciation by offering a fresh round of negotiations on the basis of that statement.

A new strategy should include providing assurances to the DPRK that the United States as well as the other major countries, including Japan and South Korea, has undertaken the strategic commitment to coexist with the regime. As proof, North Korea should feel the benefits derived from its cooperation with the world community, both political—setting up cordial relations of peaceful coexistence without prior conditions—and economic—aid, investment, and establishing ties with international financial institutions. With the North Korean authorities' consent, any aid, however, should help change the political economy of the country in a way to let the DPRK develop on its own basis by taking advantage of being integrated into the global economy. These policies should not include a hidden agenda of undermining the regime. Now that Kim Jong-un has demonstrated his desire for a measure of reform, the timing is perfect.

A paradigm of U.S.-DPRK coexistence should be worked out based on the assumption that the Pyongyang regime is here to stay and should be recognized. After that, new arrangements for a security structure for the Korean Peninsula could be discussed, with demilitarization and denuclearization remaining vital but future goals. Initially, strategic reassurances and international assistance may be granted, however idealistic that might sound, in exchange for a DPRK promise—probably a summit-level public commitment—to completely denuclearize by a target date, perhaps ten years in the future. By that time the Pyongyang leadership, maybe with a larger share of a new generation of reformists and pragmatists, resulting from the above-mentioned changes, will have to make a choice: either (1) keep its nuclear weapons but forgo all it would gain from abandoning them, including economic cooperation, security assurances, and the normalization of its international standing, or (2) abandon its nuclear weapons but gain international economic cooperation, security cooperation, and normalized international standing.

Although the U.S. role for bringing about the change is central, other players' roles are important as well. China and Russia would without much reservation support such an approach and would be helpful in promoting dialogue toward these ends, as North Korean normalization corresponds with their strategic goals in the region as well as in their own relations with the United States. Given linkage of the abduction issue to the nuclear talks, Japan's policy has often been difficult to reconcile with the other five parties, but with its DPJ government it might become more result-oriented and pragmatic. South Korea could play a vital role by supporting U.S. efforts, not pushing forward its own agenda without concern for wider goals and refraining from hostile actions against the DPRK, however irritating Pyongyang's behavior might be. Keeping the multilateral coordination mechanism intact is important—not letting Pyongyang play up contradictions between its partners. Ultimately the deal on the newly established rules of the game should receive the approval and guarantees for implementation from all the players in the Six Party Talks. A high-level political declaration and a set of bilateral, legally binding treaties on the Korean issue between each of the participants could be the basis of a final arrangement for constructing a new, more workable security architecture in Northeast Asia.

CHAPTER SEVEN

Washington's Response to an Operationally Nuclear North Korea

DAVID KANG

In the spring of 2012, the February 29 agreement between the United States and North Korea to provide food aid in exchange for progress on the nuclear issue immediately fell apart as the DPRK announced that it would test a long-range missile, as it did in April). In fact, the Korean Peninsula is in the throes of a new Cold War in which both sides engage in deterrence, name calling, and muscle flexing.[1] Once again, North Korea has engaged in bluster designed to project strength and resolve in the face of international disapproval. The North Korean nuclear issue has been the most important security issue in the region for more than two decades, and despite developments such as the death of North Korean leader Kim Jong-il and past and pending changes in leadership in South Korea, Japan and the United States, the underlying issues remain depressingly the same: how to reign in North Korea's nuclear programs and entice North Korea to open its markets and borders to greater levels of foreign interaction.[2] North Korea has been one of the most enduring foreign policy challenges facing the United States over the past half century. From a bitter and divisive war in 1950–53 through the Cold War, and now through successive nuclear crises, the United States has made little progress over the years in resolving or stabilizing its relationship with North Korea.

North Korea finds itself at a major turning point, what with the passing of Kim Jong-il and replacement by his son, Kim Jong-un; recurrent food and energy shortages; and a barely functioning economic system. The opportunities and dangers of rapid regime change or collapse in North Korea are immense. North Korea may again find a way to muddle through with its basic ruling regime and leadership intact. No matter what happens, however, the underlying task is still how to draw North Korea into the world and away from its dangerous, confrontational stance.

In the United States, most observers from across the political spectrum agree on the goal: a denuclearized North Korea that opens to the world, pursues economic and social reforms, and increasingly respects human rights. Disagreement only occurs over the tactics—what policies will best prod North Korea on the path toward these outcomes. Is it best to engage North Korea and lure it into changing its actions and its relations with the outside world, or is it better to contain the problem and coerce North Korea into either changing or stopping its bad behavior?[3]

As this process has dragged on for almost twenty years, the beliefs of both sides may have changed. While in the mid-1990s North Korea may have been willing to exchange nuclear weapons for normal diplomatic relations with the United States, leaders in Pyongyang may very well believe that events over time have shown that the United States and South Korea will never choose to live with a North Korea of any type. As for South Korea and the United States, while imagining that under certain conditions North Korea might give up its nuclear weapons was previously possible, many observers now believe that will never happen. Thus, the leadership in both countries may now believe that no real solution to the nuclear problem is possible. As a result, the real issue may not be "how to denuclearize North Korea," but rather how best to manage living with a nuclear North Korea, contain the problem, and ultimately how to enhance peaceful political and economic change in the North.[4]

North Korea is, in fact, a nuclear-weapon state. Although the DPRK has not yet managed to place a nuclear device on an intercontinental ballistic missile and prove that it can deliver that missile with any accuracy, or in any other way operationalize its nascent nuclear capability as far as we know, it has successfully detonated a nuclear device. Thus, the challenge is what to do about it. The Obama administration stated early on that it is determined to "break the cycle" of crisis escalation with North Korea. As President Barack Obama said on June 16, 2009, "There has been a pattern in the past where North Korea behaves in a belligerent fashion and, if it waits long enough, is rewarded. . . . The message we are sending them is that we are going to break that pattern."[5] Within this broad approach, the Obama administration's North Korea policy has emphasized a desire for diplomacy and the desire for close coordination with its allies.

In this chapter I consider the impact of successful operationalization of North Korea's nuclear capability on Washington, and Washington's range of options and most likely responses. These range along a continuum from doing nothing to sanctions to a blockade of various sorts to precision air strikes on suspected nuclear facilities to invasion, although not all of these may in fact be likely options, and a number would most likely be used in unison. Washington's military options are also most heavily constrained by the physical location of Seoul, South Korea—a metropolitan area of over 23 million people, and the economic, political and cultural center of the Republic of Korea—which lies just thirty miles south of the North Korean border and well within the North's artillery range. I also consider in this chapter a second set of constraints on Washington: the attitudes and policies of North Korea's neighbors—China, Russia, Japan, and South Korea. How would an operationally nuclear North Korea potentially affect and potentially complicate Washington's relations with these nations and its strategies and standing in the region?

THE MILITARY OPTION

One obvious U.S. response to a North Korean nuclear weapons program is to attack the facilities and punish North Korea. Especially if North Korea is in the early stages of operationalizing its arsenal, attacking sooner rather than later may make military sense. If North Korea does succeed in developing a functional nuclear missile arsenal, such success alone may be enough of a deterrent to dissuade the United States and its allies from attacking it.

Although North Korea spends up to 20% of its entire GDP on defense, this amounts to little more than $5 billion each year. By comparison, South Korea has been spending $20 billion or more for the past two decades, though this accounts for only about 2% to 5% of its GDP for that period (see Figures 7.1 and 7.2).

The U.S. and South Korean militaries are much stronger than the North Korean military, so although a war could be bitter and divisive, the North has little to no hope of actually prevailing in a major military confrontation. The South Korean Joint Chiefs submitted a report to the ROK National Assembly in 2008 noting that the "North Korean military does not have night fighting capability, armored vehicles cannot cross rivers, and their field guns are inaccurate."[6] The majority of North Korean tanks are T-34 and T-54/55 models, introduced during World War II and the 1950s, respectively. In addition to being fifty-plus years old, these tanks have no infrared capability and are not watertight. As to the air force, South Korean F-15K fighters have the radar capability to launch missiles against North Korea's top MiG-29 fighter before the MiG-29 can even detect the F-15K. The majority of North Korea's approximately nine hundred fighter

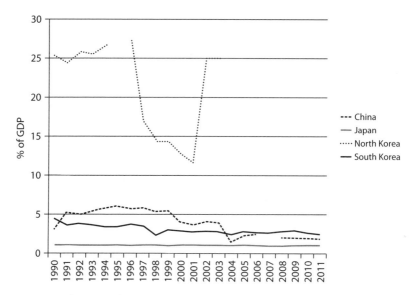

Figure 7.1 Defense spending, 1990–2011, as % of GDP. Source: National Bureau of Asian Research, "Strategic Asia Online," http://strategicasia.nbr.org/Data/CView/. Note: Neither the CIA, IISS, SIPRI, nor Jane's Defense have published North Korean data for 2005 onward.

aircraft are ancient MiG-15s and MiG-21s, introduced during the Korean War and the early 1960s, respectively.

Despite these military advantages, the United States and South Korea have no realistic military option for confronting North Korea over its nuclear weapons programs. Although the United States and ROK would eventually prevail in a war with the DPRK, the potential costs of a war are prohibitively high and deter either side from realistically expecting to start and complete a major war without utter devastation to the peninsula. Given that Seoul and its large population are so close to the North, the risk that North Korea would retaliate against Seoul is too great, given that North Korea has conventional artillery and short-range missiles within range. The former commander of U.S. forces in Korea, General Gary Luck, offered a sober but succinct estimate of the bottom line if war does break out on the Korean Peninsula: 1 million and 1 trillion.[7] That is, the costs of going to war over North Korea's nuclear program would amount to 1 million casualties and $1 trillion in estimated industrial damage and lost business. Mike Chinoy quoted a Pentagon adviser close to George W. Bush administration discussions about U.S. military options against North Korea as saying, "The mainstream view was that if any kind of military strike starts

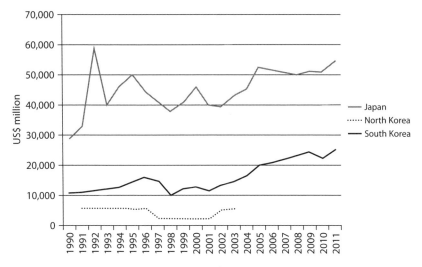

Figure 7.2. Defense spending, 1990–2011, in US$ million. Source: National Bureau of Asian Research, "Strategic Asia Online," http://strategicasia.nbr.org/Data/CView/. Note: Neither the CIA, IISS, SIPRI, nor Jane's Defense have published North Korean data for 2005 onward.

against North Korea, the North Koreans would invade South Korea, and they will cause enormous destruction of Seoul. And we are not prepared to handle all this."[8]

Even surgical strikes to take out the main Yongbyon or other reactors, another option U.S. planners would certainly consider, would have a limited impact. The DPRK voluntarily dismantled the Yongbyon reactor in 2008 as part of the 2007 Six Party Process, and it is not operational at this time, although a new light water reactor under construction on the site. Even if the reactor was operational, destroying it would only limit the extent of North Korean proliferation and would not necessarily remove any nuclear weapons from North Korea's arsenal. The outside world has little idea of where the actual nuclear material and weapons are stored or hidden; a targeted strike against the Yongbyon reactor would thus be unlikely to actually impair North Korea's military options. This point is especially true now that Yongbyon has been deactivated and the fissile material undoubtedly dispersed to other areas of the country.[9]

In sum, there is little doubt that combined U.S.-ROK forces would eventually win any war with North Korea. The key word, however, is "eventually." U.S.-ROK forces would overwhelm the DPRK's poor and obsolete forces, but the almost certain damage to Seoul and the peninsula makes this option truly horrifying. Especially as a preemptive measure, the risks are too great for most

U.S. and ROK military planners to consider seriously. Even the option of a surgical strike to take out the North's missile capabilities would have to proceed on the hope that the North would not respond.

SANCTIONS AS A STRATEGY

A less direct method of putting pressure on the North Korean regime is the use of economic sanctions, and the Obama administration is following the Bush administration by punishing North Korea with sanctions after its 2009 nuclear and missile tests. The United States is currently cooperating with UN Resolutions 1718 and 1874, both of which apply various sanctions on the DPRK, and its own Proliferation Security Initiative (PSI), aimed at interdicting any transport or exports of North Korean weapons or nuclear technology and arms to other countries.

Yet sanctions are also unlikely to achieve their stated goal of changing North Korean behavior. The problems are twofold. First, even the United States is unwilling to punish North Korean citizens by engaging in blanket economic sanctions against the North that would include basic foodstuffs and other materials. Thus, the sanctions have been targeted at the regime, focused on luxury goods and the like, but such sanctions have limited impact. Sanctions rarely force a country to change its ways; they remain more symbolic than practical for changing behavior.[10] Stephan Haggard and Marcus Noland argue, "It is highly unlikely that the sanctions by themselves will have any immediate effect on North Korea's nuclear program or on the increasing threat of proliferation. Sanctions need to be coupled with a nuanced policy that includes a strongly stated preference for a negotiated solution as well as defensive measures, of which the sanctions are only one part."[11] As Ruediger Frank concluded in his study of sanctions against North Korea, "In the long run, [sanctions] lose their impact and become a liability."[12]

The second difficulty with sanctions involves the coordination problem, which I discuss later in this chapter; neither Russia nor China is eager to push sanctions too hard on the North, and thus any sanctions the United States puts on the regime are likely to be cosmetic in nature. The only country that could realistically impose severe enough sanctions on North Korea is China. Were China to impose draconian sanctions on North Korea, it could have a devastating effect. The Chinese appear to be fairly angered at North Korea's nuclear and missile tests, and the nuclear test in particular has been a real insult to Chinese diplomatic efforts. After the first North Korean nuclear test in 2006,

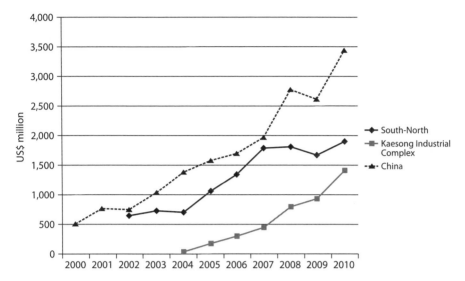

Figure 7.3. PRC-DPRK trade, 2000–2010. Source: Congressional Research Service report, China–North Korea relations, January 2010; ROK Ministry of Unification: Statistics on inter-Korean trade, January–November 2010, December 28, 2010.

China called it "flagrant and brazen" and voted with other UN Security Council members for Resolution 1718, which imposed a series of sanctions on North Korea.[13] There has also been intense debate within China about the best way to deal with North Korea and even whether North Korea remains strategically important to China.

Yet Chinese economic and political influence is quite limited. As Adam Segal noted, "The idea that the Chinese would turn their backs on the North Koreans is clearly wrong."[14] Although China has voted for the various UN sanctions (Resolutions 1874, 1718, and 1695), the Chinese also reduced the severity of those sanctions, including opposing the use of military action to enforce them. The Chinese and Russians also interpreted the sanctions in a way that rendered them to be essentially ineffective. Marcus Noland estimates that Chinese exports to the North, and even exports of luxury goods, have actually increased 140% since the imposition of sanctions.[15] Indeed, China is North Korea's main trading partner, and despite the economic sanctions imposed by UN Resolutions 1718 and 1874, trade between the two countries continues to increase. Total trade in 2008 was 41.3% greater than in 2007, amounting to between half and two-thirds of North Korea's total foreign trade (see Figure 7.3).[16] In fact, Chinese trade now accounts for between 60% and 80% of North Korea's entire foreign trade.[17]

Thus, China retains considerable economic leverage over North Korea. However, China is unlikely to use such economic pressure, nor is such pressure likely to work. China has continued to build economic relations with North Korea over the past few years, and to a considerable degree, Chinese economic policies toward North Korea have been designed to prevent instability through expanded economic assistance. That is, China faces the same problem that other countries do—how to pressure and persuade North Korea to take a more moderate stance, without pushing so hard on North Korea that it collapses. In this way, North Korea's dependence on Chinese aid limits China's ability to pressure North Korea, particularly with the new leadership in Pyongyang.

Military pressure and economic pressure are the most obvious tools to use in dealing with a nuclear North Korea, but both are also unlikely to be heavily used in practical terms. Sanctions exist now, but their application is selective, and even harsh sanctions are unlikely to cause the North Korean leadership structure to crumble. Unless North Korea attacks first, the military option is even less likely to be used. The risks are too great that North Korea could respond in a way that devastates Seoul, and thus few military planners see this as a realistic option.

ENGAGEMENT AS A STRATEGY

In exploring ways to deal with a state's undesirable behavior, the international relations (IR) literature has focused on coercive strategies, primarily deterrence or coercion.[18] Coercive strategies have tended to receive extensive attention, especially during the Cold War between the United States and the Soviet Union.[19] Rewards and punishments (carrots and sticks) are tools of both social interaction and foreign policy. However, while many of the other social sciences, such as sociology and psychology, pay equal attention to rewards and punishments, the study of international relations has tended to focus on coercion-based punishments. In coercive strategies, deterrence functions to persuade an adversary not to take a certain action by demonstrating resolve and capabilities, whereas compellence uses threats and other punitive actions to persuade an adversary to undo an action or change a course that the adversary has already taken.[20]

That IR scholars focus substantively more on coercion than inducements is somewhat surprising, because inducements and constraints both operate within a cost-benefit calculus and assumption of rational action; theoretically, they deserve equal attention. Most theories of coercive strategies are based on the presumption that a state's preferences and identities are fixed and unchanging, and conclude that only punishment can correct the adversary's destabilizing behavior. In this coercive view, because a state's preferences and interests are fixed, the adversary will refrain from a policy undesirable to other states only if the other states increase the costs that the adversary must endure to pursue the policy. According to proponents of the coercive strategies, deterrence and compellence—whether in the form of military moves or economic sanctions—raise the costs of the offending action and, in turn, modify a state's behavior.[21]

Although there is logic behind coercive strategies, and particularly economic sanctions, there is just as much skepticism in the literature about whether or not these strategies are effective.[22] Indeed, even targeted economic sanctions are rarely strong enough to modify an adversary's destabilizing behavior; the sanctions may actually reinforce that behavior by strengthening the adversary's existing preferences and identities. External pressure often strengthens the links between the regime and its public by offering a convenient external target for anger at the punishment received. Miroslav Nincic notes that "negative sanctions should undermine domestic support for a regime, but the opposite can occur if they produce a rally-round-the-flag and if, in the context of foreign besiegement, the regime's domestic opponents can be linked to hostile foreigners."[23] In this regard, economic sanctions may reinforce the adversary's regime and relevant preferences and identities, not to mention the sanctions' inability to correct the destabilizing behavior.

In contrast to the coercive strategies of deterrence and compellence, engagement is a strategy whose function is to defuse a potentially dangerous situation not through threats but through incentives. The distinguishing feature of engagement is the idea that positive inducements or the extension of benefits can produce a change in the adversary's actions, rather than the promise of harm or the imposition of current costs that raise the expense of pursuing a particular course.

Within this broad approach to engagement are two variations: conditional engagement and unconditional engagement.[24] Unconditional engagement uses available incentives for cumulative effects to ultimately transform the target state's behavior or policy preferences. This engagement may be also purely humanitarian, when a state intervenes because of a moral obligation to help citizens or to stop abuses from occurring. As Richard N. Haass and Meghan L. O'Sullivan note, unconditional engagement proceeds "without explicit agreement" that a reciprocal act would follow.[25] An exemplary case of unconditional engagement is Soviet Union president Mikhail Gorbachev unilaterally proposing to U.S. secretary of state James Baker in May 1989 that the decaying communist country would withdraw tactical nuclear weapons from Eastern Europe. Gorbachev's offer inspired the Malta Conference in December, when he and George H. W. Bush moved forward to an unprecedented agreement on nuclear arms control.[26] Also, the engaging state may provide unconditional humanitarian aid, expecting changes over time in the target state's public perception of the outside world. Despite ceaseless controversy over humanitarian aid's negative effect, such as legitimation of the target regime, aid that usually accompanies direct or indirect contacts may induce greater positive perceptions among the public regarding the engaging state.

In contrast to unconditional engagement, certain conditions that lead the target state to act in a cooperative way can also follow engagement. Perhaps the most widely studied aspect of engagement is the literature on economic interdependence, which explores ways in which expanding ties between nations tend to reduce adversarial relations.[27]

In the case of fixed preferences, engagement may affect calculations about behavior because of changes in the costs and benefits of various actions. One of the most famous examples is Robert Axelrod's solution to the prisoner's dilemma. He found that a tit-for-tat strategy of cooperative and uncooperative moves links the shadow of the future to current behavior and consequently best promotes stable cooperation among adversaries.[28]

But note that a different type of engagement seeks to transform the party, presumably over the long run, by creating new interests. This process is necessarily long-term and is vulnerable to the fact that concessions may not accompany the process in the short run, which means this form of engagement is politically vulnerable. Conditional engagement uses incentives for give-and-take practices, and it necessarily involves negotiation. As Leszek Buszynski has noted, staged engagement is a model of engagement with negotiation. On the basis of both the engaging state's and the target state's respective implementation of agreed points, the states attain a higher stage on the path to an ultimate goal that they already identified. Staged engagement involves a sequence wherein the engaging state would offer incentives in phases in response to the target state's cooperative acts. The February agreement in 2007 at the Six Party Talks has, as its framework, this type of staged engagement. Staged engagement is not the only conditional engagement. The grand deal is another model of conditional engagement; with an exchange of packages arranged through a long negotiation process, relevant partners may open a new chapter in their relationship. The Paris Peace Accords in 1973, reached after three-year-long talks for a cease-fire during the Vietnam War, is a historic example of a grand deal—a deal that broke down with North Vietnam's military occupation of the South.[29]

An increase in the benefits that the target would receive from crafting good relations can alter the target's decisional calculus in the direction of improved conduct. Furthermore, Miles Kahler and Scott Kastner note that engagement strategies "deploy economic links with an adversary in the hope that economic interdependence itself will, over time, change the target's foreign policy behavior and yield a reduced threat of military conflict."[30] In this case, economic engagement does not change state goals, but it reduces the benefits of provocative behavior while increasing the benefits of stable relations.

The theoretical discussion above sheds light on alternative ways to deal with a nuclear North Korea that would involve diplomatic and economic engagement. Dealing with the nuclear challenge, then, will most likely require more than the coercive components of sanctions and potential military strikes. This approach would include engagement, inducements, and hard negotiating from the United States. The willingness of the United States and other countries to engage in consistent negotiations with North Korea has wavered, and talks have been sporadic at best. The mood for such negotiations is often described as "appeasement" or "blackmail," and U.S. administrations are thus hesitant to appear too soft on a regime such as North Korea's.[31] As such, the situation has incrementally deteriorated over the years.

In fact, the United States has consistently stated that a range of political and economic relationships and initiatives is available to North Korea, provided that they first resolve the nuclear problem. This basic policy has spanned the Clinton, George W. Bush, and Obama administrations. For example, former secretary of state Condoleezza Rice said, "The first step is to have, from the North Koreans, a clear indication to the rest of the world and a plan for the dismantling of those programs. Much is possible after that."[32] Obama's special U.S. representative for North Korea Policy Stephen Bosworth said, "President Obama came into office committed to a willingness to talk directly to countries with which we have differences and to try to resolve those differences. This commitment to dialogue was communicated directly to North Korea in the President's first days in office. . . . It is North Korea that faces fundamental choices. . . . We will welcome the day when North Korea chooses to come out of its cave, and we will be prepared to receive them."[33]

As to encouraging economic changes in North Korea, although a decade ago North Korea began to experiment with limited opening of its markets and small adjustments to the centrally planned economy, that process largely stalled with the second nuclear crisis of 2003. On July 1, 2002, North Korea significantly adjusted the public distribution system (PDS) that had been a major element of the centrally planned economy. North Korea also adopted monetized economic transactions and changed the incentives for labor and companies.[34] North Korea also adopted a number of policies and strategies designed to increase foreign investment and trade. However, although the reforms were centrally planned and administered, they were not comprehensive. As a result, there emerged a multilayered and partly decentralized economy—prices were allowed to float, and private ownership and markets were permitted—but the state still owned most of the major enterprises and workers were controlled in many other ways.

Yet these changes were partial, conditional, and hesitant, and North Korea has been ambivalent at best about the introduction of markets. After initial surges of prices, particularly of grains, in 2005 the government partially reintroduced the PDS in grains. Although this policy ostensibly allowed the government more ability to distribute food to the most needy, it also exacerbated the difficulties of creating true price incentives in the markets. Grain prices appear to be somewhat more stable recently, but North Korea annually remains precariously close to another famine.[35] Without the full introduction of markets and the creation of alternative commercial sectors that can export goods to earn foreign with which to import food from abroad, the domestic agricultural sector in the DPRK is unlikely to ever have the capacity to feed its citizens by itself.

For its part, overall U.S. strategy toward the North Korean economy has generally emphasized isolation, although the United States has occasionally made attempts to open markets in North Korea. Pursuing economic reform in North Korea is complicated by the fact that North Korea is one of the most heavily sanctioned states under U.S. law, and removing North Korea from the sanctions list is much more difficult than it appears. Myriad laws and regulations affect U.S.-DPRK economic, cultural, and political relations, and each of them needs to be addressed individually. In fact, at least forty-two different laws restrict economic activity between the United States and North Korea.[36]

Some analysts believe that North Korea is most hesitant about opening its market because of the political challenges it would pose to the ruling regime. Others contend that opening economic relations would actually strengthen the regime and that the United States should continue to isolate North Korea. In either case, U.S. policy across administrations has been that removing sanctions and opening normal trade relations will only come *after* North Korea denuclearizes and are not the means to influence the nuclear talks. In that way, the United States has not consistently pursued economic relations as an active policy tool with which to influence North Korea.

THE STRATEGIC GEOMETRY OF THE KOREAN PENINSULA

North Korea also presents the United States with a major challenge in terms of coordinating its policies and relations with states within the complex strategic geometry of the region. The United States wants better relations with its traditional allies, South Korea and Japan, yet coordinating policies toward North Korea with these allies has proven difficult.

After a decade in which South Korea's engagement was at odds with a more coercive U.S. approach, current South Korean president Lee Myung-bak had taken a harder tack. South Korea has been more focused on reciprocity, and for the time being the two states' interests are aligned. But this was not the case in the George W. Bush and Roh administrations. South Korea is particularly worried about being left out of any U.S. actions toward the North. The Obama administration's Asia policy has been based on two basic principles: (1) emphasizing the importance of its traditional allies such as South Korea and Japan and (2) a desire for cooperative engagement with emerging powers such as China. Assistant Secretary of State for East Asia Kurt Campbell was deeply involved in a security strategy for the Obama administration that called "the U.S.-Japan alliance . . . the foundation for American engagement in the Asia-Pacific," while also "[re]affirming the importance of the U.S.-ROK alliance."[37] Secretary of State Hillary Clinton and Ambassador Bosworth have both called the U.S.-Japan alliance the "cornerstone" of stability in the region and have begun to lay out a plan that moves the alliances past their Cold War focus on deterrence of enemies to include climate change, energy security, and other out-of-area operations.[38]

Thus, in the short term, the Obama and Lee governments have held similar views toward the peninsula. Agreement is widespread among all types of analysts in the United States that the current policies are appropriate and the United States should not be offering concessions to a North Korea that has obviously violated international norms. These similar perspectives should be the cause for optimism that both countries may be able to act in concert and present a more consistent and unified approach toward North Korea. Previously North Korea could have one relationship with one country and a different relationship with a different country, so to the extent that policies and overall strategies are consistent, this step is in the right direction.

The Japanese public has been fixated on the matter of the two dozen Japanese citizens abducted by North Korea in the 1970s, which has become a major driver of Japanese policy toward the North.[39] The previous Japanese government made progress on the resolving the abductee issue a prerequisite for cooperating on the nuclear issue during the Six Party Talks, which led to difficulties in coordinating policies among the parties. How Japan's new government will act toward North Korea is still not entirely clear. Thus far, indications are that the policies will continue to be similar to previous governments, with attention to both the nuclear threat and the abductee issues.[40]

Just as important is the coordination of U.S. and Chinese policies. China has come to view the North Korea problem primarily in economic and political terms. Beijing is more concerned about North Korean *weakness*: the possibility of its collapse or chaos. Chinese analysts tend to believe that North Korea can be deterred and instead are worried about the economic and political consequences of a collapsed regime. To put the matter in perspective, should North Korea collapse, the number of refugees could potentially exceed the entire current global refugee population.[41] Even assuming a best-case scenario in which collapse did not turn violent, the regional economic and political effects would be severe.

The current question for China is to what extent its own priorities regarding North Korea may have shifted. If China decides a nuclear-armed North Korea is worse for its own interests than a North Korean collapse, China could begin to shift policy and put more pressure on the regime. Alternatively, if China continues to see instability arising from a weakened North Korea, its policies will remain roughly the same as they have over the past decade. At this point it is unclear how Chinese officials and policymakers are viewing the current situation, and how their policies will evolve in the coming months and years is unclear as well.

As noted earlier, however, it is unlikely that China would use the economic leverage that it has over North Korea, nor is it clear that such pressure would work. And China, like South Korea, must concern itself with the potential consequences of a North Korean collapse, which could include hundreds of thousands of North Korean refugees, a large and well-armed North Korean military that may not voluntarily disarm, nuclear weapons unaccounted for and uncontrolled by any central authority, and the subsequent social, economic, and cultural costs of dealing with an implosion. Thus, the prospects of China putting any significant pressure on North Korea are dim.[42]

Yet a larger view of the North Korean problem and its affect on both regional and U.S.-PRC relations offers some hopeful signs. The North Korean problem has caused China to take on a central mediating role in the region. The United States and China to cooperate closely even while their interests diverge and all the countries in the region to sit down at the same table numerous times to discuss and negotiate their differences. Although the North Korea problem remains as intractable as ever, one fortunate consequence may be greater cooperation and stability among the actors in the region—in particular, between the United States and China.

In sum, the coordination problem arises because not only is there disagreement over the best policies to pursue across diverse goals but the priorities of the states themselves are not identical. Although the United States clearly places its top priority on denuclearization, China focuses on stability, Japan on the abductees, and until the Lee Myung-bak administration, South Korea focused on economic engagement. Attempting to forge complementary policies, or at least policies that do not directly undercut each other, has proven difficult, allowing North Korea more strategic room to maneuver than the United States would ideally like.

CONCLUSION: NORTH KOREAN REACTIONS

Some observers believe that coercion will eventually cause the North to capitulate and that "just a little more" pressure on the regime will force it to submit. Past history reveals the unfortunate inaccuracy here. North Korea has little history of giving something for nothing, but the leadership in Pyongyang has a consistent policy of meeting external pressure with pressure of its own.[43] There is little reason to think that applying even more pressure will finally result in North Korea meeting U.S. demands and a de-escalation of tension.

The sad fact is that the range of coercive policy options available to the United States and other countries involved in the Six Party Talks is quite narrow. Few countries would consider military action to cause the regime to collapse, given that Seoul is vulnerable to North Korea's conventional weapons and that war or regime collapse could potentially unleash uncontrolled nuclear weapons and draw all the surrounding countries into a serious regional conflict. At the same time, until Pyongyang satisfactorily addresses the nuclear issue—

and, for Japan, the abductee issue—the United States, South Korea, and Japan are unwilling to do what North Korea wants them to do: normalize relations, which would include either an explicit or implicit security assurance from the United States, and offer considerable economic or diplomatic incentives for moderating its behavior. As a result, the United States and other regional governments are faced with a narrow band of policy choices: rhetorical pressure, quiet diplomacy, and mild sanctions.

The challenges the United States faces in dealing with North Korea are many and complex, and any imminent breakthrough appears unlikely. Moreover, these problems are likely to be exacerbated as Kim Jong-il has passed from the scene. With Kim Jong-un now on center stage, a few things have become clearer in Pyongyang, although we know very little about Kim Jong-un: he studied in Switzerland for a few years, can speak English and German, and was evidently his father's favorite. We know also that succession politics and a desire to consolidate Kim Jong-un's rule are now at the center of North Korean policy. Whether the North Korean leadership can maintain control and deal with the outside world from a position of strength in coming years remains unclear.

On the one hand, if North Korea can successfully consolidate Kim Jong-un's leadership , the regime might survive well into the future. A third generation of Kim family leadership could mean a more belligerent North Korea that is less willing to negotiate with the outside, as the young dictator proves to his own military and regime that he is strong and capable enough to lead the country. Such conditions could mean a return to more of the same depressing politics we saw under Kim Jong-il: a recalcitrant North Korea yearning for respect and recognition from the outside world.

Yet the odds of a smooth consolidation of Kim Jong-un's leadership may not be high. Kim Jong-il himself was announced as his father's successor fifteen years before he actually took office in 1994, allowing him time to build support among important internal constituencies and also creating an aura of inevitability that led North Koreans to accept him as the next ruler. Kim Jong-il also benefited from this gradual transition period in which he served under and followed his father—before the famine of the late 1990s, only a few years after the end of Soviet support for North Korea, and at the beginning of the long nuclear crisis that continues to plague North Korea's foreign relations with the world.

Given the abrupt nature of Kim Jong-un's accession to power, he faces a much more difficult situation than even his father. He has had very little time to build an expectation of inevitability within North Korea, and he, like his father, must still manage and placate the numerous competing factions, egos, and interests but without the benefit of a longer transition period and the experience and legitimacy it can provide. Furthermore, while his youth would make leadership difficult in any country—he has virtually no experience in political posts and has no proven leadership abilities—in Confucian Korean political culture he may have yet more difficulties given the emphasis on respect for age and elders. Furthermore, North Korea's economy and foreign relations are worse than ever, and the younger Kim has few financial or material reserves with which to buy support or respond to a sudden crisis. While this in and of itself does not mean he will fail, he certainly faces tremendous obstacles.

What does this mean for the future of North Korea? For years there was little reason to think that the North might actually collapse. And while Kim Jong-un may rule for the next twenty years, there is also the increasing possibility that he will be unable to manage the competing international pressures and internal factional demands. Rumors have held that another senior leader would rule as regent until Kim Jong-un has earned the trust and legitimacy that he needs to rule. The current speculation has focused most closely on Chang Sung-taek, brother-in-law to Kim Jong-il. Chang, sixty-six years old, is the vice chairman of the National Defense Commission and the head of the Administration and Guidance Department of the Korea Workers' Party, responsible for internal security and the country's police force. However, rumors about Chang have yet to be substantiated, and they still leave the regime's leadership facing the same dilemma of managing factional problems with an untested new leader.

We may be seeing the beginning of the internal collapse of the Kim dynasty, and governments, humanitarian organizations, and individuals around the region might begin reviewing their contingency plans for how to deal with the chaos that such a collapse would surely bring. Adding the challenge of collapse or transition to the long list of issues the U.S. faces with North Korea makes the difficulties even greater for a peaceful resolution of the North Korean problem.

CHAPTER EIGHT

North Korea's
Nuclear Blackmail

ANDREI LANKOV

The years that have passed since the first North Korean nuclear test of October 2006 have been full of militant rhetoric and frantic diplomatic activity. The United States has claimed a number of times that the "complete and verifiable" denuclearization of North Korea remains an important policy goal—and, indeed, the only acceptable outcome of the ongoing crisis. U.S. secretary of state Hillary Clinton, on her trip to Korea in April 2009, reiterated this position once again, stating: "Our position is when they [the North Korean leaders] move forward in presenting a verifiable and complete dismantling and denuclearization, we have a great openness to working with them."[1]

The international community is more or less supportive of this approach—at least superficially. Diplomats from a range of countries have said again and again that the "world would not tolerate North Korean nuclear weapons" and behaved as if the complete denuclearization of North Korea was the only acceptable outcome of the current crisis. Following the 2006 nuclear test, the United Nations imposed economic sanctions on North Korea, and the second nuclear test in May 2009 led to even tougher sanctions.

However, no amount of harsh rhetoric is a substitute for action. What can the United States—and more broadly speaking the world at large—really do about North Korea's nuclear capabilities? The honest answer is "not much," perhaps even "nothing." Neither the United States nor its close allies have much leverage over North Korea. Meanwhile, North Korea's decision to go nuclear reflects serious concerns of its ruling regime and can be reversed only if rewards—or punishments for noncompliance—are exceptionally high. In this chapter I demonstrate why the available leverage is insufficient and why North

Korea is likely to remain nuclear for the foreseeable future. I also suggest a possible solution while making clear that some key players in the crisis may see the solution as unacceptable.

THE RATIONALE FOR THE NORTH KOREAN NUCLEAR PROGRAM

North Korean leaders are sometimes presented in the media as madmen, people driven by some irrational or ideologically motivated desire to look dangerous and create trouble, which is not the case. Their penchant for seemingly irrational and erratic behavior is illusionary; North Korea's leaders actually know very well what they are doing. They are not madmen nor ideological zealots but remarkably efficient and cold-minded calculators, perhaps the best practitioners of Machiavellian politics to be found in the modern world.

This conclusion is obvious given what they have achieved. The seemingly irrational regime of the Kim family has survived challenges that have wiped out almost all other Communist governments. The price for this success was high: regime survival was achieved at the cost of several hundred thousand lives of North Korean commoners who perished in the late 1990s during the "arduous march" (as the North Korean media euphemistically refers to the great famine). The suffering of millions inside the country still continues and will probably continue for years to come. However, the survival of the humble population has never been high on the regime's political agenda. The top North Korean leaders care most about their own political survival.

Nuclearization of North Korea is, above all, a major part of a much broader strategy of regime survival. If one looks from this perspective, it appears almost certain that no North Korean leader would ever consider denuclearization. From Pyongyang's point of view, such a move would clearly be a mistake or, at the very least, a most imprudent decision.

For starters, the decision to go nuclear was not made overnight; the North Korean nuclear program has a long history, conceived in the late 1950s, launched in earnest in the mid-1960s, and acquiring military dimensions around 1980.[2] In other words, the nuclear weapons acquisition program is a result of decades of sacrifice, investment, hard work, and careful planning.

From its inception, the program has served three distinct political goals, each of which is quite important for Pyongyang. However, their relative significance has kept changing over time, depending on the always shifting international environment.

First, North Korea needs nuclear weapons as a powerful strategic deterrent. Kim Il-sung was impressed by the efficiency of the U.S. nuclear weapons in 1945, and the North Korean leadership believes that no foreign invader would attack them while they have a nuclear deterrent. The DPRK is deeply afraid of a foreign attack, and after the U.S. invasions of Iraq and Afghanistan, such fears can hardly be dismissed as paranoid or unfounded. The major lesson that Pyongyang seems to have drawn from the Iraqi experience is that if Iraq really had nuclear weapons, Saddam Hussein would probably still be in power.

Second, the nuclear program has domestic importance as well. The nuclear tests held in a remote mountainous area in 2006 and 2009 were actually the only visible successes of Kim Jong-il's rule. Pyongyang's propaganda now insists that the sufferings and destitution of the last two decades were, after all, a necessary sacrifice, voluntarily made by the selfless North Korean people in order to safeguard their country against their surrounding enemies—and above all, the bloodthirsty Yankees who constantly dream about destroying the entire Korean race. Surrender of nuclear weapons would, the regime might argue, render these sufferings and deaths meaningless.

The third and arguably most important goal of the nuclear program is to increase the North's ability to apply pressure on the international community or, rather, to blackmail it. In spite of their bombastic nationalist propaganda, North Korean leaders and diplomats are painfully aware that their country is not a major international player. After all, in terms of population size and economic significance, the closest analogues to their country are, of all places, such African countries as Mozambique and Ghana. At the same time, the North is burdened with an outdated and grossly inefficient Stalinist economic system that cannot even sustain itself or feed the country's population. Aid inflow is needed just to keep the system functioning, and the leaders understand that the world needs a sustainable and compelling reason to provide them with such aid.

THE INABILITY TO REFORM

The major factor that makes the North Korean nuclear program virtually inevitable is the unwillingness of the Pyongyang leaders to embark on a path of domestic reform. This unwillingness is often described by observers as "irrational" and explained away by the "shortage of information" or "misunderstanding" that allegedly exists among Pyongyang's ruling circles as regards market-oriented reforms. Unfortunately, this description offers a gross oversimplification. North Korea's unwillingness to reform is based on a perfectly rational assumption of their peculiar situation.

Indeed, the economic efficiency of a Chinese-style reformed economy is beyond doubt. The transferability of the Chinese experience, at least within the borders of the once-communist East Asia, has been proven as well. As early as the 1980s the Vietnamese emulated the Chinese reform, with equally remarkable success. Thus, optimists believe, "To avoid the potential dangers of a sudden collapse in the DPRK, it may be a better route to promote a long-term, gradual transition that seeks to encourage the forces within North Korea and the ruling regime for change. Whether that regime is another member of the Kim family or a military party collective of some sort, to further a process of economic opening and reform could lead to a subsequent path of political moderation and reform."[3] All this sounds good, and Chinese-style economic reforms might appear to be a simple and logical solution, but in the case of North Korea such reforms are inherently dangerous to the leadership. The North Korean leaders are painfully aware of China's spectacular success, but they also realize that North Korea's situation is dramatically different than China's or Vietnam's. The existence of a rich and free South Korea makes the decisive difference. The regime exists next to another country whose population speaks the same language and is officially described as "members of our nation," but those in the South enjoy a per capita income at least seventeen times (some even claim fifty times) higher than people in the North.[4]

In China and Vietnam, the affluence of the capitalist West is well known but is not seen by the populace as relevant to the problems of their own countries. For the average Chinese, a rich Japan or an affluent United States are different countries with completely different histories and cultures, and their obvious economic superiority is not a valid reason to doubt the legitimacy of China's ruling regime. U.S. or Japanese successes do not imply China's inferiority and do not cast doubt on the legitimacy of the Communist regime. With South Korea's immediate presence, however, the situation for North Korea is different.

From its inception, North Korea has gone to great lengths to present itself as a paradise in the most literal sense: a land of material prosperity and abundance. In contrast, the North depicts South Korea as a "living hell" where penniless students sell their blood to pay for books and where sadistic Yankees drive their tanks over Korean girls just for pleasure. One textbook presents North Korea's children with an enlightening picture: "A school principal in South Korea beats and drives a child from school who cannot pay his monthly fee on time."[5] In high school, North Korean children learn that "South Korea is swamped with 7 million unemployed. Countless people stand in queues in front of employment centers, but not even a small number of jobs is forthcoming. The factories are closing one after another, and in such a situation even people who have work do not know when they will be ousted from their position."[6]

These lies were necessary since the Kim Family Regime has always presented itself as another part of the same state, as the true government of a single Korea. Fundamentalist religious regimes can easily admit their economic inferiority, since the government prides itself on the alleged ability to keep its population spiritually pure so that they will enjoy rewards in the afterlife. The Kim Family Regime is different. Its claims on legitimacy and the right to govern are based on its alleged ability to deliver a better material life for its people. In 1962 North Korea's founding father, Kim Il-sung, famously promised to deliver "a house with a tiled roof, soup with meat, and silk clothes" for every North Korean. By present-day standards, these expectations are quite modest, but the regime has failed to achieve even this goal. The Marxian emphasis on material and economic success is what has made the myth of North Korean prosperity and South Korean poverty so indispensable to the regime's survival. For a long time the North Korean one-won banknote bore the inscription, "We do not envy anyone in the world!"

North Korea's leaders understood the importance of strict information control or, to put it more precisely, a self-imposed information blockade. Historically, all communist countries have tried to cut their populace off from unauthorized information from overseas, but few, if any, went to the extremes that North Korea has. The North is perhaps the only country in the world to ban the ownership of tunable radios in peacetime; all nontechnical foreign publications are accessible only by people with a security clearance, and all unauthorized contacts with foreigners are deadly dangerous.[7]

In the past decade or so, political and social changes have seriously weakened this isolation: a large-scale movement across the border with China as well as the gradual spread of foreign—above all, South Korean—movies and videos have produced remarkable changes in the North Koreans' worldview. Many North Koreans, but by no means all, now suspect that their country is poor compared to South Korea, but few people in the North realize how huge this gap actually is.[8]

Chinese-style market reforms are almost certain to be economically beneficial and would probably lead to a dramatic growth of productivity and a revolutionary increase in living standards. However, they would have an unavoidable side effect: further deterioration of the carefully constructed system of information control. This effect is unacceptably dangerous for the regime.

Those observers who extol the North Korean potential for economic reform implicitly assume that a reformed North Korean regime would still be able to suppress open dissent, while the majority of the population would be kept docile by increased living standards, augmented by a slow yet steady improvement in their political rights and individual freedoms—essentially, the situation that has existed in China and Vietnam since the late 1980s.

However, in the unique case of North Korea, the existence of a prosperous South makes such a scenario implausible. The reforms would lead to a steadily increasing awareness of South Korea's prosperity, almost literally unbelievable by North Korean standards, and would present the North Korean populace with the conviction—perhaps an illusionary one—that their manifold problems would find an easy and quick solution through unification with the South and the wholesale adoption of its social, economic, and cultural system.

The Chinese are happy with the incremental but steady improvement of their once-impoverished lifestyle, largely because they see no realistic alternative to years of hard work and gradual improvement. Whether the North Korean population, and especially its better-educated sector, would agree to endure a further decade of destitution followed by a couple of decades of relative poverty is doubtful if they were to see another, better-off Korea located just across the border, a few days' walk from North Korea's major cities. Would they agree to tolerate a highly repressive regime run, in all probability, either by scions of the ruling Kim clan or by people who once were Kim's henchmen on the assumption that this regime would someday deliver a prosperity comparable to that of South Korea? Undoubtedly not.

In a reformed system, economic efficiency rather than demonstrated political zeal would be rewarded. Combined with an unavoidable relaxation of police controls, reform would make the North Korean populace less dependent on the state's largesse, less fearful of the regime, and in the final count, less docile.

One can easily imagine how discontent about the North Korean system, as well as information about the astonishing South Korean prosperity, would first spread through the relatively well-heeled North Korean groups that are allowed to interact with South Koreans and foreigners—or that have better access to the foreign media and entertainment—and then filter down to the wider social strata. Once people come to the conclusion that they have no reason to be afraid of the usual crackdown, they are very likely to behave in the East German

style by overthrowing their government and demanding an immediate unification with their fabulously rich neighbors.

In other words, Chinese-style reforms, rather than being a way out of its economic and social woes, might quickly become destabilizing and lead to an East
German–style regime collapse. North Korea's top leaders appear more or less
conscious of this danger and hence believe that extreme caution is necessary
for their survival. As a result, they have to adhere to the old Stalinist model of
a centrally planned economy, albeit of a more extreme variety. The recent attempt to crack down on private economic activities and reduce the scale of the
markets is just another confirmation of this trend.[9]

To make things worse, the North Korean surveillance and indoctrination
systems are closely intertwined with the Stalinist economy. North Korea's surveillance operates on the assumption that every adult has a proper job with a
state-run enterprise; indoctrination and police surveillance are thus centered
on the workplace. In recent years, the North Korean authorities have made a
concerted effort to send people back to the state-run factories. In late 2008
Pyongyang attempted a full closure of the markets, but the ban was reversed
at the last minute; the currency reform of late 2009 was clearly aimed at bank-
rupting as many independent businesses as possible, since those businesses
are seen as potentially subversive. This antimarket policy does not make much
economic sense, given that most state-run enterprises no longer function and
the physical survival of the country's population largely depends on markets.
Nonetheless, the policy makes perfect political sense: when people arrive at
their factories, even if those factories have been idle for years, they again find
themselves under the authorities' watchful gaze.

This retrogressive antimarket policy damages even the limited marketization that has occurred in the last fifteen years despite the government's efforts,
but the authorities are not worried; their major concern is political stability, not
economic growth, and in the final analysis not even the physical survival of the
common people is among the regime's top considerations.

In other words, the North Korean leaders seem to be hopelessly stuck with
the inherent inefficiency of their economic model. Due to the specifics of their
position as a divided nation, they cannot handle the risks associated with a
Chinese-style authoritarian developmentalism; they cannot emulate Deng Xiaoping's "developmental dictatorship." Only one option remains open to them:
international brinkmanship. Missile development and, even more important,
nuclear projects are vital tools in such a policy.

Pyongyang has no choice but to complement its revenues with aid squeezed from the outside world. The North's leaders need generous helpings of aid—more generous than the size and importance of their country as well as the scale of its problems would otherwise warrant. They also want this aid without too many conditions attached, especially when it comes to its distribution. The aid is distributed in a manner that aims at purchasing and reinforcing support for the regime, not saving the lives of commoners, so the elite and faithful get the first and best slice. These special conditions mean that North Korea's leaders are forced to use unconventional methods to attract the aid. Risky brinkmanship and blackmail are the only options readily available to them. In order to survive, the North Korean leaders have to be, or at least appear to be, dangerous and unpredictable. Nothing serves this goal better than a stockpile of nuclear weapons.

Having nukes means that every time North Korea experiences problems, it can start making threatening noises in order to squeeze some aid from the outside world. The DPRK's leaders are afraid that without their nuclear weapons the world would become far less willing to satisfy their demands. They are probably correct. Even if the surrender of nuclear weapons is rewarded with a large payoff, this lump sum would not last forever. Meanwhile, the existence of nuclear weapons creates an opportunity for systematic and regular extortion.

WHY THE STICKS ARE NOT BIG ENOUGH

The world's diplomats seem never to tire of saying that the world "would not tolerate a nuclear-armed North Korea." Well, what can the world do to prevent such a turn of events? The talk about a "red line" that should be drawn when dealing with North Korea implies that in some cases the United States and the international community would exert pressure on the country and the North would have no choice but to surrender its nukes. The problem, however, is that neither the United States nor the international community has in their disposal means to make the pressure sufficiently strong.

For starters, the threatened use of military force against North Korea is not credible. Even putting aside the serious moral and legal considerations, a large-scale military operation in North Korea is bound to be prohibitively expensive.

Surgical strikes and air raids against nuclear installations, akin to the Israeli air raid on Iraq's nuclear research center in 1981, will not work in this case. It is too late. Once weapons-grade plutonium and nuclear devices have been manufactured, they will be safely hidden in some of the underground facilities for which North Korea is so famous. Finding the North's nuclear hiding places is virtually impossible at the moment, and even if by some miracle some reliable intelligence is obtained, it would be difficult to destroy the devices, which are hidden in massive underground fortifications.[10] The destruction of research facilities in Yongbyon or elsewhere is feasible, but this operation would not have a serious impact. After all, these facilities have fulfilled their mission. North Korea does not need many nuclear devices. It has produced enough to serve its political goals quite adequately.

Nor is a large-scale invasion by ground forces a possibility, for a number of reasons. North Korea has a rugged, mountainous terrain and a large army. If the United States and its allies were to choose to invade, their eventual victory is certain, but the price of such a victory would certainly be high.

Moreover, Washington would have serious diplomatic problems initiating such an invasion. The South Koreans are unlikely to join such an undertaking, which would be a rational choice on their part: South Korea's public prefers to live with the small possibility of a North Korean nuclear strike rather than initiate a war just thirty kilometers north of downtown Seoul—literally in the capital's northern suburbs. The massive presence of North Korean artillery in the city's vicinity virtually ensures that war, regardless of its final result, is bound to be bloody and lead to large-scale destruction of South Korea's major city. Unless faced with a clear and present danger, no South Korean government would or should be enthusiastic about supporting such a hypothetical U.S. invasion. Yet without South Korea's support, land operations would become difficult if not impossible for the United States.

In addition, one cannot rule out the fact that, in the event of a U.S. invasion, China and perhaps even Russia would cautiously support the North Korean armed forces with arms, ammunition, and intelligence. Neither China nor Russia would back a North Korean attack against the South, but in the event of a hypothetical U.S. invasion, the North Koreans would likely be seen as victims of aggression, and the Chinese would probably undertake some measures to make the situation even more difficult for their U.S. rivals. In other words, a war might be winnable for the United States or a U.S.-led coalition, but such a coalition would be difficult to build and the political, financial, and human costs of such a victory would be prohibitively high.

We are thus left with sanctions alone—such as an embargo on trade with North Korea which, as is often argued, would put the country's economy under severe strain. But the usefulness and efficiency of such sanctions are doubtful. First, a strict sanctions regime is difficult to impose since China, and to a lesser degree Russia, would be unwilling to be party to a truly rigorous (read: efficient) sanctions regime. Neither Russia nor China wants North Korea to go nuclear, but they both have other issues on their agendas, and some of those issues are more pressing than the Korean nuclear question, as I discuss in some detail below.

Another option is the use of financial sanctions, to which North Korea seems to be particularly vulnerable—as with the sanctions used or threatened during the Banco Delta Asia affair. However, the efficiency of such sanctions has never really been tested.

Perhaps the inability to maintain efficient sanctions is not as bad as it would first appear. Even in the improbable case of Chinese and Russian sabotage of the sanctions being neutralized, sanctions are not likely to influence Pyongyang's policy. North Korean society is designed in such a way as to make even efficient sanctions politically irrelevant. Normally, sanctions work in an indirect way, triggering a chain of events that indirectly influences the target nation's international behavior. However, in the North Korean case, sanctions would have negligible influence on the consumption of North Korea's top officials, generals, and dignitaries and thus would be unlikely to impact their cost/benefit calculus in any important way. In most cases, sanctions impact and influence the populations of target nations, making their lives less comfortable and more stressful. These conditions lead to a growing discontent as the public begins to blame their government for their declining living standards and other associated problems. The strategy of economic sanctions is based on the assumption that dissatisfied people will press for change in the policy that led to the international sanctions in the first place, or they will demonstrate against or even overthrow or change their government via popular revolution—or in the case of a more democratic and tolerant regime, at the ballot box.

In some other cases, dissatisfied or ambitious members of the ruling elite might also use the crisis as an opportunity to overthrow the regime, which can be achieved relatively peacefully, or it might mean a violent rebellion, depending on the time and place. However, once these dissatisfied elite members take power, they usually make concessions to have the sanctions removed.

Actually, the problems with international sanctions are well documented in the literature. For example, David Lektzian and Mark Souva elaborate on the problem of the relative immunity of nondemocratic states to sanctions: "When dealing with non-democratic countries, states should avoid broad sanctions that impose high economic costs on the population at large because most people in the country are not part of the autocratic leader's winning coalition, so the economic costs imposed on the larger population do not translate into political costs for the regime. In brief, because non-democratic leaders generally have a narrowly defined winning coalition, broad and costly sanctions will be less successful against them than against democratic countries."[11] Indeed, of all nondemocratic states currently in existence, North Korea seems to have the narrowest "winning coalition," to use Lektzian and Souva's term. Despite the tremendous changes of the past fifteen years, North Korea is not liberal enough for its people to have any influence in matters of governance. North Koreans do not vote; actually, they do vote, with a predictable 100% approval rate for a single government candidate, à la Soviet-style democratic centralism, but this is not true democracy. They do not rebel either, although this presumption seems to be changing recently, given the small-scale market riots that have become a part of everyday life.[12] The commoners are terrified and isolated; they don't have the rudimentary self-organization necessary to initiate a resistance movement, and they are still to a large extent unaware of any alternative to their mode of life. Rumors about a prosperous life outside the North Korean borders have been spreading recently, but only a minority of North Koreans understand how backward and poor their society really looks in comparison to that of their neighbors, as discussed earlier.

In other words, in the unlikely case that China sincerely cooperated with a sanctions regime—the only way such sanctions would really have any teeth—the sanctions would merely help to starve to death another few hundred thousand North Korean commoners without producing any of the desired effects. In fact, the most likely political outcome inside North Korea would be to provide additional ammunition for nationalist and anti-Western propaganda. The tiny Pyongyang elite would see the death of a few hundred thousand citizens as a regrettable but necessary price to pay for the survival of their regime.

WHY THE CARROTS ARE NOT TASTY ENOUGH

The optimists who believe that North Korea can be persuaded to abandon its nuclear weapons usually cite three major incentives that can be put on the table: monetary payments and other aid (such as building light water reactors), security guarantees, and normalization of relations with the United States. To borrow the expression of Wade Huntley, an influential soft-liner, U.S. administrations should just "sit down and talk" in order to resolve the nuclear issue.[13] The root of the current problems, the soft-liners insist, is the unwillingness of the United States to be flexible and generous enough; its approach is too militant.[14]

The aid and monetary payments are most welcome in Pyongyang, no doubt. Indeed, generous aid is necessary for regime survival. However, even a large lump-sum payment is not necessarily a long-term solution. Once the money is spent, and it would be spent quite quickly, the Pyongyang regime would have great difficulties in obtaining sufficient additional aid without its nuclear potential to act as an incentive to press the international donors. From this point of view, Pyongyang's ability to press its partners into providing relatively small portions of aid whenever necessary is more important than arranging one large payment.

Without nukes, North Korea would be just another impoverished country competing for donor attention with such places as the Sudan or Zimbabwe. Even though some aid would probably come its way, it would be on a smaller scale than is currently being received. The aid also would be strictly conditional and its distribution carefully monitored. However, in order to survive, the Kim Family Regime needs to be able to distribute its foreign aid according to its own priorities, without excessive interference from the donors. We saw this behavior during the famine, when food aid first went to the military and police and then was distributed largely among the population of Pyongyang and other major industrial centers—obviously on the assumption that riots in those areas directly threaten the regime. The population in other, more remote parts of the country sometimes received aid, but more frequently was left to its own devices. This approach led to a massive death toll in the countryside, but it also ensured that Kim and his supporters remained firmly in control.[15] The existence of the nuclear program allows Pyongyang politicians to determine the conditions under which aid should be delivered and distributed, even though some face-saving compromises with the international community seem possible.

The promises of the U.S. security guarantee are also not sufficiently attractive to change Pyongyang's behavior. Few people would doubt that North Koreans are seriously afraid of a U.S.-led invasion, a fear that seems at least partially justified. However, such security guarantees might be irrelevant for two reasons. First, North Koreans deeply distrust the United States (and, more broadly speaking, all foreigners), and they do not believe in the value of foreigners' promises, especially when they are made in democratic systems in which leaders and policies are bound to change every few years.

Second, North Korea's leaders know that their major security threat is internal not external. They are afraid of a U.S. invasion, but they are even more afraid of a domestic crisis that might lead to overthrow by their own people or elements of their own elite. Needless to say, neither the United States nor any other outside player can provide Pyongyang with a guarantee against such an outcome. One cannot imagine a U.S. president promising to send the U.S. marines to suppress a pro-democracy rebellion in Pyongyang. At the same time, the North's nuclear status at least increases its ability to fend off unwanted intervention in the event of a domestic crisis, as well as its ability to extract foreign aid and use it as they see fit. Importantly in this context, control over aid distribution might help prevent a domestic crisis or at least help the regime survive one. Victor Cha is correct when he says, "The potential for denuclearization is real, provided that the North's survival can be guaranteed."[16] However, no U.S. government would be able or perhaps even willing to guarantee North Korea's internal political stability, and this is the catch, for internal stability is where the Kim Family Regime faces the major threat to its existence.

Additionally, promises of cooperation are not particularly alluring to a regime that for many decades has done its best to remain isolated. The North Korean leaders need money, but they also suspect that exchanges with the outside world, even if conducted on their own terms, are still corrosive and ultimately destructive to their system; they might be correct. Therefore, they prefer payments and giveaways to investment, since the latter implies significant interaction between foreign investors, their goods, and North Koreans.

WHY THE UNITED STATES SHOULD NOT COUNT ON THE SUPPORT OF THE INTERNATIONAL COMMUNITY

Another important obstacle exists to resolving the North Korean nuclear issue, one that makes the North's nuclear problem even more difficult to solve: an inability to create a unified front within the international community. Apart from the United States, only a few other important players are involved: China, South Korea, Russia, and Japan. While none of these players favor nuclear proliferation and none of them want North Korea to retain nuclear capabilities, some of them have other agenda items that essentially override their concerns about North Korea's nuclear program.

Perhaps the single most important player is China, which can be described as the closest approximation to an ally of North Korea. China plays a key role in North Korea's economic exchanges. As of 2008 some 45% of all North Korean trade was with China; South Korea came second, with a 35% share, while all other countries played a minor role).[17] China is also a major provider of aid to the North; reputedly, this aid accounts for at least 40% of China's entire foreign aid budget.[18] For all practical purposes, China can also be described as the only country that shares a significant border with the North, since the DMZ is largely closed to traffic and North Korea's border with Russia is very small. Without Chinese participation, sanctions would have no effect on North Korea.

China certainly does not want a nuclear North Korea. Being a member of the nuclear club itself, China does not welcome nuclear proliferation that undermines its own unique position in the world community. Beijing also worries that North Korea's nuclear ambitions would trigger an arms race in the region, possibly leading to the emergence of a nuclear Japan and Taiwan. Citing these concerns, many optimists have expressed the decidedly unlikely hope that China will join the United States in its efforts to press or bribe North Korea into abandoning its nukes.

In spite of its aversion to a nuclear North Korea, China also has another, much more important concern: it wants to maintain the status quo on the Korean Peninsula. From the Chinese viewpoint, the problems created by the North Korean nuclear program seem less serious than any problems that might arise from North Korea's sudden collapse.

First, China would prefer to see a buffer zone between itself and the U.S. forces in South Korea, even though the strategic significance of such a buffer zone has declined markedly compared to the Cold War era. China also does not mind using the political and economic problems of North Korea to its own advantage. Chinese companies are known to be advancing into the North, taking over infrastructure and valuable mineral resources.[19] Right now, China can get the goods quite cheaply.

Beijing's greatest fear, however, seems to be the instability that North Korea's implosion would cause. Chinese diplomats worry that excessive pressure on North Korea would aggravate its endemic domestic crisis and thus produce domestic instability that might in turn lead to the regime's collapse. Such a prospect is seen as dangerous to China, since it would have to deal with refugee flows, the threat of proliferation of weapons of mass destruction, and geopolitical uncertainties of different kinds, such as smuggling of the nuclear material to or through Chinese territory.

Finally, if regime collapse were to lead to Korean unification on Seoul's terms, such a unified state would probably, albeit by no means certainly, remain a close ally of the United States, which would mean a certain deterioration in China's strategic situation. After all, sixty years ago China fought a major war to make sure that U.S. troops would not be stationed on the southern bank of the Yalu River. China worries, too, about the influence such a unified Korean state would exercise on the ethnic Korean minority in China. Quasi-official territorial claims, frequently voiced in Seoul (the so-called Kando issue), do not help to quell these worries either.[20]

No wonder Chinese policy toward the North is based on what Samuel Kim once described as a "five 'no's policy": "No instability, no collapse, no nukes, no refugees or defectors, and no conflict escalation."[21] One has to agree with Greg Moore when he describes China's dilemma (and China's dualistic approach to the North Korean nuclear issue) in the following terms: "First, the Chinese have been working hard to dissuade North Korea from advancing its long-range missile and nuclear weapons programs because they have great potential to threaten some of China's most fundamental interests—namely, regional stability, and possibly even China's economic modernization program, if worse came to worst. Second, China continues to support North Korea economically, and at times diplomatically, because a complete collapse of North Korea is not in its interest either."[22] We should probably add to this prescient remark that for Chinese policymakers, all things considered, a nuclear-armed North Korea seems to be a lesser evil than an unstable or collapsing North Korea—and perhaps even less an evil than a Korea unified under a U.S.-friendly Seoul government. This assumption is confirmed by Beijing's unwillingness to reduce the amount of aid and subsidies provided to the North, as well as by its policy of soft-pedaling on the sanctions already in place.

This approach was again made clear in October 2009, when Premier Wen Jiabao visited Pyongyang merely five months after the second nuclear test. He did not come empty-handed but brought a large aid package and promises of economic assistance and investment.[23] One could not find a better illustration of China's actual attitude to the sanctions' regime.

Another major player, Russia, is driven by a similar set of considerations. Russia is often seen as a marginal force when it comes to North Korea, which is basically true. The Russian stake in the issues is demonstrably lower than that of China. Nonetheless, one has to keep in mind the fact that Russia, holding veto power in the UN Security Council and sharing a small border with North Korea, is in a position to undermine any sanctions regime. Russia also wants to see a stable and divided Korea, since a North Korean collapse is likely to lead either to a U.S.-influenced unified Korea or the emergence of a pro-Chinese satellite regime in the northern part of the Korean Peninsula. Neither option is welcomed by Moscow, and both outcomes are less desirable than the continuing existence of a nuclear North Korea—especially because Russia, like China, does not expect North Koreans to proliferate to regimes that directly threaten Russia's own security.

Recently, in a remarkably frank statement (even if published in a rather marginal Russian-language journal), a high-ranking Russian diplomat described in the following manner Moscow's goals in Korea: "[Russian] interests require neither a strengthening of the Chinese or American influence in North East Asia nor an escalation of the U.S.-China confrontation. The maintenance of the status quo, including the continuing independence of the DPRK (irrespectively of its domestic social structure) will enable the avoidance of dramatic changes in the correlation of forces which do not serve our interests."[24] In other words, despite the considerable annoyance that North Korea's nuclear ambition causes, Russia primarily wants to maintain the status quo, including the division of Korea, because any changes to this status quo would favor either China or the United States, Russia's rivals. One should not expect Russia to be too active in bringing pressure on Pyongyang, because such pressure is almost certain to lead to a collapse of the status quo.

CONCLUSION: CONTOURS OF AN UNLIKELY COMPROMISE

Is compromise completely impossible? It seems that such is not the case, even though the road to compromise may be long and winding. An additional problem is that the only compromise solution that seems to be at least theoretically acceptable to the North Korean regime would be probably seen as unacceptable by the United States.

In order to achieve at least something, the U.S. side should abandon any illusions about North Korea's willingness to completely surrender its nuclear weapons. As it has been shown above, "complete, verifiable, and irreversible" denuclearization is an unattainable dream, at least as long as the Kim Family Regime remains in control in Pyongyang. Due to the reasons I have outlined above, North Korea needs to keep at least part of its modest nuclear arsenal. The North Koreans might compromise on certain issues, if they are paid handsomely enough, but this bottom line is nonnegotiable. As long as the Kim family stays in power, they will keep their nuclear weapons or at least maintain a level of ambiguity about their nuclear capabilities.

In these circumstances, what are the possible compromise options? To start, North Korea is likely to agree to dismantle its nuclear research facilities. After all, it does not need its old, rusty reactors anymore. Yongbyon, the North Korean nuclear research center, cannot possibly outproduce Los Alamos in the United States or Arzamas-16 in Russia, and further increasing the North Korean nuclear arsenal does not make much political sense. The Yongbyon laboratories have already produced enough plutonium for a few nuclear devices, more than enough for the dual political purposes of deterrence and blackmail. If North Koreans use these facilities to increase their nuclear armory from the six to fifteen devices they are suspected of possessing now to, say, sixty or one hundred devices, their ability to deter or blackmail will not increase five- or tenfold.[25] As a matter of fact, it will not increase much at all. Consequently, the research and production facilities have outlived their usefulness and thus can be dismantled if the payoff is sufficiently high.

This compromise might make sense if judged from the U.S. perspective, since demolishing the research facilities would diminish the likelihood of proliferation. First, the North Koreans would be unable to produce much more plutonium that could be sold overseas. Second, they would lose facilities that may be used for training their own and foreign engineers. A partial surrender of nukes might also be negotiable. Perhaps North Korea can be bribed into giving up part of its plutonium or a few nuclear devices, as long as something remains. Perhaps Pyongyang would agree to accept other measures that make proliferation less likely, thus addressing another major U.S. concern. Which types of measures would be both efficient and acceptable to Pyongyang is open to question, but perhaps surprise inspections of ships and even airport facilities would be allowed. Once again, North Korea's diplomats would require a high price for such a major concession that infringes upon their sovereignty.

Such denuclearization, however, contrary to U.S. insistence, is going to be neither complete nor verifiable. North Korea's leaders would at least need to maintain a high level of ambiguity about their nuclear capabilities—or ideally they would like to have an explicit or implicit admission that they would be allowed to keep some stockpile of plutonium and a couple of nuclear devices. The plutonium stockpile and nuclear devices would be safely hidden somewhere in its underground facilities, to serve as a deterrent and also a powerful potential tool for diplomatic blackmail.

Whether such an outcome would be acceptable to the United States remains doubtful. The United States would be expected to pay hefty fees for a downsized threat while still living with a nuclear North Korea. Perhaps such a compromise is not even advisable, as judged from the U.S. viewpoint. After all, it creates a dangerous precedent. North Korea would finally get rewarded for its nuclear blackmail: in all probability, the total price Pyongyang would extract from the United States for the above-described compromise would exceed its nuclear program spending.

This solution is imperfect and partial, to be sure. It might even be seen as unacceptable and hence rejected. Unfortunately, no other compromise appears to be on the horizon. If the above-mentioned solution is rejected, we are likely to see years of negotiations, broken promises, and false dawns—still without any tangible result—at least until the demise of the Kim Family Regime. That event appears destined for the rather distant future.

PART THREE

What's at Stake for the Nuclear Nonproliferation Regime?

CHAPTER NINE

India's Nuclear Exceptionalism and the North Korean Nuclear Case

DANIEL TWINING

India is a nuclear weapons state and a nonmember of the Nuclear Non-Proliferation Treaty (NPT). It conducted nuclear tests in 1974 and 1998 and rules out accession to either the NPT or the Comprehensive Test Ban Treaty (CTBT). India continues to produce fissile material for its nuclear arsenal and is not a party to the Fissile Material Cutoff Treaty (FMCT). The South Asian nation has developed and deployed intermediate- and long-range ballistic missiles capable of carrying nuclear payloads. Yet thanks to a civilian-nuclear cooperation agreement signed with the United States in 2007 and approved by the International Atomic Energy Agency (IAEA) and the Nuclear Suppliers Group (NSG) in 2008, India now enjoys access to the international trade in civilian-nuclear components.

In a break with nearly four decades of international nonproliferation policy, India—once the target of a rigid international embargo on dual-use and nuclear technologies overseen by the established nuclear weapons states and the nuclear suppliers' cartel—has been inducted into the international nuclear order as a legitimate nuclear weapons state. As a non-NPT member, India is unique in this regard. Does the Indian precedent undermine the nuclear nonproliferation regime? Does it subvert international efforts to contain and roll back North Korea's nuclear weapons program? Or could the Indian case actually be a model for North Korea's own nuclear normalization and acceptance by the international community?

The short answer to these questions is no. The similarities between the Indian and North Korean nuclear programs are superficial at best. Unlike North Korea, India never signed the NPT and never committed to be bound by its terms. Although it initially benefited from the diversion of nuclear materials and technology from a Canadian-designed civil-nuclear reactor,[1] India's nuclear weapons are homegrown—unlike North Korea's, whose nuclear weapons scientists received assistance at different times from the Soviet Union, China, and Pakistan. India has bound itself to the international community to pursue rules-based partnership on civil-nuclear energy production that complies with international norms—unlike North Korea, which broke out of a set of international energy-cooperation agreements in the 1990s and again in the 2000s in its pursuit of nuclear weapons. Most though not all of India's nuclear facilities are now subject to IAEA monitoring and inspection—unlike in North Korea, which has repeatedly expelled IAEA monitors, most recently in 2009. Nor has the Indian government been complicit in external proliferation—in striking contrast to North Korea, whose government has proliferated nuclear weapons designs, expertise, or materials to Syria and possibly Myanmar/Burma and whose relationship with Pakistani scientist A. Q. Khan facilitated the development of Iran's and Libya's nuclear weapons programs.[2] Unlike in North Korea, where a dynastic, totalitarian regime promotes a military-first ideology of governance, India's nuclear weapons remain firmly under democratic, civilian control. Finally, from a geopolitical perspective, India has proven itself willing to play a helpful role in stabilizing the Asian balance of power—in contrast to North Korea, whose external behavior is arguably the leading source of strategic instability in Northeast Asia.

In this chapter I present information so that readers can compare and contrast India's nuclear record against North Korea's, as my fellow contributors describe in companion chapters in this volume. I assess India's unique nuclear status as a non-NPT member that, through voluntary agreement with the main international nuclear rule-making bodies, now enjoys normal trade in civilian-nuclear components and has assumed international monitoring and nonproliferation obligations compatible with the international nuclear nonproliferation regime. I argue that India's inclusion in the international civilian-nuclear regime and its compliance with international nonproliferation commitments strengthen rather than undermine the nuclear nonproliferation regime.

Although not an NPT member, India has committed to

- Separate its civilian and military nuclear facilities and programs
- Declare its civilian facilities to the IAEA
- Voluntarily place civilian facilities under IAEA safeguards
- Sign an Additional Protocol for civilian facilities

- Continue its unilateral nuclear test moratorium
- Work with the United States to conclude a Fissile Material Cutoff Treaty
- Refrain from transferring enrichment and reprocessing technologies to states that do not have them, as well as support international efforts to limit such technologies' spread
- Secure its nuclear materials and technology through comprehensive export control legislation and through harmonization and adherence to MTCR and NSG guidelines[3]

These commitments, and the Nuclear Suppliers Group decision to normalize civilian-nuclear trade with India in return, put India in a different league than North Korea and Iran, both signatories to the NPT as non-nuclear-weapon states that nonetheless continue to actively develop nuclear weapons capabilities. The commitments also distinguish India from fellow non-NPT signatories Pakistan, which in the past has been an active external proliferator that does not enjoy trade with the NSG, and Israel, whose nuclear facilities are not subject to international safeguards. President Barack Obama's support for Indian membership in the four groups comprising the multilateral export-control regime—the Nuclear Suppliers Group, Missile Technology Control Regime, Wassenaar Arrangement, and Australia Group—demonstrates India's transition from international nuclear outlier to stakeholder in upholding a more proliferation-resistant and secure global order.[4]

India's nuclear normalization in 2008 at the hands of the IAEA, the NSG, and the individual governments that constitute them aligns India with the established nuclear powers and a number of other states that possess civil-nuclear expertise, and with the international nuclear order they uphold. In doing so, the international nonproliferation regime—which encompasses but is broader than the NPT—is stronger, rather than weaker.[5] Even if India wanted to, no clear pathway exists for India to accede to the NPT as a nuclear state. The treaty recognizes only the United States, France, Britain, China, and Russia as legitimate nuclear powers. It leaves the door to membership open only to states willing to accede as nonnuclear powers—which India clearly is not—in return for enjoying the benefits of civilian-nuclear cooperation. Moreover, Indians would be the first to point out that the NPT also legally requires the established nuclear powers to commit to eventual nuclear disarmament, which none seem inclined to do. These real flaws in the NPT should not obscure the reality that the wider international nonproliferation regime has been fortified rather than undermined by India's incorporation into it—uniquely, as a non-NPT member that has assumed many of the responsibilities, from nonproliferation to safe-guards, of the established nuclear powers.

India's nuclear normalization also advances the strategic goal of the United States and other nations of maintaining an Asian balance of power as China rises. Even for proliferation purists, this is no small matter; an international system whose rules and norms are shaped by responsible democracies in the West and Asia would likely enjoy stronger safeguards against nuclear prolifera-tion than one dominated by a Chinese superpower whose record on nonprolif-eration has been far less stringent.

In this chapter I assess India's nuclear normalization with reference to both its geopolitical and nonproliferation logics, because both have animated U.S. policy with regard to civilian nuclear cooperation with India. I also emphasize the U.S. perspective, because it was U.S. officials who conceptualized civilian-nuclear cooperation with India as a gateway to expanded strategic cooperation, and because it was the United States that sponsored India's change of status within the international nuclear order.

INDIA'S PROLIFERATION CONFLICT WITH THE INTERNATIONAL COMMUNITY, 1970–98

During the Cold War, India was alienated by Western support for a global order that appeared to discriminate against it. Unlike China, India was excluded from membership in the UN Security Council. Because China tested nuclear weap-ons in 1964, before the NPT took effect in 1970, China's nuclear arsenal was legitimized and its right to nuclear weapons and trade affirmed by the Nuclear Non-Proliferation Treaty. In contrast, India's later 1974 and 1998 nuclear tests rendered it a rogue state under international law, subjecting it to sanctions on technology trade that undercut its security and limited its economic prospects. India suffered this treatment despite its clean record on external proliferation, unlike core NPT members including the United States, which had contributed to the British and French nuclear weapons programs, and China, which con-tributed to the nuclear weapons programs of Pakistan and North Korea. In-deed, China's supply of advanced nuclear designs and components to Pakistan from the 1980s, contravening Beijing's NPT obligations while Western pow-ers looked the other way, reinforced Indian perceptions of the great powers' hypocrisy and hostility to India's legitimate security requirements. As Indian prime minister Atal Bihari Vajpayee told President Bill Clinton in 1998, China had "helped another neighbor of ours [Pakistan] to become a covert nuclear weapons state" that had "attacked India three times in the last fifty years" and had sponsored "unremitting terrorism and militancy" against India.[6]

India was the primary target of U.S. and international proliferation sanctions during the 1990s. At a 1991 nonproliferation conference, Indian officials were galled to find themselves pressured jointly by Washington and Beijing while the latter was covertly supplying nuclear weapons components to rival Pakistan. U.S. threats to impose crippling economic sanctions against India in 1995 discouraged the government of Prime Minister Narasimha Rao from testing nuclear weapons only seventy-two hours before their planned explosion.[7] In 1996, against stiff opposition from New Delhi, the United States supported a Chinese resolution in Geneva demanding that India comply with the Comprehensive Test Ban Treaty. When India did not comply, the international community imposed tough sanctions following its eventual 1998 nuclear tests. Throughout the 1970–98 period, Indian elites widely viewed their country as the victim of an international "technology apartheid" that for decades had constrained India's rise.[8] India's future president, Abdul Kalam, argued following the nuclear tests that India needed to break up the nuclear and technological "monopolies" of the great powers and the international regimes they had constructed to keep India down.[9]

U.S. POLICY IN THE 2000S: NORMALIZING INDIA AS A RESPONSIBLE NUCLEAR POWER

With the end of the Cold War, the onset of unipolarity, and a U.S. focus on containing Indian proliferation, the Clinton administration during the 1990s treated India more as a rogue state to be sanctioned and contained than as a rising world power—until India's nuclear weapons tests changed U.S. assessments of its capabilities and potential. In testing nuclear weapons, India sought to "impress the Americans with India's determination to assert itself in the world,"[10] "compel the United States to take India seriously,"[11] and "use its strategic position and resources" to encourage Washington to "bid for its support."[12] The tests therefore may be viewed as directed at the United States as much as at Indian rivals China or Pakistan, with their object being the redefinition of the terms of U.S.-India relations in ways that made a new strategic partnership possible.

New Delhi's gamble worked. Rather than intensify its previous containment of Indian power, Washington entered its most meaningful strategic dialogue with New Delhi in fifty years. According to the leaders of this dialogue, both countries' officials were educated about the strategic concerns of the other. These concerns included a mutual wariness of Chinese power, revealing a surprising convergence of interests in building a new relationship premised on Indian strength, and a common strategic outlook.[13]

In 2000, then–Texas governor George W. Bush and his advisers identified India as "a nation transforming itself into a global player" and determined that their foreign policy in office would include a greater role for a dynamic India in shaping the Asian balance.[14] Incoming national security adviser Condoleezza Rice argued that the United States "should pay closer attention to India's role in the regional balance. . . . India is an element in China's calculation, and it should be in America's, too."[15] Bush's first National Security Strategy highlighted "India's potential to become one of the great democratic powers of the twenty-first century."[16] A year later, the Central Intelligence Agency labeled India the key "swing state" in international politics, predicting that it would emerge by 2015 as the fourth-most-important power in the international system.[17]

The new Bush administration rapidly dispensed with most remaining sanctions against India stemming from its nuclear tests and set aside the nonproliferation framework that had guided Clinton administration policy.[18] Washington and New Delhi still had differences over India's nuclear weapons program. "But while in the past these concerns may have dominated our thinking about India, today we start with a view of India as a growing world power with which we have common strategic interests," asserted a State Department strategy document.[19] Undersecretary of State Nicholas Burns declared, "The United States recognizes India as an emerging world power in the 21st century, with an important role of promoting global stability, democracy and prosperity," highlighting in particular India's "large and ever more sophisticated military forces," its anticipated economic and demographic trajectories, and its democratic politics.[20]

The White House's 2006 National Security Strategy labeled India one of the main "centers of global power."[21] President Bush reportedly viewed India in the same way as his father, the United States' top envoy to Beijing in the 1970s, viewed China then—as an emerging giant whose strength and orientation could be shaped by the United States to realign the global balance of power.[22] As Ashley Tellis put it, the geopolitical (as opposed to the nonproliferation) logic behind the U.S. opening to New Delhi was to strengthen India as an independent center of power in Asia to "creat[e] an environment that provides disincentives for China to rise in any way other than peacefully."[23]

Indian leaders attested that the pronounced U.S. interest in India in the first decade of the twenty-first century was a function of India's growing power: "If there is a greater focus today on India in the U.S., it is not because India is weak, but it is because India is strong," said Foreign Secretary Shyam Saran in 2005. "We are being recognized as a country which has [an] array of capabilities, and has the potential to emerge as a very, very important power in the future."[24] Identifying "a major realignment of forces taking place in Asia," Saran said, "India and the United States can contribute to a much better balance in the Asian region."[25]

PROMOTING INDIA'S ECONOMIC AND MILITARY RISE VIA CIVILIAN-NUCLEAR ENERGY COOPERATION

In 2005 the Bush administration announced its intention to "play midwife to the birth of a new great power" by accelerating India's geopolitical rise—a declaration unprecedented in the history of U.S. foreign policy.[26] The most visible manifestation of the U.S. effort to enhance Indian capabilities was the 2007 agreement on civilian-nuclear cooperation, ratified by the IAEA and the NSG and signed into U.S. law in 2008. The broad effects of the agreement were to bring India into the international nuclear order as an accepted nuclear weapons state, bolster Indian economic growth, enable India to access advanced technologies on the international market, and enhance—rather than roll back or contain—Indian national capabilities.

Boosting India's Long-Term Growth Capacity through Civilian-Nuclear Cooperation and High-Technology Transfer

The Bush-Vajpayee summit of November 2001 produced the concept of a "trinity" of issues to advance cooperation between the United States and India: high-technology trade, civilian space cooperation, and civilian-nuclear power. In early 2003 Washington and New Delhi established the bilateral High Technology Cooperation Group to explore the further lifting of U.S. restrictions on sensitive technologies so as to enable their transfer to India. Cooperation on missile defense, including possible transfer of sensitive space launch and guidance technologies, was added to the "trinity" in 2003 to form the "quartet," and a framework agreement laying out the modalities of cooperation on these issues was announced in the Next Steps in Strategic Partnership (NSSP) agreement of January 2004.[27] The two countries declared that NSSP cooperation to strengthen India's technological, civilian space, energy, and missile defense capabilities "will increase stability in Asia and beyond."[28]

The NSSP was revolutionary in its implications: every U.S. administration since India's first nuclear detonation in 1974 had sought to deny India access to the international market in advanced dual-use technologies (many of which also have nuclear weapons–related applications) until it eliminated its strategic weapons program. The Bush administration, in contrast, "turned this approach on its head," liberalizing technology trade without demanding a rollback of India's nuclear weapons program.[29] The United States has no similar agreement with Israel or Pakistan, the other two nuclear weapons states and tacit allies that have not signed the NPT. Analysts widely attributed Washington's tacit acceptance of India's nuclear weapons program and determination to strengthen India's economic and energy capabilities by lifting restrictions on high-tech trade as part of a broader strategy of (1) enhancing India's geopolitical weight and (2) moving beyond allowing nuclear India's non-NPT status to block international cooperation with New Delhi on a range of issues.[30]

The U.S. initiative that followed in 2005 was even more significant: it was, for India, "the deal of the century."[31] In July, President Bush pledged to achieve full civil-nuclear energy cooperation between the United States and India, work with Congress to adjust U.S. laws and policies to enable the transfer of technology and assured fuel supplies to safeguarded Indian nuclear reactors, and work with the IAEA and NSG to integrate India—previously sanctioned by the international nuclear cartel for its unauthorized nuclear weapons development—as a full member of the international nuclear club, with rights equal to those of the United States and other nuclear powers. In return, India would separate its military and civilian-nuclear reactors, agree to place the latter (but not the former) under international safeguards, and commit to uphold the global nonproliferation regime as a legitimate nuclear weapon state.[32] Even as the United States was working with allies to strengthen the international nonproliferation regime—for instance, through the Proliferation Security Initiative—it was making a singular exception in that regime for nuclear-armed India.[33]

U.S. and Indian officials alike characterized civilian-nuclear cooperation, which would increase India's domestic nuclear energy–generating capacity sixfold between 2008 and 2020, as critical to India's economic development.[34] Although India had independently become self-sufficient in mastering the nuclear fuel cycle, a weak uranium resource base was its "Achilles' heel."[35] The nuclear agreement would address that weakness by assuring India of continuous, uninterrupted fuel supplies for its safeguarded nuclear reactors. By providing India with an assured source of energy supply immune from the risks of import dependence, the agreement was expected to significantly expand India's long-term economic development capacity. Prime Minister Manmohan Singh called the assured energy supply provided by the agreement a "vital national interest" without which India's rapid economic growth would be unsustainable.[36]

Perhaps more important than the expansion of India's domestic energy supply was the agreement's liberation of India from the international regime of technology sanctions, imposed as a result of India's proliferation activity dating to its "peaceful" nuclear explosion of 1974, that had severely constrained its economic development prospects. Indian strategists termed these restrictions "the global technology apartheid" that, by restricting India's access to dual-use technologies, had stood in the way of rapid economic growth.[37] External Affairs Minister Pranab Mukherjee identified these restrictions as the central roadblock to India's ability to "reposition itself in the global order" as a rising world power: "Liberating ourselves from this high-technology blockade" had been "a major objective of Indian foreign policy for decades" and was "finally at hand with the on-going implementation of our nuclear agreement with the United States."[38]

In addition to nuclear-related technologies, the deal made available to India on the international market previously denied dual-use technologies restricted by the NSG Category 2 list of sensitive technologies, with applications ranging from space flight to high-tech manufacturing to military uses.[39] "The nuclear deal is much more than about nuclear energy," reported the *Times of India.* "It's about breaking through a technology denial regime that has spread across many sectors of India's knowledge economy—from [information technology] to defense, space, pharmaceuticals, clean energy, biotech, you name it," and that had heretofore constrained India's economic development potential.[40]

Access to advanced international technologies, argued authorities in both Washington and New Delhi, was essential to India's great power aspirations. Secretary of State Rice called it part of a broader strategy "to assist in that growth of India's global power and the implications of that, which we see as largely positive."[41] It was, said Rice adviser Tellis, part of a broader U.S. design of "assisting the growth of Indian power."[42] More than an enhancement of bilateral relations, K. Subrahmanyam, the dean of Indian strategists, called the deal a vehicle for empowering India to play "the role of a balancer of power in Asia and the world." Recognizing India's strategic value, the United States—

"the originator of th[e] technology apartheid against India"—was now leading the effort to "incorporate this [rising] India into an Asian and global balance of power."[43]

Enabling the Expansion of India's Nuclear Weapons Program

That the deal was motivated by a joint ambition to strengthen India's independent capabilities was attested by the deal's implications for India's nuclear weapons program. Under the deal, India agreed to international safeguards on its civilian-nuclear facilities—but not its military ones.[44] Moreover, Washington gave New Delhi unprecedented assurances of an uninterrupted nuclear fuel supply, including the establishment of a strategic nuclear fuel reserve in India for the lifetime of India's reactors, which would render the country immune from any future cutoff in U.S. supply, a likely development under the terms of the agreement if India conducted further nuclear weapons tests.

In 2006–8, before the agreement came into force, the scarcity of domestically produced uranium and India's exclusion from the international nuclear fuel market were placing mounting pressure on the government to choose between fueling India's civilian or military nuclear reactors—but not both. Such a choice would negatively impact either India's civilian economy or its nuclear deterrent, a Hobson's choice. U.S. assurances of diverse sources of fuel supply meant that India, under the agreement, would be able to divert domestically produced uranium to its military reactors while relying on international supplies to fuel its civilian reactors. This step would allow India to stockpile spent fuel in order to provide continuity of fuel supply for its civilian and military reactors in the future—even if the United States suspended fuel shipments following an Indian nuclear test.

By assuring India of a fuel supply for safeguarded civilian-nuclear facilities —and not requiring India to safeguard its military nuclear facilities—the deal allowed India to take advantage of the fungibility of domestically produced nuclear fuel to supply its military fast-breeder reactor without risking its fuel supply for its civilian nuclear sector. India retains the sole right under the agreement to designate autonomously which facilities are safeguarded as civilian and which are free of international supervision as declared military facilities. India also remains free under the agreement to produce fissile material for nuclear weapons at the latter, unsafeguarded facilities.[45] Although Washington has civilian-nuclear cooperation agreements with other countries, none similarly grant the unrestricted right to reprocess spent fuel precisely because of its

fungibility between civilian and military uses.[46] As the former Clinton administration's top nonproliferation official stated bluntly, "The civilian-nuclear deal
will free up for India uranium needed for its weapons program."[47]

ASSESSMENT OF THE DEAL

In proposing the civilian-nuclear agreement with India, not only did U.S. officials acknowledge that India could enjoy the benefits of international nuclear
cooperation while retaining nuclear weapons capability; they actually allowed
India to improve that capability and, while securing India's commitment not
to proliferate abroad, made clear they had no intention of limiting its nuclear
weapons program. Clause 2.4 of the Indo-U.S. agreement states explicitly that
it will not impinge on India's nuclear weapons program. The U.S. congressional
report authorizing the civilian-nuclear agreement states, "U.S. peaceful nuclear
cooperation with India will not be intended to inhibit India's nuclear weapons
program. . . . India will presumably continue to produce material for its nuclear
weapons program."[48]

As Rice told Congress, "Clearly this agreement does not constrain India's
nuclear weapons program; that was not its purpose."[49] The deal does not restrict "India's right to undertake future nuclear tests, if it is necessary," Prime
Minister Singh told Parliament.[50] As U.S. nonproliferation expert George
Perkovich argued, "This deal not only lets India amass as many nuclear weapons as it wants, it looks like we made no effort to try to curtail them."[51] This critique is not entirely accurate; under the terms of the agreement, further Indian
nuclear weapons tests would lead to a suspension of international civil nuclear
energy cooperation with India. The congressional Hyde Act authorizing the
civilian-nuclear deal was clear on this point, and the State Department confirmed it in writing to the U.S. Congress.[52]

Calling the civilian nuclear agreement "absolutely unprecedented," Indian
ambassador to Washington Ronen Sen pointed out, "There has been no parallel of a single country exemption to any of the international regimes, not in the
twenty-first century, the twentieth, or in any century."[53] Under the terms of
India's bilateral nuclear cooperation agreement with the United States, Washington agreed to consult with India on the regional security conditions that motivated future nuclear weapons tests before determining whether to maintain
cooperation under the deal. The United States also pledged, in the event it cut
off fuel supply following an Indian test, to help India secure supplies from other

NSG states. Former deputy secretary of state Talbott pointed out that these terms gave India more rights than the five original nuclear weapons states. Talbott identified the Bush administration's goal of balancing China in Asia as one rationale for such leniency.[54]

Some Indian strategists and members of India's conservative political opposition argued that the deal would constrain, not enhance, the country's strategic capabilities.[55] An objective reading of the deal's benefits to India suggests that this argument is misleading: many Indian analysts and politicians who supported the deal argued that the Bharatiya Janata Party (BJP) opposition only wished that it had secured such a deal, when it was in office, with BJP leader Lal Krishna Advani privately saying he supported the deal and other party notables, including former national security adviser Brajesh Mishra, supporting it openly.[56] The scientists of the Indian Department of Atomic Energy— who had originally opposed the concept of a civilian-nuclear agreement with Washington on the grounds that it would constrain India's nuclear weapons capabilities—changed position once the final terms of the deal were agreed upon, in recognition that it furthered their long-cherished aim of expanding India's civilian and military nuclear programs alike through guaranteed fuel supply and an end to high-tech sanctions. Nonetheless, the Indian parliament's subsequent passage of a nuclear liability law that, by not conforming to international standards on liability for nuclear-reactor operators, limited the ability of U.S. companies to build and operate civilian-nuclear reactors in India reflected the blowback from the government's domestic political opposition over the terms of the U.S.-India civilian-nuclear agreement.

Critics of the U.S.-India civilian-nuclear agreement maintained that Washington sought to "give India so much for so little" in an "unbalanced" agreement. There was "a serious asymmetry in the arrangement," such critics maintained: U.S. commitments to India were tangible and immediate, whereas India made no corresponding commitments in terms of binding alliance ties or common geopolitical objectives.[57] In one sense, the critics were right: the United States sought to provide India with strategic resources that would facilitate its development of national power. Even the deal's harshest domestic critics, Communist Party (Marxist) secretary-general Prakash Karat, for example, identified the U.S. objective in these terms: "India can become a great power with the help of the United States."[58]

Yet India did make a series of commitments to the IAEA, the NSG, and their member governments on export controls and other nonproliferation obligations. These were designed to ensure that civilian nuclear cooperation with

India would strengthen rather than weaken the global nonproliferation regime. In that sense, the Indo-U.S. nuclear deal as endorsed by the international nuclear community did bind India to the common goal of upholding the international nuclear order.

EXPLAINING INDIAN EXCEPTIONALISM

U.S. policies to strengthen India's national capabilities through civilian-nuclear cooperation fly in the face of neorealist theory's contention that states are acutely focused on relative gains, even in cooperative relationships. However, India's democratic identity combined with its historical wariness of authoritarian China reassured U.S. officials. They overwhelmingly subscribe to democratic peace theory, which would suggest that India's rise as a world power would complement, not compete with, the U.S. foreign policy objectives. Indian democracy creates a U.S. comfort level in propelling the country's geopolitical rise without concern for relative gains of the kind that characterize U.S.-China relations.

The United States has invested in propelling India's geopolitical ascent in the belief that India will increasingly project its democratic values outward as it rises, and work to shape an international order informed by the same principles of peaceful pluralism that characterize Indian society. Secretary of State Rice said that the United States had a "vital interest" in India's rise as "a global power and an ally in shaping an international order rooted in freedom and the rule of law." She argued that India was "redefin[ing]" its national interests as Indians realize "their direct stake in a democratic, secure, and open international order."[59] A strong India would sustain the liberal international order that magnified U.S. power and safeguarded key U.S. interests: according to Burns, the United States was sponsoring India's ascent because "the U.S. and India share a common view of how the world should be organized."[60]

U.S. officials called India's identity as a "multi-ethnic and multi-religious and pluralistic" democracy the "foundation for our partnership in regional and global affairs," while Indian leaders declared "our common commitment to democracy, pluralism, and prosperity" the basis for Indo-U.S. cooperation on global issues.[61] In short, Indian values have made U.S. strategists comfortable promoting the rise of a new world power from the subcontinent.

At the same time, U.S. officials appeared sincere in their belief that ending the sanctions straitjacket to enable India to benefit from the international trade in civilian-nuclear components strengthened the nonproliferation regime. After its 1998 tests, India's status as a nuclear weapons state was a fact. Nor did those tests violate the NPT, which India had never signed. In no scenario short of universal nuclear disarmament (of which India had been a principled advocate since the country's founding) was India going to give up its nuclear weapons. In that light, U.S. officials and their Indian counterparts ultimately persuaded members of the IAEA and the NSG that adapting the international nonproliferation regime to the reality of India's nuclear status would strengthen it, by granting India the same rights—and imposing on it the same responsibilities—as the established nuclear powers.

These responsibilities included an array of external nonproliferation commitments, the requirement to separate its civilian and military nuclear facilities, the imposition of international safeguards on India's civilian-nuclear facilities, and institutionalized understandings that international civilian nuclear cooperation would be cut off should India test nuclear weapons.[62] As a nonsignatory to the NPT, India had previously been subject to none of these restrictions. India also possessed what its leadership frequently refers to as an "impeccable" record on nonproliferation, an assessment senior U.S. officials have repeatedly affirmed as correct.[63] India's external proliferation record is limited to the sales (and subsequent U.S. sanctioning) of several Indian companies that provided dual-use components with potential WMD applications to Iran—sales that almost certainly occurred without the knowledge of the Indian government.[64] The bar against such sales was raised much higher by the strict nuclear export-control requirements India agreed to at the behest of the NSG before India's civilian-nuclear trade was normalized.

On the question of Iran's illicit nuclear weapons development—arguably the biggest proliferation challenge of the modern era, given Iran's geopolitical position and weight—India has complied with all UN Security Council (UNSC) resolutions sanctioning Iran's nuclear activities. These include restrictions on trade and technology transfer mandated by the UNSC in 2007. At the IAEA, India has repeatedly voted to condemn or sanction Iranian nuclear activities. Prime Minister Singh has stated clearly that India is opposed to the rise of new nuclear weapons states anywhere, and that an Iranian nuclear weapons program would destabilize India's economic and strategic interests in the Middle East.[65] However, Indian leaders have rejected the implication that U.S. and European sanctions on Iran, separate from those endorsed by the UNSC, have legal force with respect to India's own exports to Iran. Although India reduced oil imports from Iran in 2012 to a level that earned it a waiver from U.S. third-party sanctions on countries doing business with Iran, American officials remained unhappy with India's ongoing commercial (nonmilitary, nonnuclear) relations with Iran.

Beyond Iran, India has also emerged as a leader in facilitating international cooperation against the danger of nuclear terrorism, which both President Obama and former IAEA director Mohammed al-Baradei have described as the leading threat to international security.[66] Since 2002 India has piloted a resolution at the United Nations on preventing terrorists from acquiring weapons of mass destruction. At the IAEA India has been active in setting and enforcing standards on physical protection of nuclear material and facilities and on combating illicit trafficking in nuclear material. India is a party to the UN Convention on the Physical Protection of Nuclear Material and its 2005 amendment.[67] At the Washington nuclear security summit convened by President Obama in April 2010, Prime Minister Singh announced the establishment in India of a new nuclear security center affiliated with the IAEA to promote proliferation-resistant nuclear energy research and development. President Obama endorsed the Indian initiative, calling it "one more tool to establish best practices" in the quest for nuclear security.[68]

"Of all the powers, India was the one most short-changed by the 1970 Nuclear Non-Proliferation Treaty. The world can no longer afford to leave it out of the non-proliferation and nuclear security tent," argues Rory Medcalf of Australia's Lowy Institute.[69] Although its nuclear weapons program was born of the "original sin" of diverting nuclear material from an international civil-nuclear reactor on its territory, India can credibly claim not to have proliferated nuclear materials or technologies to any other power as a matter of state policy. India's new international partners in civilian-nuclear trade can credibly argue that India's accession to the international nonproliferation regime has made it more robust and secure. Moreover, India's minimal nuclear deterrent, doctrine of no-first-use, and consistent support for international nuclear disarmament could be, in the eyes of some analysts, models for other nuclear weapons states, including the United States, Russia, and China.[70]

CONCLUSION: COULD NORTH KOREA BE NEXT?

Could North Korea one day follow in India's footsteps, rejoining the international community as a recognized nuclear weapons state outside the boundaries of the NPT in return for commitments to adhere to international norms and safeguards on its nuclear capabilities? North Korea's record as a serial proliferator, its history of NPT violations and other broken nonproliferation commitments to the international community, and the nature of its regime, with nuclear and missile exports a key source of hard currency for North Korea's leadership elite, suggests not.[71] A grand bargain between North Korea and the United States endorsed by the other members of the Six Party Talks—in which Pyongyang normalizes its relations with Washington and the international community in return for a series of binding security and nonproliferation commitments—was unsuccessfully pursued by both the Clinton and George W. Bush administrations.[72]

More fundamentally, North Korea's leadership believes that its nuclear weapons are necessary to manage its external security dilemmas (North Korea being surrounded by historically predatory neighbors and having previously been the target of a U.S. policy of regime change) and its internal security concerns (the fear of its own people inherent to a totalitarian regime, and the requirement to leverage its nuclear capabilities to secure international supplies of economic, food, and energy assistance in order to sustain the support of key leadership groups including the military). While India tested nuclear weapons with an eye on external military threats from China and Pakistan, its nuclear calculus was not subject to the same internal domestic calculus that continues to animate the North Korean regime. These domestic pressures cast the most doubt on Pyongyang's ability to come in from the cold on nuclear weapons, unless and until a new regime takes power that defines its interests with regard to its people and its international obligations differently.

For its part, India's adversarial relationship with Pakistan and continued targeting by Pakistani terrorist groups make it a likely target of nuclear terrorism. This danger—as well as India's aspirations to world power and inclusion in great power clubs, from the UN Security Council to the Nuclear Suppliers Group—gives India a vital stake in containing nuclear proliferation and strengthening the nonproliferation regime. India's interests are, in this sense, the opposite of North Korea's. Finally, India and the international nuclear cartel that finally opened its doors to New Delhi both have a profound interest in upholding India's nuclear exceptionalism against claims by other powers, from Pakistan to North Korea, that say they deserve similar treatment, notwithstanding their roles in proliferating nuclear expertise and materials in ways that have profoundly undermined the international nuclear nonproliferation regime, of which India can now claim to be a responsible member.

CHAPTER TEN

Global Consequences of an Operationally Nuclear North Korea

MARIA ROST RUBLEE

North Korean nuclearization has had less of an impact than predicted.[1] However, an operationalization of North Korea's nuclear capabilities may have more of an impact than has been evident thus far with the tests we've observed because of the potential for not only regional but also global repercussions. Regional consequences may include increased strains between Beijing and Pyongyang, as well as a serious consideration of an independent nuclear arsenal by Tokyo. Given the reduced credibility of the U.S. nuclear umbrella, some in Tokyo have argued that because an operationally nuclear North Korea would likely be able to target U.S. cities, some Japanese may not believe that Washington would risk San Francisco to defend Tokyo.[2] However, the consequences will ripple well beyond East Asia. The implications of a poor, isolated state effectively defying not just one but two great powers may signal the inability of the global community to constrain proliferation and weaponization.

In this chapter I discuss the direct and indirect effects of North Korean success on potential proliferants outside the region, including Syria, Myanmar/Burma, Egypt, and especially Iran. Specifically, I examine how global conditions —including the strength of the U.S., Chinese, and international reaction to North Korean weaponization—and domestic conditions—including domestic political struggles—will lead these nuclear aspirants to interpret and internalize the lessons from North Korea. In addition, I consider the ripple effects of a bolder Iran, which would undoubtedly be propelled by North Korea's success. Finally, I explore the possible impact on the Nuclear Non-Proliferation Treaty (NPT) if North Korea is able to create a fully operational nuclear weapons system.

INTERNATIONAL REACTION AND RIPPLE EFFECTS

First, however, we must assess how the reactions of the international community create ripple effects from North Korea achieving an operational nuclear force. These ripple effects do not exist separately from the global community's response; their reactions contextualize how Pyongyang and other potential proliferants "learn" what to make of the costs of nuclear operationalization. As one analyst noted, "Credibility is the word of the day. Iran already doubts the seriousness of international warnings, having seen little follow-through thus far; a feckless response to North Korea . . . will only reinforce this. The implication is obvious: Anything short of substantial sanctions imposed on North Korea will only encourage Tehran."[3] In other words, countries do not learn simply from what North Korea does. Rather, they learn from the international community's reaction to North Korea.

After the DPRK nuclear tests, analysts widely agreed that Tehran was closely watching Beijing and Moscow regarding their willingness to vote for severe sanctions.[4] In fact, while China and Russia voted for economic and military sanctions after the North Korean nuclear tests in 2006 and 2009, they worked behind the scenes to weaken the sanctions before voting took place. For example, Beijing and Moscow succeeded in making mandatory sanctions simply optional after the 2009 test.[5] There is no reason to suspect it will be any different should North Korea operationalize its nuclear stocks.

How will Iran and other nuclear aspirants learn from the international reaction to operationally ready nuclear weapons in North Korea? One way to know is compare what people say to what people do. Social psychology research shows that when actors do one thing but say another, recipients place a higher value on the action than the words. Actions create what social psychologists call "descriptive norms." "Observing others helps people understand what is 'correct' or 'normal' in a novel, ambiguous, or uncertain situation."[6] On the other hand, "injunctive norms" are verbal admonitions about proper behavior (e.g., "Don't litter" or "Don't seek weapons of mass destruction"). Therefore, when descriptive and injunctive norms conflict, actors pay much more attention to the descriptive norms. The strongest possible message is delivered when descriptive norms and injunctive norms are in sync; if international leaders say, "Seeking nuclear weapons is wrong," and then effectively punish those who do seek them, the message is quite strong.[7] Therefore, Iran and other potential proliferants will be watching to see if injunctive and descriptive norms match up should the DPRK operationalize its nuclear capability. If injunctive and descriptive norms are in conflict, nuclear aspirants will place much more weight on actions than words. For this reason, Israel has called for harsh sanctions against North Korea for defying the international community. Israeli defense minister Ehud Barak noted, "When the Iranian leadership asks themselves, 'Should we be worried or just go through the ritual of defying and cheating?' the answer depends on what happens to North Korea."[8]

For example, Washington and Beijing both have called the North Korean nuclear tests conducted in October 2006 and May 2009 "unacceptable," but neither has taken effective measures to reinforce this injunctive norm. As one expert noted, "North Korea has paid virtually no price for its intransigence."[9] What are possible outcomes in the case of operational nuclear weapons in North Korea? One unlikely possibility is that no one would react, either with words or actions. In this case, creating an operational nuclear weapons force would receive a stamp of "acceptable," unleashing a dark set of ripple effects. If the international community condemns North Korea, but takes only mild or ineffective actions, then potential proliferants will focus on the descriptive norm (operational nuclear weapons will be tolerated) as opposed to the injunctive norm (operational nuclear weapons are unacceptable). If those potential proliferants place a high value on international acceptance, then the injunctive norm may end up having more force for them. However, for many nuclear aspirants (such as Iran, Syria, and Myanmar/Burma), international acceptance is not highly prized—and in fact, rebelling against the "right" thing to do, as defined by the international community, may actually be perceived to bring more status. Only if injunctive and descriptive norms are in concert—international condemnation combined with effective multilateral action—might Iran and other potential proliferants interpret the creation of operational nuclear weapons as a risky, possibly negative act.

What is the likely response to North Korea making its nuclear stocks operational? International reaction to the DPRK's nuclear tests provides some hints. While sanctions were applied after the October 2006 test and stiffened after the May 2009 test, they have not yielded the desired results, in part because of lax enforcement. Countries that are most willing to enforce sanctions, such as Japan and the United States, are those with the least economic engagement with North Korea, making the impact minimal. Countries whose full compliance with sanctions would negatively affect North Korea, such as China and Russia, are far less willing to do so. The most important case is China, which fought for watered-down sanctions after both North Korean nuclear tests, and which has applied the sanctions much less vigorously than hoped.[10] In fact, it is estimated that North Korea could lose between $1.5 billion and $3.7 billion because of the 2009 sanctions, but only if countries forcefully applied the sanctions. UN Resolution 1874 condemning the 2009 nuclear tests does not mandate sanctions but rather calls on member states to enforce them. This lack of mandate does not bode well for the success of the sanctions.[11]

Should North Korea create an operational nuclear weapons program, the likelihood of an effective response is diminished even further. Any possible military action, already opposed by China and Russia, would likely be ruled out by the United States as well for fear that Pyongyang would launch a nuclear counterattack against U.S. troops in South Korea or Japan, or South Korea or Japan more broadly. Diplomatic measures alone would be unlikely to work, given that only sanctions have brought North Korea back to the negotiating table in the past—and with operational nuclear weapons, the country would have a much stronger bargaining position. Sanctions are the most likely option, but as noted, unless they are applied broadly and enforced vigorously by those who actually trade with North Korea, they will not be effective. The question is, will China reverse its position and both support and enforce strong sanctions?[12] On the one hand, a nuclear North Korea threatens Chinese interests, in particular because Japan may respond with a nuclear capability of its own. On the other hand, because China holds so much leverage over North Korea, by applying serious sanctions, a collapse of the regime could result. This, in turn, would likely lead to a refugee crisis in China as millions of North Koreans flee the country, as well as a reunified, democratic Korea—depriving China of its buffer between its borders and U.S. troops in South Korea. As one analyst argued about sanctions after the DPRK's May 2009 nuclear test, "China faces a choice between two evils: a nuclear North Korea or a collapsing North Korea. And a collapsing North Korea clearly represents a greater evil. This is why Beijing is negative on severe sanctions and is willing to continue providing aid to North Korea."[13] The same logic would hold true, perhaps even more so, should North Korea operationalize its nuclear stocks. In this case, while the international community would surely deliver a strong injunctive message ("Operational nuclear weapons are unacceptable"), mostly likely the descriptive norm would be in conflict ("We are not willing to take the strong measures necessary to stop countries from acquiring operational nuclear weapons"). As a result, the ripple effects of North Korean actions would likely provoke further proliferation. Given this conclusion, I turn to an examination of both direct and indirect effects of a deliverable DPRK nuclear force.

DIRECT EFFECTS: TECHNOLOGY AND ASSISTANCE

What type of direct effects beyond East Asia might be seen if North Korea successfully operationalizes its nuclear weapons? Direct effects—those that involve Pyongyang directly in the spread of nuclear technology or weapons—can be categorized into two main groups: selling of weapons or weapons technology, and technical assistance and aid.

Weapons Export

North Korean arms sales (including short- and medium-range missiles) total over $100 million a year, an important export for a country with an economy in shambles.[14] Concern has grown over the possibility that Pyongyang may attempt to sell nuclear technology or actual weapons in an attempt to gain foreign currency. If North Korea successfully creates operational nuclear weapons, the country may find it easier to locate buyers for their nuclear-related technology—as well as command higher prices—since they have demonstrated the ability to not only create and detonate nuclear weapons but also integrate them into war-fighting capability. The temptation of lucrative nuclear sales could be difficult to resist for a country under increasingly strict UN sanctions following its 2009 nuclear test.[15] If sanctions are applied with the DPRK's successful operationalization of its nuclear stocks, Pyongyang may be even more likely to sell its nuclear technology.[16]

Fear about a possible nuclear black market are exacerbated by North Korea's reputation as a "Missiles-R-Us," selling missiles to a wide range of countries, including Iran, Iraq, Pakistan, Egypt, Syria, and Yemen.[17] Other important export earnings are derived from drugs and counterfeit money. A country with such a track record may not flinch at selling nuclear technology or even weapons for financial purposes, either to other countries or non-state agents such as Al Qaeda. In May 2004, International Atomic Energy Agency (IAEA) inspectors "recovered 2 tons of uranium hexafluoride from Libya thought to have originated in North Korea."[18] Further analysis has led experts to conclude with 90% certainty that the material was sold to Libya by North Korea.[19] Uranium hexafluoride is produced for processing through gas centrifuges to create either low-enriched uranium to fuel nuclear power plants or high-enriched uranium for nuclear weapons. Indeed, the U.S. intelligence community has repeatedly expressed concern about North Korea's ability and willingness to export nuclear materials and technology.[20]

Earning hard currency is not the only reason North Korea may decide to sell its nuclear technology; revenge is another. At least twice, Pyongyang has threatened to sell or transfer nuclear weapons or technology in response to perceived U.S. slights. In April 2003 in Beijing, a North Korean foreign ministry official warned a U.S. State Department official that the country could "export nuclear weapons."[21] Two years later, Pyongyang relayed a message through a U.S. academic that "it could transfer nuclear weapons to terrorists if driven into a corner."[22] The Libyan experience illustrates that sanctions may push the DPRK into selling nuclear weapons or technology; as Malfrid Braut-Hegghammer notes, sanctions against Libya increased its isolation, which made it difficult for Tripoli to chart a more cooperative path, as well as radicalized their nuclear decisionmaking.[23] In addition, North Korea may have issued a veiled threat in 2004: at the Six Party Talks, North Korea offered to include "a ban on nuclear transfers in its nuclear freeze proposal."[24] The implied warning was that if the North Korean proposal was not accepted, the country may begin engaging in nuclear transfers.

As North Korea creates a more sophisticated arsenal, it will feel more willing to sell its nuclear technology or even weapons.[25] The motive need not be simply economics or revenge: in the case of North Korea, they are not mutually exclusive. A study of transfers of sensitive nuclear technology noted, "States are unlikely to pursue economic gains when the result undermines their own security. States may still seek economic benefits when they export sensitive nuclear technology, but they are only likely to do so when such behavior is consistent with underlying strategic conditions."[26] Countries that are most interested in illicit nuclear technology and that would be willing to conduct trade with North Korea against UN sanctions are countries unlikely to undermine Pyongyang's strategic goals.

Technical Assistance and Aid

Even if North Korea does not sell or otherwise transfer nuclear weapons to state or non-state parties, it could still destabilize the nuclear nonproliferation regime by providing technical assistance and aid to countries interested in developing nuclear weapons. Should the country successfully create operational nuclear weapons, its assistance may be in greater demand. North Korea has already shown its willingness to covertly assist countries with nuclear technology. I address two of those cases here: Syria and Myanmar/Burma.

Pyongyang's assistance to Syria's covert nuclear program began in the late

1990s, if not before, and continued until the Israeli strike of the Syrian reactor at Al Kibar in 2007.[27] In fact, U.S. intelligence officials believe that North Korean officials helped the Syrians with damage assessment and possible cover-up after the attack.[28] Damascus claimed that the facility was an "unused military building" under construction with no help from North Korea, and with no connection to a nuclear reactor.[29] However, evidence indicates otherwise:

> The images include shots taken inside what appears to be a reactor—with a grid of cylinders for control rods and refueling ports that are arrayed almost identically to those found at [the North Korean facility at] Yongbyon. Photos from outside the facility show a structure with similar roof lines, rows of windows and boxlike buildings matching the layout at Yongbyon. The dossier distributed by the [U.S.] administration describes the facility as a gas-cooled, graphite-moderated reactor that was not configured to produce electricity and was ill-suited for research. A senior European diplomat said Western intelligence services compared notes months ago and concluded that the site was a nuclear facility built with North Korean help.[30]

Although some experts have expressed skepticism that the Al Kibar facility was meant for producing weapons-grade nuclear material, few doubt that Pyongyang provided material assistance with the covert project. While North Korea was not providing a turnkey facility, they did give "design and engineering assistance, the probable supply of reactor components, and assistance in procuring items illicitly from other countries."[31] North Korea's motivation for assisting the Syrians is uncertain, because as noted earlier, ideology and economics are both enhanced by the transfers. North Korean assistance with nuclear technology to Syria is clear-cut.

The second possible case of North Korean technological aid is much more opaque: Myanmar/Burma. The DPRK and Myanmar/Burma restored formal relations in 2007, and military cooperation since then has grown extensively between the two countries. While no smoking gun exists, numerous indicators point to potential cooperation on nuclear technology. North Korean officials connected to the Syrian reactor have been sighted in Myanmar/Burma, and Japan discovered a plot to illegally export dual-use equipment to Myanmar/Burma "under the direction of a company involved in the illicit procurement for North Korean military programs."[32] Senior Myanmar/Burmese officials were suspected of secretly visiting North Korea in late 2008.[33] In addition, Pyongyang has provided technical assistance in building an extensive complex of underground facilities and six hundred to eight hundred tunnels outside Myanmar/

Burma's capital—facilities that may be linked to nuclear technology. Finally, a North Korean freighter believed to be headed to Myanmar/Burma returned to the DPRK after being shadowed by a U.S. Navy ship. South Korean intelligence believes the ship was carrying equipment related to a covert nuclear program.[34]

Members of the NPT, Myanmar/Burma, and Russia announced plans in 2001 for a ten-megawatt light water reactor for Myanmar/Burma and signed the contract in 2007, although the status of the project is unclear at present.[35] However, defectors from Myanmar/Burma claim that serious work on a secret military program is progressing with substantial help from North Korea.[36] While some have expressed skepticism regarding the defectors' assertions, Desmond Ball notes that two key detectors—unknown to each other, as far as can be ascertained—have corroborated the main pieces of the claims, which adds credibility to their story.[37] Reports indicate that the U.S. government also received information in 2006 indicating cooperation on nuclear weapons between the two countries.[38] Again, the question arises: Why would North Korea provide nuclear technical assistance to Myanmar/Burma? Up until the 2012 elections in Myanmar/Burma, the two countries shared an isolationist approach and an anti-Western philosophy, and despite sanctions against Myanmar/Burma, the authoritarian government controlled oil revenues. Thus, while the country's economy suffered from domestic corruption and international sanctions, the military dictatorship could likely divert enough money to pay for nuclear assistance.[39] For North Korea, it would be a win-win situation: hard currency and potentially oil from an anti-Western neighbor.

Recent political and economic liberalization in Myanmar/Burma make it less likely that the country would continue illicit nuclear weapons cooperation with North Korea (if indeed, such cooperation ever existed). However, the military still controls approximately 25% of the country's budget without oversight, and ongoing defense cooperation with North Korea continues to raise concerns.[40] While the country declared that it has ended all nuclear power programs, it refuses to sign the Additional Protocol (which would allow for increased inspection) and has turned down suggestions that inspections could verify that the country does not now have a nuclear weapons program.[41] Nevertheless, as the regime slowly opens to the outside world, the likelihood of nuclear weapons cooperation with North Korea decreases.

If the DPRK successfully creates an operational nuclear force, it will likely increase the amount of direct assistance the country provides to others. First, it will magnify North Korea's ability to provide assistance; its own experiences enable it to share lessons learned with other actors. In addition, successful operationalization would increase Pyongyang's credibility, in terms of both technical ability and anti-Western political skill. If UN sanctions are applied, the country could increase its marketing efforts in an attempt to make up for economic losses. While some countries may be less likely to do business with North Korea because of its rogue status (especially with UN sanctions applied), the sorts of countries seeking nuclear weapons or technology may not be deterred by such a stigma. In particular, Pyongyang would likely find a bigger customer base for nuclear technical assistance rather than for actual weapons. Libya purchased nuclear equipment from the A. Q. Khan network, but because of a lack of technical expertise, much of the equipment sat unpacked in boxes.[42] Countries that do not need technical assistance with a nuclear program are not the type to buy actual weapons or technology; they can develop it themselves. However, while states interested in North Korea's help may be more interested in technical assistance as opposed to turnkey systems or actual weapons, terrorist groups that are only interested in detonating a nuclear weapon (or threatening to do so) would likely favor the latter. Thus, both types of direct effects must be considered should the DPRK create operational nuclear weapons.

INDIRECT EFFECTS: LESSONS LEARNED

What type of indirect effects beyond East Asia might be seen if North Korea successfully operationalizes its nuclear weapons? Indirect effects—that is, effects that influence nuclear decisionmaking in other potential proliferants—are much more sensitive to the international community's reaction to the DPRK's actions. Direct effects are unlikely to be impacted a great deal by the international reaction to North Korea's creation of operational nuclear weapons, with a few exceptions as noted above. However, indirect effects are directly linked to the international community's response. If strong multilateral measures are implemented, not just announced, then other potential proliferants would likely become more cautious. Even severe unilateral actions from the United States would send a message that nuclear proliferation would more likely decrease one's security than enhance it. Indeed, any direct, effective punitive action taken against the North would raise uncertainty for those considering their own nuclear program: to what extent would that nuclear program make them a target? Social psychology research has shown that under uncertain conditions, actors are more likely to adhere to group norms.[43] In this case, potential proliferants may decide to abide by the nonproliferation norm and slow down or stop their nuclear programs.

However, direct, effective action—unilateral or multilateral—is unlikely in the case of North Korea operationalizing its nuclear forces, as noted earlier. More likely, a global response to North Korea's operationalization of its nuclear stocks would be ineffective: action from parties such as Japan and the United States are unlikely to work, given their lack of engagement with the regime already, while parties that can influence North Korea—especially China—are unlikely to implement sanctions or take direct unilateral action. In this case, the ripple effects are much stronger and more potentially damaging to the international nonproliferation regime. In particular, North Korea's possession of operational nuclear weapons would likely offer three lessons learned for nuclear aspirants, Iran in particular.

Lesson One: "Unacceptable" Is Meaningless

North Korea has been warned multiple times that its nuclear program—from the plutonium production plant at Yongbyon to missile testing to nuclear tests—is "unacceptable."[44] Even as late as May 2009, when North Korea conducted its second nuclear test, U.S. secretary of defense Robert Gates warned that "the U.S. would not tolerate a nuclear North Korea."[45] However, North Korea has not faced any significant penalties; follow-through on these threats (which started in the 1990s when Pyongyang threatened to withdraw from the NPT) has been minimal.[46] As former U.S. diplomat Mitchell Reiss noted, "North Korea has paid virtually no price for its intransigence."[47] The lesson for Tehran is clear-cut: "North Korea has refused to halt enrichment and reprocessing activities without significant penalty; this cannot help but strengthen Iran's belief that it too can defy the world. North Korea has also enlarged its nuclear arsenal against international protest, again without paying a meaningful price. . . . It should be no surprise that Tehran increasingly doubts the international community's resolve."[48]

Should North Korea marry its nuclear weapons to a missile-based delivery system—without significant repercussions—the credibility of the international community's commitment to nuclear nonproliferation would be even further eroded. If North Korea pays little to no price for creating a nuclear weapons program, testing nuclear weapons, and then miniaturizing them for missiles, Iran and other potential proliferants would be emboldened in their own pursuit of a nuclear capability, especially because Iran (and likely other potential proliferants) has declared its program peaceful, unlike the North Koreans. It will be hard for the international community to justify sharp action against Tehran or others when they can claim they are merely seeking the complete fuel cycle for domestic energy purposes, given that North Korea was allowed to openly create and possibly operationalize its nuclear stocks. As one analyst noted, "They can legitimately point to the fact that in comparison to North Korea, their behavior has been upstanding."[49]

Lesson Two: A Nuclear Weapons Program Can Strengthen Your Domestic Position

A number of IR scholars have argued that domestic political reasons can shape a country's nuclear decisionmaking.[50] North Korea is a case study in how nuclear weapons can ensure a regime's domestic survival. After the death of the DPRK's founder Kim Il-sung, his son and successor Kim Jong-il faced numerous challenges to his authority. At least two coup attempts were reported, and numerous high-level defections took place.[51] Kim Jong-il did not consolidate power until 1997, three years after his father's death, and even then many analyses suggest significant insecurity in his position given his relative lack of experience when compared to his father.[52] Analysts agree that the nuclear program has been used to shore up Kim Jong-il's position domestically, particularly with the military: "When Kim Jong-il came to power after his father's death in 1994, there were many doubts that he would be accepted, especially by hardliners in the military. Given the DPRK's economic problems since Kim Jong-il came to power, there have been doubts regarding his leadership and his control of the military. The acquisition of nuclear weapons helps to bolster his position among the military and, in North Koreans' eyes, elevates the DPRK's prestige as a major player in Northeast Asia."[53] Within North Korea, credit for spearheading the nuclear weapons program went to Kim Jong-il, and he continued to use the nuclear weapons program to bolster his position domestically.[54] Inheriting his father's political position did not mean he also inherited the political authority that his father wielded, however. Indeed, because of the severe economic crises that the country faced during his rule, Kim Jong-il had to look elsewhere for sources of political legitimacy. He did this in large part through the development of nuclear weapons and ballistic missiles, along with the confrontation with the United States that these programs created. By defying the international community, Kim Jong-il was able to stir nationalist sentiment in his favor, as well as strengthen his support among hard-liners in the military, whom some call his most important constituency.[55] North Korea's nuclear test in May 2009 has been interpreted as a means to strengthen Kim Jong-il's appointment of his son, Kim Jong-un, as his successor.[56] Operationalization of the DPRK's nuclear weapons, so that Pyongyang could strike the United States, would add additional credibility to the dynasty, something Kim Jong-un needs no less than his father. In fact, given his youth, the third Kim in the dynastic succession may need the credibility nuclear weapons can bring even more than his father did.

The internal legitimacy that a nuclear weapons program can provide may be tempting to a number of potential proliferators. With its turmoil over rigged elections in June 2009 Iran is a prime case.[57] Domestic politics have long driven Iranian nuclear policy, but the promise of using the nuclear program for domestic political authority is especially potent of late. For example, in October 2009 Tehran tentatively accepted a deal in which it would send most of its low-enriched uranium for further enrichment and then processing into fuel rods in Russia and France, respectively. However, even notable Iranian reformers— including Mir Hussein Moussavi, who lost the June 2009 election against Mahmoud Ahmadinejad under suspicious circumstances—assailed Ahmadinejad for capitulating to Western powers on Iran's sovereign right to nuclear technology. Ironically, this tactic, designed to undermine the regime's legitimacy, forced Ahmadinejad to back down on Tehran's agreement to the proposal. As of October 2012 the West and Iran are still at a stalemate on the issue. As is apparently the case in Pyongyang, nuclear politics have clearly become linked to political credibility in Iran, especially given its anticolonialism, anti-West posture.[58] Elites who compromise on the nuclear issue are now painted as traitors, whereas elites who exercise Iran's "rights" gain status.

Egypt is another country in which political elites may be interested in the political benefits of pursuing a nuclear program. Under Mubarak, Cairo had been a strong supporter of the NPT, taking an active leadership role in the United Nations on the issue; a combination of succession politics and bitterness over the Israeli refusal to give up its nuclear weapons has stirred change in the country.[59] During Mubarak's tenure, the Muslim Brotherhood had for years pilloried his regime for its failure to balance Israel's nuclear weapons. With Mubarak's overthrow and the election of Muslim Brotherhood leader Mohammed Morsi, Egypt's nuclear future is now uncertain. The Muslim Brotherhood is on record as supporting acquisition of nuclear weapons; for example, Hamdi Hassan, the spokesman for the Muslim Brotherhood parliamentary caucus, said in July 2006, "We are ready to starve in order to own a nuclear weapon that will represent a real deterrent and will be decisive in the Arab-Israeli conflict."[60] Morsi has declared that Egypt will uphold its commitments to treaties, which presumably includes the NPT. The new regime is continuing the nuclear power program started by Mubarak in 2006, pressing ahead with plans for up to six reactors at Dabaa.[61] Even under Mubarak, Egyptian officials stated that they intend to seek the full nuclear fuel cycle, which could give them access to enriched fissile material for nuclear weapons.[62] Given Morsi's assertiveness in other areas of foreign policy, one can expect that he would also endorse Egypt's right to the full nuclear fuel cycle. With the decrepit Egyptian economy and the current regime's problems with Sinai militants, the internal legitimacy conferred by pursuing a military nuclear capability could be tempting to the Muslim Brotherhood—on top of its previously indicated interest.

How would North Korean operationalization of their nuclear stocks influence decisionmaking in Iran, Egypt, or other states? The North Korean example shows that committed pursuit of a military nuclear capability can lead not only to operational nuclear weapons but also regime survival—and, in fact, a strengthened regime more resistant to domestic opposition. Such a lesson may have a profound impact on the thinking of moderates and hard-liners in Iran, where nuclear politics have become synonymous with the defense of Iran against the colonialist West. Given how close Iran is to nuclear weapons—some estimate less than a year away from a bomb[63]—DPRK success could give Tehran inspiration for the final push to finish the job. One thing seems certain: International acquiescence to operationalization of the DPRK's nuclear weapons would only encourage these and other potential proliferants.

Lesson Three: Nuclear Weapons Do Deter

For decades, Pyongyang has worried about U.S. intentions. With no formal peace treaty between the two countries after the end of the Korean War, as well as U.S. troops stationed in both South Korea and Japan, the DPRK's insecurity is both palpable and understandable. Analysis based on archival research from Soviet-bloc allies indicates that the "core motivation behind Pyongyang's nuclear saber-rattling [is] regime survival."[64] The end of the Cold War dramatically deepened this sense of vulnerability as Russia declared it would no longer provide security guarantees to North Korea, and China—undergoing capitalist reforms—no longer provided its previously unconditional support. Thus, Pyongyang had to find a way to secure itself; "In a period of three years between 1989 and 1992, the world, as Pyongyang knew it since 1948, changed beyond recognition. Such changes dictated some form of self-help security solution beyond relying on allies."[65] That the North Korean nuclear weapons program intensified during this period is no surprise.

After George W. Bush declared Iran, Iraq, and North Korea as part of the "axis of evil," and then invaded Iraq a year later, some argue the message to potential proliferators became clear. "Many analysts contend that Iran has learned an important lesson from the two other states: Without nuclear weapons, you will be attacked (Iraq), but with them, you will be untouchable (North Korea)."[66] However, this lesson is not directly transferable to Iran, because simply having nuclear weapons—without any practical means of delivery—is not enough for deterrence and may indeed provoke a preemptive strike.[67] Additionally and importantly, Pyongyang has more than nuclear weapons; it has the ability to strike Seoul with conventional weapons, as well as the probable ability to attack U.S. forces in South Korea and Japan with conventionally armed missiles. In addition, all of the major actors in the North Korean nuclear crisis opposed use of force against the DPRK, including U.S. allies Japan and South Korea, and the other Six Party Talks interlocutors, China and Russia. While Iran can unleash Hezbollah in the Middle East, Tehran is far more limited in its ability to attack the United States directly, and it does not have the ability to hurt the United States or its allies that Pyongyang does, speaking of South Korea in particular. Threatening Israel is also difficult, given Israel's ability and potential willingness to launch an immediate conventional or even nuclear response. Thus, one could argue that Iran has an even greater motivation than North Korea to acquire nuclear weapons to ensure effective deterrence against Israel, the United States, and other perceived enemies. For this reason, North Korea making its nuclear stocks operational could be a tremendous motivator for Iran to work even harder to accomplish the same goal.

AN EMBOLDENED IRAN?

If the DPRK creates operational nuclear weapons without serious consequences from the international community, the most likely and immediate ripple effect would be an emboldened Iran. Consequently, we may see two additional, negative trends: (1) deepened nuclear cooperation between North Korea and Iran and (2) a new ripple effect in the Middle East.

Pyongyang-Tehran Nuclear Cooperation

Direct and indirect effects may combine should North Korea pay little or nothing politically for operationalizing its nuclear stocks; an emboldened Iran may purchase nuclear technology directly from North Korea. Pyongyang and Tehran already trade extensively in missile technology: "Iran's ballistic missile program relies very heavily on North Korean components. . . . Three of its four known missile systems have flight characteristics essentially identical to those of North Korean missiles."[68] In terms of nuclear trade, while some experts are concerned about the possibility, others argue that Iran wants to establish indigenous capability and thus would be unlikely to purchase nuclear technology from North Korea.[69] However, nuclear cooperation may be more likely; for example, Iranian experts reportedly attended the first North Korean nuclear test.[70] Since North Korea is now working on uranium enrichment, it may be willing to share weaponization and even operationalization knowledge with Iran in exchange for assistance with uranium enrichment. Because their missiles are so similar, if North Korea can create and miniaturize a uranium-based bomb, that information could be quite valuable to Iran. (Currently, North Korea's nuclear stocks are plutonium-based, while Iran is only known to have uranium enrichment capabilities.) If Pyongyang creates operational nuclear weapons, several factors combine to make nuclear cooperation with Iran more likely, including a bolder and more eager Iran, a cash-poor DPRK, and the possibility of the two countries learning what they need from each other.

Ripple Effects in the Middle East

An emboldened Iran, possibly with nuclear ties with North Korea, may create its own, much larger set of ripple effects. If Iran is able to create and test a nuclear weapon, the prospects for a nuclear arms race will increase significantly. Iran's nuclear efforts have set off nuclear power programs in several Middle Eastern countries, including Saudi Arabia, Egypt, and Jordan.[71] The six member states of the Gulf Cooperation Council have agreed to study the feasibility of nuclear power in their countries. Turkey has also shown a renewed interest in nuclear power. While all of these countries have expressly stated that they are pursuing peaceful civilian nuclear technology, and all are working with the International Atomic Energy Agency in accordance with their NPT obligations, whether all would exclude nuclear weapons if Iran goes nuclear is not clear. As one Middle Eastern expert stated, "The Iranians have left us no option, so this is our answer to them. Arabs have no choice but to start a program under a civilian banner. You need to build the know-how, and know-how always starts with a civilian program."[72] Iran's neighbors respond this way not because they fear an Iranian nuclear attack, but rather because they resent Iran's attempt to become the regional hegemon (especially as a Persian state in an Arab region). For example, Cairo does not want to be displaced by Tehran as the lead negotiator with Israel; if this occurred, Egypt would lose regional status, which it is loathe to do.[73] Saudi Arabia is concerned for a number of reasons, including the possibility of increased Shia activism on the part of Tehran, and others in the region are worried about an excessive reaction from Riyadh.[74] Further, a nuclear Iran is likely to provoke a military response from Israel, which could lead to hardening of positions all across the region. The chain reaction—from a nuclear-operational North Korea to an emboldened nuclear Iran to nuclear reactions across the Middle East—is a long shot but unfortunately possible.

A WEAKENED NPT?

Should North Korea create a fully operational nuclear weapons system, what is the impact to the nuclear nonproliferation regime? By itself, such an achievement by North Korea is not likely to undermine the NPT. The damage done to the NPT was done when the country successfully tested a nuclear weapon; North Korea became the first NPT member country to withdraw and then explode a nuclear device.

However, the ripple effects from North Korean operationalization of nuclear weapons could seriously damage the nuclear nonproliferation regime in several ways. First, in terms of regional implications, Japan's confidence in the U.S. security guarantee may be weakened. As one former senior Japanese official said, "North Korea will eventually be able to reach the U.S. with nuclear weapons. Then the U.S. umbrella will not be trustworthy, some argue, and thus Japan should develop its own nuclear weapons."[75] While not all agree with this sentiment, concern exists in Japan about the reduced credibility of U.S. extended deterrence if North Korea can reach the United States with nuclear weapons. While a Japanese nuclear response is unlikely, it could occur.[76] Japan's creation of its own military nuclear capability would seriously undermine the NPT. Not only does Japan provide financial and technical support for the regime, it also serves as a moral bellwether; if the only country to suffer an atomic attack decides to go nuclear, other states may wonder what remains of the regime.[77]

Serious repercussions for the nuclear nonproliferation regime could also occur if either the direct or indirect effects I outlined earlier take place. If North Korea sells weapons or technology to other actors, it would undermine the regime's export controls intended to limit the sale of dual-use items that can be used for military nuclear capability, much the way the A. Q. Khan network did. Even if these importing countries do not immediately develop nuclear weapons, illegal nuclear exports may shake confidence in the voluntary export control system. If indirect effects materialize from North Korea's successful weaponization—for example, Iran becomes emboldened in its quest for nuclear weapons—the nuclear nonproliferation regime will face even more challenges. If a nuclear arms race develops in the Middle East, as discussed earlier, many will wonder if the NPT is no longer able to contain proliferation. Perceptions can create reality if state elites rush for nuclear technology because they don't want to be left behind. Iran's acquiring nuclear weapons and joining North Korea in exporting nuclear materials and technology could be the death knell of the export control system as well as the NPT.

A NEW NARRATIVE?

Perhaps the most important ripple effect of successful North Korean operationalization is the inspiration it may provide other potential proliferators. Abandoned by its allies, led by a weak successor facing coup attempts, and economically devastated by crop failures and command-economy management, North Korea persevered. To continue its nuclear program, Pyongyang had to confront multilateral diplomatic and economic pressure to abandon its efforts, yet the country managed to outwit and outplay all of its opponents. In particular, Kim Jong-il managed to resist coercion from the system's two largest powers: the United States (its enemy) and China (its friend). North Korea is the little engine that could and did. If the DPRK succeeds in creating operational nuclear weapons systems, it will have generated a new David-and-Goliath narrative, which may be quite compelling to those who also dislike the world's Goliath. Above and beyond specific lessons learned, the gripping story of North Korea overcoming all the odds and creating operational nuclear forces in full defiance of the international community—and the precedents this may set—may be for other nuclear aspirants the most appealing—and for the IAEA, the NPT, and international peace and security, the most destabilizing—ripple effects of all.

CHAPTER ELEVEN

DPRK Nuclear Challenges and the Politics of Nonproliferation

JING-DONG YUAN

North Korea's nuclear weapons program poses a serious threat to regional security and gravely undermines the international nuclear nonproliferation regime. The Six Party Talks, the multilateral process aimed at defusing and then disarming the DPRK nuclear weapons programs, achieved only partial success in getting Pyongyang to begin dismantling its nuclear facilities but largely stalled after North Korea's second nuclear test in May 2009. Will the continued impasse threaten to unravel the Nuclear Non-Proliferation Treaty (NPT), or is there a way out and the much-feared nuclear domino effect in East Asia might be avoided?

Since the second North Korean nuclear crisis broke out in late 2002, a final solution to the problem came tantalizingly close on several occasions, in particular during 2007–8, but has yet to be achieved. The prospects for resolving the issue appear dimmer still after Pyongyang conducted its second and third nuclear tests in 2009 and 2013 and the United Nations imposed Security Council resolutions and attendant sanctions on North Korea. Concerns are growing that a continued impasse could further erode the nonproliferation regime and, worse still, threaten its very survival should a nuclear domino effect in the region ensue, in addition to suspected and expanding North Korean transfers of nuclear materials and technologies to third parties.

From the very beginning—after it was revealed in 2002 that Pyongyang had been engaged in a covert uranium enrichment program, and ever since (and despite) Pyongyang's withdrawal from the NPT in early 2003—the broad international consensus was that the Korean Peninsula must remain denuclearized. Multilateral efforts have been undertaken that work toward that goal.[1] The Six-Party Talks, including China, Japan, North Korea, Russia, South Korea, and the United States, became a critical mechanism for managing and defusing the North Korean nuclear crisis and bringing about North Korean pledges to dismantle its nuclear weapons program, and even the voluntary destruction of the cooling towers at its Yongbyon facility in 2008. Six rounds of negotiation were conducted during this period, and the September 2005 joint statement and the February 2007 joint action plan brought the process closer than ever to nuclear disablement.[2]

While there was and continues to be a consensus on keeping the Korean Peninsula nuclear free, achieving that goal has not been easy due to differences among the key players over strategies, priorities, and formats of negotiation.[3] The issue before us is whether the absence of significant progress in disarming North Korea's nuclear weapons program and the lack of effective international responses to Pyongyang's continued provocation and intransigence could spell the end of the NPT as we know it. Clearly, Pyongyang's violation of Article II (in which non-nuclear-weapon states pledge not to acquire nuclear weapons) and its withdrawal from the treaty using Article X (right to withdraw for member states) without incurring punitive measures raises serious questions about the NPT and its role in nuclear nonproliferation. In this chapter I examine the potential fallout and resilience of the nonproliferation regime in the face of such grave challenges. In addition, I also look into the Six-Party Talks and suggest that the multilateral process offers unique insights into the complexity of persuading Pyongyang to give up its nuclear weapons program without triggering military confrontation on the one hand and appearing to appease the North Korean regime on the other. In the end, the most effective strategy is one that is well coordinated—with clear priorities and the right combination of incentives and sanctions—and that deals with the causes of nuclear proliferation as much as it confronts and handles its symptoms.

THE SIX-PARTY TALKS: PROMISES AND PITFALLS

North Korea's nuclear program dates back to the 1960s with assistance from the Soviet Union.[4] In 1985 Pyongyang signed the NPT, but not until January 1992 did it sign a safeguards agreement with the International Atomic Energy Agency (IAEA), which obligated North Korea to allow inspections. Subsequent IAEA inspections raised suspicions about a covert North Korean nuclear weapons program. A crisis ensued with the North threatening to withdraw from the NPT and the Clinton administration contemplating possible military actions. The October 1994 U.S.-DPRK Agreed Framework, which froze North Korea's plutonium-based nuclear program, temporarily headed off further escalation and brought the crisis under control. The implementation of the Agreed Framework, which included providing two light water reactors to North Korea, encountered various political, financial, and technical obstacles. By the time President George W. Bush came into office in 2001, the agreement was in limbo and the administration was determined to take a very different approach to dealing with North Korea than the Clinton administration took. In October 2002 the Bush administration confronted North Korea, charging that it had been engaged in a covert uranium enrichment program. After admitting to the program (this admission was later retracted, and in 2010 the program was admitted to again), Pyongyang kicked out the IAEA inspectors, withdrew from the NPT, reactivated the Yongbyon reactor, and began reprocessing plutonium. The Agreed Framework collapsed, and the second nuclear crisis began.[5]

While the international community was by and large in agreement that the Korean Peninsula should remain free of nuclear weapons, there was no consensus on how to get there. The community of nations was also confronted with a most serious challenge: never had a member state withdrawn from the NPT.[6] The Bush administration was adamant that Pyongyang should not be rewarded for its bad behavior; if anything, it should suffer the consequences of violating the norms and rules of the international nuclear nonproliferation regime. For these reasons, Washington steadfastly refused to engage in any bilateral negotiations with the North and demanded that Pyongyang first give up its nuclear program. China, however, stated its positions on the issue as follows: (1) peace and stability on the Korean Peninsula should be preserved, (2) the peninsula should remain nuclear-free, and (3) the dispute should be resolved through direct diplomatic dialogue between the United States and the Democratic People's Republic of Korea (DPRK).[7]

The Bush administration's hawkish position, including the threat of preemptive strikes, did not deter Pyongyang from adopting equally hard-line positions. Vice President Dick Cheney reportedly remarked, "We don't negotiate with evil, we defeat it."[8] Indeed, the U.S. invasion of Iraq in April 2003 only made North Korea more determined to acquire nuclear weapons capabilities, concerned that it would be the next target of regime change.[9] To prevent further escalation, Beijing shifted its position from detached onlooker to more of an engaged party. The Chinese began to exert pressure on North Korea as well as to seek to persuade Washington to show flexibility and greater realism about the situation. Chinese frustration with the North Koreans came to a boiling point when, in a rare move, Beijing cut off oil supplies to North Korea for three days in a row in late March 2003, claiming technical problems.[10] Beijing also indicated to Pyongyang that it would only guarantee its security if it met three conditions: no nukes, no threats to South Korea and Japan, and direct dialogue with the United States.[11] The first trilateral meeting between China, North Korea, and the United States was subsequently held in Beijing in April 2003.

Beijing initiated the Six Party Talks in August 2003. The Bush administration continued to refuse engaging in bilateral negotiation with North Korea, insisting that the nuclear issue was a multilateral one and therefore requiring all the affected parties to be involved, such that any negotiated outcome would then make Pyongyang accountable not just to Washington but to all participating parties.[12] As the host of the talks, Beijing laid out its new positions as follows: (1) denuclearization, (2) peninsular peace and stability, (3) dialogue and peaceful resolution of disputes, and (4) fairly addressing all parties' concerns.[13]

The multilateral process did not prove to be smooth sailing due to the huge gap between the DPRK and the United States regarding the nature and scope of the problem, approaches, sequence, and deep mistrust between the two countries, which technically remain at war.[14] At the same time, the other participants had different agendas and priorities, and the apparent lack of close coordination and agreement among the other five parties allowed Pyongyang to exploit these differences and get the concessions it sought, without committing itself to a final resolution of the issue.[15] Consequently, while there had occasionally been welcome developments that moved the negotiation toward achieving peninsular denuclearization, reconciliation, and permanent peace, the road to that final destination has proven bumpy. While the September 19, 2005, joint statement and the February 13, 2007, action plan were major achievements in the multilateral process, several significant challenges soon became apparent even before specific implementation procedures could begin, and they remain to be resolved.[16] The September 19, 2005, joint statement committed North Korea to "abandon all nuclear weapons and existing nuclear programs, and to return at an early date to the Treaty on the Non-proliferation of Nuclear Weapons and to IAEA safeguards."[17] The statement also addressed issues of establishing working groups on negotiations leading to diplomatic recognition and providing energy assistance to North Korea. The February 2007 action plan laid out plans for denuclearization and established five working groups to implement the joint statement. However, in trying to reach broad agreements, many specifics and details were deliberately left out,[18] one example being the contentious issue of the full declaration of all North Korea's nuclear programs, including its highly enriched uranium (HEU) program.

Second, the precise definition of "disablement" and the proper mechanism to verify North Korea's declarations to the IAEA would still need to be resolved before the final phase of the dismantlement process. Washington wanted to make sure that after disablement and prior to dismantlement of North Korea's known nuclear facilities, it would be difficult for Pyongyang to restart the program, as it did in early 2003 with the reprocessing of the spent fuel and reactivation of the five-megawatt graphite reactor, leading to the production of about six to eight nuclear weapons worth of fissile materials.[19]

Third, after the October 2006 nuclear test, the Bush administration redrew the red line promising strong U.S. responses should North Korea transfer nuclear materials, technology, and know-how to other countries.[20] Indeed, reports soon emerged about suspected North Korean nuclear transfers to Syria. The subsequent Israeli attack in September 2007 only intensified the speculation.[21] Preventing North Korea's nuclear exports would require more active measures of dissuasion and deterrence, such as the Proliferation Security Initiative (PSI). However, not all the parties have endorsed PSI due to its dubious legal status and implications for free navigation.[22] Critics questioned the Bush administration's North Korea policy, some congressional Republicans demanding an explanation of the Syria episode.[23] Had Pyongyang crossed the red line already, how should the administration react, what actions should be taken, and more important, what credibility was there in any North Korean commitment?[24]

North Korea conducted its second nuclear weapons test on May 25, 2009. The test came as no real surprise to most analysts; North Korea had threatened to resume its nuclear program—including tests—after the UN Security Council (UNSC) formally criticized the DPRK's April 2009 ballistic missile test as a violation of UNSC Resolution 1718.[25] That resolution, passed in the wake of the first North Korean nuclear test in 2006, had, among other moves, called on the suspension of all DPRK ballistic missile activities. What was surprising was Pyongyang's rebuff of the Obama administration's willingness for engagement. In announcing the test, North Korea's Korean Central News Agency (KCNA) noted that the DPRK had carried out a nuclear test that "was safely conducted on a new higher level in terms of its explosive power and technology of its control." The test would, according to the KCNA, "contribute to safeguarding our sovereignty and socialism and guaranteeing peace and safety on the Korean peninsula and the surrounding region."[26]

On June 12, 2009, the UNSC unanimously adopted Resolution 1874, which further tightens existing arms embargos against North Korea and increases the financial restrictions imposed on Pyongyang. Most notably the new resolution has created a legal basis for countries to interdict North Korean ships at sea suspected of items banned by this and other resolutions. According to the resolution, the May 25 test was conducted in "violation and flagrant disregard" of earlier UNSC resolutions, namely 1695 and 1718, both passed in 2006 after North Korea carried out ballistic missile and nuclear tests. UNSC Resolution 1874 also demanded that North Korea "not conduct any further nuclear test or any launch using ballistic missile technology."[27] The firm response of the UN states, as well as the other members of the Six Party Talks, to North Korea's second test put Pyongyang on the defensive, and it vowed to continue to move forward with its nuclearization. In November 2010 North Korea revealed to the outside world its uranium enrichment program, which it had long denied having. A newly constructed, modern, two-thousand-centrifuge uranium enrichment plant was built in Yongbyon to supply low enriched uranium (LEU) to feed a light water reactor under construction. Whether the program is for civilian use or for generating electricity as Pyongyang claims remains to be seen, but the dual-use nature of nuclear technology means North Korea could use it to gain the ability and materials to develop nuclear weapons.[28] While a Leap Day agreement between Pyongyang and Washington was announced on February 29, 2012, that would have North Korea cease uranium enrichment and missile tests and allow the return of IAEA inspectors in return for U.S. aid, it soon fell apart with the continuation of North Korean missile tests in April and December of 2012. Pyongyang's third nuclear test in February 2013 brought relations between North Korea and the other parties to the Six Party Talks to a new low.

COMBATING WMD PROLIFERATION:
PRIORITIES, POLITICS, AND POLICIES

The North Korean nuclear crisis and the continued impasse raise serious questions about the NPT's integrity and effectiveness. Should Pyongyang be allowed to retain its nuclear weapons, and as North Korea develops long-range ballistic missile capabilities, the growing threats that these pose not only to the United States but more imminently to its neighbors from Japan to South Korea could revive the specter of a nuclear domino in the region. These developments, coupled with North Korea's proliferation activities and the international community's ongoing tussle with Iran over its nuclear program, according to some analysts, could very much spell the end of the NPT as we know it.[29]

The North Korean nuclear crisis and the multilateral efforts to find a solution also offer a number of important lessons and indicate the challenges ahead for WMD nonproliferation at the regional and global levels. To begin with, the North Korean nuclear issue is not only a proliferation challenge but also a regional security issue that requires a comprehensive solution. Consequently, dealing with symptoms alone is never sufficient, even as it is necessary as an initial step and a matter of principle. Addressing the causes of proliferation leads to broader approaches that take into consideration such critical variables as security concerns, prestige, and national identity. Second, effective strategies require realistic targets, priorities, and good coordination, which are especially critical given the different preferences, threat perceptions, and national interests of the participating parties. Third, the allure of incentives and rewards are just as important as privation and threats of punishments.[30]

The End of the NPT?

There have been growing concerns in recent years that the international nuclear nonproliferation regime, of which the 1968 Treaty for the Nonproliferation of Nuclear Weapons (NPT) remains the core, is under significant strain given the major setbacks displayed by the 1998 Indian and Pakistani nuclear tests, North Korea's withdrawal from the NPT (2003) and its three nuclear tests (2006, 2009, and 2013), and suspicions surrounding Iran's nuclear program. In addition, what are broadly perceived by non-nuclear-weapon states as the lack of progress in nuclear disarmament, lack of progress in the entry into force of the Comprehensive Test Ban Treaty (CTBT), the continued absence of work on negotiations toward a Fissile Material Cutoff Treaty (FMCT),[31] and the failure of the 2005 NPT Review Conference all raise concerns about the survival and continuing viability of the nonproliferation regime as we know it.[32]

Within such contexts, the North Korean nuclear weapons program not only threatens regional peace and stability but poses a serious threat to the nonproliferation regime in two significant ways. First, North Korea's withdrawal from the NPT in 2003 has gone unpunished, raising serious questions about the treaty's ability to deal with noncompliance and walkout issues. Second, Pyongyang's suspected proliferation activities further erode the international community's efforts in stemming nuclear proliferation.[33] In the regional context, questions have been raised whether North Korean nuclear weapons and missile programs could trigger responses from Japan and South Korea. Both countries in the past have seriously considered the nuclear option, and it has largely been renewed U.S. defense commitments as well as pressure that have dissuaded Tokyo and Seoul from walking down the nuclear path.[34] Confidence in U.S. extended deterrence could be eroded, however, if and as North Korea continues to strengthen and weaponize its nuclear program and improve its delivery capabilities.[35] Additionally, North Korean behavior could encourage other nuclear wannabes to follow suit.[36] Finally, proliferation of nuclear materials and technologies to regions of conflict and instability, such as the Middle East, could lead states to either pursue nuclear programs of their own or take preventive actions into their own hands, as the Israeli strike of the Syrian nuclear facilities in September 2007 suggests.[37]

These dire consequences aside, North Korea's actions and Tehran's defiance regarding the pursuit of its own nuclear program point to some of the inherent weaknesses and problems of the nonproliferation regime: enforcement and dual-use issues, in addition to universality and nuclear disarmament commitments by the nuclear weapons states.[38] Fundamentally, the question is also whether the type of international nuclear order as the NPT has imposed can be sustained as it is. Basically, how can the NPT and the nonproliferation regime be sustained when the possession of nuclear weapons by some states is deemed justifiable and conducive to stability while that of others is not? In other words, the grand bargain struck in 1968 is no longer sustainable without the attendant perception of discrimination and double standards being seriously addressed, including the nuclear weapons states' own failure at nuclear disarmament despite pledges to do so.[39]

In East Asia, North Korea's challenge to the NPT has been particularly serious, not the least because of the concern over how Tokyo would respond. Japan, as is well known, has seriously considered the nuclear option. However, whether Japan will go nuclear depends on several key factors: the U.S.-Japan security alliance, the international environment, domestic developments, and Japan's strategic choice.[40] Washington has for the most part strongly opposed any Japanese intention to acquire nuclear weapons, which will likely remain U.S. policy. While the international nuclear nonproliferation regime has endured significant strain over the last few years, the international community remains united in opposing further nuclear proliferation, including that of Japan. Given Japan's reliance on overseas markets and resources, the consequences of its going nuclear would likely be severe. Also, as the only country that has suffered nuclear attacks in the past, strong popular sentiment exists in Japan against acquiring nuclear weapons.[41] The ultimate considerations would remain twofold[42] whether acquiring nuclear weapons, given the constraining factors listed above, would enhance Japan's security, and whether Tokyo remains confident in the U.S. nuclear umbrella.[43]

The U.S. attitude toward Japan's nuclear debates and its role in reining in Japanese nuclear ambition are critical. Secretary of State Condoleezza Rice's trip to Japan right after North Korea's October 9, 2006, nuclear test was an effort to shore up Tokyo's confidence in the U.S. nuclear umbrella, as well as to secure pledges from the new Abe administration that Japan would not renege on its three nonnuclear principles. Foreign Minister Taro Aso pledged to Rice that Japan had no intention of acquiring nuclear weapons, saying that Japan is not considering building a nuclear arsenal in response to the North Korean nuclear test.

That Japan and South Korea have refrained from going nuclear even after North Korea's second and third nuclear tests and are more supportive of international efforts to restrict Pyongyang's nuclear brinkmanship offers some consolation that the worst-case scenario—a nuclear domino effect in East Asia that could spell the end of the nonproliferation regime and heighten tensions in the region—has yet to transpire.[44] The other challenges to the regime warranting careful analysis are the further proliferation of nuclear materials and technologies and, in particular, the gravely serious consequence of these falling into the hands of terrorist groups at a time of growing interest in—and indeed what has been described as a nuclear renaissance of—civilian use of nuclear energies.[45] Here all is not lost; the nonproliferation regime, while under significant stress, still has the hope of being salvaged and remains resilient when assessed with regard to normative foundation, scope, and strength, among other factors.[46]

Reasons exist to remain hopeful that the nonproliferation regime can withstand the challenge, but greater efforts are clearly needed to repair the regime. The recent progress—albeit modest—with regard to the three pillars of the NPT (nonproliferation, peaceful use, and disarmament) offers some optimism. In addition, whether or not North Korean and, for that matter, Iranian nuclear programs would lead to a cascade of nuclear breakouts in other countries depends on variables more than the regimes themselves. The modest success of the May 2010 NPT Review Conference—in particular, its reaffirmation of nuclear disarmament, promotion of peaceful nuclear use, renewed efforts in addressing the Middle East issue, and the calls for strengthened nonproliferation commitments of member states—certainly offers some breathing space for the international community to reassess, amend, and strengthen the nonproliferation regime.[47] At the same time, recent discussions on nuclear proliferation suggest that states' pursuing of nuclear weapons programs depends on a multitude of factors that include threat perceptions, economic resources and technical capabilities, domestic political structures, strategic considerations, and calculations that could in turn be influenced by external variables.[48]

One of the issues that concerns most analysts and policymakers is whether North Korea's nuclear program could trigger a nuclear chain reaction in Northeast Asia.[49] As provocative and threatening as North Korea's nuclear and missile programs are, whether nuclear proliferation ensues in East Asia could be influenced by more than Pyongyang's brinkmanship. For instance, any erosion of confidence in U.S. extended deterrence to Japan and continued Chinese military buildup, coupled with the unresolved North Korean nuclear issue and the prospect of a unified Korea with nuclear weapons capabilities, could provide the perfect storm that would sway Japanese public opinions and lead Tokyo to seriously reconsider the nuclear option. If Japan went nuclear, the NPT regime would disintegrate. Likewise, a loss of confidence in the United States as a security partner and guarantor and a remilitarized Japan or a Japan seeking nuclear capabilities, in addition to the North Korean nuclear threat, would greatly influence Seoul's decisions on its nuclear options.[50]

Another concern about North Korea's nuclear weapons program is the potential for it to transfer nuclear materials and technologies to other state or non-state actors, resulting in further nuclear proliferation. There have been reports of Pyongyang's dangerous missile transfers, in particular to the Middle East, and worries are mounting that such dealings could involve nuclear items—for instance, with Iran.[51] Obviously, the Syrian case only heightens such concerns. At the same time, one could argue that with enhanced international vigilance and strengthened international and multilateral measures such as the PSI, North Korea would find it more difficult for North Korea to engage in illicit nuclear trafficking, if not experience outright and complete shutdown of its other commercially driven activities.[52]

Indeed, North Korea's second nuclear test, instead of generating another major crisis in the nonproliferation regime, has actually led the international community to renew its efforts to address some of the regime's problems and weaknesses. The second test led to the passage of UNSC Resolution 1874, which imposes yet stricter sanctions on North Korea. Moreover, the test led South Korea, after years of hesitance, to finally decide to participate in the PSI, a major U.S.-led counterproliferation effort aimed at interdicting suspected illicit trafficking of WMD-related items.[53] Indeed, if anything, the North Korean and Iranian nuclear cases have refocused the policy and analytic attention of the international community on the supply side of the proliferation ledger—that is, access to nuclear technology and assistance and how civilian nuclear cooperation could run the risk of nuclear proliferation if not properly monitored and strictly enforced where safeguards are concerned.[54] This response explains why, in recent years, multiple proposals have been put forth about controlling nuclear fuel cycles in civilian-nuclear cooperation. Restricting access to technologies related to enrichment and reprocessing critical to the production of weapons-grade fissile materials is drawing growing attention from policymakers and scholars alike.[55]

Beyond Nonproliferation

While Pyongyang might have contemplated developing its nuclear weapons program well before the first nuclear crisis of 1993–94, serious efforts were under way most likely in the late 1980s and early 1990s, when North Korea faced grave challenges in legitimacy, loss of patronage, and economic difficulties. The admission of North Korea and South Korea to the United Nations in 1991, Seoul's successful efforts to seek recognition from the Soviet Union and the Eastern European states in the wake of the 1988 Seoul Olympic Games, and the fall of the Berlin Wall and the collapse of communism in 1989 put further pressures on Pyongyang.[56] Seoul and Moscow established diplomatic relations in 1991, and in 1992 China, a longtime ally of North Korea, recognized South Korea as well. As a result, Pyongyang felt deserted, isolated, and threatened, and it began its nuclear weapons program in earnest.[57]

The fundamental issues surrounding the nuclear crisis, then, are deeply rooted mistrust between North Korea and the United States, Pyongyang's constant paranoia that the United States sought its demise, and continuing political hostility between the two. As a weaker party, North Korea has resorted to extreme measures to secure its survival and to use the nuclear card as a bargaining chip. Heavy concentration of military forces on the peninsula, especially along the demilitarized zone (DMZ), could easily result in accidental, small-scale clashes escalating to open military conflict and even war. Without addressing the legacies of the Cold War, any resolution of the nuclear issue would be difficult if not impossible and prolonged.[58]

North Korea's negotiating tactics typically include the use of brinkmanship, crisis escalation, veiled or blatant threats, and the signaling of flexibility in exchange for similar concessions from its counterpart.[59] Pyongyang's central negotiation strategy is to press for direct engagement with and recognition from the United States, including removal from the U.S. list of state sponsors of terrorism as an indication of Washington's political will, and even to entertain the idea of accepting the continued U.S. military presence on the peninsula to balance and limit Chinese influence.[60]

Without question, the most immediate driver for North Korea's nuclear weapons program is security and regime survival. Pyongyang typically would display defiance and engage in provocative activities when it is most vulnerable, which has been demonstrated in recent periods of leadership uncertainty and the Kim family succession arrangements.[61] To a lesser extent, the North's activities could be used to show off for the domestic audience the kind of achievements the isolated country can accomplish with the *Juche* (self-reliance) spirit under extreme circumstances. What is not clear—and what has remained a point of contention and debates—is whether the new North Korean regime under Kim Jong-un is willing to trade its weapons for security, economic assistance, and the return to the international community as a normal country, and if so, with what preconditions.[62] In other words, the North's pursuit of nuclear weapons and the associated policies, rhetoric, and activities are the symptoms rather than the cause of the problem. This being the case, applying the typical nonproliferation tools in tackling the North Korean nuclear issue does not suffice here. Rather, developing a multidimensional and well-integrated approach that addresses the particular issues and concerns of Pyongyang, key regional players, and the international community is imperative.[63]

Such an approach should leverage the diplomatic, economic, and military resources at the disposal of the other participating states at the Six Party Talks. In combination with political reconciliation and recognition, economic assistance, and the resolve to reject North Korean brinkmanship, Pyongyang might be convinced that a negotiated settlement would not necessarily threaten DPRK security or, for that matter, regime survival but offer significant and meaningful economic payoffs. Such an approach must also secure explicit and unequivocal pledges from Pyongyang on an agreed-upon timetable for nuclear dismantlement, leading to a complete and eventual disarmament of North Korea's nuclear weapons capabilities, with credible and enforceable verification provisions. At the same time, the promised diplomatic recognition and economic benefits, including food and energy supplies and the lifting of sanctions, should also be delivered according to agreed-upon schedules, hence depriving any excuse for Pyongyang to renege on its commitments.[64]

PRIORITIES, GOALS, AND COORDINATION

A critical step in implementing the various programs is to have priorities set right and to have clearly defined, sequential, step-by-step plans that are executable benchmarks. Trying to make linkages between issues and accomplish multiple tasks can undermine the effectiveness of the strategy and could, in fact, inadvertently delay its full implementation. In all of these, verification could be the most crucial element. Bilateral negotiation sometimes can be the most effective path to denuclearization, which in turn could be placed within a multilateral context for compliance enforcement purposes.[65]

Obviously, in dealing with North Korea, the United States, its allies, and other concerned parties always have multiple goals they want to achieve, but they must maintain their focus on the primary goal of ending the threat of the North Korean regime, either in the sense of its nuclear weapons program triggering a regional nuclear domino effect or in the form of illicit nuclear transfers to others. Other concerns, if they impede resolution of the first-order issues, should be better coordinated and perhaps sidelined or delinked from the nuclear issue. Lifting sanctions, removing North Korea from the State Sponsors of Terrorism list (which the Bush administration did in 2008), and normalizing relations could be structured in a way that encourages good behavior, compliance and implementation, and eventual resolution of the nuclear issue. Given that Pyongyang rarely lives up to its end of the bargain, verification would be critical.[66]

Failure to coordinate policies could lead to confusion and even division among allies, friends, and concerned parties, making it possible for Pyongyang to exploit such disunity. The October 2006 joint statement, for instance, threatened alliance cohesion. U.S. ambassador to Japan J. Thomas Schieffer warned President Bush that the deal, especially in which Washington was contemplating removing Pyongyang from the State Department list of countries sponsoring terrorist activities, could harm relations with Japan as long as the abduction issue remained unresolved. Indeed, after Washington removed Pyongyang from the list in 2008, Tokyo decided not to provide aid to North Korea, even though this was a major component of the multilateral deal.[67]

Another example is the October 2007 North-South Summit between former South Korean president Roh Moo-hyun and former North Korean leader Kim Jong-il, at which Seoul offered economic aid and development packages that reportedly ran up to $11 billion and signed a number of agreements with the North. South Korea agreed to fund major projects, expansion and establishment of industrial zones, and infrastructure improvements. Critics of the meeting took issue with what they perceived as one-sided largess from Seoul without requiring that Pyongyang make any progress toward denuclearization in return, even though one could argue that the latter supposed this was and would be addressed by the Six Party Talks process.[68] The significant economic aid thus promised by South Korea without linking it to progress in North Korea's nuclear dismantlement and meaningful economic reforms could have potentially undermined the goals of the Six Party Talks, which expressly emphasize "action by action"—that is, economic aid is contingent upon progress in denuclearization.[69]

The Bush administration's North Korea policy appeared inconsistent as it was sometimes divided, pitting the pragmatists who placed denuclearization as the priority against the hard-liners who advocated for regime change rather than change in regime behavior.[70] Nor was the policy well coordinated between government agencies that, respectively, had the mandates of nuclear nonproliferation, human rights, and illicit activities, among others. The timing of the Banco Delta Asia (BDA) case is a good example; the Treasury Department imposed sanctions on the Macau-based BDA for money laundering and counterfeiting activities linked to North Korean entities at about the same time that Pyongyang had just agreed to the September 19, 2005, joint statement for nuclear dismantlement. The sanctions quickly became a major stumbling block to the implementation of the September joint statement, and it took more than a year and a North Korean nuclear test before the Six Party Talks were resumed. Given its tendency to seize on any slight excuse for forfeiting its obligations, Pyongyang has taken numerous opportunities to delay, revert, and even negate its pledges and commitments as a result of the failure of the U.S. government to coordinate its DPRK policy in a more concerted fashion.[71] Differences over the lifting of economic sanctions and removal of North Korea from the list of states sponsoring terrorism are at least part of the reason for the continued impasse—as was Pyongyang's failure to present a full declaration—serving possibly as another setback in the drawn-out nuclear saga on the peninsula.[72]

Indeed, even prior to the late 2008 breakdown in dismantling North Korea's nuclear program, Pyongyang had already slowed the pace of disablement of its Yongbyon nuclear complex, arguing that the other parties failed to fulfill their parts of the agreement in terms of heavy fuel delivery. Pyongyang also claimed to have submitted a list of its nuclear facilities and activities, but Washington insisted it had yet to receive a "complete and correct" declaration of North Korean nuclear programs and activities, including its uranium enrichment program. The Bush administration also insisted that North Korea allow international (preferably IAEA) verification, even though verification was not required until a later phase under the February 2007 action plan. Meanwhile, Pyongyang hardened its position and threatened to bring the denuclearization process to a complete halt if Washington continued to demand full declaration and if fuel deliveries should fall behind schedule.[73]

Other factors also contributed to the impasse and the apparent breakdown. Technically speaking, the October 3, 2007, joint statement, committing North Korea to the year-end completion of the disablement and the declaration, may have been an unrealistic target to achieve in the first place. Nor was it any more realistic to expect the delivery of 950,000 tons of heavy fuel oil equivalent, given North Korea's limited capacity to receive it. Indeed, the Bush administration seemed less concerned with the missed deadline on disablement than with Pyongyang's failure to provide a full declaration of all its nuclear programs.

However, the declaration issue is exactly the point on which the DPRK and the United States appeared to be deadlocked. The disagreement was more about substance and interpretation of the declaration than its timing. For Washington, in addition to Pyongyang's declared spent fuel reprocessing program, declaration must include the suspected uranium enrichment programs; any extant nuclear weapons, facilities, and materials; and clarification of any proliferation activities, presumably including those involving Syria in particular. From Pyongyang's perspective, that issue was a nonstarter, for it refused to admit that it ever had a uranium enrichment program, nor would it confess to any connection with Damascus, even though many suspect that the Israeli air strike against Syria in September 2007 targeted a nuclear-related facility under construction reportedly with assistance from North Korea.[74]

Use the Right Combination to Build Trust

U.S. policy toward North Korea has leaned heavily toward punishment, sanctions, and isolation, which appear to Pyongyang to be an attempt at regime change rather than changing regime behavior. The sanctions imposed on North Korea are based either on the Trading with the Enemy Act or the State Sponsor of Terrorism list (before North Korea was delisted from the latter in 2008) only prolong hostility and animosity between the two countries without being able to address the nuclear issue or bring down the regime, since other countries, with different priorities and interests, would not be willing to push North Korea over the edge. This lack of coordination undermines the effectiveness of sanctions. The post-test sanctions have greater legitimacy, and the BDA-related sanctions appeared to have had an impact. But whatever effective impact these

sanctions could have achieved were also lost partially due to lack of coordination within the U.S. government and between Washington and other capitals.[75]

The U.S. commitment in the October 2006 joint statement to taking North
Korea off the State Department State Sponsors of Terrorism list and terminating sanctions on the DPRK under the Trading with the Enemy Act, in parallel
with the latter's actions in denuclearization, raised expectations, false hopes,
and deep concerns among various parties. Pyongyang manipulated the agreement's ambiguity in sequencing in terms of which element of the agreement
should come first and who should do what, and now Pyongyang demands that
the terms be fulfilled before it would proceed further on its obligations on disablement. Tokyo, meanwhile, became increasingly worried that North Korea
would be taken off the list prior to resolving the abduction issue.[76]

Beneath the disappointment in unfulfilled promises and differences in interpretation of obligations are decades of deep mistrust between Pyongyang and
Washington, which place different priorities in the drawn-out negotiation process. The United States has always been concerned with North Korea's nuclear
programs and its proliferation activities, while the latter is focused on how to
best secure its interests without losing—at least not prematurely—its most potent bargaining chips. While both parties claim to agree on the ultimate goal of
denuclearization, their short- to medium-term goals and the ways by which to
accomplish them remain poles apart.[77]

Inter-Korea relations today remain volatile, especially since the conservative government of Lee Myung-bak came to power in 2009. The subsequent
developments on the peninsula, including North Korea's unveiled warnings
and threats to the South and the conservative government of Lee Myung-bak
adopting a tougher line on the North, cast a shadow on the denuclearization
process. Pyongyang may simply stall and try to slow down the process, given
the growing uncertainties in inter-Korean relations now that Seoul has moved
away from the Sunshine Policy. The DPRK also dragged its feet in the waning years of the Bush administration in anticipation of a Democratic one with
which it hoped to get a better deal. Plenty of incentives remain for Pyongyang
to hold on to its nuclear programs, and its May 2009 nuclear test clearly indicates that it intends to keep that option, at least for some time to come; dealing with North Korea in the near term may have to be based on that premise.[78]
However, the March 2010 *Cheonan* incident, in which North Korea reportedly
sank an ROK naval vessel with forty-two lives lost, brought the tension on the
peninsula to a boiling point. The Lee administration was shocked by the attack

but proceeded cautiously, calling for an investigation by a multinational team rather than immediately pegging North Korea as the culprit. At the same time, Seoul suspended all inter-Korean trade except the joint venture in the Kaesong Industrial Zone. The United States and South Korea displayed their show of resolve and force by staging naval exercises while Pyongyang blasted such maneuvers as highly provocative and vowed retaliation against any aggression. Tension boiled again in November with the North Korean shelling of Yeonpyeong Island, killing a few South Korean soldiers and civilians.[79]

CONCLUSION

North Korea's nuclear weapons program and its continuing defiance of the international community, the United Nations, and the IAEA threaten to undermine the nonproliferation regime. The inability of the international community to truly impose any punitive sanctions on North Korea raises serious questions about the sanctity and enforceability of the NPT's principles and provisions. The North Korean case has important implications with regard to potential future breaches and even withdrawal by member states; deeply worrisome is the precedent set by North Korean withdrawal from the NPT without any serious consequence. But any meaningful punitive actions on previous noncompliance by North Korea would only be possible where political rather than legal consensus can be established. Once out of the treaty, North Korea is left unencumbered in its pursuit of nuclear weapons development and proliferation activities, an issue with which the international community still has to wrestle.[80] The lack of concrete signs of progress and the suspension of the Six Party Talks process since early 2009 point to the difficult tasks of reversing and deterring proliferation behavior within broader regional and international security contexts. Despite these challenges, the NPT and the nonproliferation regime it represents remain the best framework for dealing with proliferation challenges. The international community has strengthened its efforts in combating nuclear proliferation through such mechanisms as sanctions endorsed by the UN Security Council, interceptions of illicit transfers via the PSI, and coordinated policies and concerted actions aimed at persuading Pyongyang to return to the Six Party Talks.[81] The feared nuclear domino effect has not taken place, notwithstanding three North Korean nuclear tests and a series of missile tests, thanks to renewed U.S. commitments and pledges for the security of its key allies and the strategic choices made in Tokyo and Seoul to remain nonnuclear.

Crucial lessons can be drawn about the North Korean nuclear crisis and the Six Party Talks since the first crisis in 1993–94 and the second crisis and inception of the Six Party Talks in 2002–3. First is the importance of being clear and precise about the goals and commitments of concerned parties regarding North Korea's nuclear program and how to accomplish them. Ambiguity, unrealistic expectations, and failure to define the process and sequencing could cause problems and delays during implementation. Another lesson is the need to separate, rather than bundle together, the various elements and phases of the denuclearization process and prioritize them; a third lesson is to avoid linking the nuclear issue with other issues, such as the human rights situation in North Korea.

One could argue that the first step should be for North Korea to completely disable and dismantle the Yongbyon nuclear complex, followed by an accurate accounting for the weapons-grade plutonium accumulated since 2003. North Korea's suspected uranium enrichment programs and its proliferation would come next. This sequence could avoid an entanglement where differences over the scope and contents of North Korea's nuclear programs slow and even threaten to halt the entire process.

North Korea remains paranoid about threats to its security and regime survival. While succumbing to Pyongyang's unreasonable demands is tantamount to appeasement and serves no one's interests outside of the North, creating and fostering conditions that address Pyongyang's concerns and improve its economic situation and security environment may provide incentives for it to give up its nuclear programs. If the past five years of the Six Party Talks tell us anything, patience, diplomacy, and negotiation skills are fundamental to success on the long road to North Korea's eventual denuclearization.

North Korea's nuclear brinkmanship poses a serious threat to the integrity of the international nuclear nonproliferation regime, already under siege. Poorly handled, the continuing and escalating confrontation between Pyongyang and Washington could have unfathomable consequences. While the immediate concern necessarily remains defusing the pending nuclear crisis, it is never too early to think beyond nuclear nonproliferation and crisis management to develop broader strategies aimed at long-term peace and stability on the Korean Peninsula.

However, tackling nuclear proliferation alone will not suffice in creating the conditions for the region's long-term stability. A multilateral effort in security building is needed for the peninsula. While debates on how best to head off the current nuclear crisis rage on—whether through concerted international pressure, economic sanctions, or engagement and dialogue—security analysts and policymakers alike should also start thinking—or rethinking—broader strategies in addition to nonproliferation tactics. These strategies must seek to address long-term stability for the Korean Peninsula with the development of a multilateral security framework.

Finally, efforts should be made to dispel concern in Pyongyang that the rest of the nations in the region are awaiting and even pushing for its collapse and to send a clear, consistent, and unanimous message that brinkmanship does not pay. The implosion scenario and a violent collapse of North Korea are not in the interests of any of the involved parties. The Agreed Framework demonstrated the Clinton administration's serious resolve to address the nuclear issue; equally resolute should have been sincere efforts by Washington and the international community to address Pyongyang's sense of alienation and insecurity. However, implementation of the Agreed Framework from the very beginning had been hampered as a result of U.S. domestic politics. A Republican-controlled Congress elected in November 1994 was more interested in seeing the collapse of the North Korean regime, resulting in little progress at resolving the nuclear issue in the 1990s. Later, the Bush administration's initial hard-line approach did not bring about the desired result either. Here the concept of cooperative security— seeking security with rather than against one's potential adversaries—must be driven home for the DPRK. Pyongyang's concern over regime survival should be appreciated but not tolerated as an excuse for acting irresponsibly. Eventually, the linkages between humanitarian assistance, gradual and expanding economic contacts, compliance with nonproliferation norms and principles, and the mutual understanding and trust that interdependence and dialogue can promote will provide the key to untying the Pyongyang regime's knots of insecurity and fear. Only by addressing North Korea's fundamental concerns over regime survival and alleviating its impending economic crisis, while standing firm on issues of principle, can the rest of the region more effectively deal with a dangerous and unpredictable state on the verge of collapse, not to mention its involvement in potentially catastrophic international nuclear proliferation activities.

Implications and
Possible Ways Forward

GREGORY J. MOORE

I posed a number of questions at the outset of this study. Some of the answers offered in this volume bode well for peace on the Korean Peninsula and a peaceful resolution of the North Korean nuclear conundrum. Others, however, are more foreboding in nature. Here I summarize conclusions from the chapters about the implications of North Korean nuclear operationality for regional security and the nuclear nonproliferation regime, followed by a consideration of the question of whether we are being fair to the DPRK. Does any nation not deserve the right to develop adequate measures for self-defense? I include a consideration of the implications of the North Korean nuclear issue for international relations theory (and vice versa) with a focus on Realism, Neo-Liberal Institutionalism, and constructivism. I finish with some thoughts about possible ways forward toward resolving the North Korea nuclear dilemma, based on the suggestions of this volume's contributors.

FINDINGS

After an overview of the North Korean nuclear dilemma, this book has addressed the implications of North Korean nuclear operationality for regional security and the nuclear nonproliferation regime. As a general observation, none of the authors in this volume concluded in their chapters that North Korean nuclear operationality would be a positive development for regional security or the nuclear nonproliferation regime. Nor would, the contributors argue, the respective nations that are party to the matter: China, Russia, South Korea, Japan, or the United States.

First, would an operationally nuclear North Korea lead to the spread of nuclear weapons in the region? Based on the chapters here, it does not seem likely. Japan is fundamental to this question, as one of the nations that faces the most immediate threat from the DPRK, and Japan has the ability to acquire nuclear weapons if it wants to. In their chapter on Japan, Furukawa and Izumi conclude that it would take much more than operational North Korean nuclear weapons to drive Japan toward having nuclear weapons, for at least two reasons. Most important, the Japanese public still harbors a strong antipathy toward nuclear weapons, which has only strengthened in the aftermath of the 2011 earthquake, tsunami, and nuclear disasters. Another inhibitor is the continued strength and apparent stability of Japan's security relationship with the United States, which makes the argument for an independent Japanese nuclear capability more difficult to make. Bae and Choi likewise conclude that South Korea is not likely to move toward nuclear weapons in the event of North Korea's nuclear capabilities becoming operational, primarily because the North's conventional capabilities are already sufficiently threatening that an upgrade to nuclear weapons would not markedly increase South Koreans' threat perceptions; hence not enough impetus exists to overcome the "formidable antinuclear social norms"[1] in South Korea.[2] Their presentation of data regarding the public's support of the government's engagement policy and data from the Korean stock market during the period surrounding North Korea's nuclear tests lends strong support to their conclusions. Taiwan, another regional hot spot, could be impacted if Japan or South Korea were to opt for nuclear weapons. Many in Taiwan would find a nuclear deterrent useful against China's impressive display of missiles arrayed against Taiwan in nearby Fujian Province. However, given the argument presented here—that neither Japanese nor South Korean nuclear weapons are likely—Pyongyang's actions would probably not make it easier for Taipei to go nuclear. Moreover, barring the possible exception of a near warlike scenario between Beijing and Taipei, the United States would discourage such moves from Taiwan, and has in the past, because of how provocative those actions would be viewed in Beijing, and because of the likelihood that such a move would push Beijing to supplement its own nuclear capabilities, introducing a new measure of security competition to the region.

Would operational North Korean nuclear weapons lead to U.S. strikes against North Korean nuclear sites or a U.S. invasion? In his chapter on Washington's response to an operationally nuclear North Korea, David Kang concludes that despite superior South Korean and U.S. military forces, "The United States and South Korea have no realistic military option as regards confronting

North Korea over its nuclear weapons programs,"[3] primarily because of the vulnerability of Seoul, South Korea's capital, a city of 23 million people just thirty miles south of the border and well within DPRK artillery range. Kang concludes that sanctions against North Korea would have limited impact and little more than a symbolic effect. First, only sanctions that included China as a participant would really impact North Korea, and China's participation in any robust sanctions does not seem likely unless, as I discuss in chapter 4, relations between Beijing and Pyongyang seriously break down. While within the realm of possibility, the other nations cannot count on such a development, sanctions as such seem limited in utility. Second, even if Beijing did participate at some level in robust sanctions against Pyongyang, Kang argues that the effect, while potentially devastating, would not likely result in attaining the policy changes or regime change that the United States and others would like to see, given the regime's isolation and historically autarkic tendencies; a number of studies demonstrate the limited effect of sanctions in general and on North Korea in particular.[4] Still, if North Korea proceeds to full nuclear operationality, the United States, Japan, probably South Korea, and others would move toward a more robust sanctions regime than is currently in place, but again, any value other than a symbolic one is not clear. Kang notes that the United States currently has more sanctions against North Korea than almost any nation in the world, as well as over forty laws restricting U.S. economic activity with the DPRK.[5] Extant sanctions and warnings have actually not stopped North Korea from weaponizing its nuclear potential.

If North Korean nuclear operationality is not likely to lead to other states in the region acquiring nuclear weapons, or successful sanctions against North Korea, would it lead to a conventional arms race in Northeast Asia? Based on the chapters here, such an outcome appears more likely. It would certainly drive Seoul and Tokyo into a closer security relationships with Washington, and could do the same for Taipei depending on the stand Beijing takes. As Bae and Choi argue, given South Korea's present vulnerability to attack, an operationally nuclear North Korea might not induce large changes in South Korea's military posture. The same, however, cannot be said for Japan. A North Korea with operationally nuclear status would provide more ammunition for rightists in Tokyo who advocate stronger autonomous Japanese military capabilities and a harder line toward Pyongyang. If China or Russia is seen as supporting North Korea, it could also lead to harder-line Japanese positions in its relations with Beijing or Moscow as well. In the same way, South Korea would take a harder line against North Korea, and depending on China's and Russia's support of

North Korea, the South might take a harder line against them as well. North Korean nuclear operationality would also likely strengthen Japanese cooperation with the United States on anti–ballistic missile system research and deployment, and might induce Seoul[6] and even Taipei to opt in, too. All of this would be viewed as highly undesirable by Beijing and Moscow and would likely lead to higher defense spending across the region. China (and Russia) would have to respond to those increased expenditures, particularly in spending on ABM systems, as well as any hardening of positions that would come about as a result of Pyongyang's moves, especially as it regards Japan and possibly Taiwan. North Korean nuclear operationality could really shake up the existing regional alignment and increase tensions in ways that are not conducive to regional stability or continued economic development.[7]

As worrisome as the potential is of a North Korea–induced regional arms race, this volume indicates that perhaps the greatest danger posed by an operationally nuclear North Korea is the potential, or even likelihood, that Pyongyang would transfer nuclear weapons, materials, or know-how into the hands of other unreliable states or, worse yet, non-state actors such as Al Qaeda, with whom Pyongyang shares anti-American and generally anti-Western proclivities. Henry Kissinger put it well: "The spread of these [nuclear] weapons into hands not restrained by the historical and political considerations of the major states augurs a world of devastation and human loss without precedent even in our age of genocidal killings."[8] The North Korean regime has accrued a remarkable record of proliferation already—as several of the chapters here document, perhaps most pointedly the work of Maria Rost Rublee. Such proliferation includes trade or sales of nuclear know-how or materials with or to the following states: Pakistan, Iran, Syria, Libya (indirectly via Pakistan), and possibly Myanmar/Burma and pre-2003 Iraq.

Rublee argues that successful North Korean nuclear operationality would teach nuclear aspirants at least three unfortunate lessons. First, "unacceptable" is a meaningless term, alluding to statements from basically all of the other members of the Six Party Talks, as well as the IAEA and others, that North Korea's acquisition of nuclear weapons was "unacceptable." Yet to this day North Korea has not really paid any significant cost for violating the will of the international community. The second lesson is that a nuclear weapons program can strengthen a leader's or regime's domestic political position, as Kim Jong-il showed when he tried to bolster his standing with the military leadership and show the people some concrete measure of success and national pride for all their suffering. The third lesson is that nuclear weapons do in fact deter.

Rublee argues that Iran and others have taken away from the North Korean experience the impression that a nonnuclear power like Saddam Hussein's Iraq or Muammar Qaddafi's Libya is vulnerable to invasion or intervention, but a nuclear power like North Korea is not. While North Korea arguably has other things going for it besides nuclear weapons—primarily the location of its artillery and missile capabilities thirty miles from South Korea's capital—the point is well taken, particularly as regards Libya, which had a weapons program and gave it up. No doubt the North Korean leadership and the leaders of other illiberal nuclear aspirants fear Qaddafi's horrible fate.

Rublee is concerned that a North Korea with nuclear operationality could also have dire direct and indirect consequences for the nonproliferation regime. North Korean nuclear operationality could directly undermine the NPT via expanded sales of and service for nuclear weapons, nuclear weapons know-how, and the material necessary to produce nuclear weapons to states and non-state actors of concern. Another, more indirect effect would be to embolden Iran, Japan, or other states to move forward with nuclear weapons programs of their own. Iran in particular would be encouraged by successful North Korean operationality, and Iranian operationality in turn would likely spur Arab states in the Middle East to counter with their own programs given the threat a nuclear-armed Iran would pose for them. She argues that Iran's moves to date have already spurred nuclear power programs in Saudi Arabia, Egypt, and Jordan. Both Rublee and Yuan state that these circumstances, and the possible nuclearization of Iran and a state like Japan—the only nation to have ever been on the receiving end of a nuclear attack— could effectively serve as "the death-knell of the export control system as well as of the NPT."[9]

In his chapter, Yuan says that North Korea poses the most serious threat the NPT has ever faced, for two reasons. First, North Korea's 2003 withdrawal from the NPT marks the first time a member state has ever withdrawn from the treaty and then gone on to achieve nuclear weaponization, let alone operationality, but this action has gone essentially unchallenged in any meaningful way by the international community. Second, North Korea's proliferation activities to date are already a serious affront to the status of the NPT, given that the international community has found no way to either stop Pyongyang from proliferating or to hold Pyongyang accountable for having done so. Yuan concludes that North Korea "raises serious questions about the enforceability of the NPT."[10] In summary, North Korean nuclear operationality could directly or indirectly serve to cause the unraveling and collapse of the NPT and related regimes.

DOES THE DPRK NOT HAVE A RIGHT TO PURSUE
SECURITY LIKE ANY OTHER STATE?

Before going further, perhaps I should pose a question that may have been lurking in the minds of readers for some pages now. Are we being fair to North Korea? Is it not legitimate for a state to pursue its own security, particularly in North Korea's situation—as part of a Korea divided by the Soviet Union and the United States following World War II and now confronting its wealthier southern brethren and the world's foremost conventional and nuclear power? John Mearsheimer argued in 1993 that the Ukraine, then home to thousands of Soviet-era nuclear weapons on its soil, would and should maintain a nuclear deterrent.[11] Does this apply to North Korea as well? In other words, surrounded by nuclear neighbors like China and Russia and facing off against a nuclear superpower (the United States), would it not be reasonable for North Korea to acquire nuclear weapons and possibly even enhance regional stability in the process?

Generally speaking, of course a state can legitimately pursue its own security. Yet as several of the chapters here have shown, North Korea is not a typical state (being the only example of a totalitarian state in existence today), nor is North Korea's leader a typical leader (ruling autocratically by a combination of pseudo-communism, traditional Asian feudal dynastic tendencies, and modern totalitarian methods). To buttress the case that North Korea is not a trustworthy keeper of operational nuclear capabilities, I offer a brief review of some of the more important reasons that this is the case, including a consideration of North Korean involvement in nuclear proliferation, North Korean acts of terrorism in the not-so-distant past, and finally the nature of North Korea's regime and political system.

First, North Korea is a known proliferator of nuclear materials and know-how to states with poor records of responsible behavior. Rublee's chapter made this case most clearly, and I tried to do the same in chapter two. North Korea received early help on its nuclear program from China. When China grew uncomfortable with the leadership changes and undesirable tendencies in Pyongyang and ceased cooperating with the DPRK on nuclear matters, North Korea turned elsewhere for help, ultimately receiving assistance from the A. Q. Khan network in Pakistan. Evidence exists that North Korea later sold Pakistan uranium hexafluoride, a compound that can be enriched to produce weapons-grade uranium, and that Pakistan transferred it to Libya, though whether North Korea was aware of or condoned the transfer to Libya or what further dealings Pyongyang had with Tripoli is not known. North Korea has also worked closely with Iran over the years, exchanging with it missile and nuclear hardware and know-how. The U.S. invasion of Iraq also unearthed some evidence of an unrealized deal between Pyongyang and Saddam Hussein's Iraq. Hard evidence exists of active North Korean assistance with a Syrian reactor modeled on North Korea's own Yongbyon complex; Israel destroyed the Syrian installation in 2007. Some evidence also is available that North Korea might be helping Myanmar/Burma with a nuclear program, as Rublee indicates.

Second, North Korea has been involved in a number of actions of state terrorism that were linked to Kim Jong-il. For example, on October 9, 1983, in Rangoon, Burma (Myanmar), three North Korean army officers detonated a bomb in an attempt to assassinate South Korean president Chun Doo-hwan, missing President Chun but killing twenty-one South Korean officials, including four members of South Korea's cabinet, including its foreign minister, two of South Korea's senior presidential advisers, and South Korea's ambassador to Burma. The perpetrators of the bombing were captured, and confessions later revealed the details of the plot, which had likely been ordered by Kim Jong-il himself; he had taken over North Korea's clandestine espionage operations the year before.[12] North Korea was also behind the terrorist bombing of Korean Air Lines flight 858, which killed all 115 on board on November 29, 1987. Two North Korean agents posing as Japanese tourists were captured and took cyanide pills in an attempt to commit suicide. One, a seventy-year-old man, succeeded, but the other, a twenty-five-year-old female agent named Kim Hyun-hee, survived. She said their mission to destroy the KAL flight had come directly from Kim Jong-il.[13] The United States removed North Korea from its list of state sponsors of terrorism in 2008, but the regime that Kim Jong-il built still rules the DPRK. While Pyongyang has not in a long time committed any acts of terror as strictly defined, North Korea's track record of terrorism and helping states that commit or support terrorism is highly troubling.

Third, North Korea has not shown itself worthy of the burden of responsibility that goes along with becoming a nuclear weapons state as, for example, Dan Twining argues in his chapter is true of India. The North Korean political system is a totalitarian cyber-feudal military dictatorship, the regime is precariously based on a text that is largely unsupportable by known facts and led by a leader who is for the most part unaccountable to the people he governs.[14] The North Korean leadership has been known to break agreements, lie to the international community about the nature of its nuclear programs, commit acts of terror, and even use extortion in its relations with other parties, including the Chinese, as noted in my chapter four above.

For all of these reasons Kim Jong-il was a difficult and unpredictable counterpart with whom to reach agreement on matters so weighty, and the authors of this volume concur that it is best if North Korea does not acquire operational nuclear weapons. With the death of Kim Jong-il and the rise of his son, Kim Jong-un, nothing has changed in this regard. Since Kim Jong-il's death, the North Korean leadership has stated in no uncertain terms that its nuclear policies remain as before.[15] While Waltz,[16] Measheimer,[17] Alagappa et al.,[18] and others may be right about the contribution of nuclear weapons to stability and ultimately to peace and security in some contexts, although this is highly contested in the literature, none of the authors in this volume agree that a nuclear North Korea is a positive development. Nor do North Korea's neighbors.

The DPRK is still worthy of being treated as a sovereign state, and its real needs and security interests should still be taken seriously, as a number of the authors in this volume have taken pains to point out. In fact, only by addressing the DPRK's reasonable security demands—according North Korea the respect due any sovereign state, while directly addressing the problems operational North Korean nuclear weapons present the region and the international community—can a solution to the North Korean nuclear issue be found.

THE IMPLICATIONS OF THIS STUDY FOR INTERNATIONAL RELATIONS THEORY (AND VICE VERSA)

I believe this study offers several implications for international relations (IR) theory and international relations generally. As it regards IR's "isms," certainly North Korea is a difficult test case for IR's non-Realist approaches, such as constructivism, Neo-Liberal Institutionalism,[19] critical theory, and the like, given the securitization of the issues, the danger to Seoul of a "sea of fire"–type attack, and the material- and weapons-related nature of the nuclear issue itself. For these reasons the DPRK would seem to lend itself nicely to a Realist approach of some sort. Are we, however, locked into a number of Realist assumptions, such that North Korea would under no circumstances give up its aspirations for operational nuclear weapons, that the United States would under no circumstances pursue a cooperative policy option on North Korea as long as North Korea maintains its nuclear program, or that a security spiral in Northeast Asia is likely as a result?

The North Korean nuclear issue is a difficult test case for non-Realist approaches to IR, but several contributors to this volume (e.g., Hayes and Bruce, Moore, Toloraya) suggest that ways out of the North Korean nuclear morass are available. Before going further, it is helpful to note that while operating theoretically at the regional level is not possible by definition for explicitly systemic theories like Waltzian Neo-Realism or Wendt's systemic social (constructivist) theory of international politics, it *is* possible in several theoretical traditions—including other forms of Realism, Neo-Liberal Institutionalism, or constructivism at the second level of analysis.

As regards Realism, first of all, a Realist approach operating at the second level of analysis would be necessary, leaving out Kenneth Waltz's third or system-level theory of international politics. Classical Realism would work here, as would John Mearsheimer's structural Realism. Mearsheimer has discussed the notion of regional hegemons (e.g., the United States in the Americas) and the operation of a regional balance of power in Northeast Asia and elsewhere, so certainly it is not inappropriate to discuss Neo-Realist thought such as his at the Northeast Asian regional level.[20] Mearsheimer expects China in the coming few years to begin challenging U.S. supremacy in Northeast Asia, and a regional showdown is likely as a result. In his seminal 2001 work, Mearsheimer does not spend much time discussing the North Korean issue except to say that reunification of the Korean Peninsula may not lead to a more peaceful Northeast Asia.[21] However, the logic of his arguments in this work and in his Ukraine piece cited earlier lead one to conclude that North Korea would not be wise, in Mearsheimer's view, to give up its extant nuclear capabilities nor their development into operational capabilities. This would likely lead to the darker scenarios discussed by authors in this volume: a security spiral in the region, the collapse (or severe weakening) of the nonproliferation regime, and a more dangerous world in general. If one were to consider a defensive Realist position, such as the classical Realism of Henry Kissinger—as opposed to Mearsheimer's offensive Realist position—the picture is not much more optimistic. Kissinger led U.S. President Nixon to rapprochement with China in 1971–72 not ostensibly because of goodwill or idealist notions of cooperation toward a better world (though these may not have been entirely absent) but primarily because of his understanding of Realist considerations of the need for power balancing between Washington and Beijing against the Soviet Union. In North Korea's case, no such rationale exists for Washington to seek rapprochement with Pyongyang, so none is expected according to conventional Realist logic; in Kissinger's writings on North Korea,[22] no such approach is offered. Realism as an approach to this case can explain much of the posturing and antipathy extant in the DPRK-U.S., DPRK-ROK, and DPRK-Japan relationships over the years, as well as the security dilemmas North Korea has posed for South Korea and more recently (with its missiles in particular) for Japan, as well as North Korea's own security dilemma as regards the United States. However, given a Realist assessment of the North Korean nuclear issue that (1) North Korea will not likely give up its nuclear capabilities, (2) the North will not likely cease moving toward operationalization, (3) the United States is not likely to give the Indian treatment to Pyongyang, and (4) no Realist strategic logic (à la Nixon and Kissinger) exists for entente between Washington and Pyongyang, one can reach no other conclusion than that the darker, more pessimistic scenarios appear most plausible from the Realist point of view. Events may vindicate this perspective, but are things so hopeless?

Another perspective on international relations is Neo-Liberal Institutionalism[23] (hereafter referred to as NLI), along with which is associated the Democratic Peace Theory, and which approaches this case from a different angle. If North Korea were a democracy, Democratic Peace Theory would certainly hold, probably correctly, that the North Korean nuclear issue would be much easier to resolve, and in fact might not be an issue at all. Since a North Korean transition to democracy is not likely any time soon, the Democratic Peace Theory is of limited use here, except to point out that North Korea's regime type (its lack of democracy) plays an important role in the tension between North Korea on the one hand and Japan, South Korea, and the United States (all democracies) on the other.

The NLI notion of complex interdependence might be more useful. Made famous by Keohane and Nye,[24] complex interdependence is the notion that as nations trade, webs of interdependence form between them that have a number of consequences. The increasing trade and other ties and exchanges can lead to the likelihood of greater understanding and cooperation between the two sides, but more importantly perhaps, the two sides' interests become intertwined to a greater degree, and the costs of military conflict between the two sides increases, shifting the cost-benefit analysis such that war and other serious conflict become less likely. As Toloraya, Kang, and others argue in this volume, were trade relations between the nations in the region to expand to and with North Korea, such a development would bode well for peace in the region. In North Korea's case, it would likely lead to more rational, or at least less confrontational, approaches to international relations. The question remains as to whether North Korea's leadership feels confident that such economic reform and opening to trade is in the region's or the nation's interest. In this volume, while Toloraya posits that such reforms are likely, Lankov and I are more dubious, arguing that economic reforms à la Deng Xiaoping would in North Korea likely bring about political instability because of the openness and relative popular independence from the state that such reforms would ultimately create. NLI is helpful in pointing out the benefits to regional peace and security of North Korean democratization and increasing levels of economic reform and international trade, but NLI will not take us far here unless North Korea radically reforms its political system or opens up economically as China and Vietnam have. The authors here agree that such change appears unlikely in the near term. The death of Kim Jong-il and the rise of his son, Kim Jong-un, do not appear to alter this calculus but a little, for Kim Jong-un is beholden to his father's regime and legacy and does not appear now to be in any position to change his government's basic policies on economics, politics, or nuclear weapons. Assuming the continuation of a smooth consolidation of his position and authority in coming years, Kim Jong-un might embark on a series of reforms that could bring important and needed reform to North Korea. Little evidence to date indicates that this is likely, however, leaving North Korea's neighbors and the international community with the expectation that North Korea will continue on its path to nuclear operationalization.

Wendt's version of constructivism (his "social theory of international politics") can be conceived of at the regional or even dyadic (bilateral) level, as well as at the international system level (where Wendt's 1999 book operates). Thus, constructivism could be applied here as well.[25] Applying Wendt's framework to the second level of analysis is a departure from his systemic, third-level analysis of international relations, but in speaking with him in 2001, I found that he did not have a problem with using this framework at the second level of analysis. In considering Wendt at the regional or dyadic level, one might consider his Hobbesian (enemy) relational culture, Lockean (competitor) relational culture, and Kantian (friend) relational culture, applied in this case to the Northeast Asian region or to dyads in the region. As a region the Lockean (or competitor) culture pervades overall, as Wendt argues is the case in the global international system overall.[26] However, in the case of North Korea's relations with South Korea, Japan, and the United States, it would be more accurate to describe each of these dyads as Hobbesian (characterized by enmity), and relations between China and North Korea on the one hand, and between the United States, Japan, and South Korea on the other, as Kantian (or that of friends).

Wendt's framework has several implications for our study of the North Korean nuclear issue. First, we should expect that Realism will have more to say where Hobbesian relational cultures prevail, such as in DPRK-U.S., DPRK-ROK, and DPRK-Japan relations. This outcome should not be surprising given Realism's worldview and its focus on material capabilities. However, the North Korean nuclear dilemma is part of a social milieu (something Realism has less to say about) in which the North Korea nuclear issue and North Korea's Hobbesian relational cultures with the United States, South Korea, and Japan, are themselves embedded in a larger regional context of relations between China and the United States, China and Japan, China and South Korea, and other regional dyads (and, at the systemic level of analysis, the international milieu in terms of the nuclear nonproliferation regime). But all these relationships cannot be defined in Hobbesian terms. The North Korea nuclear issue does not exist in isolation; analysis of the issue consequently entails a multination, multivariate analysis, something less amenable to a Realist material-driven[27] analysis, given the diversity of factors that must be included. In other words, if Realists are correct in saying that material factors and security dilemmas drive relations between Pyongyang and Washington, certainly Pyongyang's relations with Beijing, and Washington's relations with Seoul and Tokyo, are also important considerations. These in turn introduce pushes and pulls on North Korean and U.S. policy that make analysis of the North Korean nuclear issue more complicated, even more so considering that South Korea, Japan, and the United States are democracies with regular changes of leadership and concomitant policy preferences.

Second, such a framework frees policymakers and policy analysts from a rigid approach to the security dilemmas inherent in the North Korean nuclear dilemma, and while remaining realistic about security issues, material capabilities, and so on, is more conducive to considering new ways of viewing bilateral and regional relationships, such as those suggested in the chapters here by Hayes and Bruce, myself (chapter 2), and Toloraya. Constructivism does not necessarily seek to deconstruct and discredit Realism as an approach, but to note that its appropriateness as an analytical tool is relegated primarily to cases where material factors and Hobbesian relational culture—its a priori assumptions—are preeminent. Considering the likelihood of the parties to the North Korean nuclear issue coming to agreement on a regional security framework, a new, Kissinger/Nixon-esque approach to Pyongyang by Washington—or a regional nuclear-weapon-free zone, without the balancing motives of the original Kissinger/Nixon approach—requires thinking outside the box (and *inside* the black box of state!). A consideration of the fact that not all security relationships can be reduced to the Hobbesian one, and recognition of the reality and possibility of the fluidity of dyadic relational culture shifts (e.g., from enemy to competitor in Wendtian parlance), opens up new ways of thinking about security relationships in general and the North Korean regional nexus in particular. This new kind of thinking offers hope for peaceful resolution of the North Korean nuclear issue.

POSSIBLE WAYS FORWARD

Frustrating and even depressing though the North Korean nuclear quandary can seem at times, and while the authors in this study all remain sober about the chances for peaceful resolution of the matter, this volume does offer several possible ways forward toward resolution of the issue. These appear primarily in the chapters by Hayes and Bruce (chapter 1), Moore (chapter 2), and Toloraya (chapter 7), but suggestions are offered by other authors as well.

In chapter 1, Hayes and Bruce stress the importance of establishing a Korea-Japan nuclear-weapon-free zone. Because Pyongyang has little trust in Washington, Hayes and Bruce suggest that such a zone be initiated by Seoul or Tokyo, with assurances given to Pyongyang that the United States has no nuclear weapons in the zone, nor would it transit any through ports of nation-states in the zone,. Further, South Korea and Japan would agree not to develop nor allow the deployment of such weapons on their territories, in their waters, or over their airspace. The United States would also offer security guarantees to North Korea that it would not use weapons against it, as well as other security guarantees that Hayes and Bruce argue might be sufficient enough to coax Pyongyang away from its nuclear weapons and weapons programs. Policymakers should consider this approach, although a buy-in from Washington might be more likely with a nuclear no-first-use pledge rather than a non-use pledge, for Washington certainly would want to reserve the right to use nuclear weapons to respond to a nuclear attack from North Korea on the United States, Japan, or South Korea—something that could in fact be seen as part of its treaty commitment to defend South Korea and Japan. In addition, the United States could commit to a nonaggression pledge with Pyongyang; in other words, the United States would pledge not to attack North Korea as long as Pyongyang remained within its treaty commitments and refrained from attacks on other member states.

In chapter 2 I argue that U.S. policy since the 1990s and the first North Korean nuclear crisis has failed to achieve Washington's stated goals of preventing North Korea from attaining nuclear weapons and proliferating nuclear weapons, nuclear materials, nuclear know-how, or anything else related to its nuclear program to other states or non-state actors. Consequently I propose a fresh approach for U.S. policy. I stress that the U.S. role is key here because the United States is the power that North Korea really fears, and the United States still has some leverage over South Korea and Japan. The approach is a sort of "preemptive recognition" of North Korea. U.S. policy in the past has always been to seek verifiable North Korean denuclearization *first, followed by* a treaty formally ending the Korean War, U.S. recognition of North Korea, and the establishment of full diplomatic relations between Pyongyang and the United States. Instead, I suggest that during a period of relative amicability the United States reverse the order, with a formal ending of the Korean War by treaty, full U.S. recognition of the DPRK, and the establishment of full diplomatic relations coming first, as confidence-building measures, and denuclearization would come later, perhaps in two or three years. A number of the authors, and many other observers of the North Korean nuclear impasse, have urged the United States to take such a proactive approach, as have Chinese and Russian officials, whose help is necessary to secure any agreements with Pyongyang. The argument is that if Pyongyang rejects, drags its feet, or reneges on such an offer, it would come under severe pressure from Beijing and Moscow for rejecting that which it has said it seeks for some time, and the United States would find itself in a stronger position to take a firmer stand on the issue with a greater likelihood of support from all of North Korea's neighbors. This approach might in fact provide a way out for the Kim regime, providing Pyongyang a more secure environment for the continued transition of power to Kim Jong-un, and possibly even create an atmosphere as a starting point in which the Kim regime could enact the sort of economic and political reforms China began in the late 1970s. I argue that this approach would only be appropriate during a period of relatively benign or positive North Korean behavior, but would not be appropriate immediately following provocative behavior.

Toloraya offers another way forward in chapter 7. His argument is that the only way North Korean policy will ever change is for domestic reform to deepen, and which would come primarily through economic reforms and greater trade with the outside world. While it is too early to tell at present, and continuity appears more likely at least in the short run, Kim Jong-il's death may in time open up new possibilities in Pyongyang for a fresh approach to reform within North Korea. Toloraya stresses the importance of the other members of the Six Party Talks expanding trade ties with Pyongyang. For this to happen, of course, Seoul would have to return to its softer line of the Sunshine Policy years, and the United States and Japan would have to ease trade restrictions with North Korea. In addition, Toloraya argues, Seoul, Tokyo, and Washington would need to decide if they are willing to coexist with North Korea as it is, restore the DPRK's international diplomatic standing, and offer Pyongyang security assurances in return for a North Korean pledge to denuclearize completely within a specific time period, with Toloraya suggesting ten years. In addition, Toloraya suggests that the nations in the region build on the Six Party Talks to erect a regional security architecture that would help institutionalize bilateral and multilateral arrangements conducive to peace and security among the nations in the region. He offers some good suggestions that policymakers should take seriously.

These three approaches are complementary, in fact, and could be used together. Toloraya's and my suggestions reverse the order of sequencing, offering Pyongyang diplomatic recognition, security assurances, and a regional security architecture first, with denuclearization to follow. All three approaches emphasize offering a comprehensive set of security assurances and the erection of a security architecture—or nuclear-weapon-free zone in Hayes and Bruce's case—prior to North Korea's denuclearization. This approach is realistic, for it recognizes the legitimacy of the DPRK's real security dilemma and is a goodwill gesture that has a good chance of building a sufficient level of trust that could unlock the stalled process and move things toward resolution. Lankov's chapter reminds us, however, that many obstacles remain. His warnings as to the difficulties of simultaneously meeting the needs of all six parties should be taken seriously. This said, our study ends on a note of optimism. A number of things have not yet been tried in regard to resolving the impasse surrounding the weaponization of North Korea's nuclear capabilities and the potential for full operationalization. Perhaps a number of political stars are yet to align for a solution to be found, but if several of the authors in this volume are right, there is reason for guarded optimism.

This volume demonstrates that the North Korean nuclear issue is one of the most important issues in international relations today, given the importance of the Northeast Asian region for international relations, relations between the players involved (China and the United States, in particular), the importance of maintaining the nuclear nonproliferation regime and the threat thereto posed by actions of states such as North Korea, and finally the proliferation potential that North Korea's nuclear program poses for the world. The North Korean nuclear crisis has dragged on for almost twenty years in a dangerous state of irresolution. The contributors and I hope that this volume might aid in a greater understanding of the seriousness of the issue and the perspectives of some of the actors party to the issue, and that it might offer some fresh thinking on methods of resolution. Maintaining peace and security in the region and in the world, especially given the potential for nuclear proliferation it poses, depends in no small measure on successful resolution of the North Korean nuclear crisis.

Notes

INTRODUCTION: THE PROBLEM WITH AN OPERATIONALLY NUCLEAR NORTH KOREA

1. Taken from John Hersey, *Hiroshima* (New York: Knopf, 1946), 22–23.

2. In Graham Allison, *Nuclear Terrorism: The Ultimate Preventable Catastrophe* (New York: Holt, 2005), 44; *60 Minutes*, "The Perfect Terrorist Weapon," CBS News, September 7, 1997.

3. See Siegfried Hecker, "Denuclearizing North Korea," *Bulletin of the Atomic Scientists* 64, no. 2 (May/June 2008), www.thebulletin.org/files/064002011_0.pdf, 44; and Jeffrey Park, "The North Korean Nuclear Test: What the Seismic Data Says," *Bulletin of the Atomic Scientists*, May 26, 2009, http://thebulletin.org/web-edition/features/the-north-korean-nuclear-test-what-the-seismic-data-says.

4. Peter Hayes and Scott Bruce argue in their chapter that North Korea does have the capability to use its nuclear device on its own territory to attack an invading enemy, although doing so would be highly risky for Pyongyang and in the end unlikely.

5. Nuclear weapons expert Ashley Tellis defines "weaponization" in two senses—one broader, one narrower. Here I define "nuclear weaponization" in Tellis's broader sense, but use "nuclear operationality" as he uses the term "weaponization" in its narrow sense. See Ashley Tellis, *India's Emerging Nuclear Posture: Between Recessed Deterrent and Ready Arsenal* (Santa Monica, CA: Rand, 2001), 175.

6. In response to the question of why India does not just accede to the NPT, Twining points out that the NPT is not an open treaty in the sense of allowing new members beyond the original United States, United Kingdom, France, China, and Russia (which signed on as the U.S.S.R.). Nations cannot join unless they are nonnuclear states.

CHAPTER 1: TRANSLATING NORTH KOREA'S NUCLEAR THREATS INTO CONSTRAINED OPERATIONAL REALITY

1. This list of categories is drawn from one of the few unclassified overviews of nuclear operations: A. Carter, J. Steinbruner, and C. Zraket, eds., *Managing Nuclear Operations* (Washington, DC: Brookings Institution Press, 1987).

2. See P. Hayes and S. Bruce, "North Korean Nuclear Nationalism and the Threat of Nuclear War in Korea," *NAPSNet Policy Forum 11-09*, April 21, 2011, http://nautilus.org/napsnet/napsnet-policy-forum/11-09-hayes-bruce/.

3. A good and realistic assessment comes from A. Cordesman, "Cool Heads Needed on North Korea ICBM Tests," Spacewar, July 5, 2006, www.spacewar.com/reports/Cool_Heads_ Needed_On_North_Korea_ICBM_Tests_999.html.

4. For a good technical description of the forces and technology involved, see J. Constant, *Fundamentals of Strategic Weapons, Offense and Defense Systems* (The Hague: Martinus Nijhoff, 1981), chap. 3, esp. 167.

5. P. Hayes et al., *Chasing Gravity's Rainbow: Kwajalein and U.S. Ballistic Missile Testing* (Canberra: Centre for Defense and Strategic Studies, Australian National University, 1991), http://gc.nautilus.org/Nautilus/about-nautilus/staff/peter-hayes/1991/chasing-gravitys-rain bow.pdf, 75–80.

6. "Strategic Weapon System, Korea, North," *Jane's Sentinel Security Assessment—China and Northeast Asia*, January 22, 2010.

7. Marine Corps Intelligence Activity, *North Korea Country Handbook*, MCIA-2630-NK -016-97, May 1997, www.fas.org/nuke/guide/dprk/nkor.pdf, 37.

8. Conventional electromagnetic pulse (EMP) weapons are under development in South Korea and reportedly in North Korea. The notion of a North Korean high-altitude nuclear EMP attack on the United States is a favorite notion of conservative U.S. strategic analysts— regardless, apparently, of the DPRK's inability to get a missile to work, let alone get a warhead above the United States. See F. Gaffney, "Pyongyang Goes Ballistic," National Review Online, June 20, 2006, www.nationalreview.com/articles/217987/pyongyang-goes-ballistic/frank-j-gaff ney-jr.

9. The standard unclassified reference on the complex phenomenon of nuclear EMP is in Samuel Glasstone and Phillip J. Dolan, "The Electromagnetic Pulse and Its Effects," in U.S. Department of Defense and Energy Research and Development Administration, *The Effects of Nuclear Weapons* (Washington, DC: U.S. Government Printing Office, 1977), 514–40.

10. See, for example, "NBC Capabilities—Nuclear, Korea, North," *Jane's Nuclear, Biological, and Chemical Defense*, August 12, 2010, which states that North Korea "possesses the re- sources, personnel and technology to produce radiological dispersal devices and crude elec- tromagnetic pulse (EMP) weapons."

11. For a contrasting view that provides a fantastic taxonomy of possible DPRK nuclear attacks including on South Korean cities, see B. Bennett, "Uncertainties in the North Korean Nuclear Threat," Rand documented briefing, Santa Monica, CA, 2010, www.rand.org/pubs/ documented_briefings/2010/RAND_DB589.pdf. We differ with Bennett's approach in that we consider the issue of reliability as central to which options are realistic to a DPRK decision- maker before and during a war in the peninsula.

12. See U.S. Defense Intelligence Agency, *North Korean Armed Forces Handbook*, DDI- 2680-37-77, Washington, DC, 1977), 2–33, 34, 45 (released under U.S. Freedom of Information Act to Nautilus Institute); also cited in P. Hayes, *Pacific Powderkeg: American Nuclear Dilemmas in Korea* (Lexington, MA: Lexington Books, 1990), 126–27.

13. See P. Hayes and S. Bruce, "Nuclear Competition and Korean Nationalism," paper presented at the Nautilus Institute research workshop "Strong Connections: Australia-Korea Strategic Relations—Past, Present and Future," Seoul, Korea, June 15–16, 2010, www.nautilus .org/projects/akf-connections/research-workshop/research-papers/Hayes.pdf.

14. "US–S. Korean Moves to Bring Down System in DPRK Warned," KCNA, March 26, 2010, www.kcna.co.jp/item/2010/201003/news26/20100326-04ee.html.

15. Toloraya states rather coyly later in this volume that "the DPRK becoming a de facto nuclear power probably has not increased an immediate risk of conflict in the region." Elsewhere he has been more explicit: "My opinion is that the actual use of a DPRK nuclear weapon (even if it were to prove to be operational) is highly improbable. The exception is an all-out war, and all-out war is actually deterred by the presence of nuclear potential in North Korea" (see G. Toloraya, "Russia and the North Korean Knot," *Asia-Pacific Journal*, 16-2-10, April 19, 2010, www.japanfocus.org/-Georgy-Toloraya/3345).

16. "DPRK Issues Foreign Ministry 'Memorandum' 21 Apr on Denuclearization of Korean Peninsula," KCNA, April 4, 2010, www.kcna.co.jp/calendar/2010/04/04-21/2010-0421-024.html; open source translation at www.armscontrolwonk.com/2708/seoul-purposeoriginal.

17. P. Bracken, *The Command and Control of Nuclear Forces* (New Haven, CT: Yale University Press, 1985).

18. J. Lewis, "Rethinking Extended Deterrence in Northeast Asia," paper presented at the Nautilus Institute research workshop "Strong Connections: Australia-Korea Strategic Relations —Past, Present and Future," Seoul, Korea, June 15–16, 2010, www.nautilus.org/projects/akf -connections/research-workshop/research-papers/Lewis.pdf.

19. See P. Hayes, "The Status Quo Isn't Working: A Nuke-Free Zone Is Needed Now," Global Asia, September 2010, www.globalasia.org/V5N3_Fall_2010/Peter_Hayes.html. For a detailed exposition of this concept and the many issues that must be addressed to implement such a zone, see "Korea-Japan Nuclear Weapon Free Zone (KJNWFZ) Concept Paper," Nautilus Institute, May 6, 2010, www.globalcollab.org/Nautilus/initiatives/korea-japan-nwfz/intro duction/.

20. M. Hamel-Green, "Implementing a Japanese-Korean Nuclear Weapon Free Zone: Precedents, Legal Forms, Governance, Scope and Domain, Verification and Compliance, and Regional Benefits," paper presented at the Nautilus Institute research workshop "Strong Connections: Australia-Korea Strategic Relations—Past, Present and Future," Seoul, Korea, June 15–16, 2010, www.nautilus.org/projects/akf-connections/research-workshop/research -papers/Hamel-Green.pdf.

CHAPTER 2: NORTH KOREAN NUCLEAR WEAPONIZATION

This chapter is an updated and revised version of an article originally published as "America's Failed North Korea Nuclear Policy: A New Approach," *Asian Perspective* 32, no. 4 (Winter 2008): 9–27.

1. See Dafna Linzer, "U.S. Misled Allies about Nuclear Export: North Korea Sent Material to Pakistan, not Libya," *Washington Post*, March 20, 2005; Seymour M. Hersh, "A Strike in the Dark," *New Yorker*, February 11, 2008, 58; and Christina Y. Lin, "The King from the East: DPRK-Syria-Iran Nuclear Nexus and Strategic Implications for Israel and the ROK," Academic Papers Series 3, no. 7, Korea Economic Institute, Washington, DC, October 2008, www .keia.org/sites/default/files/publications/APS-Lin.pdf. Maria Rost Rublee's chapter in this volume highlights the possibility that North Korea may be working with Myanmar on a nuclear

program, and recent revelations suggest a conventional arms nexus between Pyongyang and the junta ruling Myanmar as well (see Thomas Fuller and David E. Sanger, "Officials Seek Destination of North Korean Arms," *New York Times*, December 14, 2009).

2. James Kelly, "Dealing with North Korea's Nuclear Programs," Statement to the Foreign Relations Committee, U.S. Senate, Washington, DC, July 15, 2004.

3. For more, see Arms Control Association, "Chronology of U.S.-North Korean Nuclear and Missile Diplomacy," updated April 12, 2012, www.armscontrol.org/factsheets/dprkchron#2007.

4. See Arms Control Association, "North Korea's Uranium Enrichment Challenge," *Issue Brief V*, vol. 1, no. 36, November 22, 2010, www.armscontrol.org/issuebriefs/DPRKChallenge.

5. Martin Kalinowski, a nuclear expert at the University of Hamburg, concluded that the May 2009 test yielded a blast of about four kilotons (slightly larger than the 2006 test), smaller than the U.S. bombs dropped on Hiroshima and Nagasaki in 1945, which yielded blasts of fifteen and twenty-two kilotons, respectively (Thom Shanker and William J. Broad, "Seismic Readings Point to a Small Nuclear Test," *New York Times*, May 26, 2009). In the *Bulletin of the Atomic Scientists*, Jeffrey Park concurs. See Jeffrey Park, "The North Korean Nuclear Test: What the Seismic Data Says," *Bulletin of the Atomic Scientists*, May 26, 2009, http://thebulletin.org/web-edition/features/the-north-korean-nuclear-test-what-the-seismic-data-.

6. Lin, "King from the East," 2.

7. James Forsyth and Douglas Davis, "We Came So Close to World War Three that Day," *Spectator* (UK), October 3, 2007.

8. Hersh, "Strike in the Dark."

9. See Linzer, "U.S. Misled Allies about Nuclear Export," and Daniel A. Pinkston, "North Korea's Nuclear Weapons Program and the Six Party Talks," Nuclear Threat Initiative, Washington, DC, April 2006, www.nti.org/e_research/e3_76.html.

10. Glenn Kessler, "Bhutto Dealt Nuclear Secrets to N. Korea, Book Says," *Washington Post*, June 1, 2008, as cited in Lin, "King from the East," 2.

11. R. Jeffrey Smith, "Pakistan's Nuclear-Bomb Maker Says North Korea Paid Bribes for Know-How," *Washington Post*, July 6, 2011, www.washingtonpost.com/world/national-security/pakistans-nuclear-bomb-maker-says-north-korea-paid-bribes-for-know-how/2010/11/12/gIQAZ1kH1H_story.html?hpid=z3). See also Arms Control Association, "North Korea's Uranium Enrichment Challenge."

12. "An Israeli Lesson for North Korea?" *Economist Foreign Report*, April 22, 1993, 2; see also James Phillips, "Iran's Nuclear Program: What Is Known and Unknown," Heritage Foundation, Washington, DC, March 26, 2010, www.heritage.org/Research/Reports/2010/03Iran-s-Nuclear-Program-What-Is-Known-and-Unknown.

13. Douglas Frantz, "Iran Closes In on Ability to Build a Nuclear Bomb," *Los Angeles Times*, August 4, 2003; "Military Source: DPRK, Iran Planning Joint Development of Nuclear Warheads," *Sankei Shimbun* (Tokyo), August 6, 2003; "Iranian Nuke Experts Visited N. Korea This Year," Kyodo World Service, June 10, 2003, all cited by Lin ("King from the East").

14. James Phillips, "Iran's Nuclear Program: What Is Known and Unknown," Heritage Foundation, March 26, 2010, www.heritage.org/Research/Reports/2010/03Iran-s-Nuclear-Program-What-Is-Known-and-Unknown.

15. George W. Bush, "The President's National Security Strategy," March 16, 2006, www.state.gov/documents/organization/63319.pdf.

16. Leon V. Sigal, "Preventing a Nuclear North Korea," *National Interest*, June 23, 2011, http://nationalinterest.org/commentary/preventing-nuclear-north-korea-5518.

17. Senior State Department, C.I.A., Defense Department, and other officials, interviews with author, Washington, DC, 2002.

18. For examples, see James Mann, *Rise of the Vulcans: The History of Bush's War Cabinet* (New York: Penguin, 2004); Bob Woodward, *Bush at War* (New York: Simon and Schuster, 2003).

19. These comments are based upon various reports, but the Iraq example comes explicitly from the author's attendance at a 2004 panel on the Iraq War at the American Political Science Association's annual meeting in Chicago with a number of participants who were the best-known U.S. Iraq experts and Iraq consultants in the run-up to the war. One after another, they recounted how they had been invited to policy brainstorming sessions that Bush administration officials chaired in 2002. Once their misgivings about the war became apparent, they were effectively excluded from future such meetings.

20. See Charles L. Pritchard, *Failed Diplomacy: The Tragic Story of How North Korea Got the Bomb* (Washington, DC: Brookings Institution Press, 2007).

21. Pritchard documents these divisions well; see ibid.

22. Jeffrey Bader, *Obama and China's Rise: An Insider's Account of America's Asia Strategy* (Washington, DC: Brookings Institution Press, 2012).

23. Victor Cha, "What Do They Really Want? Obama's North Korea Conundrum," *Washington Quarterly*, October 2009, csis.org/files/publication/twq09octobercha.pdf.

24. Pritchard, *Failed Diplomacy*, 161.

25. "New" here does not necessarily mean that no one has thought of or proposed these ideas or policies before, but rather that they have not been tried.

26. See China Institutes of Contemporary International Relations, "The Security Mechanism of Northeast Asia: Reality and Prospect," *Xiandai guoji guanxi* [*Contemporary International Relations*] 12, no. 8 (2002); D. Li, "The Relations in Northeast Asia: Conflict and Cooperation," *Institute of World Economics and Politics*, Chinese Academy of Social Sciences, Beijing, 2006, www.iwep.org.cn/english/index-2.htm; and Chu Shulong, "Beyond Crisis Management: Prospects for a Northeast Asian Security Architecture," in *Security through Cooperation: Furthering Asia Pacific Multilateral Engagement*, Council for Security Cooperation in the Asia Pacific Regional Security Outlook, Canada, 2007, 13–18, www.cscap.ca/Chu%20Executive%20Summary.pdf.

27. For example, Pritchard (*Failed Diplomacy*), U.S. secretary of state Condoleezza Rice, the U.S. State Department's Christopher Hill, and even President Barack Obama have all argued for such a framework.

28. From Australia, see Peter Van Ness, "The North Korean Nuclear Crisis: Four-Plus-Two—An Idea Whose Time Has Come," in Mel Gurtov and Peter Van Ness, eds., *Confronting the Bush Doctrine: Critical Views from the Asia-Pacific* (New York: Routledge, 2005), 242–59. From South Korea, see Keun-sik Kim, "The Prospects for Institutionalizing the Six Party Talks," *Policy Forum Online*, Nautilus Institute, July 12, 2007, www.nautilus.org/fora/security/07051Kim.html.

29. If Yongho Kim is correct, it may not hurt for the United States to have a few bunker-buster-carrying aircraft parked somewhere at an airfield in South Korea at the time this new

approach was made to Pyongyang. Kim's research led him to draw a correlation between the presence of U.S. F-117s (retired in 2008, but known for their bunker-buster carrying capabilities) in South Korea and progress on talks with North Korea. His argument is that Kim Jong-il feared these bombs more than anything else, as he could be their target, and thus offered a way to hold Kim accountable. See Yongho Kim, *North Korean Foreign Policy: Security Dilemma and Succession* (Lanham, MD: Lexington Books, 2011). The newest Massive Ordinance Penetrator bunker-buster bomb, which can penetrate two hundred feet underground, is carried by the B2 bomber and would certainly fill the bill.

30. See the UK Foreign and Commonwealth Office, listing for Korea, DPRK, accessed February 25, 2012, www.fco.gov.uk/en/about-the-fco/country-profiles/asia-oceania/north-korea?profile=all.

31. As an example, see So Ki-sok, "Situation in the Korean Peninsula—A North Korean Perspective," in *Three Perspectives on Korean Developments*, PacNet no. 55, Pacific Forum, Center for Strategic and International Studies, Honolulu, HI, August 6, 2009, http://csis.org/publication/pacent-55three-perspectives-on-korean-developments.

32. Gregory J. Moore, "How North Korea Threatens China's Interests: Understanding Chinese 'Duplicity' on the North Korean Nuclear Issue," *International Relations of the Asia-Pacific* 8, no. 1 (January 2008): 1–29, and chapter 4 in this volume.

33. Here, too, see Ki-sok, "Situation in the Korean Peninsula."

34. See Pritchard, *Failed Diplomacy*, 58–59; Siegfried Hecker, "Report on North Korean Nuclear Program," Center for International Security and Cooperation, Stanford University, Stanford, CA, November 15, 2006, http://cisac.stanford.edu/publications/report_on_north_korean_nuclear_program/); and Leon V. Sigal, *Disarming Strangers: Nuclear Diplomacy with North Korea* (Princeton, NJ: Princeton University Press, 1998).

35. See Jeffrey Bader, *Obama and China's Rise: An Insider's Account of America's Asia Strategy* (Washington, DC: Brookings Institution Press, 2012).

CHAPTER 3: THE IMPLICATIONS FOR SEOUL OF AN OPERATIONALLY NUCLEAR NORTH KOREA

1. Norman D. Levin and Yong-Sub Han, *Sunshine in Korea: South Korean Debates over Policies toward North Korea* (Santa Monica, CA: Rand, 2002).

2. Gi-Wook Shin and Kristin C. Burke, "North Korea and Identity Politics in South Korea," *Brown Journal of World Affairs* 15, no. 11 (Spring 2008): 287–303.

3. "OPLAN 5027 Major Theater War-West," Global Security, page last modified May 7, 2011, www.globalsecurity.org/military/ops/oplan-5027-1.htm.

4. Tae Hyun Kim, "South Korean Perspectives on the North Korean Nuclear Question," *Mershon International Studies Review* 40, no. 2 (Summer 1996): 255–61.

5. Namkung Gon, "North Korea and Its Developing Nuclear Capability Issues in South Korean–US Public's Minds," *Journal of American Studies* 39, no. 1 (Spring 2007): 37–93.

6. Key-young Son, *South Korean Engagement and North Korea: Identities, Norms, and the Sunshine Policy* (New York: Routledge, 2006).

7. Zhiqun Zhu, "Small Power, Big Ambition: South Korea's Role in Northeast Asian Security under Roh Moo-hyun," *Asian Affairs: An American Review* 34, no. 2 (Spring 2007): 67–86.

8. Even in April 2010 in the aftermath of the sinking of the South Korean naval vessel *Cheonan*, merely 6.3% of South Korea's public demanded military means as the preferred policy option toward North Korea, according to an opinion survey by the Ministry of Unification. In the same survey, the preference for a military policy solution increased to 56% immediately after the shelling of South Korea's Yeongpyong Island in December 2010, at which time 41.1% still demanded nonmilitary options. This number is arguably an outlier, given that the general trend of public opinion from December 2002 has displayed an overwhelming preference for nonmilitary measures, such as diplomatic pressure or economic sanctions. Moreover, three months after the shelling, the policy preference for nonmilitary options returned to the dominating preference (78% according to an opinion survey by *Dong-A Daily*). One would have expected the South Korean public's preferences to have been more hawkish, given their suffering from North Korea's provocations for the last twenty years, but preference for the Sunshine Policy remains dominant.

9. Marcus Noland, "The Economic Implications of a North Korean Nuclear Test," *Asia Policy* 2, no. 26 (July 2006): 25–39.

10. Financial Supervisory Service, *Weekly Newsletter*, October 23, 2006, 2.

11. "South Korean Stock, Won Drop after North Tests Nuclear Weapon," Bloomberg, May 25, 2009, www.bloomberg.com/apps/news?pid=20601087&sid=aoiwz3EqeSUw.

12. Chung-in Moon and Davis Steinberg, eds., *The Kim Dae-jung Government and Sunshine Policy* (Seoul: Yonsei University Press, 1999).

13. Joel S. Wit, Daniel Poneman, and Robert L. Gallucci, *Going Critical: The First North Korean Nuclear Crisis* (Washington, DC: Brookings Institution Press, 2004).

14. "Containment" here is defined as the steady application of counterpressures short of war against the North's attempts to expand its nuclear capability. The definition comes from John Lewis Gaddis, *Strategies of Containment: A Critical Appraisal of Postwar American National Security* (Oxford: Oxford University Press, 1982).

15. Alexander George, *Forceful Persuasion: Coercive Diplomacy as an Alternative to War* (Washington, DC: United States Institute of Peace Press, 1993).

16. See, e.g., James Clay Moltz, "Future Nuclear Proliferation Scenarios in Northeast Asia," *Nonproliferation Review* 13, no. 3 (Fall 2006): 591–604.

17. Mitchell Reiss, "Prospects for Nuclear Proliferation in Asia," in Ashley J. Tellis and Michael Wills, *Strategic Asia 2005–06: Military Modernization in an Era of Uncertainty* (Seattle, WA: National Bureau of Asian Research, 2005), 351.

18. Paul Huth and Bruce Russett, "What Makes Deterrence Work? Cases from 1900 to 1980," *World Politics* 36, no. 4 (July 1984): 496–526.

19. Robert Jervis, "Deterrence Theory Revisited," *World Politics* 31, no. 2 (January 1979): 289–324; Richard Ned Lebow and Janice Gross Stein, "Rational Deterrence Theory: I Think, Therefore I Deter," *World Politics* 41, no. 2 (January 1989): 208–24.

20. Christopher Achen and Duncan Snidal, "Rational Deterrence Theory and Comparative Case Studies," *World Politics* 41, no. 2 (January 1989): 143–69.

21. Xide Jin, "The Six Party Talks: To Search for Common Points," *World Affairs* 9, no. 1 (2005): 26.

22. Feng Zhu, "China's Foreign Mediation and the Six Party Talks on the North Korean Nuclear Problem," *Foreign Affairs Review* (April 2008): 23–30.

23. Chung-in Moon, "Diplomacy of Defiance and Facilitation: The Six Party Talks and the Roh Moo-hyun Government," *Asian Perspective* 32, no. 4 (Winter 2009): 71–105.

24. David Baldwin, *Economic State Craft* (Princeton, NJ: Princeton University Press, 1985).

25. Robert S. Litwak, "Living with Ambiguity: Nuclear Deals with Iran and North Korea," *Survival* 50, no. 1 (February–March 2008): 91–118.

26. Leon Sigal, "North Korea Policy on the Rocks: What Can Be Done to Restore Constructive Engagement?" *Global Asia* 4, no. 2 (June 2009): 8–12.

27. Chung-in Moon and Jong-Yun Bae, "The Bush Doctrine and the North Korean Nuclear Crisis," *Asian Perspective* 27, no. 4 (Winter 2003): 9–45.

28. Republic of Korea, Ministry of Unification, "Basic Facts about Inter-Korean Relations," 2008, www.unikorea.go.kr/eng/default.jsp?pgname=LIBpublications.

29. Jacques E. C. Hymans, *The Psychology of Nuclear Proliferation: Identity, Emotions and Foreign Policy* (Cambridge: Cambridge University Press, 2006).

30. John Mueller, "Nuclear Weapons," *Foreign Policy* (January/February 2009): 44.

CHAPTER 4: BEIJING'S PROBLEM WITH AN OPERATIONALLY
NUCLEAR NORTH KOREA

This is a revised and updated version of Gregory J. Moore, "How North Korea Threatens China's Interests: Understanding Chinese 'Duplicity' on the North Korean Nuclear Issue," *International Relations of the Asia-Pacific* 8, no. 1 (2008): 1–29.

1. *People's Daily*, "China Resolutely Opposes DPRK's Nuclear Test," October 9, 2006, http://english.peopledaily.com.cn/200610/09/print20061009_310140.html.

2. Interview conducted by the author in Beijing, 2005. For this chapter I conducted a series of interviews in Beijing and Shanghai, China, in 2004 and 2005 with some of China's North Korea watchers, as well as several follow-up interviews in 2008, 2009, and 2012. Some names appear in the text, but other names do not, in accordance with the wishes of the interviewees. The interviewees come from China's best universities, the Chinese Foreign Ministry, the Chinese Communist Party, and think tanks within China's defense and intelligence communities. I am confident that the views about North Korea that these experts expressed represent those that Chinese policymakers encounter when seeking advice from China's foremost experts on North Korea; most of the interviewees were among the persons the government actually consults when seeking North Korea policy advice.

3. M. Dickie and A. Fifield, "China's Food Aid to North Korea Soars," *Financial Times*, July 21, 2006.

4. E. Pan, "South Korea's Ties with China, Japan, and the U.S.: Defining a New Role in a Dangerous Neighborhood," Council on Foreign Relations, Washington, DC, February 8, 2006, www.cfr.org/publication/9808/.

5. Scott Snyder and See-won Byun, "China-Korea Relations: Pyongyang Tests Beijing's Patience," *Comparative Connections* 11, Center for Strategic and International Studies, Washington, DC, July 2009.

6. B. Lim, "China's North Korea Trade Best Birthday Gift for Kim," *Business Week*, February 16, 2011, www.businessweek.com/news/2011-02-16/china-s-north-korea-trade-best-birthday-gift-for-kim.html.

7. Sang-hun Choe, "North Korea Rents Out Its Resources to Stave Off Reform," *New York Times*, October 25, 2011.

8. North Korea watcher in China's defense sector, interview with author, Beijing, 2005.

9. X. Yan, "Dong Ya Hepingde Jichu" [The Foundations of East Asia's Peace], *Shijie Jingji yu Zhengzhi* [*World Economics and Politics*], no. 3 (2004): www.irchina.org/news/view.asp?id=485.

10. X. Yan, *Zhongguo Guojia Liyi Fenxi* [*An Analysis of China's National Interests*] (Tianjin, China: Tianjin Renmin Chubanshe, 1997).

11. C. Lee, "Conflict and Cooperation: The Pacific Powers and Korea," in N. Eberstadt and R. Ellings, eds., *Korea's Future and the Great Powers* (Seattle, WA: National Bureau for Asian Research, 2001), 89.

12. B. Cumings, *North Korea: Another Country* (New York: New Press, 2004), 21.

13. Chinese DPRK expert, discussion with author, 2004.

14. "Juche" has been translated as "subject" or "spirit of self-reliance," but it became—and remains today—the North Korean ruling philosophy first espoused by Kim Il-sung that can be understood as "Korean self-reliance" or "Korean essentialism."

15. K. Oh and R. Hassig, *North Korea through the Looking Glass* (Washington, DC: Brookings Institution Press, 2000), 106–17.

16. The North Korean leadership seems to have been strengthening the Korean Workers' Party at the expense of the military since 2010. The Central Military Commission, which belongs to the Party, has been elevated with Kim Jong-un as its leader, since his being named Kim Jong-il's official successor in 2010.

17. At least one of China's senior North Korea watchers concurred (in an interview with the author, 2004). B. R. Myers, in *The Cleanest Race: How North Koreans See Themselves and Why It Matters* (Brooklyn, NY: Melville House, 2010), argues similarly that the DPRK has gone from leftist, communist thinking, to rightist, hypernationalist, almost fascistic thinking in recent years.

18. Toward the end of his tenure, Kim Jong-il had begun resuscitating the Korean Workers' Party, which met in the fall of 2010 for the first time in thirty years to formally endorse Kim Jong-un's ascension as heir to the Kim dynasty. It met again in April 2012 after Kim Jong-il's death to formally establish the supreme leadership of Kim Jong-un. How strong the party's position will be going forward under Kim III remains unclear.

19. J. Brook, "China Fears Once and Future Kingdom," *New York Times*, August 25, 2005; D. Goma, "The Chinese-Korean Border Issue: An Analysis of a Contested Frontier," *Asian Survey* 46, no. 6 (2006): 867–80. Koguryo was a large kingdom that straddled the China-Korean border from 37 BC to AD 668. Chinese and Koreans (North and South) each claim Koguryo as their own, though Korea historian Ned Shultz says, "Koguryo was neither Chinese nor Korean, but Koguryo" (from a discussion with author at East-West Center, Honolulu, May 24, 2004).

20. China's support of North Korea's position, or at least its agnosticism regarding blame for the two events, has infuriated South Koreans.

21. J. You, "China and North Korea: A Fragile Relationship of Strategic Convenience," *Journal of Contemporary China* 10, no. 28 (August 2001): 389–90; and *The Guardian*, "US Embassy Cables: China 'Would Accept' Korean Unification," December 1, 2010, www.guardian.co.uk/world/us-embassy-cables-documents/249870.

22. Korea Trade and Investment Promotion Agency, *A Handbook on North Korea* (Seoul: Naewoe Press, 1998).

23. J. Chung, *Between Ally and Partner: Korea-China Relations and the United States* (New York: Columbia University Press, 2007), 94.

24. Lim, "China's North Korea Trade Best Birthday Gift for Kim."

25. J. Kim, "The Political Economy of Chinese Investment in North Korea," *Asian Survey* 46, no. 6 (2006): 898–916.

26. Interview with author, China, 2004.

27. S. Kim and T. Lee, "Chinese–North Korean Relations: Managing Asymmetrical Interdependence," in S. Kim and T. Lee, eds., *North Korea and Northeast Asia* (Boulder, CO: Rowman and Littlefield, 2002), 122.

28. K. Kim, "Pyongyang, Taipei Seen to Share Feeling of Diplomatic Isolation in Nuclear-Waste Case," *Korea Herald*, February 10, 1997, 1.

29. H. Jen, "Inside Story of Vicissitudes of Sino-DPRK Relations," *Hsin Pao*, July 19, 1996, 15, in FBIS-CHI-96-140, http://wnc.fedworld.gov/; S. Kim, "The Making of China's Korea Policy in the Era of Reform," in D. Lampton, ed., *The Making of Chinese Foreign and Security Policy in the Era of Reform, 1978–2000* (Stanford, CA: Stanford University Press, 2001), 386–87.

30. International Crisis Group, *China and North Korea: Comrades Forever?*, Asia Report no. 112, February 2006, 16.

31. J. Kelly, "Dealing with North Korea's Nuclear Programs," Statement to the Foreign Relations Committee, U.S. Senate, Washington, DC, July 15, 2004; V. Cha and D. Kang, *Nuclear North Korea: A Debate on Engagement Strategies* (New York: Columbia University Press, 2003), 130–32.

32. F. Forney, "Family Feud: China's Patience for North Korea's Diplomatic Brinkmanship Has Worn Thin," *Time*, December 23, 2002, www.time.com/time/magazine/article/0,9171,400045,00.html.

33. Ibid.

34. Chinese North Korea watchers, discussions with authors, Beijing and Shanghai, 2004.

35. This news appeared in several Western news outlets, but I confirmed it with a Washington insider as well. See Jonathan Watts, "China Cuts Oil Supply to North Korea," *The Guardian*, April 1, 2003, www.guardian.co.uk/world/2003/apr/01/northkorea.china.

36. P. Pan, "China Deploys Troops on N. Korean Border," *Washington Post*, September 16, 2003.

37. Agence France Presse, "China Stopped Nuclear-Related Chemical Bound for North Korea: Japan Daily," February 21, 2004.

38. K. Bradsher and J. Brooke, "Chinese News Media Critical of North Korea," *New York Times*, February 13, 2005.

39. Interview with author, Beijing, March 2005.

40. U.S. Treasury Department, "Treasury Designates Banco Delta Asia as Primary Money Laundering Concern under USA PATRIOT Act," September 15, 2005, www.ustreas.gov/press/releases/js2720.htm.

41. J. Kahn, "North Korea and U.S. Spar, Causing Talks to Stall," *New York Times*, November 12, 2005.

42. S. Snyder, "China-Korea Relations: Kim Jong-il Pays Tribute to Beijing—in His Own

Way," in Asia Foundation/Pacific Forum Center for Strategic and International Studies, *Comparative Connections*, June 1, 2006, www.csis.org/images/stories/pacfor/0601qchina_skorea.pdf.

43. D. Kirk, "At Southeast Asia Gathering, Bid to Engage North Korea," *Christian Science Monitor*, July 28, 2006, www.iht.com/articles/2006/07/26/news/web.0726boc.php.

44. North Korea's shelling of Yeonpyeong Island was thus in response to South Korean shelling of its territorial waters, Pyongyang said in official statements.

45. Interview with author, Beijing, 2012.

46. Chinese analysts generally see Lee as too confrontational toward Pyongyang and too beholden to Washington.

47. Discussions in China, 2010–12.

48. Jane Perlez, "China-Korea Tensions Rise after Failed Venture," *New York Times*, October 20, 2012.

49. Zhu Feng, "China's Policy toward North Korea: A New Twist?," CSIS Pacific Forum PacNet no. 60, Honolulu, HI, December 8, 2010, csis.org/files/publication/pac1060.pdf.

50. A. Ang, "China Urges N. Korea Not to Test-Fire Missile," *Chicago Tribune*, June 29, 2006.

51. Associated Press, "Lips and Teeth: North Korea–China Ties Strained by Nuclear Test Vow," *International Herald Tribune*, October 8, 2006.

52. J. Kahn, "The North Korean Challenge; Angry China Is Likely to Toughen Its Stand on Korea," *New York Times*, October 10, 2006.

53. Ibid.

54. Ibid.

55. Again in February and March 2007, China cut off North Korea's oil supplies, restoring them in April; see Kyodo News Service, "China's Oil Exports to N. Korea Return to Normal in May," *Japan Today*, June 23, 2007, www.japantoday.com/jp/news/410217.

56. *People's Daily*, "China Resolutely Opposes DPRK's Nuclear Test," October 9, 2006.

57. Kahn, "North Korean Challenge."

58. Ibid.

59. L. Savage, "Bombs Away!" *Maclean's*, October 23, 2006.

60. D. Lee, "Former White House Aide Says China Considering PSI Participation," *Yonhap News*, November 15, 2006. See also S. Snyder and J. Wit, "Chinese Views: Breaking the Stalemate on the Korean Peninsula," United States Institute of Peace, Special Report, Washington, DC, February 2007. As of November 2012, however, China had not signed onto the PSI. See "Proliferation Security Initiative Participants," Bureau of International Security and Nonproliferation, Washington, DC, November 20, 2012.

61. G. Fairclough and N. King Jr., "China Banks to Halt Dealings with North Korea," *Wall Street Journal*, October 20, 2006.

62. D. Nanto and M. Manyin, "China–North Korean Relations," Congressional Research Service, Washington, DC, December 28, 2010: 19–20.

63. "China Imposes Its Own Sanctions on North Korea," *Asahi Shimbun*, June 13, 2009.

64. Chinese North Korea watcher, interview with author, China, 2004.

65. Chinese North Korea specialist, interview with author, China, 2004.

66. Y. Shi, "Chaoxian He Weiji: Lishi, Xianzhuang yu Keneng Qianjing—Qiantan Dangqiande 'Hanguo Wenti'" [The North Korean Nuclear Crisis: History, the Present Situation, Pos-

sible Prospects, and the Present "South Korea Problem"], *Jiaoxue yu Yanjiu* [*Teaching and Research*], no. 22004), www.irchina.org/news/view.asp?id=474; Yan, "Dong Ya Hepingde Jichu"; H. Chou, "Quanqiuhua Shidaide Zhongguo Zhoubian Anquan Huanjing" [China's Peripheral Security Environment in the Age of Globalization], *Shehui Kexue* [*Social Science*], no. 5, www .irchina.org/news/view.asp?id=936; J. Ren, "Dongya Duobian Anquan Jizhi: Zhongguode Kunnan yu Xuanze" [East Asian Multilateral Security Mechanisms: China's Difficulties and Choices], *Jinri Shijie* [*Today's World*], no. 10 (2005), www.irchina.org/news/view.asp?id=1111; A. Wu, "What China Whispers to North Korea," *Washington Quarterly* 28, no. 2 (Spring 2005): 35–48; X. Yu, "Zhongguo Mianlingde Anquan Weixie ji Zhanlue Xuanze Xin Sikao" [Fresh Thoughts on the Security Threats China Faces and Its Strategic Choices], *Waijiao Pinglun* [*Foreign Affairs Review*], no. 5 (2005), www.irchina.org/news/view.asp?id=1076; Y. Wang, "Good Signs from Korean Journey to a Safer Region," Institute of World Economics and Politics, Chinese Academy of Social Sciences, accessed June 20, 2006, www.iwep.org.cn/chinese/ gerenzhuye/wangyizhou/wenzhang/on%20korean%20situation.pdf.

67. *People's Daily*, "China Resolutely Opposes DPRK's Nuclear Test"; J. Chung, "China's Ascendancy and the Korean Peninsula: From Interest Reevaluation to Strategic Realignment?" in D. Shambaugh, ed., *Power Shift: China and Asia's New Dynamics* (Berkeley: University of California Press, 2005).

68. C. Hughes, "North Korea's Nuclear Weapons: Implications for the Nuclear Ambitions of Japan, South Korea, and Taiwan," *Asia Policy* 3 (January 2007): 75–104.

69. E. McVadon, "Chinese Military Strategy for the Korean Peninsula," *China's Military Faces the Future*, ed. J. Lilley and D. Shambaugh (Washington, DC: American Enterprise Institute and East Gate / M. E. Sharpe, 1999), 293.

70. U.S.-China Business Council, "U.S.-China Trade Statistics and China's World Trade Statistics," 2007, www.uschina.org/statistics/tradetable.html.

71. R. Irvine and C. Kincaid, "Japan and Nuclear Weapons," *Accuracy in Media*, June 28, 2002, www.aim.org/media_monitor_print/687_0_2_0/.

72. E. Johnston, "Fatal Accidents Damage Japan's Nuclear Dream," *The Observer*, August 22, 2004.

73. Hughes, "North Korea's Nuclear Weapons."

74. Ibid.

75. See the chapter by Izumi and Furukawa in this volume for more on this issue.

76. Hughes, "North Korea's Nuclear Weapons," 93–94.

77. Ibid., 95.

78. Nuclear Threat Initiative, "South Korea Profile," 2007, www.nti.org/e_research/pro files/SKorea/index.html.

79. Global Security, "Weapons of Mass Destruction: Taiwan," 2007, www.globalsecurity .org/wmd/world/taiwan/nuke.htm.

80. J. Tkacik Jr., "Taiwan Nukes, North Korea Nukes," Jamestown Foundation, January 6, 2004, www.jamestown.org/.

81. This conclusion is based on the comments of a senior Chinese military officer in a discussion with the author in Beijing in 2000, and as far as I know is still true today.

82. BBC, "North Korea Claims Nuclear Test," October 9, 2006, http://news.bbc.co.uk/2/ hi/asia-pacific/6032525.stm.

83. January 23, 2003, cited in K. Oh and R. Hassig, "Confronting North Korea's Nuclear Ambitions: U.S. Policy Options and Regional Implications," Institute for Defense Analysis, Washington, DC, September 2003.

84. Interview with the author, Beijing, 2004.

85. Forney, "Family Feud."

86. In 1991, residents of Northeast China's Harbin told me about the exploits of North Korean "gangsters" and "hit men" in the city.

87. U.S.-China Business Council, "U.S.-China Trade Statistics and China's World Trade Statistics," www.uschina.org/statistics/tradetable.html.

88. Liu Ming and others argue that the DPRK-as-buffer concept is not persuasive today, given U.S. capabilities and the proximity of regional bases. Interviews of Liu and others with the author, 2003, 2004, and 2011.

89. H. Chou, "Quanqiuhua Shidaide Zhongguo Zhoubian Anquan Huanjing" [China's Peripheral Security Environment in the Age of Globalization], *Shehui Kexue* (*Social Science*) 5 (2005), www.irchina.org/news/view.asp?id=936.

90. U.S.-China Business Council, "China's Top Export Destinations, 2010 ($ billion)," data from People's Republic of China, General Administration of Customs, *China's Custom Statistics*, 2010, www.uschina.org/statistics/tradetable.html.

91. Susan Shirk, *China: Fragile Superpower* (New York: Oxford University Press, 2007); G. Chen and C. Wu, *Will the Boat Sink the Water? The Life of China's Peasants* (New York: Public Affairs, 2006).

92. Yu, "Zhongguo Mianlingde Anquan Weixie ji Zhanlue Xuanze Xin Sikao."

93. "The Failed States Index," *Foreign Policy* (July/August 2007): 57. In 2009 North Korea "improved" to number seventeen on the list (see *Foreign Policy* 173 [July/August 2009]: 80–93), although the botched currency reform measures in late 2009 drove many more North Koreans into poverty. North Korea moved to number twenty-two in 2011's rankings (see *Foreign Policy*, www.foreignpolicy.com/articles/2007/06/11/the_failed_states_index_2007.

94. The latter scenario, a civil war or power vacuum in the event of a regime collapse, came up in experts' discussions with the author in China in 2004, 2005, and 2009.

95. Goma, "Chinese-Korean Border Issue." See also Dingding Chen, "Domestic Politics, National Identity and International Politics: The Case of the Koguryo Controversy," *Journal of Contemporary China* 21, no. 74 (March 2012): 227–41.

96. Chinese experts, discussions with author, 2004, 2005, 2008, and 2009.

97. Kim, "Political Economy of Chinese Investment in North Korea," 898–99.

98. S. K. Jung, "China Plans $10 Billion Investment in North Korea," *Korea Times*, February 15, 2010, www.koreatimes.co.kr/www/news/nation/2010/03/120_60827.html.

99. M. Liu, "China's Role in the Course of North Korea's Transition," in *A New International Engagement Framework for North Korea?* (Washington, DC: Korean Economic Engagement, 2004), 343.

100. S. Haggard and M. Noland, *Famine in North Korea: Markets, Aid, and Reform* (New York: Columbia University Press, 2007), 160.

101. Chou, "Quanqiuhua Shidaide Zhongguo Zhoubian Anquan Huanjing."

102. A. Scobell, *China and North Korea: From Comrades-in-Arms to Allies at Arm's Length* (Carlisle, PA: Strategic Studies Institute, U.S. Army War College, 2004), 11–13.

103. Quoted in Shirk, *China*, 123.

104. For an overview of those Talks, see J. Park, "Inside Multilateralism: The Six Party Talks," *Washington Quarterly* 28, no. 4 (Autumn 2005): 75–91.

105. Victor Cha, "What Do They Really Want? Obama's North Korea Conundrum," *Washington Quarterly* 32, no. 4 (October 2009): 119–38.

106. "North Korean Nuclear Progress: Leap of Faith," *The Economist*, March 1, 2012, www.economist.com/blogs/banyan/2012/03/north-korean-nuclear-progress.

107. Siegfried S. Hecker, "What I Found in North Korea: Pyongyang's Plutonium Is No Longer the Only Problem," *Foreign Affairs*, December 9, 2010, www.foreignaffairs.com/articles/67023/siegfried-s-hecker/what-i-found-in-north-korea.

108. L. Lin, "Chaoxian He Wentide Zhengjie yu Jiejue Qianjing" [The Crux of the North Korean Nuclear Dilemma and Prospects for Solving It], China Institutes of Contemporary International Relations, March 13, 2005, www.irchina.org/news/view.asp?id=786.

109. Y. Cheng, "Chaoxian Bandaode Heping Jincheng" [The North Korean Peninsula's Peace Process], *Yatai Zhanluechang: Shijie Zhuyao Liliangde Fazhen yu Jiaozhu* [*Asia-Pacific Strategic Arena: Major Powers and Their Relations in the Early Twenty-First Century*] (Beijing: Shishi Chubanshe, 2002), 398 (note that the Chinese and English titles are different]; Chinese experts, interviews with the author in China, 2004, 2005, 2008, 2009, and 2012.

110. Snyder, "China-Korea Relations."

111. A study of Chinese investments in North Korea reaches the same conclusion (Kim, "Political Economy of Chinese Investment in North Korea," 905). See also Sang-hun Choe, "North Korea Rents Out Its Resources to Stave Off Reform," *New York Times*, October 25, 2011.

112. See, e.g., D. Blumenthal and A. Friedberg, "Not Too Late to Curb the Dear Leader: The Road to Pyongyang Runs through Beijing," *Weekly Standard*, February 12, 2007, www.weeklystandard.com/Utilities/printer_preview.asp?idArticle=13246&R=113E5322D7.

113. On North Korean reform, see A. Lankov, "The Natural Death of North Korean Stalinism," *Asia Policy* 1 (January 2006): 95–121; I. Moon, "North Korea: Open for Business—A Bit," *Business Week*, July 26, 2004; Kim, "Political Economy of Chinese Investment in North Korea"; Haggard and Noland, *Famine in North Korea*.

114. Ceaucescu was overthrown and executed in December 1989.

115. Evans J. R. Revere, "Dealing with North Korea's New Leader: Getting It Right," CSIS Pacific Forum, PacNet no. 70A, December 27, 2011; Seung-Ho Joo, "North Korea under Kim Jong-un: The Beginning of the End of a Peculiar Dynasty," *Pacific Focus* 27, no. 1 (April 2012): 1–9.

CHAPTER 5: JAPAN'S RESPONSES TO NORTH KOREA'S
NUCLEAR AND MISSILE TESTS

This chapter started out as an expanded and updated version of an article that originally appeared as Hajime Izumi and Katsuhisa Furukawa, "Not Going Nuclear: Japan's Response to North Korea's Nuclear Test," *Arms Control Today*, June 2007, www.armscontrol.org/act/2007_06/CoverStory. With the death of Kim Jong-il and further extensive revisions, the chapter's similarity with this article has become minimal.

1. North Korea conducted a series of missile flight tests on July 5, 2006, and April 5, 2009, respectively, and the nuclear tests on October 9, 2006, and May 25, 2009, respectively.

2. Houdou Station, TV Asahi, "Opinion Poll," October 2006, www.tv-asahi.co.jp/hst/poll/200610/index.html.

3. Mitsubishi Research Institute, "Dai Sankai Shimin no Risuku Ishiki Chousa wo Jisshi" [A Third Poll to Research the Public's Risk Perception Was Conducted], July 10, 2009, www.mri.co.jp/NEWS/press/2009/2010059_1435.html.

4. Cabinet Office, Government of Japan, "Yoron Chousa Houkokusho Heisei 21-nen 10-gatsu Chousa" [A Report on the Public Opinion Poll], October 2009, www8.cao.go.jp/survey/index.html. See also Cabinet Office, Government of Japan, "Gaikou ni kansuru Yoron Chousa" [The Public Opinion Poll on Diplomacy], October 2011; www8.cao.go.jp/survey/h23/h23-gaiko/index.html.

5. Ministry of Defense, "Chart II-3-4-2, "Kako Juugonen no Bouei Kankeihi no Suii" [Change of Defense-Related Expenditure over the Past Decade], Defense of Japan White Paper, Tokyo, 2012, www.clearing.mod.go.jp/hakusho_data/2012/2012/figindex.html.

6. David C. Kang argues, "Balancing should not be the default hypothesis in international relations theory. Balancing is the expected outcome under certain conditions" (Kang, "Hierarchy, Balancing, and Empirical Puzzles," *International Security* 28, no. 3 [Winter 2003/2004], 173).

7. "National Defense Program Guidelines for FY 2011 and Beyond," approved by Japan's Security Council and the Cabinet, December 17, 2010, www.kantei.go.jp/foreign/kakugik ettei/2010/ndpg_e.pdf, 7.

8. Robert M. Gates, "America's Security Role in the Asia-Pacific" (remarks at the Eighth International Institute of Strategic Studies Asia Security Summit, the Shangri-La Dialogue, Singapore, May 30, 2009, www.iiss.org/conferences/the-shangri-la-dialogue/shangri-la-dia logue-2009/plenary-session-speeches-2009/first-plenary-session/qa/).

9. "Kanbou Choukan, Kitachousen no Kaku Jikken Choukou, 'Genjiten de Eikyou Nashi'" [The Chief Cabinet Secretary on the Prospect of North Korea's Nuclear Test, "No Impact as of Now"] *Nihon Keizai Shimbun*, November 18, 2010, www.nikkei.com/news/category/article/ g=96958A9C93819481E3EAE2E29F8DE3EAE3E3E0E2E3E29C9CE2E2E2E2;at=ALL.

10. Statement by Robert M. Gates, U.S. Secretary of Defense, remarks at the Tenth International Institute of Strategic Studies Asia Security Summit, the Shangri-La Dialogue, Singapore, June 4, 2011, www.iiss.org/conferences/the-shangri-la-dialogue/shangri-la-dialogue -2011/speeches/first-plenary-session/qa/.

11. Cabinet Office, "Jieitai, Bouei Mondai ni kansuru Yoron Chousa (Heisei 24 nen 1 gatsu)" [Public Opinion Poll Concerning Self Defense Forces and Defense Affairs (January 2012)]," March 12, 2012, www8.cao.go.jp/survey/h23/h23-bouei/index.html.

12. Statement by Hirofumi Nakasone, minister for foreign affairs of Japan, "Conditions towards Zero—'11 Benchmarks for Global Nuclear Disarmament,'" Tokyo, April 27, 2009, www.mofa.go.jp/policy/un/disarmament/arms/state0904.html.

13. Hideo Tamura, "Kaku Danto Shisaku ni 3nen Ijo" [More Than Three Years Are Needed to Produce a Prototype of Nuclear Warhead], *Sankei Shimbun*, December 25, 2006.

14. See Katsuhisa Furukawa, "Japan's Policy and Views on Nuclear Weapons: A Historical Perspective," *Jebat: Malaysian Journal of History, Politics, and Strategic Studies* 37 (2010): 1–30, http://pkukmweb.ukm.my/jebat/images/upload/Katsuhisa%20Furukawa%2037.pdf.

15. Cabinet Office, "Nankai Torafu no Kyodai Jishin ni kansuru Tsunamidaka, Shinsuiiki, Higai Soutei no Kouhyou ni tsuite" [Regarding the Publication of the Estimate of the Height of Tsunamis, the Flood Prone Areas, and the Number of Casualties in Relation to the Mega-Thrust Nankai Trough Earthquakes], August 29, 2011, www.bousai.go.jp/nankaitrough_info .html.

16. "National Defense Program Guidelines for FY 2011 and Beyond," 2–5.

17. National Institute for Defense Studies, *East Asia Strategic Review 2011*, Tokyo, May 2011, 244.

18. This point is argued in Katsuhisa Furukawa, "Nuclear Arms Control and Disarmament: Views among Japan's National Security Community," *Security Challenges* 6, no. 4 (Summer 2010): 33–54.

19. "National Defense Program Guidelines for FY 2011 and Beyond," 14.

20. These examinations include the ones carried out by a private study group of the *Anzen Hoshou Chousa Kai* [Research Commission on National Security] formed in the late 1960s, led by Osamu Kaibara, then director general of the *Kokubou Kaigi* [National Defense Council]; *Naikaku Chousashitsu* [the Study Group on Democracy in the Cabinet's Office of Research] (1967–70); *Gaikou Seisaku Kikaku Iinkai* [Foreign Policy Planning Committee] of the Ministry of Foreign Affairs (MOFA) in the late 1960s; and a group of experts called on by then defense minister Yasuhiro Nanasone (who became prime minister in the 1980s) in 1970. For further details, see Furukawa, "Japan's Policy and Views on Nuclear Weapons."

21. Sugio Takahashi, "Nuclear Issues and Japan's Security Policy," *Journal of World Affairs* 58, no. 7–8 (July–August 2010): 40–48.

22. This point was argued in Katsuhisa Furukawa, "Conditions for Japan's Nuclear Option," in James J. Wirtz and Peter R. Lavoy, eds., *Over the Horizon Proliferation Threats* (Stanford, CA: Stanford University Press, 2012), 13–32.

23. For example, then DPJ senior staff member for national security affairs Kiyoshi Sugawa presented this view in his novel *Beichou Kaisen* [*An Outbreak of U.S.-DPRK War*] (Tokyo: Kodansha, 2007), 101–9.

24. Former Japanese ambassador to Thailand Hisahiko Okazaki, one of Japan's leading strategic thinkers, has made this case. For more, see Hisahiko Okazaki, "Time to Consider a Nuclear Strategy for Japan," *Daily Yomiuri*, April 8, 2007.

25. As an example, see the work of Takuya Kubo, bureau director of defense policy for Japan's Defense Agency in the 1970s (Kubo, "Boueiryoku Seibi no Kangaekata" [A Framework to Consider the Arrangement of Japan's Defense Capabilities], Tokyo, February 20, 1971, www.ioc.u-tokyo.ac.jp/~worldjpn/documents/texts/JPSC/19710220.O1J.html.

26. For example, in the 1990s, several internal study groups in the Japanese Defense Agency examined whether Japan's nuclear option was desirable, reaching the same conclusion as the previous studies. Such a conclusion has not yet been logically challenged.

27. For example, the authoritative website GlobalSecurity.Org states, "Japan has the raw materials, technology, and capital for developing nuclear weapons. Japan could possibly produce functional nuclear weapons in as little as a year's time," accessed November 12, 2010, www.globalsecurity.org/wmd/world/japan/nuke.htm.

28. The H-IIB is a liquid hydrogen–propelled two-stage rocket employing four polibutadiene-powered solid rocket boosters, with satellite launch systems based on technologies

that could theoretically be incorporated into a warhead bus. See Furukawa, "Conditions for Japan's Nuclear Option."

29. Japan Aerospace and Exploration Agency, "Epsilon Launch Vehicle," accessed July 18, 2011, www.jaxa.jp/pr/brochure/pdf/01/rocket07.pdf.

30. See Furukawa, "Japan's Policy and Views on Nuclear Weapons." Also see Furukawa, "Conditions for Japan's Nuclear Option."

31. Hideo Tamura, "Kaku no Kuuhaku Ge" [Absence of Nukes: Part 2], *Sankei Shinbun*, December 28, 2006.

32. For more, see Donald MacKenzie, *Inventing Accuracy: A Historical Sociology of Nuclear Missile Guidance* (Cambridge, MA: MIT Press, 1993), and Sonia Ben Oguarham-Gormley and Kathleen M. Vogel, "The Social Context Shaping Bioweapons (Non)proliferation," *Biosecurity and Bioterrorism: Biodefense Strategy, Practice, and Science* 8, no. 1 (March 2010): 9–24.

33. Japanese prime minister Naoto Kan used this term in his policy speech on January 24, 2011. See Noboru Yamaguchi, "Deciphering the New National Defense Program Guidelines of Japan," Tokyo Foundation Policy Research Brief, 2011.

34. These points were argued in Furukawa, "Japan's Policy and Views on Nuclear Weapons," 23. Also see Furukawa, "Conditions for Japan's Nuclear Option."

35. Yamaguchi, "Deciphering the New National Defense Program Guidelines of Japan," 4.

36. Ibid.

37. National Institute for Defense Studies, *East Asia Strategic Review 2011*, 255.

38. Yamaguchi, "Deciphering the New National Defense Program Guidelines of Japan," 8–9.

39. National Institute for Defense Studies, *East Asia Strategic Review 2011*, 242–47.

40. Ralph A. Cossa, "Chairman's Report, U.S.-Japan Strategic Dialogue," Pacific Forum CSIS, Lahaina, Hawaii, February 25–26, 2008.

41. Senior Japanese official of the Ministry of Foreign Affairs, comment during a meeting with Katsuhisa Furukawa and a U.S. expert, Tokyo, Japan, June 3, 2010.

42. Joint Statement of the Security Consultative Committee, "Toward a Deeper and Broader U.S.-Japan Alliance: Building on 50 Years of Partnership," Tokyo, June 21, 2011, www.mofa.go.jp/region/n-america/us/security/pdfs/joint1106_01.pdf.

43. National Institute for Defense Studies, *East Asia Strategic Review 2011*, 237.

44. This is developed further in Michael J. Green and Katsuhisa Furukawa, "Japan: New Nuclear Realism," in Muthiah Alagappa, ed., *The Long Shadow: Nuclear Weapons and Security in Twenty-First-Century Asia* (Stanford, CA: Stanford University Press, 2008), 347–72.

45. For example, such issues were discussed during the Fourth US-Japan Strategic Dialogue, hosted by the Pacific Forum CSIS, Hawaii, June 29–July 2, 2012. Also, see Furukawa, "Nuclear Arms Control and Disarmament."

46. Michito Tsuruoka, "Perspective on the NPR Vol. 2," *Commentary* (National Institute of Defense Studies), May 24, 2010.

47. Furukawa, "Japan's Policy and Views on Nuclear Weapons."

48. More specifically, this treaty is the "Treaty between the United States of America and the Union of Soviet Socialist Republics on the Elimination of Their Intermediate-Range and Shorter-Range Missiles," signed by U.S. president Ronald Reagan and Soviet leader Mikhail Gorbachev, December 8, 1987, www.state.gov/www/global/arms/treaties/inf1.html.

49. For more, see Green and Furukawa, "Japan," 360.

50. Foreign Minister Okada, at a session of the Foreign Affairs Committee, Lower House, the Diet, March 17, 2010 (cited in Tsuruoka, "Perspective on the NPR Vol. 2").

51. Prime Minister Naoto Kan at the Hiroshima Peace Memorial Ceremony, August 6, 2010, Hiroshima, Japan, www.kantei.go.jp/foreign/kan/statement/201008/06aisatu_e.html.

52. Council on Security and Defense Capabilities, "Japan's Visions for Future Security and Defense Capabilities," Tokyo, October 2004, 24.

53. Ibid., 6.

54. These points are developed from the following literatures: Furukawa, "Conditions for Japan's Nuclear Option," 13–32; Hajime Izumi, "Kitachousen Mondai no Yukue to Nihon no Taiou" [Prospects of North Korean Problems and Japan's Response], *Shakai Kagaku Kenkyuu* [*Social Sciences Studies*], Institute of Social Sciences, Chukyo University 31, no. 1 (March 15, 2011): 1–36; Izumi, "Chousen Hanto no Kongo no Doukou to Nihon no Taiou" [Prospects of the Situations on the Korean Peninsula and Japan's Response], *Gaikou* 3, no. 3 (March 2010), 76–85; Izumi, "Kitachousen no Misairu Hassha de Naniga Kawaruka" [Prospect of Changes after North Korean Missile Launch], *Gaiko Forum* no. 251 (June 2009): 50–57.

CHAPTER 6: RUSSIA'S DE FACTO NUCLEAR NEIGHBOR

1. Pyongyang has even suggested that it won't denuclearize before the whole world is free of nuclear weapons. A DPRK Foreign Ministry representative stated on September 30, 2009, "In order to make the Korean Peninsula nuclear-free, it is necessary to make a comprehensive and total elimination of all the nuclear weapons on earth, to say nothing of those in and around South Korea. A prerequisite for global denuclearization is for the U.S., which tops the world's list of nuclear weapons, to cut down and dismantle them, to begin with" (Korean Central News Agency, September 30, 2009, www.kcna.co.jp/index-e.htm). In April 2010 the Foreign Ministry of the DPRK confirmed, "As long as the U.S. nuclear threat persists, the DPRK will increase and update various types of nuclear weapons as its deterrent in such a manner as it deems necessary in the days ahead" (Joshua Pollack, "Parsing Enrichment in North Korea," Arms Control Wonk, August 27, 2009, www.armscontrolwonk.com/2456/parsing-uranium-enrichment-in-north-korea); "Foreign Ministry Dismisses U.S. Nuclear Plan," Korean Central News Agency, April 9, 2010, www.kcna.co.jp/index-e.htm.

2. See Izumi and Furukawa's chapter in this volume.

3. Although a North-South naval skirmish in the disputed area of the Yellow Sea in November 2009 was probably an accident, it reminds us how easily an escalation of conflict can occur.

4. See, for example, the Russian Ministry of Foreign Affairs (MFA), "Statement by the Permanent Representative of Russia to the UN, Vitaly Churkin, in Explanation of Vote on the Draft UN Security Council Resolution on North Korea, New York, June 12, 2009," www.mid.ru/Brp_4.nsf/arh/BBED7F535D2D6CDAC32575D4002C4DD2?OpenDocument.

5. "Russian Presidential Decree on DPRK Sanctions Not to Affect Six-Party Talks: Official," Sina.com, April 2, 2010, http://english.sina.com/world/2010/0401/312274.html.

6. Vladimir Putin, "Russia and the Changing World," *Moscow News*, February 27, 2012, http://mn.ru/politics/20120227/312306749.html.

7. Michael Berk observes, "Regarding regional security, Russia does not in principle want the DPRK to gain a military nuclear capability, as this could cause a 'chain-reaction' leading Japan and South Korea to do so as well" (Berk, "Russia's Perspective on the DPRK and Regional Security," Cankor Bulletin, Canadian Institute of International Affairs, Cankor Report no. 274, Callander, Ontario, February 23, 2007).

8. Victor Cha, "We Have No Plan," Nautilus Institute, June 13, 2008, www.nautilus.org/fora/security/08046Cha.htm.

9. Russian foreign minister Sergei Lavrov, "Transcript of Remarks and Response to Media Questions by Russian Foreign Minister Sergey Lavrov at Joint Press Conference Following Talks with [South Korean] Foreign Minister Yu Myung-hwan, Moscow, 10 September 2008," www.mid.ru/brp_4.nsf/o/AA10D0AC3DED12CDC32574C1002D4BB1.

10. For example, following the DPRK threat to suspend disabling of its nuclear facilities in Yongbyon and consider restoring them to the original state, the Russian Foreign Ministry made a statement on August 26, 2008, that this decision evoked disappointment and concern in Moscow and that "all the actions in the denuclearization field by the DPRK should be accompanied by adequate political and economic support—meaning assistance to Pyongyang—including steps from the other five members of the talks. Russia fulfills its obligations fully and in a timely manner. We wish all other parties will do the same, consistently in good faith" (*Kommersant*, August 27, 2008, www.mid.ru/brp_4.nsf/o/2AAD65A3613FDDD0C325 74B200362492).

11. The key elements of this deal were, from the North Korean side, "to abandon all nuclear weapons and existing nuclear programs and return at an early date to the NPT and to IAEA safeguards," and from U.S. side, "to respect each other's [U.S. and DPRK] sovereignty, exist peacefully together and take steps to normalize their relations subject to their respective bilateral policies" (Joint Statement of the Fourth Round of the Six-Party Talks, Beijing, September 19, 2005, www.state.gov/p/eap/regional/c15455.htm).

12. See the Ministry of Foreign Affairs Spokesman's Commentary, March 10, 2009, www.ln.mid.ru/Brp_4.nsf/arh/75F0BA82CED9614CC32575750058387?OpenDocument.

13. Philip P. Pan, "After Initial Mild Reaction, Kremlin May Consider Tougher Stance on Tests," *Washington Post*, May 28, 2009, http://articles.washingtonpost.com/2009-05-28/world/36880486_1_nuclear-program-nuclear-dispute-tougher-sanctions.

14. "Russia Deploys Air Defense over N. Korea Missile Tests," Agence France Presse, August 26, 2009.

15. Russian UN permanent representative V. Churkin, speech, June 12, 2009, www.ln.mid.ru/Brp_4.nsf/arh/BBED7F535D2D6CDAC32575D4002C4DD2?OpenDocument (link inactive; accessed May 5, 2010).

16. Russian Ministry of Foreign Affairs Statement, June 12, 2009, www.ln.mid.ru/Brp_4.nsf/arh/745CC7A331A1D11EC32575D3005A08DA?OpenDocument (link inactive; accessed May 5, 2010).

17. "Russian Presidential Decree on DPRK Sanctions Not to Effect Six-Party Talks," *Global Times*, April 2, 2010, www.globaltimes.cn/world/europe/2010-04/518636.html.

18. For example, following the DPRK threat to suspend disablement of its nuclear facilities in Yongbyon and consider restoring them to the original state, the Russian Foreign Ministry made a statement on August 26, 2008, that this decision evoked disappointment and con-

cern in Moscow and that "all the actions in the denuclearization field by the DPRK should be accompanied by adequate political and economic—meaning assistance to Pyongyang—steps from the other five members of the talks. Russia fulfills its obligations timely and fully. We wish all other parties to act the same way, consistently in good faith" (*Kommersant*, August 27, 2008, www.mid.ru/brp_4.nsf/0/2AAD65A3613FDDD0C32574B200362492).

19. Alexander Vorontsov and Oleg Revenko, "Increase in Tensions on the Korean Peninsula, *Perspective*, July 7, 2010, www.perspektivy.info/oykumena/azia/vesna_2010_g__obo strenije_naprazhennosti_na_korejskom_poluostrove_2010-07-07.

20. Kim Young-hun, "Russia Charting Neutral Course in UN," *Daily NK*, June 18, 2010, www.dailynk.com/english/read.php?cataId=nk00400&num=6509; Vremya, "Punishment or Visibility: For Sanctions America needs Russia and China," May 27, 2010, http://vremya.ru /2010/90/5/254333.html.

21. Oleg Kir'yanov, "Rossiya ne smogla nazvat' prichinu krusheniya koreyskogo korablya 'Chkhonan'" (Russia Is Not Able to Identify the Cause of the Crash of the Korean Ship "Cheonan"), *Rossiyskaya Gazeta*, September 3, 2010, www.rg.ru/2010/09/03/delo-site-anons .html.

22. Russian Ministry of Foreign Affairs Information and Press Department, "Commentary in Relation to the November 23 Exchange of Artillery Fire between the DPRK and the Republic of Korea," 1626-23-11-2010, Moscow, November 23, 2010, www.mid.ru/Brp_4.nsf/arh/0 510BAB2FBA7070DC32577E4005EE381?OpenDocument.

23. Russian foreign minister Sergey Lavrov, Transcript of Remarks and Answers to Media Questions at Joint Press Conference Following Talks with Afghan Foreign Minister Z. Rasulom, Moscow, November 25, 2010, www.mid.ru/Brp_4.nsf/arh/A5F26F2320F48438C32577E60 05E4CB3?OpenDocument

24. Pak Ui-chun, "Working Visit to Russia," press release, "Working Visit to the Russian Minister of Foreign Affairs of the DPRK's Foreign Minister Pak Ui Chun," Ministry of Foreign Affairs of the Russian Federation, Moscow, December 13, 2010, www.mid.ru/Brp_4.nsf/arh/E7 4A90841A5206B8C32577F8005CE7D7?OpenDocument.

25. Statement, Ministry of Foreign Affairs of the Russian Federation, December 17, 2010, www.mid.ru/Brp_4.nsf/arh/88F67F081DD7A45EC32577FC0043FC4E?OpenDocument.

26. "N. Korea Ready to Renew Six Party Nuke Talks without 'Preliminary Conditions,'" RIA Novisti, Moscow, http://en.rian.ru/world/20110315/163010319.html.

27. Presentation and Responses to Russian Foreign Minister Sergey Lavrov to Media Questions at Joint Press Conference Following Talks with Minister of Foreign Affairs and Trade, Republic of Korea, Kim Sung-hwan, Moscow, August 8, 2011, www.mid.ru/brp_4.nsf/0/ F56D552BC969E456C32578E60057E7FD.

28. Vyacheslav Nikonov and Georgy Toloraya, eds., "Korean Peninsula: Challenges and Opportunities for Russia," *Russkiy Mir* [*Russian World*], Moscow, 2010, www.russkiymir.ru/ex port/sites/default/russkiymir/ru/fund/docs/ks210910.pdf.

29. "N. Korea Ready to Renew Six Party Nuke Talks without 'Preliminary Conditions.'"

30. For a more detailed report on Russia's current stance on the Korean issue, see Georgy Toloraya, "The Security Crisis in Korea and Its International Context: Sources and Lessons from a Russian Perspective," *Korean Journal of Defense Analysis* 23, no. 3 September 2011: 335–52.

31. Gavan McCormack, *Target North Korea* (SĐdney: Random House, 2004), 150.

32. "U.S. Chiefly to Blame for Increasing Danger of Nuclear War in Korea," KCNA, January 29, 2008.

33. The plutonium that North Korea uses for its weapons program was produced at another gas-graphite five-megawatt reactor, built by North Koreans without Soviet assistance in 1986.

34. In all fairness, recall that under South Korea's Park Chung-hee, nuclear arms were developed in secrecy, and by the end of the 1970s that program was 95% completed, which might have become the major factor causing the North Koreans to push their own program. See Yoon Won-sup, "Park Sought to Develop Nuclear Weapons," *Korea Times*, January 16, 2008.

35. V. P. Tkatchenko, "The Korean Peninsula and the Interests of Russia," *Nauka* (2000): 71.

36. KCNA reported on February 10, 2005, "We have already resolutely withdrawn from the NPT and have manufactured nuclear weapons for self-defense to cope with the Bush administration's policy of isolating and crushing the DPRK" (see Nautilus Institute, "DPRK 'Manufactured' Nuclear Weapons, to 'Suspend' 6-Way Talks for 'Indefinite Period,'" February 14, 2005, http://nautilus.org/napsnet/napsnet-special-reports/dprk-manufactured-nuclear -weapons-to-suspend-6-way-talks-for-indefinite-period/#axzz2PxfI2Xzw).

37. Nautilus Institute, "Russia on DPRK Nuclear Test," NAPSNet Daily Report, May 23, 2005, http://nautilus.org/napsnet/napsnet-daily-report/napsnet-daily-report-monday-may-23 -2005/#axzz2PxfI2Xzw.

38. Richard Weitz, senior fellow and director of the Center for Political-Military Analysis at the Hudson Institute, was probably right in suggesting at a seminar at the Korea Economic Institute in February 2010 that Russia prefers the status quo on the DPRK nuclear issue to any contingency in the impoverished, nuclear-armed communist state that could destabilize the Russian Far East: "A key issue is reconciling the sometimes conflicting stances of Russia and the United States regarding how best to realize their common goals"; quoted in Hwang Doo-Hyong, "Russia Prefers Status Quo in N. Korean Nuke to Instability: Scholar," Yonhap News Agency, Washington, DC, February 18, 2010.

39. Meeting on the Social and Economic Development of the Far East and Cooperation with Asia and the Pacific Countries, chaired by President Dmitry Medvedev, Khabarovsk, July 2, 2010, http://kremlin.ru/transcripts/8234.

40. Lee Sung-jin, "Execution Confirmed by Capital Source," *Daily NK*, April 5, 2010, www .dailynk.com/english/read.php?cataId=nk01500&num=6204.

41. The DPRK officially stated that it "will never participate in the talks any longer nor it will be bound to any agreement of the six-party talks" (KCNA, "The DPRK Foreign Ministry Vehemently Refutes UNSC's 'Presidential Statement,'" April 14, 2009, www.kcna.co.jp/in dex-e.htm; accessed May 5, 2010).

42. See discussion of the report, "North Korea Inside Out: The Case for Economic Engagement," produced by an independent task force convened by the Asia Society's Center on U.S.-China Relations and the University of California's Institute on Global Conflict and Cooperation, Nautilus Institute, October 29, 2009, www.nautilus.org/fora/security/ 09083ASTaskForce.pdf.

43. "Korea: A View from Russia," The Third Russia-Korea Forum, Diplomatic Academy,

Moscow, 2002; "Korea: A View from Russia," proceedings of the 11th Koreanologists' Conference, Institute of Far Eastern Studies, Russian Academy of Sciences, Moscow, March 30, 2007.

44. Leonid Petrov, "Russia Is Key to North Korea's Plight," *Asia Times*, July 24, 2008, http://atimes.com/atimes/Central_Asia/JG24Ag04.html.

45. For more details, see Georgy Toloraya, "The Economic Future of North Korea: Will the Market Rule?," Korea Economic Institute Academic Paper Series on Korea 2, Washington, DC, 2007.

CHAPTER 7: WASHINGTON'S RESPONSE TO AN OPERATIONALLY NUCLEAR NORTH KOREA

1. David Kang, "Korea's New Cold War," *National Interest*, December 31, 2010, http://nationalinterest.org/commentary/koreas-new-cold-war-4653.

2. Victor Cha and David Kang, *Nuclear North Korea: A Debate on Engagement Strategies* (New York: Columbia University Press, 2003). See also Jack Pritchard, *Failed Diplomacy: The Tragic Story of How North Korea Got the Bomb* (Washington, DC: Brookings Institution Press, 2007); Mike Chinoy, *Meltdown: The Inside Story of the North Korean Nuclear Crisis* (New York: St. Martin's Press, 2008); and Leon Sigal, *Disarming Strangers* (Princeton, NJ: Princeton University Press, 1998).

3. See Moon Young Park, "Lure North Korea," *Foreign Policy* 97 (Winter 1994–95): 97–105.

4. The conclusions in Andrei Lankov's chapter in this volume underline this point.

5. Joint remarks by President Barack Obama and President Lee Myung-bak, Council on Foreign Relations, Washington, DC, June 16, 2009, www.cfr.org/publication/19646/joint_remarks_by_president_obama_and_president_lee_myungbak_june_2009.html.

6. Yoo-sup Lee, "One South Korean F-15K Is Equal to Ten North Korean Mig-29s," *Maeil Gyongje*, June 19, 2009, http://kr.news.yahoo.com/service/news/shellview.htm?linkid=20&fid=515&articleid=2009061914505852598.

7. Vernon Loeb and Peter Slevin, "Overcoming North Korea's Tyranny of Proximity," *Washington Post*, January 20, 2003.

8. Chinoy, *Meltdown*, 161.

9. Recently a South Korean official claimed to be able to preemptively take out North Korean nuclear and missile sites, although the accuracy of that claim is not clear.

10. Suk Hi Kim and Semoon Chang, eds., *Economic Sanctions Against a Nuclear North Korea: An Analysis of United States and United Nations Actions since 1950* (London: McFarland, 2007).

11. Stephan Haggard and Marcus Noland, "What to Do about North Korea: Will Sanctions Work?" *Oriental Economist*, July 3, 2009, http://piie.com/publications/opeds/oped.cfm?ResearchID=1254.

12. Ruediger Frank, "The Political Economy of Sanctions Against North Korea," *Asian Perspective* 30, no. 3 (2006): 5–36.

13. David E. Sanger, William J. Broad, and Thom Shanker, "North Korea Says It Tested a Nuclear Device Underground," *New York Times*, October 9, 2006, http://query.nytimes.com/gst/fullpage.html?res=9E0CE0DC1330F93AA35753C1A9609C8B63.

14. Jayshree Bajoria, "The China-North Korea Relationship," *Backgrounder*, Council on Foreign Relations, July 21, 2009, www.cfr.org/publication/11097/.

15. Russia defined "luxury goods" loosely—as watches costing over two thousand dollars and coats over nine thousand dollars. See Marcus Noland, "The (Non)-Impact of UN Sanctions on North Korea," *Asia Policy* 7 (January 2009): 61–88.

16. Figures from Mary Beth Mitkin et al., "North Korea's Second Nuclear Test: Implications of UN Resolution 1874," Congressional Research Service R-40684, Washington, DC, July 1, 2009, 10–11.

17. Bajoria, "China-North Korea Relationship."

18. Richard Ned Lebow and Janice Stein, "Deterrence: The Elusive Dependent Variable," *World Politics* 42, no. 3 (April 1990): 336–69.

19. Barry Nalebuff, "Rational Deterrence in an Imperfect World," *World Politics* 43, no. 3 (April 1991): 313–35.

20. Terence Roehrig, *From Deterrence to Engagement: The U.S. Defense Commitment to South Korea* (Oxford: Lexington Books, 2006), 22.

21. Gary Hufbauer, Jeffrey Schott, and Kimberly Ann Elliott, *Economic Sanctions Reconsidered* (Washington, DC: Institute for International Economics, 1990).

22. Robert Pape, "Why Economic Sanctions Do Not Work," *International Security* 22, no. 2 (Fall 1997): 90–136; Daniel Drezner, "The Trouble with Carrots: Transaction Costs, Conflict Expectations, and Economic Inducements," *Security Studies* 9, no. 1 (1999/2000): 188–218.

23. Miroslav Nincic, "The Logic of Positive Engagement: Dealing with Renegade Regimes," *International Studies Perspectives* 7, no. 4 (2006): 321–41.

24. David Shambaugh suggests different variants of engagement: constructive, conditional, and coercive engagements, depending on the degree of punitive measures. See Shambaugh, "Containment or Engagement of China?" *International Security* 21, no. 2 (Fall 1996): 180–96.

25. Richard N. Haass and Meghan L. O'Sullivan, "Introduction," in Richard N. Haass and Meghan L. O'Sullivan, eds., *Honey and Vinegar: Incentives, Sanctions, and Foreign Policy* (Washington, DC: Brookings Institution Press, 2000), 4–5.

26. Lawrence S. Wittner, *Toward Nuclear Abolition: A History of the World Nuclear Disarmament Movement, 1971 to the Present* (Stanford, CA: Stanford University Press, 2003), 429–33.

27. Michael Mastanduno, "The Strategy of Economic Engagement: Theory and Practice," in Edward Mansfield and Brian Pollins, eds., *Economic Interdependence and International Conflict: New Perspectives on an Enduring Debate* (Ann Arbor: University of Michigan Press, 2003), 175–86; Joanne Gowa, *Allies, Adversaries, and International Trade* (Princeton, NJ: Princeton University Press, 1994); Dale Copeland, "Trade Expectations and the Outbreak of Peace: Détente 1970–74 and the End of the Cold War 1985–91," *Security Studies* 9, no. 1 (1999/2000): 15–58; Rawi Abdelal and Jonathan Kirshner, "Strategy, Economic Relations, and the Definition of National Interests," *Security Studies* 9, no. 1 (1999/2000): 119–56.

28. Robert Axelrod, *The Evolution of Cooperation* (New York: Basic Books, 1984).

29. After three years of Henry Kissinger–Le Duc Tho talks, the United States and Vietnam reached a cease-fire deal, for which President Nixon secretly promised that the United States would provide North Vietnam with an aid package of $3.25 billion. See Frederick Z. Brown, "U.S.-Vietnam Normalization: Past, Present, Future," in James W. Morley and Masashi Nishihara, eds., *Vietnam Joins the World* (Armonk, NY: M. E. Sharpe, 1997), 204; Stanley Karnow, *Vietnam: A History* (New York: Penguin, 1983), 698–99.

30. Miles Kahler and Scott Kastner, "Strategic Uses of Economic Interdependence: Engagement Policies on the Korean Peninsula and Across the Taiwan Strait," *Journal of Peace Research* 43, no. 5 (2006): 523–41.

31. See, e.g., Henry Kissinger, "North Korea's Nuclear Blackmail," *New York Times*, August 9, 2009, www.nytimes.com/2009/08/10/opinion/10iht-edkissinger.html.

32. Quoted on the *Lehrer News Hour*, PBS, July 28, 2008, www.pbs.org/newshour/bb/white_house/july-dec05/rice_7-28.html.

33. Stephen W. Bosworth, "Remarks at the Korea Society Annual Dinner," New York, June 9, 2009, www.state.gov/p/eap/rls/rm/2009/06/124567.htm.

34. Yukie Yoshikawa, "The Prospect of Economic Reform in North Korea," Nautilus Institute, March 2004, www.nautilus.org/DPRKBriefingBook/transition/200312NKecon.html.

35. Stephan Haggard, Marcus Noland, and Erik Weeks, "North Korea on the Precipe of Famine," Peterson Institute for International Economics, Working Paper PB08-6, Washington, DC, May 2008.

36. David C. Kang, "The Next Nuclear Agreement with North Korea: Prospects and Pitfalls: A Report of a Meeting Held October 29, 2007," National Committee on North Korea, Washington, DC, January 8, 2008.

37. Ralph Cossa et al., "The United States and the Asia-Pacific Region: Security Strategy for the Obama Administration," Center for a New American Security, Washington, DC, February 2009, www.cna.org/documents/CampbellPatelFord_US_Asia-Pacific_February2009.pdf.

38. Amelia Newcom, "Clinton to Japan: You're Our 'Cornerstone,'" *Christian Science Monitor*, February 17, 2009, http://features.csmonitor.com/globalnews/2009/02/17/clinton-to-japan-youre-our-cornerstone/.

39. Tessa Morris-Suzuki, "Japan–North Korea Relations: The Forgotten Agenda," *Asia-Pacific Bulletin*, February 10, 2009, http://hdl.handle.net/10125/7782. See also Izumi and Furukawa's chapter in this volume.

40. Leif-Eric Easley, Tetsuo Kotani, and Aki Mori, "Electing a New Japanese Security Policy? Examining Foreign Policy Visions within the Democratic Party of Japan," *Asia Policy* 9 (January 2010): 45–66.

41. *World Refugee Survey 2004*, U.S. Committee for Refugees and Immigrants, Arlington, VA, www.refugees.org/data/wrs/04/pdf/key_statistics.pdf.

42. For general corroboration and further detail on this point, see chapter 2 by Moore in this volume.

43. Leon Sigal, "Punishing North Korea Won't Work," *Bulletin of the Atomic Scientists*, May 28, 2008, www.thebulletin.org/web-edition/op-eds/punishing-north-korea-wont-work; David C. Kang, "The Avoidable Crisis in North Korea," *Orbis* 47, no. 3 (Summer 2003): 495–510.

CHAPTER 8: NORTH KOREA'S NUCLEAR BLACKMAIL

This is an updated and revised version of Andrei Lankov, "Why the United States Will Have to Accept a Nuclear North Korea," *Korean Journal of Defense Analysis* 21, no. 3 (2009), www.informaworld.com/smpp/content-db=all?content=10.1080/10163270903087147): 251–64.

1. Mark Landler, "Robust Agenda for Clinton's trip to Asia," *International Herald Tribune*, February 17, 2009.

2. For a concise review of North Korea's nuclear weapons acquisition program, see Siegfried Hecker and William Liou, "Dangerous Dealings: North Korea's Nuclear Capabilities and the Threat of Export to Iran," *Arms Control Today* 37, no. 2 (March 2007): 6–9.

3. Terence Roehrig, "Creating the Conditions for Peace in Korea: Promoting Incremental Change in North Korea," *Korea Observer* 40, no. 1 (Spring 2009): 222.

4. For details on the ongoing argument over the actual size of North Korea's GDP, see Yi Chu-chol, "Pukhan chumin-ui oepu chongpo suyong taeto pyonhwa" [The Research of Changes in North Koreans' Attitudes toward Outside World Information], *Hankuk tongpuka nonchong* [*Korean Treatises on Northeast Asia*] 46 (2008): 245–48.

5. Kang Ch'ol-hwan, "Pukhan kyokwaso sok-ŭi Namhan" [South Korea in North Korean Textbooks], in * ChosÐn ilbo*, December 7, 2001.

6. Yi Hyo-bom and Ch'oe Hyon-ho, "Pukhan kyokwaso-rul t'onghan ch'ongsonyon kach'igwan yongu: Kotung chunghakkyo kongsanchuui totok 3,4 haknyon chungsim-uro" [A Study of the Youth Value System through North Korean Textbooks: Centered around the Textbooks for "Communist Morality" for Years 3 and 4 in High School], in *Pukhan yonku hakhoebo* [*North Korean Research Association Journal*] 2 (2000): 250.

7. Research on police control and surveillance in North Korea is still in its infancy, but the basic workings of the system, outlined above, have been described many times as they are well known to every North Korean. See, for example, a detailed description of travel restrictions in Kim Sung-chol, *Pukhan tongpotului saenghwal yangsikkwa machimak huimang* [*The Way of Life of the North Korean Compatriots and the Last Hope*] (Seoul: Charyowon, 2000), 185–97.

8. The spread of videos was widely reported by refugees and the media. For a detailed account of the North Korean "video revolution," see Yi Chu-chol, "Pukhan chuminui oepu chongpo suyong taeto pyonhwa" [Research on Changes in North Koreans' Attitudes toward the Outside World Information], *Hankuk tongpuka nonchong* [*Korean Treatises on Northeast Asia*] 46 (2008): 245–48.

9. For a brief review of the North Korean counterreform policies, see Andrei Lankov, "North Korea Dragged Back to the Past," *Asia Times*, January 24, 2008, www.atimes.com/atimes/korea/ja24dg01.html.

10. In 2009 an unclassified report of the Defense Intelligence Agency stated, "Iran and North Korea protect major elements of their nuclear programs in underground facilities" (Annual Threat Assessment: Statement before the Committee on Armed Services, U.S. Senate, March 10, 2009, www.dia.mil/publicaffairs/Testimonies/statement_31.pdf, 38.

11. David Lektzian and Mark Souva, "An Institutional Theory of Sanctions Onset and Success," *Journal of Conflict Resolution* 51, no. 6 (December 2007): 849. A large part of the article elaborates on the issue and provides plentiful confirmation that sanctions are less successful when applied to nondemocratic states.

12. For a summary of recent reports on localized riots, see Stephan Haggard and Marcus Noland, "The Winter of Their Discontent: Pyongyang Attacks the Market," Peterson Institute for International Economics Policy Brief, January 2010.

13. Wade L. Huntley, "Sit Down and Talk," *Bulletin of the Atomic Scientists* 59, no. 4 (July/August 2003): 38–45.

14. Wade L. Huntley, "Threats All the Way Down: U.S. Nuclear Initiatives in a Unipolar World," *Review of International Studies* 32, no. 1 (January 2006): 49–67.

15. For a careful study of the "food diversion problem," see Stephan Haggard and Marcus Noland, *Famine in North Korea: Markets, Aid, and Reform* (New York: Columbia University Press, 2007), 108–25.

16. Victor D. Cha, "North Korea's Weapons of Mass Destruction: Badges, Shields, or Swords?," *Political Science Quarterly* 117, no. 2 (Summer 2002): 230.

17. Korean Institute for International Economic Policy, *2009 Nyonto Pukhan Taewoe kyongje chonmang* [*International Prospects for North Korea's Economy in the Year 2009*] (Seoul: Korean Institute for International Economic Policy, 2009), 2. The statistics have been recalculated, taking into account the volume of North Korea's trade with the South, which technically is not considered "international trade" in Korean statistics, and hence is treated separately. The data on the scale of the North-South trade was retrieved from the site of the Republic of Korea's Unification Ministry, accessed October 1, 2012, http://eng.unikorea.go.kr/CmsWeb/viewPage.req?idx=PG0000000541.

18. Bonnie Glaser, Scott Snyder, and John S. Park, *Keeping an Eye on an Unruly Neighbor: Chinese Views of Economic Reform and Stability in North Korea* (Washington, DC: Center for Strategic and International Studies and United States Institute of Peace, 2008), 11.

19. For a detailed review of the current state of Chinese economic advances into North Korea, see Jaewoo Choo, "Mirroring North Korea's Growing Economic Dependence on China: Political Ramifications," *Asian Survey* 48, no. 2 (March/April 2008): 344–72.

20. For the Kando issue, which tends to attract more attention in Korea when relations with China become more tense, see Choe Sang-Hun, "Tussle over a Vanished Kingdom: South Korea–China Dispute Could Affect Future Borders," *International Herald Tribune*, October 13, 2006.

21. Samuel S. Kim, "Sino–North Korean Relations in the Post–Cold War World," in Young Whan Kihl and Hong Nak Kim, eds., *North Korea: The Politics of Regime Survival* (Armonk, NY: M. E. Sharpe, 2006), 186.

22. Gregory Moore, "How North Korea Threatens China's Interests: Understanding Chinese 'Duplicity' on the North Korean Nuclear Issue," *International Relations of the Asia Pacific* 8, no. 1 (January 2008): 2–3. See also chap. 2 in this volume.

23. See Choe Sang-Hun, "China Aims to Steady North Korea," *New York Times*, October 6, 2009.

24. Georgi Toloraya and Vladimir Hrustalev, "Budushchee Severnoi Korei: stoit li zhdat' kontsa?" [North Korea's Future: Should We Wait for an End?], *Indeks Bezopasnosti* [*Security Index*] 15, no. 1 (January 2009): 100.

25. In regard to the recent estimates of North Korea's nuclear and plutonium stockpile, see, for example, Peter Crail, "NK Delivers Plutonium Documentation," *Arms Control Today* 38, no. 5 (May 2008): 25–26.

CHAPTER 9: INDIA'S NUCLEAR EXCEPTIONALISM AND THE
NORTH KOREAN NUCLEAR CASE

1. Dietmar Rothermund, *India: The Rise of an Asian Giant* (New Delhi: Stanza/Yale University Press, 2008), 58–62.

2. Gordon Corera, *Shopping for Bombs: Nuclear Proliferation, Global Insecurity, and the Rise and Fall of the A. Q. Khan Network* (Oxford: Oxford University Press, 2009).

3. Paul Kerr, "U.S. Nuclear Cooperation with India: Issues for Congress," Congressional Research Service, October 28, 2010, www.fas.org/sgp/crs/nuke/RL33016.pdf, 8.

4. "Joint Statement by President Obama and Prime Minister Singh of India," The White House, Office of the Press Secretary, November 8, 2010, www.whitehouse.gov/the-press-office/2010/11/08/joint-statement-president-obama-and-prime-minister-singh-india.

5. Christopher Ford, "To Repair, Replace, or Re-imagine the NPT Regime: Lessons from Strategic Politics in Asia," in Ashley Tellis, Andrew Marble, and Travis Tanner, eds., *Strategic Asia 2009–10: Economic Meltdown and Geopolitical Stability* (Seattle, WA: National Bureau of Asian Research, 2009), 261–94.

6. The text of Vajpayee's private letter to President Clinton justifying India's 1998 nuclear tests appeared in "Nuclear Anxiety: Indian's Letter to Clinton on the Nuclear Testing," *New York Times*, May 13, 1998, www.nytimes.com/1998/05/13/world/nuclear-anxiety-indian-s-letter-to-clinton-on-the-nuclear-testing.html.

7. Tim Weiner, "U.S. Suspects India Prepares to Conduct Nuclear Tests," *New York Times*, December 15, 1995.

8. K. Subrahmanyam, "Calling Off Deal Will Isolate India Globally," *Times of India*, August 20, 2007.

9. "Boom for Boom," *India Today*, April 26, 1999.

10. Stephen Cohen, *India: Emerging Power* (Washington, DC: Brookings Institution Press, 2001), 177.

11. C. Raja Mohan, *Crossing the Rubicon: The Shaping of India's New Foreign Policy* (New York: Palgrave Macmillan, 2004), 90.

12. Ashok Kapur, *India: From Regional to World Power* (Abingdon, UK: Routledge, 2006), 197.

13. Strobe Talbott, *Engaging India* (Washington, DC: Brookings Institution Press, 2004); Jaswant Singh, *A Call to Honor* (Bloomington: Indiana University Press, 2007).

14. Then national security adviser Stephen Hadley, explaining how Bush and his advisors viewed India during the 2000 campaign. Stephen Hadley, "Remarks to the National Bureau of Asian Research Strategic Asia Forum," Washington, DC, April 5, 2006, www.whitehouse.gov/news/releases/2006/04/20060405-11.html.

15. Condoleezza Rice, "Promoting the National Interest," *Foreign Affairs* 79, no. 1 (January/February 2000): 45–62.

16. The White House, "National Security Strategy of the United States of America," September 2002, www.whitehouse.gov/nsc/nss/2002/index.html, chap. 7.

17. Ashley Tellis, "India as a New Global Power: An Action Agenda for the United States," Carnegie Endowment for International Peace, Washington, DC, July 2005, www.carnegieendowment.org/files/CEIP_India_strategy_2006.FINAL.pdf.

18. K. Alan Kronstadt, "CRS Report to Congress: India-U.S. Relations," Congressional Research Service, Washington, DC, December 1, 2006.

19. U.S. Department of State, "National Strategy 2004–2009," cited in "U.S. for Better Strategic Partnership with 'Growing Power' India," Press Trust of India, April 18, 2005, www.ptinews.com/home.aspx.

20. Nicholas Burns, "U.S.-India Relations," prepared statement for the House International Relations Committee, *CQ Congressional Testimony*, Washington, DC, September 8, 2005.

21. The White House, "National Security Strategy of the United States of America," September 2006, www.whitehouse.gov/nsc/nss/2006/, chap. 8.

22. Matthew Cooper, "The President's Passage to India," *Time*, February 23, 2006, www.time.com/time/nation/article/0,8599,1162363,00.html.

23. Ashley Tellis, "U.S.-India Relations," remarks to the House International Relations Committee, Washington, DC, *Federal News Service*, November 16, 2005.

24. Patricia Nunan, "India/U.S. Singh Visit," *Voice of America News*, July 15, 2005.

25. Shyam Saran, "Foreign Secretary Shyam Saran's Address to the India Economic Summit," New Delhi, November 28, 2005, www.mea.gov.in//speech/2005/11/28ss01.htm.

26. Edward Luce, *In Spite of the Gods: The Strange Rise of Modern India* (London: Abacus, 2006), 281.

27. This negotiating history is covered in C. Raja Mohan, *Impossible Allies: Nuclear India, United States, and the Global Order* (New Delhi: India Research Press, 2006), and Tellis, "India as a New Global Power."

28. Joint Statement by Prime Minister Atal Bihari Vajpayee and President George Bush, "Next Steps in Strategic Partnership," New Delhi, January 13, 2004, www.indianembassy.org/pm/vajpayee/2004/pm_jan_13_2003.htm.

29. Ashley Tellis, "Lost Tango in Washington: Appreciate the Truly Revolutionary Import of the NSSP," *Indian Express*, November 14, 2004.

30. See, e.g., Condoleezza Rice, "The United States–India Global Partnership" (testimony before the House International Relations Committee, Washington, DC, April 5, 2006); Ashton Carter, "America's New Strategic Partner?" *Foreign Affairs* 85, no. 4 (July/August 2006): 33–44.

31. Mohan, *Impossible Allies*, 6.

32. Prime Minister Manmohan Singh and President George W. Bush, "India-U.S. Joint Statement," The White House, Washington, DC, July 18. 2005, www.indianembassy.org/press_release/2005/July/21.htm.

33. "Bend Them, Break Them: America and a Nuclear India," *The Economist*, October 22, 2005.

34. Amit Baruah, "Giving Our N-Program a Much-Needed Boost," *Hindustan Times*, August 13, 2007; Condoleezza Rice, "Our Opportunity with India," *Washington Post*, March 13, 2006.

35. "BARCing Up the Right Tree," *Hindustan Times*, September 3, 2007.

36. "Nuke Energy Must to Meet Growing Demand, Says PM," *Times of India*, August 21, 2007.

37. K. Subrahmanyam, "Calling Off Deal Will Isolate India Globally," *Times of India*, August 20, 2007.

38. Pranab Mukherjee, "India and the Global Balance of Power" (unpublished address to the Global India Foundation, New Delhi, January 16, 2007; text in author's possession).

39. Pramit Pal Chaudhuri, "N-Abling You to Catch More Fish and Play Harder Tennis," *Hindustan Times*, August 24, 2007.

40. Indrani Bagchi, "India's Credibility Will Take Big Hit If Deal Is Nuked," *Times of India*, August 20, 2007.

41. Bloomberg News, "Interview with Secretary of State Condoleezza Rice (as Released by the State Department)," Federal News Service, Washington, DC, May 26, 2005.

42. Ashley Tellis, "U.S.-India Relations" (remarks to the House International Relations Committee), Federal News Service, Washington, DC, November 16, 2005.

43. Subrahmanyam, "Calling Off Deal Will Isolate India Globally."

44. International Atomic Energy Agency Board of Governors, "The Conclusion of Safeguards Agreements and Additional Protocols: An Agreement with the Government of India for the Application of Safeguards to Civilian Nuclear Facilities," July 9, 2008, www.isis-online.org/publications/southasia/India_IAEA_safeguards.pdf.

45. Brahma Chellaney, "Vaunted U.S.-India Nuclear Deal Begins to Fall Apart," *International Herald Tribune*, February 13, 2006; Robert Einhorn, "The U.S.-India Global Partnership: The Impact on Nonproliferation" (testimony before the House International Relations Committee), Federal News Service, Washington, DC, October 26, 2005.

46. Baruah, "Giving Our N-Program a Much-Needed Boost."

47. Robert Einhorn, quoted in "Indo-U.S. Deal Could Lead to Arms Race, Warns Expert," *Hindustan Times*, June 27, 2007.

48. Cited in Rajesh Rajagopalan, "Swordplay in the Dark: With Regard to the U.S.-India Nuclear Deal, India's Paranoid Class Sees Enemies Where None Exist," *Indian Express*, January 3, 2007.

49. Rice, "United States–India Global Partnership."

50. Quoted in Somini Sengupta, "Defending Nuclear Pact, Indian Premier Faces Criticism," *New York Times*, August 14, 2007.

51. Quoted in Steven Weisman, "Dissenting on Atomic Deal," *New York Times*, March 3, 2006.

52. Daryl Kimball, "Text, Analysis, and Response to NSG 'Statement on Civil Nuclear Cooperation with India,'" Arms Control Association, September 6, 2008, www.armscontrol.org/node/3345; Sharon Squassoni, Fred McGoldrick, and Daryl G. Kimball, "Nonproliferation Experts Analyze State Department Responses to Congressional Questions Concerning U.S.-India Nuclear Deal," Arms Control Association, September 4, 2008, www.armscontrol.org/node/3338.

53. Quoted in Nilova Chaudhury, "Experts Say Left Helping China, Pak," *Hindustan Times*, August 21, 2007.

54. Strobe Talbott, "Good Day for India, Bad Day for Nonproliferation," *International Herald Tribune*, July 21, 2005.

55. Brahma Chellaney, "India Has Sold Its Nuclear Soul to the U.S.," *Rediff*, April 27, 2006, http://in.rediff.com/news/2006/apr/27brahma.htm; Manvendra Singh, BJP Member of Parliament, interview with author, New Delhi, September 2007.

56. Government and BJP officials, interviews with author, New Delhi, July–August 2007.

57. Carter, "America's New Strategic Partner?"

58. Quoted in Sengupta, "Defending Nuclear Pact."

59. Condoleezza Rice, "Rethinking the National Interest," *Foreign Affairs* 87, no. 4 (July/August 2008): 2–26.

60. Nicholas Burns, "U.S. Policy in South Asia" (address to the Asia Society, New York, November 27, 2006), www.asiasociety.org/speeches/06ny_burns.html.

61. "External Affairs Minister, U.S. Secretary of State Address Press Conference in New Delhi," *Hindustan Times*, March 16, 2005.

62. Nuclear Suppliers Group, "Statement on Civil Nuclear Cooperation with India," September 6, 2008, www.armscontrol.org/system/files/20080906_Final_NSG_Statement.pdf.

63. Paul Kerr, "U.S. Nuclear Cooperation with India: Issues for Congress," Congressional Research Service, February 1, 2010.

64. Dafna Linzer, "House Voted on Indian Deal Unaware of Iran Missile Sales," *Washington Post*, July 29, 2006; K. Alan Kronstadt and Kenneth Katzman, "India-Iran Relations and U.S. Interests," Congressional Research Service, August 6, 2007, 4.

65. See Prime Minister Singh's statement of March 6, 2006 to the Indian Parliament regarding India's vote at the IAEA on Iran's nuclear program, http://pmindia.nic.in/parl.htm; Daniel Twining, "India's Relations with Iran and Myanmar: 'Rogue State' or Responsible Democratic Stakeholder?" *India Review* 7, no. 1 (January 2008): 1–37.

66. The White House, Office of the Press Secretary, remarks of President Barack Obama, Prague, Czech Republic, April 5, 2009, www.whitehouse.gov/the_press_office/Remarks-By-President-Barack-Obama-In-Prague-As-Delivered/; Paul-Anton Kruger, interview with IAEA director general Mohamed El-Baradei (translated from German), September 25, 2008, www.iaea.org/NewsCenter/Transcripts/2008/sz250908.html.

67. "India to Flag Nuke-Terror Concern at U.S. Summit," *Times of India*, April 5, 2010.

68. Quoted in Indrani Bagchi, "India Plans N-Center to Drive R&D, Aims to Rope in IAEA," *Economic Times* (New Delhi), April 15, 2010.

69. Rory Medcalf, "India's Nuclear Example," *Wall Street Journal*, April 14, 2010.

70. Ibid.

71. Yuriko Koike, "North Korea's Nuclear Affair with Iran," *Moscow Times*, April 27, 2010, www.themoscowtimes.com/opinion/article/north-koreas-nuclear-affair-with-iran/404836.html. Koike is a former Japanese minister of defense and national security adviser.

72. Yoichi Funabashi, *The Peninsula Question: A Chronicle of the Second Korean Nuclear Crisis* (Washington, DC: Brookings Institution Press, 2007).

CHAPTER 10: GLOBAL CONSEQUENCES OF AN OPERATIONALLY NUCLEAR NORTH KOREA

1. Numerous analysts cautioned that a North Korean nuclear test could bring about serious consequences. See, for example, James Clay Moltz, "Future Nuclear Proliferation Scenarios in Northeast Asia," *Nonproliferation Review* 13, no. 3 (November 2006): 591–604. Regarding a possible North Korean nuclear test he notes, "The ramifications of such a test could be very serious. Japan, already moving in a strongly militaristic direction as a result of North Korea's missile tests, could be pushed over the edge and begin producing nuclear weapons. South Korea could follow suit, especially if Japan made clear moves toward the bomb. Taiwan would feel pressure, too. The United States would retain some leverage over these states, but perhaps not enough to match pro-nuclear domestic pressures in some of these countries that might become overwhelming in the face of an overt North Korean nuclear capability" (598).

See also Michael Moran, "Will Nukes March across Asia?" Council on Foreign Relations, Washington, DC, October 12. 2006, www.cfr.org/publication/11731/will_nukes_march_across_asia.html.

2. Former senior Japanese diplomat, interview with author, March 2007.

3. Michael A. Levi, "Responding to Pyongyang with an Eye toward Tehran," Council on Foreign Relations, Washington, DC, October 12, 2006, www.cfr.org/publication/11711/responding_to_pyongyang_with_an_eye_toward_tehran.html.

4. See, for example, Lionel Beehner, "The Impact of North Korea's Nuclear Test on the Iran Crisis," Council on Foreign Relations, Washington, DC, October 13, 2006, www.cfr.org/publication/11712/impact_of_north_koreas_nuclear_test_on_iran_crisis.html.

5. Neil MacFarquhar, "U.N. Security Council Pushes North Korea by Passing Sanctions," *New York Times*, June 12, 2009, www.nytimes.com/2009/06/13/world/asia/13nations.html.

6. Maria Rost Rublee, *Nonproliferation Norms: Why States Choose Nuclear Restraint* (Athens: University of Georgia Press, 2009), 40.

7. For a thorough discussion of how norms shape nuclear decision making, see ibid., esp. chaps. 2 and 6.

8. "Barak: Stopping North Korea Would Help Curb Iranian Nukes," *Jerusalem Post*, September 22, 2009.

9. Mitchell B. Reiss, "A Nuclear-Armed North Korea: Accepting the 'Unacceptable'?" *Survival* 48, no. 4 (December 2006): 105.

10. Gerard Aziakou, "UN Adopts Tougher N. Korea Sanctions," Agence France Presse, June 12, 2009.

11. Mary Beth Nikitin, Mark E. Manyin, Emma Chanlett-Avery, Dick K. Nanto, and Larry A. Niksch, "North Korea's Second Nuclear Test: Implications of U.N. Security Council Resolution 1874," Congressional Research Service, July 1, 2009, 3.

12. For a thorough examination of China's dilemma regarding North Korea's nuclear program, see Gregory J. Moore, "How North Korea Threatens China's Interests: Understanding Chinese 'Duplicity' on the North Korean Nuclear Issue," *International Relations of the Asia Pacific* 8, no. 1 (2008): 1–29. See also Stephen Haggard and Marcus Noland, "The Political Economy of North Korea: Implications for Denuclearization and Proliferation," East-West Center Working Papers, Economic Series no. 104, June 2009.

13. Andrei Lankov, "Why Beijing Props Up Pyongyang," *New York Times*, June 11, 2009, www.nytimes.com/2009/06/12/opinion/12iht-edlankov.html?_r=4. See also chap. 4 in this volume.

14. Bill Varner, "North Korea Exports $100 Million of Arms Each Year in Breach of Sanctions," Bloomberg.com, November 11, 2010, www.bloomberg.com/news/2010-11-10/north-korea-exports-100-million-of-arms-each-year-in-breach-of-sanctions.html. For an in-depth analysis of the DPRK's economy, see Dick Nanto and Emma Chanlett-Avery, "North Korea: Economic Leverage and Policy Analysis," Congressional Research Service, August 14, 2009.

15. Jack Kim, "North Korea Hints Ready to Return to Nuclear Talks," Reuters, December 10, 2009. Even North Korea's missile sales have dropped because of the international sanctions against the country. See "Acquisition of Technology Relating to Weapons of Mass Destruction and Advanced Conventional Munitions, 1 January to 31 December 2006," Office of the Director for National Intelligence, www.dni.gov/reports/Acquisition_Technology_Report_030308.pdf, 6.

16. See, for example, Charles Ferguson, "Don't Sanction North Korea," *Foreign Policy*, June 19, 2009, http://experts.foreignpolicy.com/posts/2009/06/19/dont_sanction_north_korea.

17. Graham Allison, "Hold North Korea Accountable," *Baltimore Sun*, July 23, 2006.

18. "North Korea Would Sell Nukes to Terrorists," *Washington Times*, February 5, 2008.

19. David E. Sanger and William J. Broad, "Tests Said to Tie Deal on Uranium to North Korea," *New York Times*, February 2, 2005.

20. See, for example, the 721 Report for 2005 produced by the Office of the Director of National Intelligence, "Acquisition of Technology Relating to Weapons of Mass Destruction and Advanced Conventional Munitions, 1 January to 31 December 2005," www.dni.gov/reports/CDA%2011–14–2006.pdf. A 721 Report is a biannual "Unclassified Report to Congress on the Acquisition of Technology Relating to Weapons of Mass Destruction and Advanced Conventional Munitions," which was repealed for fiscal year 2013.

21. Allison, "Hold North Korea Accountable." See also the 721 Report for 2005, 5–6.

22. 721 Report for 2005, 6.

23. Malfrid Braut-Hegghammer, "Libya's Nuclear Turnaround: Perspectives from Tripoli," *Middle East Journal* 62, no. 1 (2008): 68–69. See also Michael Collins Dunn, "MEJ Author Malfrid Braut-Hegghammer on Libya's Nuclear Rollback," *MEI Bulletin* 59, no. 1 (March 2008): 8–9.

24. 721 Report for 2005, p. 6.

25. Moltz, "Future Nuclear Proliferation Scenarios in Northeast Asia," 597.

26. Matthew Kroenig, "Exporting the Bomb: Why States Provide Sensitive Nuclear Assistance," *American Political Science Review* 103, no. 1 (February 2009): 127.

27. 721 Report for 2007 produced by the Office of the Director of National Intelligence, "Acquisition of Technology Relating to Weapons of Mass Destruction and Advanced Conventional Munitions, 1 January to 31 December 2007," www.dni.gov/reports/Unclassified%20Report%20to%20Congress%20WMD%20Covering%201January%20to%2031%20December%202007.pdf, 8.

28. Greg Miller and Paul Richter, "U.S. Opens Dossier on Syrian Facility," *Los Angeles Times*, April 25, 2008. For information on the possible cover-up after the attack, see David Albright and Paul Brannan, "The Al Kibar Reactor: Extraordinary Camouflage, Troubling Implications," Institute for Science and International Security, May 12, 2008, http://isis-online.org/uploads/isis-reports/documents/SyriaReactorReport_12May2008.pdf.

29. "UN Probes US Syria Reactor Claim," BBC News, April 25, 2008, http://news.bbc.co.uk/2/hi/7366658.stm.

30. Miller and Ritcher, "U.S. Opens Dossier on Syrian Faculty."

31. Albright and Brannan, "Al Kibar Reactor," 3.

32. Glenn Kessler, "U.S. Concerns Growing about North Korean Military Ties with Burma," *Washington Post*, July 22, 2009.

33. Julian Borger, "Burma Suspected of Forming Nuclear Link with North Korea," *The Guardian*, July 21, 2009, www.guardian.co.uk/world/2009/jul/21/burma-north-korea-nuclear-clinton.html.

34. Ibid.

35. Bertil Lintner, "Burma's Nuclear Temptation," *Yale Global,* December 3, 2008, http://yaleglobal.yale.edu/content/burma%E2%80%99s-nuclear-temptation.

36. Desmond Ball, "Burma's Nuclear Programs: The Defector's Stories," *Security Challenges* 5, no. 4 (Summer 2009): 119–31.

37. Ibid., 130.

38. William Wan, "Burma Pursued Nuclear Weapons with North Korea, U.S. Senator Says," *Washington Post*, November 25, 2011.

39. See, for example, "Burma: Economy," *CIA Factbook 2009*, https://www.cia.gov/library/publications/the-world-factbook/geos/bm.html.

40. Joshua Kurlantzick, "How Myanmar Changed and What It Means," Council on Foreign Relations, Washington, DC, February 1, 2012. See also Andrew Selth, "Burma and Weapons of Mass Destruction: Claims, Controversies and Consequences," associate paper, Future Directions International, August 2012, www.futuredirections.org.au/files/Associate%20Papers/FDI_Associate_Paper_-_09_August_2012.pdf; Sarah Weiner, "Nuclear Dialogue with the New Myanmar," Center for Strategic and International Studies, September 5, 2012, http://csis.org/blog/nuclear-dialogue-new-myanmar.

41. "Burma 'Has Given Up Nuclear Power Research' – minister," BBC News, June 2, 2012, www.bbc.co.uk/news/world-asia-18309879.

42. Mark Fitzpatrick, ed., "Nuclear Black Market Dossier: A Net Assessment," International Institute for Strategic Studies, London, 2007, 78.

43. Maria Rost Rublee, "Taking Stock of the Nuclear Nonproliferation Regime: Using Social Psychology to Understand Regime Effectiveness," *International Studies Review* 10, no. 3 (2008): 429–31.

44. See, for example, Steven B. Weisman, "North Korea's Nuclear Plans Called 'Unacceptable'; Bush Seeks a Diplomatic Solution," *New York Times*, December 14, 2002; Roger Runningen and Catherine Dodge, "Bush Calls N. Korea's Nuclear Test Claim Unacceptable," Bloomberg.com, October 9, 2006, www.bloomberg.com/apps/news?pid=newsarchive&sid=ao1_XkSfgyoM&refer=japan; Graham Allison, "Hold North Korea Accountable for Its Nuclear Arms," *Baltimore Sun*, July 23, 2006.

45. Joshua Mitnick, "North Korea's Nuclear Defiance May Embolden Iran, Israelis Worry," *Christian Science Monitor*, May 31, 2009.

46. Ibid.

47. Mitchell B. Reiss, "A Nuclear-armed North Korea: Accepting the 'Unacceptable'?" *Survival* 48, no. 4 (December 2006): 105.

48. Levi, "Responding to Pyongyang with an Eye toward Tehran."

49. Beehner, "Impact of North Korea's Test on the Iran Crisis."

50. See, for example, Scott D. Sagan, "Why Do States Build Nuclear Weapons," *International Security* 21, no. 3 (Winter 1996/1997): 54–86; Etel Solingen, *Nuclear Logics: Contrasting Paths in East Asia and the Middle East* (Princeton, NJ: Princeton University Press, 2007); Rublee, *Nonproliferation Norms*.

51. "North Korea: Leadership Succession," Global Security.org, accessed December 12, 2009, www.globalsecurity.org/military/world/dprk/leadership-succession.htm.

52. Ibid.

53. Terence Roehrig. "One Rogue State Crisis at a Time! The United States and North Korea's Nuclear Weapons Program," *World Affairs* 165, no. 4 (April 2003): 168. See also Mun Suk Ahn, "After Kim Jong-Il," *Bulletin of the Atomic Scientists*, November 16, 2009, www.thebulletin.org/web-edition/features/after-kim-jong-il.

54. Soo-Ho Lim, "Motives behind NK's Nuclear Weapons and Prospects for Denuclearization," *SERI Quarterly* 2, no. 4 (October 2009): 120.

55. Reiss, "Nuclear-Armed North Korea," 99.

56. Ibid. See also Victor D. Cha, "What Do They Really Want?: Obama's North Korea Conundrum," *Washington Quarterly* 32, no. 4 (October 2009): 125–26.

57. For a thorough examination of how domestic politics shape the Iranian nuclear debate, see Shahram Chubin, "Iran: Domestic Politics and Nuclear Choices," in Ashley J. Tellis and Michael Willis, eds., *Strategic Asia 2007–2008: Domestic Political Change and Grand Strategy* (Seattle, WA: National Bureau of Asian Research), 301–38.

58. See, for example, Suzanne Maloney, *Iran's Long Reach: Iran as a Pivotal State in the Muslim World* (Washington, DC: USIP Press, 2008).

59. For a thorough discussion of the potential change in Egyptian policy, see Maria Rost Rublee, *Nonproliferation Norms: Why States Choose Nuclear Restraint* (Athens: University of Georgia Press, 2009), 126–28.

60. Sammy Salama and Khalid Hilal, "Egyptian Muslim Brotherhood Presses Government for Nuclear Weapons," *WMD Insights*, November 2006, www.wmdinsights.com/I10/I10_ME3_EgyptianMuslim.htm.

61. Marcell Nasser, "Egypt to Move Ahead with Nuclear Power Plans," *Al-Monitor*, July 12, 2012, www.al-monitor.com/pulse/politics/2012/07/egypt-revives-plans-to-construct.html.

62. "Algeria, Emirates Plan Nonproliferation-Friendly Nuclear Programs; Egypt Keeps Fuel Cycle Options Open, Rejects Expanded IAEA Monitoring," *WMD Insights*, June 2008, www.wmdinsights.com/I25/I25_ME1_AlgeriaEmirates.htm.

63. See, for example, R. Scott Kemp and Alexander Glaser, "Statement on Iran's Ability to Make a Nuclear Weapon and the Significance of the 19 February 2009 IAEA Report on Iran's Uranium Enrichment Program," Princeton University (website), March 2, 2009, www.princeton.edu/~aglaser/2009aglaser_iran.pdf. Kemp and Glaser estimate that Iran could acquire enough fissile material for a nuclear weapon within one to three years. While three years have now passed, their estimate was criticized for being too conservative. See, for example, David Albright, Paul Brannan, and Jacqueline Shire, "Nuclear Weapon Breakout Scenarios: Correcting the Record," Institute for Science and International Security, March 18, 2009, http://isis-online.org/uploads/isis-reports/documents/Correcting_the_Record.pdf.

64. Robert S. Litwak and Kathryn Weathersby, "The Kims' Obsession: Archives Show Their Quest to Preserve the Regime," *Washington Post*, June 12, 2005.

65. Victor D. Cha, "North Korea's Weapons of Mass Destruction: Badges, Shields, or Swords," *Political Science Quarterly* 117, no. 2 (June 2002): 218.

66. Levi, "Responding to Pyongyang with an Eye toward Tehran," Levi adds that such a formulation leaves out the option of cooperation for Iran. It need not be simply a choice of develop nuclear weapons or be invaded.

67. In this case, deterrence does not refer to mutually assured destruction (MAD) through a credible second-strike capability. Rather, it refers to deterrence as "having just enough capabilities to raise uncertainty in the mind of the opponent so that it cannot neutralize you with a first strike" (Cha, "North Korea's Weapons of Mass Destruction," 217).

68. Mitnick, "North Korea's Nuclear Defiance May Embolden Iran."

69. Thom Shanker and David E. Sanger, "Making Good on North Korea Vow Will Take Detective Work," *New York Times*, October 12, 2006.

70. David A. Fulghum, Amy Butler, and Neelam Mathews, "What's Plan B?" *Aviation Week and Space Technology* 165, no. 15 (October 16, 2006): 108.

71. For in-depth analysis of neighboring countries' response to Iran's nuclear program, see Dalia Dassa Kaye and Frederic M. Wehrey, "A Nuclear Iran: The Reactions of Neighbors," *Survival* 49, no. 2 (2007): 111–28. See also James A. Russell, "A Tipping Point Realized? Nuclear Proliferation in the Persian Gulf and Middle East," *Contemporary Security Policy* 29, no. 3 (2008): 521–37; and Richard Weitz, "Gulf Cooperation Council Moves Forward with Nuclear Energy Plans," *WMD Insights*, April 2007, www.wmdinsights.com/I14/I14_ME3_GCCMoves Forward.htm.

72. Mustafa Alani, director of national security at the Dubai-based Gulf Research Center, quoted in Weitz, "Gulf Cooperation Council Moves Forward with Nuclear Energy Plans."

73. Rublee, *Nonproliferation Norms*, 126.

74. Kaye and Wehrey, "Nuclear Iran," 111–12.

75. Former senior Japanese diplomat, interview with author, March 2007.

76. Llewelyn Hughes, "Why Japan Will Not Go Nuclear (Yet): International and Domestic Constraints on the Nuclearization of Japan," *International Security* 31, no. 4 (Spring 2007): 67–96.

77. Maria Rost Rublee, "The Nuclear Threshold States: Challenges and Opportunities Posed by Brazil and Japan," *Nonproliferation Review* 17, no. 1 (March 2010): 62–63.

CHAPTER 11: DPRK NUCLEAR CHALLENGES AND THE POLITICS OF NONPROLIFERATION

1. For a fascinating account of the second North Korean nuclear crisis, see Yoichi Funabashi, *The Peninsula Question: A Chronicle of the Second Korean Nuclear Crisis* (Washington, DC Brookings Institution Press, 2007).

2. Abraham Denmark, Zachary M. Hosford, and Michael Zubrow, "Hard Lessons: Navigating Negotiations with the DPRK, Center for a New American Security," Center for a New American Security, Washington, DC, November 2009.

3. Ferial Ara Saeed, "Redefining Success: Applying Lessons in Nuclear Diplomacy from North Korea to Iran," Institute for National Strategic Studies Strategic Perspectives no. 1, National Defense University Press, Washington, DC, September 2010..

4. Walter C. Clemens Jr., "North Korea's Quest for Nuclear Weapons: New Historical Evidence," *Journal of East Asian Studies* 10, no. 1 (January–March 2010): 127–54.

5. For comprehensive analyses of the two crises, see Joel Wit, Daniel Poneman, and Robert Galluci, *Going Critical: The First North Korean Nuclear Crisis* (Washington, DC: Brookings Institution Press, 2004); Funabashi, *Peninsula Question*.

6. George Bunn and John Rhinelander, "The Right to Withdraw from the NPT: Article X Is Not Unconditional," *Disarmament Diplomacy* 79 (April/May 2005), www.acronym.org.uk/dd/dd79/79gbjr.htm.

7. Scott Snyder, "The Second North Korean Nuclear Crisis: Assessing U.S. and DPRK Negotiation Strategies," *Pacific Focus* 22, no. 1 (March 2007): 49–52; Bates Gill and Andrew Thompson, "A Test for Beijing: China and the North Korean Nuclear Quandary," *Arms Control Today* 33, no. 4 (May 2003): 12–14.

8. Warren P. Strobel, "Vice President's Objections Blocked Planned North Korean Nuclear Talks," Knight Ridder Washington Bureau, December 20, 2003, quoted in Snyder, "Second North Korean Nuclear Crisis," 50.

9. Robert S. Litwak, "Living with Ambiguity: Nuclear Deals with Iran and North Korea," *Survival* 50, no. 1 (February–March 2008): 91–118.

10. Gady A. Epstein, "From Beijing, Stern Words for an Uneasy Ally," *Baltimore Sun*, March 28, 2003; Jonathan Watts, "China Cuts Oil Supply to North Korea," *The Guardian*, April 1, 2003.

11. Ching Cheong, "China Offers North Korea Security from Any US Attack," *Straits Times*, May 3, 2003.

12. Gilbert Rozman, "The North Korean Nuclear Crisis and U.S. Strategy in Northeast Asia," *Asian Survey* 47, no. 4 (July/August 2007): 601–21; Snyder, "Second North Korean Nuclear Crisis," 52–56.

13. Edward Cody and Anthony Faiola, "North Korean Ends 'Candid' China Visits," *Washington Post*, April 22, 2004.

14. Andrei Lankov, "Why the United States Will Have to Accept a Nuclear North Korea," *Korean Journal of Defense Analysis* 21, no. 3 (September 2009): 251–64; Lankov's chapter in this volume; and Siegfried S. Hecker, Sean C. Lee, and Chaim Braun, "North Korea's Choice: Bomb over Electricity," *The Bridge*, Summer 2010, 5–12.

15. Linus Hagström, "Normalizing Japan: Supporter, Nuisance, or Wielder of Power in the North Korean Nuclear Talks?" *Asian Survey* 49, no. 5 (September/October 2009): 831–51; Leszek Buszynski, "Russia and North Korea: Dilemmas and Interests," *Asian Survey* 49, no. 5 (September/October 2009): 809–30; Denny Roy, "Parsing Pyongyang's Strategy," *Survival* 52, no. 1 (February–March 2010): 111–36.

16. International Crisis Group, "After the North Korea Nuclear Breakthrough: Compliance or Confrontation?" Asia Briefing no. 62, April 30, 2007, www.crisisgroup.org/library/documents/asia/north_korea/b62_after_the_north_korean_nuclear_breakthrough_final.pdf.

17. U.S. Department of State, "Joint Statement of the Fourth Round of the Six-Party Talks," September 19, 2005, http://2001-2009.state.gov/r/pa/prs/ps/2005/53490.htm.

18. Victor Cha, *The Impossible State: North Korea, Past and Future* (New York: CCCO, 2012), 261–70.

19. Siegfried S. Hecker, "Denuclearizing North Korea," *Bulletin of the Atomic Scientists* 64, no. 2 (May/June 2008): 44–49, 61–62.

20. Siegfried S. Hecker and William Liou, "Dangerous Dealings: North Korea's Nuclear Capabilities and the Threat of Export to Iran," *Arms Control Today* 37, no. 2 (March 2007): 6–11.

21. Leonard S. Spector and Avner Cohen, "Israel's Airstrike on Syria's Reactor: Implications for the Nonproliferation Regime," *Arms Control Today* 38, no. 6 (July/August 2008): 15–21.

22. James Cotton, "The Proliferation Security Initiative and North Korea: Legality and Limitation of a Coalition Strategy," *Security Dialogue* 36, no. 2 (June 2005): 193–211.

23. Christina Y. Lin, "The King from the East: DPRK-Syria-Iran Nuclear Nexus and Strategic Implications for Israel and the ROK," Academic Papers Series 3, no. 7, Korea Economic Institute, Washington, DC, October 2008, www.keia.org/sites/default/files/publications/APS-Lin.pdf; Spector and Cohen, "Israel's Airstrike on Syria's Reactor: Implications for the Nonproliferation Regime."

24. Danielle Pletka, "A Pushover for Pyongyang," *On the Issue*, May 2008, www.aei.org/ar ticle/27951; John R. Bolton, "Bush's North Korea Nuclear Abdication," *Wall Street Journal*, May 8, 2008; Evans J. R. Revere, "The North Korea Nuclear Problem: Sailing into Uncharted Wa ters," *American Foreign Policy Interests* 32, no. 3 (May 2010): 183–90.

25. Jae-Soon Chang, "NKorea Threatens Nuclear, Missile Tests," Associated Press, April 29, 2009, www.breitbart.com/article.php?id=D97S4DRG0&show_article=1.

26. "KCNA Report on One More Successful Underground Nuclear Test," KCNA, May 25, 2009, www.kcna.co.jp/index-e.htm.

27. "Security Council Imposes Tougher Sanctions on DPR Korea," UN News Center, June 12, 2009, www.un.org/apps/news/story.asp?NewsID=31121&Cr=dprk&Cr1=.

28. Siegfried S. Hecker and Robert Carlin, "North Korea in 2011: Countdown to Kim il-Sung's Centenary," *Bulletin of the Atomic Scientists* 68, no. 1 (January/February 2012): 53, http:// cisac.stanford.edu/publications/north_korea_in_2011_countdown_to_kim_ilsungs_cente nary/; Siegfried S. Hecker, "Where Is North Korea's Nuclear Program Heading?" *Physics and Society* 40, no. 2 (April 2011): 5–9.

29. Patrick Clawson, "Nuclear Proliferation in the Middle East: Who Is Next after Iran?" in Henry D. Sokolski, ed., *Taming the Next Set of Strategic Weapons Threats* (Carlisle, PA: Stra tegic Studies Institute, U.S. Army War College, 2006), 27–39; Gary Samore, "The Korean Nuclear Crisis," *Survival* 45, no. 1 (Spring 2003): 7–24; Andrew Scobell and Michael R. Cham bers, "The Fallout of a Nuclear North Korea," *Current History*, September 2005, 289–94; Sammy Salama and Heidi Weber, "Arab Nuclear Envy," *Bulletin of the Atomic Scientists* 63, no. 5 (September/October 2007): 44–49, 63.

30. Bennett Ramberg, "Living with Nuclear North Korea," *Survival* 51, no. 4 (August–Sep tember 2009): 13–20.

31. In December 1993 the UN General Assembly adopted by consensus a resolution rec ommending the negotiation of a nondiscriminatory, multilateral, and internationally and effectively verifiable treaty banning the production of fissile material for nuclear weapons or other nuclear explosive devices, which became known as a Fissile Material Cutoff Treaty (FMCT). However, differences over the scope of the treaty have so far prevented the Confer ence on Disarmament from agreeing on a program of work and the setup of a committee for negotiation of the treaty.

32. Sharon Riggle, "Could the Non-Proliferation Treaty Collapse? The Uncertain Road Ahead," *Disarmament Forum* 1 (May 2000): 29–38, www.fas.org/nuke/control/npt/news/1-00 -eriggle.pdf; Harold Müller, "A Treaty in Troubled Waters: Reflections on the Failed NPT Review Conference," *International Spectator* 40, no. 3 (July–September 2004): 33–44; George Perkovich, "The End of the Nonproliferation Regime?" *Current History* 105, no. 694 (Novem ber 2006): 355–62; Mario E. Carranza, "Can the NPT Survive? The Theory and Practice of US Nuclear Non-proliferation Policy after September 11," *Contemporary Security Policy* 27, no. 3 (December 2006): 489–525; Tom Sauer, "The Nonproliferation Regime in Crisis," *Peace Re view* 18 (July 2006): 334–35.

33. Joshua Pollack, "North Korea's Nuclear Exports: On What Terms?," A 38 North Spe cial Report, October 14, 2010, http://38north.org/wp-content/uploads/2010/10/38North_SR9_ Pollack2.pdf. See also Mark Fitzpatrick, "Stopping Nuclear North Korea," *Survival* 51, no. 4 (August–September 2009): 5–12; Peter Crail, "NK-Syria Nuclear Connection Questionable,"

Arms Control Today 37, no. 8 (October 2007): 35–36; Spector and Cohen, "Israel's Airstrike on Syria's Reactor."

34. Kurt M. Campbell and Tsuyoshi Sunohara, "Japan: Thinking the Unthinkable," in Kurt M. Campbell, Robert J. Einhorn, and Mitchell B. Reiss, eds., *The Nuclear Tipping Point: Why States Reconsider Their Nuclear Choices* (Washington, DC: Brookings Institution Press, 2004), 218–53; and Jonathan D. Pollack and Mitchell B. Reiss, "South Korea: They Tyranny of Geography and the Vexations of History," in Campbell, Einhorn, and Reiss, *Nuclear Tipping Point*, 254–92; Yuri Kase, "The Costs and Benefits of Japan's Nuclearization: An Insight into the 1968/70 Internal Report," *Nonproliferation Review* 8, no. 2 (Summer 2001): 55–68.

35. Michael J. Green and Katsuhisa Furukawa, "Japan: New Nuclear Realism," in Muthiah Alagappa, ed., *The Long Shadow: Nuclear Weapons and Security in Twenty-First-Century Asia* (Stanford, CA: Stanford University Press, 2008), 347–72; Kang Choi and Joon-sung Park, "South Korea: Fears of Abandonment and Entrapment," in Alagappa, *Long Shadow*, 373–403; Mike M. Mochizuki, "Japan Tests the Nuclear Taboo," *Nonproliferation Review* 14, no. 2 (July 2007): 303–28; and Masa Takubo, "The Role of Nuclear Weapons: Japan, the U.S., and the 'Sole Purpose,'" *Arms Control Today* 39, no. 9 (November 2009): 14–20.

36. Chung Min Lee, "The Evolution of the North Korean Nuclear Crisis: Implications for Iran," Proliferation Papers, Institut Français des Relations Internationales, Paris, Winter 2009.

37. Leonard S. Spector and Deborah R. Berman, "The Syrian Nuclear Puzzle," in William C. Potter, with Gaukhar Mukhartzhanova, ed., *Forecasting Nuclear Proliferation in the Twenty-First Century: A Comparative Perspective*, vol. 2 (Stanford, CA: Stanford University Press, 2010), 100–128. See also Spector and Cohen, "Israel's Airstrike on Syria's Reactor"; Lin, "King from the East"; Chaim Braun and Christopher F. Chyba, "Proliferation Rings: New Challenges to the Nuclear Non-Proliferation Regime," *International Security* 29, no. 2 (Fall 2004): 5–49.

38. For a comprehensive discussion of the nonproliferation regime and the various issues involved, see Leonard S. Spector, "The Future of the Nonproliferation Regime," in Jeffrey A. Larsen and James J. Wirtz, eds., *Arms Control and Cooperative Security* (Boulder, CO: Lynne Rienner Publishers, 2009), 113–47; and Rebecca E. Johnson, "Arms Control, Universality, and International Norms," in Larsen and Wirtz, *Arms Control and Cooperative Security*, 215–31.

39. William Walker, "The Absence of a Taboo on the Possession of Nuclear Weapons," *Review of International Studies* 36, no. 4 (November 2010): 865–76, and Walker, "Nuclear Enlightenment and Counter-Enlightenment," *International Affairs* 83, no. 3 (2007): 431–53. For a critique of Walker's thesis, see David S. Yost, "Analyzing International Nuclear Order," *International Affairs* 83, no. 3 (2007): 549–74; Joachim Krause, "Enlightenment and Nuclear Order," *International Affairs* 83, no. 3 (2007): 483–99.

40. Etel Solingen, "The Perils of Prediction: Japan's Once and Future Nuclear Status," in Potter with Mukhatzhanova, *Forecasting Nuclear Proliferation in the Twenty-First Century*, 131–57; Jacques E. C. Hymans, "Veto Players, Nuclear Energy, and Nonproliferation: Domestic Institutional Barriers to a Japanese Bomb," *International Security* 36, no. 2 (Fall 2011): 154–89.

41. For more, see Izumi and Furukawa's chapter in this volume.

42. After a careful analysis of Japan's interests, public opinion, and policy history, Izumi and Furukawa in this volume draw the same conclusions.

43. James L. Schoff, "Realigning Priorities: The U.S.-Japan Alliance and the Future of Ex-

tended Alliance," Institute for Foreign Policy Analysis, Cambridge, MA, March 2009; Steven Pifer et al., "U.S. Nuclear and Extended Deterrence: Considerations and Challenges," Brookings Arms Control Series Paper 3, Brookings Institution, Washington, DC, May 2010, 29–36.

44. Llewelyn Hughes, "Why Japan Will Not Go Nuclear (Yet)," *International Security* 31, no. 4 (Spring 2007): 67–96; *Hajime Izumi and Katsuhisa Furukawa*, "Not Going Nuclear: Japan's Response to North Korea's Nuclear Test," *Arms Control Today* 37, no. 6 (July/August 2007): 51–56; Izumi and Furukawa's chapter in this volume. On South Korea, see Scott Snyder, "South Korean Nuclear Decision Making," in Potter with Mukhatzhanova, *Forecasting Nuclear Proliferation in the Twenty-First Century*, 158–81.

45. International Security Advisory Board, Department of State, "Report on the Implications of the Global Expansion of Civil Nuclear Power," Washington, DC, April 7, 2008; Justin Alger, "From Nuclear Energy to the Bomb: The Proliferation Potential of New Nuclear Energy Programs," Nuclear Energy Futures Paper no. 6, Centre for International Governance Innovation, Waterloo, ON, September 28, 2009, www.cigionline.org/sites/default/files/Nuclear_Energy_Futures%206.pdf. See also Charles D. Ferguson, "Potential Strategic Consequences of the Nuclear Energy Revival," Proliferation Papers no. 35, Institut Français des Relations Internationales, Paris, Summer 2010; "On the Global Nuclear Future," special issues of *Daedalus* 138, no. 4 (Fall 2009) and 139, no. 1 (Winter 2010).

46. Joseph F. Pilat, "The End of the NPT Regime?," *International Affairs* 83, no. 3 (2007): 469–82; Jeffrey Fields and Jason S. Enia, "The Health of the Nuclear Nonproliferation Regime: Returning to a Multidimensional Evaluation," *Nonproliferation Review* 16, no. 2 (July 2009): 173–96.

47. Rebecca Johnson, "Assessing the 2010 NPT Review Conference," *Bulletin of the Atomic Scientists* 66, no. 4 (July/August 2010): 1–10; Deepti Choubey, "Future Prospects for the NPT," *Arms Control Today* 40, no. 6 (July/August 2010): 25–29; Lewis A. Dunn, "The NPT: Assessing the Past, Building the Future," *Nonproliferation Review* 16, no. 2 (July 2009): 143–72.

48. See Potter with Mukhatzhanova, *Forecasting Nuclear Proliferation in the Twenty-First Century*. Other major contributions include Etel Solingen, *Nuclear Logic: Contrasting Paths in East Asia and the Middle East* (Princeton, NJ: Princeton University Press, 2007); Jacques E. C. Hymans, *The Psychology of Nuclear Proliferation* (New York: Cambridge University Press, 2006); Hymans, *Achieving Nuclear Ambitions: Scientists, Politicians, and Proliferation* (New York: Cambridge University Press, 2012); Steven Meyer, *The Dynamics of Nuclear Proliferation* (Chicago: University of Chicago Press, 1986).

49. Joseph Cirincione, "The Asian Nuclear Reaction Chain," *Foreign Policy* 118 (Spring 2000): 120–36.

50. Elizabeth Bakanic et al., "Preventing Nuclear Proliferation Chain Reactions: Japan, South Korea, and Egypt," Princeton University Woodrow Wilson School of Public Affairs, Princeton, NJ, January 2008, http://wws.princeton.edu/research/pwreports_f07/wws591f.pdf.

51. Hecker and Liou, "Dangerous Dealings"; Siegfried S. Hecker, "From Pyongyang to Tehran, with Nukes," *Foreign Policy*, May 26, 2009, http://experts.foreignpolicy.com/posts/2009/05/26/from_pyongyang_to_tehran; Justin Muzinich, "The Nuke in the Cargo Hold," *Policy Review* 162 (August/September 2010): 83–92.

52. Hazel Smith, "North Korean Shipping: A Potential for WMD Proliferation?," Asia Pacific Issues no. 87, East-West Center, Honolulu, February 2009; Sheena Chestnut, "Illicit Ac-

tivity and Proliferation: North Korean Smuggling Networks," *International Security* 32, no. 1 (Summer 2007): 80–111.

53. Lee Chi-dong, "S. Korea Plays PSI Card to Counter N. Korea's Brinkmanship," *Yonhap News*, May 26, 2009, http://english.yonhapnews.co.kr/national/2009/05/26/76/0301000000AEN20090526005200315F.HTML. On PSI, see Mary Beth Nikitin, "Proliferation Security Initiative (PSI)," Congressional Research Service Report for Congress RL34327, Washington, DC, January 8, 2010.

54. Erik Gartzke and Matthew Kroenig, "A Strategic Approach to Nuclear Proliferation," *Journal of Conflict Resolution* 53, no. 2 (April 2009): 151–60. This article introduces a number of articles in this special issue of the journal. See also Matthew Fuhrmann, "Spreading Temptation: Proliferation and Peaceful Nuclear Cooperation Agreements," *International Security* 34, no. 1 (Summer 2009): 7–41.

55. Masahiko Asada, "Strengthening the Nuclear Non-Proliferation Regime: Proposals and Problems," *International Spectator* 44, no. 1 (March 2009): 67–79; Oliver Meier, "The Growing Nuclear Cycle Debate," *Arms Control Today* 36, no. 9 (November 2006): 40–44.

56. For a detailed discussion of the inter-Korean competition for status and legitimacy, see David C. Kang, "Status and Leadership on the Korean Peninsula," *Orbis* 54, no. 4 (Fall 2010): 546–64.

57. See Joseph Cirincione, Jon B. Wolfsthal, and Miriam Rajkumar, eds., *Deadly Arsenals: Nuclear, Biological, and Chemical Threats* (Washington, DC: Carnegie Endowment for International Peace, 2005), 279–93; Michael J. Mazaar, *North Korea and the Bomb* (New York: St. Martin's Press, 1995); Jacques E. C. Hymans, "Assessing North Korean Nuclear Intentions and Capacities: A New Approach," *Journal of East Asian Studies* 8, no. 2 (May–August 2008): 259–92.

58. Saeed, *Redefining Success*. See also Richard C. Bush, "The Challenge of a Nuclear North Korea: Dark Clouds, Only One Silver Lining," Policy Papers no. 23, Brookings Institution, Washington, DC, September 2010.

59. Scott Snyder, *Negotiating on the Edge: North Korea Negotiating Behavior* (Washington, DC: United States Institute of Peace Press, 1999).

60. John W. Lewis and Robert Carlin, *Negotiating with North Korea: 1992–2007* (Stanford, CA: Center for International Security and Cooperation, 2008), http://iis-db.stanford.edu/pubs/22128/Negotiating_with_North_Korea_1992–2007.pdf.

61. Martin Fackler and Mark McDonald, "North Koreans Bolster Power of Ruler's Kin," *New York Times*, September 28, 2010, www.nytimes.com/2010/09/29/world/asia/29korea.html; Donald Kirk, "North Korea's New Dawn with Kim Jong-un," *Christian Science Monitor*, October 5, 2010.

62. Choe Sang-Hun, "North Korea Resumes Work on Nuclear Reactor, Group Says," *New York Times*, May 17, 2012; Victor D. Cha, "What Do They Really Want?: Obama's North Korea Conundrum," *Washington Quarterly* 32, no. 4 (October 2009): 119–38; Michael J. Green, "The Perilous Case of Kim Jong Il," *National Interest*, September/October 2009, 36–42.

63. Jung-hoon Lee and Chung-in Moon, "The North Korean Nuclear Crisis Revisited: The Case for a Negotiated Settlement," *Security Dialogue* 34, no. 2 (June 2003): 135–51.

64. Stephan Haggard and Marcus Noland, "Engaging North Korea: The Role of Economic Statecraft," Policy Studies 59, East-West Center, Honolulu, 2011; Leon V. Sigal, "North Korea

Policy on the Rocks: What Can Be Done to Restore Constructive Engagement?" *Global Asia* 4, no. 2 (Summer 2009): 8–12.

65. International Crisis Group, "After the North Korea Nuclear Breakthrough."

66. Gregory J. Moore, "America's Failed North Korea Nuclear Policy: A New Approach," *Asian Perspective* 32, no. 4 (October 2008): 9–28; and Moore, chapter 2 in this volume; Joel S. Wit, "Enhancing U.S. Engagement with North Korea," *Washington Quarterly* 30, no. 2 (Spring 2007): 53–69.

67. Glenn Kessler, "Envoy Warns N. Korea Deal Fallout," *Washington Post*, October 26, 2007.

68. Chung-in Moon, "Reflection on a Summit," Global Asia Forum, undated, www.glo balasia.org/Global_Asia_Forum/Reflections_on_a_Summit.html.

69. Aidan Foster-Carter, "North Korea–South Korea Relations: Summit Success?" *Comparative Connections* 9, no. 3 (October 2007), http://csis.org/files/media/csis/pubs/0703qnorth korea_southkorea.pdf; Ralph A. Cossa, "North-South Summit: Potential Pitfalls Ahead?" *Pac Net* 41 (2007), www.csis.org/media/csis/pubs/pac0741.pdf.

70. "U.S. Seeks NK Regime Transformation," *Korea Times*, December 9, 2004.

71. Victor Cha, a former National Security Council official in the George W. Bush administration, offers a different account and interpretation of these developments. He argues that the BDA case had already been determined even prior to the September 2005 meetings of the Six Party Talks, at which the historic joint statement was reached (Cha, *Impossible State*, 263–67).

72. Helene Cooper, "Bush Rebuffs Hard-Liners to East North Korean Curbs," *New York Times*, June 27, 2008; Bill Powell, "N. Korea Reneges on Nukes—Again," *Time*, August 27, 2008, www.time.com/time/world/article/0,8599,1836612,00.html?xid=rss-world.

73. Dan Eggen, "Doubts about Nuclear Verification Keep N. Korea on List of Terrorist States," *Washington Post*, August 12, 2008.

74. Spector and Cohen, "Israel's Airstrike on Syria's Reactor."

75. Stephan Haggard and Marcus Noland, "Engaging North Korea: The Efficacy of Sanctions and Inducements," in Etel Solingen, ed., *Sanctions, Statecraft, and Nuclear Nonproliferation* (New York: Cambridge University Press, 2012), 232–60; Dingli Shen, "Can Sanctions Stop Proliferation?" *Washington Quarterly* 31, no. 3 (Summer 2008): 89–100.

76. Masahiro Matsumura, "Simpleminded or Farsighted?—The US' Handling of North Korea," Nautilus Institute Policy Forum Online, July 15, 2008, www.nautilus.org/fora/ security/08054Matsumura.html.

77. Cha, "What Do They Really Want?"; Denmark, Hosford, and Zubrow, "Hard Lessons."

78. Bennett Ramberg, "Living with Nuclear North Korea," *Survival* 51, no. 4 (August–September 2009): 13–20.

79. Leon V. Sigal, "Primer—North Korea, South Korea, and the United States: Reading between the Lines of the *Cheonan* Attack," *Bulletin of the Atomic Scientists* 66, no. 5 (September/ October 2010), 35–44.

80. Wade L. Huntley, "Rebels without a Cause: North Korea, Iran, and the NPT," *International Affairs* 82, no. 4 (July 2006): 723–42.

81. Choe Sang-Hun, "North Korea Stance on Nuclear Plan Unchanged," *New York Times*,

February 25, 2012; Blaine Harden, "U.S. Envoy: No Commitment by N. Korea on Future Talks," *Washington Post*, December 10, 2009.

CONCLUSION: IMPLICATIONS AND POSSIBLE WAYS FORWARD

1. See Bae and Choi, chap. 3, this volume.

2. This does not preclude the possibility that South Korean public opinion could shift with North Korean provocations, such that the reintroduction of U.S. tactical nuclear weapons to South Korea could prove an acceptable short-term solution or bargaining chip for Seoul to consider.

3. See Kang, chap. 7, this volume.

4. Ibid.; see endnotes 7, 8, 9, and 19 for that chapter.

5. Ibid., n. 34.

6. Seoul is so close to North Korea that ABM systems would not provide much protection for it, nor would ballistic missiles likely be used against it, but ABM defense might provide some protection for Busan and other areas in southern South Korea.

7. For more detailed depictions and discussions of possible Northeast Asian regional alignments, see Gregory J. Moore, "Constructing Cooperation in Northeast Asia: Historical Northeast Asian Dyadic Cultures and the Potential for Greater Regional Cooperation," *Journal of Contemporary China* 22, no. 83 (September 2013).

8. Henry Kissinger, *On China* (New York: Penguin Press, 2011), 496.

9. See Rublee, chap. 10, this volume, p. 217.

10. See Yuan, chap. 11, this volume, p. 219.

11. Mearsheimer was wrong about the Ukraine keeping its nuclear capabilities, for all of them were returned to Russia between 1994 and 1996. See John J. Mearsheimer, "The Case for a Ukrainian Nuclear Deterrent," *Foreign Affairs* 72, no. 3 (Summer 1993): 50–66.

12. Don Oberdorfer, *The Two Koreas: A Contemporary History* (New York: Basic Books, 2001), 142.

13. Ibid., 183. Oberdorfer interviewed Miss Kim.

14. I refer here to many of the claims of the North Korean regime about the history of the ruling Kim family, particularly as they surround the birth and rise of Kim Jong-il. For more, see Kongdan Oh and Ralph Hassig, *North Korea through the Looking Glass* (Washington, DC: Brookings Institution Press, 2000), and B. R. Myers, *The Cleanest Race: How North Koreans See Themselves—and Why it Matters* (Brooklyn, NY: Melville House, 2010).

15. Choe Sang-hun, "North Korea Stance on Nuclear Plan Unchanged," *New York Times*, February 26, 2011, www.nytimes.com/2012/02/26/world/asia/north-korea-stance-on-nuclear -plan-unchanged.html?ref=asia.

16. See Scott Sagan and Kenneth Waltz, *The Spread of Nuclear Weapons: A Debate Renewed*, 2nd ed. (New York: W. W. Norton, 2002).

17. John J. Mearsheimer, "Case for a Ukrainian Nuclear Deterrent."

18. See Muthiah Alagappa, ed., *The Long Shadow: Nuclear Weapons and Security in Twenty-First Century Asia* (Stanford, CA: Stanford University Press, 2008).

19. Here, Realism and Liberalism (or Neo-Liberal Institutionalism) are capitalized to distinguish them as theoretical IR approaches distinct from their other, more common usages.

20. John J. Mearsheimer, *The Tragedy of Great Power Politics* (New York: Norton, 2001).

21. Ibid., 374.

22. For example, see Henry Kissinger, "North Korea's Nuclear Blackmail," *New York Times*, August 10, 2009.

23. While an argument can be made that Liberalism, Neo-Liberalism, and Neo-Liberal Institutionalism are treated by some in IR as independent of each other, I treat them here as one tradition, rolling them together and applying one label: Neo-Liberal Institutionalism.

24. Robert Keohane and Joseph Nye, *Power and Interdependence*, 4th ed. (London: Longman, 2011).

25. See Alexander Wendt, *Social Theory of International Politics* (Cambridge: Cambridge University Press, 1999). For Wendt's cultures applied to the dyadic (bilateral) level, see Gregory J. Moore, "Not Very Material but Hardly Immaterial: China's Bombed Embassy and Sino-American Relations," *Foreign Policy Analysis* 6, no. 1 (January 2010): 23–41; and Gregory J. Moore, "Constructing Cooperation in Northeast Asia: Historical Northeast Asian Dyadic Cultures and the Potential for Greater Regional Cooperation," *Journal of Contemporary China* 22 (September 2013).

26. Wendt, *Social Theory of International Politics*, 285.

27. I argue here and elsewhere that Realism is a material-driven project, something many of Realism's leading thinkers have argued as well. In this piece, "Not Very Material but Hardly Immaterial," the following Realist examples are highlighted as emphasizing the prevalence of material factors: Kenneth Waltz, *Theory of International Politics* (Reading, PA: Addison-Wesley, 1979), 131; Robert Jervis, "Realism in the Study of World Politics," *International Organization* 52, no. 4 (Autumn 1998), 74; John David Singer and Melvyn Small, "National Military Capabilities Data," Version 3.0: 1816–2001, Correlates of War Project, University of Michigan, Ann Arbor, 1995; John David Singer, Stuart Bremer, and John Stuckey, "Capability Distribution, Uncertainty, and Major Power War, 1820–1965," in Bruce Russett, ed. *Peace, War, and Numbers* (Beverly Hills, CA: Sage, 1972), 19–48; Mearsheimer, *Tragedy of Great Power Politics*, 55–57, 369; Randall Schweller, *Unanswered Threats: Political Constraints on the Balance of Power* (Princeton, NJ: Princeton University Press, 2006), 150; Gideon Rose, "Neoclassical Realism and Theories of Foreign Policy," *World Politics* 51, no. 1(October 1998): 144n72; ; and a new Realist author of interest, Yuan-kang Wang, *Harmony and War: Confucian Culture and Chinese Power Politics* (New York: Columbia University Press, 2011).

Index

ukraine & russia

a fraternal rivalry

anatol lieven

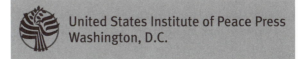

United States Institute of Peace Press
Washington, D.C.

United States Institute of Peace
1200 17th Street NW
Washington, DC 20036

©1999 by the Endowment of the United States Institute of Peace. All rights reserved.

First published 1999

Printed in the United States of America

The paper used in this publication meets the minimum requirements of American National Standard for Information Sciences—Permanence of Paper for Printed Library Materials, ANSI Z39.48-1984.

Library of Congress Cataloging-in-Publication Data
Lieven, Anatol.
    Ukraine and Russia : a fraternal rivalry / Anatol Lieven.
      p. cm.
    Includes bibliographical references and index.
    ISBN 1-878379-87-9 (pbk. : alk. paper)
    1. Ukraine—Relations—Russia (Federation) 2. Russia (Federation)—Relations—
Ukraine. 3. Nationalism—Ukraine. 4. Nationalism—Russia (Federation) I. Title.
    DK508.57.R9L54 1999
    303.48'2477047—dc21   99-12974
                                                      CIP

Ukraine and Russia

To my wife, Sasha,
with my dearest love

CONTENTS

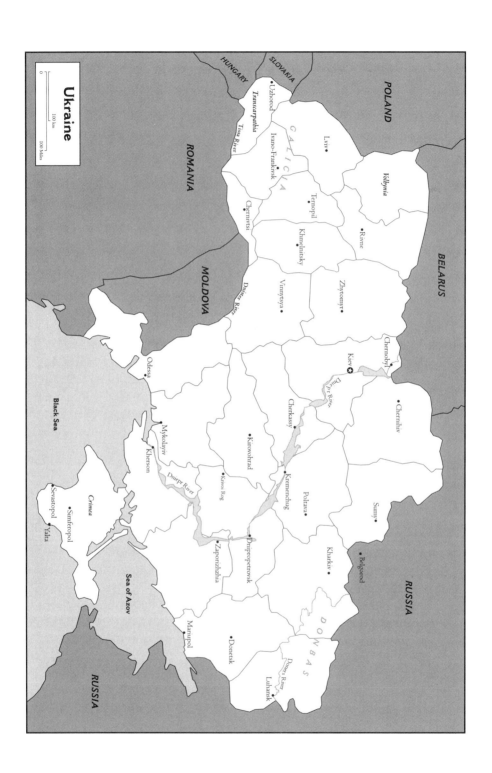

FOREWORD

In the near future, the North Atlantic Treaty Organization (NATO) will address the question of further enlarging its membership beyond the most recent additions of Poland, Hungary, and the Czech Republic. The politics of incorporating former adversaries into the Atlantic Alliance has raised considerable controversy, but as NATO's borders stretch eastward from East-Central Europe toward the former republics of the Soviet Union, subsequent rounds of deciding on new members will undoubtedly prove even more divisive.

The logic of NATO enlargement inevitably brings up the issue of Ukraine. In turn, because of its history and demography, it is well-nigh impossible to speak of Ukraine's membership in any Western organization without serious consideration of Russian sentiments. Ukraine already has a special agreement with NATO, much along the lines of the alliance's special agreement with Russia. However, Ukraine has not actively pursued NATO membership, perhaps reflecting its special relationship among other Soviet successor states with the Russian Federation. Nevertheless, Ukraine's foreign minister recently stated that his country's membership in both NATO and the European Union would contribute to the expansion of democracy and stability in Europe.

As recently as mid-1998, Deputy Secretary of State Strobe Talbott declared that "should Ukraine one day decide to seek entry into the alliance, the door will remain open." Underlying such reassurances by the West's foreign policy establishments is the view of Ukraine as occupying a crucial position in the geopolitics of Eurasia—a country that can serve as a buffer between the new democracies of Eastern Europe and a Russia with an uncertain democratic future. To be sure, Ukraine's very size and position in the Eurasian political landscape make it, in Sherman Garnett's phrase, "the keystone in the arch" of the transatlantic security architecture. Moreover, besides the concern over a former Soviet republic that still possessed a threatening arsenal of Soviet nuclear weapons, Western observers believed that this was the Soviet successor state among those with sizable ethnic Russian minorities that faced the most violent future.

As Anatol Lieven explains in *Ukraine and Russia: A Fraternal Rivalry,* Russia's objections to the transformation of Ukraine into a "buffer state" that once again demarcates the Eurasian political space go beyond the extension of NATO up to its borders. He argues that a concerted effort on the part of the West to make Ukraine a member of the Atlantic Alliance while excluding Russia would seem to unravel perforce the historical, political, and social bonds that have been forged between the two countries over the course of centuries. Such an effort, he explains, attempts to counter a Russian threat to the independence and security of Ukraine—and Europe—that is more hypothetical than extant.

In fact, Lieven contends, Ukraine's acceptance of a Western policy of actively pulling Ukraine into NATO would surely sharpen the appearance of an anti-Russian ideology on the part of the Ukrainian government, thereby severely threatening relations not only between Russia and Ukraine, but also between Russians and Ukrainians in Ukraine. In other words, as Lieven concludes, if Ukraine's value to transatlantic security lies in the country's continued internal stability, such an assertive policy of NATO enlargement in this direction would lead to exactly the kind of result the West wishes most to avoid.

Before conducting the initial research for this book as a 1996 senior fellow in the Institute's Jennings Randolph Program for International Peace, the author spent many years as a journalist for *The Times* of London, covering the democratic revolutions in the former Soviet Baltic republics and the turmoil of transition in the former communist states of East-Central Europe. In *Ukraine and Russia,* Lieven employs the same kind of insightful reportage and a skillful analysis of the region's convoluted history and politics to examine the relationship of these two intertwined Slavic countries. As he explains, the ethnic relationship between Russia and Ukraine is complex: An ethnographic map of Ukraine would indicate distinct Russian- and Ukrainian-speaking areas of settlement, yet it would also show a pervasive intermingling—and intermarriage—of both groups throughout much of the country. Centuries of Russian influence and decades of Soviet rule have established a significant Russian community in Ukraine. However, the ethnic closeness of these two groups has allowed the Russification of much of the country. Moreover, as Lieven points out, most of the "Russian" community's members in Ukraine can be more aptly described as "Soviet" immigrants. As such, they have more identification with the Russian *people* than with any sort of state-centric Russian nationalism.

Such a portrait of ethnic tolerance is bound to differ markedly from the image of Ukraine held by most Western policymakers. Certainly, it is a different image than U.S. national security officials held at the time of the Soviet Union's dissolution. Many of these officials steeled themselves for a violent clash soon after Ukraine's independence, as Soviet controls suddenly disappeared. In his 1991 visit to Kiev, just shortly before Ukraine's independence, President Bush urged Ukrainians to work against "suicidal nationalism," seemingly telling the country to exercise its post-Soviet independence cautiously, lest Moscow destabilize Ukraine by mobilizing a putative "fifth column" of ethnic Russians in Ukraine's eastern and southern regions.

That scenario is exaggerated, Lieven argues—especially now, given the Russian government's apparent lack of will to exert its influence in the major Russian-speaking regions of the country. Although he acknowledges a certain lassitude in Russian officialdom to try to exert much influence at all following its debacle in Chechnya and the economy's steady deterioration, one of Lieven's central themes in this work is that the closeness of "Russians" and Ukrainians works against such a scenario of ethnic polarization and political extremism in Ukraine. Although there are strains of nationalist sentiment among the country's major ethnic groups, the concept of a "nation" for both of them is still somewhat undefined.

This is not to say, however, that Ukraine does not face serious domestic problems that could increase tensions between its two major ethnic groups. As Lieven concludes, the most serious threats to Ukraine's stability come from within. Indeed, despite the affinity between the two countries, Lieven emphasizes that Ukraine and Russia are also distinct rivals. In the post-Soviet experience, Ukraine is exercising its independence in various ways, and Ukrainians are realizing their own national identity, including a resurgence of the Ukrainian language in education and government. As the Ukrainian state begins the arduous process of identifying its nation, Lieven argues, it should realize that maintaining such a level of ethnic tolerance will require nation-building programs that integrate the country's major Russian-speaking population. In other words, the task of nation-building in post-Soviet Ukraine must embrace a civic nationalism that aims toward inclusiveness, not an exclusive ethnic nationalism that could also very well provoke a reaction from Ukraine's much larger neighbor to the east.

As the author of this work explains, however, there are formidable challenges to such a civic nation-building project. Ukraine's economy continues on a downward slope, a trend that is accelerated by pervasive corruption and half-hearted attempts at economic reform. The Kuchma administration clearly has not fulfilled its promises of economic growth and prosperity, and the recent rise in popularity of the country's leftist parties means that if Kuchma is defeated in the 1999 presidential elections, the Ukrainian economy probably will fare no better under any of his likely successors. Furthermore, Ukraine's political geography is distinguished by regional fiefdoms that compete for central power in Kiev. These two factors have contributed to a strong regionalism and regional loyalties in Ukraine. While such loyalties dampen the prospect of a Ukraine rent by ethnic nationalism, this does not mean that the country is not vulnerable to ethnopolitical manipulation on a mass scale. In fact, as Lieven points out, as Ukraine's economic problems grow more acute, some of the country's regional political clans could resort to ethnic scapegoating to increase their political capital.

Yet the area of Ukraine that poses the greatest potential danger is one that means a great deal to both governments and that has served for centuries as a nationalist rallying cry for Russian politicians—the Crimean Peninsula. Crimea has a high concentration of ethnic Russians, but unlike members of the Russian-speaking population in the country's east, those of southern Ukraine are not that close to their Ukrainian neighbors. In fact, Crimea is the one region of Ukraine where one can speak of a Russian secessionist movement. Crimea also has a controversial administrative legacy, stemming from Khrushchev's transfer of the peninsula from Russian to Ukrainian jurisdiction in 1954. The headquarters of the former Soviet Black Sea Fleet remains in the Crimean port of Sevastopol, and dividing up the fleet under the agreement that accompanied the 1997 Russian-Ukrainian Treaty on Friendship, Cooperation, and Partnership (the "basic treaty") leaves open the possibility of removing this military stronghold from Russia's control twenty years hence. The reversion of the fleet's base to Ukrainian control could spell the end to a major source of employment for this region's ethnic Russians—at a time when Kiev must also accommodate thousands of

Crimean Tatars who are returning to their homeland after the forced relocation of the Stalinist era. The Russian government is loath to relinquish control of the fleet and its base, which have served as a defensive outpost against Turkey, Russia's historic rival; the Russian people themselves have an equally strong attachment to the peninsula.

Although both the Russian and Ukrainian legislatures have ratified the basic treaty, Russia's Federation Council (the legislature's upper house) conditioned its approval on Ukraine's ratification of the agreement on the disposition of the Black Sea Fleet and leasing arrangements for its Sevastopol base. As this book goes to press, Ukraine is expected to approve the agreement, but it is not unreasonable also to expect that the treaty and the terms of the agreement on Sevastopol and the Black Sea Fleet will continue to serve as a campaign issue in Ukraine's October 1999 presidential elections and Russia's presidential polls, scheduled for the following year. Already, some Russian politicians campaigning to succeed President Boris Yeltsin have seized upon the issue of the treaties. Ukraine's entry into NATO's ranks obviously would have grave consequences for the Russia-Ukraine basic treaty, the author notes, as well as for the future of conflict avoidance on the Crimean Peninsula.

Ukraine and Russia: A Fraternal Rivalry is the latest product of the Institute's ongoing examination of the Soviet Union's dissolution and the resulting problems of sovereignty and national identity. The case of Ukraine has also been addressed in the Institute's Series on Religion, Nationalism, and Intolerance in senior scholar David Little's *Ukraine: The Legacy of Intolerance* (United States Institute of Peace Press, 1991). On Russia's relations with former Soviet republics in general, the Institute has also published the late Galina Starovoitova's Peaceworks report *Sovereignty after Empire: Self-Determination Movements in the Former Soviet Union* (No. 19, October 1997), and Martha Brill Olcott's *Central Asia's New States: Independence, Foreign Policy, and Regional Security* (United States Institute of Peace Press, 1996). On security issues, among the titles the Institute has recently published are James Goodby's *Europe Undivided: The New Logic of Peace in U.S.-Russian Relations* and David Yost's *NATO Transformed: The Alliance's New Roles in International Security,* both published by the United States Institute of Peace Press in 1998. In late 1999, the Press will feature among its distinguished authors former Institute fellow Peter Reddaway and his analysis of Russia's economic reforms and their effect on the country's democratization and political stability.

The Institute also expects to publish former fellow Igor Zevelev's forthcoming study of the Russian Federation's policies toward major Russian communities in the "near abroad." In the cases of the Baltic states and Kazakstan, the history of the Russian communities in these former Soviet republics has been relatively brief, compared to that of the Ukrainian-Russian relationship. Ukraine and Russia, as Anatol Lieven masterfully explains in the following pages, have had a much longer and much more complex coexistence. Foreign policymakers should understand the multifaceted and enduring nature of their relationship as they ponder the future of European security and the roles these two countries will play in it.

Richard H. Solomon
President
United States Institute of Peace

PREFACE

This work is based on material gathered during nine visits I made to Ukraine as a correspondent for *The Times* of London between 1993 and 1995, and on a three-month research trip to Ukraine in the summer and autumn of 1995, which was funded by grants from the Leverhulme Trust and Nuffield Foundation. It was written during my time in Washington, D.C., from January 1996 to January 1997 as a senior fellow at the United States Institute of Peace. I am grateful to all these institutions for their generous support. The opinions expressed in this work are naturally my own, and none of these bodies bears any responsibility for them.

My analysis of the Ukrainian-Russian relationship is rooted in a reading of this region's history. However, while I hope it is academically respectable, this is not primarily an academic work; rather, it is a personal view based on my experience and observations of the region. In particular, the amount of space I have given to direct quotations from people I have interviewed may seem unusual. For this I make no apology. The citizens of Ukraine today are after all not inhabitants of ancient Egypt, whose opinions and beliefs must be pieced together from archaeological evidence. They are living people with voices of their own and things to say that are often more interesting than the views of distant analysts.

The people in both Ukraine and Russia who extended their hospitality or helped my wife and me in other ways during our stay are too numerous to list. Among Western correspondents, however, Anna Reid of the *Daily Telegraph,* Matthew Kaminski of the *Financial Times,* and Alexis Rowell of the British Broadcasting Corporation deserve special thanks. I would also like to thank Sherman Garnett of the Carnegie Endowment for International Peace, Dominique Arel of Brown University, and Andrew Wilson of London University for their helpful advice.

Note on Transliteration

In this work I have used, as a rule, the Ukrainian form of the names of people and places in Ukraine, except in rare cases where another form (Latinate, Polish, or Russian) has had a long-standing presence in English, as with "Kiev" or "Galicia." In these cases I have put the Ukrainian form in parentheses where appropriate. I have made an exception where individuals are clearly identified as members of the Russian, Jewish, or Tatar minorities; for these cases I have used their individual forms, with the Ukrainian form in parentheses where appropriate. In quotations of reported speech, I have followed the forms used in the source itself.

INTRODUCTION

Russia and Ukraine are united in my blood, my heart, my thoughts. But from friendly contacts with Ukrainians in the camps over a long period I have learned how sore they feel. Our generation cannot avoid paying for the mistakes of generations before it....

We must prove our greatness as a nation not by the vastness of our territory, nor by the number of nations under our tutelage, but by the grandeur of our actions....We must leave the decision to the Ukrainians themselves—let federalists and separatists try their persuasions.

—Alexander Solzhenitsyn, *The Gulag Archipelago*

This book contains two main arguments. The first is that the existing sense of national identity of most inhabitants of Ukraine (as of 1998), although very unwelcome to Ukrainian radical nationalists and Russian imperial nationalists—indeed, precisely *because* it is unwelcome to them— contributes greatly to the stability and unity of independent Ukraine, the peace and security of the region, and therefore to the interests of the United States and the West in general.

The reason for the unhappiness of both Ukrainian and Russian nationalists is, paradoxically enough, the same. As will be described in the course of this book, centuries of common history have led ordinary Ukrainians and their Russian neighbors in most parts of Ukraine to be very close in culture, language, behavior, and attitudes. For Ukrainian nationalists, particularly those from the specific culture of the western Ukrainian region of Galicia, this affinity makes it very difficult to convince the mass of ordinary Ukrainians to support their version of narrow, ethnocentric, often chauvinistic Ukrainian nationalism.

As for Russian imperialists, although they frequently refer to the closeness of ordinary Russians and Ukrainians as an argument for a union between the two states, in fact this closeness is working against their hopes. In the past, when the state was dominated by Russia, the lack of clear distinctions between Russians and Ukrainians contributed to Ukrainians easily becoming Russified. Today, with the state being Ukrainian, this lack of distinction is helping more and more Russians to become to a considerable extent Ukrainianized, in terms of gaining fluent command of the Ukrainian language and developing a real loyalty to a civic version of Ukrainian patriotism. This makes it very difficult to turn the Russians of Ukraine into a rebellious "fifth column," working to destabilize Ukraine and bring it under Russia's subjugation—all of which is both good in itself and very much in the West's interest.

The second argument stems from the first. It is that Russia and Ukraine, although separate nations, are also closely linked. These links have not just been forged over the centuries by Russian, then Soviet, governments but have also developed "organically" through millions of human contacts over hundreds of years, resulting in very important aspects of common psychology, religion, culture, language, and historical identification.[1] These aspects of shared identity are changing and will go on doing so, but this both is and ought to be a gradual process. It can be encouraged, but not forced, by the Ukrainian state. The desire of most inhabitants of eastern and southern Ukraine for close relations with Russia was reconfirmed by the results of the March 1998 Ukrainian parliamentary elections—an increased vote for the Communists and Socialists.

With regard to Western policy, therefore, this book recommends a certain caution. It is certainly very desirable to give various kinds of aid in an attempt to strengthen the Ukrainian economy, on which in the end the stability, unity, and even independence of Ukraine will chiefly depend —while recognizing that as everywhere else in the world, economic reform and economic success will depend on the Ukrainians themselves.

The lack of such economic reform to date and the deepening economic crisis and economic hardship in Ukraine are a dark background to the factors I describe; they also give grounds for concern that if they continue for a long period, as now seems probable, Ukrainian politics may not remain forever as peaceful as they are at present. In the course of 1998, the Kuchma administration began to show signs of a willingness to step outside the law in order to target opponents and hold onto power. Meanwhile in Russia, all the optimistic promises of a coming boom have once again come to nothing, and the approach of the presidential elections of the year 2000 and the succession to Yeltsin are fraught with uncertainty and danger.

I argue that in these circumstances, to see Ukrainian independence mainly in terms of an anti-Russian stance, and to encourage Ukraine to move in this direction, could have disastrous results, because it would be against the wishes of a very large proportion—indeed, as of 1998, a majority—of Ukraine's own citizens. It would also not serve the vital national interests of the United States in this region, interests which lie above all in the fostering of democracy, peace, economic development, and stability, not in favoring particular nationalist agendas.

The reason the United States has a vital interest in the prevention either of a Russo-Ukrainian conflict or an internal Ukrainian one should be obvious but is worth restating here. Several countries in the Transcaucasus have been racked by war without this having much effect on the West; but Ukraine, with 52 million people, is very much larger and also borders on two countries which will soon be North Atlantic Treaty Organization (NATO) members, Poland and Hungary. Conflict involving Ukraine and Russia would have a destabilizing effect on the whole of Europe.

The threat of such conflict has greatly receded since the May 1997 Russia-Ukraine Treaty on Friendship, Cooperation, and Partnership. The most important aspect of the basic treaty was that after years of negotiations and disputes which occasionally reached the edge of violence, Russia and Ukraine agreed on how to divide up the Black Sea Fleet and its main base at Sevastopol, with Russia renting most of the base for twenty years. This agreement will be examined at more length in chapter 4.

While a direct Russian-Ukrainian fight over Sevastopol is still not impossible in the more distant future, such clashes—like the Iraqi invasion of Kuwait—have been very much the exception in the world in recent decades. Much more common has been some combination of internal unrest with outside sponsorship and pressure. This is why the internal stability of Ukraine, and the peaceful, gradual, and voluntary integration of the Russians of Ukraine into the Ukrainian polity, are also vital Western interests.

Russian officials have privately threatened that if Ukraine seeks to join NATO, then Russia will use the Russian minorities in Ukraine to destabilize and even destroy the country. As this book will strongly emphasize, the potential for such deliberate destabilization among the Russians of Ukraine (and of other Soviet successor states) has been greatly exaggerated; it appears even more fanciful in the context of the acute economic downturn that has once again struck both Russia and Ukraine since August 1998. Nonetheless, it is true both that this is indeed Russia's most powerful weapon in Ukraine, and that the extent of its power will depend as much on future Ukrainian governments—in their treatment of the Russian minority—as on actions by Moscow. It is also true that a Ukraine and Russia both endlessly condemned to severe poverty, social stagnation, and pervasive official corruption cannot but in the long run generate political instability that may take on a chauvinist cast.

THE STRUCTURE OF THIS WORK

Experts on Ukrainian and Russian history may wish to skip the first chapter, which sketches the history of the region up to the present. For reasons of space, this is necessarily a brief and fairly superficial overview. I should also stress that this book is not intended as a work of professional historiography and cannot attempt to be a thorough history of Ukraine. Rather, it is a book about aspects of contemporary Ukraine and Ukrainian-Russian relations by a journalist who has spent long periods in the region. As such, I have had to exercise brevity in presenting the religious history of Ukraine and the very important but also very complicated relationships among the different Orthodox patriarchates, the Uniates, and the Roman Catholics.

Furthermore, because of this work's contemporary focus, the first chapter pays only limited attention to the Polish-Ukrainian relationship, even though this relationship was of critical importance in shaping Ukrainian history and western Ukrainian culture, and even though much of modern Ukrainian nationalism (especially of course in areas long under Polish rule) was formulated in opposition to Polish claims. The transfer of Galicia and Volhynia from Poland to Soviet Ukraine by Stalin, and the subsequent deportation of most of its Polish minority, mean that today the Polish-Ukrainian relationship is far more straightforward than the Russian-Ukrainian one. While nostalgia for the lost lands certainly does exist in Polish society, only a tiny fringe of extreme Polish nationalists have called for the return of these lands. It is quite impossible now and for the foreseeable future that the Polish parliament would declare Lviv a Polish city—in the manner that the Russian parliament has declared Sevastopol a Russian city more than once.

Despite this and other large gaps in my historical account, some historical background is necessary for any serious study of the Ukrainian-Russian relationship today. This is because the centuries of common rule have been obviously crucial in shaping the contemporary identities of Ukrainians and Russians and the relationship between them. Moreover, the nature of several key periods and episodes during this long history has long been a source of contradictory propaganda for Russian and Ukrainian nationalists, both of whose accounts need to be treated with extreme caution. The first step in avoiding being trapped by narrow and biased versions of Ukraine and Russia today must therefore be an attempt to examine their history objectively.

This is obviously even more true of the Soviet period. Stalin's rule in particular imposed the most outrageous suffering on Ukraine and to a lesser extent on Russia, a subject which has also become a matter of bitter dispute between historians and pseudo-historians. The Soviet period, and in particular the vast migration into Ukrainian industrial cities of both Ukrainian and Russian peasants, also in effect created modern Ukrainian society as it exists today across much of the country.

The second chapter looks more closely at contemporary Ukrainian society, focusing on relations between Ukrainians and Russians, on mutual images and prejudices, on the various kinds of Ukrainian national identity, and on the reasons for the lack of a strong sense of a Russian national identity among the Russians in Ukraine. This chapter contains three theses, which are central to the book.

The first is that as a whole, the "Russians" in Ukraine (as in most of the other former Soviet republics) are not really Russians at all; rather, they are Russian-speaking Soviet immigrants. Second, this being so, it follows that there is naturally little to distinguish these "Russians" from their equally Sovietized Russian-speaking Ukrainian neighbors. (In the crucial case of language, for example, while the great majority of Ukrainians in most of the country speak fluent Russian, 34 percent of Russians in 1989 already claimed to speak fluent Ukrainian.[2] In any case, many people in this region speak Surzhik, a sort of mixed Russian-Ukrainian dialect.) Third, the immigrant nature of these "Russian" populations, added to the atomizing and depoliticizing effects of Soviet rule, helps make it very difficult for them spontaneously to generate social, political, or labor organizations to defend their economic, political, or national interests.

Chapter 2 also analyzes the national feeling of Russian-speaking Ukrainians, such as President Leonid Kuchma, and argues that while this sentiment is less culture-based than the nationalism of Galicians from western Ukraine, or that of the Ukrainian-speaking nationalist intelligentsia, Russian-speaking Ukrainians have in fact retained a real sense of loyalty to Ukraine—a feeling that, since independence, has become the main foundation of the new Ukrainian state.

Chapter 3 looks at the different regions of Russian-speaking Ukraine and briefly describes their distinct histories and characters. It also analyzes the rule of local elites, or "parties of power," and the nature of their influence and their priorities in the Ukraine of the mid-1990s. It argues that while most of these elites are hardly convinced Ukrainian nationalists, they now have very good reasons of pragmatism and self-interest for respecting the authority of Kiev; hence, a Russian government bent on destabilizing Ukraine (which has not been the case so far)—even if it were to adopt a ruthless strategy—would be hard put to find local allies. I suggest, however, that the unprincipled greed of many of these elites means that there is a risk of them falling out bitterly over the division of state wealth and patronage, and that the defeated party might then at some stage try to appeal to ethnic sentiment to revenge itself on its victorious rivals.

The possible exceptions to this rule are examined in chapter 4. Crimea and especially Sevastopol contain a Russian population that has a different origin and character from that of the rest of Ukraine; for one thing, it is much less closer to the Ukrainians. There also exists between the local Russians and the Crimean Tatars a degree of ethnic hostility quite unlike the attitudes of most Ukrainians to their Russian neighbors and vice versa. This means that Crimea is the only part of Ukraine where one can imagine future violence of the kind that racked the Transcaucasus and Yugoslavia in the early 1990s.

This chapter will also examine the town and the "question" of Sevastopol, which is a case on its own because of both the presence of the Black Sea Fleet and the immense emotional importance that Russians attach to keeping a stake in this city. If Crimea is the only place in Ukraine where one can imagine spontaneous ethnic violence, Sevastopol is perhaps the only place outside Russia for which one can imagine many ordinary Russians willingly going to war. This is remarkable, for—as the Chechen war has amply demonstrated—the Russian people of today are hardly in a warlike mood or anxious to seek bloody conflict with their neighbors.

The fifth chapter analyzes the reasons for the weak, ambiguous, and undefined nature of Russian nationalism and the Russian national identity today against the background of history and with reference to recent events in the Russian-Ukrainian relationship and in areas such as Chechnya, which are outside the immediate scope of this book. It suggests that Russia today is much less dangerous to its Western neighbors than many commentators have assumed, and that this is not just because of its current physical weakness but also for cultural, social, and psychological reasons.

The conclusion examines Western policy toward Ukraine and Russia in the context of the expansion of NATO and (perhaps) of the European Union. It argues strongly that rather than trying to build up Ukraine as a buffer against Russia—as some Western analysts and officials would advocate—the interests of the West, of peace, and of the peoples of Ukraine will be served by encouraging Ukraine's economic development, national independence, and democratic state building, as well as by encouraging friendly and peaceful relations between Ukraine and Russia, because such relations are desired by a majority of Ukrainian citizens and are also in the interests of the whole region.

THE ARGUMENT

On the whole, therefore, my conclusions about the future of Ukraine are optimistic. Assuming that Ukraine achieves a reasonable degree of economic progress, that ethnic tensions with the Crimean Tatars can be restrained, and that the dispute over Sevastopol can be managed peacefully—admittedly big assumptions—I believe that the threat from Russia will be slight, and that the great mass of Russians in Ukraine can be integrated into the new state.

However, it is vital to stress that the peaceful and democratic development of Ukraine will be possible in the long run only if the version of Ukraine and Ukrainian culture presented to the Russians of Ukraine remains on the whole moderate and integrationist, rooted in civic nationalism and not in ethnicity or a narrowly nationalist version of the Ukrainian tradition, and if the Ukrainian state is not seen by large segments of its population to have gone out of its way to create a breakdown of relations with Russia (however, if a Russian regime were seen as principally guilty in this regard, that might be a different matter).

Finally, as chapter 5 will strongly emphasize, Ukraine's stability depends in part on Russia not developing an ethnic chauvinist version of Russian nationalism nor seeking to spread its appeal to Russians beyond Russia's borders.

In light of these tentative conclusions, I would like to endorse the following 1993 statement by a group of Ukrainian and Russian-Ukrainian scholars, published in the journal *Politichna Dumka*. The statement was written under the administration of President Leonid Kravchuk, at a time when the combined threat from Ukrainian nationalist policies and conflict with Russia looked much greater than at the time of this writing. Nonetheless, its arguments are still worth emphasizing for the future, particularly because the authors' statement on the lack of a direct military threat from Russia has since been entirely borne out by the Chechen war—both by the miserable performance of the Russian army and the extreme lack of enthusiasm of the Russian population and military alike for military adventure.

> The threat to Ukraine [from Russia] does not exist in the classical military sense. But that does not mean that one should completely reject the idea of a strategic threat in other ways....
>
> Pursuing classical "balance of power" tactics against Russia would result in the unnecessary economic and psychological exhaustion of Ukraine and could well lead to the state's collapse from an internal threat....
>
> A belief that Ukraine should consistently oppose Russia on the international stage is erroneous. It would be more reasonable and beneficial to move toward the European Union and the non-military structures of NATO independently but in parallel....
>
> A non-confrontational strategy concerning Russia is warranted still more by the domestic circumstances of Ukraine.... Ukraine's national security is not threatened by Russian military expansion, but by Russia's potential use of social, cultural and psychological means....
>
> The contradictions and dynamics in Russian-Ukrainian relations are similar to those when you try to separate two Siamese twins.... There is no event in world history which parallels in complication the phenomenon of Russian-Ukrainian combined separation and co-existence, both in its quality and in its sheer scale.... There is an almost organic entangling of tasks.
>
> Neither Ukraine's security nor favorable conditions for her development as a nation are possible without deep and sincere neighborly relations with Russia. Long-term confrontation is also ruled out for internal cultural and psychological reasons (and this is also true of Russia).

Therefore Kiev faces the tremendous task of rebuilding its centuries-old relationship with Moscow on a qualitatively new basis while also acquiring the means to defend its own interests. . . .

Hence the involvement of non-Ukrainians in the process of Ukrainian nation-building should be considered an important precondition for that process's success. . . .[3]

1

UKRAINE AND RUSSIA
United and Divided by History

Russia and most of Ukraine are linked historically through two long periods of common rule, which between them make up the greater part of the history of the East Slavic peoples.[1] In any study of the Ukrainian-Russian relationship as it enters the twenty-first century, some portrayal and analysis of this history is therefore essential. In the words of Alexander Motyl, "Ukraine cannot be understood in isolation from Russia, but, by the same token, Russia cannot be understood in isolation from Ukraine. The two countries define each other in a way that few others do. *The historical interconnections between Ukraine and Russia have penetrated every aspect of their current relationship.* Their relations are therefore complex and are likely to remain so for the foreseeable future."[2]

Moreover, as noted in the introduction, nationalist intellectuals on both sides endlessly seek in history for arguments and justifications. The propagation of a new version of Ukrainian history—with or without strongly anti-Russian tendencies—has been seen as a crucial part of Ukrainian nation building by both Ukrainian nationalists and Western analysts (previously, this was also true of the need to set forth a version of Ukrainian history which repudiated Polish historical claims).[3]

The importance of such a state-led reconstruction of historical "truths" is especially important in the cases of Ukraine and Russia because, in the words of Volodymyr Kulyk, "Unlike the Baltic Republics, where the continuity of identity and even statehood was not disrupted during the fifty years of Soviet rule, or Armenia, where a high level of national homogeneity and integration provided good prospects for the revival

11

and development of tradition, Ukraine and Russia did not maintain a continuity and in essence had nothing to revive."[4]

Meanwhile in Crimea and some other Russian-speaking parts of Ukraine, local Russian intellectuals, backed by academics and nationalists in Russia itself, are producing their own conflicting versions of events. Such historical disputes may seem academic, but because they contain implicit territorial claims, in other parts of the world they have frequently contributed to the outbreak of bloody wars.

The points at issue between the Ukrainian and Russian nationalists extend from the ninth century through the Middle Ages and the Russian Empire and into Soviet rule. As in Yugoslavia and much of the rest of the world, the most bitter insults that nationalists on either side can hurl at each other are also drawn not from present disputes, but from historical crimes and sufferings. As will be seen, so far the mass of the population in Ukraine is a great deal less affected by such historically derived sentiments than in Yugoslavia; but if in the future—God forbid—hatred does develop between the two peoples, historiography will bear its share of the blame

CHRONOLOGY: NINTH–THIRTEENTH CENTURIES

Mid–Ninth Century: East Slavic tribes come under the rule of Scandinavian warriors and traders, the Varangians. The ruler of Novgorod, Riurik, gives his name to the subsequent dynasties in Kievan Rus and later Muscovy.

860: Askold and Dir, Varangian rulers in Kiev, lead raid on Constantinople.

878: Oleg (Helgi), Varangian prince of Novgorod, seizes control of Kiev and makes it the chief Varangian base, where he rules until 912. The lands under Kiev's hegemony come to be called "Rus." The Varangians lead their Slavic vassals in attacks on the Byzantines and wars against the Turkic nomads of the eastern and southern steppes.

980–1015: Rule of Vladimir (Volodymyr) "the Great." In 989, after forming an alliance with Constantinople, he converts from paganism to Orthodox Christianity.

1037: Establishment of the Orthodox metropolitanate of Kiev, founded from Constantinople and initially staffed by Greeks. The area of Kiev's domination covered most of what is now Ukraine, Belarus, and European Russia.

Eleventh Century: Gradual disintegration of the Kievan polity amid feuding among the rulers of the constituent city-states. Novgorod becomes independent.

1240: Capture of Kiev by the Mongols (Tatars); destruction of the Kievan confederation. With the exception of Galicia and Volhynia in the West, the Riurikid princes become vassals of the Mongols.

THE DISPUTE OVER KIEVAN RUS

Russian and Ukrainian nationalist historians are currently engaged in a struggle for exclusive possession of the supposed legacy of Kievan Rus, although it is only fair to add that there is also a considerable number of historians in both countries who agree on many issues, and that most of the populations in both countries view this question and other historical-national disputes with complete indifference.[5]

Nonetheless, many nationalists on both sides—but especially among the Ukrainians, given their greater insecurity and perceived need to build up the ideological and historiographical bases of their statehood —are literally obsessed by this issue, and it figures strongly in the ideology of extremist parties in both countries. Ukrainian nationalists argue for a continuity of ethnic and cultural tradition in the old Kievan Rus heartland, and that the Russians of Muscovy by contrast are mainly descended from Finno-Ugric tribes. They also argue that while Kievan Rusian culture may have existed in the northern principalities of Suzdal, Vladimir, and later Moscow, this was "Asiatized" and changed beyond recognition by centuries of Mongol domination.

Since the eighteenth century at least, official Russian historians for their part have argued both that the political and religious legitimacy of Kievan Rus was passed on to Moscow by its Riurikid princes and through the Moscow patriarchate, and that many of the actual inhabitants of the Kievan Rusian core area fled north to the forests of what is now Russia to escape from the Mongols. It has also been common in Russia to argue that it is the Ukrainians, while undoubtedly living in the old Kievan territory, who were changed over the centuries by the impact of Lithuanian and Polish domination, so that the true cultural tradition was continued in Muscovy.[6]

Part of the debate on the legacy of Kievan Rus is a dispute over the extent to which medieval Muscovy actually had a conscious project of "gathering in the lands of Rus." For contemporary Russian intellectuals, the belief that the Muscovite grand princes were committed to this is part of their claim that Muscovy was the only legitimate and conscious heir of Kievan Rus, and that the Russian state inherited this mantle. They argue that the grand princes of Moscow were after all very consciously descended from St. Vladimir and the other rulers of Rus, and it was on this that their dynastic legitimacy rested.

The most extreme claim stemming from this argument is that the Ukrainians do not really exist as a nation, and are just a "Little Russian" branch of the general Russian stock, destined by history, religion, and culture to come under the rule of Muscovy. This was the official position of the imperial Russian state before 1917, and to the fury of many Ukrainians, it is still widely held in Russia today. A milder version of it is the view, taught as official dogma under the Soviet Union, that the Ukrainians, Belarusians, and Russians are historically "brother nations," all deriving from Kievan Rus, and closely linked by language, religion, culture, and shared history.

It must be stressed, however, that there is a very important difference between the official Russian imperial doctrine in the last decades of the empire, which was that the Ukrainians were "the same" as the Russians, and that of the Soviets, which was that the Ukrainians were "similar" or "brothers." The first eliminated any idea of Ukrainian independence, ever—and indeed Ukrainian independence from the Russian Empire could not have been achieved without massive bloodshed (as was indeed the case during and after World War I); the latter admitted the theoretical possibility, and in the end allowed the reality.

It is amusing to note that some Ukrainian neofascists, belonging to the UNA/UNSO (the Ukrainian National Assembly and the linked Ukrainian National Self-Defense Organization) movement, in fact accept the idea of the basic unity of the East Slav peoples—if only because of their obsession, which they share with their Russian equivalents, that their country should be a great military power and not just another state among equal states. A particularly gruesome version of this attitude was expressed to me by Oleksandr Nadtoka, a leader of UNSO in Donetsk, who said,

> Our program says that Ukrainians are used to being a great power, and we will restore that to them. . . . We are for the union of all the East Slavs, all the descendants of Kievan Rus, because after all our fellow Slavs are closer to us than Jews or Americans. But it must be clearly recognized who are the senior heirs of Rus, who have preserved its traditions most faithfully. So we say that Kiev, not Moscow, must be the capital of

Eastern Slavdom, because Moscow has become a city of international Jewish capital.[7]

However misused by Soviet ideology and Russian imperialism (or even by UNSO), the basic assumption of Russians and Ukrainians being closely related peoples jointly descended from Kievan Rus might seem to an outsider no more than common sense; there is after all no logical reason that two, three (including Belarus), or indeed many more states should not legitimately derive from medieval Rus and have many traditions in common. After all, if Novgorod had survived as an independent state (as it did until almost the end of the fifteenth century), Muscovy would have had an East Slav Orthodox, "Russian"-speaking rival older and more historically distinguished than itself; if Galicia had emerged as an independent Catholic-oriented state, either in the Middle Ages or in the twentieth century, there would have been another "Ukrainian"-speaking state descended from Kievan Rus.

Serious contemporary Western historians have little truck with either nationalist version. Thus Simon Franklin and Jonathan Shepard, in their history of Kievan Rus, do not even bother to discuss the Ukrainian-Russian controversy, but very sensibly write in their introduction,

> This book is and is not an account of a thing called Russia. The further we pursue the thing into the past, the more misleading our modern vocabulary becomes. Only in nationalist fantasy can the word "Russia" stand for a kind of platonic form, immanent even when invisible, constant in essence though variable in its historical embodiments. . . . The story of the land of the Rus could continue in one direction towards modern Russia, or in other directions towards, eventually, Ukraine or Belarus. The land of the Rus is none of these, or it is a shared predecessor of all three. Modern state identities are irrelevant here, as are the distinctions between modern national identities.[8]

The statement by many contemporary Ukrainian historians that Kievan Rus was a "Ukrainian state" is therefore as absurd as that by Russian historians that it was a "Russian state"—a view reflected in the once standard work by the Russian émigré George Vernadsky, entitled simply *Kievan Russia,* and in the Russian transformation of the ancient chroniclers' description of Kiev as "The Mother of the Cities of Rus" into "Mother of *Russian* cities," a phrase used endlessly in Soviet and contemporary Russian writing.[9] (It is interesting that just as the Russians have tried to turn the whole of Rus into "Russia," so in their mildly derogatory slang term for Russians, *Moscali,* the Ukrainians have responded by cutting the Russians down from Russians into mere "Muscovites"—as indeed they were generally known to the outside world before the union with the Ukrainian Cossack hetmanate in the seventeenth century).

Generations of scholars in the West have now demonstrated that while ethnic differences may be primordial, the identity of most modern nations in the full sense is very much a product of the past few centuries, and cannot be read back into earlier epochs. From this point of view, it makes as much sense to talk about a Ukrainian or Russian state or nation existing a thousand years ago as it would be to talk of the empire of Charlemagne as a "French state" or that of Alfred the Great as a "British state."

■ CHRONOLOGY: THIRTEENTH–SEVENTEENTH CENTURIES

1264: Foundation of Lviv; kingdom of Galicia-Volhynia reaches its apogee.

1299: Metropolitan of Kiev leaves the city and settles in the principality of Vladimir (near Moscow in what is now Russia); Kiev's religious and cultural supremacy over Rus draws to a close.

1344–1349: Lithuania annexes Volhynia, and Poland annexes Galicia; last independent Riurikid Orthodox principalities in what is now Ukraine cease to exist. In 1356, Lviv adopts Magdeburg Law.

1362: Lithuanian army defeats the Mongol Golden Horde, and Lithuania gains control of Kiev and most of what is now Ukraine.

1380: Muscovite army under Grand Prince Dmitry Donskoy defeats the Mongols at Kulikovo; Moscow gains ascendancy over the other principalities of north and northeastern Rus.

1385: Union of Krevo (Krewo) between Poland and Lithuania. Grand Prince Jogaila (Wladislaw Jagiello) of Lithuania marries Jadwiga of Poland and converts his realm from paganism to Catholic Christianity.

1471: Muscovite forces capture Novgorod and destroy last independent northern Orthodox Slavic state.

1552–1557: Tsar Ivan IV (the Terrible) of Muscovy conquers the Tatar khanates of Kazan and Astrakhan. Russian conquest of Siberia begins.

1569: Union of Lublin; state (as well as dynastic) union of Poland and Lithuania; strengthening of the power of the Catholic church in the Polish-Lithuanian lands.

1596: Union of Brest. A large minority of Orthodox clergy in the Polish-Lithuanian lands accept the supremacy of the pope while retaining their own liturgy and traditions. They become known as the Uniates, or "Greek Catholics." Relations between the Orthodox majority in the former Rus lands and the Polish-Lithuanian state worsen. The Zaporozhian Cossacks develop in the steppes between Poland-Lithuania and the Crimean Tatar khanate.

1598–1613: End of the Riurikid dynasty in Muscovy; attempt by Poles and Lithuanians to conquer Muscovy is defeated. Romanov dynasty ascends to the throne.

1637: Zaporozhian Cossack revolt against Poland-Lithuania employs slogans in defense of Orthodoxy. Following defeat, many Orthodox peasants flee from Polish rule to the Muscovite lands in eastern Ukraine.

1648: Cossack rebellion led by Hetman (Cossack leader) Bogdan Khmelnitsky leads to general uprising of Orthodox peasantry and gentry. Polish armies are defeated. Polish and Jewish inhabitants of the Rus lands are massacred.

1649: Khmelnitsky enters Kiev and proclaims a new Rus state.

1651–53: Cossack failures in battle with the Poles.

1654: Treaty of Pereiaslav between Khmelnitsky's representatives and those of Tsar Alexei of Moscow (whose title now reads Tsar and Autocrat of All Great and Little Rus). Cossacks and Ukrainian gentry accept union between their lands and those of Muscovy and rule of the tsar.

THE DISPUTE OVER THE RUSSIAN-UKRAINIAN UNION OF 1654

Ironically enough, it has been suggested that Ukrainians themselves may have played a significant role in encouraging the Muscovite state to see itself as the heir of Rus and protector of all the Orthodox. In the late sixteenth and seventeenth centuries, a number of prominent Orthodox monks from Ukraine moved to Muscovy, as part of a movement of many thousands of Ukrainian and Belarusian nobles and peasants who preferred the rule of the Orthodox tsar to that of the Poles.[10] The Kievan Orthodox patriarchate had moved north into what is now Russia after Kiev's destruction by the Mongols, and from its foundation in 1448 the metropolitanate of Moscow had claimed ecclesiastic jurisdiction over all of Rus.

Bitterly hating Polish Catholic rule, these Ukrainian religious figures idealized the tsars of Muscovy as Orthodox monarchs and helped formulate an ideology which justified their rule over all the Orthodox Rus ("Rus" until the eighteenth century was the word still used by Ukrainians to denote both themselves and the Belarusian subjects of Poland). This Ukrainian influence also played a role in persuading the leaders of the intensively conservative, inward-looking Muscovite Orthodox church that they must carry out reforms to bring themselves out of the cultural isolation in which they had lived under Mongol domination and into line with Orthodox practice and learning elsewhere, precisely so as to bolster their claim to lead the whole Orthodox world.[11]

The ferocious reaction against these changes on the part of much of the Muscovite clergy and laity helped produce the Great Schism, which claimed thousands of victims and did permanent damage to the Russian Orthodox church and its authority in Russian society. By undermining the traditional, intensely and monolithically religious Muscovite state and culture, the Schism also helped pave the way for Peter the Great's Westernizing program in the decades that followed. The latter, while it Europeanized the Russian elites, also divided them from the Russian masses and helped lay the foundations of future revolt and finally revolution. The Schism could therefore be called one of the greatest of the many sacrifices that Russians were to make over the centuries in the search for empire and "gathering-in of the lands of Rus."[12]

Modern Ukrainian and Russian nationalist historians have differed sharply about the precise meaning and nature of the process by which most of Ukraine did in fact come under the rule of the tsars of Russia (the title "tsar," from Caesar, was adopted by the grand princes of Muscovy in the sixteenth century as a sign of their claim to be the successors of the emperors of Constantinople. Under Peter the Great, the title was officially replaced by the more European-sounding "imperator," or emperor).

The sixteenth and seventeenth centuries marked the development of the Zaporozhian Cossacks, Ukrainian-speaking frontiersmen who settled beyond the rapids (*za porozhe*) of the river Dnieper (in Ukrainian Dnipro, in Russian Dnyepr), to the south of Kiev. They had an uneasy relationship with the Polish rulers of Ukraine; on the one hand, the Cossacks helped protect the Polish frontier and the settled lands in what is now northern and western Ukraine from the Crimean Tatars (vassals of the Ottoman Empire), whose raids until the late eighteenth century kept the steppes of southern Ukraine largely uninhabited.[13]

On the other hand, like much of the Ukrainian Orthodox population in general, the Cossacks resented the rule of the Catholic Poles, and in particular, the increasing use by Polish landlords of Jewish managers and intermediaries to raise rent and services from the Ukrainian peasantry. The Cossack elites wanted the king of Poland to recognize them as part of the nobility, with all the privileges this entailed, and to provide for a large standing Cossack army. The Cossacks also pursued contacts with Muscovy, which in the sixteenth and early seventeenth centuries had expanded southward to include "Sloboda Ukraine," the Ukrainian-speaking area around Kharkiv (founded in 1656) to the east of Kiev.

In 1596, relations between the Polish state and most of its Orthodox subjects worsened still further when a large section of the Ukrainian and Belarusian Orthodox clergy recognized the authority of the pope in the Union of Brest, while retaining the traditional Orthodox liturgy. Thus was born the Uniate church, which was to play a critical role in shaping the culture and identity of Galicia and Volhynia, and giving these regions an identity wholly separate from that of Orthodox Russia.

However, the Uniates were bitterly denounced as apostates by a majority of the Orthodox in Ukraine, and the Union of Brest may have played a part in encouraging the latter still further to look to Moscow for protection and leadership. Even in the present day, the Uniate-Orthodox split remains highly important under the surface in Ukraine. It plays a role in distinguishing the west of Ukraine culturally from the east and south, and it also contributes to the splits within the ranks of the Ukrainian nationalist forces.

With Orthodox Ukrainians increasingly inflamed by religious, economic, and political grievances, the first decades of the seventeenth century saw a series of Cossack risings against the Poles. In 1648, under the leadership of Hetman Bogdan Khmelnitsky, the Cossacks rose in a cumulative revolt, which initially aimed at extracting concessions, rather than at ousting Polish rule altogether. They were joined by a large part of the Ukrainian population, in a movement inevitably accompanied by large-scale atrocities against the local Jewish and Polish populations. (These atrocities, combined with the later role of Ukrainians in pogroms during the Russian Civil War and in the Nazi Holocaust, have resulted in a common Jewish stereotype of Ukrainian nationalists comparable to radical Ukrainian nationalists' stereotypes of Russians, or to Russian images of the Tatars—which is not of course to say that any of these stereotypes are justified).[14] The Cossacks captured Kiev and launched campaigns into what are now western Ukraine and Poland, but in the following years they came under heavy pressure from Polish counteroffensives.

Faced with the choice of seeking help from the Muslim Ottoman sultan or the Russian Orthodox tsar, they chose to look to Muscovy, which already ruled over Sloboda Ukraine, to the east of Kiev. A key part in this decision was played by the leaders of the Orthodox church in Ukraine, who as already mentioned had come to regard the tsar as natural leader of the Orthodox world. In 1654, at the town of Pereiaslav, Khmelnitsky and his followers swore allegiance to Tsar Alexei, who thereby changed his title from "Tsar of All Rus," to "Tsar of All Great and Little Rus."

Little Rus (Malaya Rus)—like Great Rus, a term of Byzantine ecclesiastical origin—was the designation which until the later nineteenth century was used by most Ukrainians of the Russian Empire to describe their homeland. The term was appropriated by the Russian state, and in the nineteenth century came to be seen by Ukrainian nationalists as demeaning ("Rusian" was formerly used as a vague general term to describe all the Orthodox East Slavs, including those non-Slavic, Lithuanian princes who had converted to Orthodoxy rather than Catholicism in the course of the Middle Ages).[15]

One reason is that, very suggestively, the Russian Empire which had succeeded the tsardom of Muscovy had replaced the ancient word "Rus" with the new one "Rossiya," or Russia, and designated Ukraine (not then generally called Ukraine) as not Malaya Rus, but Malaya Rossiya. From being a recognized sharer in the patrimony of ancient Rus, "Ukraine" was thereby clearly designated a subordinate province of a new state entity (albeit on old foundations), Russia. Viewed from this perspective, it may well be asked who did more to destroy the idea of a united Rus: the Ukrainian nationalists who eventually rose to vindicate Little Rus's claim to a separate identity, or the Great Russian imperialists, who with their obsession with autocracy, absolutism, centralization, and standardization, destroyed the possibility of a voluntary and respectful union between the heirs of Rus.

For in 1654, in return for the Cossacks' allegiance, the tsar had guaranteed the rights of the Cossacks, the status of the Cossack nobility, and the freedom of Ukrainian towns to elect their own municipal governments. The Orthodox church in Ukraine and Belarus came under the "blessing" of the patriarch of Moscow, but was promised freedom from direct interference. Later, these claims and others were included in a "Code of the Rights of the Little Rus People," completed by Ukrainian jurists in 1743 largely on Polish models.

A magnificent equestrian statue of Khmelnitsky in Kiev, erected during the Russian Empire, commemorates this—in a symbolism deeply irritating to contemporary Ukrainian nationalists—by having the rider point with his mace of office toward Moscow.

The Pereiaslav treaty was in no sense conclusive; for another seventy years, successive Cossack hetmans swung back and forth between support for Russia, Poland, and even the Ottoman Empire. Not until Peter the Great's victory over the Swedes and their Cossack allies at Poltava in 1709 were Kiev and the left-bank Ukraine firmly secured by Russia; and not until the partitions of Poland at the end of the eighteenth century did most of the rest of Ukraine pass into Russian hands.

Nonetheless, the Pereiaslav accession has always been of great symbolic importance, at least in Russian and Soviet propaganda, and it used to be the key "legal" question (insofar as law has any meaningful place in such debates) in the Ukrainian-Russian relationship. For Ukrainians—not just nationalists, but those who hoped for an autonomous Ukraine in alliance with Russia—this was simply a personal union between two states, under the rule of one monarch, but with quite separate administrative, judicial, educational, and even military institutions and traditions (the Zaporozhian Cossack host and the forces of the hetmanate survived for more than a century under general Russian command).

Ukrainians point out correctly that such personal unions were common in medieval and renaissance Europe, and by no means implied the merging of the states concerned. They also point out that the promises made by Tsar Alexei amounted, although this was nowhere explicitly stated, to a guarantee of effective legal and administrative autonomy for that part of Ukraine which Khmelnitsky brought under the rule of the tsars (only a small part, of course, of the "Ukrainian" territory later accumulated by the tsars and Soviets). With the partial exception of the rights of the Cossack nobility, all these promises were later broken by Alexei's successors; naturally enough in the view of Ukrainian nationalists, these broken promises render the Pereiaslav agreement itself null and void.

For Russians, in the past and even today, Khmelnitsky's "submission" simply signified the "reunification of the lands of Rus," destined by religion and history, into one state and under the rule of one monarch. The inconvenient details of the agreement itself are generally passed over in silence; indeed, it has been suggested that the Muscovite state, with its traditions of autocracy, absolutism, and the complete absence of legal estates and rights, was simply incapable of grasping the notion of a binding contract between the monarch and part of his people, and that this incomprehension has persisted in Russian attitudes to this day.

Both sides in this debate have a tendency to twist the evidence. Ukrainians exaggerate the extent to which the part of Ukraine under Khmelnitsky's brief rule was really a "state," even by seventeenth century East European standards. They downplay the key importance of the Orthodox Ukrainians' religious identification with the Orthodox tsar, in an era when religion was a considerably more important focus of loyalty than linguistic "nation," and when "Church Slavonic" was (and still is) the common language of the Orthodox church in both Russia and Ukraine.[16]

The Russians, however, have had to ignore much weightier evidence, suggesting that while Ukraine was certainly not a "nation" in the modern sense by the seventeenth century, Ukrainians already possessed many of the attributes which in the nineteenth and twentieth centuries have gone to lay the foundations of nationhood for other countries in Europe: a widely different historical experience; particular traditions, institutions, and customs; and the existence of a separate language, albeit divided into different dialects.

Moves by the Russian government in the 150 years after Pereiaslav to remove all separate Ukrainian institutions were therefore undoubtedly a crime as well as a mistake. In particular, Catherine the Great's introduction of the Great Russian form of serfdom into the Ukrainian lands was bitterly resented by the Ukrainian peasantry, whose feelings were summed up in these lines from a popular song: "Kateryna, Devil's Mother, what have you done? To the wide steppe and the free land you have brought destruction."[17]

It is, however, worth pointing out that rather than indicating something particularly imperialist in the Russian national tradition, these moves by the government in St. Petersburg formed part of a general European trend in the later nineteenth century, usually dubbed "enlightened despotism." A key aspect of this trend, whether in Russia, Austria, Prussia, or Spain, was the attempt by royal governments to strengthen and centralize state power and in the process break down local traditions of political autonomy and linguistic difference.

These disputes continue to underlie the Ukrainian-Russian relationship and are bitterly argued over by historians (and still more by pseudo-historians, a species produced in droves by both nations). However, for most Ukrainians, Russians, and Ukrainian-Russians the disputes are of limited significance. Much more important is the experience of Ukraine and Ukrainians under Russian and Soviet rule, an experience which has crucially shaped Ukraine and the Ukrainians, and has indeed created this country and its society in their present forms. Barring an economic miracle—of which there are sadly few signs at present in either Ukraine or Russia—Ukraine will remain for a long time to come a post-Soviet society, and understanding the Soviet experience in its Ukrainian form will be crucial to understanding Ukraine. Oddly enough, despite the atrocious suffering inflicted by Soviet rule under Lenin and especially Stalin, the common Soviet experience, for reasons that will be explained, tends to unite rather than divide most contemporary Ukrainians and Ukrainian-Russians.

■ CHRONOLOGY: SEVENTEENTH–TWENTIETH CENTURIES

1657–86: Ukrainian and Polish lands are ravaged by repeated wars between Poles, Cossacks, Russians, Swedes, Turks, and Tatars. Drastic weakening of Polish-Lithuanian state occurs. Podolia and Bratslav are conquered by Ottoman Turks.

1659: Union of Hadiach attempts to recreate the Polish state as a tripartite commonwealth with Lithuania and the Cossack-Rus lands. The union is rejected by most of the Cossacks and is never implemented.

1667: Treaty of Andrusovo. Poles and Russians agree to divide Ukraine along the line of the Dnieper River, with Kiev remaining in Russian hands. Eclipse of the Cossack state.

1687–1709: Hetmanate of Ivan Mazepa.

1689: Peter I (the Great) ascends throne of Russia. In 1721 he gives himself new title of Emperor (Imperator) of All the Russias. His costly wars against Sweden and the Ottoman Empire, westernizing reforms, and vast building projects alienate the Cossacks.

1708: Hetman Mazepa rebels against Russia and allies with King Charles XII of Sweden.

1709: Swedish and Cossack forces are defeated by Russians (and pro-Russian Cossacks) at Poltava. Russian government appoints puppet hetman and drastically reduces Ukrainian autonomy.

1734–40 and 1769–74: Russian army is victorious in wars with Ottoman Empire. Southern steppes (the "Dikoye Polye") are opened to settlement.

New cities are founded in the conquered territory, including Yekateri-noslav (now Dnipropetrovsk), Sevastopol, and Odessa.

1775: Russian troops occupy and abolish the Zaporozhian Cossack *sich* (base). Zaporozhian Cossack lands are annexed to the province of "New Russia." End of the last remnants of Ukrainian autonomy within the Russian Empire. Introduction of Russian serfdom into Ukraine.

1792: Black Sea Cossack host, renamed Kuban Cossack host, is transferred to northern Caucasus to fight the Muslim mountaineers.

1793 and 1795: Second and third partitions of Poland divide remaining Polish-ruled Rus lands between Russia and Austria, which takes Galicia. Uniates increasingly escape Russian persecution by moving to Galicia.

1835: Completion of the integration of the Cossack and Ukrainian nobility into that of Russia.

1840: The Ukrainian nationalist poet Taras Shevchenko publishes his first major work, *Kobzar.* Beginnings of Ukrainian national movement (initially cultural) in Russian Ukraine.

1850s: Appearance of the Hromada Ukrainian cultural societies.

1863: Valuyev Decree. The Russian government, alarmed by growing Ukrainian nationalism among intellectuals in Ukraine and the rebellion in Russian Poland, bans publication of religious and educational books in the Ukrainian language. Persecution of the Uniates in Russian Ukraine is intensified.

1900: Founding of the Revolutionary Ukrainian Party.

1905: Revolution in Russia and Ukraine forces reforms which allow Ukrainian parties to function openly, although under police supervision.

1914: Outbreak of the First World War.

UKRAINE: A COLONY OR A PARTNER OF RUSSIA?

In the context of the contemporary relationship between ordinary Ukrainians and ordinary Russians, the key question about Ukraine in the Russian Empire is, to what extent was Ukraine a Russian "colony," or to what extent by contrast was it a junior partner in the Russian Empire? To put it another way, if we repeat the comparison, already made in this book's introduction, of Russia to England, its imperial contemporary, then was Ukraine its Ireland, or was it its Scotland?[18] And in this century, was the Soviet Union simply a new version of the Russian Empire, as Ukrainian nationalists claim, or was it a state based on a Communist ideology and party which to some degree at least transcended nationality?

Under the empire of the tsars, the subjection of Ukraine is obvious. In the course of the eighteenth century, its autonomous institutions and laws were progressively abolished by the tsars, and in the later nineteenth century, even the use of the Ukrainian language (like the Gaelic language for long periods in both Ireland and Scotland) was banned in state schools and most publications. The Uniates, who like the Irish Catholics were suspected of being a potential fifth column, were severely persecuted. In this sense, Ukraine was like Ireland.

On the other hand, for the great majority of Ukrainians who were Orthodox by religion, there was no barrier whatsoever to entry into the Russian elite and to rising to its highest ranks. Indeed, under Catherine the Great, and to a lesser extent her successors, there was a deliberate and successful attempt by the tsars to promote members of the Ukrainian and Cossack nobility so as to "co-opt" them and win their loyalty, for "the chink in the armor of the Little Russian *shlyakhetstvo* (from *szlachta*, the Polish for gentry) ... was their passionate desire to be given the same status in the Russian Empire as the Russian *dvoryanye* (nobility)."[19] This resembled the policy followed toward the Tatar, Georgian, and Baltic German nobility, but with the great added advantage for the tsars that the Ukrainians were already "Russian" Orthodox. Members of Ukrainian families such as the Razumovskys and the Bezborodkos became favorites at court and among the richest landowners in the empire.

These were the great names, but countless "small people" also went from Ukraine to Russia to earn their fortunes, or did so through military service, so that Moscow today is as full of Ukrainian names as London is of Scottish ones. This process is indeed still continuing, as the higher wages to be earned in Russia today draw in hundreds of thousands of Ukrainian workers every year, above all to the construction trade. My own wife's stepfather and two half-sisters are of Ukrainian descent, but are otherwise completely "Muscovites," although when their friends wish to tease them, they say they are "obstinate as sheep"—reputedly a Ukrainian characteristic.

Culturally, an appeal was made under tsarism, and in a more muted way under communism during and after the Second World War, to the common heritage of Orthodoxy, descent from Kievan Rus, and the tsar's "liberation" of Orthodox lands from the rule of Catholic Poland. Indeed, in the very narrow worldview of the traditional Russian peasantry, focused not on nationality but on loyalty to tsar and Orthodoxy and resentment of landlords, it is obvious that dividing lines from Ukrainian peasants must have been very blurred, since they worshipped the same religion, obeyed the same tsar, and hated the same landlords. Assimilation, first of the elites and then of much of the rest of the population, was also greatly helped by the closeness of the Russian and Ukrainian languages.

This policy helped produce generations of loyal Ukrainian military and bureaucratic servants of the Russian Empire (such as, for example, General P.I. Kondratenko, killed in the defense of Port Arthur against the Japanese in 1905) and cultural figures such as Nikolai Gogol, strongly aware of his Ukrainian (or rather "Little Russian") identity, but writing in Russian and profoundly loyal to the idea of East Slav unity under the rule of the Orthodox tsar, and the ancestors of the poet Anna Gorenko, better known as Akhmatova.[20]

To the land-hungry Ukrainian peasantry, after the end of serfdom in 1861, the Russian Empire offered by the late nineteenth century vast new lands for colonization in Siberia and Central Asia. Just as a telephone book in many parts of Canada and New Zealand will turn up more Scottish names than English, so the Ukrainians more than the Russians settled large areas of the Russian east. Most important, the Russian imperial army, by defeating the Tatars and the Turks, opened up for settlement, mainly by Ukrainians, the so-called "Wild Field" (Dikoye Polye), the steppes north of the Black Sea.

Officially called "New Russia" (Novorossiya) under imperial rule, this area is considered by Russians as belonging to them by right because the Russian army conquered the land from the Turkish infidel, and it was settled under Russian imperial rule (of course if that argument were accepted, former colonial powers could claim half the world). A milder sentiment, in terms of support for a more varied Ukrainian and Ukrainian-Russian identity, linked to Russia, was expressed by Arnold Hugel, a Russian-Jewish academic in Kharkiv:

> What is Ukraine after all? Present-day Ukraine is the territory of the Ukrainian SSR [Soviet Socialist Republic], a Soviet creation. Of this, traditional Ukrainian lands make up perhaps 40 percent. The whole of the south and east were never Ukrainian or Russian before the late eighteenth century. They were the Wild Field, conquered by Russia under Catherine the Great. And as to this area, Slobodskaya Ukraine, around

Kharkiv, this was from the very beginning of settlement here a mixed Ukrainian-Russian territory, so why should it suddenly change its nature now, after four hundred years?[21]

Thus in 1917, the Russian provisional government strongly opposed extension of the authority of the autonomous Ukrainian government, or Rada (Council), to the provinces of Kharkiv, Yekaterinoslav (Dnipropetrovsk and Donetsk), Kherson (Odessa), and Tauride (Nikolayev and Crimea), on the grounds that these provinces were not Ukrainian in character and had not been part of the autonomous hetmanate or Sloboda Ukraine.

Finally, Ukraine was clearly not an economic colony in the traditional sense. Because of climate and history, Ukrainian agriculture and the Ukrainian peasantry were always richer than those of Russia, and by the end of the nineteenth century, Ukraine had also become one of the main industrial centers of the empire (although the capital for this industry was to a great extent neither Ukrainian nor Russian, but West European). In these senses, Ukraine's relationship to Russia was like that of Scotland to England, clearly subordinate but with elements of partnership in, identity with, and profit from the imperial enterprise, and this relationship continued under Soviet rule.

In one sense—and this was also true under Soviet rule—Ukraine was like neither Ireland nor Scotland. Under British rule, neither of these countries had political autonomy as such, but both were ruled by laws and administrative practices different from those of England. In the Scottish case, this was because as part of the Act of Union between Scotland and England, and so as to reduce Scottish discontent, the Scottish legal system, the independent Presbyterian church, and the traditional system of local administration were left intact.

In Ireland, it was just the opposite. Because of a well-justified fear of Irish rebellion, Ireland throughout British rule was ruled by laws and administrative practices far more authoritarian and arbitrary than those of England and than English society would have tolerated.

In the Russian Empire, however, the whole intention and result of tsarist centralizing and standardizing measures from the eighteenth century on was that Ukrainians came to be governed by exactly the same institutions and laws as Russians. With the admittedly important exception of the laws affecting the use of language, in terms of personal rights and freedoms—or rather the universal lack of them—it was impossible to tell who were the "colonizers" and who the "colonized," and this was also true in the economic field.

This was of course also quintessentially true under Communist rule, which bore down equally on the individual rights of all its citizens. This is of critical importance in understanding the attitude of contemporary Ukrainians to Russia and Russians. The fact that a Ukrainian could see no difference between the way the state was treating him and the way it was treating his Russian immediate neighbor meant that resentment against the policies of the Russian and Soviet governments did not carry over into ethnic hostility to Russians—or at least much less than was the case in other European empires.

An ordinary Russian industrial worker, whether under imperial or Soviet rule, was also in no way economically better off than the Ukrainian at the next machine, nor did he feel racially superior, nor did the Ukrainian see him as in any way living a superior life, or resent him for this. At the level of personal experience, Soviet Ukraine was not a "colonial" society in this way, and so it is hardly surprising that it did not produce an "anticolonial" reaction among most Ukrainians. As a result, in the words of Andrew Wilson, "The majority of the population who voted for independence [in 1991] clearly associate themselves not with the nationalist movement or the independent Ukrainian governments of 1917–1920, but with the heritage of Soviet Ukraine."[22]

■ CHRONOLOGY: 1917–1921

April 1917: Revolution in Russia overthrows tsarist administration. In Kiev, Ukrainian nationalist organizations form the Rada, which vies for power with local Soviets and "bourgeois" groups.

October 1917: Bolsheviks seize power in Petrograd and Moscow.

November 20, 1917: Rada proclaims Ukrainian Republic. Soviet Ukrainian government formed in Kharkiv.

February 9, 1918: Soviet forces capture Kiev. Treaty of Brest Litovsk between Central Powers and Soviet government allows German-Austrian occupation of Ukraine.

March 1, 1918: Rada forces, backed by Germans and Austrians, recapture Kiev.

April 28, 1918: Rada government is overthrown by Germans and replaced with puppet government of Hetman Pavlo Skoropadsky. Peasant attacks on landlords and occupying forces spread across Ukraine. Anarchist forces, led by Nestor Makhno, appear on the southern steppe.

November 11, 1918: Germany signs armistice with Western allies. German forces withdraw from Ukraine. Skoropadsky is overthrown by Ukrainian national forces, who proclaim independent republic. Fighting between new Polish and Ukrainian forces in former Austrian Galicia leads to victory for the Poles.

February 1919: Soviet forces capture Kiev, which they hold thereafter except for brief periods of rule by White Russians and Poles. Ukrainian national forces are driven into western Ukraine.

October 1920: Poland signs armistice with Soviet Russia and disbands Ukrainian national forces on its soil. Consolidation of Soviet rule in Ukraine.

THE CIVIL WAR AND THE SOVIET VICTORY

The standard explanations for the failure of the independence movement during the early twentieth century dwell on the small size of the nationalist intelligentsia; the Russified nature of the—in any case also small—Ukrainian urban population; and the lack of developed national feeling among the peasantry, especially in the south and east. Throughout the conflict, many areas of Ukraine were in fact "whirlpools of peasant anarchism," in W. H. Chamberlin's phrase, rather than regions of clear-cut conflict among Bolsheviks, nationalists, and Whites.[23]

This is all true, but it is also worth stressing the "positive" aspects of the Bolshevik appeal to Ukrainians: notably radical socialism and the promise of genuine autonomy within a true federation, which would allow a flowering of Ukrainian culture. The Bolsheviks could hardly have prevailed so easily against the national forces if they had not themselves been able to draw on some aspects of Ukrainian national feeling among their largely Ukrainian peasant forces.

Such a flowering of Ukrainian culture did occur later under the rule of the Ukrainian "national communists" in the 1920s.[24] It led both to a great strengthening of the use of the Ukrainian language in literature, schools, and official institutions. Indeed, so determinedly did the Ukrainian Communist leader Mykola Skrypnyk push his Ukrainian national program that he even pushed for the linguistic and educational rights of the large Ukrainian populations in parts of Russia and Central Asia, and sought a kind of informal "protectorate" over them.

As a result of this genuine furthering of national interests, some representatives of the independence movement returned to Soviet Ukraine

—notably Myhailo Hrushevsky, father of modern Ukrainian historiography and brief president of independent Ukraine. However, he was later exiled to Russia by Stalin and died in 1934, and in the subsequent purges, the national communists were ruthlessly destroyed by Stalin, and a new era of Russification set in.

An interesting example of the degree of independence and national feeling retained by the Ukrainian Communist intellectual elites until the end of the 1920s is provided by the minutes of a meeting in February 1929 between Stalin and representatives of the Ukrainian Writers' Union, who uttered strong expressions of national feeling and criticized Russian Communist attitudes to Ukraine and Ukrainians.[25]

At the meeting, Stalin was forced to respond to these criticisms with politeness and even deference—for which he took a frightful revenge in the years that followed. Very few of the Ukrainian writers who attended that meeting survived the next decade. However, Ukrainian never sank back to the low level it had occupied in the last years of imperial rule, and—within the suffocating bounds of Communist ideology—some official space for a Sovietized official Ukrainian culture remained.[26]

A good summary by an eyewitness of the reasons for both the failure of the independence movement and the Soviet appeal to many Ukrainians is provided by Petro Grigorenko—a reliable source, since he later became a courageous and strongly anti-Soviet dissident, sympathetic to Ukrainian nationalism. He was born in a village in what is now the Zaporizhzhia (in Russian, Zaporozhia) region to the north of the Black Sea—part of the region conquered and settled under Russian imperial rule, with the result that the region was ethnically mixed, with Bulgarian, German, Jewish, and Russian villages as well as Ukrainian.

In the second chapter of his memoirs, suggestively entitled "I Learn of My Nationality," he describes how during the Civil War,

> People in our village knew little about the struggle for Ukrainian independence or the Ukrainian nationalist movements. . . . Our attitude towards both the Central Rada and the Hetman [Skoropadsky] was hostile. People felt that both groups had been put in power by the Germans. However, with the establishment of Soviet rule in Ukraine, the then autonomous and nationally minded Ukrainian Communist Party began an official policy of spreading Ukrainian culture and identity through the schools and cultural organizations, and from them, I learned that I belonged to the same nationality as the great Shevchenko, that I was Ukrainian.[27]

Similar sentiments are echoed by Victor Kravchenko (see below).

For much of the Civil War, the dominant force in Grigorenko's home area was neither Ukrainian nationalists, nor Bolsheviks, nor White Russians, but Nestor Makhno's Anarchists—who were mostly Ukrainians and owed a great deal to the Ukrainian Cossack tradition, but did not present themselves as Ukrainians (or Russians) politically.[28]

The classic Russian literary account of Ukrainian nationalism during this period—an account typical of attitudes to the history of Ukrainian nationalism on the part of Russian intellectuals, and with a certain added impact on them of its own—is *The White Guard* of Mikhail Bulgakov, who spent the Civil War in Kiev, where he was born. His description of the city is the greatest to date in literature.

His description of the Ukrainian nationalist forces, however, while extremely powerful, is essentially a diaboliad. It was because of his evident prejudice against Ukrainian nationalism that Bulgakov was bitterly criticized at the meeting of the Ukrainian Writers' Union mentioned above. Members of the union demanded that his play *The Days of the Turbins* (the basis for *The White Guard*) be taken off the stage in Moscow because of its anti-Ukrainian attitudes.

Bulgakov usually calls the nationalists collectively "Petlyura," after their principal leader—a mysterious, demonic figure who is never seen but is suggested through the stories and legends which swirl around him in the popular imagination. The nationalist forces are presented as a blind force of peasant fury, with no real program but anti-Semitism, and led by disappointed rural schoolteachers who surge into Kiev out of the darkness, then after a few weeks of anarchy, looting, and murder disappear again from the stage and from history.

THREE FACES OF SOVIET RULE

It was in the Soviet period that Ukraine experienced its greatest sufferings of modern times: the terrible famine of 1933, induced by Stalin's Communist regime to break peasant resistance to collectivization (and also, to a lesser extent, nationalist opposition to Soviet rule); the purges of the 1930s, which wiped out both the Ukrainian leadership which had fostered the national revival of the 1920s and a very large part of the Ukrainian cultural intelligentsia; the horrors of the Second World War and the Nazi occupation; and the Stalinist repression of western Ukraine which followed.

On the other hand, however terrible for the people of Ukraine, Soviet rule was from the point of view of Ukrainian nationalism Janus-faced: It also united most Ukrainian-speaking areas and established for the first time a theoretically and to some extent actually autonomous territorial state, called Ukraine. This state then used those theoretical rights under the Soviet constitution to help break up the Soviet Union; after the Soviet collapse, it became the independent republic of Ukraine. From the 1930s, this theoretically autonomous state was of course intended by the Soviet regime in Moscow to be a Ukrainian national space drained of Ukrainian national content; nonetheless, in that space, certain national feelings were preserved.[29]

By expelling most of the Polish minority in western Ukraine, Stalin —cynical though it may sound to say this—also unwittingly laid the groundwork for generally good and uncomplicated relations between Poland and Ukraine after the latter achieved independence in 1991. Poland, in sharp contrast to the period 1918–22, has been strongly supportive of Ukrainian independence and territorial integrity.[30]

These relations would have been much more difficult if a large Polish-Ukrainian minority had been demanding extra rights and looking to Warsaw for support. In this brutal fashion, Stalin can be said to have ended three centuries of intermittent Ukrainian-Polish conflict and left Ukraine much freer to strengthen its independence against Russia, without having to fear a threat from the west. The absence of a Polish threat also deprives Russian national imperialists of what used to be one of their strongest arguments for Ukrainian union with Russia—the need to unite to resist this alleged menace. Even so, many West Ukrainians remain thoroughly paranoid about Poland, as witnessed by the decision in October 1996 to deny visas to a group of Polish veterans of the wartime Home Army, who wanted to visit Ukraine to erect a memorial to comrades killed fighting Nazis and Soviets (and Ukrainian nationalists, although this fact was not emphasized). Ukrainian officials argued that the Poles had territorial claims.[31]

On three occasions—in the 1920s, to a more limited degree under Ukrainian Communist Party First Secretary Petro Shelest in the 1960s, and in the years immediately before the Soviet collapse—the government of Soviet Ukraine launched "Ukrainianization" (or rather re-Ukrainianization) programs in education and state service which, although later reversed by Moscow in the 1920s and 1960s, helped to strengthen Ukrainian identity and preserve the Ukrainian language in areas where it otherwise might have been supplanted by Russian.

The Soviet regime in Ukraine, and even to an extent in Russia, also emphasized particular symbolic Ukrainian cultural figures—most notably the nineteenth-century poet Taras Shevchenko, whose enormous stat-ues are to be found in virtually every Ukrainian city—while trying to suppress their anti-Russian side and emphasize their "progressivism." During the Second World War, to reward victorious Soviet Ukrainian generals Stalin created the Order of Khmelnitsky, the equivalent of the orders of Suvorov and Kutuzov for the Soviet army as a whole.[32]

A good example of the Soviet propaganda image of Shevchenko, and the lessons it tried to teach concerning the legitimacy of Soviet rule in Ukraine and the relationship of Ukrainians to their Russian "elder brothers" is to be found in the introduction to the English translation of his collected poetry (published in 1989):

> When a people has the courage to put its pride in its pocket and reject its own national ambitions, to accept criticism and draw lessons from it, this is the most convincing evidence of its moral health and good pros-pects for the future. Shevchenko's objective attitude towards his own people shows that internationalism was an integral part of his views. This explains why true Russians never identified czarism, attacked by Shev-chenko, with Russia, in the same way as true Poles were never insulted by Shevchenko's anger with the Polish nobility.
>
> One need only be reminded of his cordial friendship with his Russian brethren. He bore this noble feeling throughout his life and passed it down to us to be forever preserved and promoted.
>
> Even in his younger years Lenin singled out Shevchenko as a spokes-man of his people. . . . [H]e saw Shevchenko as a great revolutionary democrat, one of those true internationalists who . . . lives laying the foun-dations to a union of nations which is unique in the history of mankind and under whose skies we are now working and progressing.[33]

Stalin took the provinces of Galicia and Volhynia from Poland in 1939 and joined them to Ukraine, thus fulfilling an old dream of Ukrainian nationalists, although hardly as they would have wished. In the long run, this proved a fatal move from the Soviet point of view. Like the Baltic states, Galicia proved an area that could not be suppressed or assimilated by Soviet and Soviet Russian culture. It had never been part of the Russian Empire, and under Austrian and Polish rule its people had had far more opportunities for civic and political organization than the subjects of the tsar. Galicia is also largely inhabited by Uniates, who feel no lingering religious affinity to Russia and have the bitterest memories of past persecution.

In the past ten years, Galicia has been the heartland and base of Ukrainian radical nationalism, and the protest movement by Ukrainian nationalist parties whose main base was Galicia played an important role in pushing the Ukrainian Communist leadership toward separation from the Soviet Union. Since independence, these parties have strongly opposed closer relations with Russia and official status for the Russian language in Ukraine. The threat of Galician protests appears to have been one reason that in 1994 the newly elected Ukrainian president, Leonid Kuchma, did not follow through on his campaign promise to grant this status.

▪ CHRONOLOGY: 1921–91

1920–27: Period of "national communism" and the "New Economic Policy" in Soviet Ukraine.

1922: Founding of Soviet Union.

1923: Initiation of "Ukrainianization," especially of the education system, and of "indigenization" of the Ukrainian Communist Party.

1924: Myhailo Hrushevsky, former president of the Rada, returns to Kiev.

1928–1932: First Soviet Five-Year Plan.

1929: Stalin launches collectivization of agriculture. Already by March 1930, some 250,000 Ukrainian kulaks are shot or deported. Hundreds of thousands more follow over the next two years.

1930–34: Ukrainian Communist Party and academia are purged of "nationalist" elements. Ukrainianization is brought to an end. Ukrainian Orthodox church is suppressed.

1933: Collectivization and forced food collection lead to artificial famine in Ukraine, the Russian Cossack lands, Kazakstan, and elsewhere. In Ukraine, between 4.5 million and 8 million people die. Millions more leave the countryside for the cities.

1936–38: The worst years of Stalin's purges. Most of the leading elements of the Ukrainian Communist Party and intelligentsia are executed or imprisoned.

1938: Study of Russian is made obligatory in all Soviet schools.

1939: As a result of the Molotov-Ribbentrop Pact with Nazi Germany, the Soviet Union invades eastern Poland (following the German invasion in the west). The Ukrainian-speaking areas are annexed to Soviet Ukraine.

1941: Germany invades Soviet Union. Most of Ukraine is quickly overrun.

1941–45: Soviet-German War. Some 4 million civilian inhabitants of Ukraine, including up to 1 million Jews, are killed by the Nazis as part of the Holocaust for being Communist sympathizers or in reprisal for partisan operations, or die as a result of forced labor. Around seven hundred towns and 28,000 villages are wholly or partly destroyed. Around 1.5 million Ukrainian soldiers are killed while serving with the Soviet army or die of starvation and maltreatment in German POW camps. Soviet partisans and Ukrainian nationalist partisans in the Ukrainian Insurgent Army (UPA) are both active in western Ukraine, drawing German reprisals.

1945: Transcarpathia (to 1918 Austro-Hungarian; to 1939 Czechoslovak) is annexed to Soviet Ukraine. For the first time, all the main Ukrainian-speaking lands are united in one state.

1945–47: Most of the Polish population of western Ukraine is deported to Poland on Stalin's orders.

1945–54: UPA partisans continue the struggle against Soviet rule in western Ukraine.

1953: Death of Stalin.

1950s–60s: Extensive industrialization of Ukraine, which ceases to be a mainly rural country.

1963–72: Petro Shelest is first secretary of the Ukrainian Communist Party. He carries out a cautious policy of Ukrainianization.

1972: Shelest is removed and replaced by the hard-line Volodymyr Shcherbytsky, who rules Ukraine until 1989. Resumption of Russification.

1985: Mikhail Gorbachev becomes general secretary of the Soviet Communist Party.

1986: Explosion at Chernobyl nuclear plant north of Kiev contaminates large areas of Ukraine.

1988: Mass demonstrations against Soviet rule begin.

1989: Ukrainian is declared sole official language. Shcherbytsky is dismissed.

1991: Collapse of the Soviet Union. Ukraine becomes independent state.

THE DEBATE OVER THE FAMINE OF 1933

The most tragic and the most hotly disputed episode in the often dreadful history of Soviet Ukraine was the famine of 1933, induced by the Soviet state in the course of the collectivization of agriculture. In this famine millions of inhabitants of Ukraine died, along with millions of others from across the Soviet Union: Russians, especially from the Cossack areas; Volga Germans; and especially Kazaks. Estimates for the number of dead in Ukraine range up to 8 million, although the true figure may be around 5 million—which would still be more than 15 percent of the population of Ukraine at that time, a death rate with few parallels even in the great famines of East Africa in recent decades.

This was one of three great famines in Soviet times, the first being in 1921–22, the third in 1946; the worst effects of the first, however, were felt in Russia, along the Volga.[34] The end result, together with the Second World War and the purges, has been Russian, Ukrainian, Belarusian, and other populations that are very much lower today than they would have been otherwise, but with the Ukrainians (with the Kazaks and the Cossacks) coming off worst.

Unlike the other two great Soviet famines, that of 1933 was undoubtedly, in Robert Conquest's phrase, a "terror famine," with no natural causes and deliberately induced to break the resistance of the Soviet peasantry, and especially the peasants of particular regions and ethnic groups, to collectivization and Soviet rule. In Ukraine, as in west Siberia and the Cossack regions, resistance to collectivization was much stronger than in the central Russian provinces. This was above all because unlike most Russian peasants, the farmers of the former areas had possessed their own fixed homesteads and had never traditionally lived in communes where the land was regularly redistributed.

There can be no doubt, therefore, that Ukraine, like the Russian Cossack lands, was singled out for especially ruthless treatment. In the case of Ukraine, the "terror famine" was also part of Stalin's moves to destroy Skrypnyk and the Ukrainian "national communists," whom he regarded as a threat to his own rule.

In the words of Stanislav Kossior, the secretary of the Ukrainian Communist Party Central Committee, to a group of Communist officials, "The peasant is adopting a new tactic. He is refusing to reap the harvest. He wants the grain to die in order to choke the Soviet government with the bony hand of famine. But the enemy miscalculates. We will show him what famine is."[35]

The famine of 1933 is also viewed by more radical Ukrainian nationalists as a specific genocide (or ethnocide) against the Ukrainian nation, akin to the Nazi German genocide against the Jews. Because they regard the Soviet Union as a continuation of the Russian Empire, many also argue, either implicitly or quite openly, that this was a specifically Russian action.[36] A typical statement of this kind is the following by the writer Mykola Riabchouk:

> There were two large-scale holocausts in twentieth century Europe, one of them implemented by the Nazis against the Jews, and another one by the Bolshevik-Russian regime against the Ukrainians. . . . The Prussian and the Russian approaches, though different in form, were quite similar in their essence. . . . "[C]lass struggle" is only a bleak euphemism for a much more profound and essential process in Soviet Russia (or the so-called "Soviet Union")—re-establishment and expansion of the old Russian Empire.[37]

This accusation causes the most deadly offense among Russians who hear it—especially, of course, to those whose own relatives suffered or died under Stalin or who feel deeply the damage Stalinist rule did to Russia; it is also vehemently criticized by patriotic but objective and academically distinguished scholars such as Professors Roman Szporluk and Bohdan Krawchenko.

These scholars point out that while overall Ukraine suffered much worse than Russia from the famine, specific regions of Russia where resistance to communism had been greatest (notably the Cossack areas of the Don, Kuban, and Orenburg) did in fact suffer as badly as Ukraine; that collectivization broke the spirit and traditions of the Russian peasantry just as surely as it did those of the Ukrainians, just as Stalin's purges decimated the Russian intelligentsia equally as those of other nationalities; that in Ukraine itself, there was no attempt to single out local non-Ukrainian (Russian, German, Bulgar, or Jewish) farmers for better treatment, and that there is no evidence that their casualties were proportionately lower than those of their Ukrainian neighbors; that ethnic Ukrainian Communists themselves played a leading part both in organizing collectivization in Ukraine and in the Soviet regime as a whole, so that the word *genocide* in this case appears an absurdity. *Genocide,* as in the Nazi Holocaust against the Jews or the Hutu massacres of the Tutsi in Rwanda, is an attempt to wipe out the race concerned, to kill every member of it—which was obviously not Stalin's intention with the Ukrainians. He meant to subjugate them, not wipe them out. The Nazis did mean to wipe out the Jews, and in parts of Europe they did indeed kill almost every one of them. It therefore would have been logically absurd—a contradiction in terms—for self-declared Jews to have served in high ranks of the Nazi Party and the SS; whereas numerous self-declared Ukrainians rose to high rank of the Stalinist Soviet Union. Finally, Stalin himself, and several of the chief organizers of collectivization, were not in fact ethnic Russians, nor did they act in the name of Russia.

One of the most vivid and terrifying accounts of the famine is by Victor Kravchenko, a Ukrainian who was a Communist Party official in a Ukrainian village during the famine and later defected to the West. He describes in detail both the famine's horrifying dimensions and the fact that it was deliberately created to break the peasantry's resistance to collectivization and by implication Soviet rule. However, Kravchenko never calls the famine a "Russian genocide"; he clearly presents it as a Communist and Stalinist crime.

Equally important, to accuse the Russian nation of genocide against the Ukrainians is to miss the whole point of Russian attitudes to Ukraine (a point which Ukrainian nationalists themselves emphasize and criticize in other contexts). This is that the core of Russian ambitions in Ukraine, and the greatest Russian threat to Ukraine, lies in the fact that Russians do *not* regard Ukrainians as aliens but as a people who are closely related to or even identical with the Russians themselves and therefore belong in one state or confederation with them.

For a consciously Russian regime to decide to exterminate the Ukrainians would therefore be about as ideologically consistent as Hitler deciding to wipe out not the Jews, but the Saxons or Bavarians. Like other contemporary European empires, tsarist Russia in the nineteenth century did carry out operations of "ethnic cleansing" against populations in the Caucasus and Central Asia—but these were Muslim tribal peoples, not Slavic Orthodox (this does not of course make the operations any more morally acceptable, whichever Europeans were doing it).

It must be said that the "genocide" version of the famine has not been adopted by the Ukrainian state or by the most reputable Ukrainian historians, and it has not been included in most of the new standard Ukrainian history textbooks for use in schools. Members of President Kuchma's administration, as well as liberal Ukrainian intellectuals, have expressed their strong opposition to this version of what happened. Yet it continues to have wide currency among the nationalist intelligentsia, including some within the Ministry of Education, among Ukrainian émigrés in the West, and in the publications of state-subsidized nation-alist cultural organizations such as Prosvita. Quotations from their books and articles on this subject are sometimes deliberately translated and reprinted in the Russian-language press with a view to encouraging hostility to Ukrainian nationalism.

One curious feature of the way that the famine has been "remem-bered" is that the most bitter writing on the subject has emanated from western Ukraine—which at the time of the famine was under Polish rule and therefore did not experience it. This anomaly has been explained as the result of the sheer traumatization caused in Soviet Ukraine by the famine and its appalling death rate.

THE IMPACT OF THE SECOND WORLD WAR

Another factor in diminishing the impact of the famine seems to have been that eight years after it came the German invasion and the Second World War. This overshadowed memories of the famine with new horrors and sufferings—the war cost Ukraine even more deaths than the famine, at least if the figures for the deaths of Jewish inhabitants in the Holocaust are included. The war also created a new myth as a basis for Soviet rule in Ukraine—the myth of the liberation of Ukraine from Nazi German tyranny by a heroic Soviet army in which Ukrainians played a key part alongside the Russians and other nations and contributed great mili-tary leaders such as Marshal Yeremenko, defender of Stalingrad.

The power of this myth came from the fact that—unlike most Soviet propaganda—it did have a basis in truth. While many west Ukrainians fought for Ukrainian independence in the ranks of nationalist guerrilla forces, and others served in the German army, police, and SS, much larger numbers were conscripted into the Soviet army (including the fathers—both of whom were killed in action as Soviet officers—of the first two presidents of independent Ukraine, Leonid Kravchuk and Leonid Kuchma). Considerable numbers of other Ukrainians joined Soviet partisan units.[38]

Moreover, because of Nazi atrocities in Ukraine (more than 250 Ukrain-ian villages were destroyed with all their inhabitants, compared to 1 in France), and their evident racial contempt and hatred for the Ukraini-ans as a Slavic people, there seems little doubt that most Ukrainians did welcome the Nazi defeat and the return of the Soviet army. Given what we now know about Nazi plans for the racial subjugation and colo-nization of Ukraine, it is also clear that Ukrainians were, on balance, quite right to do so. Ukraine would not have received independence from the Nazis with the ease it did under Mikhail Gorbachev, even assuming that a recognizable "Ukraine" survived prolonged Nazi rule at all.

A visit to the Museum of the Second World War in Kiev, with its long table set with soldiers' canteens, each with the identity card and death notice of a Soviet soldier, is therefore a genuinely moving experience because of the immense losses suffered by the Russian, Ukrainian, and other troops of the Soviet army, but also because these troops did after all spare the world, and Ukraine, a greater evil.

The fiftieth anniversary of the end of the war, in May 1995, gave interesting evidence of how differently the war, and by extension much of the history of the Soviet Union, is regarded in different parts of Ukraine. In Lviv (in Polish, Lwow; in Russian, Lvov; and in Yiddish and German, Lemberg), capital of Galicia, the commemoration was akin to that in the Baltic states. In other words, while limited mention was made of German atrocities, much more attention was given to celebrating the Organization of Ukrainian Nationalists and its partisan wing, the UPA, and to condemning the Soviet victory, portrayed overwhelmingly as an alien invasion and conquest which ushered in a new period of national subjugation and Communist tyranny.

In the huge, mainly Russian-speaking cities of eastern Ukraine, equally predictably, the war was commemorated in almost exactly the same way it was in Russia, of course with emphasis on local heroes and episodes. There was virtually no attempt to give a more shaded picture or to point out that Soviet victory also brought the return of Stalinist terror.

But what was really striking was that this was also true of the national celebrations in Kiev. Except for the fact that they were in the Ukrainian language, and emphasized the role of Ukrainian commanders and soldiers, in content the exhibitions and displays were almost identical to those in Moscow (however, the style was different). Obviously as a result of policy on the part of the Kuchma administration—marking a clear break from the approach under the previous president, Leonid Kravchuk —almost no mention was made of the activities of the Ukrainian nationalist forces.

This was, it must be said, a major historical falsification, since these forces played a very important part in the fighting in western Ukraine. Like their equivalents in the Baltic states, they went on fighting against Soviet rule for almost ten years after the war ended. The partisans' heroic endurance, and the atrocities committed by the Soviet regime in the course of antipartisan operations, did a great deal to keep Ukrainian nationalism and hatred for Soviet rule alive in the areas most affected. The last partisan units surrendered only after Stalin died, and some former guerrillas remained at large in the woods until the 1960s.

THE SOVIET UKRAINIAN IDENTITY

This brings out a key point about the background to Ukrainian national attitudes and political behavior today: that in their degree of identification with the Soviet Union, most Ukrainians were in an intermediate position. They did not see the Soviet Union as completely their state, as did most Russians and Belarusians, but nor did they see it as wholly alien, as did the Balts and Galician Ukrainians. Unlike the Georgians and Armenians, they did not have a strong sense of a cohesive and glorious national culture older than that of Russia, let alone the Soviet Union; and unlike the Muslim peoples, they did not have religious and social traditions which created a wall between them and Soviet Russian culture.

Ukrainians, as already stated, did not suffer from discrimination under the Soviet Union as long as they spoke Russian in public (and usually in private as well) and identified with communism and the Soviet state. The officer corps of the Soviet army in the 1980s is estimated to have been around one-third Ukrainian; and in Ukraine itself, Ukrainians held senior (and responsible) positions in the party and state systems, to a markedly greater degree than the "titular nationalities" of other republics.

Thus in 1955–1970, with 74.9 percent of the Ukrainian Soviet Socialist Republic's population at the end of that period, ethnic Ukrainians provided a staggering 100 percent—every single member—of the secretariat of the Central Committee, all of the republican first secretaries and prime ministers in that period, all of the first secretaries of the Komsomol and all the chairmen of the trade unions, 93 percent of the most senior Communist officials, and 89 percent of senior ministers. They even provided half of the chairmen of the republican KGB, which in other republics was a role strictly reserved for Russians.[39] In other republics with large Russian minorities (such as Latvia and Kazakstan), a much higher proportion of the senior party and state posts was always reserved for Russians (or loyal Ukrainians).

The very different figures for Ukraine reflect the fact that the Soviet Russian leaders trusted and identified with the Ukrainians to a far greater degree than they did with any other nationality (at least since the Latvians and Jews in the 1920s). These figures also partly reflected a deliberate intention under Khrushchev, with his long Ukrainian experience, to turn Ukrainians into the "second big brothers" in the USSR. This intention was also responsible for his transfer of Crimea to Ukraine in 1954. It also allowed Ukrainian Communist Party first secretary Petro Shelest to begin a moderate Ukrainianization of the education system and media in Ukraine, an act which played an important role in preserving the Ukrainian language in some areas where it otherwise might have died out, such as Dnipropetrovsk.

This Ukrainianization was brought to a halt by Moscow after 1972, and Shelest was replaced with the hard-line Volodymyr Shcherbytsky —something which, to judge by my conversations with former Soviet Ukrainian officials, caused great and enduring resentment even among completely orthodox and loyal Ukrainian Communists. However, while Shelest's removal was followed by a limited removal of his supporters, they were replaced mostly with other Ukrainians. There was no attempt to replace Ukrainians with Russians throughout the Ukrainian SSR leadership. This was partly because Brezhnev himself had spent a critical part of his career as first secretary of Dnipropetrovsk, accumulating in the process a largely Ukrainian bureaucratic clique around him, including Shcherbytsky and the later Soviet president, Nikolai Podgorny (Mykola Pidgorny).

These men were conservative Communists and mostly—although not exclusively—Russian-speaking. All the same, throughout much of the Soviet Union under Brezhnev, representatives of the titular nationalities were making discreet strides toward local dominance, above all in "symbolic" institutions such as the republican Supreme Soviets, but also to a very real degree within the Communist hierarchy. The growing looseness and corruption of Brezhnevite rule also led, as is well known, to a slippage of central control.[40]

Most Ukrainians who thought about these matters appear to have resented not so much the Soviet Union as such, as their subordinate position within it. They wanted more equality with the Russians, more power to make their own decisions and less forced obedience to the dictates of the Soviet government in Moscow; but these attitudes were widely held among Ukrainian (and Ukrainian-Russian) state officials, economic managers, and even Communist officials who in other ways regarded themselves, and indeed genuinely were, loyal to the Soviet system and Communist ideology.

There was also a degree to which these men jumped to nationalism in 1989 precisely to defend their own rule of Ukraine against the rising tide of "democracy" (as it then appeared) in Russia, as well as to try to co-opt and limit the Ukrainian nationalist forces, whom the authorities literally a few weeks before had been busy suppressing (the Brezhnev-ite leadership in Ukraine had always been lukewarm about Gorba-chev's reforms and had covertly sabotaged many of them). They acted in the spirit of Lampedusa's self-interested, opportunist but perceptive Sicilian nobleman during Italy's national revolution: "For everything to stay the same, everything has to change."

An analogy could be drawn to the Skoropadsky government of 1918. Its leaders were former members of the tsarist elite and would never have led a revolt against the tsar; but they were also conscious of their Ukrainian descent. After the fall of the monarchy, they took power in Ukraine largely to ward off the spread of Bolshevik revolution and redistribution of property; however, some at least also became, it would appear, sincere Ukrainian patriots. Although themselves frequently Russian-speaking (or even of ethnic Russian origin, such as General Vsevolod Petrov), they introduced a sweeping program of Ukrainian-ization of the school system and bureaucracy.

THE SOVIET UKRAINIAN LEGACY

Today, a typical representative of the former Soviet elite turned Ukrainian patriot is the second president of Ukraine, Leonid Kuchma. A Russian-speaking Ukrainian from Chernihiv (in Russian, Chernigov) in north-central Ukraine, under Soviet rule he rose to high rank in the state managerial sector, becoming director of the huge Yuzhmash missile plant at Dnipropetrovsk, in east-central Ukraine, and then prime minis-ter under Kravchuk.

In common with most other directors of major Ukrainian industrial plants (especially of course those in the military-industrial complex), Kuchma believed strongly in the necessity of preserving close economic relations and open borders with Russia—and probably still does, if this can be achieved without placing Ukraine under undue Russian influ-ence, let alone control.

Before independence, Kuchma showed no recorded signs of Ukrainian nationalism, and in the elections of 1994 he campaigned on a platform of friendship with Russia and official status for the Russian language. At his inauguration in July 1994, he declared that "Ukraine is histori-cally part of the Eurasian economic and cultural space" (in other words, related to Russia and other former Soviet republics), whereas his predecessor, Leonid Kravchuk, had emphasized Ukraine's "European" character and alignment.[41]

Nonetheless, Kuchma has become a genuine Ukrainian patriot, has learned to speak fluent Ukrainian, and has continued Ukrainianization, although in a more moderate and diplomatic way than under his predecessor—and this is not from opportunism alone, or from fear of the anger and mobilizing capacity of the Galician and other radical nationalists. Although these factors played a part, the main point is that it was one thing to obey orders from a government in Moscow which in theory and under the Soviet constitution at least reflected the interests of the whole union and in which Ukraine had an equal stake; to take orders from the new, purely Russian government of Boris Yeltsin would be something else, and quite unacceptable.

One reason for Kuchma's popularity with many Ukrainians was made clear in an exchange during a television debate with President Leonid Kravchuk during the presidential election campaign of 1994. Posing a question, one of the audience members sneered at Kuchma for speaking such poor Ukrainian. Kuchma replied haltingly, "That I speak poor Ukrainian is my misfortune, which I am trying to rectify; but it is a misfortune I share with many of my fellow countrymen." Because a majority of inhabitants of Ukraine at that time (and perhaps still today) considered Russian their mother tongue, while perhaps also feeling guilty about this at some level, Kuchma's honest response won support, while Kravchuk's arrogant and patronizing tone—exactly what Russian-speaking Ukrainians loathe in the radical nationalists in general and the Galicians in particular—cost him sympathy and votes. However, it is important to note that Kuchma might well not have won votes from this episode if he had simply justified speaking bad Ukrainian—he had to declare his determination to improve it, something he has since done with striking success. By 1996, Kuchma (publicly at least) insisted on using only Ukrainian.

In this context, it is interesting to examine the results of an opinion poll in the Russian-speaking areas of Ukraine in May 1994, carried out by the reputable Democratic Initiative Center.[42] This poll produced evidence of strong disillusionment with Ukrainian independence and desire for a revival of the Soviet Union. However, this did not mean a preference for the *Russian* as opposed to the Ukrainian state. To a question about living standards and other matters, 76 percent answered that things were better in Russia, but when asked about the future of Crimea, 48 percent said that it should stay part of Ukraine, against 10 percent who said it should go to Russia, and 16 percent who said it should become independent.

When asked what people they generally identified with, only 3 percent said "the people of Russia," against 34 percent who said "the people of the former Soviet Union or the CIS [Commonwealth of Independent States]," 34 percent "the people of Ukraine," and 23 percent the people of their particular region. This is a striking lack of identification with Russia, given that 38 percent of those polled gave their nationality as Russian, against 56 percent Ukrainian (although 62 percent of the total gave Russian as their native language). Equally striking is that so many Ukrainians failed to give "the people of Ukraine" as their first answer. This area may not be "Russian," but it continues to feel strongly Soviet.

UKRAINIAN ELECTORAL BEHAVIOR, 1991–94

The complicated Ukrainian attitude to the Soviet Union was reflected in a series of votes in the months leading up to the end of the Union in 1991. It is important to note that, as a result of "Russifying" and migration processes going back some three hundred years, 22 percent of the population of Ukraine (11.4 million people) were listed in the census of 1989 as Russian by nationality—although, as I shall point out in the next chapter, this definition needs very careful analysis. The proportion of Ukrainians in the population varied from 51 percent in Donetsk in the east, and only 26 percent in Crimea, to 90 percent in Lviv in the west. Central regions such as Chernihiv and Cherkassy also had Ukrainian majorities of over 90 percent, but many of these populations gave Russian as their mother tongue.

Overall, although 72 percent of the country was Ukrainian (37.4 million), more than one-third gave Russian as their mother tongue (this figure would be larger still, if not for the inclusion of Jews, Greeks, Bulgars, and other minority populations). This meant that Ukraine on achieving independence had a small majority—52 percent—of its population who did not in fact speak Ukrainian as their first language—nothing very unusual in international terms, but a source of acute pain and worry for Ukrainian nationalists, who fear that unless the use of Ukrainian is strengthened, Ukraine will become like Belarus, with neither political nor cultural identity (probably an exaggerated fear, for after all, Ukraine's autonomous cultural and political traditions are far stronger than those of Belarus).

In March 1991, in a referendum called by Mikhail Gorbachev, 70.5 percent of Ukrainians who voted (in an 80.2 percent turnout) did so to preserve the Soviet Union as "a renewed federation" (today on the basis of this vote, Soviet loyalists—ranging from Gorbachev himself to Communists in Ukraine and Russia—continue to argue that the dissolution of the Union at the end of the year was illegal and undemocratic).

However, an even higher proportion of Ukrainian voters, in a simultaneous republican poll, declared themselves in favor of Ukrainian sovereignty within the Union. Strikingly, support for Ukrainian "sovereignty" was extremely high in the "Russian" and "Russified" areas of eastern and southern Ukraine, with Crimea voting 84.7 percent in favor, and Donetsk, 86.2 percent. However, local Communist authorities may have influenced this response.

In Galicia, the overwhelming majority of people voted against the Union. In a third poll, held only in the three Galician regions, 89.9 percent voted for complete independence and the end of the Union.[43]

On December 1, 1991, the Communist-turned-nationalist administration of former Communist Party first secretary Leonid Kravchuk called a referendum on Ukrainian independence, which produced a 90 percent vote in favor. The eastern and southern regions were less enthusiastic than the west, but still turned out strong yes votes (84 percent in Donetsk, 85 percent in Odessa). The exception was Crimea, with only 54 percent in favor—still a majority. These votes are the basis for the democratic legitimacy of independent Ukraine—however much some voters later regretted their yes votes.[44] In simultaneous presidential elections, 61.6 percent cast their votes for Kravchuk, against 29.5 percent for the combined candidates of the "national-democratic" parties, who did not help their cause by splitting three ways.

By May 1994, according to the opinion poll carried out by the Democratic Initiative Center in Kiev, 47 percent of people polled in southern and eastern Ukraine declared that if allowed to vote again on independence, they would vote against. Twelve percent said they would not take part, and just 24 percent now declared they would vote for independence. These figures were closely linked to economic suffering and pessimism, with 60 percent of people polled saying either that Ukraine would fail to overcome its economic crisis within five years, or that it would never do so. This was closely linked to anger that the promises by Kravchuk and the nationalists of rapid prosperity as a result of independence had turned into a ludicrously bad joke. East Ukrainian feelings are not assuaged by the fact that when they complain about being deceived, nationalists call them "denationalized sausage heads who vote with their bellies," as Volodymyr Pavliv, editor of the Lviv magazine *Post Postup',* put it.[45]

As a result of this shift in attitudes, during the next presidential elections in June 1994 there was a much clearer and potentially dangerous split in Ukraine between the nationalist west and the mainly Russian-speaking east and south, with the nationalist parties throwing their weight behind "the first president of independent Ukraine," Kravchuk, against the alleged "Russophile" Kuchma, and Kravchuk running on a strong platform of defending Ukrainian independence and the Ukrainian language against Russia and its allies in Ukraine.

Thus in the second round of the elections in Crimea, 90 percent were for Kuchma and just 8.9 percent for Kravchuk; in Donetsk the figure was 79 percent to 18.5 percent; but in Lviv, it was 93.8 percent for Kravchuk and just 3.9 for Kuchma, and in Volhynia, 83.9 to 14. The much greater population of the big eastern and southern cities gave the national victory to Kuchma, by a convincing margin of 52.1 to 45.1 percent. This reflected above all the decline of the economy and living standards under Kravchuk, at a much steeper rate than in Russia, and the hyperinflation of Ukraine's provisional currency, the karbovanets.

What alarmed both Western observers and Ukrainian nationalists was that Kuchma had indeed campaigned on a "pro-Russian" ticket, both in terms of relations with Russia and of official status for the Russian language, and that the country seemed to have split along dangerously clear geographical lines over these issues. However, the lines were not in fact so clear: The broad band of central regions (and some southern ones, such as Odessa) produced much more mixed and balanced results.[46]

However, the 1994 result in the Russian-speaking areas also reflected considerable anger with the anti-Russian nationalist and especially Galician cast given the administration under President Kravchuk. It also led observers—and of course many of the voters concerned—to ask why these regions had voted so strongly for independence in 1991. The 1998 Ukrainian parliamentary elections led to an even stronger vote for the Communists and Socialists in the east and south, while the total vote for the nationalist parties was almost unchanged, remaining overwhelmingly restricted to Galicia and Kiev.

One reason for these votes in the Russian-speaking areas in December 1991 was of course that the Union had already for all intents and purposes collapsed, and that the president of Russia as well as the government of Ukraine were calling for its abolition. However, it is important to note that the words *independence* and *sovereignty* were very little understood by many ordinary people in the Soviet Union at that time (outside specific areas such as the Baltic states, Galicia, and Moldavia).

It was not uncommon to hear people declare they were for "independence," then later in the conversation hear them say, "Of course, I want independence within the Soviet Union." Many East Ukrainians and Crimeans who voted for Ukrainian independence understood it to mean full political autonomy and economic independence from Moscow's dictates; they certainly did not think it would mean customs barriers with Russia, a collapse of interrepublican trade, separate currencies, and divided and potentially hostile armed forces.

The mixed attitude of Ukrainians to the Soviet Union is also reflected in official policy toward the sharing out of Soviet assets; for while one strong strand of official and unofficial historiography, described above, regards the Soviet Union as a Russian empire and Ukraine as a colony, Ukrainian demands for a share of the Black Sea Fleet have been based on the premise that Ukraine was a form of partner in a dissolved common enterprise. This is also true of some of the Ukrainian arguments about Sevastopol as a "city of Russian glory" on the basis of its defense by the Soviet army in 1941–42. Ukrainians point out with justice that the Soviet army was not a Russian army, and that Ukrainians played a key part both in that army and in the defense itself. This is entirely true— but it does lay them open to the charge of a certain inconsistency.

2

UKRAINIANS AND RUSSIANS IN INDEPENDENT UKRAINE

It should already be apparent that the common picture of a "Russian-speaking east Ukraine" against a "nationalist west" needs to be qualified in several ways. Above all, the "Russian diaspora" in Ukraine, and for that matter in other republics as well, is neither truly Russian nor a diaspora in the usual historical and international sense of the term. Instead, Russians in Ukraine can best be understood as people left behind by the Soviet Union, very unsure of their own identity, but more closely linked to their Ukrainian home than to their Russian homeland. Even without the high (and in the cities almost universal) degree of intermarriage between Russians and Ukrainians, the country would be ethnically mixed, with members drawn from almost every European republic of the former Soviet Union. It is very unlikely that most of the population would be responsive to attempts from Moscow to stir up revolt—unless in the meantime the internal Ukrainian political situation had changed radically, which is not at all likely in the short to medium term.

That there are very important differences between the Russian-speaking and the "nationalist" parts of Ukraine is indubitable. However, it would be a mistake to follow radical Ukrainian nationalists in assuming that just because Russian-speaking Ukrainians or the Ukrainian "Russians" themselves speak Russian, they are ipso facto antinational or anti-Ukrainian. Intellectuals from these backgrounds say that they do not have a "weaker" Ukrainian feeling than the Galicians, but a different and equally legitimate one. In the words of one of them, "Gogol may not have written in Ukrainian, but that doesn't mean he was a worse Ukrainian than Shevchenko, and he was certainly a much better writer."

Many of the Western fears—and Russian hopes—surrounding the Russian population in Ukraine have been based on the misperception that this is a "Russian diaspora." On the strength of this belief, Western intelligence agencies have expressed concern in the past that the Russians in Ukraine might secede or put great pressure on the Ukrainian state to enter a new union with Russia (for example, the U.S. intelligence community's 1994 assessment of Ukraine's political situation).[1] As noted in the introduction, Russian officials for their part have privately threatened that if Ukraine takes a strongly anti-Russian stand in its foreign policies—for example, by seeking to join NATO—the Russian government will "activate" the Russians in Ukraine in such a way as to divide, weaken, and possibly destroy the Ukrainian state.

More "Sovietized" than "Russified"

To understand the Soviet Union's "Russification" policy and its legacy in eastern and southern Ukraine, it is crucially important to understand how this process differed from official Russification policy under the Russian Empire. In recent decades, what took place was mainly *Soviet modernization,* expressed through the medium of the Russian language. Although official propaganda, as expressed in all school textbooks, certainly emphasized the "unbreakable brotherhood" of Russia and Ukraine, it did not necessarily attach Ukrainians to a specifically Russian national identity.

The "Russians" in Ukraine are concentrated in the south and east of the country, although many also reside in Kiev, and smaller numbers in cities elsewhere in central and western Ukraine. They live together with and intermixed with very large numbers of Russian-speaking "Ukrainians," to the extent that it is often very difficult to disentangle the two. The spread of the Russian language to these groups was the work of state policies of "Russification" under the tsars and the Soviets, but greatly aided—as with such processes elsewhere in the world—by factors of modernization, personal advantage, and intermarriage.

Ukraine's "Russians" are the product of two major population movements. The first was from the 1790s to the 1820s and consisted of Russian peasants who either moved voluntarily or were resettled by their Russian landlords on the newly conquered and previously almost uninhabited steppes to the north of the Black Sea to open them for farming (the majority of the settlers were of course Ukrainians from the contiguous Ukrainian provinces, but important numbers of German colonists and Serbs and Bulgars fleeing Ottoman rule in the Balkans also established themselves in this region).

The second and larger wave of Russians into Ukraine was made up of peasants and workers who came to the great mines and factories that began to open in Ukraine from the 1870s on. Interrupted by the revolution and civil war, this flow resumed during Stalin's forced industrialization.[2] The reason Russian, rather than Ukrainian, peasants headed for the Ukrainian cities for several decades had to do with Ukrainian peasant attitudes, the roots of which are too complex to be discussed here. Ukrainian peasants under tsarism often preferred to move thousands of miles to Kazakstan or Siberia to go on farming, rather than fifty miles to the nearest city to work in a factory. The result today is that while more than half of the population of the east Ukrainian city of Donetsk is of Russian origin, more than half of the names on the telephone list of the governor's office in the Russian Far East's Vladivostok are Ukrainian.[3]

Under Soviet rule, Ukrainian peasants joined the flow into the industrial cities, which are overwhelmingly situated in the south and east of Ukraine because of the presence of coal and iron ore mines and easy access to the Black Sea ports and the Russian interior. Four of Ukraine's six largest conurbations are situated in the south and east, one (Kiev) in the center, and one—by far the smallest (Lviv)—in the west. This gives numerical and electoral weight to the Russian-speaking areas, which brought the Russophone Leonid Kuchma to power in 1994.

The newly arrived Ukrainian workers were progressively Russified by the Soviet state education system (which for most of the Soviet period allowed Ukrainian-language schools in the countryside and small towns while trying to keep the cities Russian-speaking); by the effects of working in "all-Union" (that is, Moscow-controlled) factories, where the language of administration was Russian; and by intermarriage and social contact with the Russian-speaking population. They were not "denationalized," as many Ukrainian and Western writers say, because they had not been "national" before.

However, it was not merely the Ukrainians who did not necessarily become Russian as a result of the Soviet education process; to an extent, this was also true of the Russians themselves. Not just the Ukrainian peasants, but the Russian ones as well, were to a considerable extent "prenational" in the first decades of this century, and they did not think of their identity primarily in terms of nationality—largely because, being illiterate (unlike their West European or Japanese counterparts), they had no exposure to a modern national written culture and state educational system. The entire modern education and cultural shaping of these newly urbanized populations therefore took place in a Soviet context, and these populations remain to this day Soviet, rather than Russian or Ukrainian, in their basic cultural and social attitudes. They were truly, in the Communist phrase, "cooked in the workers' pot."

THE LACK OF CIVIL SOCIETY

Moreover, thanks to Soviet totalitarian rule, these populations did not develop institutions of civil society—and as of 1998, such institutions are developing only with extreme slowness, in Russia as in Ukraine. This is obviously having an adverse effect in terms of inhibiting the growth of genuine democracy and preserving the rule of deeply corrupt, short-sighted, and incompetent elites. However, it has also had the effect of limiting the capacity of these populations to develop new identities for themselves, identities which might lead to increased tension with Kiev. Vassily Lyakh, a teacher in Dnipropetrovsk (and head of the museum dedicated to the theosophist Madame Blavatsky, who was born in the city, then called Yekaterinoslav, in 1831), describes this situation:

> Russian cultural and social organizations here simply don't exist. Back in 1992, there was a group of local businessmen, teachers, and so on, who wanted to create a society for local Russian culture, but somehow the energy ran out and nothing happened. Maybe because it was in response to Ukrainianization, and since then this has turned out to be slower and less terrifying than we thought. . . . It is the same in other cities, I have heard—Russian clubs and societies are small or nonexistent.
>
> Only the Ukrainians and Jews here have national organizations. The Jewish ones are financed and organized from abroad, and the Ukrainian ones by the Ukrainian state. Russian attempts here have received no help whatsoever, certainly not from Russia, either state or private. Maybe it is something to do with Russians not really feeling like a nation in the way that other nations do. . . . For example, I have heard that even in the United States, the Russians are the only emigrant group that doesn't have a serious national organization of their own.[4]

In addition, the lack of a capacity for spontaneous organization from below has been of critical importance in limiting social protest against the mass deprivation resulting from economic reform. A key factor in the lack of such protest has been the weakness of the trade unions and the workers' lack of faith in them. In an area such as eastern Ukraine, mass labor protests might take on a national or at least regional coloring, especially if the situation is mishandled by the government in Kiev.

So in terms of general stability and security in the area, the lack of a civil society has not been a bad thing entirely. Its absence is, for example, one reason the oft-made parallel between the Russians of today and the inhabitants of Weimar Germany is not appropriate. The Germans had a long tradition of political mobilization from below, without which the rise and triumph of the Nazis would have been impossible.

Thus a critically important reason for the lack of organized resistance to Ukrainianization in eastern Ukraine—even where it has been seriously resented—is that the Russian intelligentsia in Ukraine, including the teachers, quite simply lack the organization, tradition, and experience of spontaneous protest to mobilize themselves or Russian parents, while the state retains quite enough authoritarian means and attitudes to deal severely with any individual teacher or small group of teachers that goes too far in its protests.

As it is, the lack of civil society's institutions and organizations and the general atmosphere of political passivity, apathy, and cynicism have created an inertia that has sustained Ukraine. If Ukraine in its present borders had not existed, not many people in eastern and southern Ukraine would have wanted to invent it; but equally, now that they live in an independent Ukraine, very few of them have the energy to run the immense risks involved in trying to dismantle it.

This raises the question of whether all this will change as (or if) these areas do in fact grow closer to Europe and develop civic institutions. A nascent Western-style attitude to some of these questions is apparent in the words of Valery Ruban, a Russian-speaking municipal deputy in Kharkiv:

> I'm a Ukrainian taxpayer and as such I have the right to demand that my taxes go to pay for a school for my children in my native language, which is also the language of 85 percent of the people in this city. But the Soviet tradition is of the state looking at us as slaves—do this, do that—and the people going on sleeping, and accepting that. The new Ukrainian state is no different. How could it be? It's still run by the very same Soviet bureaucrats! So far, only about 5 percent have woken up and are actually trying to make something of this new "democracy" and protesting when their interests are harmed.[5]

More bitter were the words of Dmitry Kornilov, a Russian nationalist activist in Donetsk, but they were words that I have heard echoed in different forms by both democratic activists and Ukrainian nationalists:

> The parties of power here, the bureaucrat-politicians and their business allies, are terrified of political parties, which would mean that elections would lead to genuine changes of power—*their* power. So they do everything possible to stop them emerging, and that also of course suits the Ukrainian state. This has been most evident in Crimea since the Ukrainian state stepped in. You can see there how the media constantly repeat the line that ordinary people should not be involved in politics, because this is the business of the wise, experienced leaders. Our business is to govern you, and you should just think about women, TV, beer, and the beach. You don't even have to vote—we'd be much happier if you didn't, because that will just prove how ignorant and unfit for politics you are.[6]

Very similar criticisms of the "parties of power"—although from a totally opposite standpoint—were expressed to me in March 1994 by Dymitro Ponomarchuk, a spokesman for the Ukrainian nationalist party Rukh. Ponomarchuk also said that the existing ruling elites were trying to stifle all political organization and mobilization from below. As of 1998, there is no sign that this picture has changed or is changing.

The question is, if the rest of the population in Donetsk and other cities woke up, could its unhappiness in fact (as Mr. Kornilov would wish) take a Russian national form that threatens Ukraine? And would local Ukrainians (as Mr. Ponomarchuk would wish) develop a strongly Ukrainian ethnic consciousness, possibly threatening relations with their ethnic Russian neighbors?

Certainly, if the institutions of civil society were to develop without being accompanied by the kind of economic change that significantly raises the living standards of the mass of the population and creates local governments more responsive to the needs of ordinary people, then at some stage in the future there may well be serious social unrest. For it seems very unlikely that people who are capable of mobilizing and, presumably, are increasingly aware of the economic success of Poland and other former Communist countries would accept indefinitely either their present miserable conditions or the rule of local governments composed of an odious mixture of former Soviet bureaucrats, "businessmen," and outright criminals, most of them motivated solely by the desire to get rich at the expense of state and people. Of course, when trouble like this looms, it can easily be exploited by forces that want to increase national tensions. Nonetheless, the indications are that in this region such a development of national hostility is a long way off—and there are grounds for hope that it will not develop at all.

UKRAINIANIZATION

The lack of national tensions at present does not mean that some aspects of Ukrainianization have not created deep irritation in the Russian-speaking areas. One example that has proved deeply divisive in other national contexts (for example, the Hungarians in Slovakia) is the Ukrainianization of state services and—even more important—the school system, ushered in by the Soviet Ukrainian language law of 1989, which made Ukrainian the sole official language.

These measures are understandable in view of what was done to the Ukrainian language under Russian and Soviet rule, but it would be hard to deny that they have an undemocratic aspect. In the 1994 presidential elections, a majority of Ukrainians voted for Kuchma, whose platform clearly opposed such Ukrainianization measures. The measures are also opposed by overwhelming majorities in particular areas of Ukraine, such as Kharkiv. A French aid worker in Kharkiv summed up the situation as of 1995 as follows:

> In twenty-five years' time, it seems likely that everyone here will speak Ukrainian fluently and be able to use it for public purposes, even if they still use Russian continually at home and in their offices.
>
> As of now, though, there's no doubt that the language issue here is a very real problem. Kravchuk was not re-elected to a considerable degree because of his Ukrainianization policy, and people voted for Kuchma in part because of his promises to defend the Russian identity. That doesn't necessarily mean that people want an official status for Russian in Ukraine as a whole, but they certainly want Kharkiv to be able to make its own rules.[7]

Ukrainian as the sole official language of Ukraine has been enshrined (despite firm electoral pledges to the contrary by President Kuchma) in the 1996 constitution. However, as of 1998, regional and local governments in eastern and southern Ukraine continue to use Russian for internal purposes and for communicating with the citizenry; whether this is "legal" or not is a matter of debate.[8]

In education, the stated aim of the Ukrainianization program introduced under President Kravchuk and left in place by Kuchma is to

increase the number of Ukrainian-language schools to match the proportion of "ethnic Ukrainians" in the population (72 percent) by the year
2000 (although the more radical nationalists would like to go further
and make 90 or even 100 percent of schools Ukrainian-language).

Dominique Arel observes that under Kravchuk the "Ministry of Education advanced policies . . . very much in line with an ethnolinguistic
conception of Ukraine. . . . [T]he signals were unmistakably at odds
with the proclaimed civic conception of the state."[9] These policies were
accompanied by rhetoric from nationalist intellectuals (including those
attached to the ministry itself) about Russian being a "foreign" language and the "language of the colonizers"—notions inevitably deeply
disturbing to Russians and insulting to many Ukrainian speakers of
Russian.[10] Russian-speakers counter that since Russian has had a presence in parts of Ukraine since the sixteenth century, and since one of
Ukraine's greatest writers, Gogol (among many others), wrote in Russian, to call the language "foreign" makes little sense.

Particularly wounding to the Russian and Russian-speaking cultural
intelligentsia was the decision, made under Kravchuk and maintained
under Kuchma, to teach Russian literature in schools and universities
—including Russian-language ones—as part of "world literature" classes;
"Ukrainian literature" classes would not cover the works of Russian
writers.[11]

Although at the beginning 25 percent of the "world literature" courses
were devoted to Russian-language writers, Education Minister Anatoly
Pohribny indicated that this proportion would be reduced as Russian
teachers retired. As some of these teachers pointed out to me, this
places Gogol, a Ukrainian Russian-language writer, or Mikhail Bulgakov,
or Isaac Babel—the latter two, respectively, a Russian and a Russian-
Jewish writer in Ukraine—in a strangely anomalous position, especially
of course regarding their works set in Ukraine.

Under Kuchma, the official rhetoric from the government (although
not from all its representatives) has greatly diminished, and the program
itself has also slowed somewhat. So far, it has been barely implemented
at all in Donetsk or Crimea, and very little in Kharkiv; but it is proceeding fast in Dnipropetrovsk, and in Kiev the program is largely complete
(assuming that the Russians are to be left a share of schools equivalent
to their population), advancing from only 20 percent of schoolchildren
in 1988 to 54.7 percent in 1994. In 1994, 46 percent of institutions of
higher learning throughout Ukraine were still Russian-language, but
this was still a major drop from Soviet times.[12]

The dispute over language and education has caused considerable grumbling among many Russian-speaking teachers and intellectuals, but almost no public protest in the form of demonstrations or strikes. One reason is the belief among many "Russians" that this move is basically historically and morally justified, even if they think it is being carried out in a crude, hasty, harmful, and insulting manner. Fair-minded Russian intellectuals do recognize that a situation in which only a single Ukrainian-language school existed in all of Donetsk in the last year of Soviet rule hardly could have been allowed to continue. They worry, however, that if more radical Ukrainian plans are fulfilled, one day there may be only one symbolic Russian school there, regardless of the wishes of Donetsk's people. For example, Larisa Trojan, who approved of the ultimate goal of moderate Ukrainianization, told me, "Because under Kravchuk the radical Ukrainian nationalists raised the question of restricting the Russian language so crudely and offensively, they created a reaction where none was necessary. . . . They have Bolshevik attitudes, or those of Bandera"—the reference was to Stepan Bandera, the World War II–era radical Ukrainian nationalist leader. "They want to change everything immediately, by decree, and anyone who opposes them must not be engaged in debate, but simply got rid of." [13]

This view very much reflected the spirit of the (centrally appointed) education chief of Dnipropetrovsk, Lydia Polutsiganova, a history teacher for twenty years and a Soviet official for ten. On local objections to the pace of Ukrainianization, she replied curtly, "It's not my job as a state official to study local national proportions or local opinions. I have been told to make 72 percent of schools Ukrainian-language, and that's what I'll do. Open the law and read it. I'm not going to discuss it with you or anyone else." [14]

Alexander Morzhov, a Russian math teacher (with a Ukrainian mother) in Dnipropetrovsk, reacted to this approach:

> I am Russian but speak Ukrainian better than my wife, who is Ukrainian; but I can't teach in it; my pupils would immediately feel there was something wrong, false, missing. . . .
>
> This attempt to force everyone into Ukrainian is a crime against education. It will produce a generation of semiliterates, especially in the sciences.
>
> It's also very bad for the Ukrainian language, which I love. When I hear Kuchma and his like trying to speak it, I don't know whether to laugh or cry—they simply murder it, and that is also true, naturally, of many of the teachers in these new Ukrainian language schools. . . .

You're right, Ukrainianization is not wholly unjustified in view of what happened in the past, but it is a very complicated business from every point of view and should be approached with care and thought and consideration for the wishes of parents and teachers. Instead, all these old Communist officials like Polutsiganova, who used to be the most dogmatic and authoritarian of Marxists, have gone on as before, beating people over the head, but now in the name of the nation.[15]

A rather typical response by a Russian-speaking Ukrainian to Ukrainianization of the content (as opposed to the language) of teaching came from Yuri Chumanchenko, a well-off businessman in Dnipropetrovsk (with a Russian wife who is also partly Ukrainian—in other words, a very familiar east Ukrainian mixture). Early in our conversation he criticized the Russian government and state, saying "they always want to be big brother to the Ukrainians, but instead of behaving like a brother, the Russian government today is simply trying to gouge out every advantage for Russia." But on the subject of Ukrainianization, he said,

My son had to pass an exam here in order to get into school in England, so we sat down together to look at the new school textbooks here. Whether in Russian or Ukrainian, they are full of terrible Ukrainian nationalism. They just took the old Soviet line and stood it on its head. Everything that was good is now bad, everything that was bad is now good, Russia has always been an enemy of Ukraine, and so on—all the way back to God knows when. We couldn't bear to read them, we wanted to throw them away. It is partly the fault of the old bureaucrats, who have changed their state loyalty but not their behavior. In the old days they ordered us to be Communists, now they are ordering us to be nationalists. Perhaps after a generation or so they will have died out and we will be able to live normally.[16]

Despite such irritation, the Ukrainianization issue does not cause as much worry to Russians as might be expected. In part, this stems from the fact that Ukrainian is not, after all, a completely different language, like Estonian; it is very easy for a Russian to learn. As one Ukrainian nationalist deputy exploded when a Russian colleague claimed that the requirement to speak Ukrainian in the parliament constituted oppression, "Even an elephant could learn to speak Ukrainian in five years!" As previously noted, even before independence more than a third of Russians in Ukraine claimed to speak Ukrainian fluently, and more than half had some knowledge of it.

Thus it seems like poetic justice that just as the linguistic and cultural closeness between Russians and Ukrainians once worked in favor of

Russification as a state policy, it is now working for moderate Ukrainianization. Another key factor that both results from and contributes to this closeness is the degree of intermarriage between Russians and Ukrainians in the great cities of the east and south, where the overwhelming majority of local Russians have a close Ukrainian relative and vice versa. Not only does this greatly limit the potential for the development of local ethnic hatred, it also means that even local Russians or part-Russians who speak almost no Ukrainian will remember a Ukrainian-speaking parent, grandparent, uncle, or aunt; their prejudices against learning the language are diminished accordingly. Small personal factors like this may not show up in statistics, but they are of the most crucial importance nonetheless, and they are reflected in the speed with which Russians in many parts of Ukraine are in fact learning Ukrainian.

Some of the sting has also been taken out of the language issue because both Russian and Ukrainian are to some extent being sidelined by English, a phenomenon exemplified by Mr. Chumanchenko's son, on his way to a boarding school in England. In both Ukraine and other postimperial contexts, a major fear among parts of the educated classes, and among ambitious people in general, is that shifting education into the "native" language will "provincialize" it and cut them off from access to—and jobs in—the wider world (to take a North American example, much like the fears of English-speakers in Quebec). In Ukraine, this is particularly true in the sciences, mathematics, engineering, and related disciplines, in which education and technical training were conducted entirely in Russian during the Russian imperial and Soviet eras; as a result, the Ukrainian language lacks not only a specialized literature but also in many cases an established vocabulary in these fields. Moreover, a critical question is what kind of culture will be presented to Russians and Russian-speaking Ukrainians who are now learning Ukrainian. I will return to this question in chapter 5, where I discuss the question of a civic versus an ethnic Ukrainian identity and state loyalty.

A related question concerns modernization. In the field of literature and the arts, Ukrainian has suffered from a perceived and, indeed, a real provincialism because of the supremacy of Russian but also to an extent because of the approach of the nationalist intelligentsia. In the words of an exasperated Bohdan Krawchenko,

> The Galicians in particular have suffered from an unwillingness to modernize their literary culture, and this harms their ability to attract people from other areas, and Russian-speakers in general. How long can they go on and on in their writing about the beautiful Ukrainian skies? I hate it

with a passion! . . . If we are to develop a modern Ukrainian culture, attractive to all the people in Ukraine, we have to struggle against the legacy of Ukrainian populism and 1930s-style integral nationalism. And this is happening. There is a already a new generation of writers and poets, and some even criticize Shevchenko![17]

To understand the seriousness of these writers' sacrilege, one has to understand that portraits of Shevchenko, ritually draped in strips of traditional embroidery, now occupy the places in schools and government offices around Ukraine that used to be inhabited by the immortal Lenin. Grigory Nemiria, head of the Open Society Institute in Donetsk, agreed with Krawchenko: "The biggest problem with our nationalists is that they want to go forward looking backwards. We are still waiting for someone like de Gaulle, a nationalist who would be a hero for the present generation, not the old idols of nationalist culture. . . . Look at our hetmans whom they praise so much. Ukrainians were so proud of them that at one point we had five of them at the same time! Some of them called in the Turks, others the Russians."[18] Or in the words of Semyon Gluzman, a Ukrainian-Jewish psychologist and former dissident who spent several years in the Soviet camps,

> As with most Jewish families here, my family spoke Russian, identified with the Russian language and culture, and feared Ukrainian nationalism, which we identified with hatred of Jews and with past atrocities. . . . But during my time in the camps, when I met and made friends with young Ukrainian dissidents with a deep sense of justice and idealism, I began to understand the tragedy of what had been done to Ukrainian culture under Soviet rule. When Ukrainians came from the villages to Kiev, they automatically tended to lose their culture, because it was treated as being not even second-rate but third-rate, systematically belittled and sidelined. . . .
>
> But I have also to recognize that Ukraine today is divided between two linguistic cultures. What it will be like in twenty or two hundred years, I don't know; but if Ukrainian has extended itself across the whole country, that will mean also that it has become a different Ukrainian. These nationalist idiots who march about shouting can't extend their culture across the whole country. It will have to become a modern European culture before it can spread. . . . So far much of it has inevitably been a kind of peasant shivaree.
>
> Today, for example, an intelligent Ukrainian intellectual can only look at Ukrainian state television with pain—primitive, fake "folk-dances," fake "experts," fake history, or rather a kind of Punch and Judy show.[19]

Yevgeny Zakharov, head of Folio Publishers in Kharkiv, said that as of 1995 the Ukrainian literature was making very little progress in most of Ukraine, for economic as well as cultural reasons: "Most of our publication, whether of original works or translations from foreign languages, is in Russian, because books in Ukrainian just don't sell. Every book in the Ukrainian language, even the very best, is economically deadly for us. That is why up to 95 percent of publication in Ukrainian is subsidized by the state. The quality of translation from English into Ukrainian is also often very poor, which is another reason why people prefer to read translations into Russian."[20]

The off-putting aspects (for national minorities and Ukrainian liberals) of much of traditional Ukrainian literature, including the official curriculum, may not matter so much if some of the most dynamic and determined elements among both Ukrainians and Russians are concentrating above all on learning English as their passport to the wider world. As Yekaterina Karpenko, a Russian-speaking teacher in Kharkiv, told me with a sigh, "They aren't reading either Pushkin or Shevchenko anymore, if they can help it. The bright ones are all reading in English—not Dickens, of course, but computer manuals and business guides."

HISTORICAL PREJUDICES AND MUTUAL INSULTS

Many Ukrainian intellectuals have seen the teaching of a new version of Ukrainian history as a key to creating a new sense of national identity among Ukrainians, and to dispelling many of the Soviet and Russian myths that they had been taught under Soviet rule. Anatoly Pohribny, the deputy education minister under Kravchuk in 1992-94, declared explicitly that "education should be directly subordinated to the demands of building an independent Ukrainian state."[21] Something like this is also implied in Yeltsin's call in 1996 for the formulation of a new "Russian National Idea."

The question in Ukraine, of course, is what version of Ukrainian history and historical identity is to be taught, and what effect this will have not just on ethnic Ukrainians, but also on Ukraine's large and politically crucial "Russian" minority. According to Andrew Wilson, modern Ukrainian historians risk further polarizing contemporary politics by inverting the traditional Russian-Soviet historical schema and emphasizing a history of conflict rather than cooperation.[22] For apart from the strongly anti-Russian feelings of many historians who were formerly nationalist dissidents or sympathizers under Soviet rule, another problematic element in both Russian and Ukrainian contemporary historiography is that so many of the new nationalist historians, especially in official institutions, are former official Soviet historians. As such, they were not only cut off from new international currents of historical thought, but in many cases they are quite simply accustomed to both preaching state dogma and making the search for and criticism of "enemies of socialism" (or today, of the nation) an essential part of their work.

The way in which some Ukrainian Communist historians in particular have swung around virtually overnight to a crude and simplistic anti-Russian nationalism (just as many Communist historians in Russia have become Russian national chauvinists) is really not a pretty sight, and it does not increase the respect of the Russian intelligentsia in Ukraine for the state intellectual apparatus. In the words of Larisa Trojan, deputy editor of the Russian-language (but patriotically Ukrainian) newspaper *Kievskiye Vyedomosti,* which she described as "a paper for Ukrainians reading in the Russian language": "Now they are accusing us Russian-speakers of being treacherous *Moskali*—all those old party officials from the Academy of Sciences and the Soviet newspapers who used to spout Marxism-Leninism and bend to the slightest breeze coming from Moscow. It's much easier for them simply to change a few words in their language and to become Ukrainian nationalists than it is for them to learn how to be professional journalists or scholars." [23]

It is only fair to add, however, that the standard short history of Ukraine approved for use in Ukrainian schools is a translation of the work by the Ukrainian-Canadian historian Orest Subtelny. It is balanced, objective, and of high scholarly quality, and this reflects the generally calm and balanced approach of the Ukrainian administration under Leonid Kuchma to both Ukrainian nationalism and relations with Russia. [24]

Of course, real sentiments, not just cynical careerism, underlie Ukrainian academic attitudes to the question of Kievan Rus, and these sentiments carry real political importance. The idea of sharing the ninth through the thirteenth centuries with the Russians is made intolerable for many Ukrainians by the general and continuing Russian assumption, stated or unstated (and explicit in both Soviet history textbooks and many of the new post-Soviet Russian ones), that if the East Slavic nations are brothers, the Russians are the elder brothers and thus deserve the role of leadership. Ukrainians today see this sentiment inspiring Russian policies for the future of the Commonwealth of Independence States, as well as projects such as that of Alexander Solzhenitsyn's for a new East Slav union.

The Russian pose (sometimes false, but often quite genuine) of benign, patronizing, slightly bewildered, and disappointed goodwill, like that of an uncle hurt by his erring nephew's ingratitude, is deeply irritating for many Ukrainians, even for that very large number who do in fact see the Russians as a closely related people (or who are personally closely related to Russians).

At a more popular level than Solzhenitsyn's, an amusing but typical example is the Muscovite woman who asked me one day with genuine distress, "I've just read that Ukraine is bigger than France and has almost as many people. That can't possibly be true, can it?"

In an effort to distance themselves from the Russians, and to rebuff Russian territorial claims, while not losing the mantle of descending from Kievan Rus, for the past hundred years Ukrainian nationalist historians and propagandists have been stating that it is the Ukrainians who are in fact the only legitimate descendants of Rus, because the Russians allegedly derive not from Slavs, but from Slavicized Finno-Ugric and Turkic tribes, and because the Muscovite state tradition is derived not from that of ancient Kiev but that of the Tatars. Connected to this is the claim that the Ukrainian areas always retained a closer connection to the West and an unambiguously "pro-Western" cultural orientation.

These arguments have elements of truth, but as far as the "ethnic" argument is concerned, they are rendered somewhat ridiculous by the simultaneous claim of these Ukrainian historians that the Ukrainians, by contrast and in face of all the evidence, are a "pure" ethnos, derived from the stock of Kievan Rus and settled in the same place "since the Neolithic Age."[25] Of course, neither Russians nor Ukrainians—nor any other European nation—can be described in any sense as a "pure" ethnos, and the whole argument has a distinctly racist tone about it. It should also be noted that ethnicist arguments are the exclusive property of the radical Ukrainian nationalists; even Russians nationalists in Ukraine do not reply in kind, or not yet anyway.

One branch of Ukrainian historiography and nationalism therefore does indeed owe much to old commonly held European nationalist attitudes, preserved in Ukraine by isolation under Soviet rule, but they are attitudes that have been widely regarded in the West since the Second World War as dangerous and potentially catastrophic, and that would now, if generally adopted, tend to divide and alienate Ukraine from the main currents of Western thought. (Amusingly, one point on which Ukrainian and Russian nationalist historians agree is in angrily rejecting the view—held by most Western historians and strongly supported by the evidence—that Kievan Rus was established under the leadership of Scandinavian Vikings, or Varangians, rather than purely by the Slavs.)

These debates are thoroughly abstract as far as the vast majority of everyday Ukrainians and Russians are concerned, but it would be wrong to think that they are therefore devoid of contemporary meaning. Some of the implications of Russian claims to primary descent from Kievan Rus are obvious in Russian ambitions of leading a new union of East Slavic peoples. Less clear, but clearly menacing, are the statements of Ukrainian nationalist historians, such as Yaroslav Dashkevych, that only Ukrainians are ethnically descended from the people of Kievan Rus, and that apart from them, Crimean Tatars and Karaites (a tiny Jewish sect) are indigenous peoples of Ukraine, and that all the others—Jews and others as well as Russians—are "immigrants."[26]

These conflicting claims have been accompanied by insults that have made them even more mutually intolerable. Thus a traditional Russian view of Ukrainian cultural and linguistic differences from the Russians is that they are due to the fact that the feeble, defenseless Ukrainians, lacking the Russian state to protect them, allowed themselves to be "Polonized" (that is, heavily influenced by their Polish overlords, who were also one of Russia's greatest historical rivals).

This Russian view applied with especial force to the Uniates, Orthodox East Slavs in what is now Belarus and Ukraine. In the sixteenth century Uniate bishops accepted the supremacy of the pope to bridge the gap between Poles and "Rusians" and to gain favors from the Polish state. Viewed by Russians (and in the past, by many Ukrainians as well) as traitors to religion and nation, Uniates have been persecuted by both Russian and Soviet regimes. They are now concentrated in Galicia (in Ukrainian, Galychyna), in western Ukraine, and are partly responsible for that region's specific brand of Ukrainian nationalism.

As to modern Ukrainian nationalism, a common Russian view used to be that it was "an invention of the Austrian General Staff"—in other words, that it has no traditional or historical base, but was devised by the Austro-Hungarian Empire before the First World War to divide and weaken Russia. This absurd theory is still held by many older Russians.

On the other side, the most wounding Ukrainian insult against the Russians has been the one about Tatar influence—in its most extreme form, that Russians are "Asiatic savages," as several of my acquaintances in Lviv and among the Ukrainian emigrants in the West have described them (including a leading Ukrainian-Canadian lawyer in Kiev, who would no doubt be appalled if anyone used such language in Canada to describe an ethnic minority).

Stemming from such an extreme view is the conviction that Russia conquered, exploited, and tormented Ukraine—quite opposite the view of Russians, who believe that Russia peacefully assimilated Ukraine, added greatly to its land, and protected it against Poles, Turks, and Germans.

These are the views of ideologists on either side. As for most ordinary Ukrainians and Russians, although they have a mildly satirical view of each other with certain undercurrents of hostility, it must be said that the hostility is relatively mild by international and historical standards, and operates mainly at the level of humor, sometimes affectionate. There is a great difference between Russian jokes as told by most Ukrainians and the much more biting—indeed racist—ones told by Balts, for example.

This difference is partly explainable by the fact that just as in large areas of Ukraine, Russians and Ukrainians are deeply intermarried, so in Russia itself, there are large numbers of Ukrainians who have become completely Russified, to the degree that if they are acknowledged as Ukrainians, it is only at the level of a mildly humorous stereotype without much ethnic bite. Jokes of this kind, by Kievans against the people of Novgorod and so on, apparently go back more than a thousand years.[27]

The Russian stereotype of the *khokhol* (a mildly derogatory term derived from the top knot that the Ukrainian Cossacks used to wear) is one of an obstinate, slow, sly but unaggressive, mild, and not bad-hearted provincial peasant. According to Jeffrey Brooks, in the *lubok* and other popular literature of Russia before 1917, Ukrainians are usually simply identified as Russians: "When the Ukrainians were mentioned specifically as an ethnic group, it was either as defenders of the southern borders of Russia, or they were stereotyped as likable, thick-headed clowns."[28]

Similarly, many Russians and Russian-speaking Jews—and some Russian-speaking Ukrainians, at least in the past—consider the Ukrainian language as an amusing peasant dialect, spoken by "Yvan and Maryna from the collective farm" and without the beginnings of a serious modern literature—something like the way Lallans (Lowlands Scots) is seen by the English, or Frisian by the Germans. The Russian imperial interior minister Vyacheslav von Plehve (himself of German origin) expressed an extreme but not atypical form of this prejudice when, upon banning publication of the Bible in Ukrainian in 1904, he declared that "the extreme paucity of the Little Russian language makes it entirely unfit to express abstract notions in general and the lofty truths of the Revelation in particular."[29]

By contrast, the general Ukrainian historical stereotype of the *Moskal* (Muscovite) is that of an overbearing, brave, drunken, sentimental, dirty, sometimes brutal, sometimes licentious, but also not an invariably or necessarily bad-hearted individual, often a soldier. (In the eighteenth and nineteenth centuries, *Moskal* was in fact synonymous with *soldier,* presumably because soldiers of the imperial army were the only Great Russians that most Ukrainian peasants ever saw.)

It is only when one comes to stereotypes of the Russians among the Galicians in the far west of Ukraine, and Russian stereotypes of the West Ukrainian "fascists," that real ugliness and hatred spread from individuals to take in the mass of the population on both sides, involving both general stereotypes and real or invented memories of particular atrocities or unpleasantnesses directed against either the individuals concerned or their ancestors, friends, or neighbors in the past.

These perceptions mark a key difference between the situation in the mixed Ukrainian-Russian areas of Ukraine and that in Croatia and Bosnia before the outbreaks of the wars there. In many areas of those former Yugoslavian republics, terrible ethnic atrocities had been perpetrated on all sides (although especially by the German Nazis and their Croat Ustashe allies) during the Nazi occupation and the Chetnik and Communist resistance in 1941–45. Even more important, those atrocities in many cases were committed by members of neighboring communities, well known to their victims. Such intimacy of violence is evident, for example, in the memoirs of Milovan Djilas, and it was to be true again during the wars from 1991 to 1995.

In Ukraine from 1941 to 1945, the situation was quite different. In Yugoslavia, Nazi atrocities were overwhelmingly directed against the Serbian populations of Croatia and Bosnia (and of course against the Jews); in Ukraine, the Nazi terror tended to fall indiscriminately on the Russian minority and on the ethnic Ukrainian majority. Across most of the country, the experience of the Second World War therefore did not establish a legacy of Ukrainian-Russian hatred among neighbors. Memories of ethnic atrocities do exist in western Ukraine, where the Ukrainian national forces sometimes targeted local Russian communities (which were, however, very small). Fear of and hatred for the followers of Bandera were deliberately fostered among the Russians of Ukraine under Soviet rule. On the other hand, in 1939–41 and after 1944, the hand of Soviet repression—usually in the form of the Soviet secret police, who were either Russians or at least Russian-speaking—fell with particular savagery on the Ukrainians of western Ukraine, where anti-Soviet feeling was strongest and nationalist partisans fought with heroic determination until the early 1950s.

Fortunately, as I have already pointed out, Galicia lies at the opposite end of Ukraine from the main concentrations of the Russian population, most of which is thus shielded from the strongly anti-Russian feelings of the Galicians, just as the Galicians are shielded from having large numbers of Russians living among them. Russians in Galicia these days keep very quiet, and many have left since 1991, while Ukrainians in the Donbas are overwhelmingly non-nationalist and mainly Russian-speaking.

However, there are Ukrainian nationalist "cultural" organizations that are working to change this benign ignorance among the Russians of eastern and southern Ukraine—notably Prosvita, which ostensibly exists to promote Ukrainian language and culture, but which is also responsible for a good deal of extreme nationalist propaganda of a kind designed to worry and anger Russians. While Prosvita is apparently the biggest non-party organization in Ukraine, its more than one hundred thousand members are overwhelmingly in Kiev and western Ukraine. Its offices in eastern Ukraine are very small and generally obscure, except when a local Russian-language paper reprints some especially egregious insult that Prosvita has issued. Thus in Kharkiv, the deputy chairman of the local Prosvita organization, Bogdan Fik, told me,

> In the Ukrainian genocide and all their other crimes, the Communists always carried out a policy based on Great Russian chauvinism and the great power ambitions of the Russian people. . . .
>
> Worst of all is that Russian rule and Russian immigration has damaged our genotype. Everything that you see here—lack of order, dirty toilets—is the result of racial assimilation. Because once a man has been drawn away from his ethnos, his traditions, his language, he can no longer behave decently in any way or find a decent place in the world.[30]

In a city with a Russian majority, and 85 percent Russian-speaking (as of 1995), these did not seem to me wise words. In other parts of the world, with more excitable populations, such a statement might have already incited violence, or been used to do so. However, in both Kharkiv and Donetsk, it was striking that both the local publications of Prosvita and the local Russian nationalist papers obviously had very little financial backing (claiming a lack of both Ukrainian and Russian state interest) and were printed on paper of such poor quality as to be often barely legible. The papers of parties backed by the local business establishment, by contrast, were expensive and glossy, visible proof of not only the local economic balance of power but to a considerable extent the political one as well.

Broken Promises

There are two points for possible concern over Ukraine's future, even though their danger should by no means be exaggerated. The first relates to economic progress and prosperity—and, more important, their spread throughout the population at large. Every single opinion poll conducted in Russia and Ukraine over the past three years has shown the overwhelming majority of respondents ranking living standards and economic stability high above "national" issues (Galicia and Crimea being partial, but only partial, exceptions). The only concern that comes close to these issues in most polls is a concern for peace and a fear of war and civil war. The concern for what more idealistic or nationalist observers dismissively call "sausage issues" was indeed reflected in the results of the 1991 referendum for Ukrainian independence in the Russian-speaking areas.

However, the question of open borders with Russia is also frequently mentioned in response to both formal and informal polls—and is of tremendous importance, both economic and familial, to people in border regions such as Kharkiv (which was previously the unofficial capital of a huge region embracing several southern Russian provinces) and Luhansk. The existing customs controls are already very unpopular, although Russia is seen, quite rightly, as equally responsible for them. If there were ever an attempt to introduce a visa regime, like that of the Baltic states, there might well be a serious outburst of anger.[31]

Even more important was the promise by President Leonid Kravchuk and other Ukrainian leaders (encouraged by naive, foolish, or politically interested Western "economists") that an independent Ukraine would rapidly become prosperous, at a much faster rate than Russia.[32] This seemed plausible to Ukrainians, aware of the natural riches of their republic (especially in agriculture, thanks to the better climate) and of how much of this had been taken away by the central Soviet state and never returned in any form. Of course, for reasons that are by now too well known to need repeating, such an optimistic scenario was also nonsense.

By the end of 1993, under President Kravchuk's rule, the situation in eastern Ukraine and Crimea was developing in such a way that, had it continued, really serious trouble might have occurred sooner or later.

The reasons were partly Kravchuk's alliance with the radical national-ists, especially in education and the military, and tension with Russia over the Black Sea Fleet. Much more important, however, was the fact that the Ukrainian economy and living standards were declining at a much faster rate than those in Russia, while the currency was collapsing much faster into hyperinflation. People in border areas could see that their neighbors on the Russian side were beginning to live visibly better than them. If this had continued for several more years, it would have been very surprising had a secessionist movement not emerged.

Under President Kuchma, however, the currency has been stabilized, the most irritating aspects of Ukrainianization dropped, and relations with Russia softened. Ukraine is proceeding at an economic level which, although worse than that of Russia, is not deteriorating much faster (and economic hardship in Ukraine is softened to some extent by the better climate, allowing people to grow more of their own food).

The combination of these two factors—but especially the second—has created a widespread sense of betrayal among ordinary people in much of southern and eastern Ukraine, a feeling of having made a key decision, with critical and mostly evil results for their own lives, on the basis of false promises.

In the words of an acquaintance in Dnipropetrovsk, Sergei Seriogin, "In 1991, before the referendum, a friend from the local Rukh [nation-alist organization] went around saying, 'Vote for independence, and you'll see. In a few years we'll be so rich we'll be locking our doors with sausages.' Now when we meet I ask him, 'Eaten any nice keys recently?' He doesn't like it at all, but it's his own fault."

This disillusionment has contributed to a feeling of the pointlessness of democracy, a feeling which has also been strengthened somewhat by President Kuchma's promises to the Russian-speaking areas of Ukraine before the last elections. Kuchma was clearly elected on a platform of granting an official status for the Russian language at the national level, better relations and more-open borders with Russia, and a Ukrainian constitution with more powers for the regions (the phrase "federal sys-tem" was sometimes mentioned). None of these promises has been kept. While better relations with Russia have been partly frustrated by Russia's own actions, and a federal system was perhaps unworkable under current circumstances, Kuchma has simply gone back on his word on the language issue, partly under pressure from Ukrainian nation-alists, and partly perhaps out of his own growing identification with the Ukrainian state and language.

This partial retreat is quite understandable and also perhaps inevitable; so bitter is the opposition of the Galicians to official status for Russian that to have pushed this through might have led to very serious and destabilizing trouble. But one must also recognize that since this promise played a key part in getting Kuchma elected, it is not surprising that his Russian former supporters feel cheated.

It is disappointing that few Western diplomats with whom I spoke in Kiev saw anything wrong in principle, or dangerous in practice, in Kuchma's failure to keep this democratic promise, so far have some of them come to identify with aspects of Ukrainian nationalism.

A THREAT OF UNREST?

Given the underlying bitterness with Kiev's broken promises, on top of extreme hardship, it is not inconceivable that a mass movement of social protest might emerge somewhere in Ukraine in the future and take on a national cast.

However, this would probably take place only if a large segment of the local elites had also for some reason lost faith in their ability to get what they wanted from Kiev. To a limited degree, this happened in the mass strikes by coal miners in the Donbas in the summer of 1996, which combined two essential elements: the genuine and quite understandable fury of the miners at the fact that their wages were months in arrears, at conditions in the mines, and at rumored plans for mass closures and layoffs; and the fact that the local party of power had not only been largely excluded from patronage in Kiev, but that parts of it were under criminal investigation for their wholesale plundering of the state budget when their representative, former mine director Yukhum Zviagilsky, was acting prime minister under Kravchuk.

The situation was then made worse by the Kiev authorities' heavy-handed response to the strikes, a response motivated in part precisely by fears that the movement was headed in the direction of separatist or at least autonomist demands. However, despite the level of economic hardship and the real anger involved, it is impressive that the miners did not raise Russian national demands and calls for secession from Ukraine. As the miners explained, they do not see themselves as "Russians" in this sense, and the local elites, while anxious to put pressure on Kiev, had no desire for a rebellion and civil war.

An analogy for the future course of regional politics in eastern Ukraine may perhaps be the Indian union. Over the past fifty years,

India has experienced repeated regional, seminationalist movements in Gujarat, Tamil Nadu, and elsewhere in other parts of the country that have often centered on language issues. In West Bengal and Kerala, regional sentiment has mingled with social protest to produce support for the Communists. Yet local elites and leaders of these movements have known how to control their followers to stop well short of a demand for secession—and to some extent the whole process has become a means for particular areas, and their elites, to extract subsidies and bureaucratic positions from the central state. This game is understood by all sides; played according to certain well-defined rules; and kept within bounds partly by certain underlying factors of common religion and culture. Where these factors are weaker than elsewhere, as in Sikh Punjab, a game that begins according to the rules can get badly out of hand, with tragic and bloody consequences.

Finally, there is a question of Moscow's future policy toward Ukraine's Russians. At present, the Russian government has very few allies in eastern Ukraine, whatever some officials and "experts" in Moscow may deceive themselves into thinking. The Soviet Union had many, and would still have them if it could realistically be resurrected; but as explained, this is not the same thing as supporting today's Moscow. The large but crippled Soviet-loyalist Communist Party in eastern and southern Ukraine, and the tiny but sometimes intellectually relatively prestigious Russian nationalist groups, are united in opposition to the national government in Kiev, but otherwise they are completely opposed.

The Communists want the whole of Ukraine to reenter a close union with Russia, but on an equal basis. They are totally opposed to any area of Ukraine splitting off to join Russia and have generally backed successive Ukrainian governments over the issues of Crimea and Sevastopol. In the words of Alla Alexandrovskaya, secretary of the Kharkiv Communist Party in 1995,

> We want to see a new federation between Russia and Ukraine, but we certainly don't advocate breaking away Ukrainian territories and giving them to Russia. The question of Crimea needs to be solved at a higher level, through a new union. Similarly, though we are for a federal system within Ukraine, with real power being given to the regions, we don't want to create regional autonomies along linguistic lines. That would be to divide neighbor from neighbor and would be very dangerous for Ukraine.[33]

The Russian nationalists would also like such a union, much like the type advocated by Solzhenitsyn (minus Galicia, which they regard as "foreign" because it was not part of Russia before 1917 and is also largely not Orthodox). Failing this, however, they want to take from Ukraine as much "historically Russian" territory as possible—namely Crimea, "New Russia," and the Donbas.

The split between these two political tendencies has been one subsidiary reason for the weakness of both. Another reason is that both have been strongly hostile to the Yeltsin government and unlikely to call on it for support. The Communists regard him as one of the arch-destroyers of their beloved Soviet Union, the nationalists as a traitor to Russian national and imperial interests. Yet this raises the question whether a future Russian administration under a new president, one untainted by responsibility for the death of the Soviet Union, might have more success in trying to appeal to the Ukrainian Russians.

This question also arises because, as of the end of 1998, the Russian government had not really tried at all to stimulate a sense of "Russian-ness" in the Russians and Russian-speakers of this region, or to mobilize them against Kiev. None of the traditional means had been used: no covert funds to Russian political, social, or cultural organizations (or if such funds were distributed, to judge by the results they must have been pitifully small); no subsidized youth groups or historical societies; no attempt to set up consulates, despite appeals from local people and apparent willingness in Kiev; not even money to pay the debts of Russian television companies in Ukraine, by far Russia's biggest cultural influence, to rebroadcast Russian programming in the region.

This Russian failure in the field of television would be astonishing in a government genuinely committed to stirring up the "Russians" of Ukraine or even trying to consolidate their identity. In May 1994, 85 percent of the people in southern and eastern Ukraine—in other words, including many Ukrainian-speakers—said they liked watching the Russian state channel Ostankino, against just 21 percent for the Ukrainian first channel (not surprisingly, in view of that channel's paralyzing dullness). This is especially important because a majority of people also said that they got most of their political information through television—and Ukrainian nationalists have been full of (partly justified) criticisms that Russian television's reporting of issues such as Crimea is full of anti-Ukrainian bias. In the words of a Kharkiv-based journalist, Alexei Nestnov of the BBC Ukrainian Service,

> If a civil society here does develop, it will have to come from within and from the new business classes. . . . So far, Russian influence has played no role—there are no new Russian-backed associations, even cultural ones,

no organized attempts to maintain links. If I were in the Russian government and had their ambitions toward Ukraine, I would play this card much more wisely and thoroughly. It's extraordinary—they haven't even bothered to open a consulate here, though they promised long ago. They won't even pay for Ostankino, which is by far their biggest source of influence here. In the economic field, they simply seem to be pursuing Russian interests. There is no industrial policy toward this region, no attempt to retain ties to Russia and affection for Russia by encouraging exports to Russia from the Kharkiv-based factories, for example.[34]

This Russian failure remained the case throughout 1998 (and was also mentioned in the case of Dnipropetrovsk by Vassily Lyakh, quoted earlier). It is particularly striking when one compares it to official Russian statements about support for the "diaspora." Official Russian policy was formalized in "fundamental guidelines," a series of approaches published in August 1994. In the former Soviet Union and the West, the most widely noticed points were those stressing the need to defend Russian rights (albeit in accordance with international law) and draw the attention of international organizations to any violations. However, there was also a list of practical measures to support the Russian language and Russian culture in the "diaspora," including continuing broadcasts from Russia; support for local Russian-language television, radio, and newspapers; aid for Russian cultural societies and social organizations; and the foundation of new Russian schools and universities. These measures are similar to the approach of other states toward their compatriots in neighboring countries (for example, Hungary today, Weimar Germany in the 1920s).

The only problem is that, like so many grand Russian state policies announced in recent years, almost none of this has actually been put into effect. The only visible measure of Russian support for the Russians of Ukraine has been a provision to allow students from Sevastopol to study at Moscow University on the same basis as Russian citizens, and even this initiative was more the responsibility of Moscow mayor Yuri Luzhkov than of the Russian government.

Again, some aspects of this failure have been truly remarkable. For example, by far the most powerful, and the most popular, link between Russia and the diaspora has been Russian television. One of the very few noneconomic demonstrations I have seen in eastern Ukraine was in August 1995 against a decision to cut off rebroadcast of a much-loved Russian children's program *Good Night Children* (much like *The Muppets*) on the excuse that Ostankino had not paid its debts. It may be difficult to imagine the program's protagonist—Khryusha, a fictional pig—as presenting a very serious threat to the Ukrainian state, but stranger things have happened in history. The point here is that the Russian state has not even *tried* hard to preserve Khryusha and his friends as "agents of influence" in Ukraine.

Moreover, there has been no evidence whatsoever—not even circumstantial—for any attempt to use violent covert operations (assassinations, or "wet" operations, or even *provocatsii*) to try to cause destabilization and increase hatred and unrest; for example, by attacking Ukrainian nationalist targets in eastern Ukraine.

Despite all the talk among some circles in both Kiev and the West about Russian neoimperialism, Russian pressure, and Russian threats, in fact Russian policy toward Ukraine has been extremely restrained and moderate—if only because the Russian government lacks both the means and the will for a tougher policy. Under the weak and corrupt rule of Boris Yeltsin, the government has had the greatest difficulty achieving sufficient unity, discipline, and indeed vision in its own ranks to formulate any coherent policy at all, in any field.

RELIGION

In the past, the issue of religious allegiance was of course a critical factor in the political development of Ukraine and the state loyalties of its people. Indeed, for premodern populations, it was *the* critical issue, the one that did the most to shape people's later national identification. In Ukraine, the Uniate church played the leading role under Polish and Habsburg rule in shaping the distinct culture and identity of Galician Ukrainians. In other parts of Ukraine, the common loyalty to Orthodoxy was the key issue in leading Ukrainians to accept Russian rule, and in shaping the cultural closeness that is so evident among the Ukrainians and Russians of the great cities of eastern and southern Ukraine.

Today, however, the importance of this factor has greatly diminished, for the simple reason that religious belief has declined. After a brief but intense flareup of religious observance in the last years of the Soviet Union and the first years of independence, by 1994 fewer than 30 percent of Ukrainians were declaring in opinion polls an allegiance to any of the traditional churches, with the falloff most evident among those of Orthodox heritage.[35]

This waning of religious allegiance is also true in Russia and most of the other European former Soviet republics, where people of a religious bent are just as likely to join a new evangelical church or exotic cult as they are to return to the faith of their grandparents. This is partly a result of the legacy of Soviet rule, but more important, of a general pattern of modernization that has affected the whole of industrialized Europe.

The Christian religious divisions of contemporary Ukraine are too complicated to be discussed in any detail in a book of limited length. Basically, ever since the expulsion of Poles from the country, there has been a three-way division of religious affiliation in Ukraine. In Galicia (but spreading to other parts of Ukraine) are the Uniates (Greek Catholics), whose origins were described in the previous chapter. Orthodox in liturgy, but loyal to the pope, they are exclusively ethnic Ukrainians and tend to be heart-and-soul Ukrainian nationalists. Their stronger commitment is shown by the fact that in opinion polls, the numbers professing the Uniate faith are around 20 percent of the total number of those expressing a traditional Christian religious belief, although, as a proportion of the population, people of Uniate descent are much fewer. Because of their links to Ukrainian nationalism, the Uniates were savagely persecuted under Stalin, who confiscated their churches and gave them to the Orthodox. Today, this has led to repeated clashes, as the Uniates try to recover their stolen property from Orthodox congregations, and has split the religious dimension of Ukrainian nationalism down the middle.

Until the early 1990s, the Orthodox church in Ukraine was simply the Russian Orthodox church, loyal to the patriarch of Moscow. Under the Ukrainian Republic of 1917–20, an independent (Autocephalous) Ukrainian Orthodox church was set up. The church was crushed under Soviet rule, but it survived in the Ukrainian emigration. A new Autocephalous church was founded after Ukrainian independence in 1991 by Metropolitan Filaret of Kiev, with the encouragement of President Kravchuk; this church is also exclusively ethnic Ukrainian.

As of 1998, however, around three-quarters of parishes and believers remain loyal to the Ukrainian branch of the Russian Orthodox church. This church of course contains both Ukrainian and Russian believers. The progress of the new Autocephalous church has been hindered by continuing deep splits with the Autocephalous church of the emigration and its followers in Ukraine, who accuse the Kiev patriarchate and especially Patriarch Filaret of being former KGB agents, morally corrupt, and much too close to the former Communist authorities.

Clashes over the occupation of church property have led to violence between Orthodox and Uniates and between Autocephalous

Orthodox and Russian Orthodox. The truth is, however, that the "worshippers" on either side have been, in general, too elderly to do each other much harm. The exception has been when political groups have become closely involved in the conflict.

Thus in July 1996, the Autocephalous church attempted to bury its recently deceased patriarch, Volodymyr, in the cathedral of St. Sophia in Kiev, which is the source of a dispute between the church and the Russian Orthodox, because the government had said the church could not use the cathedral. When riot police blocked the way of the funeral procession, young activists belonging to the Ukrainian neofascist movement UNA/UNSO tried to push through, using the coffin lid as a shield. The police lashed out with indiscriminate force, and several dozen people were injured. The patriarch was then buried in the pavement outside the main gate of St. Sophia, a spot that has now become a shrine for the Autocephalous church. I witnessed this scene myself and felt as if I had been transported back many centuries.[36]

This incident caused a tremendous furor in the press and political circles, but when I visited churches in the countryside east of Kiev—those loyal to Moscow and those loyal to Kiev—the worshippers did not seem to care much, apart from cursing the politicians. Indeed, most of the more elderly worshippers in particular seemed unclear about what the whole church split consisted of anyway. The rest of the population was almost wholly indifferent to the religious issue involved. When the monument to Volodymyr was unveiled in July 1996, some fifteen hundred people attended—a large crowd by Ukrainian standards, but tiny in proportion to Kiev's approximately 2.5 million inhabitants.[37]

In the first months of the Kravchuk administration, the state gave strong support to the Autocephalous church, but backed off to some extent after failing to get recognition from the patriarch of Constantinople (the titular leader of Orthodox everywhere) and failing to win over most Ukrainian Orthodox believers. Under Kuchma, the state has taken a decidedly neutral line. In his words, "Appeals are again being heard for the government to set down a policy on religion. Behind this are attempts to press for a state church, to create divisions between one church that is ours and another that is alien. But our policy is to create equal conditions for all churches and ensure peace between all confessions."[38] After the clash over the patriarch's funeral, Kuchma declared, "We must not return to an earlier, discredited course of redistributing churches and church property and groundlessly taking it away from one and giving it to another. This cannot and must not be the sphere of state activity. . . . In Ukraine, just as in any other democratic country, the church is legislatively separate from the state and is totally independent of it in its religious activity."[39]

Many Ukrainian nationalists vehemently disagree with this position and believe in having a national church. However, their case is weakened by both the Uniate-Orthodox split, which makes a national church, as such, an impossibility, and a certain incongruity about the whole idea of creating a state-backed national church at the beginning of the twenty-first century, in an age when the great majority of Ukrainians are no longer Christians in any real sense. (Both the Autocephalous church and the Russian Orthodox church have denounced the increasing presence of Protestant evangelical missionaries from the West.)

Both the Russian state and, later, the Communist Party used the Orthodox church to further their imperial aims, and a great many Russians today—from Boris Yeltsin and Yuri Luzhkov on down—are also using Orthodoxy either for essentially state and nonreligious reasons (for example, to strengthen the Russian national identity) or simply for their own personal political ends (for example, Luzhkov's rebuilding of the monstrous Cathedral of Christ the Savior in Moscow). The situation is the same in Ukraine, with the difference that the ethnic nationalist element is much stronger. Thus Oxana Khomchouk, a Ukrainian church historian at the Ukrainian Academy of Sciences, told me,

> I have always been an atheist, but I baptized my son in the Autocephalous church because I believe that in this time all true Ukrainians, whether or not they are believers, should do everything to create one Ukrainian national church independent of Moscow. If Ukraine is to be an independent, united country, it must have an independent, united church, just like every other nation. . . . What matters is the inner understanding of the national idea, which for me is a kind of religion. . . . The Russians in Ukraine of course want to stay with the Moscow church so as to continue their imperial rule, and the only Ukrainian Orthodox believers in Ukraine who do not see this and want to stay with the Moscow patriarchate are stupid *babas* [grandmothers] who just don't want anything to change.[40]

This passage illustrates a frequent problem with more radical Ukrainian nationalists, already alluded to in this chapter with reference to culture. They tend to think that for Ukraine the path of Western modernity and development simply means getting away from Moscow. They do not realize that very often their own ideas risk pulling Ukraine in a half-circle, away from the modern West and back toward a much older and darker Europe, not Russian or Soviet, but also not to be remembered with much nostalgia. Compared to this, Kuchma's looks the more modern and progressive vision—especially since, in the end, religious allegiance will not in fact decide Ukraine's fate one way or another. All it can do is add a certain extra and unnecessary element of irritation to relations between Ukrainians and Russians in Ukraine.

3

THE RUSSIAN-SPEAKING
AREAS OF UKRAINE

To understand the Russian-speaking areas of Ukraine, and indeed the country as a whole, one must recognize that Ukraine is very regionalized, not in a formal and constitutional sense, but in terms of sentiment and the real structures of power. Many Ukrainians could still be plausibly described as *tuteshni*—that is to say, as people whose primary identification is with their locality rather than with their state or "nation."[1] Or as a Western diplomat in Kiev put it to me in an April 1994, off-the-record conversation,

> No one can really say what is happening in Ukraine, or where the country as a whole is heading—as you can in Poland, for example—because no one can grasp the country as a whole. The different areas are totally different. The people in some of them hardly know each other, and the politicians have completely different priorities. That doesn't mean the country will break up—what happens is that the center and the regions circle slowly around each other, trying to extract concessions. What it does mean, though, is that it makes it even more difficult to carry out economic reform—coherent economic reform, let alone radical reforms. There are just too many different interests involved, all of them powerful, and none of them capable of gaining overall dominance.

In this way, Ukrainians—and Ukrainian-Russians—across much of the country have retained some of the features of their premodern peasant ancestors. A key reason for this is that Soviet rule encouraged strong feelings of identification with the city on the one hand and the whole Soviet Union on the other, but weak ones with Ukraine. As already pointed out, this was also true for Ukrainian-Russians, who identified neither with Russia nor Ukraine, but with their city and with the whole Union. In the words of Grigory Nemiria about the Donbas,

> For the Donbas, the real economic and political center was the Soviet one, in Moscow. Kiev was just the regional administrative center, not of great importance. So when we became independent, there had to be a major and very difficult re-evaluation of which center to look to. It was made even more complicated by the fact that for us here, regional identity was always more important than national identity. The fact that you came from the Donbas was more important than that you were Russian or Ukrainian; so of course the breakup of the Soviet Union also meant a raising of this regional identity and loyalty. . . . In any case, most people here honestly couldn't say what they are ethnically, because most families, like mine, are mixed.[2]

The Russian-speaking areas of Ukraine do have certain features in common, as described in the last chapter, but they are very far from being united in terms of either political or economic interests, except in their strong but unfocused dislike of the radical nationalists; this feeling was shown in the vote for Kuchma in 1994. But when it comes to the mobilization of these sentiments into stable parties or public protests, it must be stressed that since independence there has not been a single regional party or movement, whether in defense of political, economic, or linguistic interests, that has spanned the whole area. Instead, one of the most bitter feuds within the Ukrainian political elite since independence has been fought out between the dominant political-economic groups (or "parties of power," as they are known in the former Soviet Union) of the eastern regions of Donetsk and Dnipropetrovsk (in Russian, Dnyepropetrovsk).

A FORTUNATE GEOGRAPHY: GALICIA AND CENTRAL UKRAINE

Those who have seen a clear black-and-white divide between east and west Ukraine have missed three important elements of Ukrainian political geography: the fact that nationalist Galicia does not make up the whole of "west Ukraine" and that its specific variant of nationalism has very limited cultural and economic appeal outside its own region, the critical importance of central Ukraine, and the divisions within the whole of the Russian-speaking area.

What is often described as "west Ukraine" in more superficial Western analyses really only applies to Galicia and to a lesser extent Volhynia—

the two provinces that were part of Poland until 1939 and in the case of Galicia had previously been subject to Austria (and had been under Catholic influence since the Middle Ages). Galicia also suffered a brutal Russian military occupation during the First World War, followed by a ruthless Soviet antipartisan struggle after 1944.

As repeated election results have shown, it is only in these regions (and to some degree in the city of Kiev, because of its large concentration of nationalist intelligentsia and civil servants) that support for a radical, ethnic-based, and potentially antidemocratic version of Ukrainian nationalism is really overwhelming. This is not true even of the immediately neighboring regions, whether Transcarpathia on the Hungarian border to the southwest of Galicia, or Khmelnitsky and Zhytomyr to the east. Furthermore, Galicia is relatively small: The city of Lviv had a population of 787,000 according to the census of 1989; but the Donbas (Donetsk and Luhansk together) had a population of more than 7 million.

Consequently, many genuinely patriotic Ukrainians elsewhere in Ukraine regard radical nationalism as a specifically Galician product, heavily influenced by the Polish and Uniate tradition, and culturally and historically separate from the rest of (Orthodox or previously Orthodox) Ukraine. A common insulting term for the Galician nationalists in eastern Ukraine is "the *Pans*," after the Polish word for "mister" and previously for "lord" (this is especially hurtful because the Galician Ukrainian nationalists actually originated and spent much of their history in bitter struggles with the Poles).

Critics also point out—and quite rightly—that Galician nationalism is not "more Western" simply because it is geographically closer to Central Europe; the Central Europe from which Galician nationalism derived was that of the 1890s to the 1930s, and isolation under Soviet rule has hindered its modernization.

Galician and Galician-style Ukrainian nationalism today does indeed retain certain worrying features of the extreme "integral" nationalism of the 1930s. These elements were played down in the late 1980s and early 1990s, when the nationalist umbrella organization Rukh seemed to have a brief chance of appealing to a majority of Ukrainians and of coming to power. However, with Rukh's failure, extremist platforms have resurfaced in some of the various nationalist parties.[3]

The result is not just that aspects of Galician Ukrainian nationalism today remain worryingly extreme and ethnicist,[4] but also that Galicians are actually behind, not ahead of the rest of the country when it comes to some aspects of economic reform—as the International Finance

Corporation found to its surprise in the case of privatization. Having set up its first regional project office in Lviv because it assumed privatization would go fastest there, it then discovered that it was actually in the east where the local administrative elites showed the greatest interest (or rather, self-interest) and dynamism in this regard.

One aspect of this Galician distinctiveness is language: Galicians sometimes claim to speak the "purest" Ukrainian, and this has been reiterated by some Western observers. In fact, the Ukrainian dialect on which modern literary and educational Ukrainian has been based is situated not unnaturally in the center of the country, in the region of Poltava. The people of that region regard the dialect of Galicia as a heavily Polonized version of Ukrainian, just as they regard the language spoken in much of eastern and southern Ukraine, Surzhik, as a cross between Ukrainian and Russian —which indeed it is.

It is this central region of Ukraine—and not the west or the east— that has provided the dominant elements in the Ukrainian administrations since independence (both Presidents Kravchuk and Kuchma come from this region, as do all of their likely successors), and could be said to have saved the country. If Galicia and the Russian-speaking areas of Donetsk or Kharkiv—let alone Crimea—had been geographically contiguous to each other, the unity and peace of Ukraine would have been in serious doubt, given the very real hatreds that exist between the ordinary people of these areas.

But in the words of Grigory Nemiria, sweeping his hand over a map, "Fortunately, Lviv is at that end, Donetsk at this end, and there is all this space in-between." The two areas are separated by a broad belt of territory, five hundred miles wide and stretching from Khmelnitsky to Dnipropetrovsk, in which most of the people, although ethnically Ukrainian (and mostly Ukrainian-speaking) and committed to Ukrainian independence, have a much milder and less ethnic version of Ukrainian nationalism and a much calmer and friendlier attitude toward Russians. Thus in 1994, while Kravchuk got more than 60 percent of the vote in Galicia and Volhynia, and Kuchma a majority in the east and south, neither candidate achieved a majority in the eight central regions.

THE "PARTIES OF POWER"

Just as "western Ukraine" is by no means a unitary region, so political power and popular attitudes and identities in the mainly Russian-speaking east and south are divided among several different centers of roughly equivalent importance in terms of population (except for the Donbas, which is much bigger) and political weight. Even politically aware people in these regions are astonishingly ignorant of what is happening next door, so to speak. As of 1998, this included the small number of active Russian nationalists, whom one would have expected to have a strong interest in cooperation or at least exchange of information.

The regions have their own separate political elites, usually called the "parties of power," and different political "clans" grouped around particular industries and economic interests (sometimes criminal), particular leaders, or both. The elites in different regions have also developed their own banks, which in turn have gained control of major sectors of both industry and the media, both in their own region and in Kiev. One of the most powerful examples to date has been Privatbank of Dnipropetrovsk, which provided financial backing for the political clan of Pavlo Lazarenko and, in turn, benefited from his time as prime minister.

Although they contain many former Communist officials, these groups do *not* represent the Communist Party. Ukraine's Communist Party (together with the more centrist Socialist Party) has by far the largest support of any party in eastern and southern Ukraine. It is the only mass political organization—but except to an extent in Luhansk, Communists do not hold any share of local power (even in Donetsk, they held just 15 out of 75 seats on the local council as of 1998). The party is now made up of the hard-line (or, if you will, consistent and honest) Communists who did not abandon the party during its collapse and banning in 1991. They lost their state posts and did not benefit from privatization; therefore, they have remained poor. Many of them are in fact recent recruits to the senior ranks of the party itself, precisely because they were idealists who had joined in response to the early promise of Gorbachev's perestroika and then became disgusted as their superiors used their positions to leave the sinking Communist ship and enrich themselves under the new order.

This cadre tends to come from the struggling local professional classes, badly hit by the collapse of state wages and services. They are also Soviet loyalists, not Russian nationalists, and appear sincere when they say they want a union with Russia on terms of equality. They seem to be undergoing a certain process of "social-democratization," not in terms of their ideology, which largely remains mastodonic, but because their exclusion from both central and regional power has turned them *faute de mieux* into representatives of local protest over social issues such as payment of pensions, closure of kindergartens, and decay of public services. This activism alone has been enough to give them a certain prestige in the local populace, even among those who do not share their belief in either the resurrection of the Soviet Union or their statist economic policies.

The four main centers of Russian-speaking Ukraine—Dnipropetrovsk, the Donbas, Kharkiv, and Odessa—will be described below; because of their special character and international importance, Crimea and Sevastopol are covered separately in chapter 5. For brevity's sake, I have excluded from this survey smaller centers, such as Mariupol and Zaporizhzhia, which also have their own distinct clans and leaderships.

These regional centers are often in rivalry for power in Kiev. In particular, the feud between the Dnipropetrovsk and Donbas groups, each linked to organized crime, has contributed to the only serious social unrest in Ukraine since independence and, perhaps, to the country's only political violence. This, regional struggle for central power, rather than influence from Moscow or even local Russian sentiment as such, could prove the biggest threat to political stability if these groups try to stir up nationalist passions to defend their own positions or fight their way back into power.

There is little likelihood of that happening as long as a local party of power has a reasonable share of influence with and patronage from the central government. But in June 1993, a feeling among local elites in the Donbas that they were being cut out of central power combined with economic discontent among the region's coal miners and anger at Ukrainian nationalism to produce a major strike, which publicized the miners' economic demands but also had political overtones.

The strike helped cause the dismissal of Prime Minister Kuchma, a former factory director from Dnipropetrovsk, and his replacement as acting prime minister in September 1993 by Deputy Prime Minister Yukhum Zviagilsky, a former mine director from Donetsk and representative of the Donbas party of power. Upon acquiring the premiership, Zviagilsky promptly set about removing Kuchma's Dnipropetrovsk appointees from the central bureaucracy.

One of the problems about the new elites in both Russia and Ukraine, and a major potential cause of instability, is that they are greedy —and greedy to an irrational extent that sometimes goes so far that it threatens their own interests. By May 1994, talk of Zviagilsky's corruption was so widespread that President Kravchuk replaced him. After Kuchma was elected president in July 1994, he launched an investigation of Zviagilsky and his clan, and Zviagilsky fled to Israel just ahead of the lifting of his parliamentary immunity. (He returned in March 1997 after his immunity was restored.) The Kuchma administration arrested some smaller players and in turn purged the central administration of Zviagilsky's Donbas appointees, returning Dnipropetrovsk men to Kiev. However, members of the Zviagilsky clan remained in power in the Donbas, now led by Vladimir Shcherban, former director of a state shop, whom Zviagilsky picked to be deputy mayor and who later became governor of the region. Shcherban also took over the leadership of Zviagilsky's local commercial interests. Leaders of these interests used their bureaucratic and political power to divert state subsidies and privatized companies into their own pockets, thereby getting a stranglehold on much of the local private sector.

By the autumn of 1996, the dominance and indeed near monopoly of the central government by this Dnipropetrovsk group was seen by some Western observers as threatening economic progress and even political stability. This had become even more the case after Kuchma's old associate Pavlo Lazarenko, the former head of the regional administration and deputy prime minister in the first two years of Kuchma's administration, became prime minister of Ukraine in May 1996. Lazarenko had already introduced around 60 officials and politicians from his group into the central ministries and presidential apparatus. By August 1996 this number had jumped to 160; by autumn, it reportedly rose to more than 200.[5]

Lazarenko was originally director of a collective farm and therefore, like former president Kravchuk, from a more culturally Ukrainian and Ukrainian-language rural background. However, the rural ex-Soviet elites are also some of the most economically conservative and antireformist groups in the country, and Lazarenko's influence in the central government has helped stifle economic change through both conservatism and corruption.[6] Certainly the mayor of Dnipropetrovsk, Mykola Shvets, and other senior officials whom I interviewed in the city (all members of Lazarenko's clan) in August 1995 gave the impression of being completely Soviet in spirit by way of their denial of unpleasant but obvious truths (such as that the salaries of teachers and other state employees in the city were months in arrears), their complete lack of ideas about economic reform, and their authoritarian attitude toward carrying out state policies.

Sherman Garnett, who described the Lazarenko clan's influence as "bloodsucking," declared in October 1996 that "this group from Dnipropetrovsk is choking off benefits that should be trickling down to normal folks by lining their own pockets. They are prolonging the agony of the change that Ukraine is trying to make by a systematic looting of assets."[7] Just as Zviagilsky was accused of making tens of millions of dollars from exporting state coal and from selling cheap subsidized Russian oil on the world market and pocketing the difference, so the greatest accusations of corruption against Lazarenko focused on his decision to allocate a large share in the state-controlled import of natural gas to a Dnipropetrovsk company, Unified Electrical Systems, run by an old associate. A government-ordered reorganization of gas distribution in May 1996 reportedly made UES one of just two Ukrainian companies allowed to sell gas to industry and also granted it tax exemptions as an importer of essential goods. Other regions were infuriated—especially the Donbas, which is the biggest gas user in Ukraine and has its own local gas company, Intergaz. As a result of the reorganization, the firm was effectively bankrupted. The episode was typical of how the semi-Soviet, semicapitalist nature of the post-Soviet "market economy" in Ukraine (as elsewhere in the former Soviet Union) has allowed corrupt monopolies to flourish.[8] In such a fashion, Ukraine forms part of a pattern of "crony capitalism," which has undermined many national economies and has contributed greatly to the recent wave of economic crises around the world.

With the combination of his traditional power in the region and his newly acquired ability to use central power and patronage, Lazarenko was able to exercise an extremely tight control both over appointed officialdom and over which candidates run for office in Dnipropetrovsk, with the result that the great majority of local elected officials are his allies or clients. The managers of the local industrial plants are also closely tied to him, and this administrative-managerial elite has gone into private commercial and financial activity, creating private banks—most notably Privatbank, founded by Dnipropetrovsk industrial managers and now a major financial power in Ukraine. Through these new financial institutions and the administration of state contracts and loans, this administrative-managerial elite has come to control much of local private business.

In June 1996, the party of power in Donetsk, led by Vladimir Shcherban, head of the local administration (sometimes dubbed "governors"), struck back by orchestrating another major strike by the miners. Whether by the leaders' own design, or because in the meantime miners' anger, misery, and frustration had worsened, this strike was much larger and included blocking roads and railway tracks by demonstrators.

The government replied with a heavy hand, arresting hundreds of strikers and accusing them of "threatening Ukraine's territorial integrity," although demands for local autonomy and closer relations with Russia, while present, had been secondary to economic grievances such as mine closures and pay arrears. Vladimir Shcherban was dismissed as governor and replaced by an unelected central appointee.

Lazarenko also suggested publicly that the movement in Donetsk was behind a June 1996 car-bomb assassination attempt. Assuming that this was a real attempt, and not (as many suspected) a faked attack by Lazarenko's men intended to justify a state crackdown in the Donbas, Lazarenko's assertion may have been the case in a sense—not because the striking miners had anything to do with the bombing as such, but because the Donetsk party of power is intertwined with the region's private sector, which is intertwined, in turn, with organized crime. These groups were very angry indeed with the prosecution of Zviagilsky and his associates, with Lazarenko's policy toward Donetsk, and finally with the gas contract. Whatever the truth behind the assassination attempt, there was nothing faked about an incident at Donetsk airport a few weeks later. Yevhen Shcherban (apparently no relation of Vladimir, but closely linked to him), head of the major local group of companies Dyelo Vsyekh and also reportedly the biggest boss of local organized crime, was shot dead with his wife. The assailants have not been found.

These kinds of parties of power are to be found all over Ukraine and Russia, although rarely are they either as tight and disciplined or as wealthy and powerful as the Dnipropetrovsk party of power has become under Kuchma and Lazarenko. However, while these "old-new" elite groups across the former Soviet Union have benefited enormously from their ability to twist privatization and other free-market processes through their grip on the post-Soviet government and bureaucracy, their close links to the local administrations and central state officials also leave them vulnerable to shifts in political power.

For example, it is thought that private banks in both Russia and Ukraine, including some of those regarded as the most powerful, are in fact highly dependent on government accounts and "soft" loans, extracted from the state treasury by a mixture of influence, favors, and outright corruption. This gives the central government and, to a lesser extent, local governments tremendous power, and it means that the financial elites simply have to involve themselves in politics if they wish to survive. Their situation can be compared in some respects to that of English noblemen in the fifteenth and sixteenth centuries, as portrayed by Shakespeare. One wonders why they always came to the royal court and got themselves involved in intrigues and civil wars, when this so often resulted in their losing not just their lands but their heads. Why didn't they just sit quietly in the countryside cultivating their estates? The answer is that in a basically lawless society, they didn't dare be cowards. Much of their wealth depended on royal favors, grants, offices, and monopolies, which could be secured only by a presence in court politics. Moreover, even in their own regions, the noblemen were surrounded by a ring of enemies hoping for their downfall and intriguing at court themselves to bring this about; nobles could ward off these plotters only with the help of central protection and patronage.

Then again, there was always the possibility that a local elite who was thoroughly excluded, threatened, and infuriated or a group of outsiders would go outside the elite system altogether and call on the hungry and perennially discontented peasantry to rise in revolt. The analogy in the case of Ukraine would obviously be an excluded local group stirring up mass protest, either for an economic cause, local autonomy, or—in the very last but, fortunately at present, very remote eventuality—secession and union with Russia. Such an "appeal to the masses" has already occurred twice in the Donbas miners' strikes, once in 1993, and again more seriously in the summer of 1996.

The very tightness and exclusiveness of such post-Soviet parties of power, with their grip on so many aspects of local life, means that outsiders who become wealthy without their patronage, but who are excluded from the official patronage they enjoy, resent them extremely and develop a passionate desire to get a grip on state power themselves. According to Sherman Garnett, it has been estimated that real political and economic power in Ukraine is enjoyed by a group of men (almost all are male) which may number as few as two hundred.[9]

This narrowness of this group of "ins" naturally creates a great ring of disappointed and aspiring "outs" in the regions. Maneuvers among the different parties of power for office and influence in Kiev also give such regional outsiders the chance to develop powerful central allies of their own—the exemplification of Tip O'Neill's maxim that "all politics is local." In the words of a cynical local journalist in 1995,

> Today, one pack of wolves is feasting on the body of the state, and very happy about it; but outside the ring, there are always other wolves waiting. At the moment, they can do nothing, because they are isolated. But what if they combine in a pack of their own, with support from the center? After all, we are supposed to be a democracy. The Party of Power

can influence elections, it can buy them, it can even rig them to some extent, but it can't control them completely. Some day, the outsiders will get their chance.[10]

In Dnipropetrovsk, a classical example of such an "outsider" is Gennady Balashov, a local Russian businessman and would-be politician who was narrowly defeated by a representative of the party of power in the 1995 mayoral elections. Balashov owns a chain of shops, fast-food establishments, slot-machine halls, and a discotheque, and is hoping to buy major shares in local industry as part of the slow-moving privatization process. "The local elite will certainly try to block me, and given the way privatization here works," he observed, "they have plenty of opportunities to keep it in their own pockets."

Although obviously a wealthy man on a local scale, Balashov considers himself a representative of small businessmen against the "barons," the men who can use their state connections to make the really big profits, which come from energy and raw materials exports. He ran for mayor on a platform of populism, anti-elitism, defense of the Russian language, and a mild kind of Russian national sentiment allied to local patriotism —a desire to restore the glories of the Yekaterinoslav of the past. His shops all have names that reflect this history, such as Potemkinskaya and Yekaterinskaya. In his words,

> I am a Russian, but my mother is Ukrainian and I do not consider myself a Russian nationalist. I have given my shops these names because they reflect our traditions here in Dnipropetrovsk. If we had kept the name of Yekaterinoslav, we would also have kept that city's wealth and glory. Today, I travel all over the world, and I keep seeing how people don't like or respect Russians; but I also see signs of how Russia before the revolution was a great country, and then when Russians traveled they were indeed respected. . . .
>
> I strongly support an official status for the Russian language, at the very least at the regional level, not just because it is the language of so many people here, but because it has been a central part of the life of this city since its foundation. . . . But despite all the wrong actions of the nationalists, there are no ethnic divisions or tensions here as yet. Most people are like me, a mixture of Russian and Ukrainian, as this town has always been. And if only for that reason, many of us favor a new Union, or at least a close relationship between Russia and Ukraine. . . .
>
> If the central government here goes on with forced Ukrainianization, then there could one day be a problem. The population here is peaceful, but then up to now, no one has tried to mobilize them, to stir them up. Russia herself has shown no interest in this. But if the day came, then

Moscow might well be able to create some kind of movement in east Ukraine with money and support, because many people here are really fed up, and find a new Bogdan Khmelnitsky to lead it.[11]

A clear implicit threat—and perhaps a personal dream of which he may not have been fully conscious—lies behind Balashov's words. Whether he and people like him would ever take the risk of actively supporting an alliance with Moscow seems questionable, especially in view of their own Ukrainian family ties, but it is obviously worth keeping in mind, especially since, as Balashov said, Russia has not yet even tried to play this card. For the moment, however, it seems more likely that such "outsiders" would look for allies in Kiev—for example, rivals to succeed Kuchma for the presidency, such as former prime minister (and former Ukrainian KGB chief) Yevhen Marchuk, or Lazarenko himself.

From the point of view of Ukrainian—and Russian—political stability, the other thing to remember about businessmen-politicians such as Mr. Balashov is that they live in a very violent world in which their own chances of personal survival are less than those of soldiers in many wars. Getting into the back of Balashov's car one time, I found myself sitting on a sawed-off, pump-action shotgun. His bodyguards were all armed, and during the election campaign for mayor, shots were fired into his house as a warning. In the case of Yevhen Shcherban, as noted, the shots were not a warning.

If the contract killings that are so much a part of the business world do spread into politics on a major scale, not only will instability in itself be a result, but they could also open the way for Moscow to use such violence as a cover for covert destabilization operations of its own—should the Russian government ever decide on or be provoked into adopting such a strategy.

DNIPROPETROVSK

The political base of Lazarenko and Balashov lies halfway down the great river Dnieper in east-central Ukraine and was once another great center of Soviet industry. In Dnipropetrovsk (population 1.18 million; region, 3.9 million)[12] the main product of its great combine harvester factory these days is the "Kravchushki" (an unflattering reference to President Kravchuk and his hapless stewardship of the Ukrainian economy), the small metal luggage carts Ukrainians use when they travel to Odessa, Moscow, and even Istanbul to buy goods to resell at home. In the nearby town of Novomoskovsky (New Moscow), I passed one after another immense heap of pots and pans being sold by the roadside; the local kitchenware factory, unable to pay its workers with money, had like so many others reverted to paying them in kind.

The city of Dnipropetrovsk is largely Russian and overwhelmingly Russian-speaking, but as a whole this area is less Russified than other parts of the east and south. This is partly because it is closer to the traditionally Ukrainian areas and further from Russia, which meant that after the defeat of the Tatars it was settled by a more purely Ukrainian population, and partly because to some extent it was settled by Ukrainians even before the Tatar defeat, as the nearby elites (*starshyna*) of the Zaporozhian Cossacks turned from their seminomadic, piratical ways to settled agriculture in the eighteenth century. Pride in the Zaporozhian tradition is strong in the region and has been exploited by the Ukrainian nationalist parties.

Like its neighbors, Kirovohrad and Dniprodzerzhynsk, this city is an extreme rarity in the former Soviet Union in that it still bears the name of a leading Communist—Grigory Petrovsky, interior minister of the USSR's Russian republic, president of Soviet Ukraine, and a man with a great deal of both Ukrainian and Russian blood on his hands—and there are no official plans to change this. Stranger still, the first two towns are named after Russians, and the third after a Pole, "Iron Felix" Dzierzinski (in Russian, Feliks Dzerzhinskii), founder of the Soviet secret police.

The reason is that these cities lie in the largely unpopulated steppe that was conquered and settled in the later eighteenth century by the tsars, who gave the cities they founded in this region their own names or those of their spouses: Dnipropetrovsk was Yekaterinoslav, founded by Prince Potemkin in honor of Catherine the Great, and contains a large and beautiful cathedral of St. Catherine in her honor; Kirovohrad was Yelisavetgrad. A third city in this area was Alexandropol, named after Alexander I; in Soviet times this was given the good Ukrainian name of Zaporizhzhia, after the nearby rapids on the river (now submerged by a great artificial lake) and the Cossacks who used to live "beyond" them.

The names of the other cities are of course deeply embarrassing to Ukrainian nationalists and hurtful to local people with a sense of what Communist rule did to Ukraine, but it is now very difficult to rename them. Yekaterinoslav, for example, was briefly named Sicheslav by the Ukrainian government in 1918, after the Cossack base (or *sich*) that used to be in the region. Ukrainian nationalist intellectuals claim to have found evidence that Dnipropetrovsk was founded 360 years ago but differ on what it was called.

Some local people have also suggested a neutral compromise, such as "Dniproslav" (just as Donetsk, after being called "Stalino" from 1924 to 1961, was renamed after its river). Many local Russian intellectuals, however, say that the cities must revert to their old imperial names, which are after all bound up with much of their history. This is very difficult not just for Ukrainian nationalists but for the Ukrainian state, because it might serve as an argument for Russian nationalists who claim that because this area was conquered and settled by Russia, it is in some sense "Russian land."

The strong local Communist Party, for its part, of course wants the city names to remain as they are. Thanks to party members, and a general local feeling of not wanting to be dictated to by "those ——— *Pans,*" a massive statue of Lenin still stands (as of 1995) in the main street, as indeed he most likely still stands in all the cities of eastern Ukraine—a curious thing in a state where one branch of its national ideology now accuses the state he founded of having committed "genocide" against Ukraine.

The arguments concerning the names sometimes have their comical side. Thus Vadim Ryzhkov, a local journalist favoring the "Dniproslav" compromise, wrote an article in a local Russian-language newspaper in 1995 satirizing both sides (but especially the Ukrainian nationalists) by suggesting mischievously that the only "authentic" and "original" name was that of a Tatar fort that once stood nearby, called Koidaq, which he claimed means "Sheep's Hill," and that this therefore ought to be the name of the city. This produced a letter from representatives of the local branches of Rukh and Prosvita, Yvan Shulik and Serhii Dovgal, seemingly incoherent in their apoplectic rage, accusing Ryzhkov of "[c]ontributing to the degradation of society. . . . We consider that he is guilty of harming public morale and national harmony, serving the Russian empire, increasing public misery, diverting the moral orientation of the people from their historical-national roots, which is reflected in the unbelievable rise in crime, other aspects of degradation, evil lies."[13]

In other parts of the world such words might be the prelude to bullets, but in Dnipropetrovsk most local people did not seem to take the whole question seriously, or indeed to be very interested in it. I talked on the street to a group of three middle-aged men, old friends—a math teacher, an engineer, and a "scientific worker." All three were a mixture of Ukrainian and Russian, and all had voted for Kuchma in the presidential election. They disagreed on the name, the teacher saying, "I don't see the point of change—nobody remembers who Petrovsky was anyway—but if they insist, let's have a referendum and see what the majority thinks." The engineer wanted to go back to Yekaterinoslav, "a fine old name, with a fine sound." The scientist wanted to compromise on Dnyeproslav, "so that they'll all stop arguing about it." Yet, as they all agreed, "It's certainly not going to make us quarrel. It's really not important, and God knows we've got better things to worry about." They all referred to the activists and politicians on the different sides as "them," as if they were aliens pursuing obscure quarrels on a distant planet.

DONETSK

This region represents by far the biggest concentration of population in the whole of Ukraine. Including neighboring and closely linked Luhansk, the "Donbas" contains a total of more than 7 million people (Donetsk city, 1.12 million), or almost 16 percent of the whole population of Ukraine in only two of its twenty-five regions. They are 44 percent Russian, and in 1989 two-thirds gave Russian as their native language.

In the past, this was also the most powerful economic region of Ukraine, but the decline of its worn-out, expensive coal mines is increasing arrears of wages, unemployment, poverty, and casualties among those still at work. As equipment wears out and safety rules are ignored, Donbas coal has become the most expensive in Europe in terms of lives lost per million tons mined—in 1995, 4.7 lives, to be precise. During that year, 345 Donbas miners were killed and another 6,700 injured.[14]

I myself reached the coal face at the Tenth Capitolina mine by crawling for some two hundred yards on my hands and knees, and this is by no means the oldest and most decrepit mine. Before going down, I promised the chief engineer that I wouldn't break anything. "Oh, that's all right," he replied grimly, "It was all broken long ago." The miners of the Donbas work in conditions that would break most men and do not encourage a respect for human life. If they ever really get angry and rally behind a cause, they could be very dangerous indeed.

So far, discontent in the region has been mainly economic. The area saw four serious general strikes by the miners from 1989 to 1998, the first two in Soviet times—which did much to undermine the Gorbachev government and, indirectly, to destroy the Soviet Union—the last two against governments of independent Ukraine.[15] Even if, as stated, these strikes have been partly the result of maneuvers by the local party of power, this is only one part of the explanation. In fact, the surprising thing (examined in the next chapter) is that the Donbas has not seen *more* social protest. Part of the reason for the relative lack of protest is that the miners know all too well that the pits are worn out and what an impossibly large amount of money it would take to restore most of them. This gives a certain meaninglessness to their protests, but that does not diminish their misery or their anger with Kiev.

Another reason for the miners' failure to develop a strong political movement of their own, independent of party of power games, may be that Donetsk is an extreme case in terms of its identity as a city, which is almost entirely Soviet. It was founded in 1869 by a Welsh mining entrepreneur, John Hughes of Merthyr Tydfil, commissioned by the Russian government to develop the Donbas coal fields, and (uniquely) was named after him—Hughesovka, or in Russian and Ukrainian, Yusovka.[16] (In the Soviet period it became first Stalino, and when that went out of fashion, it was given the bland name of Donetsk, after the local river, in 1961.) Under the tsars, the city and region even lacked both a provincial administration and an elected local council, both of which sat in Yekaterinoslav.

The Donbas's great development and glory came under Soviet rule, when it was officially dubbed the "Boiler Room of the Whole Union" (Vsyesoyuznaya Kochegarka). But today, the evidence of its unplanned and chaotic growth, as well as the peasant origins of its workers, can still be seen in the sprawling suburbs of one-story cottages where much of the population lives.

These cottages are surrounded by gardens of an acre or two, which thanks to the fertile soil of the steppe (when it can be watered) and the generally warm climate, are bursting not just with potatoes and cabbages, as in Russia, but with fruit and vegetables of every kind, often with chickens cackling in the background and sometimes even a pig. The wives, mothers, and children of the miners tend these plots, as do the miners themselves in their increasing periods of unemployment. Those who live in blocks of flats in the center often have such allotments separately.

The importance of these gardens for supporting the people and maintaining social peace in Ukrainian (and southern Russian) cities such as Donetsk simply cannot be exaggerated. In many cases, the gardens can provide a family with most of the food it needs (except for bread, sugar, and so on) to survive the winter, with some left over for barter. Without them, given the rapid decline of the mines, much of the population might by now be virtually starving—and at that point, a revolutionary situation would be a real possibility.

Larisa Trojan, the daughter and granddaughter of Donetsk miners, described the spirit and identity of the miners in Soviet days, and their anomie today:

> In Soviet days, the slogan was always "Glory to Work. Glory to the Worker," meaningless perhaps, but it gave people a sense of meaning, of pride. Today there is nothing. Their entire identity, their being has been kicked away. . . .
>
> We had a song, "The Miners Are the Shock Troops of Labor." The miners were the aristocracy of the workers, with good pay by Soviet standards, and the *stakhanovites* [miners who overfulfilled production quotas] were the aristocrats of the miners. Of course, conditions were always tough, and they have got tougher and tougher as the mines have got older and the equipment has worn out. . . .
>
> The miners also had real power within the Soviet system; they showed that at the end, by helping to bring down Gorbachev. But though you may not know this, they also helped to bring down Khrushchev, thirty years ago. The two things that really did him in—and allowed Brezhnev and his group to move against him—were, first, that he had lost the confidence of the armed forces through his military cuts and, second, that he had alienated the miners of Donetsk by trying to cut overtime payments, because even then he saw that the Donbas mines were old, not profitable. . . . Don't think the miners don't remember what power they used to have. . . . I was talking to Dmytro Pavlychko, the nationalist poet, about the suffering of the miners today, and he said in a very high-minded tone, "Of course, this is true, but don't you realize that people must be encouraged to endure hardship so as to build our independent state?" and I replied, "Don't *you* realize that for seventy years people have been told to endure bitter hardship for the sake of an abstract idea, an undefined glorious future. They're tired of it. How can you go and ask this again?"[17]

Today, Donetsk remains a Soviet coal town, and its people's anomie and bitterness at their present sufferings is exacerbated by an uncomfortable awareness that by their great strikes in 1989 and 1991 the Donbas miners did a good deal to help bring about the destruction of the Soviet Union—the only state to which their city really belonged and which had a real use for them.[18]

Donetsk never was a city in any sense that would have been understood by previous ages: Like some former industrial cities in North America, the place is simply a temporary encampment of the Industrial Revolution's nomadic forces. Today it is, economically, a Soviet ghost town, but still inhabited by a million people. In the words of Leonid Savonov, of the Twenty-First Petrovskaya mine, "Our region is dying fast, but we have somehow to go on living."

An attempt has been made by some local Russian historians, backed by colleagues in Russia, to show that this was the territory of the Don Cossacks and, therefore, really belongs in Russia. Ukrainian historians for their part have asserted that it was first Kievan and then Zaporozhian Cossack land. The truth seems to be that before the late eighteenth century it was barely cultivated at all, and Zaporozhians, Don Cossacks, Crimean Tatars, and Nogai Tatars all rode across it, fought one another, and intermittently grazed their flocks there. By the late nineteenth century, it had acquired a Ukrainian-speaking peasant population, although this was not very numerous.[19]

Of rather more contemporary significance was the Bolshevik-influenced Donetsk–Krivoi Rog "republic" of the spring of 1918, which rejected the authority of the Ukrainian Rada and attempted briefly to hold out against the German and Austrian occupation of the area before being forcibly incorporated in the German-backed Ukrainian "hetmanate" state. This history is sometimes used (for example, in the pages of the local Russian nationalist paper *Donetsky Kryazh*) as an argument for seeking to create a Donbas autonomous republic within Ukraine, on the Crimean model, or even to secede and join Russia. Such academic arguments, based on a detailed but highly selective reading of local history, are very much in vogue among segments of the Russian intelligentsia in eastern Ukraine, some of whom have taken to amateur local history in a big way, partly out of long-standing personal interest, and partly in reaction to Ukrainian claims.

The odd—but in fact very typical—thing is that these people resemble local Ukrainian intellectuals under Soviet rule (with the difference of course that the latter had to be much more careful about what they said). They are politically marginalized, and the academics on state salaries are also often economically marginalized, increasingly desperate, and therefore increasingly bitter. They are also frightened of becoming culturally marginalized through Ukrainianization. All these factors together produce odd obsessions, quirks, and bitterness.

In most areas, such as Dnipropetrovsk, these people really are completely incidental to the lives of their cities. However, their arguments should not be dismissed as completely without political significance, especially in the Donbas. Autonomist demands surfaced during both the 1993 and 1996 strike movements, and the Donetsk and Luhansk regional councils voted in support of these calls. A local plebiscite tacked on to the presidential elections in 1994 also produced a 90 percent majority for official status for the Russian language.

However, as the previous chapter has described, the regional identity of the Donbas at present is not a Russian one, but a Soviet one inextricably linked to one profession, the miners. In this sense, it is by no means necessarily "anti-Ukrainian." The region's identity is, however, very specific and very different from that of other regions of Ukraine (for example, Russian-speaking eastern ones, let alone Galicia).

The danger—already clear in the summer of 1996—would be if a mixture of elite politics; social and economic despair; fury at Kiev's economic policies; resentment at Ukrainianization; and miners' solidarity, discipline, and toughness were to combine in a very strong local autonomy movement. Even that would not be so dangerous if Kiev reacted in a restrained way; but any violence from the center could well create an outburst and produce exactly the "Russian" result that both Ukrainian nationalists and Russian-Ukrainian loyalists fear the most.

People in Donetsk are now deeply hostile to the idea of Ukrainian independence. (The region's Russian-speakers call Independence Day by its name in Ukrainian, because as many of them say, "It's not our holiday.") However, very few people I talked to there, with the exception of the small number of outright Russian nationalists, have any idea of what to put in its place, except for the Soviet Union—a dream which, for more and more people, is fading. On Independence Day in August 1995, the crowd celebrating it was tiny, consisting of around 150 people out of a population of more than a million, but so too was the crowd called by Russian nationalist groups to protest the celebration. The Communist-backed "Internationalist Movement" meeting in honor of the Soviet Union was slightly larger, but only slightly, and was made up mainly of pensioners complaining about their pensions being in arrears. The truly important and symbolic local celebration remains "Miners' Day." In the typical words of an older miner at the Petrovskaya, a man whom his companions addressed respectfully as "Petrovich,"

> If we can help it, we don't want anything to do with either Ukrainian or Russian nationalists. They will bring us nothing but evil—they have already, look at how we live. Who are they to defend me from, these defenders of my national rights? My mother was Russian—are the Ukrainians to defend me from her? My father is Ukrainian—should I ask the Russian army to save me from him? Should I support that drunken

swine Yeltsin, who shoots at his own parliament? I will drink to Bogdan
Khmelnitsky, who united our two peoples. But where today will we find
such a man?

ODESSA

At the other end of southern Ukraine, on the Black Sea coast near the
border with Moldova, is Ukraine's greatest port, Odessa (city population,
1.1 million; region, 2.6 million), which used to be the second-biggest
port of both the Soviet Union and the Russian Empire. Its past wealth
survives in the imposing neoclassical mansions and art nouveau apart-
ment blocks dating from Russian imperial times. From its origins—
founded and given its classical name under Catherine the Great in
1794 by the Duc de Richelieu, a French émigré in the Russian service
—Odessa was a cosmopolitan and ethnically mixed city, with a relatively small Ukrainian presence.[20]

Although always overwhelmingly Russian-speaking, the most notable part of the city's population, and the one with which it is most
often identified, has historically been the Jews, whose life and society
before and during the Russian Revolution were immortalized by Isaac
Babel and other writers. Although the city's Jewish population is considerably reduced today, there are still many Jewish businessmen in the
city (some of them returned émigrés) who have close commercial and
cultural links to Jewish Odessan émigrés in Israel and the United
States. Odessa has also been famous as a center of Soviet and now
international organized crime—and, of course, of Soviet humor.

Although small Russian nationalist groups exist in Odessa, calling for
restoration of the "New Russia" (Novorossiya) region, their influence is
very limited. On the whole, the political and commercial elites (the
two are of course closely intertwined) and indeed most of the population regard Ukrainian rule calmly, although without any great affection
or respect.

The people and the city of Odessa as a whole have so far suffered
badly from the disintegration of the Soviet Union. This can be seen in the
steep drop in trade through the port, from 85 million metric tons in
the last year of Soviet rule to just 51 million tons in 1995.

However, it must be pointed out that this is *officially reported*
trade—a good deal more goes unreported. Furthermore, while the city
as a whole may have suffered—and this is evident from the condition
of public services, the pay arrears of teachers, the terrible conditions

of pensioners—the end of Communist rule has of course provided far greater opportunities for personal enrichment. The chief beneficiaries have been a relatively small number of former officials and new businessmen, but it is also true that because of its commercial traditions (even, covertly, under Soviet rule), much of the rest of the population has been able to take some advantage of the new system. Odessa in the early 1990s saw the fastest development of private shops (whether privatized or newly founded) of any city in Ukraine, usually selling imported consumer goods that had made their way in through the port.

While there is regret for the loss of the huge Soviet territory that used to be Odessa's commercial hinterland, as long as no sudden or radical Ukrainianization takes place, and as long as trade and personal contacts with Russia remain relatively easy, it is difficult to see any disruptive political movement taking place in Odessa. In the words of a local journalist,

> This is a commercial center, and for most people here money comes first, second, and third. It always did, under Soviet rule as well—half the town lived directly or indirectly off the stuff the seamen brought back from the West to sell.
>
> People here may not much like the Ukrainian state, but they'd never be so foolish and reckless as to carry out some kind of revolt against it. If Ukraine were to go into an economic plunge again, as in 1993, then there might be some talk, but you've got to remember, this isn't Donetsk or Kharkiv, on the Russian border. We're the wrong side of Ukraine here. If Ukraine broke up, we'd be stuck out on a geographical limb like Kaliningrad, and most of our trade would vanish. Nobody here wants that. Open borders with Russia, free trade, yes. That would obviously be very good for Odessa. But our bosses here don't have any illusions about Russia; they know that the problems today on the borders are just as much the Russian government's fault as that of the Ukrainians, that Moscow is pursuing Russian economic interests, not some sort of humanitarian cooperation.[21]

KHARKIV

Kharkiv (in Russian, Kharkov) in northeastern Ukraine (city population 1.6 million; region, 3.2 million), a mere fifteen miles from the Russian border, has a very different history and historical identity from all the other parts of the country. This is the part of Ukraine with the oldest connection to the Muscovite and Russian states, dating from the establishment of the Belgorod defensive line against Crimean Tatar raids into Russia, beginning in 1571. Kharkiv itself was founded in 1656 and grew into the capital of "Sloboda Ukraine," and unofficially, under both tsars and Communists, of a group of Russian (but to this day partly Ukrainian-speaking) provinces to the north. For much of the Russian imperial period it was the largest city between Moscow and the Black Sea and was considerably bigger than Kiev.

Because of this history, its closeness to the border, and strong personal ties of intermarriage with people in Russia, the establishment of border controls and visas between Russia and Ukraine has caused particular bitterness in Kharkiv (as also in Donetsk, Luhansk, and Mariupol), and was mentioned by several local people in my informal sampling of opinion. Asked what would happen if the Ukrainian side attempted to introduce a visa system, three people replied that this was the one thing that would produce a very strong and potentially violent movement of protest in an otherwise politically apathetic population. One of them described the customs controls at the border as "like something out of a film of the Civil War—White bandits attacking a train; uniformed hooligans burst in, demand vodka and money, then disappear again." This is of course a vast exaggeration, but the irritation is real enough—though he did admit that the Russian border guards are just as corrupt as the Ukrainian ones.

In 1805, Alexander I founded a university here (Russian-language, of course), the fourth in the empire. In both the Russian imperial and Soviet eras, Kharkiv was also a major military center, with a large officers school. Under Soviet rule, the city became a major center of the military-industrial complex, with the second-biggest tank factory in the Union and an electronics center, Khartron, which produced the guidance systems for nuclear missiles as well as for the Soviet space program; as a result, there is a major concentration of technical intelligentsia in the city. These plants reported directly to the all-Union ministries in Moscow, and in general Kharkiv had rather limited contacts with the Ukrainian government in Kiev.

Because of its past, Kharkiv has the most "Russian" (as opposed to "Soviet"—an important distinction, as already noted) feel of all the major Russian-speaking cities in Ukraine. After Odessa, it also has the grandest architecture and the most pleasant and civilized urban atmosphere. From the tsarist period, it has great official buildings in the neoclassical style; art nouveau merchant mansions, such as the "House of the Golden Fish" from 1903; and a beautiful city park. From Soviet times dates the main square, supposedly the largest enclosed urban space in the world, lined with some striking buildings from the 1920s and 1930s.

An enormous modern opera house in Kharkiv is also one of the largest in the former Soviet Union. A surprising number of old houses survived the Second World War, when control of the city changed hands no less than six times. Altogether, the city gives the impression of being too big and imposing for its present reduced circumstances, and this is something of which its people are bitterly aware.

A certain anti-Kiev (rather than anti-Ukrainian) feeling endures from the years 1918 to 1934, when Kharkiv was the capital of Soviet Ukraine. Furthermore, local elites actually are not that glad to be reporting to Kiev, where they are big fish, rather than to Moscow, because Kharkiv was in fact quite a big all-Union fish in the old days, given its military and scientific importance. This sense of marginalization should not be exaggerated. Kharkiv probably contains more articulate Russian intellectuals than elsewhere in Ukraine; they are not yet articulating anything like revolt or secession, although there is certainly deep irritation with aspects of Ukrainianization.

Alexei Nestnov said the following about the national culture—or, rather, the lack of it—of people in the Kharkiv area (the interview was in 1995, but things do not seem to have changed significantly since):

> On the whole, people here wouldn't want to make a clear choice between Ukraine and Russia, if this could be avoided. And they themselves don't distinguish clearly between what is Ukrainian and what is Russian. If you enter a house here, you can't say whether it is a Ukrainian or a Russian home—in any case, families are often mixed. If it is a Ukrainian intellectual family, there might be a collection of Ukrainian literature, but this would be rare.
>
> Houses are decorated in a different way, depending on whether they are Ukrainian or Russian. If there are some "traditional" Ukrainian decorations, then they may just as well be hung up by local Russians. In the villages, of course, it is different. There, people have kept more genuine traditions, songs, ornaments, and so on. But they don't really think of them as national traditions, but as local ones—it's the *tuteshni* feeling, not nationalism. . . .
>
> On the whole, people here always liked the image of Russia that they received from Russian television, Russian culture, and so on. But since October 1993, and still more since Chechnya, there has been a change. People here are very peaceable, they hate the idea of war and political violence. So, whereas people here—including many local Ukrainians— used to call themselves Russians, now this is not so popular. But people here still don't call themselves Ukrainians, so you could say they don't know what to call themselves.[22]

There is deep unhappiness in Kharkiv over the dire economic situation and the prospects of what used to be highly prestigious Soviet high-tech industries. Many in the city spoke wistfully of the possibility of reviving the Soviet space program on a Ukrainian-Russian basis, "because it's obvious that the Russians can't succeed without us, and on our own we're nothing."

However, it is also evident in Kharkiv—as in Odessa and indeed throughout eastern Ukraine—that a new generation of local politicians is appearing. Its members are drawn largely from the younger generation of Communist officials and state managers, but are now closely linked to local private business; indeed, thanks to privatization, which they strongly favor, many have become wealthy (openly or covertly) businessmen themselves. Publicly at least, they profess strong loyalty to the Ukrainian state, and it is very difficult to see them rebelling against it unless a move were made to strip them of local power, or if the Ukrainian economy once again started to deteriorate much faster than Russia's. They also profess to feel, more or less sincerely, primary loyalty to their own cities and their populations.

Representative of this new class is the intelligent and dynamic mayor of Kharkiv, Yevgeny Kushnarev, who in February 1997 was made chief of the presidential administration in Kiev—a shrewd move by President Kuchma, because it not only co-opted a popular local leader from Russian-speaking Ukraine but also went some way toward balancing the great and much-resented influence of the Dnipropetrovsk clan, led by Lazarenko and to some extent by Kuchma himself.

When I interviewed him in August 1995, Kushnarev described himself as a "European-style Social Democrat." His close links to the government in Kiev may help explain his strongly centralist line. If excluded from influence and favors, he might have adopted a somewhat different approach—as he conceivably could in the future if he were cast out again from the charmed circle. Others in Kharkiv mentioned the history of Sloboda Ukraine as a basis for local autonomy. In an interview with me, however, Kushnarev was careful to draw a sharp line between, on the one hand, his desire to defend the Russian language in his area and to pursue special economic links and agreements with neighboring Russian regions and, on the other hand, any question of a divided state loyalty. In his words,

I think it would be wrong for Ukraine to pursue a softer policy toward Russia over the Black Sea Fleet and other issues. Any softness is taken by

Russia as weakness. Moscow has never treated the other republics as equals, and I can tell you that from my own experience. I am a Russian, my parents were from Smolensk, but I love my country, Ukraine, and obey the Ukrainian government....

As to the question of tariffs on trade with Russia, that's a different matter, which must be worked out in a way that benefits both sides.... Ideally, we would like to create a special border zone stretching from here to Belgorod [in Russia], with low tariffs and relaxed controls, to stimulate trade. We can't hope to keep all of Kharkov's industries going, though we must try to save the best; but I believe our main hope lies in becoming a center of trade and financial exchange between Russia and Ukraine, and a base for joint banks and financial-industrial groups.

However, for this I see no need for Kharkov to be an autonomous region or Ukraine to become a federal state. Historically, the only basis for this would be in the case of Crimea and to a certain extent Galicia. I think we need a unitary, civilized state to carry out the necessary economic reforms, ensure a stable currency, and so on—like France under de Gaulle. Then later, perhaps, we can decentralize to some extent....

On language, every region should have the right to give official status to Russian, but this should not be understood as meaning federalism. I sympathize with Ukrainianization, but it depends on how it is done. Russian will remain the language of interethnic communication here for a long time to come. In 1990, when I was elected, there were only two Ukrainian-language schools in Kharkov, and now there are fifty; but the university, that's a different matter. There we need to go very slowly and carefully or we will destroy our intellectual traditions and potential and infuriate our people.... Yes, maybe the law says that it must change in three or five years, but if they try to do this kind of thing by decree, they will create just the sort of anti-Ukrainian, nationalist, or Communist movement of protest that we all want to prevent.[23]

Above all, it is important to remember that even those politicians and business leaders in eastern Ukraine who are most in favor of close ties to Russia have become progressively more disillusioned with the Yeltsin government's policies toward Ukraine. There was particular anger with what was seen as ruthless Russian trade policies, intended to maximize Russian advantages while crippling the competition. Indeed, while I heard some expressions of respect for retired General Aleksandr Lebed and one or two other Russian opposition politicians (mostly those opposed to the Chechen war, but emphatically excluding Vladimir Zhirinovsky), literally nobody—not one single person—I spoke with in eastern and southern Ukraine, whether Russian or Ukrainian, expressed any liking or admiration for Boris Yeltsin.

Among the state industrial managers, typical was the attitude of Alfred Kozlovsky, the manager of the giant steel pipe factory in Dnipropetrovsk (formerly named after Karl Liebknecht). He began by cursing the nationalists and saying that close ties to Russia were essential for Ukrainian industry. But then he continued as follows:

> For fifty years, we exported gas to Russia at rock-bottom state prices. Now we are dependent on Russia, and Russia continually gouges higher prices and cuts us off when we can't pay. This isn't a brotherly, humane, or partnerlike attitude. If they want partnership with us, they should allow us to buy gas at Ukrainian prices. In my view, it's an attempt to force our production costs and our prices higher than those in Russia, because at the moment our products are cheaper and we are outselling them.... Kuchma has created all the conditions for normal cooperation with Russia, now it is up to Russia to do the same and not keep trying to exclude our goods [at this, he spat loudly into the wastepaper basket].... Russia is behaving very badly, very greedily. After all, we are all Slavs, brother peoples.[24]

This goes to the heart of the matter: A great many people in eastern and southern Ukraine would like a close and equal union with Russia, and certainly want very close and open relations with ordinary Russian people, without strict border controls or national hostility. But if the Russian state tries to push its own interests at the expense of Ukraine, then even these "pro-Russians" find themselves firmly on the Ukrainian side.

4

CRIMEA AND SEVASTOPOL

THE UKRAINIAN ONION

The lack of Russian state interference in Ukraine has been especially striking in the case of Crimea because of the much stronger passions involved in the Crimean issue—in both Russia and Crimea itself—and the much greater apparent opportunities for the Russian government to use this issue against Ukraine.[1] There have of course been statements by individual ministers on the "Russianness" of Crimea, repeated votes by the Russian parliament in support of the Russian national movement in Crimea and of a return of Sevastopol to Russia, and interventions by opposition politicians. Under Yeltsin, however, the state has taken no practical action, except in trying to retain control of most of the Black Sea Fleet and its base. Moreover, the question of Sevastopol was shelved by the agreement that accompanied the 1997 Russia-Ukraine basic treaty (which has been ratified by both legislatures, but with the condition by the upper house of the Russian parliament that Ukraine also ratify the fleet treaty).

As long as circumstances do not change radically, this situation is likely in my view to remain the same under Yeltsin's probable successors; for after Chechnya, today's Russian political leaders are by no means anxious for military adventure, and a good deal of the opposition's interest in Crimea has seemed to many observers to stem largely from political opportunism and a desire to harm and embarrass the administration.

However, Russian national feelings over Crimea must not be ignored, for they do have a genuine basis both in history and in demography: 67 percent of the Crimean population today is Russian; half of the 25 percent Ukrainian population consider Russian to be their native language; and Crimea was, after all, transferred from Russia to Ukraine without the slightest attempt to consult its inhabitants.

The hopes and ambitions of the Russians of today's Russia for Ukraine may be described as something like an onion—albeit an unnatural, mutant onion, with a stone in the middle. The outermost skin, by now obviously peeling and largely discarded, is the belief that Ukrainians and Russians are one people; then comes the belief that they are closely related peoples, destined to live in some form of union; then the belief that the eastern and southern parts of Ukraine ("New Russia") are historically part of Russia and not Ukraine; then the belief that Khrushchev's transfer of Crimea to Ukraine was unjust, and that Crimea legally still belongs to Russia.

Finally, there comes the stone: the belief, held by the overwhelming majority of Russians who consider the issue, that the city and naval base of Sevastopol are simply Russian, a part of Russian national territory and Russia's national patrimony, and that even if they should not be annexed from Ukraine, Russia must keep a permanent stake and military presence there. All the other beliefs are already fading, or can be in effect compromised away; the question of Sevastopol, however, may be one on which in the end there can be no compromise, despite the provisional twenty-year lease agreed on in May 1997.

The questions of Crimea and Sevastopol are obviously linked. Sevastopol is situated in Crimea, and the two were transferred together from Russia to Ukraine in 1954, although the Russian Duma now claims that Sevastopol, as a military port, was administered under Soviet rule —not by the Russian then the Ukrainian governments, but by the Union government—and was therefore in a separate category. More important, the emotional and political problems surrounding Sevastopol and Crimea are rather different from problems related to other Ukrainian regions, and they give rise to different dangers.

THE CRIMEAN TATARS

Among more honest and less nationalist Russian intellectuals, there is a recognition that while Crimea was never Ukrainian, it was also for the greater part of its history not Russian either.[2] The oldest remaining people to have been settled there are the Pontic Greeks, whose presence goes back three thousand years or more; they are by now tiny in both numbers and political significance, partly as a result of deportations under Stalin.

Far more important today are the Crimean Tatars, rulers of Crimea from the thirteenth century until the Russian annexation of 1783.[3] The beautiful Ottoman-style palace of their khans still stands in the old capital of Bakhchiserai. Over the following century and a half, their proportion of the population was reduced by emigration to Turkey and by the immigration of Slavic settlers. Under Soviet rule, they were given a role as the titular nationality of the Crimean Autonomous Republic of the Russian Federation; but during World War II, Stalin deported the entire remaining population to Central Asia, seeking revenge for the collaboration of some of them with the Germans, and perhaps also fearing their possible cooperation with the Turks in the event of a future Soviet-Turkish war, which at that time he may have been considering. Almost 20 percent of those deported are estimated to have died from starvation, exhaustion, and disease in the first eighteen months of exile. Crimea's autonomous status was abolished, and it was reduced to the level of an ordinary region. Unlike the Chechens and other deported peoples, and despite a continuous movement of protest and agitation for which many Tatars received long prison terms, the Tatars were not permitted to return to their homeland after Stalin's death.[4]

It was only under Mikhail Gorbachev—and not until 1989, four years into his rule—that the Soviet state moved to right this terrible wrong, and soon afterwards the Soviet collapse meant that although the legal and police restrictions on Tatar returns were lifted, the Tatars received almost no Soviet state aid for their return, and very little from the new and struggling Ukrainian state. Meanwhile, of course, Tatar houses and lands had long since been occupied by Russian and Ukrainian settlers—a source of intense bitterness to the Tatars of today. Some 250,000 of them now live in Crimea, mostly in virtual shantytowns. Another 150,000 or so are still supposed to be in Uzbekistan and elsewhere, either because they have settled down there, they are waiting for better economic times in Crimea, or they are deterred by the high fee the Uzbek government demands for permission to emigrate from the country. According to official Ukrainian figures, as of December 1997, only 52 percent of Tatar returnees had proper housing, and only 23 percent had regular jobs (although of course very many have part-time or unregistered work, often in the black market).[5]

In January 1994, I drove through the former Tatar capital, Bakhchiserai, with Server Umerov, a Tatar leader who had been minister of construction in Soviet Uzbekistan. He gestured to the right and the left as we drove:

All these houses were Tatar before 1944. Now they are occupied by Russians and Ukrainians, and our people are living in shacks and cowsheds. Over there was the *madrasseh* [religious school]—it was demolished. There was the cemetery—also flattened to build a school. It is impossible to estimate how much property was stolen or destroyed, of course along with millions of animals. Nonetheless, we are not asking for our own homes back—though we have the right to—because we are merciful people. But in compensation for what was taken, we are demanding that 40 percent of the regional privatization fund should be allocated to the Tatars, to help us resettle in what is after all our own land.[6]

The Tatars are led by dedicated, determined, and honest leaders, steeled by years in Soviet prison camps. Because of the long campaign to return home and overwhelming unity on the most important national questions, the Tatar community as a whole has an extremely impressive capacity for political mobilization. On the fiftieth anniversary of the deportation, on May 18, 1994, around two hundred thousand people, or 80 percent of the entire Tatar population, marched in commemoration. On a number of occasions, demonstrations of more than one hundred thousand have taken place—far more than any Russian demonstration in the region, or anywhere else in the lands of the "Russian diaspora."

Crimean Tatar demonstrations have also been responsible for the only instances of mass violence in Crimea since independence. In October 1992, after police had bulldozed an "illegally built" Tatar settlement in the town of Alushta and arrested and beat up Tatar protesters, a Tatar crowd stormed and briefly occupied the Crimean parliament, overwhelming the police guards and forcing the government to order the release of the Tatar detainees. In June 1995 in the town of Feodosia and neighboring areas, Tatars protesting against the extortions of Russian gangsters from Tatar shopkeepers and the murder of Tatar traders launched attacks on Russian-owned shops and businesses thought to be mafia controlled, and clashed with police. Two Tatars were killed when the police opened fire.[7] In the words of Nedir Bekirov, chief of the political section of the Tatar Mejlis (the standing committee of the Tatar "parliament"), in August 1995,

> Over the past year or so, traditional criminality in this region has been replaced by a new type, resembling I suppose that of America in the 1930s. A key aspect of it is the takeover of the authorities and political groups by criminal forces. We, as an ethnic minority, have been among the main sufferers from this marriage, and despite all our protests both

to Kiev and the government here, nothing was done. . . . Finally the
boundaries of our tolerance were exceeded. The murders of Tatars made
it obvious that we were not under the protection of the law, and that if
we try to go though the justice system, the legal authorities themselves
will save the murderers.[8]

Another underlying reason for the riots, however, was undoubtedly
frustration that the Ukrainian government had not kept its promises to
increase aid to the Tatars and raise their political status, even after it had
essentially overthrown Crimea's pro-Russian Meshkov administration,
which the Tatars had so resolutely opposed. The riot was soon followed
by the announcement by Kiev of a new program of support, although
much of this involved attempts to raise money from Turkey and the Arab
world. Kiev's previous promises to the Tatars had been partly a bribe
to gain their support against the Crimean Russian movement, and the
Tatars gave it fully and gladly (thereby increasing anti-Tatar feelings
among the Russians). Throughout 1997 the Tatars continued to complain
of lack of help from Kiev, and even that the Ukrainian government was
making it hard for Tatar returnees to acquire Ukrainian citizenship.[9] In
the Ukrainian parliamentary elections of 1998, this led to tens of thousands of Tatars being disenfranchised, and more angry protests.

The chairman of the Tatar Mejlis, Mustafa Cemiloglu (Djemilev), a
former dissident who spent fifteen years in Soviet camps and personally a very impressive individual, told me,

> The Russian nationalists here know that the only force that can prevent
> their movement to join Russia is the Tatars. . . . We will never agree to
> join Russia. It is true that the Ukrainian government has so far done little
> for us, but we lived under Russia for two hundred years, and you see
> what it has brought us. The Russian state says that it is the heir of the
> Soviet Union, but it only wants the benefits of this. It accepts no respon-
> sibility for the crimes the Soviet Union committed against us and other
> peoples. . . .
>
> So we want to stay as an autonomous republic within Ukraine, but
> not as at present; we want an autonomy like those of the Russian Feder-
> ation, based on the core [original] nationality, but with stronger rights
> and guarantees for us as the people of state, and not less than one-third
> of the seats in the parliament.[10]

But Kiev has to tread very carefully on this issue. In the first place, the
Ukrainian minority in Crimea is just as worried by the Tatars as are the
Russians, for the good reason that they were also settled in stolen Tatar
property under Soviet rule; they fear Tatar attempts to recover it and

they are just as opposed to the Tatar demands for a Tatar Autonomous Republic. Common hostility to the Tatars is indeed a strong force uniting the Russians and Ukrainians of Crimea.

More to the point, for Kiev to move in the direction of full support for the Tatars would be the one thing that could restart the Crimean Russian secessionist movement and perhaps turn it into an outright revolt. Partly with Kiev's backing, the Tatars have received weighted representation in the Crimean parliament, their own television programs, and a small amount of state aid, but that is all. So Kiev continues to sit on the fence, and the Tatars, in their makeshift houses on the bare hillsides, continue to look down into the valleys at their former homes and seethe with anger.

The Russian-Tatar relationship in Crimea, unlike that between the Russians and Ukrainians in most of the rest of Ukraine, does contain the potential for violence in the future, because it is rooted in old hatreds, ethnic and religious differences, and present issues that affect ordinary people on both sides (unlike the arguments of the rival nationalists over the Donbas, for example, which leave the great majority of ordinary people there utterly indifferent). The Tatars understandably enough bitterly resent the Russian majority and its occupation of their homes. The Russians fear Tatar attempts to recover their former property; revenge for their past wrongs; and the links between the Tatars and Turkey, Russia's historical enemy and a regional power of which Russians are becoming increasingly afraid. In the words of Leonid Grach, head of the Crimean Communist Party (and claiming to be a Soviet internationalist, not a Russian nationalist), "I am not against the Tatars as such, but because they are looking to Turkey for support, and I see Turkish influence and Turkish expansionism as extremely dangerous for the whole world. That is why I stand for a united Black Sea Fleet, because I want forces in this region that could defend our Slavic countries from this Turkish threat. . . . Do you know that Turkey is already selling tourist maps showing Crimea as part of Turkey, as it was three hundred years ago?"[11]

Of course, the risk is that at some stage, it will be precisely this Tatar example—and not hostility to Kiev—that will lead the Russians to countermobilize. I heard talk to this effect among Russian nationalists in Crimea during a visit in September 1995. In the words of one of them, "Every time the Tatars have a riot or a big demonstration, Kiev gives them something. That's what we have to learn." Fearing precisely this, the Ukrainian government has been very cautious about supporting the Tatars and their political claims, but this in turn runs the risk that it will be the Tatars' patience that will finally snap. This is the hope of some of the extreme nationalist groups in Galicia, such as UNA/UNSO, who would dearly love to encourage the Tatars to "take back" Crimea from the Russians, but so far the Ukrainian government has been successfully limiting their activities, and their actual support and influence is in any case small. However, in November 1997, the Tatars did forge an electoral alliance with Rukh, a more moderate Ukrainian nationalist party.[12]

The Examples of Crimea and Transdniestr

Of all the regions of the Russian diaspora, just two have generated serious secessionist movements—Crimea and the Transdniestr region of Moldova. In Transdniestr, the revolt of local Russians under the hardline Communist leadership led to the establishment of a separate region, which up to 1998 has preserved a sort of independence. In Crimea, the movement for an independent or fully autonomous territory linked to Russia collapsed in 1995, although it is possible that the movement may be revived in the future.

The first thing to remember about Transdniestr and Crimea is how unusual they are. No other areas of the "Russian diaspora," not the Donbas, not northern Kazakstan, not Narva in Estonia, have generated serious secessionist movements. Crimea is distinct from the other Russian-speaking areas of Ukraine for four main reasons: Crimea is the only area of Ukraine with an absolute majority of Russians (and a Ukrainian population that is also overwhelmingly Russian-speaking) thanks to state-encouraged immigration under both the tsars and Soviet rule; Crimea was transferred to Ukraine from Russia in 1954 without the local population being consulted; Crimea retains strong ties to Russia, stemming from the facts that much of the population immigrated from Russia after World War II, and that the Crimean economy was critically dependent on the tourist trade from Russia and has been badly hurt by the disintegration of the Soviet Union; and the people of Crimea are angry at the economic suffering that has followed Ukrainian independence.

Taking all these factors together, there seemed to be good reason to think that Crimea would generate an unstoppable movement for separation from Ukraine, with terribly dangerous consequences for the whole region. The fact that the Russian secessionist movement in Crimea proved so feeble in the end is an important indicator of the weak mobilizing capacity of the Russian diaspora as a whole.

The successful separation of Transdniestr might be taken as an argument that this is not necessarily the case, but the separation of this region occurred under unique circumstances. For in the creation of the Transdniestrian state, two key factors were present that cannot be duplicated in the future, or at least not in anything like the same way. The first is that all the essential groundwork for Transdniestr's separation from Moldova was done between 1989 and 1991, when the Soviet Union and a united Soviet Communist Party and central state were still in existence.

Local Communist officials, state managers, and official trade unions played the central, essential role in mobilizing the "Russians" of Transdniestr against Moldovan nationalism, and in organizing separate Transdniestrian authorities and armed forces. They were encouraged to do so by hard-line Communists in the Soviet leadership in Moscow, and the Soviet state protected them from Moldovan retaliation. Finally, the Soviet Fourteenth Army was stationed in Transdniestr. When the Moldovans finally did launch an armed attack on Transdniestr, beginning in May 1992, Soviet troops under the command of General Aleksandr Lebed intervened swiftly and decisively to help the Transdniestrians and end the fighting under the pretext of "peacekeeping."

Today, as the previous chapter emphasized, the Soviet Communist Party and its attendant organizations no longer exist. This means that the institutions to organize the local Russians are missing. Equally important is that there are no chains of command or links of official patronage leading back to Moscow. Thus, even if the Russian government wanted to organize future secessions—of which there is no sign at present—it would lack most of the means to do so.

Finally, while the Russian armed forces are still stationed in Crimea (and to a much lesser extent in Kazakstan, but in no other areas of the diaspora), their position today is very different from what it was in Transdniestr in 1992. There, everything was still in a state of flux, with the Soviet Union only a few months dead. The Transdniestrian forces (undoubtedly with Soviet military help) had been built up to the point where they were able to resist for several weeks without the Russian army becoming directly and obviously involved. That then gave Lebed the chance to present his forces as "neutral peacekeepers" with some appearance of plausibility.

In Crimea in 1995 the situation was very different, and this will be even more the case in the future. The Crimean Russians had far fewer opportunities and much less time than the Transdniestrians to create their own armed forces. This means that if the Russian forces had wished to intervene to help them, they would have had to do so much earlier and much more blatantly than in Transdniestr, with no serious chance to present themselves as "peacemakers," and in circumstances where the diplomatic cost to Moscow of armed intervention would have been vastly higher than was the case in Transdniestr.

THE COURSE OF THE CRIMEAN RUSSIAN MOVEMENT FOR SECESSION

In January 1991, with the Soviet Union still in existence but its authority clearly waning, a referendum in Crimea led to a 93 percent vote (on an 80 percent turnout) for making Crimea a full union republic (in other words, separate from both Ukraine and Russia). A compromise was reached whereby the Ukrainian parliament agreed to make Crimea an autonomous republic, the only one in Ukraine.

After the collapse of the Soviet Union and the establishment of Ukrainian independence, more and more Crimean Russians started to demand a complete break from Ukraine and union with Russia— although this was not clear-cut Russian nationalism, for it was also mixed up with a desire for the restoration of the Soviet Union as a whole. Phrases often heard in the region during this period were "Crimea should be a bridge between Ukraine and Russia" and "Crimea should be the foundation stone of a new Union."

Hostility to Ukraine was fueled by the Russo-Ukrainian dispute over the Black Sea Fleet. A great many Russians in Crimea—especially of course in Sevastopol, the peninsula's largest city—strongly identify with the fleet, in which a considerable number of them served. Expressions of support by Russian opposition politicians, and a vote of the Russian Supreme Soviet on July 9, 1993 declaring Sevastopol part of Russia, encouraged locals to believe in Russian support, although they would have done better to note that this declaration was really part of the bitter and ultimately bloody chess game between the Supreme Soviet and the Yeltsin administration, and that it was promptly denounced as illegal by Yeltsin and the Russian Foreign Ministry.

By the end of 1993, anger with Kiev had grown sharply as a result of the economic crisis, much deeper at that time than the crisis in Russia; hyperinflation; and the Ukrainian nationalist rhetoric of the Kravchuk administration. A series of votes by the Crimean parliament—promptly declared illegal by the Ukrainian government—increased Crimean autonomy, and in January 1994 Crimean presidential elections led to the victory (with 73 percent of the vote) of Yuri Meshkov as president of Crimea. A local legal official (allegedly with former KGB links), Meshkov campaigned on a platform of union with Russia, although he moderated his stance somewhat after being elected. Only one of the other six candidates, Crimean parliament chairman and former regional Communist Party first secretary Nikolai Bagrov, had campaigned for continued union with Ukraine. He received 23 percent of the vote. In March, a referendum called by Meshkov produced a 78.4 percent vote for a vaguely defined "sovereignty," and 82 percent for the establishment of joint Russian-Ukrainian citizenship.[13] The support of the great majority of the population of Crimea at that time for some form of union with Russia is hardly therefore in doubt.

However, it is equally true that a great part of Crimea's dissatisfaction with Ukraine was for economic reasons. Meshkov himself told me during the election campaign, "What is happening in Crimea is not a growth of Russian nationalism but that people are losing everything they have worked for, are suffering from desperate shortages, and see the only hope of stability and prosperity in close links with Russia. I do not regard myself as a Russian nationalist—my mother is Ukrainian. I just see that the interests of our republic dictate that we be part of the Russian economic zone."[14]

When it became clear that Meshkov could do nothing to improve the economic situation, his popularity waned fast; by April it had dropped to barely 40 percent, according to opinion polls. Sergei Makarov, a shopkeeper in Simferopol, expressed a very common attitude—echoed by several of his neighbors with whom I spoke—in May 1994 when he told me, "I voted for Meshkov because I believed his promises, that we would join with Russia and things would improve. But now I see that nothing has changed, we are worse off than ever. And there is also talk that Meshkov is building a fine new house for himself, that his followers are stealing. All that has happened is that the name of the leader has changed, Meshkov for Bagrov. All politicians are thieves, in my opinion."[15]

Clearly, a "national movement" whose voters' patience, loyalty, and discipline do not last even four months is not exactly very well motivated. The contrast with the kind of loyalty and determination shown by other national movements in the former Soviet Union—by Balts, Armenians, Abkhazians, or Chechens—is almost ludicrous.

Meshkov was soon bitterly at odds with the Crimean parliament, despite the fact that the great majority of its members had also been elected on pro-Russian tickets. Such splits have occurred in almost every former Soviet republic where any semblance of democracy has been allowed, from Russia and Armenia to Kyrgyzstan. It is nonetheless surprising that the crisis between president and parliament in Crimea occurred so quickly, and at a time when the crisis with the Ukrainian government was at its height.

At the heart of the political crisis among the Russian political forces in Crimea lay the battle over economic policy, with the struggle for control and privatization of state property in the background. Meshkov made a serious mistake when he appointed as his prime minister Yevgeny Saburov, an economist from Moscow (although his family came from Crimea) and former Soviet Russian deputy prime minister. While an able man with a real understanding of economic reform and the practical constraints on Crimean moves, Saburov also proved to be a very unpleasant individual who infuriated local Russian politicians with his open Muscovite contempt for them as ignorant provincials. (This resentment of Muscovite arrogance is widely felt in provincial Russia as well as Ukraine.)

Much more important, the appointment of Saburov and five other ministers from Moscow (out of seven in the whole cabinet) cut the local elites off from sources of local patronage and, above all, from access to privatization (although as it turned out, none occurred under Meshkov's rule). Saburov had no local political base of his own to counter this growing hostility and was too politically inept (and had too little time) to create one.

Finally, if Meshkov had hoped to strengthen his ties to Moscow and thus gain Russian official support for his movement by appointing Saburov, he was completely mistaken. Even before the start of the war in Chechnya in December 1994 began to obsess Moscow's attention, the Russian government had held Meshkov and the Crimean secessionist movement at a very long arm's length. Evidently out of fear of the appalling crisis, both with Ukraine and the West, that would result from Russian-Ukrainian violence in Crimea, the Russian government refused to encourage Meshkov in any way. Instead, Moscow continued to pursue negotiations with Kiev on the division of the Black Sea Fleet (although apparently using the Crimean Russian movement as an extra lever). The Russian government's desire for good relations with Kiev, and the belief that this would yield results, was of course strengthened by Kuchma's victory over Kravchuk in July.

The Yeltsin administration refused even to meet Meshkov officially, and as far as I know he never met Yeltsin, former prime minister Viktor

Chernomyrdin, or former defense minister Pavel Grachev at all, even in private. When he went to Moscow in February 1994 (and reportedly again in April), he was not allowed to meet a single Russian minister in public, and he was told firmly in private to moderate his line. Saburov, too, firmly opposed the more radical Crimean Russian nationalists and secession, and tried to find compromises with Kiev. In an interview with me in late May 1994, Saburov expressed bitter disappointment with Russia's lack of support:

> If the Ukrainian financial blockade continues, do you think Russia will pay our bills? There's about as much chance of the United States doing so.... Since 1991 Russia has pursued an isolationist policy without any serious concern for the positions of Russians outside Russia's borders. There's been some talk, but that's all. This so called "Russian imperialism" now exists only in the pages of your newspapers....
>
> It's true I have friends in the Russian government, but they can do nothing to help us. Russia has her own problems, they say.[16]

As he told the Crimean parliament that afternoon, while deputies bombarded him with demands for state assistance for their areas, factories, and farms; wild proposals for a Crimean currency; and questions about Russian aid, "You have to recognize that we are on our own. The Crimean budget and the economic survival of Ukraine depends on this parliament, no one else. You are looking for a wizard, but I'm not a wizard, or some force to come in from outside and save you, but no such force exists."

Politicians and groups in the Russian Duma gave rhetorical support, but that was all (and in the case of Russia's Communists, their rhetoric was also moderated by the urgent desire to stay on good terms with the Ukrainian Communists, who as noted do not favor Crimean secession). Meanwhile, Crimea's dependence on Ukraine for water, electricity, and transport links was being ruthlessly emphasized by a drought that left local agricultural interests (heavily represented in the parliament) howling for compromise with Kiev to increase Ukrainian water supplies.

Interestingly, even the leader of the government-backed Russian Union of Cossacks, Ataman Viktor Ratiyev, whom I interviewed in Simferopol in May 1994, took a moderate line on relations with Ukraine, stressing the need for peaceful compromise. This was a very different approach from that previously taken by the Cossacks in Moldova and Abkhazia. In part, as Ratiyev himself said, this may have been because of a deep unwillingness to risk war with Ukraine; but it was also, in my view, almost certainly because he had received orders to this effect from his paymasters in the Russian government. He was also obviously doing his best to keep the local "Cossack" volunteers (in any case, few in number and apparently unarmed) led by Lieutenant Colonel Viktor Melnikov, to the same line.

In Ratiyev's words, which were very different indeed from the things he had been saying in Transdniestr two years earlier,

> Our policy is to show that the Cossacks of Crimea, Russia, and Ukraine are one people and are committed to peace and stability in Russia and Ukraine. We promise that where there are Cossacks there will be no conflict. . . . .
>
> We support the efforts of Presidents Yeltsin and Kravchuk to bring about a peaceful resolution of the Crimean problem. We believe that the people of Crimea have the right to decide their own fate and to become a full republic of a new union, but in present circumstances, they should exercise their sovereignty within Ukraine. God grant that there should be no war between Russians and Ukrainians, because we are one people. I say this to you with particular emphasis, because my wife is Ukrainian.[17]

THE COLLAPSE OF THE RUSSIAN SEPARATIST MOVEMENT

Relations between Meshkov and Kiev inevitably deteriorated fast. In March 1994, Kravchuk declared illegal a plebiscite on Crimean sovereignty, and in May he did the same for the sovereignty declaration by the Crimean parliament. The election of Kuchma in July—with overwhelming (83 percent) support from Crimean voters—made little difference, and the new Ukrainian president went on firmly vetoing Crimean laws that were in conflict with the Ukrainian constitution. In May, a Western correspondent described Crimea as "one of the worst of the ethnic flashpoints left over from the former Soviet Union."[18]

By summer, however, Meshkov and the Crimean parliament were already at each other's throats. In September, Meshkov ordered the parliament dissolved and briefly sent police to lock its doors. Kuchma was able to pose as a neutral mediator, urging both sides to find a "civilized solution." Meanwhile, outbreaks of cholera and diphtheria in the region killed several dozen people and increased disenchantment with the government.

At the end of September, the parliament voted to strip Meshkov of almost all his powers. The following month, in a move to win Kiev's support against Meshkov, the parliament voted 63-0 to choose as the new prime minister (replacing Saburov) Anatoly Franchuk, father-in-law of Kuchma's daughter and a close friend of the Ukrainian president.

The standoff continued for months, until the following March. With Russia's attention distracted by the Chechen war, the Ukrainian government and parliament moved against Crimean autonomy, abolishing the 1992 constitution and the office of Crimean president, and placing the Crimean government under direction from Kiev, with the right of veto over the choice of prime minister. Ukrainian troops disarmed Meshkov's small bodyguard, the only armed force at his command (since no steps had been taken to create a Crimean Russian national guard).

Belatedly, Meshkov and the parliamentary majority drew back together and appealed to Moscow; but just three days later, Russian deputy premier Oleg Soskovets visited Kiev as part of an attempt to sign a Russian-Ukrainian treaty, and described Crimea as Ukraine's "internal affair"—for which the Russian government was thanked by Kuchma. Indeed, Russia's own campaign against Chechen separatism would have made support for Crimea utterly inconsistent, and this was openly recognized in Moscow.

In Crimea itself, only a few hundred mostly elderly Russians protested against the Ukrainian move, and the parliament ruled out any attempt at mass mobilization. In July, it tried to dismiss Prime Minister Franchuk as too pro-Ukrainian, but was forced to abandon this move under pressure from Kiev.[19] He was eventually forced out six months later.

Among the reasons for the lack of violent protest in Crimea against the Ukrainian takeover are that the military failure of the Russian army in Chechnya was a terrible shock, and the television pictures of the bloodshed and destruction a salutary warning to the few hotheads who had dreamed of an armed rebellion against Ukraine. There was also a feeling that by going into Chechnya, the Russian government had once again shown its lack of concern for Crimea, and had in fact opened the way for the Ukrainian government's intervention and takeover.

The old Soviet managerial elites, who dominated the Crimean parliament, proved far more interested in fighting with Saburov over the privatization of state property (which of course they wanted themselves) than in risking a real showdown with Kiev, especially without Moscow's support; this was and is also the interest of the immensely powerful Crimean mafia groups, who are closely linked to the local elites.

Meshkov himself proved an extremely, indeed almost comically, incompetent leader and administrator. In many ways, both in his behavior and in his relations with Moscow, Meshkov recalled the president of Belarus, Alexander Lukashenko. Of course, Moscow was much politer to Lukashenko, as the leader of a large, strategically vital, and internationally recognized state. But the Russian government also proved completely unwilling, or unable, to consolidate his friendship by giving him the subsidies he kept asking for.

Most important of all, however, was the fact that in the end the mass of Crimea's Russian population, although it had voted for independence, did not mobilize in support of it—unlike the Balts or the Ukrainian nationalists. If the Crimean parliament had been regularly surrounded by crowds of tens of thousands of people ready to die in Crimea's defense, the Ukrainian government would not have been able to intervene without risking serious bloodshed and consequent Russian state intervention. In fact, pro-independence demonstrations even at the height of the movement never amounted to more than ten thousand people at the very most, and only very rarely numbered more than a thousand. Most of the time the "crowd" outside the parliament consisted quite literally of a half dozen old ladies. This is hardly the stuff of which revolutions are made.

CRIMEA AND UKRAINE SINCE 1995

It would be a mistake, however, to think that the Crimean problem has gone away entirely. The years 1996-1998 saw repeated friction between the Crimean parliament and Kiev over the extent of Crimean autonomy and the appointment of Crimean prime ministers.

Underlying this friction has been an economic situation in Crimea that has continued to deteriorate even faster than in Ukraine as a whole. In September 1997, Prime Minister Franchuk said that the first eight months of that year had seen different sectors of Crimean industry decline between 46 and 60 percent, and that in many fields Crimea's economic decline had been the fastest of any region of Ukraine.[20] In particular, the vitally important tourism sector remains utterly crippled. One reason is the lack of a Russian or Ukrainian middle class. Newly well-off Ukrainians and Russians now go to the West for their holidays; the new poor cannot afford to go to Crimea or anywhere else.

To attract Western tourists, Crimea would need huge investments, which could come only from Western firms; but these are frightened off by official corruption and mindless bureaucracy (as elsewhere in Ukraine); the unstable political situation; and perhaps most important, the iron grip that local mafia groups have over local property, especially in the potentially lucrative tourism sector. Throughout 1997 and 1998, organized criminal groups continued to fight over the spoils, with the number of contract killings running far higher than anywhere else in Ukraine.

With the exception of the anti-NATO protests during the joint U.S.-Ukrainian military exercise Operation Sea Breeze in August 1997 (discussed further in the conclusion), the biggest demonstrations in Crimea in 1996–98 were not against Ukrainian rule or for union with Russia—although these continued at intervals, especially in Sevastopol—but against unpaid wages and pensions. In April 1996, riot police dispersed some three thousand teachers who were blocking roads in protest of their wages being up to six months in arrears. In November 1997, military pensioners blocked roads and railway lines. In January 1998, around six thousand teachers struck and demonstrated again, with their wages now ten months in arrears despite repeated official promises.[21]

It is not difficult to see how at some point such economic discontent could be mobilized once again behind demands for greater autonomy or union with Russia. However, this is in my view not likely to happen for a long time: The collapse of 1994–95 was complete and humiliating; the hostility between the Russian and Ukrainian governments over Sevastopol has been suspended under the 1997 Russia-Ukraine basic treaty; and as already pointed out, the mobilizing capacity of the Russians in Crimea is low. Furthermore, while the economic situation is very bad, for the moment at least it is not much worse than in Russia. Nonetheless, if there should be a return to the position of 1992–94, when Ukrainian living standards were visibly a good deal worse than in Russia and declining faster, then thoughts of separatism would almost automatically be revived.

Finally, as of 1998, there had been no basic reconciliation between the government in Kiev and a great majority in the Crimean parliament, which in turn does seem to reflect the views of most of the inhabitants of Crimea. Instead, there was clash after clash. Some of these were over matters of real substance, such as the repeated disputes over the appointment of Crimean prime ministers. In other cases, both sides seemed to be picking fights for no good reason. This was true of repeated attempts by the Crimean parliament to make Crimea follow Russian, not Ukrainian time (in other words, an hour earlier), and of sharp cuts by the Ukrainian government in Russian-language broadcasting to Crimea (Tatar-language broadcasting was also cut). In April 1997, the retransmission of Russian public television to Sevastopol was stopped altogether, touching off yet more local protests.

The political autonomy of Crimea has been severely reduced; in fact, the line of both Kiev and Kiev's representatives in Crimea has been that Crimea's autonomy should be almost entirely economic. In the words of Crimean deputy prime minister (later prime minister) Arkady Demydenko in September 1995, "I think our constitution should contain provisions for autonomy, but with a strong vertical structure of authority and command, from the president of Ukraine down to the government of Crimea, so that clashes cannot occur. Crimean autonomy should be purely economic, and in this field we should have full control over our own decisions, as long as these do not conflict with the laws of Ukraine."[22]

In March 1996, the Crimean parliament appealed to the Council of Europe and the Organization for Security and Cooperation in Europe, declaring that, "as a result of Ukraine's actions, the autonomous Republic of Crimea no longer possesses any characteristics or functions of an autonomy."

This was an exaggeration as far as economic powers were concerned. In the spring of 1996, Crimean Russian elites, strongly backed by public opinion, had successfully resisted a new Ukrainian constitution that seemed to imply the abolition of Crimea's autonomy—although they were forced to accept several clauses that abolished Crimea's claims to sovereignty (for example, one that deleted references to "Crimean citizens," as opposed to "Ukrainian citizens in Crimea").[23]

Nonetheless, the Crimean appeal proved to have a real basis in fact. In February 1997, after Kuchma had vetoed the parliament's attempt to replace Demydenko (who had replaced Franchuk a year before) as prime minister and choose a new speaker, Ukrainian officials announced that henceforward the Ukrainian presidency would make *all* official appointments in Crimea. The new speaker of the parliament (nominated by Kiev), Anatoly Gritsenko, declared, "The new leadership of the Crimean parliament consists of people who share and accept the policies of the Ukrainian president and parliament"—in other words, not those of the Crimean parliament they were heading. At the same time, Valery Pustovoytenko, chief of staff of the Ukrainian government (and later prime minister), expressed his support for Demydenko in less-than-enthusiastic terms: "[Mr. Pustovoytenko] stressed that . . . Arkady Demydenko has failed to achieve, during his year in office, any improvement in the work of the government. However, he noted that Demydenko would remain in his position."[24]

The absurd thing about this dispute was that the parliament wanted to replace Demydenko with ex-prime minister Franchuk, who could not by any stretch of the imagination be described as anti-Ukrainian. In other words, this was not a dispute about a separatist threat, but a quarrel over power. In the end, in June 1997, Kuchma did agree to reappoint Franchuk, but only after making clear that it was his decision, not the Crimean parliament's.

After the events of 1994–95, it is certainly understandable that the Ukrainian government should want to keep a tight grip on the Crimean administration for a considerable time. Nonetheless, repeatedly vetoing decisions by the local legislature and backing regional governments more for their loyalty than their competence cannot be a basis for stability or good relations—or, of course, democracy—in the long run.[25]

In early 1998, Kiev decided by decree to dismiss the elected municipal government of the Crimean resort town of Yalta and place the town directly under Kiev's jurisdiction. Western diplomats in Kiev told me that this move was almost certainly motivated mainly by a desire to control the privatization of Yalta's real estate.

There has therefore been a well-based fear in Crimea that without any autonomous political power as a defense, former Soviet property in Crimea—especially the hotels and sanatoriums—would simply be seized as "Ukrainian state property" by the Kiev elites for their own use and profit. In the words of Vassily Stefanyuk, head of a Simferopol advertising agency, in 1995, "Under the surface, tremendous battles are going on among the bureaucrats, the politicians, and the mafias, here and in Kiev, for the division of state property. Everyone knows that if you don't get your hands on something, you'll be a poor man in the future. So everyone who can is grabbing something."[26] In the end, it would appear that the Kievan and Crimean elites were able to agree on dividing much of the property between them and their mafia backers.

That the Crimean government and political groups were by 1995 acting as a front for criminal groupings was stated as a fact by the great majority of political observers with whom I spoke in Crimea. Leonid Pilunski, head of the Helsinki Citizens' Assembly (for encouraging people's awareness of their legal rights) and no sort of Russian nationalist, told me that "Crimea today is simply ruled by criminals, it is a criminal state. Behind every political group, government, or opposition, there stands a criminal one." This, he said, was one reason—apart from their own personal stupidity—that Meshkov and Saburov suddenly found themselves so isolated in the summer of 1994. They had simply not taken into account the critical struggle for property. "They thought they were playing chess, and they suddenly found themselves playing draughts—without knowing the rules."[27]

SEVASTOPOL—"CITY OF RUSSIAN GLORY"

Sevastopol is not an ancient Russian city; it was founded on the orders of Catherine the Great in 1784 after the Russian conquest of the Crimean Tatars. Established near the ruins of the ancient Greek city of Chersonesus, Sevastopol was given a Greek name meaning "City of Honor." Yet Sevastopol is older than most American cities—several decades older than the great American naval ports of Pearl Harbor and San Diego, for example (or rather, the American possession of San Diego, which was previously a Spanish and then a Mexican town).

As stated, even for Russians who regard the loss of all the other former Russian territories with relative indifference, Sevastopol is simply Russian. In conversation, Russians often describe it as the last straw: "We have given up so much, and now this as well." In the words of a Russian student at Moscow State University, "Look at how many magnificent lands the Ukrainians have taken from us, and then Sevastopol on top of that. Instead of making so much anti-Russian noise, they should be thankful for what they've got, and sit as quiet as mice." It is only fair to add, however, that she ruled out any Russian war with Ukraine:

> No one in Russia actually wants to fight Ukraine and send their sons to die there, for Sevastopol or anywhere else. We don't hate the Ukrainians. They're just annoying, that's all. . . . And all this Russian talk of Ukraine not really existing, that the Ukrainians say they're so worried about— yes, it exists, but it's just kitchen-table talk. In practice, every Russian with any sense knows that Ukraine is independent and will stay independent. They know that to take away that independence they'd have to fight, and no one wants to fight, on the contrary most Russians want good relations with Ukraine, that's the whole point. The bitterness is over particular issues, like Sevastopol. If we could solve these, relations and attitudes would get much better, I'm sure.[28]

Before he became prime minister, Russian foreign minister Yevgeny Primakov expressed the pragmatic and moderate Russian view on Sevastopol as follows, in March 1997:

> My opinion is that we must not advocate any territorial claims against
> Ukraine, absolutely not. . . . Any territorial claims by Russia could really
> set us against each other, and any kind of conciliation would be very,
> very far removed. It would be a tragedy both for Russia and Ukraine. But
> you have to understand that deep in the heart of every Russian there is
> a belief that Sevastopol is a Russian city. We suggest as a solution a long-
> term lease of Sevastopol as the base for the Russian Black Sea Fleet.[29]

Russians point out, with some justice, that if Khrushchev had not transferred Sevastopol to Ukraine in 1954, the independent Ukrainian state after 1991 would certainly never have dreamed of asking for it, or indeed for Crimea, as these were by no stretch of the imagination ever Ukrainian territory, and had never been portrayed as such even by the most strident Ukrainian nationalists (although they were briefly claimed by the Rada in 1917).

In private, many Ukrainian officials themselves admit as much: "Who would ask to swallow a hedgehog?" as one of them glumly put it to me. Instead, their most forceful and effective arguments are that existing borders and Ukrainian territorial integrity must be respected; looking at some of Russia's own restive regions and undefined frontiers, they point out that these principles are also important to Russia itself. This argument is partially accepted in Moscow, and helps explain Russia's passivity with regard to the Crimean issue.

It is not that most Russians, or even Russian politicians, spend large amounts of time worrying about Sevastopol, or that they want to annex it, if necessary, through war. The sentiment against fighting Ukraine is overwhelming. Nonetheless, if pressed, an overwhelming majority of Russians will say that it is a Russian city, and that Russia must retain a *permanent* stake there through the guaranteed presence of the Russian Black Sea Fleet.

These sentiments have been reflected in repeated votes in the Russian Supreme Soviet and, since 1993, the Duma, declaring that the 1954 transfer was illegal, and affirming that Sevastopol is a Russian city—declarations which have been rejected by the Yeltsin administration. In April 1997, the Russian Federation Council (the upper house of parliament) proposed a joint Russian-Ukrainian administration of Sevastopol, touching off another furious response from Kiev. This is particularly striking because, unlike the directly elected Duma, the Council is made up of regional governors and representatives of Russia's autonomous republics—that is to say, people with a strong stake in stability and peace.

It is also highly instructive in this context that Moscow mayor Yuri Luzhkov, a prime contender to succeed Yeltsin as president, has repeatedly declared his support for a Russian presence in Sevastopol. During a highly inflammatory visit in January 1997 (made despite warnings by the Ukrainian foreign ministry that his presence was undesirable), Luzhkov declared, "No Russian will feel comfortable until Sevastopol is returned to the Russian Federation. . . . Sevastopol is a city of Russian glory. It was and remains a Russian city and we should defend its right to be a Russian city."[30]

These remarks were promptly disavowed by the Russian government. It is very unlikely that if he became president, Luzhkov, an archpragmatist if ever there was one, would ever want to go to war over Sevastopol. But he is one of Russia's most skilled politicians, with a fine feel for the public's pulse. If he thinks that there is electoral capital to be made out of Sevastopol—even after the signature of the basic treaty and leasing agreement of 1997—the rest of the world should take notice.

An additional reason for the politically dangerous nature of the Sevastopol issue is that the Russian population of the city (which has a significant total population of 366,000, according to the 1989 Soviet census —twice as much, for example, as the predominantly ethnic Armenian enclave in Azerbaijan's Nagorno-Karabakh region, and almost as many as Chechnya's capital city of Grozny) is perhaps much more easily mobilizable than Russians elsewhere in Crimea, let alone in the rest of Ukraine. For one thing, they are conscious of being the overwhelming majority; second, they are to a greater extent genuinely ethnically Russian and less intermarried with the Ukrainians; and third, because so many of them are naval veterans, they have a much stronger sense of Russian identity and military patriotism, partly because the Soviet navy preserved much more of a sense of continuity from the Russian imperial fleet and its traditions than did the Red Army.

After the debacle of 1994–95, the city's political leadership is by no means in a radical mood, especially because it is deeply in debt to the Ukrainian government for energy and other supplies. In the words of a senior municipal official, speaking off the record,

> The bulk of the Russian population here is Russian and feels Russian; I am a Russian myself. I lived for forty years in the Soviet Union and found its dissolution, and all these new [borders], extremely painful as well as very harmful for the interests of our people. . . . I wish we could all live peacefully and harmoniously in something like the European Union. I deeply fear the threat of a Ukrainian-Russian conflict—though it does

not look likely, thank God—and I am very worried when I hear all this nationalist talk of us being a buffer against Russia. Think what that would do to us here; it would make our position completely impossible. No one here wants rebellion and war, and we certainly don't want to be pulled into anyone else's wars. . . .

It's true that a great many local people would still like independence from Ukraine. But that's like my daughter saying, "I want to be independent, but you must go on feeding me"—it's just not realistic. As a Ukrainian civil servant, paid by Ukraine, I have little choice in my actions. If Russia would give Sevastopol a large sum of money to pay our debts to Ukraine and our municipal wage bill, then, between us, I might give you a different answer. But Russia has problems of her own.

Although even here they are not willing to provide open or covert subsidies as a result of their feelings, the reasons Russians attach more importance to Sevastopol than any other ethnically Russian area of the former Soviet Union have to do with both history and current strategy, but more with the former. Strategically, Sevastopol retains its importance as a naval base in the event of a conflict with Turkey. Rivalry with Turkey in the Black Sea region focuses especially on conflicting plans for the transport of oil and gas from the new Caspian Sea fields to the outside world. Turkey advocates a route (currently supported by the United States) through Georgia and Turkey to its Mediterranean port of Ceyhan; Russia's preferred route would bring Caspian oil to its terminal at Novorossisk and then across the Black Sea to either Bulgaria or Romania. Russia's perception of a Turkish threat has grown with the very uncomfortable awareness that because of Russia's precipitous military decline, its forces are now inferior to those of Turkey in this region.[31] In some far-off, theoretical future, Sevastopol might also be the base once again of a "blue water" fleet capable of sending squadrons to the Mediterranean and the Indian Ocean, although at present such an eventuality looks utterly remote.

At present the Russian navy, particularly the Black Sea Fleet, is quite simply falling to pieces, with its ships being cannibalized to keep others even partly seaworthy. Ukrainians say with glee that in ten years, the "problem" of the fleet will no longer exist because it will simply have sunk quietly to the bottom of the sea. Yet this quip ignores the fact that the fleet involves not just ships but also major air force and air defense units as well as a marine infantry of fifteen hundred troops.

As for the Russian naval command, its current plan is to adjust to reality by converting the Black Sea, Baltic, and probably even Far Eastern

Fleets into much smaller, but hopefully efficient, coastal defense forces, leaving only the Northern Fleet with any "strategic" capability.

Much more important is the moral and emotional significance of Sevastopol's history. The city is partly seen as a symbol of the Russian Empire and the Russian navy at the height of their achievement and glory, and as a base from which Russian fleets sailed out to do victorious battle against the Turks.

Above all, however, Sevastopol is seen as a symbol of brave and stoic Russian *resistance* in two great historic sieges. The first was in 1854-55, when Russian forces held out for eleven months against the attacking armies of France, Britain, and Turkey. Three Russian commanders were killed in succession while leading the defense, and the battle entered Russian literary history through the work of Leo Tolstoy, who served there as a junior artillery officer.

Of even greater emotional weight for Russians (who forget that this was not a purely Russian battle) is the defense of Sevastopol against the Germans for ten months in 1941-42, one of the most heroic episodes of the Second World War. Outnumbered and outgunned, the surrounded Soviet forces fought almost literally to the last man and the last patch of ground, returning in 1944 to sweep the Germans from Crimea. In particular, the defense of 1941-42 was the greatest epic in the history of the elite marine infantry.

Between them, these battles over a few dozen square miles of land cost around 1.2 million lives from all the armies involved—more than the losses of the British Empire on all fronts in the First World War, far more than both sides in the American Civil War, and more than the United States in the First and Second World Wars combined. For Russians, the battles over Sevastopol are almost as weighty in military lore as the sieges of Stalingrad and Leningrad.

When Westerners say that all this is in the past and that Russians should "snap out of it," it is difficult not to smile. Britain, it may be remembered, not so long ago fought a small but bloody war for a group of strategically worthless, almost uninhabited "ice-cold bits of rock" (as President Reagan called them) in the South Atlantic; France clings to various expensive and useless outposts that remind it of past glory; and the United States has engaged in a deeply emotional internal debate about whether to hand over the Panama Canal, thereby risking serious damage to its relations with Latin America. In other words, there is nothing very unusual or "aggressive" about Russia's stance over this issue, the more so because—it must be repeated once again—

Sevastopol for Russians is not just a remote naval base, but a part of Russian national territory. Not Guantánamo Bay, but San Diego. Of course, this may change with time. In the words of one Moscow-based military attaché from a NATO country in 1995, "I don't know if the Russians would go to war for Sevastopol, but there's no doubt whatsoever that it is of enormous emotional significance to them. A Russian city, built by Russians, inhabited by Russians, defended by Russians. Twice defended, twice lost, twice regained—one of their great heroic episodes. The British would have said just the same about Gibraltar forty years ago. But now, of course, most British couldn't give a damn."[32]

Russian public opinion polls show a majority of Russians opposed to the stationing of Russian troops outside Russia if this is liable to lead to armed clashes and the loss of Russian lives. But Sevastopol is not regarded as "outside Russia," and contemporary history suggests that while weary former imperial nations will in the end give up *imperial* territory without a fight, they may fight very hard to keep *national* territory.

Sevastopol is indeed just about the only territory outside Russia's borders for which one can imagine Russian soldiers and the Russian population actually wanting to fight and being willing to fight hard; even then, for this to happen, they would have to see Russia as having been directly attacked. As Chechnya shows, the very tired, apathetic, and deeply unmilitary Russian people and their extremely cynical, demoralized, and disorganized armed forces are really in no mood for a fight if they can help it.

At certain moments over the past seven years, the question of the Black Sea Fleet did seem to bring Russia and Ukraine close to armed violence. However, this threat has now been suspended at least—and, we must hope, ended altogether—by the 1997 Russia-Ukraine basic treaty and the accompanying agreement on the division of the fleet and its bases.

The treaty lasts for ten years and guarantees the sovereignty and territorial integrity of both countries. Both sides undertake not to form alliances with third states to be used against each other, and promise not to allow their respective territories to be used for threats to the other's security. They also promise to resolve all disputes between them peacefully.[33]

Concerning Sevastopol, it was agreed that Russia would lease the main fleet installations for twenty years at a rent of around $100 million a year. This is to be drawn from Ukraine's huge unpaid debt to Russia for oil and gas supplies, estimated to have reached more than $3.5 billion as of 1997. The Ukrainian navy keeps a presence at Sevastopol, being based in the subsidiary Streletskaya Bay. Ukraine had previously agreed to sell its 50 percent share of the ships and shore-based forces to Russia, and is left with about 18 percent of the whole.[34]

This seems a reasonable compromise. The length of the lease is much less than the Russians had been demanding previously (ninety-nine years was a time frame I often heard proposed in Moscow), but considerably longer than more radical Ukrainians had been insisting on. The rental is far higher than the Russians previously had been willing to pay—but then, most sensible Russians had long given up hope of the Ukrainians ever repaying most of their energy debts in any case.

The Russian side made one very important concession in agreeing that the Ukrainian navy could continue to be based alongside Russia's in Sevastopol itself. For years, the Russians had been insisting that the Ukrainian squadron move to one of the lesser military ports in Crimea, such as Balaclava. However, with the points of dispute between the two fleets now cleared up, their presence in the same port need not necessarily lead to friction—as long as the general geopolitical situation does not change. Yet it should be remembered that the agreement does not appear to have been popular with most of Sevastopol's populace, who had been hoping for an exclusively Russian presence.[35]

It is important to note, however, that this agreement has not solved the Sevastopol problem for good; it has only suspended it for twenty years. The agreement has a provision that the lease can be extended for five years if both parties agree, but after that the whole agreement would have to be renegotiated.

The view of many senior Ukrainian officials—and, of course, of nationalist politicians—is that the lease should not be renewed and the Russian navy should leave. Indeed, this is implied in Articles 17 and 92 of the Ukrainian constitution, passed in July 1996: The first categorically forbids the stationing of foreign troops in Ukraine; the second, a rather contradictory article that was passed with Sevastopol in mind, allows military bases, but only for limited periods.[36]

At present, most Russians, and certainly most Russian naval officers, have no intention of ever moving the fleet from Sevastopol, whatever the Ukrainians may say. In the words of Lieutenant Commander Andrei Krylov of the Black Sea Fleet,

> Russia has agreed again and again to divide the fleet with Ukraine. Of course, we in the fleet don't like it, but we have loyally accepted the decision. We have made agreement after agreement, and each time the

Ukrainian government has extracted some concession from Russia and then gone back on their word. Naturally this makes us mistrustful. . . . Also, we simply can't share the base at Sevastopol with the Ukrainian fleet—you see how it is. It would be like cats and dogs, endless arguments, damaging the interests of both fleets and of the town. Much better if they move to another base. . . .

We have recognized this as Ukrainian territory—though of course many still privately disagree, but that is not the issue. We are not challenging their sovereignty. The point is that this is and has always been a Russian naval base, and both we and the great majority of the people of Sevastopol—who also have a right to be heard—want it to remain so forever.

If we lose bases elsewhere, we can always restore them. If we leave here, we would have left for good. And no Russian naval officer is going to leave Sevastopol.[37]

The vast majority of Black Sea Fleet officers appear strongly committed to Russia and opposed to a Ukrainian takeover, even when Russia sacks them. Thus in the first three months of 1996, more than fifteen hundred officers of the fleet lost their jobs as a result of "restructuring" (or, as one might say, a belated recognition of reality) by the Russian defense ministry. Despite assiduous wooing and job offers by the Ukrainian navy, only seventy of them, or less than 5 percent, volunteered for the Ukrainian service.[38]

Of course, an awful lot can happen in twenty years. First of all, the fleet itself is going to be reduced to a shadow of its former self, as aging ships are retired (or simply sink at their moorings) and are not replaced—although this presumably will not be the case with the air defense squadrons and the marines. Whatever some may believe about an "unchanging Russian imperial character," the Russian people may indeed come to resemble the British and lose interest in such overseas outposts (although, once again, the Falklands is a cautionary example in this regard). The people of Sevastopol may come to accept Ukrainian rule. Or, on the other hand, future Ukrainian governments and political leaders may decide that the Russian fleet is not doing any great harm just sitting there, after all, a view that already appears to be shared by most ordinary Ukrainians.

Any or indeed all of these things may happen over the next two decades. However, they will not happen automatically; in the meantime, the West in my view should be using this long breathing space to cool down the feelings of both sides about Sevastopol and the fleet.

Frankly, by far the best thing for Western security, for the interests of Russia and Ukraine, and—last but not least—for the people of Sevastopol itself would be if both Russians and Ukrainians were simply to forget about the place.

THE RUSSIAN AND UKRAINIAN ARMED FORCES

As of 1998, neither the great bulk of the Ukrainian armed forces nor the vast majority of Russian officers have the slightest desire to fight each other, which may prove to be the greatest factor of all in guaranteeing "security" in this area.

During my visits to Crimea during the most tense period of the Crimean separatist movement in 1994 and 1995, I conducted an informal opinion poll on the streets, questioning some seven Ukrainian officers and officer cadets from the Ukrainian army and Black Sea squadron, and five Russian officers from the Black Sea Fleet about the danger of armed conflict between Russia and Ukraine over Crimea. Every one of them replied not just that this was highly unlikely, but that they themselves and the great majority of their comrades were absolutely against any conflict and strongly supported compromise solutions.

This was a striking difference from my experience with attitudes in other parts of the former Soviet Union where conflicts developed—for example, Georgian and Abkhazian responses in Abkhazia before the outbreak of fighting there. It meant that in Crimea, there was far less danger that violence might start spontaneously in chance encounters between edgy and bitterly hostile armed men on either side. I am convinced that this played a key role in preventing the outbreak of violence on the peninsula.

It may be instructive in this context to quote two sets of remarks to me, one by General Aleksandr Lebed in February 1994, when he was commanding the Russian Fourteenth Army in Transdniestr, the other by a Ukrainian captain in the summer of 1995, whom I met by chance on a train and who was speaking off the record. I asked both men if they thought there was a danger of war between Russia and Ukraine and, if so, how their respective armies would fight.

In General Lebed's opinion,

> The Fourteenth Army will never fight against Ukraine, and I don't believe the Russian army as a whole will either. For example, I myself am half Ukrainian, and my three deputy commanders are all Ukrainians. The Russian army officer corps today is about 30 percent Ukrainian, just as

the Ukrainian army is at least 30 percent Russian—whatever these words mean, because we are so intermarried that really it's impossible to say who is what exactly, and we never thought about it. We will never fight each other. Of course, there are problems in Crimea, for example, because it was historically Russian territory and the people there feel Russian; but it can and must all be sorted out peacefully. A Russian invasion to divide up Ukraine? No—out of the question.[39]

According to the Ukrainian officer, Vadim, to whom I quoted Lebed's remarks,

Only a tiny minority of officers, even in our officers' union, actually want to fight Russia. Most would agree with Lebed. It's quite true that we are closely related: I served for much of my career in Russia, and of course many of my closest friends are Russians. I come from a military family, my wife is Russian, my sister is married to a Russian officer and they are stationed in Leningrad [sic] now. . . .

As to how the Ukrainian army would fight in a war with Russia—and a war really isn't likely, thank God—to be honest, I think that would depend on how the war started. If it seemed as though a nationalist Ukrainian government had gone out of its way to provoke the Russians, and if at the same time they were ramming Ukrainianization down our throats and sacking good officers so as to appoint nationalists and political timeservers, and at the same time paying us a pittance—like what happened in 1992 and 1993, say, but even worse—then I think the army might just fall to pieces if it was asked to fight. But if on the other hand it was obviously Russia that was attacking us, say if some madman like Zhirinovsky came to power and started threatening us and demanding or invading Ukrainian territory, maybe trying to throw us out of Crimea by force, then I think Ukrainians would be so angry they would fight very hard. I would, certainly. After all, Ukraine is my home. I won't allow anyone to disturb its peace, to kill its people. But we really don't want to fight Russia, and I'm convinced the vast majority of Russians don't want to fight us either.[40]

The viewpoint of the strongly nationalist former Ukrainian defense minister, General Kostiantyn Morozov, whom I also interviewed in 1995, was of course quite different. In his words,

The basis of the state must be the Ukrainian nation, and all state policies should be based on this principle. In some fields, we may have to go slowly about this to avoid angering the Russian-speaking areas, but the army is a special case. Here we can't delay. Of course, people of all nationalities in Ukraine should have the right to serve in the army, but only if they accept Ukraine as their only homeland and feel no other loyalties.... There must also be a rapid move to the Ukrainian language and a Ukrainian cultural basis for the military. I regarded and still regard the Union of Officers as a very positive force in that regard....

Our soldiers must be ready to defend their country against every aggressor and in all circumstances, which is only possible if it has a deep conviction of its national tasks. At the beginning, when I was defense minister, we had such a policy. When we chose cadres for senior positions, we made our criteria active patriotism as well as professionalism. We examined their past careers, their families, what they did and where they lived, and their attitudes to Ukraine and Ukrainian history.... We did not ask them specifically if they would be ready to fight Russia; we just wanted to make sure that they would fight any enemy of Ukraine if necessary. That is required of soldiers in every army of the world, and we should ask it of ours as well.[41]

This is a military view that is understandable and, as the general said, almost universal. However, it must also be said that—in my view—in the past century in Europe we have seen more than enough examples of nations that believed their security lay in national armies not just trained to fight each other, but also psychologically conditioned to hate and fear each other, after the fashion of the members of the Ukrainian officers' union mentioned by the general and their attitudes to Russia.

Thus Captain Yevhen Lupakov, head of the officers' union in the Ukrainian Black Sea Fleet, told me, "Russians are a people who throughout their history have practiced ruthless and barbarous aggression against their neighbors, and I don't believe they have changed. How can you ask us to trust them? Of course we have to be ready to fight them if necessary, and our troops have to be educated for this."[42]

The union has called for officers of Ukrainian origin to leave the Russian armed forces, because "Moscow colonizers are planning aggression against Ukraine."[43] Similar attitudes about "Ukrainian nationalists" —not about Ukrainians as a people—are to be found among a few ultranationalist Russian officers.

However, such "security" has often proved wholly illusory in the past. Given this melancholy history, it may be worth at least trying an experiment to see whether mutual security is not better guaranteed by two opposing armies that do not hate and fear each other, do not want to fight each other, and do not in fact very much want to fight anybody —even were either of them at present in any state to do so.

5

Ukrainian and Russian Nationalisms and National Identities in the 1990s

Ethnic and Civic Versions of Ukrainian Nationalism

The point about the Ukrainians and Russians not wanting to fight each other leads naturally to another central question posed by this work, a question that concerns the nature and future development of Ukrainian and Russian national identities and national feelings. Equally important is the question of what is the *desirable* course of their development, from the point of view of not only the West but of these people themselves.

General Morozov and Western proponents of the "buffer state" project would say that Ukraine's only hope of achieving a real national identity, as well as true independence and security, is by differentiating itself sharply from the culture and ideology of Russia and by greatly increasing Ukrainian ethnic nationalism. In the words of the Ukrainian-American scholar Yaroslav Bilinsky, "As victims of physical and cultural genocide, the Ukrainians could and should insist on being given the benefit of the doubt in their attempt to widen and deepen the majority ethnic basis of the new Ukraine, particularly in the circumstance of a very aggressive tendency on the part of the old dominant Russian minority to take over positions of power in the newly independent and not quite consolidated country. To build Ukraine as a non-ethnic based civil society has not worked out."[1] The crucial question Bilinsky leaves unanswered, however, is *which* Ukrainians? The majority who voted for Kuchma's bilingual program in 1994 and against radical Ukrainian nationalism?

As Andrew Wilson has pointed out, this kind of thinking has led Ukrainian nationalists, even those professing democratic ideals, to send out "mixed signals" in certain crucial areas as to whether individual preferences or even democratic majorities should necessarily be respected if these run up against what the nationalists perceive as the "vital interests of the nation." This dilemma especially pertains to the status of the Russian language in Ukraine, and to "positive discrimination" in favor of Ukrainian.[2] This approach was cogently criticized by Vladimir Grinev, who declared in 1993, "We cannot accept the proposition that it is first necessary to build a state, and only after that can we think of democracy. With that kind of attitude, God knows what kind of a state—authoritarian or even fascist—we might build."[3]

The approach advocated by Bilinsky would in fact be akin to the process by which most European nation-states were formed in the nineteenth century and would indeed, therefore, be the "natural" path of Ukrainian national development. It would also be a mistake in my view and perhaps a very disastrous path. After all, "classical" European state and national formation also took place through repeated wars and violent national hostilities, leading in this century to two monstrous catastrophes which destroyed Europe's greatness. It is disappointing to find some members of the Ukrainian diaspora in the West returning to their homeland bearing such messages.

At present, this tendency also seems not just unnecessary but actively counterproductive from the point of view of Ukrainian state building and the consolidation of independence. For, as I have pointed out repeatedly in this book, while Ukraine has not become a civil society, the Ukrainian state so far has been much more stable and cohesive than many of its own supporters feared—certainly more so than U.S. intelligence agencies predicted in their 1994 National Intelligence Estimate —and this has surely been a boon not just to Ukraine itself but to the region and indeed the world. Internal ethnic peace and harmony, based on an avoidance of just such ethnicist policies as recommended by Bilinsky, have therefore not detracted from but contributed to the building of the Ukrainian state and hence Ukrainian independence. In any case, if Russian elites in Ukraine are disallowed from seeking power within the Ukrainian system, then where will they seek it?

An ethnonationalist development of the Ukrainian state would not only destabilize Ukraine internally, it could also contribute to the great misfortune of Russia itself developing in such a direction—that is to say, of Russian national consolidation along ethnic lines—and of this leading to similar reactions in neighboring nations. Needless to say, such a process would bring ruin to the entire region.

Under President Kuchma and his likely successors, and under the elites who now rule Russia, there is little likelihood of this happening. Kuchma's Ukrainian nationalism is far from being ethnicist or intolerant. On the contrary, it is mostly moderate, civic, integrationist, and has indeed successfully appealed to many of the Russian and Russian-speaking elites of eastern and southern Ukraine (although a narrower and harsher strain of nationalism resides among certain state elements, especially in the education ministry).

However, it is also true—as the more radical nationalists charge—that this version of nationalism, while inoffensive, does in some ways lack content and spirit; and there is always the risk that these nationalists will go on providing Ukrainian nationalism with a content that is hostile to the Russians, particularly given problems—such as the Sevastopol question—in relations between Russia and Ukraine, and the perhaps inevitable tendency of anyone ruling Ukraine to feel the need to mark the state off from Russia.[4] "Integrationist," after all, is not exactly the same thing as "inclusive." A widespread view among neutral observers of nation building, as well as nationalists themselves, is that, "the nation-building process does not involve solely 'positive' identification—'What we are'—but also, *and perhaps primarily* 'negative' identification —'What we are not.'"[5]

And herein lies a danger. For one might foresee a future in which the Russian-speaking "Ukrainians," and indeed many of the "Russians," are integrated into the "Ukrainian nation," but at the cost of excluding substantial minorities, with a much firmer Russian "counteridentity" of their own. If 85 percent of Ukrainians were to develop a stronger Ukrainian consciousness, but at the price of 15 percent developing a stronger Russian consciousness, and if this 15 percent were concentrated in Crimea and the Donbas, the result would be not more, but much less internal stability and unity for Ukraine. This problem has been sensitively analyzed by Alexander Motyl, who points out that "Although inclusionary Ukrainian nationalism is certainly preferable to the exclusionary variety, and is not necessarily inconsistent with a state-based national identity, it too views the ethnically Ukrainian nation as the cornerstone of state-building."[6] Motyl recommends instead the state-based Ukrainian nationalist thought of the early twentieth-century Ukrainian political philosopher Vyacheslav Lypynsky, as revived by the contemporary historian Yaroslav Hrytsak. Yet Motyl ruefully acknowledges that given the hostility of contemporary Ukrainian nationalists to Lypynsky, the proponents of such ideas "are in for a rough time."

Lypynsky, a conservative Ukrainian patriot, politician, and historian who had supported Skoropadsky, criticized the Ukrainian national movement of 1917–20 for its failure to appeal to non-Ukrainians, and argued that this had been a key reason for its defeat. He appealed for territorial —not ethnic—patriotism and was a strong opponent of the ethnic-based (and quasi-fascist) "integral nationalism" which gathered strength among Ukrainian nationalist organizations in the 1930s.[7]

One could also recommend that the new Ukrainian state take a leaf from the book of the old Russian imperial state's propaganda in Ukraine, which certainly demonized certain Ukrainian "traitors," such as Hetman Ivan Mazepa, for example, who rebelled against Peter the Great. But the Russian state could not possibly have been so successful in attracting Ukrainian loyalty if it had treated the whole Ukrainian tradition in this way. Instead, the approach emphasized elements of common identity, religion, history, and culture (although, of course, Russian propaganda also highlighted the presence of common enemies—Poles, Turks, Germans, and to a lesser extent, Jews).

Fortunately, some of the basis for a more positive and vibrant, but inclusive, Ukrainian patriotism clearly distinct from that of Russia is present today, and this basis is recognized by many ordinary Russians and Russian intellectuals in Ukraine. Partly it centers on the fact that Ukraine today is more peaceful than Russia and does not have ambitions to play the role of a military great power; another part derives from Ukraine's much stronger European character than Russia's in the past—if only this can be given some reality in the future. The first aspect was summed up for me by Vilen Gorsky, head of an institute for the study of public opinion in Kiev:

All these arguments about history are the work of small groups of nationalist intellectuals; ordinary people, whether Russians or Ukrainians, don't give a damn. History as such won't lead to serious trouble between Russia and Ukraine. . . .

Actually, Ukraine in this way is much luckier than Russia, though the Ukrainian nationalists don't see it, precisely because it doesn't have this great load of history weighing on it: our glorious ancestors, empire, great power status, the National Idea, the salvation of the world. . . . This leaves people here freer to concentrate on just trying to live in a civilized way. And educated, intelligent Russians here are beginning to feel that, and to be grateful to be in Ukraine. . . . It's like in Britain, I believe: The more you keep thinking about your glorious past, the less you can cope with the modern world.[8]

Among ordinary Russians, a feeling of relief to be in Ukraine was given a tremendous boost by the bloody and disastrous Russian war in Chechnya, whose horrifying images were of course shown on all of Ukraine's television channels. These images came on top of disturbing media coverage of the bombardment of the Russian parliament in October 1993, and of the involvement and losses of Russian troops in Tajikistan and other regional conflicts.

While not as articulate as Gorsky's explanation, the sentiment of a Russian housewife in Kharkiv expresses a widespread and very important recognition: "I may not be too happy in this independent Ukraine, but at least I'm glad that my son will never have to go and risk his life in some stupid war in the Caucasus because politicians in Moscow tell him to."[9]

This feeling may be of more than temporary importance in bolstering a Russian sense of identification with Ukraine, because it ties in with the traditional Russian stereotype of the Ukrainians mentioned previously: the image of them as slower, milder, gentler, and less prone to violence than the Russians. Of course, as is the case with any other stereotype, this image is open to question, and it clashes head on with another Russian stereotype, that of the savage, bloodthirsty Galician "Banderovite" (it also clashes with both the Ukrainian and the Russian image of the Zaporozhian Cossacks, not a notably gentle lot). Nonetheless, as an enduring, deeply rooted image, it is a useful basis on which a more strongly felt Ukrainian patriotism can be built, and it has apparently been confirmed by recent events.

Such an image ties in well with the deep though unformulated antimilitarism of ordinary people throughout Ukraine and Russia, and it reflects a sentiment based on the fear of war, a general demilitarization of attitudes resulting from modernization and demographic change, and an aversion to the atrocious conditions of military service.

This antimilitarism was perhaps expressed in Russian-Ukrainian attitudes to President Leonid Kuchma, even after faith in him had begun to wane. In the words of a journalist from Dnipropetrovsk in August 1995,

Kravchuk made all those big speeches on television about the Ukrainian nation and its history and culture, declaring that everything is fine, we are sailing ahead to a glorious future—and in the end it just infuriated people, it became a joke given the way things had really turned out. Whereas Kuchma sits there with his head in his hand, and he says, more or less, "We're sinking; it's really quite awful. But we shall all have to do our best to save ourselves." He gives a gentle, rather gloomy impression, like Ia in *Vinni-Pukh* [Eeyore in *Winnie the Pooh*]. He doesn't blame anyone or look for scapegoats and enemies. For all I know, it may be a complete pose. But people here seem to like it. The Ukrainians are a mild, calm people on the whole, without so much of the Russian tendency to strong leaders and violent solutions.[10]

Or as Maria Antonova, a scientist now working for a living in Donetsk's market, put it in August 1995—probably also reflecting the impact of Chechnya and the nose-dive in Yeltsin's popularity—when I quoted these remarks to her,

Yes, that may be so, but let me tell you we're all getting pretty tired of Kuchma holding his head and saying how bad everything is. We know how bad things are a lot better than he does. His job is to *do* something about it. . . . But all the same I must admit, he is not a cruel or violent man. He is probably corrupt, like all the rest, but he is civilized and cultured, and I don't think he would ever kill lots of people or oppress them. . . . We are disappointed that he has not kept his promises over the Russian language and so on, but I don't think that is because he is anti-Russian. It is just that he is weak, he is afraid of those nationalists and Galicians and all the trouble and even violence they might cause if they don't get their own way as always.[11]

The other factor involves Ukraine's supposedly greater cultural closeness to Europe. In the Baltic states, the recognition by local Russians (however grudging) that the Balts have a "higher civic culture" and are "closer to Europe" has been of critical importance in their passive acceptance of the new situation there. Three hundred years ago, parts of Ukraine also had a much freer and more developed civic culture than Russia, but this has been largely obliterated by the intervening years of Russian and Soviet rule; and, as already noted, the Galician tradition does little to sustain such a culture. Nonetheless, if Ukraine could create vibrant and prestigious civic institutions, this would also attract real local Russian loyalty—although probably only if, as in the Baltic states, it were combined with a real and visible promise of economic progress and equal distribution of its benefits among the population. Unfortunately, as of 1998, such progress is almost wholly lacking.

But perhaps even this failure to reform does not matter so much as long as Ukraine's economy does not once again fall far behind Russia's. If the economic circumstances of 1993 were to repeat themselves and continue for a long period, Ukrainian unity and stability undoubtedly would be endangered in the long run, even if Russia did not lift a finger. On the other hand, if Ukraine were to make major economic and cultural progress toward the West while Russia lagged further and further behind, then—as in the Baltic states—this would not only strengthen the Ukrainian state but would go a long way toward consolidating the loyalty of the Ukrainian Russians. As of 1998, however, there is no sign of this happening.

It is worth restating that the "Russian diaspora" in Ukraine, so often and so mistakenly viewed as a Muscovite fifth column in waiting, is neither truly Russian nor a diaspora in the usually accepted sense of the word. In fact, neither the "Russians" nor the very large number of Russian-speaking Ukrainians in eastern and southern Ukraine feel any great loyalty to *the Russian government*, and they are gradually developing a genuine allegiance to Ukraine. What they do feel is a genuine attachment to *the Russian people* and thus a strong desire to maintain close and friendly—but also equal—relations with Russia. The Russian language, and the separation of state from ethnicity throughout Russia's history, gives Russians in Ukraine an opportunity to express this linkage clearly. Their spokesmen often say, "*My Russkiye, no my ne Rossia-nye*" ("We are [ethnic] Russians, but we are not Russian citizens"—or perhaps, since citizenship is a concept which has had little meaning in most of Russian history, "We do not belong to the Russian state."

In the words of Dmitri Vydrin, a senior member of President Kuchma's staff and a typical representative of the (large majority) of Russian intellectuals in Kiev who now identify with independent Ukraine,

> Relations between the Russian and Ukrainian states may be cold, but relations between the two peoples, and between individuals, are warm. However, one of the greatest evils of post-totalitarian society is that there are so few contacts, especially economic and cultural, independent of the states. In normal civil societies ordinary citizens would play the biggest part in such contacts, and Ukrainian-Russian relations would benefit.... As long as the problem of relations between Ukraine and Russia remains on the level of state contacts, it will remain insoluble. It will only be solved when the chief lobbyist is not an official, but a businessman, with his own permanent and pragmatic interests in a good relationship.[12]

In December 1995, Vydrin was forced to resign from the presidential staff for expressing such sentiments in a book, in which he declared that Ukraine should foster its "Eurasian" links as well as look to the West.[13] This was exactly the platform on which Kuchma was elected in 1994, but it is unacceptable to many more radical Ukrainian nationalists, who fear that good relations between Ukraine and Russia cannot possibly be equal and that Moscow will, as in the past, seek to use them to subordinate Ukraine.

THE "RUSSIAN THREAT TO UKRAINE"

By late 1998, it has surely become blindingly obvious that the direct Russian threat to Ukraine is at present and will be for a long time to come very slight indeed—as long as Ukraine itself can maintain political stability and unity and some measure of economic growth. The extraordinary defeat in Chechnya has savagely underscored Russian military weakness, and lack of both money and will among Russia's elites means that there is no prospect of seriously remedying this for the foreseeable future, especially given the renewed economic crisis that hit Russia in August 1998. Russia may perhaps one day be able to create small but efficient special forces, but nothing like the kind of army necessary for a war with Ukraine. In any case, as I have pointed out, the great majority of Russian soldiers do not have the slightest desire to fight their neighbor.

From 1992 to 1994, economic pressure stemming from Ukraine's dependence on Russian oil and gas also failed completely to bend successive Ukrainian governments to Moscow's will. One reason for this failure was that the oil and gas pipelines running across Ukraine toward the West meant that Ukraine could siphon off its needs from Russian exports. Russia simply could not cut off supplies to Ukraine without also cutting off its biggest source of export earnings, which are much more important to the new Russian elites than are the dreams of a restored union or Russian empire.

Finally, there is no evidence that the new Russian elites are nearly as obsessed with Ukraine as the statements of Russian nationalists would suggest. In the words of Sherman Garnett, "Despite mutual suspicions and a conflicting sense of where the relationship ought to be headed, both [Russia and Ukraine] have shown a high degree of moderation and pragmatism when it counted."[14] The Russian government has also generally treated Russia's own economic advantage as more important than hopes of continued or renewed union, beginning with the January 1992 decision by the Gaidar government to carry out a currency reform separating Russia from the other former Soviet republics. The new relationship between Russia and Ukraine was codified in their 1997 basic treaty.

There have been fears that private economic relations, and especially Russian investment, threaten Ukraine with Russian "neocolonial" influence, but these fears, too, are probably mistaken; after all, the Russian state no longer controls Russian businessmen—and cannot even get them to pay taxes. Moreover, by late 1998, several of the largest Russian financial-industrial groups were virtually bankrupt. It seems very unlikely, therefore, that a Russian government would be able to persuade them to risk their own interests to act as agents of Russian state influence. Why should they?

However, there remains an indirect Russian threat to Ukraine, via the Russian population there, especially in Crimea. As I hope this book has made clear, this threat is much weaker than has been suggested by Russian officials and nationalists and feared by Ukrainian nationalists and some Western observers. The Russian state has not yet tried to exploit it, and these populations themselves lack the traditions and institutions to mobilize on their own. Both of these facts mark a clear difference, for example, from the position of the German population beyond Germany's borders during the period of the Weimar Republic, let alone after the Nazi rise to power. The German populations had deep-rooted cultural and social institutions and a formidable mobilizing capacity, and they also received strong support from the German state.[15]

Nonetheless, it would be wrong to assume that no future threat to Ukrainian stability and unity from the Russians of Ukraine will ever exist. As Rogers Brubaker has written, the political behavior of such ethnic communities is conditioned by what he calls a "triadic nexus": partly by their own internal dynamics, partly by influence from the ethnic metropolis (in this case, Russia), and partly by the behavior of the government and the ethnic majority in the state where they live. A tragic example of this nexus was the Serbian minority in Croatia.[16] Their revolt in 1991 was produced by a mixture of their own traditions, memories, and fears; of manipulation and encouragement from the Milosevic government in Serbia; and of the chauvinist behavior and rhetoric of the new Tudjman government in Croatia and the Croat nationalist parties. So in the Ukrainian case, how the political behavior of the Russian population develops will depend critically on the behavior of future governments in Kiev and how they define the Ukrainian state.

It should also be emphasized that for the Ukrainian state to treat Russian culture and the Russian language in Ukraine with generosity is not only expedient but also just, whatever may have been past Russian crimes against the Ukrainian language and culture. Russians in Ukraine and indeed many Russian-speaking Ukrainians do represent a tradition in Ukraine which goes back at least to the sixteenth century, when Muscovy first absorbed what is now part of Ukraine; in the sense of shared culture and religion, the tradition goes back much further. "Russification" in Ukraine was, as Ukrainian nationalists argue, mainly the result of Russian imperial rule, but in other international contexts, following the fall of other European empires, the generally accepted feeling has been that both time and cultural achievement bring a certain legitimacy; to repeat, the Russian-speaking element in Ukraine's history goes back hundreds of years and has produced a number of distinguished writers, including Gogol.

THE RUSSIAN NATIONAL IDENTITY

Finally, there is an aspect of both the Russians of Russia itself and the Russians outside Russia that will be of critical importance for the future, and on which the behavior of the Ukrainian state can have a decided effect for good or evil. This is the question of Russian national identity, of how Russians define themselves and the Russian state. Up to 1998, this identity has been complicated and ambiguous and has proved very weak when confronted with the changed circumstances that have followed the collapse of the Soviet Union. Compared to most of their neighbors, Russians in fact often find it very hard to say what being Russian really means.[17]

A key feature of this ambiguous identity—and one for which we should be profoundly grateful—is that Russians have not in the past seen themselves as an ethnic nation, after the manner of Balts, Caucasians, or most Ukrainian nationalists. The danger is that precisely these examples on their borders may lead the Russians to adopt this type of self-definition. If Ukraine were to head in an ethnic nationalist direction it would be almost impossible for Russia to avoid a reaction in the same direction, which could have disastrous results for the whole region. As I hope this book has made clear, the internal peace and stability of Ukraine depends critically on Russian and Ukrainian neighbors *not* developing sharply defined and opposing national identities—and that is also true of other areas of mixed settlement, both outside and inside Russia.

In the past, Russia was never a Russian national state as such, and Russian loyalties attached to institutions which, although they embodied large elements of "Russianness," were not purely Russian: the Orthodox religion, the tsar, Marxism, the Communist Party, the Soviet Union. Before 1917, the official census reported not Russians, Ukrainians, Poles, and so on, but Orthodox and Catholic; the people of state were defined by religion, not language or ethnicity.

A curious contemporary example of this attitude came at a May 1993 meeting of the Russian Assembly, an ultranationalist group, which took place with the participation of the Moscow patriarchate. The assembly resolved, not unpredictably, that "the term 'Russian' is a generic concept that includes Great Russians, Little Russians, and White Russians," in other words, Ukrainians and Belarusians. However, the assembly also declared that people of a completely different ethnicity, such as Tatars or Jews, could become "Russian" simply by being baptized into Orthodoxy.[18] The assembly gave voice to fantastic plans for the creation of new great empires, but these were not ethnic fantasies. Professor Alfred Rieber points out:

> With the exception of the extreme right-wing parties, after 1905, the overwhelming majority of Russian political organizations were multi-ethnic in composition. (The Black Hundreds were, despite their notoriety, never more than a small and ultimately ineffectual movement.) This tradition also survived into the Soviet period. Although there were cases in which the tradition was brutally violated, it was never repudiated in principle or altogether abandoned in fact. Taken together, these conclusions suggest that historically speaking there are grounds for an alternative outcome that avoids widespread, endemic civil war throughout the borderlands.[19]

Or in the words of Vadim Ryzhkov, a Russian historian and journalist from Dnipropetrovsk,

> Russians are not nationalists in the Baltic or Galician sense. For one thing, they have absorbed so many other ethnic groups that they really have become a kind of "super-ethnos," and then the Soviet state sucked away all their national feeling into itself. They have a very weak national consciousness, but have—or had—a very strong state or imperial consciousness. That is why when their state is taken away they are so incapable of acting or organizing parties to defend their interests—and then

of course the local parties of power are taking good care that *no* popular parties of any kind should appear, because that would threaten them
and their exploitation of the state.[20]

Under Soviet rule, of course, the Russian identity became more bound
up than that of any other people with that of the Soviet Union (although
the Ukrainians, and certainly the Belarusians, also suffered from such an
identity to a lesser extent). The Communists, especially during and after
the Second World War, exploited Russian symbols and traditions, but in
the process also overworked them, transformed them, debased them,
and ended by alienating them to some extent from the Russians themselves, so that after "independence" in 1991, there was a feeling that, in
the words of Stanislav Govorukhin, "Russia is a puzzling, unknown
country. It has turned out that we know nothing about her."[21]

In the context of Russian-Ukrainian relations, the important thing to
remember is that while Soviet propaganda exploited underlying Russian imperial sentiments, it did not give them explicit voice or embody
them in its official ideology. During the period of Soviet totalitarianism,
no more than a handful of Russians were in a position to step outside
the official ideology and subject it to analysis and criticism, the more
so of course in that it played so skillfully on some of their own much
older, deep-rooted, and unanalyzed assumptions. A key to understanding
the way the Soviet Union collapsed therefore is precisely that Russians
did *not* see it as a "Russian Empire," but a Communist-misgoverned
union of nations in which, they believed, they were exploited even
more than the others.

This view was reflected in the various "internationalist" movements
that were created in certain republics—notably the Baltic states and
Moldova—during the last years of the Soviet Union to combat local
nationalism, defend the rights of the local Russian-speaking minorities,
and preserve the union. "Internationalism" in this sense could well be
seen as a cover for local Russian interests, just as on the world stage it
was a cover for Soviet power. However, it was far from being a cover
simply for Russian nationalism, and more important, it was not seen as
such by the ordinary Russians involved.

They were encouraged in this belief by the fact that several leading
members of non-Russian (but Russian-speaking) minorities, especially
Jews, joined these movements out of an understandable historic fear of
local nationalism, and used the language of internationalism (in Latvia,
for example, Tatyana Zhdanok and Irina Litvinova). In other words, the
Russians involved were not consciously using internationalist rhetoric

as a cover for their own national aims. It may have been a lie, but it was one they believed themselves. Nor, as chapter 1 pointed out, were the great majority of Russians in most of the republics a "colonial elite," even to the extent, for example, that this was true of the poorer Pieds Noirs in Algeria, who were still far above the economic level of the vast majority of Muslims.

This explains both why the Russians of Russia and also of Ukraine (notably the miners) helped the Soviet *state* to collapse, and why they were so surprised that some form of Soviet *union* did not survive. Far from seeing it as an empire, they really had swallowed Soviet propaganda about it being a brotherly and voluntary union. In this way, Russian attitudes can be compared to some of the more naive and optimistic hopes of British people in the 1940s and 1950s about the British Commonwealth; it was not a mistake that the tougher-minded French were ever likely to make.

Moreover, the Russian elites, and even the Russian people as a whole, in the course of Muscovy's huge expansion from the fifteenth to the twentieth centuries came to incorporate very large numbers of non-Russians, who adopted the Russian language without becoming fully "Russian," a process greatly accelerated under Soviet rule. This makes the kind of race-based ethnonationalism characteristic of many of the Baltic or West Ukrainian radical nationalists extremely difficult to develop, even should the Russian state wish to develop such an identity, which so far it has not. For it is important to remember that Russia today is a real federation, in which at least some of the other peoples, notably the Tatars, enjoy a high level of both practical autonomy and real freedom to develop their own cultures.

The official self-image of Russia today also contains aspects that can be compared to the way in which India, for example, has elevated the idea of "multiethnicity" and an officially recognized multiplicity of religions and cultures to the level of a state principle, although this last idea also contains strong elements of deceit, self-deceit, and conscious or unconscious hypocrisy in both countries.

None of the major Russian parties today (with the partial exception of Vladimir Zhirinovsky's, now fortunately in eclipse) espouses a narrowly ethnicist version of Russian nationalism. Instead, the image, derived from Soviet culture, is that of the Russians "leading" a voluntary alliance of other peoples. General Aleksandr Lebed and other Russian politicians dubbed "nationalist" (or even "ultranationalist") in the West have spoken repeatedly of the Russian Federation as a "multinational" state, and Lebed—and indeed the Russian government—have spoken of Islam and Buddhism, along with Orthodox Christianity, as Russia's "traditional" religions, which the state should foster and support.[22] (This obviously does *not,* however, necessarily imply democracy, and is quite compatible with a more or less benevolent dictatorship.)

Clearly, this Russian self-image is to a great extent a myth, and often a hypocritical one, when it comes to the real past history of Russia, but it has been of great importance in moderating Russian political attitudes to Russia's ethnic minorities, such as the Tatars and Yakuts. (The Caucasians are in a somewhat different case, for the specific reason of Russians' dislike of their highly visible commercial and criminal activity.) Equally important in this regard has been Russia's ambitions for leadership or hegemony within the former Soviet Union, a hegemony which cannot today or for the foreseeable future be based mainly on coercion; rather, it must have a genuine element of consent and mutual interest. Obviously, it would be impossible for a Russian government on the one hand to have such a program and on the other hand to take up a narrowly ethnic chauvinist position at home.

RUSSIAN ATTITUDES TOWARD THE "NEAR ABROAD"

Neither past identification with the Soviet Union, nor present ambitions mean that "in the prevailing view of Russians, the whole of the USSR was the real Russia."[23] While Russians—and the Russian government—do regard the whole of the former USSR as "a sphere of vital Russian interests" (and, in most cases, as a would-be Russian sphere of influence), they have a very wide range of attitudes toward the different republics and areas, and of hopes concerning them. Not many places outside Russia, and not all places within Russia (Chechnya, for example) are regarded by ordinary Russians viscerally as part of "the Russian land." A Chechen mountain does not feel like a Russian birch forest, and most of the Russian soldiers with whom I talked privately in Chechnya admitted that in fact this was not "Russian land."

As to the other lands, different attitudes swirl around in the Russian psyche, sometimes mixing, sometimes not: ambition and fear of bloodshed and financial sacrifice, desire for a new federation and fear of Islam, a feeling of "Eurasian" identity and a feeling of European superiority to the "Asiatics." In Ukraine, a Russian naval base in Sevastopol is definitely Russian; a baroque square in Lviv is definitely not. What exactly is Kiev?

Only in the minds of Russian or Western ideologues is any of this simple or "monocausal"; human psychology does not work that way, especially in times of rapid and profound transition.

Who better than Ryszard Kapuscinski to describe this kind of imperial cognitive dissonance? In his *Imperium,* the Polish journalist and author tours the Soviet republics that would become independent shortly after his travels. While most Russians may believe their country should continue to rule over this vast territory in some way, Kapuscinski notes that those same Russians indeed had a difficult time grasping the "Russianness" of the Soviet Union's expanse. "I was aware how much Moscow differs from the rest of the country (although not in everything)," writes Kapuscinski, "and that enormous areas of this superpower are an immeasurable terra incognita (even for the inhabitants of Moscow)."[24]

In such a view, Uzbekistan is a strategic ally–cum–client state, but very few Russians at heart want to live once again in the same state as Uzbeks, whom they fear both for their growing numbers and their Islamic religion. Tajikistan's border with Afghanistan, guarded by Russian troops, is regarded as Russia's military-strategic border, and also an ideological border in the sense of keeping out "Islamic fundamentalism" — much as Americans have in earlier times regarded the Elbe or the Thirty-Eighth Parallel in Korea; it is *not* regarded as Russia's ethnic, cultural, or in any real sense *national* border. However, the Russian attitude to another part of Central Asia, Russian-settled northern Kazakstan, is quite different; this area is regarded in more or less the same way that Americans see the Dakotas—as a previously almost uninhabited land to which the Russians brought settled agriculture and "civilization." Where, then, does Russia's "real" border run?

The Russian attitude toward Kazakstan again differs completely from the Russian attitude toward the Baltic states and the question of the Russian minorities there. The Balts are generally viewed as genuinely independent, developed European peoples; Russian anger is directed at the *uses* of their independence, in terms of policy toward the Russian minorities and overtures toward military alliance with the West (but not, it should be noted, toward membership in the European Union, to which Russia does not object).

Concerning Ukraine, Russians also have an entirely different set of attitudes, and the conflicts between them have been partly responsible for the ineffectiveness and sometimes near paralysis of Russian policy toward Ukraine. Thus while most Russians regard Sevastopol as

"Russian land" in the strict sense, they have a much looser attitude toward most of Ukraine, which they regard as not "Russian," but as a land with a mainly common history and inhabited by "younger brothers" of the Russians. As for Galicia, Russians regard it as "foreign" in almost the same way they do the Baltic states, but without the grudging respect that Russians often accord the Balts because of their economic and civic achievements.

The complex mixture of Russian attitudes toward Ukraine is to be found in the writings of Solzhenitsyn, a quotation from whose *Gulag Archipelago* stands as the epigraph of this study. He differs from most Russians in having (or having once had) more sympathy for Ukrainian nationalism, thanks to his friendships with Ukrainian dissidents. However, as the following passage from one of his recent works makes clear, this has been largely dissipated by the belief that the nationalists themselves are now exercising power in an "imperial" fashion by ruling over unwilling Russian areas which do not historically belong to them, and trying to "Ukrainianize" their populations (it should be said in defense of Solzhenitsyn's honesty and consistency that he has also called for Russia to allow the independence of the Chechens and any other nation that really wants to leave the Russian Federation):

> Leaving aside the swift turnabout of Ukraine's Communist chieftains, we have seen the Ukrainian nationalists, who . . . cursed Lenin, sorely tempted from the first by his poisoned gift, and eagerly accepting the false Leninist borders of Ukraine (including even the Crimean dowry of the petty tyrant Khrushchev). Ukraine, like Kazakhstan, immediately set out upon a false imperial path.
>
> I do not wish the burden of great power status upon Russia, nor upon Ukraine.
>
> I sincerely express my best wishes for Ukrainian culture and distinctiveness, and genuinely love them; but why do they begin not with the restoration and spiritual strengthening of their national nucleus, not with cultural work within the boundaries of the Ukrainian population and territory proper, but with an impulse to become a great power?
>
> I suggested solving all national economic and cultural problems within a single Union of eastern Slavs, and still regard this as the best solution, for I do not see any justification for splitting millions of ties of friendship and family by new international borders. . . . [But] in the same essay I stipulated that of course no one must dare forcibly to keep the Ukrainian people from secession, and there must be a guarantee of full minority rights.[25]

This passage contains almost the full range of Russian attitudes regarding Ukraine: There is a pan-Slavic "love" of Ukraine and desire for union with it, but there is also a Russian nationalist implication that Ukraine is presently, in a quasi-imperial fashion, occupying some lands that are in fact Russian and has no right to try to "Ukrainianize" their people; in particular, there is resentment about the transfer of Crimea. Unlike Solzhenitsyn's previous work, there is very little on past Russian imperial crimes against the Ukrainians.

There is also respect for Ukrainian nationalism and Ukraine's right to independence, if that is what Ukrainians really want, but this respect is coupled with the implication (by no means wholly incorrect) that Ukraine received independence in 1991 not through the will of its people, but as a result of the self-serving and hypocritical maneuvers of the then "Communist chieftains." There is an appeal to the importance of human ties between Russia and Ukraine, and a renunciation of the use of force to keep them together.

This last view is shared by the great majority of Russians (including Russian officers) and is consistent with Solzhenitsyn's view of the Ukrainians as "younger brothers." The renunciation of force to hold Russia and Ukraine together is crucial in giving Ukraine a considerable measure of security from attack; at the same time, such a view is implicitly denied to Kazaks, for example, whom neither Solzhenitsyn nor most other Russians would view as "brothers."

The differences between Russian attitudes to the other former Soviet peoples are of vast importance in conditioning likely Russian responses to their possible future behavior. Thus the Russians of Latvia and Estonia proved remarkably quiescent in the face of policies that removed most of their political rights; banned the public use of their language; and in the case of Latvia, are now even moving against their rights in the field of education—despite the fact that a majority of Riga's population is of Russian origin!

However, it should be recalled that, in the first place, most Russians were always well aware that the Balts were somehow "different." The common phrase for them in the Soviet era was "*nash zapad*" ("our West"), which stresses that they belonged not only to the Soviet Union, but also to the West; in other words, they were not seen as simply "part of Russia." Many Russians always had a deep respect for higher Baltic civic culture, and this has been even more true in recent years. That has obviously never been the case with Kazakstan or Ukraine.

Second, since their achievement of independence in 1991, the Balts have drawn closer and closer to the West, thanks to their successful reforms and their striking and very visible economic progress. As a result, Estonia has already been welcomed into the first group of states to begin accession negotiations with the European Union, and the other two Baltic states have good hopes of following soon. The Russian business elites in the Baltic states share in these hopes and the growing wealth.

Little of this progress, alas, is true of Ukraine as of 1998, and there are not many signs that it will be true in the future. This means that the Russians of the Baltic states will accept discrimination from the Balts to an extent it is impossible to imagine them swallowing from Ukrainians. If some future Ukrainian government were so reckless as to adopt Latvian-style measures against the Russian minority, the Russians of Ukraine would revolt, with consequences for the region and for Europe that cannot be foreseen but which could well be disastrous. At present, such a Ukrainian policy looks extremely unlikely. Western policy should be to make sure it stays that way.

CONCLUSION
Implications for Western Policy

What are the implications for Western policy of the material presented in this book? The question must be posed, because the formulation of a Western strategy in this region is becoming more and more important as NATO plans its expansion eastward. By the year 2000, NATO members are expected to include Poland and Hungary, two of Ukraine's neighbors to the west. In the foreseeable future, NATO will probably include Romania, another neighbor, and perhaps the Baltic states as well. Meanwhile Russia, partly in response to NATO's progress eastward, seems to be making stronger efforts to form a union with Belarus—although as of 1998 it appears that this will not go much beyond rhetoric because of the deep unwillingness of the Russian elites to make real sacrifices for the sake of propping up the ruinous Belarusian economy.

The need for a clear Western strategy toward the western areas of the former Soviet Union, and a clear sense of Western interests and goals, is especially important because of Russia's present military and economic weakness and the state's inability to fulfill its most basic tasks, such as revenue collection and payment of wages on time. Following the Russian defeat in Chechnya and the renewed economic crisis in 1998, an impression is growing in the West that Russia is in fact too enfeebled and irresolute to oppose Western plans, however provocative to Russians.

Given that this belief co-exists with deep instinctive hostility to Russia in many circles in the West, there is a danger that the West may be led into dangerous attempts to exploit Russian weakness—dangerous because they will cause enduring resentment in Russia, for which the West will

153

pay a heavy price if Russia ever recovers; because the West may be led as a result into making major moral commitments in areas where its real interests and degree of genuine readiness for sacrifice and commitment are actually slight; and, finally, because the West's very involvement may encourage precisely the development that it ought most to fear.

As for the Ukrainian government, in 1995–96 it moved from its previous position of opposing NATO expansion—because of the danger that this would redivide Europe and implicitly consign Ukraine either to a second-class Europe or even to Russia's sphere of influence—to one of cautiously welcoming it. However, Ukrainian spokesmen continued to express (at least in public) the wish that the expansion should have a mainly political, not military, character and that it should not involve the stationing of new forces or nuclear weapons in the new member states.

In these circumstances, the first and most obvious questions to be asked are whether Ukraine itself should be invited to become a member of NATO at some stage (something the Kravchuk and Kuchma administrations have not asked for, although they have favored close cooperation with NATO short of membership), and what the implications for Ukraine and Russia will be if NATO expands without seeking to include Ukraine.

Zbigniew Brzezinski thinks that Ukraine should indeed be invited to join NATO and the European Union. Yet, as the following passage makes clear, he does not believe that *successful* domestic reform is an essential precondition for membership. Desirable, yes, but not essential: "Sometime between 2005 and 2010, Ukraine, especially if in the meantime the country has made significant progress in its domestic reforms and has succeeded in becoming more evidently identified as a Central European country, should become ready for serious negotiations with both the EU and NATO."[1]

This passage ignores the real situation in the country—not least in the extraordinary optimism of the belief that Ukraine, given its economic record so far, could be ready for negotiations with the EU in seven years' time.

In my view, there are just three contingencies that could make NATO membership for Ukraine a good idea, either for the West or for Ukraine itself. The first is if Russia were simultaneously invited to join. However, this would completely transform the existing alliance and its raison d'être. If this did happen, it could only be for one of two reasons. On the one hand, NATO might become what its own propaganda sometimes says that it is becoming: a broad pact for common security and the advancement of democracy and economic stability, with no designated enemy or common military purpose. In this case, however, including Russia and Ukraine in NATO would duplicate the existing Organization for Security and Cooperation in Europe to a considerable extent.

On the other hand, NATO might remain what it was founded to be and what it has largely remained up to the present, especially in the minds of the applicants from Eastern Europe: a pact for common military defense; that is to say, an alliance to fight a war, should this become necessary. However, NATO as a military defensive alliance could expand to include Russia only if it had become the military component of a united Western-Russian front either against China or the Islamic world.

Such scenarios at present look unlikely; however, they are not wholly to be discounted. I have met with far more outlandish ones emanating from the think tanks of various Western security agencies. In the Middle East, there is an obvious danger—albeit not a critical one as yet—that Turkey may swing in an Islamist and anti-Western direction, thereby dealing a terrible blow to the West's security structures in the region. If so, U.S. policy in the Transcaucasus, for example, will have to swing 180 degrees, and the need for partnership with Russia will become blindingly apparent.

In the Far East, if China uses its growing economic (in spite of the region's financial crisis) and military strength to seek confrontation with the United States over Taiwan and Korea, then once again the need to woo Russia will become increasingly apparent to U.S. policymakers. In these circumstances, ten or fifteen years from now it may seem entirely reasonable to invite Russia and Ukraine simultaneously into NATO, assuming that Russia's leaders are still in a mood to consider their own real interests and have not been so infuriated by Western policy that they go out of their way to side with China.

The second contingency which would justify NATO membership for Ukraine (in this case without Russia) would be if Russia had become an open, determined, and powerful enemy of the West and of Ukraine —for example, by forming a close and effective alliance with China aimed at attacking American influence in various parts of the world, and also by making real efforts to subvert Ukraine from within. Despite the rhetoric of some Russian politicians, none of this has happened so far. If it does, there will indeed be a strong case for expanding NATO against Russia.

is it really necessary?

Until it does, however, the argument will be all the other way. For nothing could be so calculated to drive Russia into implacable opposition to the West, and a frantic search for anti-Western allies—any allies —as a NATO that included Ukraine and did not include Russia. For Russians, this would be conclusive evidence of Western contempt and rejection, as well as a Western attempt simultaneously to isolate and subordinate them. It would create a European order which would fester for generations in the hearts of Russians, and which all patriotic Russian politicians—of every political stripe—would feel it their bound duty to destroy.

Moreover, there is the critical question of whether Western electorates are really prepared to send their nations' soldiers to fight in defense of Ukraine as a fellow NATO member. In the case of Poland, the Czech Republic, Hungary, Romania, and Slovenia this is purely theoretical, because there is no chance of their being attacked. There is also very little chance of this in the case of Ukraine—unless it were to seek unilaterally to eject the Russian fleet from Sevastopol. Unfortunately, NATO membership, or even strong NATO support short of membership, is exactly what might encourage a future Ukrainian government to think that it might be able to get away with this after the twenty-year Russian lease of the base expires.

Finally, there would be a case for NATO membership for Ukraine without Russia if the Ukrainians had progressed as far as the present candidates—the Poles, Czechs, and Hungarians—toward Western Europe in terms of further economic reform, democratization, and the creation of a civil society. The case would be strengthened if Russia in the meantime had failed to progress in these directions, still more, of course, if Russia had fallen into internal chaos and become a source of instability for its neighbors.

Unfortunately, although both Ukraine and Russia have made progress in holding and respecting democratic elections, both lag badly behind in terms of the institutionalization of democracy; the creation of genuine civil societies; and above all, the achievement of effective economic reforms and stable economic progress.

Unlike Russia, Ukraine admittedly had been able to avoid involvement in attempts at the bloody suppression of secessionist movements; but then, the anti-Ukrainian Russian separatists in Crimea showed nothing like the determination, courage, and uncompromising radicalism of General Dudayev and his successors in Chechnya. Should the Russians of Crimea ever develop such a spirit (God forbid), we shall have to see whether a future Ukrainian government will react with greater wisdom and humanity than the Yeltsin administration.

Therefore, at present and for the foreseeable future, there is no case for inviting either Ukraine or Russia to become members of NATO, and this is indeed the consensus of the great majority of U.S. and West European policymakers. However, there exists at the same time a strong feeling in certain circles that even without full membership, Ukraine should be built up as a form of buffer state against Russia and encouraged by all means to distance itself from Russia economically, politically, and culturally. This is also, of course, the view of many Ukrainian nationalists.

But one of the approaches of the Ukrainian nationalists (backed by some Ukrainian emigrants in the West) in their effort to distance Ukraine from Russia and deal with the alleged Russian threat is also itself inadmissible and a threat to peace and stability. This approach is to increase Ukrainian hatred of Russia and Russians by propaganda that blames the Russian people and the Russian national tradition for the crimes not just of imperial Russia but also for all those of the Soviet Union against Ukraine, and to brand the Russians and the Russian language in Ukraine as "foreign" and implicitly or explicitly hostile.

A striking feature of both more radical Ukrainian nationalists and some anti-Russian Western analysts is their inability to distinguish between the Russian state and the Russian people. This is something Ukrainians in eastern and southern Ukraine are usually careful to do, stressing that their dislike for Yeltsin's government does not mean that they dislike or distrust their own Russian neighbors.

Attitudes among West Ukrainian nationalists can be very different. As one of them told an Agence France-Presse correspondent in 1997, "NATO is our best guarantee of security and independence. . . . Russians are imperialists. It has been in their blood for centuries and that will not change." Another, the actress Joanna Nilivok, told the same correspondent that "All Ukraine suffered from Russian imperialism. . . . [T]he Russians did everything they could to destroy our culture."[2]

I myself heard such talk again and again among more radical Ukrainian nationalists and Ukrainian emigrants in North America, one of whom described Russians to me as "a threat to civilization." This attitude has been echoed by some American opinion makers who support NATO expansion. Syndicated columnist George F. Will, for example, wrote that "expansion is in the Russians' DNA."[3] It is not hard to imagine what sentiments like these will do for ethnic harmony in

eastern and southern Ukraine, if they are ever seen to be endorsed by
the Ukrainian state.

The desire of some Western thinkers and policy advocates to turn
Ukraine into a buffer state against a feared (or presumed) resurgence of
Russian imperialism also risks taking on board some of these Ukrainian
nationalist sentiments and strategies; indeed, since an effective Ukrainian
buffer state would have to have much stronger borders with Russia
than is now the case, and since at present such a tougher border regime
would be utterly unacceptable to most of the Ukrainian, as well as
Russian-Ukrainian, inhabitants of the Ukrainian border regions, it follows that they would either have to be overruled, or their amity toward
Russia and Russians would have to be turned into ones of hostility.

Since in fact no imminent threat of Russian aggression or expansion
exists, this in my view is an unnecessary, foolish, and even a wicked
project. It increases the most important potential threat to Ukraine,
which is an internal one; in any case, the last thing Eastern Europe needs
is yet another dose of national hatred where little at present exists. It
also offends democracy by ignoring the real people of Ukraine and
their 1994 vote for Kuchma and a program of national reconciliation,
in favor of a nationalist construct—an abstruse, undefined, theoretical
"Ukrainian People," whose national interests allegedly take precedence
over the real interests and wishes of everyday Ukrainians. This attitude,
explicitly stated in the passage by Yaroslav Bilinsky quoted in the previous chapter, has terrible antecedents in European and world history.
The duty of the West by contrast is to support democracy, which commonly means respect for the wishes of the existing electorate, not
some nationalist-platonic ideal of what this electorate ought to be and
to think.

Finally, an attempt to turn Russia's neighbors into a *cordon sanitaire*
against Russia—especially if this results in fostering anti-Russian nationalism—could produce exactly what the West should fear most, a reaction
in Russia and the Russian diaspora that would turn Russian nationalism
from its present, largely nonethnic, definition to an ethnic one, sharply
differentiating Russians from other peoples, both within Russia and in
neighboring states.

Analogies for such a process can be found in the way that Turkish
political elites in the first three decades of this century abandoned
their old Ottoman identity, based on imperial loyalty and religious adherence, for ethnic Turkish nationalism, whose greatest leader and the-
orist was Kemal Ataturk. The disastrous results for Turkey's own ethnic

minorities, as well as for one neighboring state with a Turkish minority (Cyprus), should need no emphasis. If Russia, and Russians in the Russian "diaspora," should develop such an ethnic identity, the dangers would be infinitely greater. When Brzezinski advises Russia to "emulate the course chosen by post-Ottoman Turkey, when it decided to shed its imperial ambitions and embarked very deliberately on the road of modernization, Europeanization and democratization," he should remember what this supposedly benign path has meant for Kurds, Armenians, and Greeks—and what, in Russia's case, it would mean for Tatars and Ukrainians.[4]

A project of making Ukraine into a buffer is also unnecessary because Ukraine performs this role adequately simply by existing as an independent and internationally recognized state. At present, there are no signs whatsoever that Russia would be able to overthrow Ukrainian independence, let alone somehow pass through Ukraine to threaten the rest of Europe.

Indeed, Russo-Ukrainian relations in 1997 appeared to take a historic step in the right direction, with the signature of the Russia-Ukraine basic treaty. This in turn was made possible only by the resolution (or, rather, suspension) of the dispute over the Black Sea Fleet and control of its base at Sevastopol.

This accord, which involved major Russian concessions, can be put down in part to NATO's expansion and Russia's desire to consolidate friendly relations with Ukraine and diminish Ukrainian perceptions of a Russian threat, which might drive the Ukrainians further toward NATO. These Russian overtures could well be called a positive side-effect of NATO expansion.

However, the news reports that have spoken of a "solution" to the Sevastopol question are mistaken. As chapter 4 pointed out, the problem has not been solved. Rather, it has been frozen for twenty years, after which there is no way of predicting what line either side will adopt on Russian use of the base. In the meantime, passions on both sides may have cooled—or they may not have. And an attempt to turn Ukraine into a Western military ally would inevitably imply support for the Ukrainian position on Sevastopol. If Western policymakers ever do prove so reckless as to involve their nations in the Sevastopol issue— other than as peacemakers and sponsors of a reasonable compromise involving both Ukrainian territorial integrity and a Russian military presence—this disputed city could one day prove to be the stone that upsets the entire Eurasian applecart, and regional peace, economic development, and democracy in both Russia and Ukraine will all go tumbling to the ground.

It may seem very unlikely that NATO would in fact ever go this far, given its strong distaste for dangerous and long-term commitments elsewhere; certainly the great majority of the U.S. military establishment would be against it.

On the other hand, exactly such a NATO engagement was the original official scenario of Operation Sea Breeze, the joint U.S.-Ukrainian military exercise discussed briefly in chapter 4. Under this scenario, U.S. troops were to land on the Ukrainian coast, not far from Sevastopol, to help the Ukrainian government suppress a secessionist movement backed by military intervention from "State Orange"—a "neighboring power."

After vehement protests not just from Moscow but from Russians in Crimea, the scenario was changed to one of disaster relief, but the diplomatic damage had been done. The Crimean parliament denounced the exercise and the U.S. Marines were met with hostile demonstrations. In the words of one sergeant, "Rarely have the marines been met with signs like that. It hit them like a concrete block. Everywhere else we've been recently, in Bulgaria and Romania, people have been so welcoming."[5]

The scenario was the Ukrainian government's idea, not Washington's, but it is extraordinary that Washington accepted it and asked Ukraine to change it only after Russian protests. For not only was this grossly offensive to Russia, at exactly the moment when it had agreed to shelve the Sevastopol issue largely on Ukraine's terms, but it also increased tension in the region and led to some of the biggest demonstrations since the collapse of the Crimean separatist movement— which is surely not meant to be the point of such exercises. Most important of all, the original scenario was also fundamentally a *lie*. For, as noted, it is actually very unlikely that in a real crisis NATO would in fact come to the help of Ukraine with ground forces. Indeed, the false promise of help could well lead the Ukrainian government to harden its position in a way that could have disastrous consequences. Something very much like this happened in Bosnia between 1992 and 1994, and the Bosnian Muslims learned the foolishness of taking up rigid (even if morally wholly justified) positions on the basis of U.S. hints of military support.

Fortunately, such support is unlikely to be necessary in the case of Ukraine. As demonstrated by the March 1997 Clinton-Yeltsin summit in Helsinki (and underscored by the economic crisis of 1998), Russia is simply too weak to oppose NATO expansion to Central Europe (as opposed to areas of the former Soviet Union) or indeed to threaten the West directly. Moreover—and this is of critical importance—the new Russian economic elites have a vital interest in maintaining working relations with the West. Most of their wealth ultimately comes from the export of Russian raw materials to the West. Unless Russia is really driven to the wall, or Russians outside Russia get involved in a situation that gives Moscow no choice but to intervene, it will do nothing that might provoke serious Western trade sanctions against Russia.

The West should certainly strongly emphasize Ukrainian independence, territorial integrity, and the inviolability of borders. It should also do its utmost to help strengthen the Ukrainian economy and state, while recognizing that, as elsewhere, its capacity is limited; in the end, real economic progress depends on the Ukrainians themselves—and so far, they have made an appalling mess of it.

However, Western policymakers should not use this help to try to turn the Ukrainians in an explicitly anti-Russian direction, and talk of a Ukrainian "buffer state" should be firmly rejected. First, because it is unnecessary, since Russia is not a threat to Europe. Second, because this could threaten Ukraine's own ethnic peace, on which in the end everything else depends.

The West must recognize that the links between the Ukrainian and Russian peoples (rather than the states) have not been forged solely or even mainly by decree from above. They have developed organically, and if they are to be weakened, it should be allowed to happen through a similarly slow, natural process of attrition, without *diktats*, and without the stirring up of new ethnic hatred where none has so far existed. Harmony between Ukrainians and Russians in Ukraine is the cornerstone of stability not just of Ukraine but of the entire region. As such, it is also a truly vital interest of the West in general and the United States in particular.

Ukraine, Russia, and Washington, D.C.

NOTES

INTRODUCTION

1. To take one small but telling example, marking both off from the West Europeans, neither the Russian nor the Ukrainian language has any word that truly corresponds to *privacy*. I am indebted to Semyon Gluzman for this insight. See also Svetlana Boym, "Everyday Culture" in *Russian Culture at the Crossroads: Paradoxes of Postcommunist Consciousness*, ed. Dmitri N. Shalin (Boulder, Colo.: Westview, 1996), 167, 183 (note).

2. According to the 1989 Soviet Census.

3. Olexander Dergachev et al., "Post-Communist Ukraine: Contradictions and Prospects for Socio-political Development," *Politichna Dumka* (January 1993): 136 ff.

1. UKRAINE AND RUSSIA: UNITED AND DIVIDED BY HISTORY

1. For a survey of this theme, see Peter J. Potichnyj, *Ukraine and Russia in Their Historical Encounter* (Edmonton, Alberta: Canadian Institute of Ukrainian Studies, 1992).

2. Alexander J. Motyl, *Dilemmas of Independence: Ukraine After Totalitarianism* (New York: Council on Foreign Relations Press, 1993), 5; emphasis added.

3. For the importance of historiography in Ukrainian nation building, see Zenon Kohut, "History as a Battleground: Russian-Ukrainian Relations and Historical Consciousness in Contemporary Ukraine," in *The Legacy of History in Russia and the New States of Eurasia,* ed. Frederick S. Starr (Armonk, N.Y.: M. E. Sharpe, 1994). For the uses of historiography to fuel potential Russian-Ukrainian territorial disputes, see Serhii M. Plokhy, "Historical Debates and Territorial Claims: Cossack Mythology in the Russian-Ukrainian Border Dispute" and Catherine Wanner, "Historical Narratives, Personal Narratives: Ethnographic Perspectives on Nationness in Post-Soviet Ukraine" in "Peoples, Nations, Identities: The Russian-Ukrainian Encounter," special issue of *The Harriman Review* 9, nos. 1–2 (Spring 1996).

4. Volodymyr Kulyk, "The Search for Post-Soviet Identity in Ukraine and Russia and its Influence on the Relations Between the Two States," *The Harriman Review* 9, nos. 1–2 (Spring 1996).

5. For a study of the meaning of Kiev and especially of its religious status in the Ukrainian tradition, see Omeljan Pritsak, "Kiev and All of Rus: The Fate of a Sacral Idea," *Harvard Ukrainian Studies* 10, nos. 3–4 (1986).

6. For a fairly typical late Soviet Russian view, see Boris Rybakov, *Kievan Rus* (Moscow: Progress Publishers, 1989). For a Western academic denial of the commitment of medieval Muscovy to recovering the Kievan legacy, see Edward L. Keenan, "On Certain Mythical Beliefs and Russian Behaviors" in *The Legacy of History,* ed. Starr.

7. Interview with the author, Donetsk, March 22, 1994.

8. Simon Franklin and Jonathan Shepard, *The Emergence of Rus 750–1200* (London: Longman, 1996).

9. For a brief but highly insightful analysis of the contemporary Ukrainian-Russian relationship in historical perspective, see John Morrison, "Pereyaslav and After," *International Affairs* 69, no. 4 (1993). For a discussion of the presentation of the Pereiaslav Treaty and other questions of Ukrainian-Russian history in Soviet historiography, see Stephen Velychenko, *Shaping Identity in Eastern Europe and Russia: Soviet-Russian and Polish Accounts of Ukrainian History, 1914–1991* (New York: St. Martin's Press, 1993).

10. See Keenan, "On Certain Mythical Beliefs."

11. See Frank Sysyn, "The Formation of Modern Ukrainian Religious Culture," in *Church, Nation, and State in Russia and Ukraine,* ed. Geoffrey Hosking (New York: St. Martin's Press, 1991).

12. For a classic Russian perception of the sacrifice of the old united Russian society for the sake of empire, see "The Ukrainian Problem" in Prince Nikolai Trubetskoy's *The Legacy of Genghis Khan,* ed. Anatoly Liberman (Ann Arbor, Mich.: Michigan Slavic Publications, 1991).

13. For a brief, nonspecialist account of the Zaporozhians, see Albert Seaton, *The Horsemen of the Steppes: The Story of the Cossacks* (London: Bodley Head, 1985), 41–46, 73–95 and passim.

14. For a sophisticated and honest recent collection of attempts to approach the often tragic Jewish-Ukrainian historical encounter, see the essays in Howard Aster and Peter J. Potichnyj, eds., *Ukrainian-Jewish Relations in Historical Perspective* (Edmonton, Alberta: Canadian Institute of Ukrainian Studies, 1990).

15. For a translation of the text of the Pereiaslav agreements, see Paul Robert Magocsi, *A History of Ukraine* (Toronto: University of Toronto Press, 1996), 214–15.

16. A classic account of the importance of pre-existing religious affiliations in the formation of modern national allegiances and unions between peoples (in this case Anglo-Scottish) is Linda Colley's *Britons: Forging the Nation 1707–1837* (London: Pimlico, 1992).

17. Quoted in Isabella de Madariaga, *Russia in the Age of Catherine the Great* (New Haven, Conn.: Yale University Press, 1981), 579.

18. This question is raised in the essay by Professor D. C. B. Lieven, "The Russian Empire and the Soviet Union as Imperial Polities," *Journal of Contemporary History* 30, no. 4 (October 1995).

19. Madariaga, *Russia in the Age of Catherine the Great,* 309.

20. For an analysis of Gogol the Ukrainian, see George Luckyj, *Between Gogol and Shevchenko: Polarity in the Literary Ukraine* (Munich: W. Fink, 1971). For a portrait and analysis of another nineteenth-century "Little Russian" (but also proudly "Ukrainian") writer, see Luckyj's *Panteleimon Kulish: A Sketch of His Life and Times* (New York: Columbia University Press, 1983). To pursue the Scottish analogy, Gogol in this sense could be compared to Sir Walter Scott (who indeed influenced his "Taras Bulba"), a very proud Scot who was nonetheless deeply committed to union with England, with the difference that in Gogol's case there was more emotion and less calculation than in Scott's. Later, sentimental novels set in a folkloric Scottish rural setting—the so-called "Kailyard school"—had their exact parallel in Russian-language novels set against the Ukrainian folkloric background of the *khutor,* or farmstead.

21. Interview with the author, Kharkiv, August 5, 1995.

22. Andrew Wilson, "The Donbas Between Ukraine and Russia: The Use of History in Political Disputes," *Journal of Contemporary History* 30, no. 2 (April 1995).

23. W. H. Chamberlin, *The Russian Revolution,* vol. 2 (Princeton: Princeton University Press, 1935; reprinted 1987), 221. See also Magocsi, *A History of Ukraine,* 498–99.

24. For the Ukrainianization period of the 1920s, see James E. Mace, *Communism and the Dilemmas of National Liberation: National Communism in the Soviet Ukraine, 1918–1933* (Cambridge, Mass.: Harvard University Press, 1983), and George Y. Shevelov, *The Ukrainian Language in the First Half of the Twentieth Century (1900–1941): Its State and Status* (Cambridge, Mass.: Harvard University Press, 1989).

25. See Leonid Maximenkov, ed., "Stalin's Meeting with a Delegation of Ukrainian Writers on 12 February 1929," special issue of *Harvard Ukrainian Studies* 16, no. 3/4 (June 1992).

26. Taras Shevchenko, *Selected Poetry,* trans. Jon Weir et al. (Kiev: Dnipro Press, 1989), 11. An excerpt from Shevchenko's poem "Kateryna" reveals his real feelings about the Russians:

> O lovely maidens, fall in love,
> But not with Muscovites,
> For Muscovites are foreign folk,
> They do not treat you right.
> A Muscovite will love for sport,
> and laughing go away;
> He'll go back to his Moscow land
> And leave the maid a prey
> To grief and shame.

27. Petro G. Grigorenko, *Memoirs,* trans. Thomas P. Whitney (New York: W. W. Norton, 1982), 13, 14.

28. For Makhno's movement and its background in this region, see Paul Avrich, *The Anarchists in the Russian Revolution* (Ithaca, N.Y.: Cornell University Press, 1973).

29. For the importance of Soviet rule in institutionalizing national territories and even identities, see Ronald Suny, *The Revenge of the Past: Nationalism, Revolution, and the Collapse of the Soviet Union* (Stanford, Calif.: Stanford University Press, 1993), and Rogers Brubaker, *Nationalism Reframed: Nationhood and the National Question in the New Europe* (New York: Cambridge University Press, 1996), especially 23–54.

30. See Ian Brzezinski, "Polish-Ukrainian Relations," *Survival* 35, no. 3 (1993).

31. Angela Charlton, "Ukraine Denies Visas to Polish War Veterans," Associated Press, October 9, 1996.

32. See Velychenko, *Shaping Identity,* especially 135–55.

33. *A Selection of Taras Shevchenko's Poems,* trans. and with an introduction by Boris Oliynik (Moscow: Progress Publishers, 1987). It should hardly need stressing that this Soviet account of Shevchenko's views about Russia and Russians is rampant nonsense.

34. The standard work in English on the famine in Ukraine remains Robert Conquest's *The Harvest of Sorrow: Soviet Collectivization and the Terror-Famine* (New York: Oxford University Press, 1986). See also Bohdan Krawchenko and Roman Serbyn, eds., *Famine in Ukraine, 1932-33* (Edmonton, Alberta: Canadian Institute of Ukrainian Studies, 1986). For contemporary accounts, see Victor Kravchenko, *I Chose Freedom: The Personal and Political Life of a Soviet Official* (New York: Charles Scribner's Sons, 1946), 91–131; Grigorenko, *Memoirs;* and Wasyl Hryshko, *The Ukrainian Holocaust of 1933,* ed. and trans. Marco Carynnyk (Toronto: Bahriany Foundation, 1983).

35. Grigorenko, *Memoirs,* 36.

36. For a summary of Ukrainian nationalist literature on the famine, see Wilson, "The Donbas Between Ukraine and Russia."

37. Mykola Riabchouk, "The Elimination of a People," *The Ukrainian Weekly* (Toronto), January 22, 1995.

38. On the Ukrainian nationalist movements and partisans in World War II, see John A. Armstrong, *Ukrainian Nationalism* (Englewood, Colo.: Ukrainian Academic Press, 1990).

39. Figures in Paul Kolstoe, *Russians in the Former Soviet Republics* (London: Hurst, 1995), 177.

40. For an analysis of the way that the titular nationalities were able to strengthen their position in the later decades of Soviet rule, see Suny, *The Revenge of the Past,* especially 84–127.

41. See Dominique Arel and Andrew Wilson, "Ukraine Under Kuchma: Back to Eurasia?" *RFE/RL Research Report* 3, no. 32 (August 19, 1996).

42. Democratic Initiative Center, *A Political Portrait of Ukraine: Results of a Public Opinion Poll of Citizens in the South and East of Ukraine* (Kiev: Democratic Initiative Center, May–June 1994).

43. The figures are from Roman Solchanyk, "The Referendum in Ukraine," Radio Free Europe/Radio Liberty, *Report on the USSR,* March 29, 1991.

44. Figures from *RFE/RL Research Report* 1, no. 13 (March 27, 1992).

45. Interview with the author, Lviv, August 25, 1993.

46. For the 1994 election results, see Arel and Wilson, "Ukraine Under Kuchma."

2. UKRAINIANS AND RUSSIANS IN INDEPENDENT UKRAINE

1. A summary of the 1994 National Intelligence Estimate was provided by Daniel Williams and R. Jeffrey Smith, "Dire U.S. Forecast for Ukraine Conflict," *International Herald Tribune,* January 26, 1994.

2. For a general view of the position of the "Russians" outside Russia as of 1995, see Neil Melvin, *Russians Beyond Russia: The Politics of National Identity* (London: Royal Institute of International Affairs, 1995), especially 78–99 for Ukraine. See also Kolstoe, *Russians in the Former Soviet Republics.* For shorter analyses, see Subtelny, "Russocentrism," and Igor Zevelev, "Russia and the Russian Diasporas" along with the comment on it by Gail Lapidus in *Post-Soviet Affairs* 12, no. 3 (1996). For an overview of the importance of regional politics in Ukraine, see Grigory Nemiria, "L'etat et les Regions," *L'Autre Europe,* nos. 30–31 (1995).

3. On the basis of this, members of the Ukrainian neofascist organization UNA/UNSO have suggested that the Russian Far East and parts of Kazakstan really ought to become Ukrainian territories.

4. Interview with the author, Dnipropetrovsk, August 13, 1995.

5. Interview with the author, Kharkiv, August 3, 1995.

6. Interview with the author, Donetsk, August 27, 1995.

7. Interview with the author, Kharkiv, August 3, 1995.

8. On the language question in 1994–95, see Yaroslav Bilinsky, "Primary Language of Communication as a Secondary Indicator of National Identity: The Ukrainian Parliamentary and Presidential Elections of 1994 and the Manifesto of the Ukrainian Intelligentsia of 1995," *Nationalities Papers* 24, no. 4 (1996). On the situation as of 1996, see Ustina Markus, "The Bilingualism Question in Belarus and Ukraine," *Transition,* November 29, 1996.

9. Dominique Arel, "Ukraine: The Temptation of the Nationalizing State," in *Political Culture and Civil Society in Russia and the New States of Eurasia,* ed. Vladimir Tismaneanu (Armonk, N.Y.: M. E. Sharpe, 1995), 177. See also his "Language Politics in Independent Ukraine: Towards One or Two State Languages," *Nationalities Papers* 23, no. 3 (1995).

10. Author's interview with Yvan Drach, Kiev, July 21, 1995.

11. See Kolstoe, *Russians in the Former Soviet Republics,* 182–83.

12. Figures in Arel, "Ukraine: The Temptation of the Nationalizing State," 176.

13. Interview with the author, Kiev, April 2, 1994

14. Interview with the author, Dnipropetrovsk, August 11, 1995.

15. Interview with the author, Dnipropetrovsk, August 14, 1995.

16. Interview with the author, Dnipropetrovsk, August 13, 1995.

17. Interview with the author, Kiev, July 20, 1995.

18. Interview with the author, Donetsk, August 28, 1995.

19. Interview with the author, Kiev, July 29, 1995.

20. Interview with the author, Kharkiv, August 6, 1995.

21. Quoted in Andrew Wilson, *Ukrainian Nationalism in the 1990s: A Minority Faith* (New York: Cambridge University Press, 1997), 157; this work gives a short but highly useful and perceptive survey of the historiographical arguments on both sides through the years. See also David R. Marples, "New Interpretations of Ukrainian History," *RFE/RL Research Report* 2, no. 11 (March 12, 1993).

22. See Andrew Wilson, "National History and National Identity in Ukraine and Belarus," in *Nation Building in the Post-Soviet Borderlands: The Politics of National Identities,* ed. Graham Smith et al. (New York: Cambridge University Press, 1998); and Andrew Wilson, "Myths of National History in Belarus and Ukraine," in *Myths and Nationhood,* ed. Geoffrey Hosking and George Schöpflin (London: Hurst, 1997).

23. Interview with the author, Kiev, July 8, 1995.

24. Orest Subtelny, *Ukraine: A History* (Toronto: University of Toronto Press, 1988).

25. For a summary of these views, see Wilson, "National History and National Identity," in *Nation Building in the Post-Soviet Borderlands,* ed. Smith et al.; and Wilson, "Myths of National History," in *Myths and Nationhood,* ed. Hosking and Schöpflin. Such claims of primordial habitation of the national area are common to nationalist historians from a great many countries.

26. Yaroslav Dashkevych, "Ukraine and the National Minorities," *Derzhavnist,* no. 3 (1991): 24–27, quoted in Markus, "The Bilingualism Question."

27. George Vernadsky, *Kievan Russia* (New Haven, Conn.: Yale University Press, 1948), 309.

28. Jeffrey Brooks, *When Russia Learned to Read: Literacy and Popular Literature, 1861–1917* (Princeton, N.J.: Princeton University Press, 1985), 228.

29. Quoted in Shevelov, *The Ukrainian Language,* 44. As Shevelov indicates elsewhere, this was to some extent true before the revolution simply because due to its banning from public life and the education system, Ukrainian had never developed a vocabulary for many concepts, especially in science and in the field of modern politics and administration (p. 220). Vocabulary for these concepts entered the language during the period of the struggle for independence and in the first years of Soviet rule.

30. Interview with the author, Kharkiv, August 7, 1995.

31. See for example the passages concerning the new borders in interviews with Donetsk miners and their families in Lewis H. Siegelbaum and Daniel J. Walkowitz, eds., *Workers of the Donbass Speak: Survival and Identity in the New Ukraine, 1989–1992* (Albany, N.Y.: State University of New York Press, 1995). Those protesting against the effects of the borders included Valery Samofalov, one of the leaders of the 1989 strike and seemingly among the most democratically and progressively minded of the miners' leaders.

32. See, for example, Jürgen Corbert and Andreas Gummich, *The Soviet Union at the Crossroads: Facts and Figures on the Soviet Republics* (Frankfurt: Deutsche Bank Economics Department, 1990).

33. Interview with the author, Kharkiv, August 6, 1995.

34. Interview with the author, Kharkiv, August 4, 1995.

35. For an overview of religious-political developments in Ukraine as of 1995, see the essays by Bohdan Bociurkiw, Vasyl Markus, and Serhiy Bilokin in *The Politics of Religion in Russia and the New States of Eurasia,* ed. Michael Bourdeaux (Armonk, N.Y.: M. E. Sharpe, 1995).

36. See Lida Poletz, "Police Beatings at Funeral Shock Ukrainians," RTN, July 18, 1995.

37. See Ron Popeski, "Ukraine Opens Monument to Dead Patriarch," RTN, July 14, 1996.

38. Yuri Kulikov, "Ukraine's Kuchma Rules Out State Orthodox Church," RTN, March 15, 1996.

39. Ukrainian Radio, July 26, 1995; translated in the British Broadcasting Corporation's *Summary of World Broadcasts,* July 28, 1995.

40. Interview with the author, Kiev, August 1, 1995.

3. THE RUSSIAN-SPEAKING AREAS OF UKRAINE

1. Wilson, *Ukrainian Nationalism in the 1990s,* 195.

2. Interview with the author, Donetsk, August 22, 1995.

3. See Wilson, *Ukrainian Nationalism in the 1990s.*

4. Ibid.

5. See the articles by Vyacheslav Pikhovshek in *Most,* no. 46 (1995), 1, 4–5, translated in *FBIS Daily Report/Central Eurasia,* December 19, 1995; and in *Kievskie vedomosti,* May 28, 1996, 3-4, translated in *FBIS Daily Report/Central Eurasia,* May 28, 1996.

6. See Jane Perlez, "On Ukraine's Economic Path, Clique Mans Roadblocks," *New York Times,* October 18, 1996.

7. Ibid.

8. James Rupert, "Regional Tensions Trip Up Ukraine's Quest of Stability," *Washington Post,* October 27, 1996.

9. Sherman Garnett, *Keystone in the Arch: Ukraine and the New Political Geography of Eastern and Central Europe* (Washington, D.C.: Carnegie Endowment for International Peace, 1996).

10. Interview with the author, Dnipropetrovsk, August 14, 1995.

11. Interview with the author, Dnipropetrovsk, August 16, 1995.

12. All statistics in this chapter are from the 1989 (and last) Soviet census.

13. *Dnyepropetrovsk,* August 11, 1995.

14. *OMRI Daily Digest,* August 15, 1996.

15. For an oral history of the 1989 and 1991 strikes and their background, see Siegelbaum and Walkowitz, *Workers of the Donbass Speak*.

16. On Hughes, see Theodore H. Friedgut, *Iusovka and Revolution* (Princeton, N.J.: Princeton University Press, 1989); Gregory Guroff, ed., *Entrepreneurship in Imperial Russia* (Princeton, N.J.: Princeton University Press, 1983); and Emrys G. Bowen, *John Hughes* (Cardiff: University of Wales Press, 1978).

17. Interview with the author, Donetsk, August 2, 1995.

18. For a picture of the Donbas miners between the strikes of 1989 and 1993, with extensive interviews, see Siegelbaum and Walkowitz, *Workers of the Donbass Speak*. It includes many valuable insights into the reasons for the failure of the democratic protest movement of 1989 to consolidate itself into effective long-term structures—either political or trade unionist—and the growing irritation of the miners with the new Ukrainian state. For a comparison with the character and behavior of steelworkers in the Urals industrial city of Magnitogorsk, see Stephen Kotkin, *Steeltown USSR: Soviet Society in the Gorbachev Era* (Berkeley, Calif.: University of California Press, 1991).

19. For a survey of the historiographical battles over the Donbas, see Wilson, "The Donbas Between Ukraine and Russia." See also his "The Growing Challenge to Kiev from the Donbas," *RFE/RL Research Report* 2, no. 33 (August 20, 1993). For the condition of the Donbas before Hughes, I am partly relying on family history. My great-grandfather owned an estate covering part of what is now the city of Donetsk.

20. For the origins, growth, and character of Odessa during its first 120 years under the Russian Empire, see Patricia Herlihy, *Odessa, A History: 1794-1914* (Cambridge, Mass.: Harvard University Press, 1986).

21. Interview with the author, Odessa, October 10, 1995.

22. Interview with the author, Kharkiv, August 4, 1995.

23. Interview with the author, Kharkiv, August 8, 1995.

24. Interview with the author, Dnipropetrovsk, August 13, 1995.

4. Crimea and Sevastopol

1. For an overview of the different aspects of the Crimean issue (mainly from a Ukrainian point of view), see Maria Drohobycky, ed., *Crimea: Dynamics, Challenges, and Prospects* (Washington, D.C.: American Association for the Advancement of Science, 1995), and David Marples and David F. Duke, "Ukraine, Russia, and the Question of Crimea," *Nationalities Papers* 23, no. 2 (June 1995).

2. For the contemporary political organization and program of the Tatars, see Mustafa Cemiloglu, "A History of the Crimean Tatar National Liberation Movement: A Sociopolitical Perspective," in *Crimea*, ed. Drohobycky; and Andrew Wilson, *A Situation Report on the Crimean Tatars* (London: International Alert, 1994). See also James Rupert, "Tatars Return to an Inhospitable Home in Crimea," *International Herald Tribune*, January 11, 1996.

3. For the history of the Crimean Tatars, see Alan Fisher, *The Crimean Tatars* (Stanford, Calif.: Hoover Institution Press, 1978).

4. See Robert Conquest, *The Nation Killers* (London: Macmillan, 1966); Aleksandr M. Nekrich, *The Punished Peoples* (New York: W.W. Norton, 1978); and Alexander Solzhenitsyn, *The Gulag Archipelago,* vol. 3 (New York: Harper & Row, 1978), 386–98 and passim.

5. See the December 8, 1997 release from Unian, the Ukrainian news agency, quoting Ukrainian deputy premier Valery Smoly; translated in *Summary of World Broadcasts,* December 10, 1997.

6. Interview with the author, Bakhchiserai, January 25, 1994.

7. See Gennady Potapenko, "Two Die in Riots by Tatars," Associated Press, June 26, 1995.

8. Interview with the author, Simferopol, August 29, 1995.

9. Associated Press, November 29, 1997.

10. Interview with the author, Simferopol, May 25, 1994.

11. Interview with the author, Simferopol, August 28, 1995.

12. "Rukh and Tatar Mejlis Agree," Unian, November 7, 1997; translated in *Summary of World Broadcasts,* November 8, 1997.

13. For the 1994 elections, see Andrew Wilson, "The Elections in Crimea," *RFE/RL Research Report* 3, no. 25 (June 24, 1994).

14. Interview with the author, Simferopol, January 26, 1994.

15. Interview with the author, Simferopol, May 23, 1994.

16. Interview with the author, Simferopol, May 25, 1994.

17. Interview with the author, Simferopol, May 29, 1994.

18. Peter Conradi, *The European,* May 27, 1994.

19. See "Crimean Supreme Soviet Revokes No Confidence Vote," Interfax, August 2, 1995; translated in *Summary of World Broadcasts,* August 4, 1995.

20. See "Crimea's Economy in Steep Decline," RIA Novosti, September 30, 1997; translated in *Summary of World Broadcasts,* October 10, 1997.

21. For the first teachers' protests, see Associated Press, April 8, 1996; for the protests by military pensioners, see Unian, November 26, 1997; translated in *Summary of World Broadcasts,* November 28, 1997. For the second teachers' strike, see RIA Novosti, January 13, 1998; translated in *Summary of World Broadcasts,* January 15, 1998.

22. Interview with the author, September 15, 1995.

23. *Monitor,* May 21, 1996.

24. See "President Kuchma Will Make All Crimean Appointments," Unian, February 10, 1997; translated in *Summary of World Broadcasts,* February 12, 1997.

25. For the clash over the replacement of Demydenko and Gritsenko, see "Crimean Parliament Sacks Pro-Ukraine Speaker," Agence France-Presse, February 6, 1997, and "Ukraine's Crimea Region Elects Pro-Kiev Leader," Reuters, February 13, 1997. For the parliament's next attempt, see "Crimean Parliament Replaces Chief Executive," Associated Press, April 9, 1997.

26. Interview with the author, Simferopol, September 15, 1995.

27. Interview with the author, Simferopol, September 13, 1995.

28. Interview with the author, Moscow, October 18, 1994.

29. See "Primakov: Russia Must Not Make Territorial Claims on Ukraine," Agence France-Presse, March 1, 1997.

30. See Reuters, January 17, 1997, and Associated Press, January 20, 1997.

31. As of 1993, the Turkish army numbered 503,000 to Russia's 1.7 million, but the latter number was already only on paper and since then the Russian forces have declined steeply to some 1.2 million by the end of 1996. Moreover, of course, the Russian forces are spread over the entire country, not concentrated in the south. While the Russian navy is falling to pieces and not being replaced (the Black Sea Fleet has received no new warships since 1991), the Turkish navy in 1992 embarked on a modernization program with American assistance, just as the Turkish army received from the United States 1,200 surplus NATO tanks at a special discounted price.

32. Interview with the author, Moscow, October 3, 1995.

33. See "Main Points of Russia-Ukraine Accords," Agence France-Presse, May 31, 1997.

34. See "Calm on the Black Sea: Russia and Ukraine Resolve Dispute," *International Herald Tribune,* May 30, 1997, and "Facts About the Former Soviet Black Sea Fleet," Associated Press, May 28, 1997.

35. See "Crimea: Residents Disagree With Black Sea Deal," Tass, May 30, 1997.

36. See "Ukrainian Official Says No Automatic Extension of Crimean Naval Base Lease," Unian, May 29, 1997; translated in *Summary of World Broadcasts,* May 31, 1997.

37. Interview with the author, Sevastopol, September 2, 1995.

38. *OMRI Daily Digest,* March 18, 1996.

39. Interview with the author, Tiraspol, March 29, 1994.

40. Interview with the author, August 11, 1995.

41. Interview with the author, Kiev, September 6, 1995.

42. Interview with the author, Sevastopol, January 28, 1994.

43. *Za Vilnu Ukrayinu,* February 2, 1995; translated in *Summary of World Broadcasts,* February 11, 1995.

5. NATIONALISMS AND NATIONAL IDENTITIES IN THE 1990S

1. Bilinsky, "Primary Language of Communication."

2. Wilson, *Ukrainian Nationalism in the 1990s,* 151, 153–57.

3. Quoted in *Politichna Dumka* 1 (1993): 136.

4. See for example Ilya Prizel, "The Influence of Ethnicity on Foreign Policy: The Case of Ukraine," in *National Identity and Ethnicity in Russia and the New States of Eurasia,* ed. Roman Szporluk (Armonk, N.Y.: M. E. Sharpe, 1994).

5. Michael Shafir, "Ukraine as a Nation and as a State," *Transition,* September 6, 1996; emphasis added.

6. Motyl, *Dilemmas of Independence,* 80.

7. See "The Political and Social Ideas of Vjacheslav Lypynskyj," *Harvard Ukrainian Studies* 9, nos. 3/4 (December 1985); and Wilson, *Ukrainian Nationalism in the 1990s,* 42–44.

8. Interview with the author, Kiev, June 26, 1995.

9. Interview with the author, Kharkiv, August 4, 1995.

10. Interview with the author, Dnipropetrovsk, August 13, 1995.

11. Interview with the author, Donetsk, August 23, 1995.

12. Interview with the author, Kiev, July 20, 1995.

13. Dmitri Vydrin and Dmitri Tabachnik, *Ukraine on the Threshold of the 21st Century: A Political Overview* (Kiev: Lybid, 1995).

14. Sherman Garnett, "Ukraine: Europe's Crucial Frontier," paper to the Aspen Institute conference on U.S. relations with Russia and Ukraine, August 18–24, 1996. The paper was based on Garnett's book, *Keystone in the Arch.*

15. For the German minority in interwar Poland, see Richard Blanke, *Orphans of Versailles: The Germans in Western Poland* (Lexington, Ky.: University of Kentucky Press, 1993).

16. Brubaker, *Nationalism Reframed,* 55–76.

17. See Gregory and Alexander Guroff, "The Paradox of Russian National Identity," in *National Identity,* ed. Szporluk.

18. This declaration is quoted by John Dunlop in "Religion and Empire Saving," one of the essays in *The Politics of Religion in Russia and the New States of Eurasia,* ed. Michael Bourdeaux (Armonk, N.Y.: M. E. Sharpe, 1996), 15–16.

19. Alfred J. Rieber, "Struggle Over the Borderlands," in *The Legacy of History,* ed. Starr, 85–86.

20. Interview with the author, Dnipropetrovsk, August 15, 1995.

21. From the film, "The Russia We Have Lost," directed by Stanislav Govorukhin.

22. Aleksandr Lebed, press conference, Moscow, June 24, 1996.

23. Roman Szporluk, "Statehood and Nation-Building in the Post-Soviet Space," in *National Identity,* ed. Szporluk, 10.

24. Ryszard Kapuscinski, *Imperium* (New York: Alfred A. Knopf, 1994), 87.

25. Alexander Solzhenitsyn, *The Russian Question at the End of the 20th Century* (New York: Farrar, Strauss and Giroux, 1995), 90–91.

CONCLUSION: IMPLICATIONS FOR WESTERN POLICY

1. Zbigniew Brzezinski, *The Grand Chessboard: American Primacy and Its Geostrategic Imperatives* (New York: HarperCollins, 1997), 84.

2. Jean Baroud, "Ukrainian Nationalists' Dream of Entering NATO," Agence France-Presse, July 8, 1997.

3. "Westward Ho—And Soon," *Washington Post,* June 13, 1996.

4. Brzezinski, *The Grand Chessboard,* 119. See also John Keegan, "Tales of Combat to Come," *Washington Post Book World,* December 1, 1996.

5. Ian Mather, "NATO Plays in Russia's Backyard," *The European,* September 4, 1997; see also Mykhailo Yelchev, "Ships Arrive in Crimea for Controversial Exercises," RTN, August 23, 1997. For a response by a leading Russian democrat, see Sergei Yushenkov, "Russia Has Point on NATO," *The Moscow Times,* August 28, 1997; and Dmitry Zaks, "Russians Bristle at NATO Sea Breeze," *The Moscow Times,* August 26, 1997.

INDEX

Anatol Lieven is editor of *Strategic Comments* and expert on post-Soviet affairs at the International Institute for Strategic Studies in London. For many years Lieven was a journalist, serving as a Moscow-based correspondent for *The Times* of London and in Central Europe for the *Financial Times*. Lieven is the author of *Chechnya: Tombstone of Russian Power* and the prize-winning *The Baltic Revolution*. In 1996, Lieven was a fellow in the Jennings Randolph Fellowship Program at the United States Institute of Peace.

JENNINGS RANDOLPH PROGRAM FOR INTERNATIONAL PEACE

This book is a fine example of the work produced by senior fellows in the Jennings Randolph fellowship program of the United States Institute of Peace. As part of the statute establishing the Institute, Congress envisioned a program that would appoint "scholars and leaders of peace from the United States and abroad to pursue scholarly inquiry and other appropriate forms of communication on international peace and conflict resolution." The program was named after Senator Jennings Randolph of West Virginia, whose efforts over four decades helped to establish the Institute.

Since 1987, the Jennings Randolph Program has played a key role in the Institute's effort to build a national center of research, dialogue, and education on critical problems of conflict and peace. More than a hundred senior fellows from some thirty nations have carried out projects on the sources and nature of violent international conflict and the ways such conflict can be peacefully managed or resolved. Fellows come from a wide variety of academic and other professional backgrounds. They conduct research at the Institute and participate in the Institute's outreach activities to policymakers, the academic community, and the American public.

Each year approximately fifteen senior fellows are in residence at the Institute. Fellowship recipients are selected by the Institute's board of directors in a competitive process. For further information on the program, or to receive an application form, please contact the program staff at (202) 457-1700.

Joseph Klaits
Director

UKRAINE AND RUSSIA
A FRATERNAL RIVALRY

This book is set in the typeface Garamond; the display type is Albertus. Cover design by The Creative Shop; interior design by Joan Engelhardt and Day Dosch. Page makeup by Helene Y. Redmond of HYR Graphics. Map designed by Kenneth P. Allen. Copyediting and indexing by EEI Communications, Inc. Peter Pavilionis was the book's editor.